MW00794819

Kings and Queens

MACMILLAN

PROFILES

Kings and Queens

MACMILLAN LIBRARY REFERENCE USA
New York

Macmillan Library Reference USA
1633 Broadway
New York, New York 10019

Manufactured in the United States of America

Printing number
1 2 3 4 5 6 7 8 9 10

Cover design by Berrian Design

Library of Congress Cataloging-in-Publication Data

Kings and queens.
p. cm. — (Macmillan profiles)
Profiles of 170 rulers.
Includes bibliographical references (p.) and index.
ISBN 0-02-865375-0 (alk. paper)
1. Kings and rulers Biography Dictionaries. 2. Queens Biography Dictionaries. I. Macmillan Library Reference USA. II. Series.
D107.K54 1999
920.02—dc21
[B] 99-37943
CIP

Front cover clockwise from top: Queen Elizabeth II (Corbis/Bettmann); Emperor Hirohito (Corbis/Bettmann); King Fahd (Corbis/Bettmann); King Cetewayo (Corbis/Hulton-Deutsch Collection)

This paper meets the requirements of ANSI/NISO A39.48-1992 (Permanence of Paper)

Contents

Preface

Macmillan Profiles: *Kings and Queens* is a unique reference featuring over 170 profiles of notable monarchs, past and present, from around the world. Macmillan Library Reference recognizes the need for reliable, accurate, and accessible biographies of important figures in world history. The Macmillan Profiles series can help meet that need by providing new collections of biographies that were carefully selected from distinguished Macmillan sources. Macmillan Library Reference has published a wide array of award-winning reference materials for libraries around the world. It is likely that several of the encyclopedias on the shelves in this library were published by Macmillan Reference or Charles Scribner's Sons. All biographies in Macmillan Profiles have been recast and updated for a younger audience by a team of experienced writers and editors. Thirty new biographies were commissioned to supplement entries from original sources.

The goal of *Kings and Queens* is to present an inspiring introduction to the life and times of kings, queens, emperors, empresses, czars, czarinas, emirs, sultans, pharaohs, and other royal rulers from ancient times to the present. Students will learn about history and culture as they are drawn into stories of imperial life in opulent castles, court intrigue, enchanting romance, arranged marriages, wars and revolutions, assassinations, and more. The article list was based on the following criteria: relevance to the curriculum, importance to history, name recognition for students, and representation of as broad a cultural range as possible. In addition, *Kings and Queens* includes a biography of the current royal ruler of every country that remains a monarchy at the end of the twentieth century. The article list was refined and expanded in response to advice from a lively and generous team of librarians from high schools and public schools across the United States. The result is a balanced, curriculum-related work that brings these historical figures to life.

FEATURES

Kings and Queens is part of Macmillan's Profiles Series. To add visual appeal and enhance the usefulness of the volume, the page format was designed to include the following helpful features:

- Time Lines: Found throughout the text in the margins, time lines provide a quick reference source for dates and important events in the life and times of these important men and women.
- Notable Quotations: Included throughout the text in the margins, these thought-provoking quotations are drawn from interviews, speeches, and writings of the person covered in the article. Such quotations give readers a special insight into the distinctive personalities of these royal rulers.
- Definitions and Glossary: Brief definitions of important terms in the main text can be found in the margins. A glossary at the end of the book provides students with an even broader list of definitions.
- Sidebars: Appearing in shaded boxes throughout the volume, these provocative asides relate to and amplify topics.
- Pull Quotes: Inserted throughout the text in the margins, pull quotes highlight essential facts.
- Suggested Reading: An extensive list of books, articles, and Web sites about the monarchs covered in the volume will help students who want to do further research.
- Index: A thorough index provides thousands of additional points of entry into the work.

ACKNOWLEDGMENTS

We thank our colleagues who publish the Merriam Webster Collegiate Dictionary. Definitions used in the margins and many of the glossary terms come from the distinguished Webster's Collegiate Dictionary, Tenth Edition, 1996.

The biographies herein were written by leading authorities at work in the field of world history. *Kings and Queens* contains over 75 photographs. Acknowledgments of sources for the illustrations can be found on page 479.

We are also grateful for the contributions of the following inimitable team of librarians who helped compile the article list. Their knowledge of school curriculum and reader interest was invaluable in shaping a volume of optimum usefulness to middle- and high school students.

Rosalie Daniels, Mann Magnet Junior High, Little Rock, Arkansas
Dennis Donnelly, Hoover High School, San Diego, California
Kathy Labertew, Clairemont High School, San Diego, California
Dottie Renfro, Madison Middle School Library, Richmond, Kentucky

This work would not have been possible without the hard work and creativity of our staff. We offer our sincere thanks to all who helped create this marvelous work.

Abd al-Rahman Khan

1844–1910 ● RULER OF AFGHANISTAN

Abd al-Rahman Khan Barakzai (also known as Abd er-Rahman) ascended the Afghan throne during the second British invasion of Afghanistan. Embarking on a relentless policy of centralization of power, he weathered four civil wars and a hundred rebellions during his reign (1880–1910).

He was the grandson of Dost Mohammed (r. 1826–39; 1842–63), the founder of the Barakzai dynasty. At the age of thirteen, he was given his first appointment, and he showed his talent when assigned, later on, to command the army of the northern region, of which his father was governor. Playing an active role in the five-year war of succession, he twice won the throne for his father and an uncle before being defeated by yet another uncle, Sher Ali (r. 1863–66; 1869–79). Forced to leave, Abd al-Rahman spent eleven years in exile in the Asiatic colonies of Russia. His opportunity came in 1880, when Britain's invading forces, shaken by the intensity of Afghan resistance, were casting for a candidate acceptable both to them and to the resistance. In return for British control over Afghanistan's foreign relations, he was recognized as the ruler, in July 1880, and assigned a **subsidy** by Britain.

Abd al-Rahman Kahn weathered four civil wars and a hundred rebellions during his reign.

subsidy: a grant or gift of money.

In the wake of Britain's invasion, multiple centers of power had emerged in Afghanistan, with two of Abd al-Rahman's cousins controlling major portions of the country. He rejected offers to share power, defeating one cousin in 1880 and the other in 1885, and emerged as the undisputed ruler of the country. His next challenge was to overcome the clans, whom he subdued, in a series of campaigns between 1880 and 1896. He imposed taxation, conscription, and adjudication on the defeated clans. His policies encompassed all linguistic and religious groups but took a particularly brutal form in the case of the Hazaras.

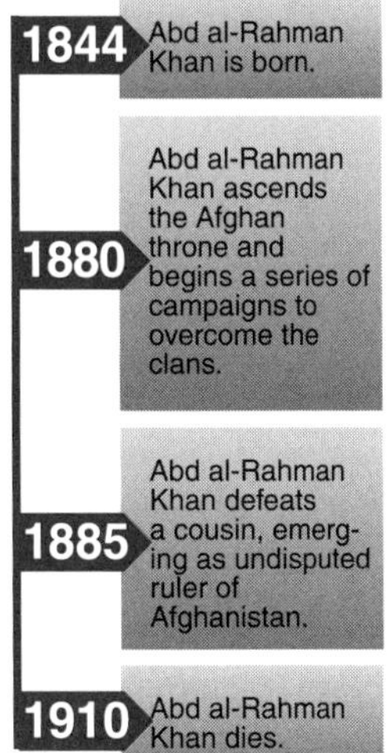

To establish his centralizing policies, he transformed the state apparatus. The army, chief vehicle of his policies, was reorganized and expanded, and the bulk of the state revenue was spent on its upkeep. Administrative and judicial practices were bureaucratized, with emphasis on record keeping and the separation of home and office. He justified these policies on religious grounds, making *shari'a* (the law of Islam) the law of the land, and nonetheless turning all judges into paid servants of the state.

Abd al-Rahman was able to concentrate on consolidating his rule at home because of Britain's and Russia's desire to avoid direct confrontation with each other. Afghanistan became a buffer state between the two empires; they imposed its present boundaries. Playing on their rivalry, Abd al-Rahman refused to allow European railways, which were touching on his eastern, southern, and northern borders, to expand within Afghanistan, and he resisted British attempts to station European representatives in his country. Toward the end of his reign, he felt secure enough to inform the viceroy of India that treaty obligations did not allow British representatives even to comment on his internal affairs.

When he died, he was succeeded by his son and heir apparent, Habibollah Khan, who ruled until 1919. ◆

Abdullah ibn Husayn

1882–1951 ● KING OF JORDAN

Abdullah, born in Mecca (in present-day Saudi Arabia), was a son of Husayn ibn Ali. On his eleventh birthday, he went to Constantinople (now Istanbul) to join his father, who had been summoned by the sultan. In 1908 Husayn was appointed Sharif of Mecca, over the objections of the Committee of Union and Progress (the Young Turks). Between 1910 and 1914 Abdullah represented Mecca in the Ottoman parliament.

The Turkish authorities tried to strip Husayn of his administrative (but not religious) duties when the construction of railroad and telegraph lines made direct rule from Constantinople possible. Husayn resisted, and he was in danger of dismissal when the dispute was shelved due to the outbreak of World War I.

In February 1914 Abdullah met Lord Kitchener, then minister **plenipotentiary** to Egypt, and asked him if Britain would aid Sharif Husayn in case of a dispute with the Turks. Abdullah also met with Ronald Storrs, the Oriental secretary at Britain's consulate in Cairo. This meeting led to a subsequent correspondence between Storrs and Abdullah that later developed into the Husayn–McMahon correspondence, an exchange in which certain pledges were made by Britain to the sharif concerning an independent Arab kingdom (with ambiguous boundaries) in the Fertile Crescent.

plenipotentiary: invested with full power.

The Turks tried to persuade Husayn to endorse the call for **jihad** against the Allies, but he delayed until June 10, 1916, when the Arab revolt was declared. Abdullah was entrusted with the siege of the Turkish garrisons in Taif and Medina. His brother Faisal, meanwhile, scored quick victories in Syria. Faisal set up an independent Arab kingdom with its capital at Damascus toward the end of 1918; the French drove him out two years later. Meanwhile, Abdullah was defeated in an important battle with the Wahhabi followers of ibn Saud. Britain placed Faisal on the throne of Iraq, which had been slated for Abdullah.

jihad: a holy war waged on behalf of Islam as a religious duty.

One key to understanding Abdullah is his deep loyalty to Islam, which in his mind was linked to the notion that God had favored the Arabs with a unique position as the carriers of culture and faith. For him, Arabism was inseparable from Islam and meaningless without it. His family, which claimed a direct line of descent from the Prophet Muhammad, provided the crucial link between the two.

Another key to an understanding of Abdullah's personality is that, as a rule, he sought cooperation, even in the midst of conflict. He preferred bargaining to fighting, and he constantly formulated value-maximizing strategies in which he compromised with his adversaries so that all sides might stand to gain from the outcome.

Although Abdullah strove for unity, he engaged in nation building on a limited scale when unity was unattainable. When he appeared with a small band of armed followers in Madaba, after the French had ousted his brother Faisal from the throne of Syria in 1920, he was intent on leading Syrian political refugees, members of the Istiqlal party still loyal to Faisal, and the **bedouins** he could muster in a bid to wrest Arab rights in Syria from the French. With T. E. Lawrence acting as a go-between, he negotiated a deal with the new British colonial secretary, Winston Churchill, under which Abdullah agreed to administer Transjordan for six months, beginning on April 1, 1921, and was granted a subsidy by Britain. One consequence of this was to remove Transjordan from the sphere of applicability of the Balfour Declaration.

bedouin: a nomadic Arab of the Arabian, Syrian, or north African deserts.

Abdullah took over the administration of an arid plateau with a population of about 235,000, largely bedouin, poor, and uneducated, a land with some two hundred villages, half a dozen towns, and no major cities. Governmental services were virtually nonexistent. When he died, he left a nation-state comparable with others in the Middle East, although lacking in financial independence. The period from 1924 to 1940 was one in which central administration was developed, with Palestinians gradually replacing Syrians. An exemplary land program gave farmers property security unmatched in the Fertile Crescent. In 1925 the Ma'an and Aqaba regions were effectively incorporated into Transjordan (they had technically formed part of the Hijaz). In the same period, the bedouins, who had preyed on the **sedentary** population, were successfully integrated into the state, for which John Bagot Glubb, the organizer of the Desert Patrol, was largely responsible.

sedentary: settled; remaining in one location.

In 1928 Transjordan acquired an organic law under which Abdullah gained recognition in international law. It also provided for constitutional government and a legislative council, but Abdullah had wide authority to rule by decree, under the guidance of Britain. Although Transjordan remained militarily dependent on Britain, on March 22, 1946, a treaty was concluded whereby Britain recognized Transjordan "as a fully independent state and His Highness the Amir as the sovereign thereof." Following a name change, the Hashemite kingdom of Jordan concluded a new treaty with Britain in 1948.

Through years of dependency on Britain, Abdullah fell behind the times, continuing to reflect the Ottoman empire in which he had grown up: **dynastic** and **theocratic**, Arabs accepting foreign suzerainty under compulsion. He was out of step with Palestinian and secular Arab nationalism as well as Zion-

dynastic: relating to a succession of rulers of the same line of descent.

theocratic: relating to the government of a state by those regarded as being divinely guided.

ism. He sought to use British influence to forge Arab unity rather than to get rid of the British as a first step toward unity. British residents, notably St. John Philby and Percy Cox, drove a wedge between him and Syrian members of the Istiqlal party, who had perceived the Hashemites as champions of Syria's independence from France. When Abd al-Rahman Shahbandar, a nationalist Syrian leader who had been a longtime supporter of Abdullah, was assassinated in July 1940, Abdullah's base of support in Syria died with him.

Abdullah could accept a Jewish homeland only in the context of the old **millet** system: as a minority with a large degree of autonomy within a kingdom that he ruled. Zionists found this totally unacceptable but valued his accommodating approach to the problem. Yet he was a pioneer of Arab–Jewish understanding. He accepted the Peel Commission Report of 1937, which recommended partition of Palestine, even if he did not embrace a Jewish state. He also publicly accepted the 1939 white paper on Palestine, which was favorable to the Arabs. It has been said that he was driven by personal ambition, hoping to incorporate the Arab portion of Palestine within his domain, yet it is clear that he saw himself as an Arab acting for the Arabs. As his grandson King Hussein pointed out, Abdullah realized that the Jewish community in Palestine was only the tip of the iceberg and that the balance of forces dictated compromise. Abdullah met with Golda Meir, who was acting on behalf of the political department of the Jewish Agency, on November 17, 1947, and it was agreed that Abdullah would annex the Arab part of Palestine under the UN partition plan but would not invade the Jewish part.

millet: a grass cultivated for its grain that is used for food.

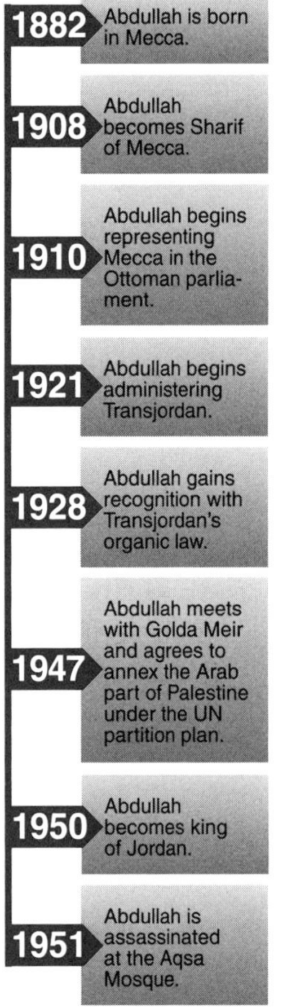

When the British mandate ended on May 14, 1948, the Jews declared the creation of a Jewish state, and war broke out with the Arabs. The Arab Legion (Jordanian army) occupied what came to be known as the West Bank; Britain accepted this as long as Abdullah kept out of the Jewish zone; when Jewish forces and the Arab Legion clashed over Jerusalem, which was to have been designated an international zone, Britain cut off arms supplies and spare parts, and ordered all of its officers to return to Amman. The Arabs held on to East Jerusalem, but the Arab Legion had to withdraw from the towns of Lydda and Ramle, which laid Abdullah open to charges of betrayal. In the final analysis, his strategy salvaged territory for the Arabs that may one day serve as the basis for a Palestinian state.

Abdullah initiated a conference in Jericho at which the Palestinian participants expressed a wish to join in one country with Jordan. Parliamentary elections were subsequently held in the West and East Banks, with twenty seats assigned to each. Parliament convened on April 24, 1950, at which time Palestinian deputies tabled a motion to unite both banks of the Jordan. This was unanimously adopted. Abdullah became king of a country that now included the holy places in Palestine, with a population of 1.5 million, triple the population of Transjordan alone.

Abdullah was assassinated at the Aqsa Mosque on July 20, 1951, by a handful of disgruntled Palestinians believed to be working with Egypt's intelligence service. ◆

Abdullah II

1962– ● KING OF JORDAN

In 1999 Jordan's King Hussein stunned the world by announcing that his son Abdullah, not his brother, Hassan, would succeed him.

Two weeks before he died from cancer in 1999, Jordan's King Hussein stunned the world by announcing that his son Abdullah, not his brother, Hassan, would succeed him as ruler of the Hashemite Kingdom of Jordan. The king's reversal astonished many, but perhaps no one was as surprised as Crown Prince Hassan, who had been in line for the throne since 1965. Hassan might have seen it coming; the young Abdullah had been the crown prince once before, until he was three. Then in 1965, amid rumors of an assassination attempt, King Hussein decided to make his younger brother, Hassan, the crown prince, in case a more immediate transfer of adult power became necessary. (Hussein's grandfather, Abdullah I, was assassinated in the doorway of the al Aqsa Mosque in Jerusalem in 1951. Fifteen-year-old Hussein was standing beside him and was hit as well, but the bullet ricocheted off a medal that his grandfather had insisted he wear.)

Abdullah ibn al-Hussein was born in 1962, the eldest son of King Hussein and his second wife, the English-born Toni Avril Gardiner, renamed Muna (Arabic for "My Wish"). The king and Princess Muna (she preferred not to be made a queen) divorced in 1972. Through his father's lineage, the Hashemite dynasty, Abdullah is related through forty-three generations of eldest sons to the prophet Mohammed, the founder of Islam. Abdullah was educated at the Deerfield Academy in Amherst, Massachusetts. He is said to have told his fellow students, before they learned otherwise, that his father owned a telephone company. Abdullah was later enrolled in the British military academy at Sandhurst, where his father had studied. After his military training, Abdullah took yearlong courses in international studies at Oxford and Georgetown universities.

"Hussein's soul will remain with us and among us and will not go away from our hearts and souls, and we shall preserve Hussein's legacy in building and in giving, with all loyalty and sincerity, for the sake of Jordan."

King Abdullah, on the death of his father, King Hussein, 1999

Like his father, the prince in his early bachelor years was a sort of gentleman adventurer who enjoyed action and risk. Well equipped by his military training, Abdullah was an accomplished marksman, a deep-sea diver, and a pilot of helicopters and jet fighter planes. He liked fast cars, and won the Jordanian National Rally one year.

Abdullah worked his way up through the ranks of the military, without any obvious preferential treatment, eventually becoming commander of the Jordanian Special Forces. In May 1998 Abdullah and other special forces commandos fought a battle outside Amman with four gunmen who had murdered an Iraqi diplomat and about a dozen others. The Jordanian soldiers got their men, though one commando died in the battle. No one witnessing the scene would have imagined that one of the commandos would be their king within a year.

Power was transferred to Abdullah on February 6, 1999, eight days after his thirty-seventh birthday, and twelve days after being named crown prince by his ailing father. Abdullah was sworn in as regent by Prime Minister Fayez Tarawneh after the twenty-two-member Cabinet voted unanimously to approve him as Hussein's successor. Abdullah was sworn in to fill a "**constitutional vacuum**" because his father, who was being kept alive on a respirator after his lungs, liver, and kidneys had failed, was deemed unfit to rule.

constitutional vacuum: absence of a legitimate functioning ruler.

Abdullah's most immediate need upon taking office was to provide continuity, but there was a widespread sense that the government would not continue without some shifting of personnel. There were questions about how Abdullah would handle certain officials who owed their positions to his uncle Hassan, the former crown prince. Indeed, one of Abdullah's early acts in office was to remove four generals from their posts, though the generals, all over sixty, had reached retirement age. One of the generals, Tahsin Shurthom, who was second in command of the army and one of the negotiators of the 1994 treaty

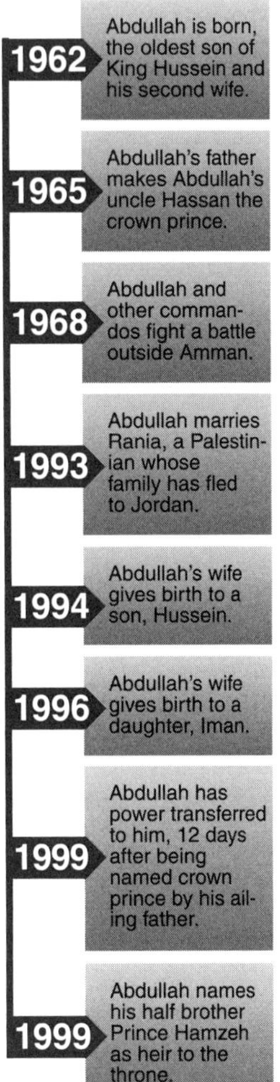

with Israel, had been one of Abdullah's mentors in the army, and the two are said to have a good relationship.

One of the questions early in Abdullah's reign, besides his management of the Jordanian government, concerns how he will deal with any challenges from the opposition Muslim Brotherhood. The Brotherhood opposes Jordan's peace agreements with Israel, and boycotted Jordan's general election in 1997, complaining of state media strictures and alleged threats against its candidates. Even before Abdullah was crowned king, the Muslim Brotherhood asked to meet with him to present its demands for the dissolution of Parliament and the calling of new elections—actions that are within the king's power.

Abdullah's management style is described as inclusive rather than divisive, and he is widely expected to be a unifier, like his father. However, in order to have the strength to unify and include opposition elements, he will first have to consolidate his base of power, a foundation that only the passage of time can provide. Like any successor to a popular ruler, Abdullah must keep a balance between appearing too aggressive and too weak. Within months of his accession he had already met with the major Arab leaders, and was visited by Center Party leader Yitzhak Mordecai, a candidate in the 1999 elections for prime minister of Israel.

Some observers familiar with Middle East politics are confident in Abdullah's prospects for stability because he was a career army officer for eighteen years and has the allegiance of the military and the bedouin tribes, who make up most of the Jordanian military. In addition, Abdullah has a common touch, as his father did; one of the complaints about Crown Prince Hassan was that, however experienced he might be, he was elitist.

In June 1993 Abdullah married Rania, a Palestinian whose family had fled to Jordan after Iraqi forces invaded Kuwait in August 1990. Queen Rania was born in Kuwait in 1970 to Palestinian parents from the West Bank of Tul Karem. She received a bachelor's degree in business administration at the American University in Cairo in 1991. Abdullah and Rania have a son, Hussein (b. 1994), and a daughter, Iman (b. 1996). Abdullah's marriage to a Palestinian may help his standing among the Jordanian general public, of whom 70 percent are Palestinian.

Abdullah's very first act in office—a move widely praised and sure to ease tensions within the royal family—was to name Queen Noor's eldest son, Prince Hamzeh, as heir to the throne.

Crown Prince Hamzeh bin Hussein was born in Amman on March 29, 1980. Reportedly it was the late king's wish that Hamzeh succeed Abdullah: Hamzeh was King Hussein's favorite son, and frequently appeared beside his father at meetings with foreign leaders. ◆

Akbar

1542–1605 ● MOGUL EMPEROR

Akbar, named Jalal-ud-Din Muhammad Akbar, was the grandson of Babur, founder of the Mogul empire and son of the second Mogul emperor, Humayun; he was also a descendant of Genghis Khan and Tamerlane. At the time of Akbar's birth Humayun had been defeated by an Afghan usurper, Sher Shah, and was forced to flee his capital, Delhi. Akbar was born in exile in the city of Umarkot in Sind. By the time he ascended the throne at age fourteen his father had managed to restore a section of his empire under a Persian protectorate. Within only two decades, Akbar had expanded his inheritance to its original boundaries and beyond. The name Akbar, Arabic for "great," was adopted to describe this man noted for his military, administrative, and religious achievements and his warm, humane personality.

The name Akbar, which means "great" in Arabic, was adopted to describe the emperor's military, administrative, and religious achievements, as well as his warm, humane personality.

Akbar's first task on taking over the kingdom was to defeat all rival claimants to the throne. Chief among these was the Hindu minister Hemu, whom he defeated at Panipat. Akbar went on to conquer the territories of his father's original kingdom and the surrounding areas. By 1562 he had conquered the Punjab, Hultan, Ganges, and Juman basins from Panipat to Allahabad, Gwalior, Ajmer, Kabul, and Rajputana. He consolidated his authority over the influential Hindu region of Rajputana by making a series of marriage alliances with the local royal family. By 1576, he had conquered Malwa, Clitor, Ranthambhor, Kalinjar, Gujarat, and Bengal. In his last wave of conquests (1586–92), he overran Kashmir, Sind, Baluchistan, Kandahar, part of Orissa, the Deccan, Khandesh, Berar, and Ahmadnagar.

Akbar was not only a remarkable military leader but was also a notable administrator. He had surveyors measure the land area

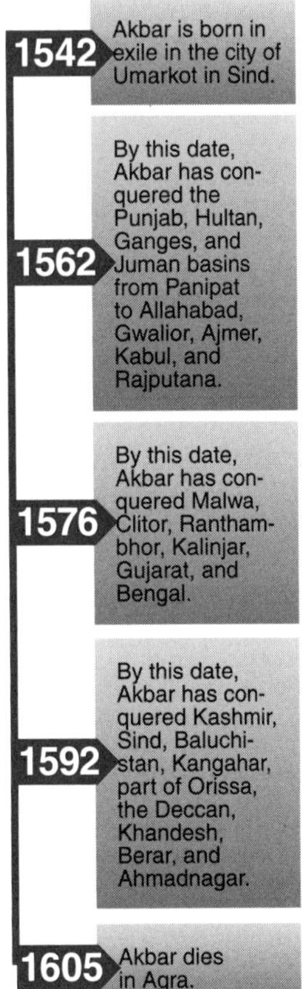

of the empire so that land revenues could be accurately calculated, then divided the territory in fifteen *subas*, or provinces, to ease administration. Many of his administrative reforms were adopted by the British in later years. Despite the Mogul Empire's devout Islamic culture, he allowed for complete freedom of religion for all his subjects. Many Hindus were appointed to prominent positions and he did away with the hated *jizya*, a poll tax levied on all Hindus making religious pilgrimages.

Akbar himself came to doubt many of the important precepts basic to Islam. He preferred reason to the written word of the Koran and saw validity in other religious beliefs, particularly those of Hinduism (he believed in the transmigration of souls upon death rather than the traditional Muslim belief in a heavenly paradise). His split with Islam was nearly total when he rewrote the fundamental prayer of that religion to read, "There is no God but Allah, and Akbar is his vice-regent." On three occasions he summoned Jesuit missionaries to teach him the principles of Christianity but each time rejected fundamental Christian beliefs such as heaven, the Trinity, and the incarnation of Christ. His interest in religious beliefs led him to convene a council of sages of all the major religions of India. Akbar then chose from each religion those beliefs which appeared most reasonable to him and incorporated them into a new religion, the *Din-i-Ilahi* (Divine Faith), which was to unify his empire but came to nothing. He erected houses of worship, *ibadat khana*, in which members of all religious persuasions could worship.

Although Akbar was illiterate, each evening he had his servants read to him. He established an extensive library of twenty-four thousand books containing works translated from many languages and staffed his court with noted intellectuals.

Akbar was unwilling to forego the pleasures allowed him by his position. He had a stable of five thousand elephants and it was said that his harem numbered five thousand but this figure probably included eunuchs and slaves in addition to wives, concubines (said to number three hundred), and many young children. Akbar had seven children by his consort: his sons Salim, Murad, and Danyal, and four daughters. Toward the end of Akbar's reign, Salim rebelled against his father but the two were reconciled shortly before Akbar's death in Agra in 1605. ◆

Akhenaton

C.1379–1362 B.C.E. ● PHARAOH OF EGYPT

Akhenaton, the son of Amenhotep III and his commoner wife, Tiy, was one of the greatest religious reformers of the ancient world; he is often credited with being the first **monotheist**. Physically very weak and thin, with a bulging pot belly, Akhenaton was very different from his father, a remarkable builder and hunter. Rather than spend his time at the hunt or at other physical activities common to Egyptian princes, Akhenaton was an intellectual who spent much of his youth poring over Egyptian religious texts.

monotheist: a person who follows the belief that there is but one God.

At the time of his ascent to the throne, Egypt's Eighteenth Dynasty was undergoing radical social changes. The country was an economic and military power which ruled Nubia, Palestine, and Phoenicia, as well as Upper and Lower Egypt. Extensive foreign trade allowed for other cultures to make their mark on Egyptian society and many Egyptians had adopted modes of dress and habit unfamiliar to the otherwise isolated Egyptian culture. Even the pharaoh had become little more than a figurehead monarch, removed from mundane matters of state. The pharaohs had relinquished their authority in favor of priests and bureaucrats who administered religious and secular rites and laws, for which they received great wealth and prestige.

Rather than spend his time at the hunt or at other activities common to Egyptian princes, Akhenaton was an intellectual who spent much of his youth poring over Egyptian religious texts.

Egyptians worshiped an immense pantheon of gods and goddesses, each requiring its own rituals. The gods of Egypt were generally depicted in human or animal form, often combining elements of the two. Two important gods were Re, worshiped in Heliopolis, and Amon, worshiped in Thebes; there was animosity between the adherents of these two gods. A few years before Akhenaton's birth a new deity, Aton, appeared in the Egyptian pantheon. Aton was originally depicted similarly to Re, as a human figure with the head of a falcon and a sun disk over his head; the whole figure was surrounded by a coiled serpent. Gradually the human and animal elements of Aton disappeared, leaving only the sun disk to represent the god.

Akhenaton assumed the throne sometime during the latter years of his father's reign. Immediately upon coming to power he began to promote the worship of Aton. The temple of Re-Harakhte, in the royal capital of Thebes, was abandoned for new temples erected to Aton at Karnak. Unlike the older temples, which were dark, imposing edifices containing majestic statues of the gods and their subjects, the new temples were less imposing and well lit by windows. Aton, the sun disk, had to be worshiped where his rays could reach. Much of the ritual was performed in the open air. The ritual was less developed than that of other gods; rather than consisting of a series of commandments and ceremonies, it demanded of its adherents merely to be grateful to Aton for the life that they were given. There was no tradition of divine rewards and punishments.

> *"You made the earth as you wished, you alone,*
> *All peoples, herds, and flocks;*
> *All upon earth that walk on legs,*
> *All on high that fly on wings,*
> *The lands of Khor and Kush,*
> *The land of Egypt."*
> Akhenaton's *Hymn to Aton*

Akhenaton became a zealous champion of Aton. In the sixth year of his reign, he changed his name from Amenhotep ("Amon is satisfied") to Akhenaton ("he who serves Aton"). His capital was moved from Thebes, the city sacred to Amon, to Amama, renamed Akhetaton, meaning, "place of Aton's power." A crusade was waged against the old gods: their statues were destroyed, and their names were erased from temples and documents. Their images were replaced with those of Akhenaton and his consort, Nefertiti. The traditional funeral hymn was rewritten; references to Osiris, god of the dead, were replaced with the name of Akhenaton; Akhenaton composed new hymns to Aton.

The new city of Akhetaton was a remarkable architectural feat, containing wide boulevards, villas, gardens, and pools. At the center of the city stood an open temple to Aton. The city was decorated with a new style of art in which the subjects were depicted as they appeared rather than being idealized by the artist. Akhenaton was depicted with all his physical defects and Nefertiti was shown as a hag, in a style that was closer to caricature than art.

reactionary: ultraconservative in politics.

Akhenaton was not a radical reformer. He had returned the monarchy to its former potency, causing him to be regarded by many as a **reactionary**. New nobles were created to replace the old aristocrats, leading to dissent among Egypt's leading families. In his zeal for religious reform, Akhenaton had neglected commerce and the military and his administration was infiltrated by corrupt officials. Many of his former subjects and allies in Africa and Asia were abandoned. During the twelfth year of his reign, the queen mother visited Akhetaton to warn him of the slow disintegration of his kingdom. He apparently accepted her advice; he was separated from Nefertiti and promoted Smenkhare, his son-in-law and possibly his younger brother, to a leading role in the administration of Egypt. Akhenaton, who was sickly, died soon after. He was succeeded briefly by

Smenkhare and then by Tutankhaton. Tutankhaton rejected the reforms of his predecessor, restoring the old gods to their former eminence. He himself changed his name to Tutankhamen, in honor of Amon, the god Akhenaton had tried to destroy. ◆

Akihito

1933– ● EMPEROR OF JAPAN

Akihito is the emperor of Japan and head of the world's oldest royal dynasty. He became Japan's 125th emperor upon the death of his father, Emperor Hirohito, on January 7, 1989. Japan is a constitutional monarchy and Akihito holds no actual powers of government, but he performs a number of ceremonial duties specified in Japan's constitution. As Japanese emperor, he is also the chief **Shinto** priest. Akihito has won the respect of many around the world for his dedication to the cause of peace. The name chosen to represent his reign is *Heisei*, which means achieving peace.

Shinto: the indigenous religion of Japan consisting chiefly in devotion to the emperor as a descendant of the sun goddess.

Akihito Tsugunomiya was born on December 23, 1933, to Emperor Hirohito and Empress Nagako. The name *Akihito* means shining pinnacle of virtue. *Tsugunomiya* means prince of

Japanese emperor Akihito, (left) and his wife, Empress Michiko (right), with their son, Crown Prince Naruhito, and his wife, Princess Masako, in 1993 in Tokyo.

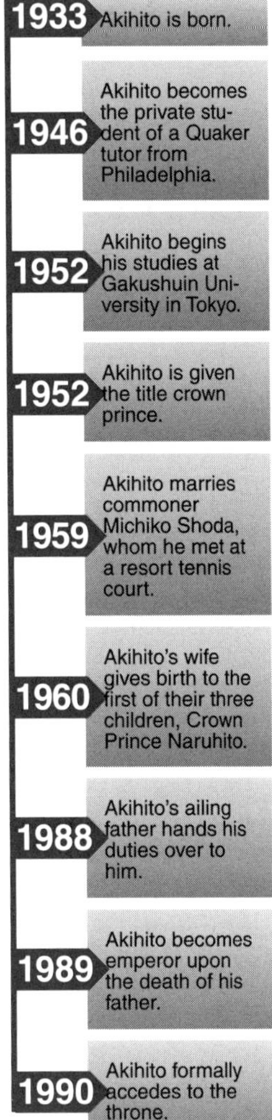

the august succession and enlightened benevolence. Akihito was the fifth of seven children born to his parents and the first of two sons. According to imperial custom, he was separated from his parents at the age of three and was raised by nurses, tutors, and protective chamberlains who saw to his needs. The young prince was only allowed to visit his parents on weekends. When he was six, Akihito was sent to Gakushuin (Peers' School) in Tokyo, where most of his classmates were from privileged aristocratic families. Akihito remained at the school until near the end World War II (1939–45), when he was sent out of Tokyo to escape the bombing raids of the Allied Forces fighting Japan.

Emperor Hirohito surrendered to the Allies in 1945. Afterward, the Allies wrote a new constitution for Japan that stripped the emperor of his powers to govern and put all political power into the hands of elected representatives. On January 1, 1946, in a dramatic announcement that stunned the Japanese people, Hirohito formally renounced all claims that he was divine. For hundreds of years, the Japanese had worshiped their emperor as a divine descendent of Amaterasu Omikami, the sun goddess and the most important Shinto deity. Hirohito's announcement signaled a dramatic shift toward democratization in postwar Japan. From that time on, Akihito's life changed significantly, and he was liberated from the life of isolation that he might otherwise have received as the son of god-king, and he began to spend increasingly more time with his peers. As part of an effort to groom him for a new, democratic age, Hirohito arranged for Akihito to study with an American tutor, Elizabeth Gray Vining, a Quaker from Philadelphia. Vining taught Akihito from 1946 to 1950, and she is said to have profoundly influenced the prince by nurturing his independent thinking.

In 1952 Akihito began his studies in political science and economics at Gakushuin University in Tokyo. In November of that year, he came of age and was formally declared rightful heir to the throne and given the title "crown prince." In early 1953 the crown prince interrupted his studies to take a fourteen-country tour of North America and Europe, where he represented Japan at the coronation of Queen Elizabeth II in England.

By that time, the imperial court had begun its hunt for a suitable bride for Akihito. The court chose hundreds of possible candidates of noble bloodlines. But Akihito broke with tradition and decided to marry a commoner, Michiko Shoda, whom he had met on a tennis court at a summer resort called Karuizawa. Michiko was the daughter of Hidesaburo Shoda, the president of a flour company, and a graduate of Tokyo's fashionable Sacred Heart Women's University. She initially rejected Akihito's proposal, fearful of the loss of freedom that would come from an imperial marriage and concerned about her acceptance among the aristocracy. But after Akihito's repeated calls and relentless wooing, Michiko agreed. Thus began a period in Japan in the 1950s known as the "Michi Boom," which was characterized by tremendous popular interest in the imperial throne and the engagement of the crown prince and Michiko.

The imperial court had begun its hunt for a suitable bride for Akihito; the court chose hundreds of possible candidates of noble bloodlines, but Akihito broke with tradition and decided to marry a commoner.

Akihito and Michiko were married on April 10, 1959, in a Shinto ceremony on the grounds of the Imperial Palace. According to tradition, the emperor and empress did not attend the ceremony, but they watched it on television from a nearby building. After the wedding, some of Michiko's fears were realized when some aristocrats and government officials appeared reluctant to accept her, but Michiko prevailed. Departures from royal traditions continued throughout their marriage. At Michiko's insistence, a small kitchen was installed in her home so that she could bake for her family. Japanese aristocratic women typically never even enter a kitchen, much less cook in it. The royal couple also decided to raise their children themselves instead handing them over to chamberlains. Akihito and Michiko raised three children: Crown Prince Naruhito, Crown Prince Aya, and Princess Nori. Their oldest son, Naruhito, who was born in 1960, is heir to the throne, though Aya is eligible for succession as well.

In the 1980s Akihito increasingly assumed his father's duties and took his place on state visits. In 1988 the ailing emperor, who suffered from pancreatic cancer, passed all his imperial duties to the crown prince. The emperor died the following year, and Akihito became emperor. He announced that he would devote the new imperial reign to Japan's further development and the promotion of peace on earth. After a series of more than ten ceremonies, including the royal funeral of Hirohito and special ceremonies for ascending to the throne, becoming the chief Shinto priest, and inheriting the imperial treasures, Akihito formally acceded to the throne in 1990, one year and ten months after his father's death.

Emperor Akihito's duties have included signing official documents, greeting foreign dignitaries, and presiding over certain important Shinto religious ceremonies. He and the empress frequently travel out of the capital to observe local affairs in other parts of the country and to come into contact with the Japanese people. Akihito also takes time to pursue his personal interests, which include sports, marine biology, and music. The emperor and his family are all accomplished musicians, and the emperor plays a cello.

Some Japanese people oppose the emperor system because it represents a uniquely privileged institution in what is supposed to be a democratic society.

Like many monarchs throughout history, Emperor Akihito has faced opposition from people within and outside of his country. Some Japanese people have been opposed to the emperor system because it represents a uniquely privileged institution in what is supposed to be a democratic society. World War II veterans in Europe have demonstrated against his visits and have demanded apologies from him for Japan's actions during the war. Akihito traveled to a number of countries in the 1990s to apologize publicly for the wrongs committed by his country during World War II and for Japan's occupation of various countries in the early 1900s. For these apologies and other actions to promote peace and democracy, Akihito has remained a popular figure around the world. ◆

Alaric

370–410 ● KING OF THE VISIGOTHS

A descendant of the Balthi, one of the leading Goth families, Alaric was born on an island in the delta of the Danube River. In his youth the Visigoths were forced to migrate westward because of attacks from the Huns at their rear. The Eastern Roman emperor, Theodosius the Great, took on the Visigoths as **mercenary** forces and Alaric became a commander in Theodosius's army. Upon the death of Theodosius in 395 Alaric hoped to receive a more important position in the government of the new Eastern emperor, Arcadius, but was disappointed. In 397, however, he attained a much greater position when the Visigoths elected him as their king. Turning toward Greece he sacked Corinth, Argos, and Sparta, sparing Athens only in return for a heavy ransom.

mercenary: hired for service in the army of a foreign country.

After Alaric was defeated by the Western Roman general Flavius Stilicho, Arcadius commissioned him to move north toward Italy; Alaric accordingly proceeded to establish a Visigoth kingdom in Illyricum. His attempted invasion of Italy in 402 was again rebuffed by Stilicho. Honorius, the Western Roman emperor, subsequently convinced Alaric to join forces with him in what he believed would be an inevitable war with the Eastern Empire. The death of Arcadius in 408 preempted the projected attack on the East, and Alaric demanded four thousand pounds of gold as indemnity. He was paid at Stilicho's insistence but Honorius subsequently had Stilicho executed. Alaric invaded Italy, besieged Rome, and demanded a large ransom. In 409 a second siege resulted in Rome's capitulation and the deposing of Honorius. When the emperor regained power within a year, Alaric invaded Rome for the third time and captured the city in 410. Traitors opened one of the gates and when Alaric gave his forces six days to take what they wanted, they proceeded to sack the city. This event sent shock waves throughout the Roman world and was seen as the end of Roman civilization. Alaric had intended to go on to invade north Africa, but died before he could act on his intentions. ◆

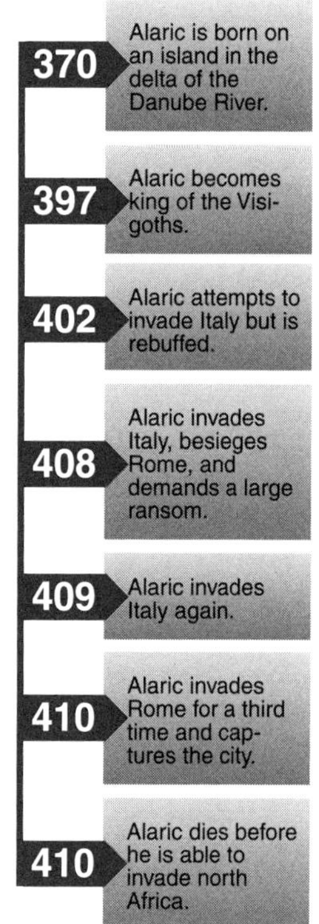

Albert II

1934– ● King of Belgium

Albert II of Belgium did not plan to be king. His older brother, Baudoin, had been trained as crown prince, and assumed the throne of Belgium in 1951, following the abdication of their father, King Leopold III. In fact, King Baudoin would become Europe's longest reigning monarch. However, when Baudoin died suddenly on August 9, 1993, without an heir, the throne went to his younger brother, Albert. Many expected Albert to abdicate in favor of his son Philippe, who had been groomed for the job, but Albert stepped forward as a strong leader with decades of experience in various aspects of Belgian government and business.

King Albert II (second from left) and Queen Paola (left) of Belgium entertain King Carl and Queen Silvia of Sweden in 1994.

During World War II, the Belgian royal family fled to France and Spain, then was deported to Germany and Austria.

King Albert II was born with the title Prince of Liège on June 6, 1934, at the Château du Stuyvenberg in Belgium's capital, Brussels. He is the son of King Leopold III and Queen Astrid, born Princess of Sweden, who was killed tragically in an automobile accident in Switzerland just a year after Albert's birth. Albert completed his studies despite a tumultuous childhood spent partly in exile during World War II. In 1940 the Belgian royal family fled to France and Spain, then was deported to Germany and Austria. Albert finished his studies in Geneva, Switzerland, before returning to Belgium with his father; older sister, Princess Josephine-Charlotte; and brother, Crown Prince Baudoin.

Unencumbered by the royal duties that consumed his older brother, Albert II launched a career in international business and philanthropy. From 1962 until his assumption of the throne in 1993, Albert served as President of Honor of the Council of Administration of the Belgian Office of External Trade. In this capacity, he presided over worldwide economic missions and promoted external trade among Belgian companies. Before becoming king, Albert had already conducted nearly a hundred foreign visits to encourage foreign investment in Belgium. The Prince Albert Fund for the Training of External Trade Specialists recognizes the king's contribution in this field. In addition to his role as trade ambassador, he was named president of the

General Board of the General Bank for Savings and Pensions, and as president of the Belgian Red Cross.

King Albert II is married to Paola Ruffo di Calabria, daughter of the Italian prince Fulco Ruffo di Calabria and Countess Louisa Gazelli. The couple met in 1958, when Albert was attending the funeral of Pope Pius XII and the coronation of Pope John XXIII in Rome. Albert and Paola were married a year later. Throughout her tenure, Queen Paola has demonstrated a keen interest in issues of social welfare in Belgium. Together the couple has three children, Crown Prince Philippe (born April 15, 1960), Princess Astrid (born June 5, 1962), and Prince Laurent (born October 19, 1963).

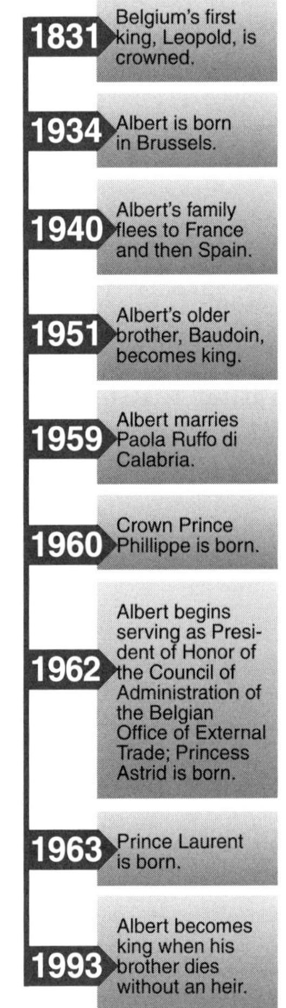

Crown Prince Philippe serves as Duke of Brabant until he is crowned king. Educated at Oxford and Stanford Universities with degrees in constitutional history and political science, he is currently a commissioned officer in the Belgian Air Force. Philippe succeeded his father as president of the Belgian Foreign Trade Office in 1993, and actively promotes international exchange in Belgium. Princess Astrid, married to the Archduke of Austria-Este and mother of four, succeeded her father as head of the Belgian Red Cross. Prince Laurent serves as a military officer.

The Belgian royal house is relatively young among European courts; Albert II is only the sixth king of Belgium. The country won its independence from the Netherlands after a Revolution in 1830. Its first king, Leopold of Saxe-Coburg, was chosen to rule under a constitution that significantly limited royal power. The country annually celebrates the crowning in 1831 of its first king, Leopold, on July 21.

Belgium is a federal parliamentary democracy under the jurisdiction of a constitutional monarch. The king appoints a prime minister, who is then approved by the Belgian Parliament. The monarch also appoints justices to the Supreme Court, where they serve for life. Finally, he serves as commander-in-chief of the Belgian armed forces, holding the rank of lieutenant general and vice admiral. The royal family hosts state visits by foreign dignitaries, and also serves as an international liaison with other governments.

King Albert II's leadership in the arenas of international business and relations has served his country well, as in recent years, Brussels has become a major European capital, hosting the headquarters for the European Community, NATO, and other international organizations. ◆

Alexander I

1777–1825 ● CZAR OF RUSSIA

The son of Czar Paul I and grandson of Catherine the Great, Alexander I was born in Saint Petersburg. He was raised in the liberal atmosphere of his grandmother's court, where he received a Western education under the tutelage of Frédéric César La Harpe, a Swiss revolutionary. This education was not in keeping with the military training usually provided to a future heir to the throne, nor were La Harpe's republican sentiments compatible with the aristocratic upbringing Alexander received from his reactionary father. Even as a youth Alexander felt torn by the conflict between his grandmother's liberalism and his father's extreme conservatism.

Alexander became czar in 1801, after his father was murdered in a coup.

Czar Paul was wary of his son's flirtations with liberalism and planned to disinherit him. His unpopular opposition to Catherine's reforms, however, soon led to his downfall and Paul was deposed and murdered in a coup of which he had prior knowledge; on March 12, 1801, Alexander became czar.

Upon assuming the throne, Alexander began a major campaign to modernize Russia along the model of post-revolutionary France. He gathered several of his friends along with his tutor, La Harpe, in a so-called Secret Committee which set lofty goals for itself, including emancipation of the serfs, the promotion of industry, and the creation of a constitutional monarchy. A constitution was written that was partially implemented but for the most part the committee was a failure and was soon abandoned. Despite his liberal leanings Alexander was an **autocrat** who envisioned himself fulfilling the role of an enlightened **despot**. He interfered in all proposed reform legislation and often imposed his reforms on a reluctant populace. La Harpe, who soon realized that he had failed to mold Alexander according to his own philosophies, left Russia and returned to Switzerland.

autocrat: a person ruling with unlimited authority.

despot: a ruler with absolute power and authority.

Upon assuming the throne Alexander proclaimed Russian neutrality in the European wars, but this, too, was short-lived. Napoleon, who had previously cited Alexander as an example of the enlightened despot he wished to emulate, threatened European stability. In 1804 Russia joined Britain, Sweden, and Austria in a coalition against France. Alexander found himself at war; his armies were unprepared and easily defeated at

Austerlitz, Eylau, and Friedland. But rather than humiliate Russia, Napoleon concluded with Alexander the Treaty of Tilsit on July 7, 1807. The treaty created an alliance between France and Russia against Britain. Alexander was now free to fulfill his own territorial ambitions. He wrested Finland from Sweden in 1809 and added the Ottoman province of Bessarabia in 1812. The next year he successfully concluded a nine-year war with Persia by annexing most of Georgia. Yet despite the military advantages offered Alexander by the treaty, the Tilsit agreement was unpopular among the people. France's isolation in Europe had been extended to Russia; trade suffered and the economy faltered. In 1812 Russia finally abrogated the treaty. The French response was immediate; on June 24 of that year Napoleon invaded Russia. The war between France and Russia was disastrous for both sides. The French made rapid advances across Russian territory and soon reached Moscow. The city was set afire and this act of barbarism so infuriated Alexander that he refused to reach any accord with Napoleon. The French were left no option but to begin a disastrous retreat; they were ill-provided for the bitter cold of a Russian winter and countless French troops died in what is considered the turning point of Napoleon's career. Although Russia had been thoroughly despoiled by the French invasion, its unwillingness to succumb to the French was considered the first great victory against Napoleon. Russia emerged from the war as the major European power at the Congress of Vienna (1814–15).

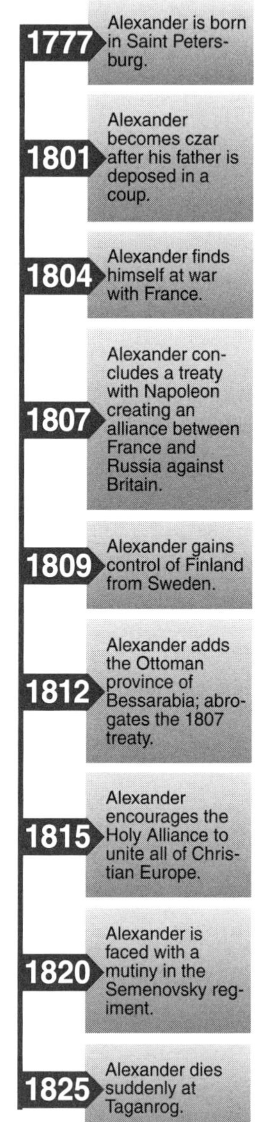

During Napoleon's Hundred Days bid to regain his empire, Russia joined the Quadruple Alliance with Austria, Britain, and Prussia. At Alexander's behest this alliance served as the nucleus of the short-lived Holy Alliance, formed on September 26, 1815, to unite all of Christian Europe.

It has been said that the flames of burning Moscow served as a spiritual inspiration for Alexander. He underwent a religious transformation in which he tried to govern Russia according to divine will. Religious figures suddenly became prominent in his administration, often to the detriment of the country.

Alexander did not fulfill any of the ambitious projects he had set for himself upon assuming the throne and his final years were spent in morose religious speculations. Nor could he find consolation in his family life. He had married the German princess Louise of Baden-Durlach when he was only sixteen years old. The Empress Yelizaveta Alekseyevna, as she came to be known, had only one child, a girl, who died in infancy. For many years Alexander carried on an affair with Maria Naryshkina; only toward the end of his life did his grief over the child's death reconcile the czar with his empress.

The final years of Alexander's reign were no less stormy than the early years. In 1820 he was faced with a mutiny in the Semenovsky regiment, the same regiment he had commanded as prince and which had carried out the coup that brought him to the throne. In 1825 Alexander received news that the Greeks had rebelled against the Ottomans. Despite the previous agreements not to interfere in the internal affairs of Europe, Alexander set out to help. On the way he died suddenly at Taganrog. His close friend and adviser Klemens Metternich remarked, "The novel is over; history begins." Alexander was succeeded by his brother Nicholas I. ◆

Alexander II

1818–1881 ● CZAR OF RUSSIA

As a boy Alexander II received the standard education accorded to a member of the royal family, studying humanities, history, statecraft, and military science. In 1841 he married the German princess Marie of Hesse-Darmstadt, who adopted the Russian name Maria Alexandrovna and bore him six sons and two daughters.

> ***"Better to abolish serfdom from above than to wait till it begins to abolish itself from below."***
> Alexander II, 1856

Alexander II succeeded his father to the throne of Russia in 1855 during the disastrous Crimean War (1854–56). Seeing the effects of the war on Russia, Alexander sued for peace after the fall of Sebastopol. Although he was a kindly and sentimental monarch Alexander had no original ideas on how to run his country, which was already showing signs of defeat on the battlefield, and often vacillated between the opinions of his various advisers. Although Alexander was a conservative he recognized the need for economic reforms in Russia so as to fully exploit the country's rich natural resources. He believed that the Crimean fiasco was symptomatic of a widespread deterioration of the economy and of the morale of the people.

On February 19, 1861, Alexander took great strides to end the morass into which Russia was sinking. He issued a proclamation ushering in the "Era of Great Reforms." His manifesto called for changes in all aspects of the Russian administration. Practices of government finance were called into question and amended and the judicial system was reorganized along the pattern of the French system. He ordered universal military training in which all members of society—nobles and peasants—underwent similar regimentation and instruction. Towns and rural districts received a degree of local autonomy allowing them to collect taxes for their own use. Progress was made in the areas of civil liberties and academic freedoms.

The most important element of Alexander's proclamation, however, was the emancipation of the serfs. Until that time approximately three-quarters of the Russian population lived as serfs, indebted to aristocratic landlords. Alexander believed that maintaining the people as serfs was actually counterproductive because all their labors benefitted others, thereby discouraging them from producing more and improving their lot. At the same time, the liberation of the serfs was a dangerous move in that it would enrage those aristocrats whose livelihood depended on retaining this system. Alexander therefore moved slowly and cautiously in his plan, first introducing committees "for improving the position of peasants" in the outlying provinces of Poland and Lithuania. As the new idea slowly took root it was expanded to include other Russian provinces and additional freedoms, eventually leading to total emancipation. Historians debate whether Alexander intended that the liberated serfs would remain dependent on the upper classes, or whether he envisioned the eventual formation of communal councils to oversee the land. Whatever his true intentions, Alexander's reforms were popular and earned him the title of Czar Liberator.

Alexander's popularity was not long-lived; both sides of the political spectrum attacked him. The reactionaries complained that he was discarding the sacred traditions of Russia and overrunning the traditional structure of a well-functioning society; the radicals and liberals protested that the long-needed reforms were too slow and insufficient. Even Alexander's entourage began criticizing him with impunity. Continued agitation by peasants and intellectuals led to further unrest. One growing movement, the Nihilists, with their total rejection of the traditional standards of Russian society, threatened to undermine the regime. Alexander became disillusioned with his earlier reforms and rejected many of them. He centered his efforts on restoring Russia's pride, which he did by a successful series of

"We thus became convinced that the problem of improving the condition of serfs was a sacred inheritance bequeathed to Us by Our predecessors, a mission which, in the course of events, Divine Providence has called upon Us to fulfill."
Alexander II, Emancipation Manifesto, March 3, 1861

conquests in the Balkans, the Caucasus, and Asia. In the Russo-Turkish War of 1877–78 he managed to regain South Bessarabia, Kars, and Ardahan, territories lost to Turkey in the Crimean War. Yet Alexander's victories were overshadowed by his disillusionment over the failure of his reforms; his disappointment developed into severe depression by 1880 and the government of the country passed into the hands of Count Mikhail T. Loris-Melikov, Alexander spent most of his time at leisure, preoccupied with a love affair with Princess Yekaterina Dolgorukaya. Following the death of the Czarina Maria Alexandrovna, Alexander married the princess in a secret ceremony.

Alexander never relinquished his dream of reforms. On March 1, 1881, he drove through the streets of Saint Petersburg on his way to grant further political concessions. A bomb was thrown at his carriage and Alexander was killed. Following the assassination, his program of reforms was rejected by Alexander III, his son and heir. As a French diplomat said at his funeral, "A liberator's is a dangerous job!" ◆

Alexander III

1845–1894 ● Czar of Russia

The attitude of Alexander's regime can be summed up in the words of one of his advisors, who referred to parliamentarianism as "the great lie of our times."

Because Alexander III was the second son of Czar Alexander II he was trained for a military rather than an imperial career. The sudden death of his older brother, Nikolay, when Alexander was twenty put Alexander into the position of heir, a role for which he was ill-prepared. He was a stocky, surly individual, not adept at statecraft or diplomacy. His disposition was further coarsened by his tutor, K. P. Pobedonostev, a fanatic Russian nationalist and reactionary. In 1866 Alexander married his brother's fiancée, Princess Dagmar of Denmark, who assumed the Russian name of Maria Fyodorovna. He became czar in 1881 following the assassination of his father.

Unlike his liberal father, who earned the title Czar Liberator for the concessions he made to the people. Alexander III followed the advice of Pobedonostev and rejected his father's reforms. The autonomy granted to the rural districts, cities, and peasant communes or *zemstvos*, was revoked. All decisions, even those affecting the appointment of provincial midwives, were placed under the direct authority of the czar. The attitude of Alexander's regime can be summed up in the words of one of his advisors, who referred to parliamentarianism as "the great lie of our times."

Alexander III was a chauvinistic Russian nationalist who sought to unify his far-flung empire through a policy of Russification. Russian was enforced as the sole language of instruction in the schools, including those in the Baltic provinces, Poland, and Finland. The Russian Orthodox Church, whose power Alexander II had reduced in the provinces, was reinstated as the sole legitimate religion. Jews in particular were singled out for harsh treatment, often despite the protests of foreign governments. Others who suffered were aristocrats in the Baltic provinces and Poland, who had earlier received a charter from Alexander II permitting them to practice their own religions. One such noble, Mikhail B. Barclay de Tolly, of Scottish descent, had his child baptized according to the Lutheran rite. When asked by Alexander how he dared baptize his children according to that rite, Barclay quoted the law of Alexander II. On the spot, Alexander rescinded the law. Despite Alexander's warnings, Barclay baptized his second child according to the Lutheran rite; he was promptly dismissed from the royal guard and army.

Alexander prided himself on being like his subjects. His behavior was often childish and boorish, showing utter disregard for the opinions of his advisers and the sentiments of his subjects. He was the object of assassination plots; for instigating one of these plots Vladimir Ilyich Lenin's elder brother, Vladimir, was hanged in 1887. At the same time, Alexander was capable of magnanimous gestures to benefit his countrymen. In one instance he provided eighteen million rubles of his own money to relieve impoverished villages. He was often surrounded by competent advisors, notably his interior minister, Count Mikhail T. Loris-Melikov, who supported the establishment of a cabinet and basic laws as a forerunner to a constitution. These ideas were quickly rejected by the czar; Loris-Melikov was replaced by Count Nikolay R. Ignatiev, a reactionary pan-Slavist.

Alexander continued the policy of Russian expansionism in Asia and the Far East but avoided major military conflicts. One of his important decisions was the abrogation of the traditional Russo-German Alliance in favor of a new Franco-Russian

Alliance, concluded on December 31, 1893. This alliance paved the way for Russian participation in World War I on the side of the Allies. Alexander died suddenly on October 20, 1894, shortly after the conclusion of the new alliance. He was succeeded by his ill-fated son, Nicholas II. ◆

Alexander the Great

356–323 B.C.E. ● MACEDONIAN EMPEROR

His great reputation is based on his military genius, his remarkable conquests of the East, and his zeal to promote Hellenism in the lands that he conquered. He was the son of Philip II of Macedonia and Olympias of Epirus. When he was thirteen his father engaged Aristotle to tutor him in poetry, drama, and politics; the scholar gave Alexander a thorough education, also stimulating his interest in science, medi-

Alexander the Great appears in profile on an ancient Greek coin.

cine, and philosophy. There was some friction between Alexander and his father as the latter's various marriages left the question of Alexander's succession to the throne uncertain. When Philip was murdered in 336 B.C.E., Alexander, not yet twenty, wasted no time ascending the throne and executing his rivals.

From his father Alexander inherited an excellent army and a war against Persia. He went immediately to Thessaly, where partisans of independence had gained ascendancy, and reestablished Macedonian control of Greece. Then, having had himself elected general of all the Greeks in the campaign against Persia, he moved quickly to counter the defecting Thracians and en route back to Greece crushed the threatening Illyrians. Finally he hastened back to Thebes, which had revolted in his absence. There he set an example which brought the other Greek states into abject submission by destroying the city and selling its citizens into slavery.

In the spring of 334 B.C.E. Alexander resumed the battle against Persia. He set out with an army of forty thousand Greek and Macedonian troops and crossed the Hellespont. At the Granicus river, near Troy, he achieved a brilliant victory against a large army of Persians and Greek mercenaries and turned to a now-submissive Asia Minor while Darius II of Persia advanced into Syria. Alexander won a historic victory against him at Issus in November 333 B.C.E. and, rejecting the Persian king's peace offers, turned toward Phoenicia. He defeated and destroyed Tyre, then went on to Palestine and besieged Gaza. Next came his conquest of Egypt and the foundation of the new city of Alexandria, which was to become the literary, scientific, and commercial center of the Greek world. In Egypt he went to the Oasis of Siwa to consult the oracle of Ammon, god of the sun, and was hailed there by the high priests as the son of Ammon—a title usually accorded to pharoahs—which confirmed his belief in his divine origin.

Darius had meanwhile reorganized his forces but Alexander won another victory against him at the battle of Guagamela in October 331 B.C.E. After securing the Iranian city of Susa with its store of treasures, he completed his destruction of the Persian empire after a mere three years of warfare by making his way to Persepolis, the Persian capital; there he plundered the royal treasury and burned the city.

As the Persian empire had once included part of western India, Alexander crossed the Indus River in 326 B.C.E. and marched through the Punjab, but his army refused to continue advancing indefinitely. Alexander told them, "Go home and tell them that you left Alexander the Great to conquer the world alone." However, only a quarter of his original army returned with him to Persia. The return to Greece, by sea to the Persian Gulf and overland across the desert, was fraught with difficulties.

His reign after his return was increasingly autocratic and execution for misconduct was not uncommon. He also incurred Macedonian disfavor by attempting to enforce a policy of cooperation with the Iranians, adopting Persian ceremonial at court, himself marrying the daughter of Darius, and encouraging his soldiers to take Iranian wives. The Macedonians finally rebelled when he tried to incorporate Iranians into the army, but a reconciliation was reached at Opis in the summer of 324 B.C.E.

In Egypt, Alexander the Great went to the Oasis of Siwa to consult the oracle of Ammon, god of the sun, and was hailed there by the high priestess as the son of Ammon.

After a year spent organizing and surveying his empire, Alexander spent his final months planning further conquests and expeditions. He died in Babylon of a severe attack of fever and was buried in Alexandria, leaving his empire "to the strongest." Having failed to appoint a capable successor, however, he contributed to the breakup of the empire he had so brilliantly consolidated.

An excellent soldier and military strategist, Alexander was flexible and resilient and won his soldiers' devotion by leading them into battle and often incurring injuries in the process. His conquests inaugurated a new period in history by extending the influence of Greek civilization and opening the doors to Greek traders and settlers who followed in the wake of his army, often settling in one of a number of "Alexandrias" he had founded along his march. Not surprisingly, legends about him abounded and a romance of which he was hero appeared in Egypt c.200 C.E. and became widely popular in the Middle Ages in western European languages.◆

Alfred

849–899 ● KING OF THE WEST SAXONS

The youngest of the five sons of Aethelwulf, Alfred was crowned in 871 on the death of his brother Aethelred. He came to the throne in the midst of a Danish invasion. Although he defeated the Danes at Ashdown in 871 and prevented their invasion of Wessex, they attacked again in 875 and 878 and this time encountered no effective resistance. His country overrun, Alfred retreated to Atheleny in the marches of Somerset and reassembled his army. In 878 he defeated the Danes at Edington, in Wiltshire. The country was now split into two: a Danish part, northwest of the London-Chester road, and the Anglo-Saxon part dominated by Wessex. In 886 he conquered London and with the submission of Northumbria, he ruled all England. In the years of peace that followed Alfred devoted himself to his kingdom. He strengthened his fortifications and his navy and enforced compulsory military service—measures which proved invaluable when the Danes returned in 893 and were forced to withdraw after four years of battle.

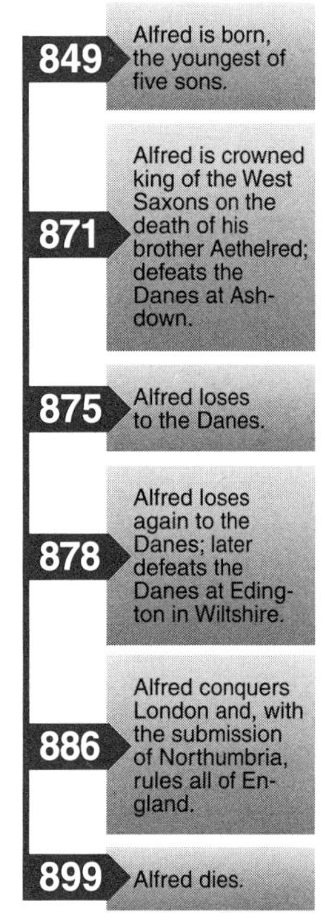

Alfred's successful resistance to the Danes marked him as the first Anglo-Saxon leader to repel Scandinavian invasions in England and although he did not succeed in freeing all the territories from Danish rule, he laid the foundations for the unification of England. During periods of peace, brief though they were, he was also notable for codifying the law, establishing unity, and reforming the administration of the kingdom by extending and consolidating the shire system of local government.

Alfred also contributed greatly to the education of his people by encouraging the monasteries as centers of learning and establishing a school for nobles in his own court. Himself a talented writer, he translated several works and encouraged the translation of all philosophical and theological works from Latin into Anglo-Saxon, thus promoting the development of Anglo-Saxon into a literary language. ◆

Amanollah Khan

1892–1960 ● KING OF AFGHANISTAN

Amanollah (also called Amanullah Barakzai) launched a *jihad* (holy war) against Great Britain and declared Afghanistan's independence from Britain in 1919. He

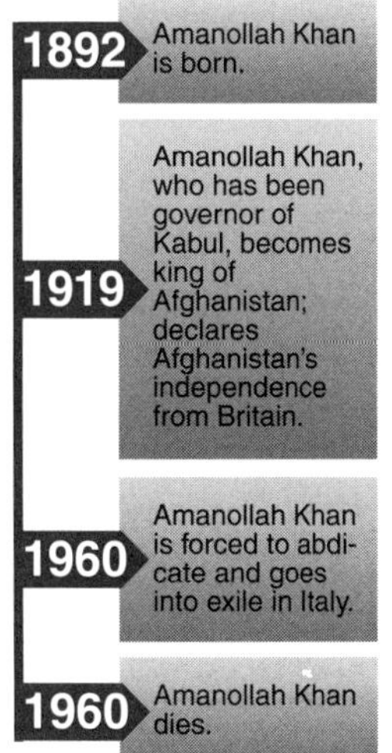

embarked on an ambitious program of modernization, introducing secular reforms and education.

He was the third son of Habibollah Khan (r. 1901–19), who was assassinated. Amanollah, then governor of Kabul, convinced the army and power elite to prefer his claim to the throne over that of his brothers and uncle. In May 1919 he went to war against the British administration and at the end of a one-month campaign, was able to negotiate control of his country's foreign policy (which his grandfather Abd al-Rahman Khan had surrendered). He welcomed recognition of his regime by the then new and revolutionary government of the Soviet Union; however, he soon turned to countries without territorial designs on Central Asia, establishing ties with France, Germany, Italy, Japan, and the Ottoman empire. He failed to initiate official relations with the United States.

Advised by Ottoman-educated Afghans and impressed by Ottoman Turkey's example, Amanollah embarked on his own scheme of development. First he promulgated a constitution and convened three *loya jirga* (grand assemblies, composed of various segments of the power elite) to ratify his important decisions. Second, he systematized the administrative divisions of the country into a territorial hierarchy of subdistricts, districts, and provinces. The centrally appointed administrators at each level were assisted by a locally elected consultative body. Third, he replaced iltizam (tax farming) with directly collected taxes in cash. Fourth, he tolerated a free press, entrusted the intelligentsia with responsible positions in the government, and spent a major portion of the revenue of the state on the expansion of education.

These reforms proved to be enduring. However, he alienated his subjects with more symbolic policies such as the mandatory unveiling of Afghan women and the imposition of European attire on civil servants and schoolchildren. Simultaneously, he canceled the monetary and symbolic **sinecures** enjoyed by the leaders of the clans and the headmen of villages. Furthermore, his new tax policies weighed heavily on agricultural producers and were unpopular in the countryside. Opposition was organized under the symbolic defense of the values of Islam and spearheaded by leaders of the religious establishment. Leaders of clans and social bandits also played an important role. He might have overcome the challenge had he paid more attention to his army—but he had neglected its welfare and was

sinecure: a position that requires little or no work and usually provides an income.

unable to prevent soldiers from joining the several revolts that broke out simultaneously in 1928. He was forced to abdicate in May of 1929 and went into exile in Italy. ◆

Amenhotep III

1417–1379 B.C.E. ● PHARAOH OF EGYPT

Amenhotep, son of Thutmose IV, was one of the great builders and reformers of the Egyptian Eighteenth Dynasty. His full regal name was Amun-Hotpehek-Wase. There is some speculation that Amenhotep's mother was not an Egyptian but a Mittani princess. This would have been extraordinary for the time, given the **insular** attitudes of the Egyptian ruling classes. It is known that his wife, Tiy, was a commoner, another break from tradition for a dynasty whose kings regularly married their sisters so as not to contaminate the royal stock.

insular: reflecting a narrow, provincial viewpoint.

While still a youth, Amenhotep was placed under the tutelage of Yuya, master of the horse. Not only did Yuya teach the prince the art of war, he inflamed his passion for the hunt. One legend reports that while still a young child, Amenhotep succeeded in capturing a large herd of wild cattle.

It is known that Amenhotep's wife was a commoner, which was a break from tradition for a dynasty whose kings regularly married their sisters so as not to contaminate the royal stock.

After acceding to the throne Amenhotep turned his attention to advancing Egyptian prestige among neighboring states. The Amarna tablets tell of embassies established and trade being carried on with the other powers of the time, notably Assyria, Babylonia, the Hittites, and the Mittani. Much of the wealth garnered by Amenhotep went to embellish his capital, Thebes.

His royal complex of palaces and harems encompassed eighty acres. In addition, he had constructed for Tiy a huge artificial lake measuring thirty-seven hundred by seven hundred cubits. The vast temples of Karnak and Luxor are also credited to Amenhotep.

His tranquil reign and the extensive trade carried out in his name transformed Thebes into a thriving cosmopolitan city. This spurred dissatisfaction among many of the nobles and priests, who regarded an isolated Egypt as indispensable to their own interests.

Pyramids at Giza

The three largest pyramids of ancient Egypt, built during the 2500s B.C.E. as royal tombs for Fourth Dynasty pharaohs, still stand on the west bank of the Nile River at Giza, near Cairo. The northernmost, oldest, and largest of the three pyramids was built for Khufu (Cheops in Greek). Called the Great Pyramid, Khufu's tomb is 755 feet in length at the base of each of its four sides and covers almost 13 acres. The sides are aligned correctly with the four compass points. Before the Great Pyramid lost its original limestone casing, it was 481 feet tall; today it stands at 451 feet. The pyramid was built of some 2.3 million limestone blocks, which weigh an average of about 2.5 tons. According to the ancient Greek historian Herodotus, the Great Pyramid was built by 100,000 laborers over 20 years. The middle pyramid was built for Khafre (Chefren in Greek). It is about 708 feet on each side and was originally 471 feet high. The southernmost pyramid, and the last to be erected, was that of Menkaure (Mycerinus in Greek). The smallest of the three, it measures 356 feet per side with an original height of 218 feet.

Amenhotep ruled Egypt for thirty-eight years. Contemporary portraits from the final years of his reign show him to be ailing. Some scholars have suggested that his son and heir, Akhenaton, ruled jointly with his father in the last years of his reign. Upon his death Amenhotep was buried in the funerary temple he had already prepared for himself. Although the temple was the largest of its kind, all that remains of it today are enormous statues, the Colossi of Memnon. ◆

Arthur

SIXTH CENTURY ● KING OF THE BRITONS

Arthur is traditionally known as a sixth-century king of the Britons. Discussion of the origins of Arthur is of long standing. He is the hero or, later, the central figure of a large body of literature in most western European languages but most especially in the medieval forms of French, German, English, and Welsh. He is consistently portrayed as a British ruler, and there is no doubt that his origins are to be sought in early Welsh sources and to a lesser extent in Breton and Cornish literature.

The evidence for Arthur's historical existence is meager and difficult to evaluate. Chapter 56 of the ninth-century *Historia Brittonum (The History of the Britons)*, usually attributed to eighth-century historian "Nennius," places him in the context of the first period of the attacks on Britain by the Germanic invaders, in the second half of the fifth century, and lists twelve of his famous victories. The chronicle now known as *Annales Cambriae (The Annals of Wales)* notes under the year 518 the Battle of Badon as an Arthurian victory, probably the same as that which closes the Nennian list, and under 539 the Battle of Camlan, in which Arthur and Medrawd fell. (Medrawd, also called Mordred, is Arthur's rebellious nephew, whose abduction of Queen Guenevere led to the catastrophic final Battle of Camlan.) The Nennian notes and the chronicle entries probably derive from the same northern British source of the eighth century and are the earliest testimony to a historical

Camelot

According to medieval folklore and literature, the court of King Arthur, a Celtic ruler in sixth-century Britain, was located in Camelot. From that base, Arthur and his Knights of the Round Table reputedly led the struggle to defend England against Saxon invaders. Whether a real Camelot existed is uncertain, although some amateur archaeologists claim to have found its location not far from London.

Whether real or not, Camelot became an enduring symbol of virtue and nobility. During the Middle Ages, King Arthur and his Knights of the Round Table were held up as flawless practitioners of the medieval ideals of chivalry and courtly love. The ideals of Camelot have been perpetuated in the modern world, notably in Alfred Lord Tennyson's long narrative poem *Idylls of the King* (written between 1859 and 1885), and the opera *Parsifal* (1882), by Richard Wagner. In the twentieth century, the story of Camelot has been retold in T. H. White's novel *The Once and Future King* (1958) and in Alan Jay Lerner and Frederick Loewe's Broadway musical *Camelot* (1960). After the assassination of President John F. Kennedy in 1963, many of his admirers came to regard his White House as a modern-day Camelot, characterized by what was perceived as the charm, grace, intelligence, and wit of the president and his wife, Jacqueline, and by Kennedy's defense of freedom abroad. The incorporation of the Kennedy administration into the Camelot legacy demonstrates the latter's durability and adaptability to changing times.

Arthur. The places referred to in the list of battles cannot be securely located, and not all are to be associated with Arthur; but the list probably represents the remnant of a pre–ninth-century Welsh poem that contained a catalog of some of Arthur's traditional victories. Together with a **eulogistic** reference to Arthur in another Welsh poem, *Gododdin*, from northern Britain, these early allusions suggest the development of a fifth-century British leader into a popular heroic figure celebrated in song. (The *Gododdin* reference cannot be dated more accurately than to the sixth to ninth century.) The British author Gildas, however, writing about 540, does not name Arthur, although he celebrates the Battle of Badon; nor do other major historical sources, such as *The Anglo-Saxon Chronicle* or eighth-century British historian Bede, refer to him, so that some doubt as to King Arthur's historical existence must remain.

eulogistic: commendatory; praising.

Stories of Arthur, like many other northern British heroic legends, were relocated in early medieval Wales and achieved great popularity even before the arrival of the Normans in the eleventh century opened the way for this material to become a major component in the **chivalric** literatures of western Europe. Welsh poems from before 1100, stories in the *Historia Britonum*,

chivalric: relating to medieval knighthood.

and material in some saints' lives of the eleventh and twelfth centuries all testify to a variety of tales being told about Arthur and to the fact that the hero was beginning to attract to himself legends and heroes from other cycles. In Nennius's work Arthur and his dog Cabal hunt the boar Porcum Troit, a story more fully developed in the eleventh-century Welsh tale *Culhwch and Olwen*, and stories of Arthur in this latter source have already become associated with topographical features. Poems in the *Black Book of Carmarthen* and the *Book of Taliesin*, both from the thirteenth century, portray Arthur as the leader of a band of renowned warriors, Cei and Bedwyr foremost among them, who fight with monsters, hags, and giants and who carry out a disastrous expedition against the otherworld to free a prisoner. The twelfth-century *Life of Saint Gildas* contains the story of the abduction of Arthur's wife by Melwas and her imprisonment in the Glass Island. These are the elements, together with some personal names, that seem to represent the earliest stratum of the Arthurian legend and that reappear in contemporary terms throughout its later forms.

There is more than one tradition of Arthur's end besides that of his death at Camlan. One that is attested early is his removal to the Isle of Avalon to be healed of his wounds and to await the call to return. At the end of the twelfth century the monks of Glastonbury claimed to have discovered the graves of Arthur and his wife at their abbey, but this seems never to have found popular acceptance. Arthur's role as the awaited hero remained a political force throughout the Middle Ages among the Celtic peoples of Wales, Cornwall, and Brittany. The later stages of his legend as the chivalrous king who was head of Camelot and the Round Table and instigator of the search for the Holy Grail belong to the realm of literary history. ◆

> ***"Yet some men say in many parts of England that King Arthur is not dead, but had by the will of our Lord Jesu into another place; and men say that he shall come again, and he shall win the holy cross. I will not say it shall be so, but rather I will say: here in this world he changed his life."***
>
> Thomas Malory, *Le Morte d'Arthur*, c. 1470

Asoka

C.273–232 B.C.E. ● EMPEROR OF INDIA

Asoka was one of the hundred sons of Bindusura and the grandson of Chandragupta, the first Mauryan emperor of northern India. Asoka was serving as viceroy of Ujjain in Malwa at his father's death. Bindusura's death prompted a bloody war of succession; Asoka was the only son to survive. Some historians choose to point to contemporary records in which Asoka shows his concern for his brothers and sisters as discrediting the legend. There was, however, an unexplained four-year gap between his father's death and his own coronation.

Little information is available on the early years of Asoka's forty-year reign. Some thirteen years after his accession Asoka attacked Kalinga near the Bay of Bengal in an attempt to expand his realm. Despite his military victory Asoka was appalled by the carnage of war. There were 100,000 casualties and 150,000 prisoners were taken; millions more may have died from famine and disease. The sight prompted a radical transformation in Asoka. Whereas he had previously enjoyed the life of a royal prince, the memory of Kalinga inspired him to adopt the philosophy of *ahimsa*, or noninjury of living things. Asoka abandoned the hunt and became a vegetarian. He provided for his subjects by planting trees, digging wells, and building hospitals and began exporting medicinal herbs to many of the neighboring states.

"Beloved-of-the-Gods, King Piyadasi, speaks thus: To do good is difficult. One who does good first does something hard to do. I have done many good deeds, and, if my sons, grandsons and their descendants up to the end of the world act in like manner, they too will do much good. But whoever amongst them neglects this, they will do evil. Truly, it is easy to do evil."

From the Fifth Edict of Asoka

Asoka adopted the *dharma*, Buddhist laws encouraging respect for one's parents and teachers, charity, honesty, moderation, and tolerance of all people. He exhorted his officials to treat his subjects as if they were his own children. Although Asoka's empire was the largest that the dynasty would know, he abandoned military conquests, preferring to send missionaries abroad in a program he referred to as "conquest through faith." (He did not, however, disband the army, nor did he abolish capital punishment.) Asoka's missionaries reached as far as Greece in Europe, Egypt in Africa, and Burma and Ceylon in Asia.

In his own realm Asoka established a group of educators, the *dharma-mahamatras*, who roamed the country preaching the teachings of the Buddha. He is said to have built 8,400 temples, some of which can still be seen. Perhaps his greatest achievement was carving the teachings, called edicts, of the *dharma* on countless cave walls and pillars throughout the kingdom. These records provide historians with a thorough understanding of Asoka's reign. They are highly ornate monuments, polished by a technique that has yet to be reproduced, written in both Pali and local languages. The writings designate Asoka as *Devanampiya* (Beloved of God) and *Piyadashi* (One concerned about the welfare of his subjects).

Little is known about Asoka's personal life. He was apparently **polygamous** but only one wife, Kalivaki, is known. Two of his children, a son, Mahendra and a daughter, Sanghamitra, may have been missionaries in Ceylon. Asoka was not succeeded by his oldest son, Tivara; however, two grandsons,

polygamous: having more than one mate at a time.

Dasaratha and Samprati, divided the empire after Asoka's death. They were unable to consolidate their power and within fifty years the Mauryan empire had crumbled.

Some scholars are skeptical as to whether Asoka actually embraced Buddhism. Although he adhered to the *dharma*, there is no record of other important Buddhist principles, such as the Four Noble Truths and the Eightfold Way, being promoted during his reign, while the principles of *dharma* and *ahimsa* are common to Buddhists, Jains, and Hindus. These scholars claim that Asoka was actually the founder of a new universal faith combining the pacifist principles common to all Indian religions. Some legends contradict this claim, telling that Asoka spent his final years attempting to prevent schisms developing in Buddhism. ◆

"Whoever praises his own religion, due to excessive devotion, and condemns others with the thought 'Let me glorify my own religion,' only harms his own religion."
From the Twelfth Edict of Asoka

Atahualpa

C.1498–1533 ● INCA RULER

Atahualpa was Inca ruler at the time of the Spanish Conquest of Peru in the 1530s. Little accurate information exists about the life of Atahualpa—even his date and place of birth are uncertain. Some suggest that he was born in the imperial center of Cuzco, others that he was from Tomebamba (present-day Cuenca, Ecuador). His father was Huayna Capac, the last undisputed ruler of Tahuan-Tinsuyu, the Inca empire; his mother was a favorite secondary wife from the north. Huayna Capac died unexpectedly from smallpox that swept into the Andes ahead of the Spanish.

The Andean practice of succession was not based on primogeniture; any male child from the principal or any of the secondary wives could become *último* Inca (ruler). The division of Cuzco into separate halves (*hanan* and *urinsaya*) with a divided government and the importance of the cults of the lineages (*panacas*) of previous Inca rulers complicated the question of

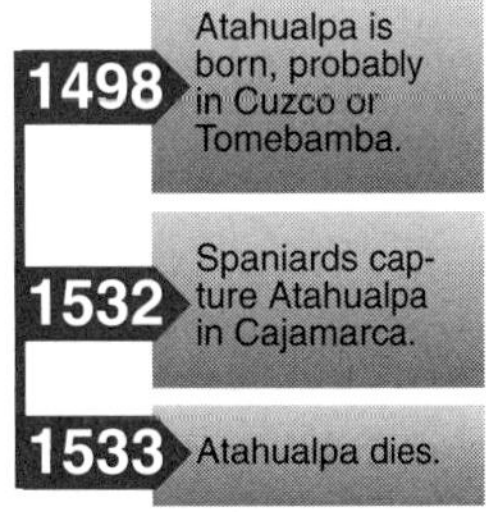

succession. As he lay dying, Huayna Capac was repeatedly asked by elder advisers about the succession. It seems he favored his youngest child, Ninan Cuyochi, who, unfortunately, also contracted smallpox and died. Huayna Capac's second choice was probably Huascar, his son with Ragua Ocllo. Initially the Cuzco religious and political elite supported Huascar. Indeed, the Cuzco leadership proclaimed him heir after Huayna Capac's death. But as Huayna Capac shifted into and out of a coma in his last hours, he also named Atahualpa, a favorite from the north, who had promising military potential. Atahualpa, with the support of great military commanders, moved southward in an attempt to secure control of Tahuantinsuyu. Victorious, Atahualpa's forces captured Huascar outside Cuzco and imprisoned him. General Quizquiz went into Cuzco, attempting to obliterate completely the Huascar faction.

Such was the political scene in the realm when the handful of Spaniards under Francisco Pizarro arrived on their third expedition of 1531. Atahualpa had left commander Rumiñavi in charge of Quito and Chalicuchima in control of the central Andes while he, along with a few thousand troops, traveled to the city of Cajamarca in northern Peru to rest and enjoy the thermal baths nearby. There he was captured by the Spanish on November 16, 1532. After realizing the European thirst for gold, Atahualpa offered, as ransom, to fill a room with gold, and twice with silver within two months. Pizarro and the other Europeans were astounded, as shipments slowly began to make their way into Cajamarca from throughout the realm. With the completion of the ransom (a total of about 13,420 pounds of 22½-carat gold and 26,000 pounds of good silver), the quandary of what to do with the Inca ruler increased. Atahualpa began to mistrust the promise of release and had probably ordered his commanders Rumiñavi and Chalicuchima to move toward Cajamarca. But the Spanish convinced Chalicuchima to enter Cajamarca where they took him prisoner.

Atahualpa offered to fill a room with gold and twice with silver within two months as ransom to his Spanish captors.

Ultimately, a group that included royal officials and the recently arrived Diego de Almagro persuaded Pizarro that it was dangerous to keep the Inca captive and that he should be executed. The principal Atahualpa defenders, Hernando de Soto and Hernando Pizarro, were away at the time the mock trial took place. Atahualpa was charged with ordering while in jail the execution of his half brother and preparing a surprise attack against the Spaniards, charges for which he was found guilty and sentenced to die at the stake. Friar Vicente de

Valverde succeeded in converting Atahualpa to Christianity, and therefore the Inca was garroted instead of burned. In later years myths evolved that he would return and usher in a new age during which the yoke of the invaders would be overthrown. ◆

Attila the Hun

c.406–453 ● Ruler of the Huns

In 433 Attila succeeded his uncle Rua as king of the Huns, a Mongol tribe from Asia that had slowly migrated westward, driven to leave by exhausted soil and their own enemies. Living off cattle and war, they had subjugated some of the German tribes while other tribes, fleeing them, had been driven to seek sanctuary within the Roman Empire which they later subdued. Rua left his kingdom, which at the time of his death extended from the Don River to the Rhine, to his two nephews, Bleda and Attila.

History does not provide accurate information about Attila. The Roman historians of the day were so twisted by hatred of what he had already done and fear of what he might do that they seem to be describing a demon rather than a human being. Attila's use of psychological warfare—such as using exaggerated reports of his cruelty to immobilize his enemies with terror or encourage them to surrender—may have contributed to this hatred.

Roman historians during Attila's time were so twisted by hatred of what he had already done and fear of what he might do that they seem to be describing a demon rather than a human being.

Attila was illiterate but extremely intelligent, his conquests depending more on cunning than force, and he ruled his people by playing on their superstitions. He was not the savage that his Roman opponents termed him, often showing more honor, justice, and mercy than they did. He lived simply, ate and drank moderately, and had many wives, but did not indulge in Roman-style debauchery.

The first eight years of Bleda and Attila's reign were mostly spent warring with other barbarian tribes, which gave the Huns control in Central Europe. Bleda's ambitions and role in these conquests are unknown. Attila wanted to rule all of Europe and the Near East. Both the Eastern and Western Empires paid him

a yearly tribute, protection money against his depredations, saving face by claiming it was payment for services rendered. In 441 his troops defeated Constantinople's army, threatening Constantinople itself until the Eastern emperor promised to triple his yearly tribute.

The decaying, decadent Rome of Attila's day was a tempting target. The shrinking native population left rich farmland uncultivated while the wealth accumulated from centuries of conquest and exploitation created a high standard of living attractive to barbarians seeking new land to accommodate their expanding population. The empire's contracting borders meant that it no longer had access to the raw materials, particularly grain, on which it was dependent, and it no longer had dependable markets for its goods. Barbarians who had been settling along the frontiers for centuries, immigrating individually or by official invitation of the emperor, had become Romanized. The German tribes outside the empire were primarily Christian and, after five centuries of contact with Rome, also aspired to the acquisition of Roman culture. Rome's army and administration were mostly in German hands. Assassination had become the most common way for emperors to gain power.

Attila became the most powerful man in Europe when Bleda was murdered in 444 (rumor had it that Attila was responsible for Bleda's death). His conquests continued and in 447 the Huns invaded the Balkans, sacking towns and enslaving thousands. They wreaked such devastation that the Balkans were ruined for centuries and the Danube ceased to be the main route for East-West trade, to the detriment of the cities along its banks.

The two Roman emperors, Theodosius II and Valentinian III refused to continue to pay Attila tribute and Attila seized the pretext offered to him by Honoria, Valentinian's sister, to attack. Banished to Constantinople after her seduction by a **chamberlain**, Honoria sent a ring to Attila with an appeal for help. Attila promptly declared that the ring was a proposal of marriage entitling him to both Honoria and a dowry of half of Europe. When this demand was refused, he declared war. In 451 he joined forces with the Franks and the Vandals and marched into Gaul, sacking, burning, massacring, and striking terror into the hearts of its inhabitants. It took the combined might of the Visigoths and Rome in the Battle of the Catalaunian Plains, one of the bloodiest battles of history to secure an indecisive

chamberlain: an attendant on a sovereign or lord in his bedchamber.

victory for Rome. The Roman forces were too exhausted and divided to go after Attila when he retreated.

In 452 Attila invaded Italy itself, destroying and looting. Attila could have reached Rome virtually without opposition—the road was open before him—but his army was suffering from plague and food shortages. He had a conference with an imperial delegation consisting of Pope Leo I and two senators. Exactly what happened at that conference is unknown, but Pope Leo took credit for Attila's immediate retreat. Attila left, threatening to return in the spring if his demands for Honoria were not met. While waiting for the bride who would bring him half an empire, Attila celebrated his marriage with another young woman, Ildico. He put aside his usual restraint and drank and feasted. He then died during the night of a burst blood vessel, choking on his own blood. Chaucer recalled the event in *The Canterbury Tales*, "Looke, Attila, the gret conquerer . . . / Deyde in his sleep, with shame and dishonor, / Bledynge ay at his nose in dronkenese."

Attila could have reached Rome virtually without opposition—the road was open before him—but his army was suffering from plague and food shortages.

His kingdom was divided among his sons but they were unable to maintain control of their subject peoples because of jealousies and conflicts among themselves. They eventually succeeded where the two Roman Empires had failed: they destroyed Attila's empire. ◆

Augustus

63 B.C.E.–14 C.E. ● FIRST ROMAN EMPEROR

Augustus's mother was the daughter of Julia, Julius Caesar's sister. Upon his father's death in 59 B.C.E. Augustus was adopted by Julius Caesar; though originally named Gaius Octavius, he received the name Gaius Julius Caesar Octavianus after Caesar's death.

"I found Rome a city of bricks and left it a city of marble."
Augustus Caesar, reported by Seutonius

The news of Caesar's death and of being designated the main heir in Caesar's will reached Augustus while he was studying in Apollonia. He was only nineteen when Caesar was murdered but determined to avenge the death and secure his own political position. His rival Mark Anthony was defeated in a campaign at Mutina and Augustus won popular support by paying the legacy promised the people in Caesar's will out of his own pocket when Mark Anthony refused to surrender Caesar's property or pay the legacy.

In 43 B.C.E. Augustus made peace with Anthony and a triumvirate was formed between them and the Roman general Lepidus. They signed an agreement whereby each swore to give up in death any friend who was demanded as a victim by the others; this pact led to the deaths of 300 senators and 2,000 knights. Cicero, for whom Anthony had a personal hatred, was not spared.

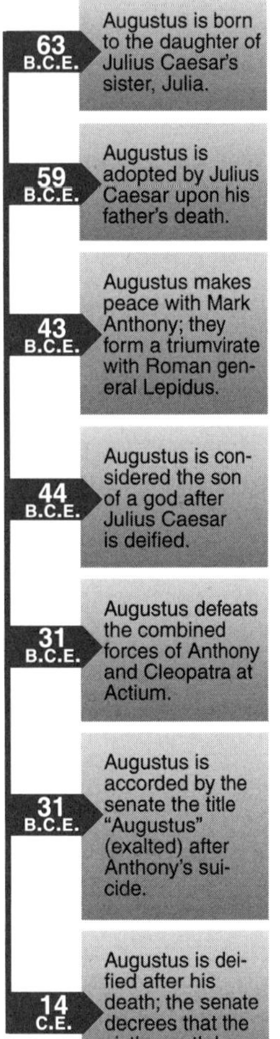

The following year Caesar was officially deified and Augustus was regarded as a god's son. That year, too, the triumvirate defeated the forces of Marcus Junius, Brutus, and Gaius Cassius at Philippi. Their victory consolidated their control of the Roman world, which they proceeded to divide up among themselves, according the west to Augustus, the east to Anthony, and Africa to Lepidus. Lepidus was soon deposed and the empire redivided among the two others (Anthony by now had married Augustus's sister). While Anthony alienated the Romans by his fondness for things Egyptian, among them Cleopatra, Augustus made himself popular among the people and aristocracy of Italy by his temperance, adherence to Roman ideals, generosity in the realm of public building, and the opportunities he offered for advancement. Under the pretext of attacking Cleopatra he instigated a propaganda war against Antony; one ploy was the publication of Anthony's will, which left inheritances to Cleopatra's children and requested burial in Alexandria. In 31 B.C.E. he defeated the combined forces of Anthony and Cleopatra at Actium; with Anthony's suicide, he became the sole master of the Roman world and was accorded by the senate the divine title of "Augustus" (exalted).

Although the peace he had achieved was preserved within the empire, Augustus did successfully wage war against Africa, Asia, Gaul, Spain, and Dalmatia. Within the empire he sought to resolve various problems of society and state. He hoped to achieve a revival of Roman morals through the encouragement of marriage, an increasing birthrate, and a reduction in luxury. Laws were passed to diminish slavery and improve the position of freed slaves. For administrative purposes, the country was organized into *regiones;* military reforms were also implemented. Thus he achieved the so-called *pax Augusta* for his empire, fostering the internal peace, law, and security which brought prosperity to his citizens.

Augustus was a patron of the arts and a friend of Ovid, Horace, Vergil, and Livy; the Augustan age was known as one of literary and artistic triumphs.

Although married three times, he had no heir and thus reluctantly left the throne to his stepson Tiberius. After his death he was deified. By a decree of the senate the sixth month was named Augustus (today August) in his honor. ◆

Bajazet (Bayezid) II

C.1447–1512 ● OTTOMAN EMPEROR

The elder son of Emperor Mehmed II, Bajazet was noted for his consolidation of Ottoman power and his infamous law whereby, upon assuming the throne, the new emperor was to dispose of his brothers and their children so as to insure an unsullied reign. Although Mehmed did not appoint a successor, it was assumed he favored his younger son, Jem, over Bajazet. Both filled administrative positions as provincial governors but Bajazet was an intellectual who avoided combat in favor of academic pursuits; Jem was more inclined to war. Mehmed's grand **vizier** endorsed Jem's claim to the throne, but Bajazet, who had forged matrimonial ties with leading **janissaries**, received their support and assumed the throne.

vizier: a high executive officer of the Ottoman empire.

janissaries: soldiers in an elite corps of Turkish troops organized in the 14th century and abolished in 1826.

In the ensuing civil war Jem declared himself emperor at Bursa, but his reign lasted only eighteen days. Bajazet proved himself a capable military commander and Jem was forced to flee. He did not want to kill his brother, but Bajazet rejected Jem's proposal that the empire be partitioned between them. Bajazet suggested that Jem live in retirement in Jerusalem. Jem waived Bajazet's offer and sought sanctuary with the Knights Hospitalers stationed to the island of Rhodes.

Until his sudden death in 1495, Jem remained a threat to Bajazet. Both the pope and France saw in Jem an ally to lead

them in a successful crusade to regain Jerusalem. Although nothing came of these plans, Bajazet remained alert to the impending threat and did little to consolidate his father's conquests, refusing to lead his armies to a distance where his authority could be challenged (in fact, Bajazet was the first Ottoman emperor not to lead his armies into battle). Nonetheless, he succeeded in subduing Bosnia (1483) and extended his authority to the banks of the Dniester (1484) and from there to Crimea. A truce was signed with King Matthias Corvinus of Hungary, securing his northern European boundary.

Much of Bajazet's reign was spent improving the economic situation of the empire, ailing as a result of his father's policies. He put an end to the devaluation of the currency and restored private lands that had been confiscated. When King Ferdinand and Queen Isabella of Spain expelled their Jewish community in 1492, Bajazet welcomed the refugees to Turkey, recognizing them as the nucleus of a much-needed middle class.

Bajazet's reign witnessed the rise in Safavid Persia of the mystical Muslims, the Sufis; many of the Turcoman tribesmen in Anatolia were influenced by this movement. Known as the Kizil Besh (red hats), they threatened both the Ottoman and Mameluke empires, leading Bajazet to make border concessions to the Mamelukes in Syria to rid himself of these tribesmen.

Only after Jem's death was Bajazet able to focus his attention on the empire's principal rival, Venice. The Turkish navy was expanded, and Bajazet gained control of the eastern Adriatic coast, conquering Lepanto, Modon, Coron, and Navarino. Peace was signed with Venice in 1503, but Venice was never able to regain its former glory because the vast Ottoman navy now controlled the Mediterranean basin.

In his final years, Bajazet sought to defeat the Safavids. At the time he favored his son Ahmed, who shared his temperament, as his successor, but when Ahmed adopted the practices of the Kizil Besh, Bajazet was forced to recognize his headstrong son Selim as heir. Before the war with the Safavids was concluded, Selim deposed his father and exiled him to Demotika. Bajazet died en route; it is supposed that Selim had him poisoned. His legacy to Selim was a mobile army and a dominant navy. ◆

Beatrix

1938– ● QUEEN OF THE NETHERLANDS

For more than a century, women have reigned in the Kingdom of the Netherlands. After the abdication of her mother, Queen Juliana, on April 30, 1980, Princess Beatrix Wilhelmina Armgard was crowned as the fourth female monarch in a row to rule Holland. Her domain comprises the twelve provinces of the Netherlands, as well as the Caribbean islands of Aruba and the Netherlands Antilles (consisting of Bonaire, Curaçao, Saba, St. Eustatius, and St. Maarten).

Born on January 31, 1938, at Soestdijk Palace in Baarn, Queen Beatrix was the first child of Queen (then Princess) Juliana and Prince Bernhard. From 1940 to 1945, while the Netherlands was occupied by German troops, the royal family lived in exile in the United Kingdom and in Ottowa, Canada. During this difficult period, two sisters were born, Princesses Irene (born 1939) and Margriet (born in Canada in 1943).

Queen Beatrix was educated in the Netherlands, earning a law degree from Leiden University in 1961. There she studied subjects appropriate for a head of state, including politics, history, languages, international affairs, and economics.

On March 10, 1966, Princess Beatrix married the German diplomat Claus von Amsberg. From 1967 to 1969 the princess gave birth to three sons: Crown Prince William Alexander, Prince Johan Friso, and Prince Constantijn. The Netherlands is a hereditary monarchy, and the oldest child succeeds the throne upon the death or abdication of the reigning monarch. Beatrix's eldest son, Crown Prince Willem-Alexander, will hold the title Prince of Orange until he is crowned king as Willem IV. Born on April 27, 1967, he completed a degree in history at Leiden University. He also was commissioned as an officer in the Royal Navy, serving on board several ships. More recently, he completed pilot training in the Royal Netherlands Air Force. Princes Johan Friso and Constantijn are also active in official royal activities, including state visits and diplomatic missions.

> ***"A democratic society is founded on trust between its citizens and its leaders, and between citizens themselves. Changes, at home and abroad, place heavy demands on our resilience and our capacity to preserve and strengthen the cohesion of our society."***
>
> Beatrix II, speech from the throne, 1998

Queen Beatrix is the latest monarch in a long line of the Dutch royal House of Orange, founded by William of Orange (1533–84), who led the fight for independence from Spain. When a new constitution was drafted in 1848, it ushered in the constitutional monarchy that forms the basis for Dutch government today. Although the queen exercises certain authority, her powers are limited by the Constitution, ensuring that governmental powers are shared between the monarch, the prime minister, and the parliament. Amsterdam is the official national capital, but the seat of government is The Hague, where the royal family has resided since 1981 in Huis ten Bosch Palace.

The queen is responsible for several major political appointments within the Dutch government. She appoints the prime minister, generally choosing the leader of a majority coalition. The queen also appoints the vice prime ministers as well as the Cabinet. She also nominates justices to the country's Supreme Court (the Hoge Raad), who serve for life. A Council of State—composed of the queen, the crown prince, and counselors—are consulted on administrative policy by the executive and legislative branches of government. Like other European monarchs, the queen conducts state visits abroad and receives foreign dignitaries in the Dutch royal palaces. Beatrix has regularly toured the Caribbean Dutch territories to study and aid in economic and social development in those regions.

Queen Beatrix has taken a proactive role in official affairs of the state, spending much of her day meeting with ministers, studying and signing state documents, and receiving members of parliament. The queen also officially opens the yearly session of parliament each September. From her throne, she delivers a speech outlining the policies of the government for the new year.

Queen Beatrix has demonstrated a special interest in social welfare and health care. The Princess Beatrix Fund supports victims of debilitating diseases, including polio and other muscular disorders. Along with Prince Claus, the queen has donated money to assist disabled children in the Netherlands and the Netherlands Antilles. In addition to monetary contributions, the queen has taken leadership roles in the European

Working Group, which develops volunteer work in Asia and Africa, and in the National Youth Fund and UNICEF. She regularly visits the provinces under her jurisdiction to learn about social, economic, and environmental issues affecting her subjects. The country celebrates Queen's Day on April 30, the anniversary of Beatrix's coronation. ◆

Bhumibol Adulyadey

1927– ● King of Thailand

Bhumibol Adulyadey is the king of Thailand and the longest reigning monarch in Thai history. His name is also spelled Phumiphon Adunyadet, which means strength of the land, incomparable power. King Bhumibol is the ninth sovereign in the Chakri dynasty and is called Rama IX. He reigns as a constitutional monarch, a position that limits his power as a ruler. As head of state, he maintains only an advisory role in the government. The prime minister actually heads the government. The king's role is also to uphold religion in Thailand. Despite the king's limited authority in government, King Bhumibol is a unifying force in the nation, and he has served as mediator and conciliator in a number of political conflicts over the years.

"The task of bringing peace and happiness to the country is not about making everyone good. But it is about promoting good people, enabling them to govern the country, and about preventing people who are not so good from obtaining positions of power."

Bhumibol Adulyadey, 1969

The soft-spoken Buddhist king has a reputation for hard work and devotion to the Thai people. He has won the admiration of many and has become one of the world's most respected monarchs. The Thai people have an almost religious reverence for their king, evidenced in part by the display of his portrait in most of the country's homes and businesses. King Bhumibol is also an accomplished jazz composer and musician who has played with such musical giants as Benny Goodman, Duke Ellington, and Louis Armstrong. He is also a sportsman, photographer, painter, and inventor of agricultural machinery.

Bhumibol Adulyadey was born in Cambridge, Massachusetts, on December 5, 1927. His father was Prince Mahidol, brother of the King Prajadhipok, and his mother was Princess Sangwalya Mahidol, who was born a Thai commoner. At the time of Bhumibol's birth, Prince Mahidol was studying medicine

King Bhumibol in 1946, the year he ascended to the Thai throne.

at Harvard University in Cambridge, and his mother was studying nursing. The family returned to Thailand in 1928 after Prince Mahidol completed his medical training. Then, in 1929, Prince Mahidol died. Bhumibol and his older brother Anand were sent to Switzerland for their education.

"The Thais are intelligent but they lack the opportunity to increase their knowledge and competence. Many intelligent Thai people who had a chance to acquire higher learning have already proven themselves equal to, or even superior to, people in similar positions in developed countries."

Bhumibol Adulyadey, 1981

In 1935 King Prajadhipok abdicated after a military coup in 1932 that ended 800 years of absolute monarchy in Thailand. An absolute monarchy gives the ruler unlimited power. The throne went to Bhumibol's older brother, Anand Mahidol, who was ten years old at the time. A regency was installed to govern until the king came of age, and Bhumibol and King Anand continued their education in Switzerland. The boys visited Thailand briefly in 1938 and 1939. During much of World War II (1939–45), a pro-Japanese puppet government controlled Thailand, and the two brothers did not return to their homeland again until after the war in late 1945, by which time King Anand had come of age.

In 1946 the young king was found shot dead in the palace in Bangkok. Whether the death was accidental or an assassination has never been publicly clarified. Bhumibol then became successor to the throne. A regency ruled for him while he completed his education in law and political science at the University of Lausanne in Switzerland. Bhumibol had been scheduled to ascend the throne in 1947 after the ceremonial cremation of his brother, and according to religious tradition, his lighting of the king's funeral pyre. But another military coup led to a period of political instability that caused the ceremony to be postponed. A royal court astrologer later chose March 2, 1949, as the appropriate date for the crowning, but Bhumibol's difficult recovery from an automobile accident in late 1948 postponed the date yet again. Finally, on May 5, 1950, Bhumibol was formally crowned king of Thailand.

King Bhumibol's first years of rule occurred during a series of military dictatorships that began in 1948 and lasted until 1973. But rather than retreat into the obscure role of a ceremonial figurehead, the king immersed himself in development projects that have come to include agriculture, home industry, and rural development projects, environmental programs, and such hill-tribe projects as developing substitution crops for the lucrative opium poppy. Over the years, he has also intervened in a number of political crises, most notably in 1973 and 1992, when violent conflicts between pro-democracy demonstrators and the military government led to the deaths of dozens of demonstrators and threatened to tear the country apart. His mediation quickly brought an end to each of these crises.

Bhumibol Adulyadej married Mom Rachawong Srikit Kitiyakara, also spelled Mom Rajawongse Sirikit Kittiyakara, a distant cousin, in 1950. The king and queen have four children. From oldest to youngest, they are Princess Ubol Ratana, Crown Prince Maha Vajiralongkorn, Princess Maha Chakri Sirindhorn, and Princess Chulabhorn. Princess Maha Chakri Sirindhorn is tremendously popular and has been given the title crown princess to qualify her for succession to the throne. But the king is expected to pass the throne to his only son, Crown Prince Maha Vajiralongkorn. ◆

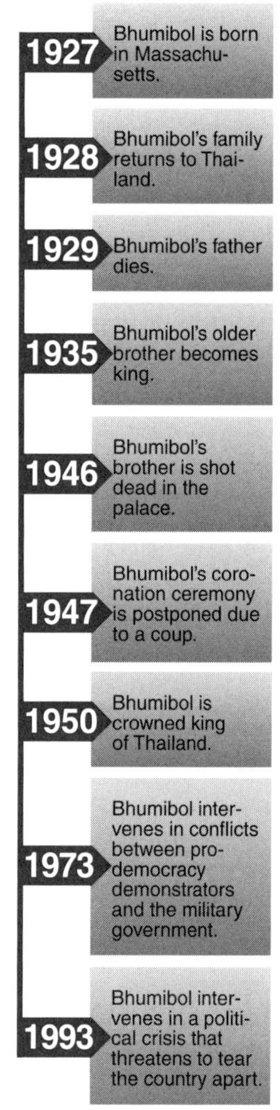

Birendra Bir Bikram Shah Dev

1945– ● King of Nepal

As influence from the modern world seeped into the remote and mountainous nation of Nepal, Birendra Bir Bikram Shah Dev was the king whose job it became to lead his nation from an ancient kingdom to a constitutional monarchy. The transition was rocky, as protestors died, coalitions rose and fell, and a rough new path was carved. But today the Nepalese people have a voice in ruling their nation.

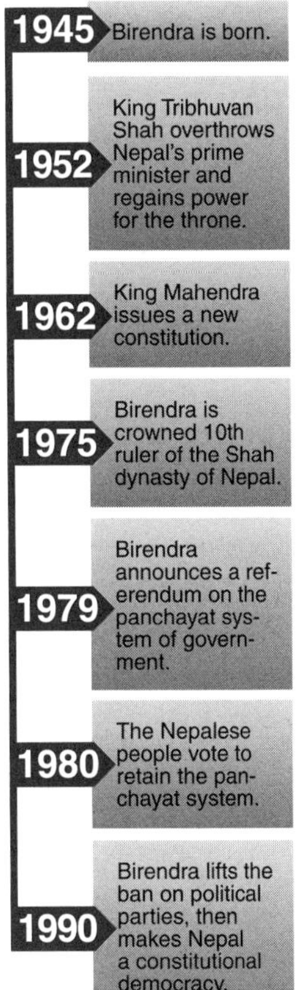

Birendra, born in 1945, became the tenth ruler of the Shah dynasty of the Kingdom of Nepal when he was crowned in 1975. Nepal lies in southern Asia, with Chinese Tibet to its north and India touching its east, south, and west borders. In the mid 1700s, the area that is now Nepal consisted of three kingdoms when a bold warlord, Prithvi Narayan Shah, descended upon the kingdoms and unified them under his rule. Thus began the Shah dynasty, which rules Nepal to this day.

From 1846 to 1951 the monarchy became merely symbolic, while power resided with a hereditary prime minister. But in 1951 King Tribhuvan Shah, Birendra's grandfather, overthrew the prime minister and regained power for the throne. When Tribhuvan died in 1955, his son Mahendra Bir Bikram carried on his father's efforts to create a constitutional monarchy. Mahendra created Nepal's first democratic constitution, and the Nepalese held their first elections for a two-house parliament. But a dissatisfied Mahendra suspended the elected parliament and banned political parties. In 1962 he issued a new constitution and established a nationwide system of assemblies called *panchayats* that he controlled.

King Mahendra died in 1972, and Birendra was crowned in 1975 at the age of thirty. Birendra inherited a major struggle within Nepal. While Birendra tried to maintain the panchayat system, reformers worked to undermine it. Birendra created programs to strengthen the panchayat and to extinguish the power of underground political parties in rural areas, but his efforts failed.

Students initiated political agitation in the late 1970s, and serious riots broke out in 1979. These events forced King Birendra to act. On May 24, 1979, he announced that there would be a national referendum in which the people could decide to support or reject the panchayat system of government. This proposed vote was the first time in modern history that the king had consulted his subjects. In May 1980 the Nepalese people voted by a narrow majority to retain the panchayat system, but with some changes. The major change was that the National Assembly would be elected by popular vote. The first such election took place in 1981, though political parties were still outlawed.

At the beginning of 1990 the panchayat system still dominated Nepal. With lightning speed, though, the system crumbled and was destroyed. Throughout Eastern Europe, the Soviet Union, and several Asian countries, democratic movements were reshaping the world. These movements inspired the

Nepalese people in their struggle. In 1990 the Movement for Restoration of Democracy (MRD) was formed to create a multiparty system, improve economic conditions, and restore democracy. In February of that year, mass demonstrations, police retaliation, mass arrests, and labor strikes rocked Nepal's major cities. After several violent demonstrations, including one outside the royal palace, Birendra lifted the ban on political parties on April 8, and on April 16 he issued a royal proclamation to dissolve the panchayat system. Birendra named a prime minister, and a multiparty coalition government took office. In November 1990 Birendra proclaimed a new constitution making Nepal a constitutional monarchy. In May 1991 Nepal held its first truly free elections in thirty-two years. The Nepali Congress Party won a majority, and Girija Prasad Koirala became prime minister.

In 1990 mass demonstrations, police retaliation, mass arrests, and labor strikes rocked Nepal's major cities.

The great exhilaration of their new democracy began to wear down as Nepal continued to struggle through the 1990s to establish a stable multiparty government. No single party was able to create a majority, so many incompatible coalitions formed and crumbled. By 1999 Koirala had returned as the seventh prime minister since 1991.

Throughout the turmoil King Birendra retained the affection of his people. In shops and homes all over Nepal once could find his picture posted. He is a Hindu and of the Indo-Aryan ethnic group, as the constitution requires. The Nepalese believe their king is a manifestation of the Hindu god Vishnu. The birthday of Birendra, December 28, is a national holiday. Birendra lives in the capital city of Kathmandu. Nepal is one of the least economically developed nations in the world, but it is rich in culture and natural beauty. Most of Nepal's 21 million people farm or raise livestock in rural areas. Climbers come to Nepal from around the world to scale the peaks of the Himalaya Range, of which Mount Everest is the highest. ◆

Robert Bruce

1274–1329 ● SCOTTISH KING

Robert Bruce bore the same name as his grandfather, a claimant to the Scottish throne after the death of Margaret Maid of Norway in 1290. Edward I of England supported the rival claim of John Baliol in return for recognition of

Edinburgh Castle

Edinburgh Castle was built around 1070 on a rock overlooking Edinburgh, Scotland. It sits atop the remains of other structures, some dating back to 1000 B.C.E. Malcolm III and Margaret were the first Scottish king and queen to live in the castle, and it served as the home of many future Scottish monarchs. Mary, Queen of Scots gave birth to her son, James, in the castle; he later became James VI of Scotland, as well as James I of England.

The castle was besieged repeatedly during Scottish internal struggles and Scottish-English conflicts, and had to be rebuilt many times. The only part of the original castle that remains is St. Margaret's Chapel, which both attackers and builders considered a sacred spot. Today Edinburgh Castle is a historic monument visited by a million tourists each year; the castle also serves as the home of the Scottish Division, a military garrison. Scotland's crown jewels (an ancient crown, scepter, and sword of state) are on permanent display at Edinburgh Castle. The castle also houses a giant fifteenth-century cannon called the Mons Meg.

suzerainty: the dominion of a superior feudal lord.

English **suzerainty**. Baliol, however, had no intention of paying fealty to Edward. In 1295 he signed the Auld Alliance with France in a bid to assert Scottish independence. Edward responded by devastating the country and capturing its royal symbols, among them the Stone of Destiny, believed to have been Jacob's pillow, upon which Scottish kings were crowned.

With Baliol exiled to Normandy the revolt was resumed by William Wallace and supported by the native Scottish aristocracy led by Robert Bruce and John Comyn. Edward's military prowness and personal rivalry among the Scottish nobles doomed the revolt. After a crushing defeat at Falkirk in 1298, Wallace fled to France, leaving Bruce and Comyn in command of the disheartened forces. Rivalry among the two resulted in Comyn nearly killing Bruce in a brawl in 1299. At the same time, Bruce shared the Anglo-Norman descent of the English nobility and possessed extensive estates as far south as London. His defection to Edward in 1302, therefore, came as no surprise. In fact, Bruce believed that it was not yet time for Scotland to rise in revolt.

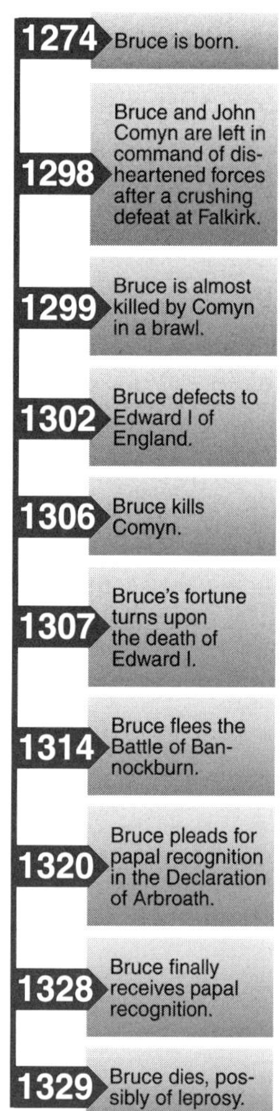

For four years, Bruce feigned fealty to England. By 1306, believing that the disastrous defeats of the past were forgotten, he approached several rebel leaders to probe their readiness to resume hostilities. At a church in Dumfries he described his plans to Comyn, but the animosity between them still lingered. Threatened with betrayal, Bruce killed Comyn. Bruce now faced opposition from both Edward's and Comyn's supporters. Although the country was as yet ill-prepared for war, Bruce fled to Scone and, with the support of the local clergy, declared himself king (Robert I).

When news of the revolt reached Edward, he swore never to rest until Bruce had been punished. Bruce and his supporters were hounded incessantly; once captured, they were treated callously. A brother was hanged and a sister was suspended in a cage from the walls of Berwick Castle. Only at the last minute was Bruce's twelve-year-old daughter spared a similar fate. Bruce himself only narrowly eluded capture. The Scottish MacDougal family still possesses a brooch supposedly ripped off Bruce's shoulder in battle. The fugitive king was in despair when, hiding in a cave, he watched a spider spinning its web. Swinging from a slender strand, it narrowly missed the cave's wall several times before finally succeeding in attaching the thread. The spider's perserverance was said to have inspired Bruce to continue the struggle.

His fortune turned upon the death of Edward I in 1307. The new king, Edward II, lacked his father's military acumen, while under Wallace, Bruce had mastered the necessary guerilla tactics for fighting larger forces. Major assaults were often conducted at night. Bruce's men, disguised by dark cloaks, would creep up to the walls of English castles, scale them, and force an entry. Even some of his opponents began supporting Bruce covertly. A secret entrance to Edinburgh Castle was revealed by an aristocrat who used it to visit his mistress in town.

By 1314 only the countryside surrounding Stirling remained in English hands. Bruce's brother Edward, in command of the besieged local castle, agreed to surrender to the English if he was not relieved within a year. British chroniclers claim that one hundred thousand English troops surrounded the castle. Twenty thousand is more likely, and no less a significant adversary to Bruce's six thousand men. Edward, however, disregarded the local topography, vital for Bruce's guerrilla tactics. The road to Stirling ran through a forest, below which was a boggy field traversed by several sluggish streams known as burns. By one such stream lay the village of Bannock. In the first day of the Battle of Bannockburn, Bruce repelled Edward twice. Scottish troops attacked the English horses; their enormous corpses prevented English mobility in the bog. On the second day Edward mistakenly placed his archers behind his soldiers, ultimately denying them the protection of a hail of arrows. While the Scottish decimated the imposing English forces, Edward fled so hastily that his contemporaries claim he could not even "make water." Scotland was now completely independent.

Scottish troops attacked the English horses; their enormous corpses prevented English mobility in the bog.

Although Bruce had the support of the Scottish clergy, the pope still supported English suzerainty even after Edward himself disclaimed his rights to Scotland in 1323. Bruce pleaded for papal recognition in the Declaration of Arbroath (1320), but it was not received until 1328. Shortly after, Robert Bruce died, possibly of leprosy.

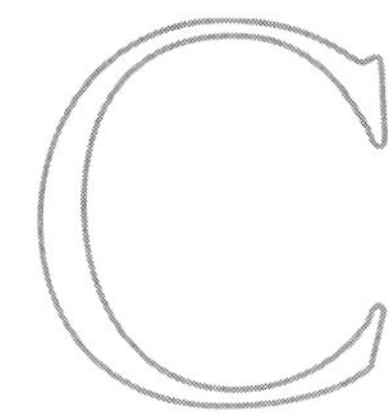

Carl XVI Gustaf

1946– ● KING OF SWEDEN

King Carl XVI Gustaf rules the twenty-four provinces that make up the kingdom of Sweden. The seventy-fourth King of Sweden, he has ruled since 1973, when he succeeded his older brother on the Swedish throne.

Carl XVI Gustaf Folke Hubertus was born on April 30, 1946, at Haga Palace in Stockholm. By that time, his parents, King Gustaf V Adolf and Queen Sibylla of Sachsen-Coburg-Gotha, had already borne five children: Crown Prince Gustaf VI Adolf and the princesses Margaretha, Birgitta, Désirée, and Christina. Gustaf VI Adolf ruled Sweden for twenty-three years following his father's death in 1950. When Gustaf VI Adolf himself passed away on September 15, 1973, his twenty-seven-year-old brother, Carl XVI Gustaf, became king.

King Carl's commitment to the natural world derives from a deep interest in outdoor life cultivated since childhood.

As is traditional in most of Europe's royal families, by the time Carl XVI Gustaf took over the throne, he had completed a rigorous education with private tutors, boarding school, and academic studies at the University of Uppsala. He also undertook military training in Sweden's army, navy, and air force. Carl XVI Gustaf was eventually commissioned as a naval officer with duties on board several ships within the Swedish Navy's fleet. In addition to this training, the king acquired economic and diplomatic experience with official visits and tours of duty at Swedish embassies and international organizations throughout Europe and Africa.

King Carl XVI Gustaf married Silvia Sommerlath on June 19, 1976. The couple had met during the 1972 Olympic Games

in Munich, Germany, where Silvia—daughter of a German father and Brazilian mother—served as an interpreter. The couple has three children: Crown Princess Victoria (born July 14, 1977), Prince Carl Philip (born May 13, 1979), and Princess Madeleine (born June 10, 1982). In 1982 the royal family moved their primary residence from the Royal Palace of Stockholm to the more remote Drottningholm Palace, a residence with a long history for the Swedish royal family.

After centuries of agnatic succession, in which only males served as Swedish monarchs, in 1980 the provisions of the original 1819 Danish constitution were amended to allow women to assume the throne. Under this rule, Princess Victoria Ingrid Alice Désirée, eldest child of King Carl XVI Gustaf and Queen Silvia, will succeed her father. The princess's training includes foreign language instruction in Germany, France, and the United States, as well as specially designed study programs to familiarize her with the details of the Swedish parliament (the Riksdag) and other aspects of the government.

The Swedish monarchy is among the oldest in the world, tracing its heritage back more than a thousand years. Carl XVI Gustaf is part of the Bernadotte dynasty, which has ruled Sweden since 1818. Today, the king's duties are primarily ceremonial, and unlike his royal counterparts in the neighboring countries of Denmark and Holland, the Swedish monarch does not appoint the prime minister, cabinet, or Supreme Court judges. Those traditionally royal powers were curtailed beginning in the last half of the nineteenth century, when the exact provisions of Sweden's constitutional monarchy took shape.

However, the king serves as Sweden's official head of state and commander-in-chief. In accordance with the 1974 Constitution Act, which sets forth the exact powers of the monarch, he ceremoniously opens the country's parliament each year, and is active on several of its committees concerning foreign affairs. An annual budget for the head of state is allocated by the Riksdag, and the royal family pays taxes like other Swedes. The king is Sweden's foremost representative in foreign relations, making regular state visits abroad. The Swedish royal family also hosts foreign officials to Sweden. On a regular basis the king makes official visits to local businesses, government, and educational and charitable institutions throughout the country.

Upon his accession to the throne, King Carl XVI Gustaf adopted the motto "For Sweden . . . With the Times," expressing his intention to merge the traditions of the Swedish monarchy with the exigencies of a modern society. As part of this mission, the king has demonstrated a special interest in preserving the environment. His commitment to the natural world derives from a deep interest in outdoor life cultivated since childhood, including a love for scouting, hunting, and sailing. In 1972 he took a leading role in the United Nations Conference on the Environment in Stockholm. In 1988 he became chairman of the World Wide Fund for Nature (WWF), and established an international environmental colloquium held annually at the Royal Ulriksdal Palace in Stockholm. ◆

Catherine de Médicis

1519–1589 ● QUEEN OF FRANCE

Wife of one French king (Henry II) and mother of three (Francis II, Charles IX, Henry III), Catherine de Médicis was a dominant figure in French politics for almost twenty years. A daughter of Lorenzo II de Medici, she was orphaned at an early age and was educated in a convent. Her marriage at fourteen to the future Henry II of France in 1533 came as a result of a political maneuver between Pope Clement VII and Francis I. During her husband's reign Catherine did not take part in politics, being eclipsed by his mistress Diane de Potiers, the woman who dominated his life. After ten years of childlessness, Catherine bore him nine children. She also stayed in the background during the one-year reign of her son Francis II (1559–60). However, with the accession of her second son, the ten-year-old Charles IX, she became regent of France and retained her hold on the government even after the king attained maturity.

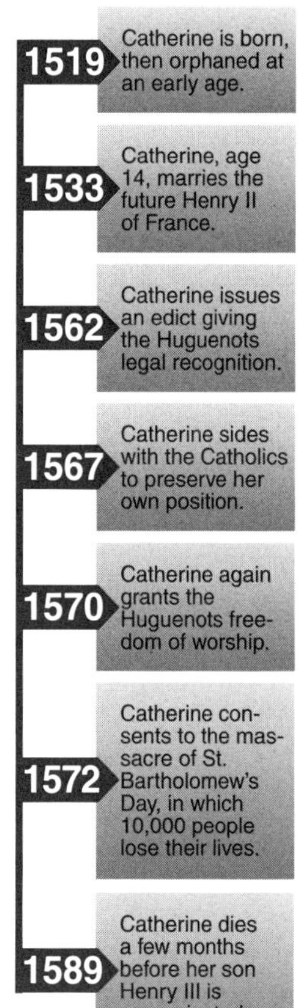

Catherine pursued a moderate policy at the beginning, backing the conciliatory chancellor Michel de L'Hospital. Her attempt to keep a delicate balance in French religious life was evident in the edict of January 1562 which, for the first time, gave the Huguenots legal recognition, allowing them to gather for prayer outside walled cities. However, this policy failed with the massacre of sixty Huguenots during a religious service at Vassy by troops of Francis, duke of Guise, which sparked the first of the religious wars of France (1562–98). Caught between the two warring parties, Catherine adopted an opportunistic position aimed at preserving her own position and that of her children. In 1567, following the attempt of the Huguenots to capture the king at Meaux, she went over to the Catholic side but in 1570, when she suspected the Guises, who were the leaders of the extreme Roman Catholic party, of dealing with the king of Spain, Philip II, she issued the Edict of Saint-Germain, which again granted the Huguenots freedom of worship. She then clashed with the Huguenot leader, Gaspard de Coligny and, alarmed at the influence he had acquired at the court, tried to solve the problem by concocting a plot for his assassination. Coligny was shot and wounded; two days later servants of the Guises burst into his house and killed him. His murder signaled the beginning of the massacre of Saint Bartholomew's Day (1572), to which Catherine consented, and in which, it is estimated, 10,000 people lost their lives. This turned out to be a political blunder since it eliminated the advantage that Catherine had as a third party representing royal authority. She continued to be involved in politics during the reign of her third son, Henry III (1574–89), who made political mistakes of his own. Catherine died a few months before he was assassinated by a fanatical Dominican friar. ◆

Catherine II

1729–1796 ● CATHERINE THE GREAT, EMPRESS OF RUSSIA

Catherine II, also known as Catherine the Great, came to power in 1762 after a military coup deposed her eccentric husband, Peter III, who was murdered by the brother of Catherine's lover Count Orlov. She probably did not authorize Peter's murder, but this event did not contribute to the legitimacy of her rule; nor did the fact that Catherine was a German princess who had converted to Russian Orthodoxy on her arrival at the Russian court of the Empress Elizabeth. From the outset, however, Catherine showed herself determined to rule absolutely—not as regent or consort—and managed to do so successfully for over thirty years.

Arriving at the court of Peter the Great's daughter Elizabeth in 1744 at the age of sixteen, the German-speaking Calvinist Princess Sophie from the Prussian court of Stettin was required to change her religion, language, and even her name in order to be deemed suitable for the Russian throne. She had come to marry Elizabeth's seventeen-year-old nephew and heir, who was impotent and played with toys in bed. At first she thought of suicide but found consolation in reading and horseback riding. She proved remarkably adaptable and survived the numerous intrigues and humiliations of Elizabeth's rule until, at the age of thirty-four, her burning ambition to rule Russia was realized in a coup d'etat organized by her lover Grigori Orlov in which her husband, then reigning as Peter III, was murdered.

Intelligent, lively, and witty, Catherine was an astute manipulator of public opinion and made every effort to consolidate her hold on the Russian throne. She presented herself as a devotee of the Enlightenment, which was then sweeping Europe, and patronized its philosophers. Spokesmen for the Enlightenment such as Denis Diderot and Voltaire (with whom she corresponded) believed that people are naturally free and equal and should be encouraged to educate themselves to improve their situation. This optimistic world view did not, however, necessarily encompass democratic government, as social reform was thought to be best undertaken by autocratic rulers. Naturally, many monarchs, among them Catherine, seized upon this philosophy as a pretext for wielding absolute authority. Tension inevitably occurred during her reign between the humane reforms she was genuinely committed to instituting and the repression necessary to maintain a system of government as totalitarian as that in Russia.

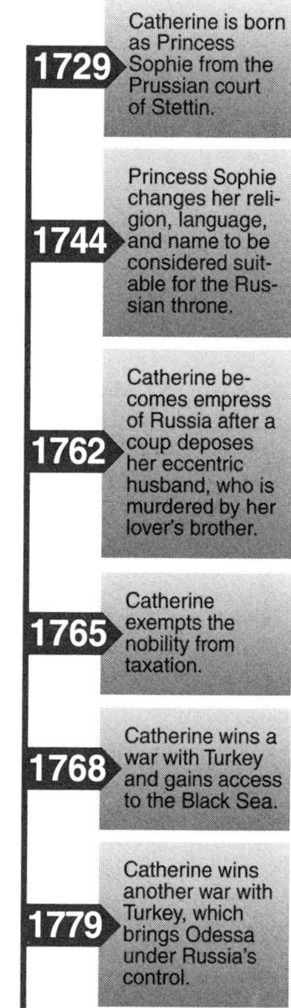

Certainly, the backward, unwieldy, and impoverished landmass which constituted the eighteenth-century Russian empire at the beginning of Catherine's reign was not open to any realistic form of democratic government. Russian rulers traditionally ruled by decree, personally authorizing every government decision. Catherine tried early in her reign to institute some kind of limited parliamentary debate by convening a commission to codify the Russian law. She frequently wrote of her sympathy for the oppressed masses and tried to abolish torture and encourage the humane treatment of servants. Despite these and other humanitarian measures, Catherine's reluctance to allow any weakening of her personal control of government led to inevitable repression. Intellectuals such as the writer Alexander Radishchev who dared to criticize her rule were exiled and had their work suppressed. The great Cossack rebellion of 1773–75 was harshly put down. The near-success of this rebellion also convinced Catherine of the impossibility of freeing the serfs,

Russia's peasant class that was legally tied to the land they worked on and considered the property of their noble owners. Indeed, Catherine strengthened the power of the nobility; in 1765 they received exemption from taxation.

Catherine's foreign policy was vigorous and innovative. She pursued many of the same aims as her predecessors, securing Russia's borders and ensuring outlets to the sea. During her reign she engineered the partition of Poland no fewer than three times and positioned an ex-lover, Stanislas Poniatowski, on the Polish throne. By the end of her reign Poland had ceased to exist. On the Asian front Catherine fought two wars with Turkey; the first, in 1768, resulted in the Treaty of Kuchuk Kainardji, whereby Russia gained access to the Black Sea, permitting her to annex the longcoveted Crimea in 1783. From 1787–92 another successful war with Turkey, ending in the Treaty of Jassy, brought Odessa under Russian control. As a result of these territorial gains the empire's population jumped from nine to twenty-nine million, making Russia a formidable power. The removal of Poland and the Tartar state, which had acted as buffers between Russia and western Europe, also increased Russia's interest in European affairs. The empire formed under Catherine the Great was to constitute a continual strategic threat for the next two hundred years. The seeds were also sown for ongoing ethnic problems with the assimilation of millions of non-Russian Ukrainians, Poles, and Tartars who bitterly resented Russian rule.

During Catherine's reign the seeds were sown for ongoing ethnic problems with the assimilation of millions of non-Russian Ukrainians, Poles, and Tartars who bitterly resented Russian rule.

Catherine's economic policy was linked to her territorial expansion; immigration was encouraged; fur, mining, and textile industries set up; and export duties abolished to encourage trade. She tried to encourage the development of towns in the hope that this would lead to the establishment of an educated middle class, as was the case in Europe. Progress was, however, slow in the rural, sparsely populated majority of the empire. Of European origin herself, Catherine tried to instill in the nobility an admiration for European culture. She also exploited Russian traditions when it suited her and cultivated a personality cult, encouraging her subjects to think of her as their little mother.

There is no shortage of vivid stories concerning Catherine's personal life and penchant for young lovers. In fact, for most of her life she was very restrained, taking her first lover, thought to be the father of her eldest son, later Paul I, in desperation after her own marriage remained unconsummated. By the time the Empress Elizabeth died, Catherine was apparently deeply involved with her second lover, Grigori Orlov, who engineered her coup and fathered two of her children. Orlov was succeeded by the cavalry officer and later field-marshal Grigori Potemkin, to whom she appears to have been most deeply attached and whom she entrusted with many important missions. Only in the last fifteen years of her life, growing increasing lonely and frightened for the future, did Catherine embark on the promiscuity that so shocked contemporary and later historians.

Opinion remains divided as to whether Catherine the Great was a power-hungry monster or a gifted liberal ruler. She appears to have been genuinely devoted to improving the lot of her adopted country, and by the standards of her time she deserves to be considered one of the most powerful and positive influences in Russian history. ◆

Charlemagne

742–814 ● CHARLES THE GREAT, KING OF THE FRANKS

Son of Pepin III the Short and grandson of Charles Martel, Charlemagne was crowned king, together with his brother Carloman, in 753. At his father's death the realm was divided between him and his brother but soon after, conflict arose between them. At the death of Carloman in 771 Charlemagne became sole king. He eliminated Carloman's family and used the alliance between it and Desiderius, king of the Lombards, as a pretext for invading Italy, ostensibly to extend military help to the Roman church. In 774 he conquered Pavia and was crowned king of the Lombards. Pope Adrian I also granted him the title Patrice of the Romans, which he bore in addition to his two royal titles, authorizing him to intervene in the temporal affairs of Rome under the formal authority of the pope. Returning to his realm Charlemagne embarked on a war against the Saxons (led by his most powerful enemy, Witlekind) which lasted more than thirty years, until 804. Saxony was conquered step by step and its population forcibly Christianized. In his ordinance of 777 draconic measures were prescribed, including the death penalty for opposing conversion. In 787 he responded to a call of Muslim rulers in northern Spain, who were fighting against the Ummayads of Córdoba, and led a raid into Spain.

"Let no one in our forests dare to rob our game which we have already many times forbidden to be done. And now again we firmly decree that no one shall do this any more."

Capitulary (laws) of Charlemagne, 802

The only results of this expedition were the destruction of Pampelona (Pamplona), capital of the Christian kingdom of Navarre, and the retaliation by the Basques, who wreaked havoc on the rearguard of his army in the Pass of Roncesvalles. But for Charlemagne's military and diplomatic skills, the defeat might have provoked a general revolt by the Saxons. Having crushed his opponents, Charlemagne proceeded to change the structure of his kingdom: in 789 he promulgated a decree aimed at realizing the ideal Christian kingdom, based on the biblical concepts of the Holy People and Sacred Monarchy. The Franks were represented as the heirs of ancient Israel and the Chosen People, while Charlemagne was portrayed as a new King David. His subjects were ordered to swear allegiance to him, every revolt or sign of infidelity being considered an offense against religion. The church was incorporated in the royal system as part of the government subservient to the monarch.

Among Charlemagne's conquests were the duchy of Bavaria (788), the frontier territories of Brittany and the Slavs on the Elbe; but here Charlemagne contented himself with imposing his overlordship. From 797 to 799 he attacked the Avars and conquered their kingdom, enriching his treasury with the booty; once, he had 4,500 captives executed. After many conquests, the idea of a Christian empire was broached at Charlemagne's court. The idea was first given public expression at the council held in 794 at Frankfurt, where many decisions on ecclesiastical and lay reforms of the kingdom were made. The condemnation of Adoptionism, a heresy originating in Spain and that of the decisions of the Council of Nicaea II (787) concerning images left Charlemagne appearing to be the sole leader and defender of Christianity. Then, too, the publication of the *Caroline Books* (a treatise attributed to Charlemagne containing a criticism of the Iconoclasts) was intended to discredit Byzantium and Empress Irene and also to create a new status for Charlemagne. After the death of Adrian I, Charlemagne recognized the new pope, Leo III, and in a letter to him attempted to clarify the division of power, limiting the pope to prayers. A revolt against Leo that compelled him to flee from Rome served Charlemagne's intentions. He received the pope at his camp at Paderborn, where the army was mobilized against the Saxons, and promised to come to Rome to clarify the situation. In 799, after having seen to the completion of his palace at Aix-la-Chapelle (Aachen), which was modeled on the Byzantine imperial palace, he led an expedition to Rome, intending to arbitrate between the pope and his accusers. Leo skillfully prevented this intercession by successfully defending himself against the accusations and positioned himself as Charlemagne's equal. At the Christmas Mass of 800 he crowned Charlemagne emperor of the Romans, to the great disappointment of the Frankish king, who sought a more powerful title such as emperor of the Christians. In 802 Charlemagne, who was never to return to Rome, began to organize his empire on religious principles, taking into account the feudal structures of society. He tried to win recognition of his imperial title by the Byzantine Basileus, obtaining it only in 812; his conflict with Byzantium led him to develop relations with the caliph Harun ar-Rashid of Baghdad.

> ***"We decree that throughout our whole realm no one shall dare to deny hospitality to the rich, or to the poor, or to pilgrims: that is, no one shall refuse shelter and fire and water to pilgrims going through the land in God's service, or to any one travelling for the love of God and the safety of his soul."***
>
> Capitulary (laws) of Charlemagne, 802

The last years of Charlemagne's reign marked the beginning of his empire's disintegration. Because his empire lacked an effective administrative structure, Charlemagne tried to govern by obtaining his vassals' and counts' **fealty**, but this system was not very efficient and signs of local independence emerged despite the emperor's great prestige. Moreover, the long and continuous wars ruined the free peasants, who began to shirk their military duties. As a result, the first Scandinavian raids were disastrous for the counties along the coast of northern France and the Low Countries.

fealty: the fidelity of a vassal or feudal tenant to his lord.

Charlemagne was a man of contradictions. He adopted the lifestyle and customs of his German ancestors, speaking the Frankish idiom of Austrasia and wearing traditional Frankish clothes—a leather vest or linen tunic. However, Greek was heard at his court and he was a patron of the arts and letters, encouraging the spread of knowledge throughout his empire despite the fact that he did not know Latin. He gathered scholars and intellectuals at his palace of Aix-la-Chapelle and was responsible for the Carolingian Renaissance. Charlemagne took an active part in discussions of the palace academy and was considered after his death to be the patron saint of learning and universities. Yet while demanding a perfect moral life from members of his family and banishing to monasteries those who sinned, he continued to entertain concubines. Nevertheless, Charlemagne became a legendary figure through the centuries, with all the good deeds of his dynasty coming to be associated with his personality.

Subsequent generations were greatly influenced by his depiction in the *Song of Roland*. Charlemagne's romantic image inspired the concept of imperial dignity and also served as a model to Napoleon.◆

Charles I

1600–1649 ● KING OF ENGLAND

> ***"Never make a defence or apology before you be accused."***
> Charles I, letter to Lord Wentworth, 1636

Born in Dunfermline, Scotland, the second son of James VI of Scotland (later James I of England), Charles I (Charles Stuart) was a sickly child and not expected to live long; he did not speak until he was five and could not walk until he was seven. He grew up in the shadow of his elder brother, Henry, the heir apparent. Henry had the fine physique and prowess that Charles lacked but he fell ill and died in 1612. Charles's favorite sister, Elizabeth, left home to marry a German monarch. Thus deprived of his closest friends, Charles grew up quiet and introverted. He was small in stature and spoke with a Scottish accent and a noticeable stammer. A man of strong religious sentiment, he was a loyal husband to his queen, Henrietta Maria (sister of King Louis XIII of France), and a devoted family man. James VI of Scotland also became king of England in 1603 and Charles succeeded him as ruler of the two kingdoms in 1625, but his reserved nature and lack of political judgment or diplomatic skill prevented him from cultivating strong bonds with his subjects.

A monarch distant from his people and insensitive to social and political currents, Charles became overly dependent on stronger personalities in his court. He initially came under the influence of the duke of Buckingham, the court favorite of his father. Buckingham's dashing appearance, wit, and talent for flattery captivated the young king but disgusted many of his countrymen. With Buckingham's assassination in 1628, the king turned for support to the queen, catering to her every whim, which ranged from acquiring a pack of pet monkeys to having a dwarf in full armor jump out of a pie and stand at attention at the dinner table. Her extravagances did not meet with the approval of a populace which was also highly suspicious of her Catholicism. The king's love of fine art and his patronage of painters like Anthony Van Dyck and Peter Paul Rubens gave him an honored place in the development of the arts, but to certain of his subjects money spent on paintings and tapestries seemed a criminal waste.

Charles was a firm believer in the divine right of kings to rule. He placed no trust in his parliament, which he viewed as little more than a tool for raising taxes, failing to recognize that this institution had assumed an independent power and within its ranks were many men of Puritanical religious views and ideas of political liberty in conflict with his own. For eleven years he sought to rule without their assistance and imposed on the country arbitrary taxes to finance ill-conceived and ultimately futile wars with France and Spain.

In 1639 King Charles's attempts to impose a book of common prayer on his Presbyterian Scottish subjects led to a short war in which his forces were defeated. He was forced to summon parliament again to raise funds to pursue the campaign in Scotland. The obedience he counted upon was not forthcoming, for parliament denounced his autocratic approach to government and sought to impeach his leading counselors. One of the king's closest advisers, the earl of Strafford, was impeached, sentenced, and executed and Charles was powerless to save him. Parliament passed, by 159 to 148 votes, a Grand Remonstrance condemning the king's misrule. Plans were set in motion to eliminate the king's control of the army and he feared that the queen would be impeached because the strong feeling against the rise of Catholic influence at court. Desperately trying to assert the authority he believed he still possessed, in 1642 the king went in person with four hundred men to arrest five members of Parliament he accused of treason; the five escaped and the incident served to highlight his weakness.

Efforts to settle the conflict peacefully failed. In London the sentiment of the people was with parliament and King Charles moved his court north to York. The queen traveled to Holland to pawn the crown jewels; the honor of the monarchy would not stand before the pressing need for funds.

After a series of minor skirmishes, King Charles's armed forces and those of his rebellious Parliament met in a major confrontation at Edgehill in 1643. Before the battle Charles told his soldiers, "Your king is both your cause, your quarrel and your captain. The foe is in sight. . . ." For the first half of what became the English Civil War, the king's forces held the advantage but this was never exploited in a move on London, the capital. From 1645 the tide turned with a major Royalist defeat at Naseby to an army headed by Lord Fairfax and Oliver Cromwell. By 1646 the king was surrounded in Oxford but managed to escape in disguise to his old enemies, the Scots, encamped at Newark. The following year an agreement was reached between the Scottish commanders and parliament and the king was handed over. His attempts to forge alliances with the various parties to the conflict were in vain; he was placed on trial at Westminster for treason. In his trial and execution he displayed a strength of character that would have served him well in earlier years. He refused to recognize the court, claiming that no earthly tribunal could judge him; his death warrant was signed by Cromwell. Charles went to his death a proud man; he asked for shirts to wear so that he would not shiver in the frosty January air, saying, "If I tremble with cold, my enemies will say it was from fear; I will not expose myself to such reproaches." Convinced of the justice of his cause, the sight of the sharp ax and block did not frighten the king, as he said with conviction, "I go from a corruptible to an incorruptible crown, where no disturbance can take place." ◆

"If I tremble with cold, my enemies will say it was from fear; I will not expose myself to such reproaches."

Charles I, before his execution, 1649

Charles II

1630–1685 ● KING OF ENGLAND AND SCOTLAND

The eldest surviving son of King Charles I, Charles II (Charles Stuart) was in many ways the opposite in character to his ill-fated father. Tall and handsome with an outgoing personality, devoted to the pursuit of physical pleasures, Charles developed the flexibility to steer a safe course between the conflicting religious and political interest groups threatening to tear the country apart.

In 1645 King Charles I sent his sons, Charles and James, to France, perhaps fearing that the course of the Civil War would turn against him. Prince Charles returned in 1650 and led an abortive invasion of England from Scotland. Final defeat came in 1651 at the battle of Worcester, where the prince distinguished himself with his courage in the fray. One contemporary described how Prince Charles led out the army and engaged it himself, charging at the head thereof many several times in person, with great courage and success. Despite the talents he displayed in his role as army commander, the battle did not go his way and the parliamentary army entered the city. There is an account of Prince Charles escaping from his lodging by the back door as a parliamentary officer entered by the front.

There followed six weeks of life on the run from the victorious parliamentary forces with a £1,000 price on his head at a time when many families lived on £50 a year or less. Prince Charles utilized his skills as an actor, traveling around disguised as a gentleman's servant. He stayed at a series of safehouses owned by Royalist sympathizers, often Roman Catholics. On one occasion that has since been entered into legend, he hid in an oak tree while soldiers searched the surrounding area. Another time he had to take his horse into a smithy to be shoed. He asked the smith for news of the battle of Worcester and the smith told him the good news of the defeat of the Scots but regretted that that rogue Charles Stuart had not yet been captured. Prince Charles, in his role as a Midlands farmer, commented that he thought Charles Stuart deserved to be hanged more than any other for initiating the invasion and the smith commended him for speaking like an honest man.

Prince Charles escaped to a long and poverty-stricken exile in France. In 1658 the Lord Protector of England, Oliver Cromwell, died. There followed a period of political uncertainty with growing fears of anarchy. In this climate, one of Cromwell's leading generals, George Monck, invited Prince Charles to return and accept the English crown. He entered London in triumph in 1660 on his thirtieth birthday. The people were anxious to put behind them the conflict of previous years and desired a return to the stability that once characterized the country. The new King Charles II responded by adopting a conciliatory tone toward those who had opposed his father in the Civil War. The men immediately involved in the regicide were brutally executed and Oliver Cromwell's body exhumed and disgraced, but to others clemency was extended and there was a period of widespread satisfaction with the new king's rule; this did not last.

The king's policy of religious tolerance was opposed by a significant segment of the population, who feared that it would

> ***"This is very true; for my words are my own, and my actions are my ministers."***
> Charles II, reply to John Wilmot, Earl of Rochester

open the way for a revival of Roman Catholic power. Charles became involved in a war with the Netherlands over commercial jealousies; although England won two victories, the Dutch admiral, M. A. de Ruyter, sailed up the Thames in 1667, burning several warships, while Charles was occupied with his mistresses. The king's popularity was also adversely affected by the 1670 Treaty of Dover with King Louis XIV of France. In return for an alliance against the Dutch, Charles promised to become a Roman Catholic and was promised military help if his subjects turned against him. His connection with the king of France and suspicions about the activities of his queen in advancing the Catholic cause eroded the popular support he enjoyed at his restoration. When his queen, Catherine, failed to produce an heir, fear intensified as it became clear that the king's Catholic brother, James, would succeed him. Such fears were amplified by claims in 1679 of the existence of a Popish plot to murder Charles and place James on the throne. Between the years 1679 and 1681 the king almost lost control over the government but through adroit maneuvering he restored his influence and ended his reign in a strong position.

The return of the royal court brought again to London the color that had been lacking during the years of parliamentary rule. The king had little inclination to involve himself with the details of his administration pursuing instead his private interests. He began to rebuild his father's plundered art collection and brought to England a taste for French music and furniture. He had a keen interest in science and encouraged the formation of the Royal Society in 1662, a scientific research foundation still active today. It is recorded that he stayed up one night observing an eclipse of Saturn through a telescope and his interest inspired others. The king was also a lover of parks and gardens, going daily to London's Saint James's Park to feed the ducks and greeting his subjects with the raising of his hat along the way.

Charles had married the Portuguese princess Catherine of Braganza in 1661. Though he always behaved in a courteous manner toward her, his affections were elsewhere. The queen failed to produce an heir to the throne but the king had scandalized respectable society by having at least fourteen illegitimate children by a succession of mistresses, some noblewomen, but others actresses, like the famous Nell Gwynne (one of his last utterances was "Don't let poor Nelly starve"). His attitude toward women is indicated in his remark on being told that his mistress Barbara Villiers had converted from Anglicanism to Catholicism. The king is reported to have said "he never concerned himself with the souls of ladies, but with their bodies, insofar as they were gracious enough to allow him." Daniel Defoe summed up Charles's reign as follows:

> The royal refugee our breed restores,
> With foreign courtiers and with foreign whores,
> And carefully repeopled us again,
> Throughout his lazy, long, lascivious reign. ◆

Charles V

1500–1558 ● GERMAN EMPEROR, KING OF SPAIN (AS CHARLES I)

Charles's reign was fraught with the difficulties of retaining his many territories and authority in the face of the growth of Protestantism, increasing French and Turkish pressure, and the opposition of a hostile pope. The son of Philip I of Castile and grandson of Emperor Maximilian I, Charles numbered many other Catholic kings and queens of Europe among his close kin: his maternal grandparents were Isabella I of Castile and Ferdinand II of Aragon. He was raised by his aunt, Margaret of Austria, regent of the Netherlands. His regimented upbringing left him little opportunity to form close relationships, a circumstance responsible for his cool and aloof personality which at best inspired respect rather than admiration.

> ***"I speak Spanish to God, Italian to women, French to men, and German to my horse."***
> Charles V, attributed

At fifteen Charles assumed rule over the Netherlands, and a year later he became king of Spain when his grandfather Ferdinand died. Insensitive to Spanish traditions, Charles instituted what virtually constituted foreign rule over the country, freely exploiting its resources to further his own ends. When he became king of Germany and was elected emperor-designate in 1519 (finally being crowned emperor by the pope in 1530) he gave his spiritual mentor, Adrian of Utrecht (later Pope Adrian VI, a supporter of the *devotia moderna* religious movement which arose in late fifteenth century Holland) the unenviable task of administering Spain as his regent. A revolt of the Castilian cities soon followed.

A zealous and pious Catholic, Charles struck the first blow in his battle against Protestantism, then gaining force in central

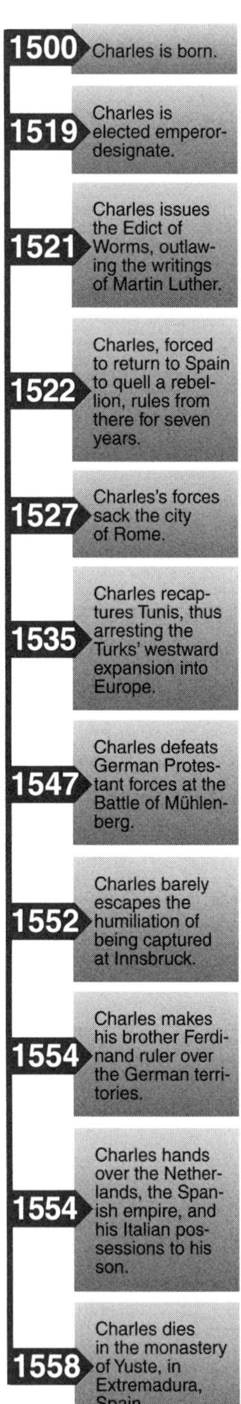

Europe, with the 1521 Edict of Worms, which outlawed the writings of Martin Luther. In 1522, however, he was forced to return to Spain to quell a rebellion and ruled from that country for the next seven years, achieving a rapprochement with the rebellious nobles and adopting the Spanish language, customs, and manners as his own. After his institution of a far stricter degree of administrative centralization there than elsewhere in his empire, Spain became his primary base. Spanish troops served him loyally, while the treasure fleets from the New World helped fund his operations throughout Europe.

Charles's reign was marked by persistent disputes with Francis I of France, a manifestation of the struggle between the houses of Habsburg (represented by Charles) and Valois to secure hegemony in Europe. In 1525 Francis was captured and forced to marry Charles's sister Eleanor, but he reneged on the terms of the Treaty of Madrid and, with the backing of the anti-Habsburg Pope Clement VII, continued to assert his claim to Burgundy. During a 1527 campaign against the pope, Charles's forces sacked the city of Rome; in 1536 Charles traveled to Rome to challenge Francis to single combat, an offer the latter refused. It was only the more pressing need to unite against the incursions of the Ottoman Turks that prompted the two warring monarchs to engineer an agreement whereby Charles gave up his claims to Burgundy in exchange for Francis's relinquishing his interest in Milan and Naples.

Charles first arrested the Turks' westward expansion into Europe by recapturing Tunis in 1535, a year after its conquest by the enemy. But the cost to him was great, and he became increasingly plagued by the inadequacy of his financial means to preserve his holdings, let alone indulge any dynastic ambitions he might entertain. Thus, his 1543–44 campaign against a resurgent Francis was severely hampered by his shortage of money. Its outcome, though, was successful in that the French king surrendered territory in Canada and agreed to the convocation of a general church council (the Council of Trent) to consider reform, which Charles had been calling for since the mid-1530s.

Charles saw reform as the church's only means to check the spread of Protestantism, which threatened to become especially virulent within his own kingdom; Protestant German princes formed the Schmalkaldic League in 1531. With the backing of the Council of Trent, he went to war against the League, defeating its forces at the Battle of Mühlberg in 1547. However, instead of receiving the credit he regarded as his due for having reasserted the Catholic cause, Charles was criticized by Pope Paul III for tolerating Protestants in Augsburg. Frustrated and angered by perpetual papal opposition, Charles allowed his religious zeal to wane.

Charles's efforts to settle the succession on his son, the future Philip II, so enraged the German Catholic princes that they allied against him with Henry II of France. Unable to prevent the consequent loss of some of his imperial possessions to France in 1552, Charles barely escaped the humiliation of being captured at Innsbruck that same year. Tired by the constant effort of maintaining his patrimony and dispirited by the election of another hostile pope, Paul IV, Charles made his brother Ferdinand ruler of the German territories in 1554; handed over the Netherlands, Spain and its empire, and his Italian possessions to Philip; and retired to the monastery of Yuste, in Extremadura, Spain, where he died soon afterward.

"I make war on the living, not on the dead."
Charles V, when advised to hang Luther's corpse from the gallows, 1546

Given the difficulties of attempting to maintain such extensive possessions, Charles's endeavors were impressive as much for their manner as their scope. An able and forceful statesman, he demonstrated a moral uprightness and sense of personal honor that commanded respect. However, the twenty-eight million ducats in debts he incurred are evidence of the inadequacy of his means. Exploitation of the riches of the Spanish empire in the New World was in its infancy, and Charles was forced to borrow money from the great financial centers of Antwerp, Augsburg, and Genoa at crippling rates of interest. After his death, his former domains were rife with dissent, highlighting the magnitude of his achievement in controlling them. ◆

Charles VII

1403–1461 ● King of France

Usually described as a man of weak character, Charles VII had a long, eventful reign. He was the eleventh child of Charles VI and Isabella of Bavaria, and became regent of France in 1418 when his father went mad. His position was precarious: the English army was in possession of a large territory in northern France and the French nobility was divided into two factions, the Burgundians and the Armagnacs.

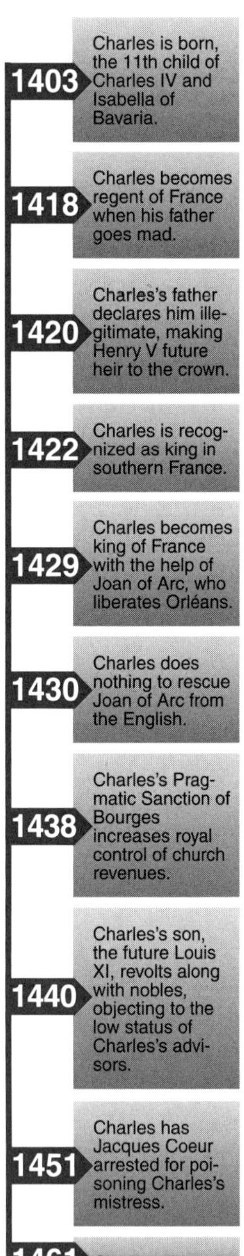

In 1419, at a conference in Montereau, the Armagnacs murdered the duke of Burgundy, John the Fearless, at a meeting where the dauphin (the future Charles VII) was present, thus forcing the Burgundians into the arms of the English. Charles's insane father, who came under the influence of the Burgundians, then accepted the Treaty of Troyes (1420) whereby he declared his son illegitimate and designated Henry V of England regent and future heir to the crown of France. Yet after Charles VI's death in 1422 the dauphin was recognized as king in southern France; however, he was almost powerless and under the influence of his Armagnac councilors. He eventually recovered the occupied parts of his kingdom thanks to the nationalist movement on his behalf inspired by Joan of Arc. In 1429 she led the French troops against the English, who were besieging the city of Orléans, and liberated it. This opened the way to Rheims where, in the ancient traditional ceremony, Charles was crowned on July 17, 1429. Joan of Arc had given the king confidence in himself and he became known as Charles the Victorious. However, the king and his advisers decided to do nothing to rescue Joan of Arc when she was captured and handed over to the English in May 1430.

In 1435 Charles concluded the Peace of Arras with Philip the Good of Burgundy. The reconciliation strengthened him vis-à-vis the English and in 1436 he was able to take Paris. This was followed by a period of military standstill in which unruly bands roamed and terrorized the countryside. In the course of these years the king introduced many reforms in the tax system and in the army and, in 1438, issued the Pragmatic Sanction of Bourges, which restricted the authority of the pope over the French church and increased royal control of church revenues.

During this part of his reign Charles was served by a group of loyal advisers, among them the merchant and banker, Jacques Coeur, whom Charles made master of the royal mint and employed as diplomat and administrator of the royal finances. The fact that his advisers were of relatively low social standing caused resentment among the great nobles, who were joined by his own son, the future Louis XI; their revolt (1440) was suppressed.

Charles's mistress Agnès Sorel was influential in court life and also involved herself in political matters. She bore the king four daughters. Her death, soon after the birth of her fourth daughter, was rumored to have been caused by poisoning. The dauphin was suspected but more than a year later, in 1451, Jacques Coeur, whose great wealth had provoked the jealousy of important members of the royal court, was accused. Charles VII ordered his arrest and confiscated his property.

After twenty years of struggle, Charles VII succeeded in driving the English out of the kingdom. At the time of his death only Calais remained in English hands. ◆

Charles XII

1682–1718 ● King of Sweden

Charles XII acceded to the throne of Sweden when only fifteen years old after the death of his father Charles XI, assuming power almost immediately. He was a bright, energetic prince with an aptitude for languages and mathematics but his true love was sport, and he excelled in riding and bear hunting. Fascinated with military history, he sought ways to further Sweden's control of the Baltic region.

At age eighteen Charles left Sweden at the head of his armies, never to return to his capital. His first target was Denmark, which had threatened the independence of Sweden's traditional ally, Frederick, duke of Holstein-Gottorp. With Denmark easily crushed, Russian czar Peter the Great and King Augustus II (the Strong) of Poland feared that Charles would now turn against them. Peter was also seeking an alternative maritime outlet for his growing empire to replace the difficult Arctic route. To establish a Baltic outlet, Russian troops occupied Swedish Livonia and Estonia. Some 40,000 Russian troops were stationed at Narva, in Estonia, to protect the new acquisition. Charles led 10,000 men to Narva where, under the cover of a raging blizzard, he stormed the center of the Russian defenses. This headstrong assault was an extraordinary success; unable to identify their attackers because of the snow, the Russian camp divided into two detached sections. Countless terrified Russians fled the battlefield only to drown in the Narva River. By the battle's end, the number of captured Russians actually outnumbered their Swedish assailants, forcing Charles to release everyone except officers.

Charles led 10,000 men to Narva where, under the cover of a raging blizzard, he stormed the center of the Russian defenses.

The Russian defeat left Charles with three options: the immediate invasion of that country, suing for peace on his own

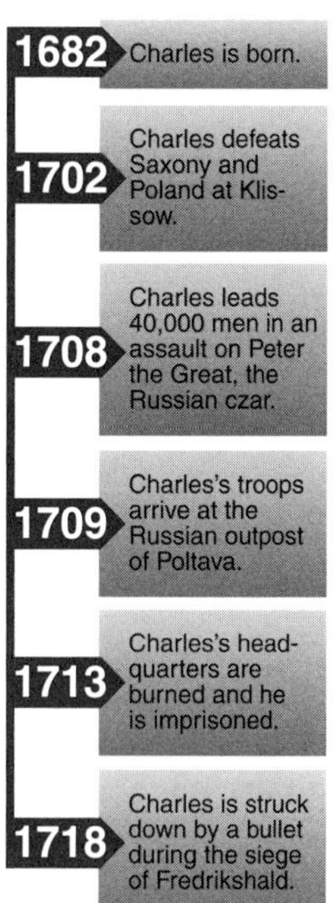

hegemony: extreme influence or authority over others.

terms, or invading Poland. He chose the last, mistakenly underestimating the popularity of the German-born Augustus. Charles's decision was made without consulting his officers, who suspected him of loving war for war's sake. Charles felt closer to his troops, preferring the simple uniform and boots of a common soldier to royal garb and fashionable wigs. He admired the rank and file and believed that all competent officers must rise from it. When a young corporal of noble blood applied for promotion, Charles refused to grant the favor and demanded that he first serve in the ranks so as to learn to appreciate his future charges. No one dared question the victorious king, described by one contemporary as "awe-inspiring and almost sinister."

Charles utilized original tactics in his war against Poland. The dreaded Caroline cavalry charge, in tight formation and with sabres drawn, was responsible for the defeat of the combined forces of Saxony and Poland at Klissow in 1702. Charles replaced Augustus with pro-Swedish Stanislas Leszczynski. Augustus escaped to Saxony but was finally defeated in 1706.

Charles, although described by some as an impetuous adventurer, was the most powerful king in northern Europe. He had spent considerable time in Poland trying unsuccessfully to encourage Prussia to participate in an invasion of Russia. Russia would always threaten his Baltic **hegemony**, he believed, unless he attacked its very heartland by invading Moscow, a strategy shared with Napoleon and Adolf Hitler. Peter's reconquest of Livonia and his construction of a new city there, Saint Petersburg, prompted Charles to lead 40,000 men in an assault on the czar, supported by Ukranian Cossack leader Ivan Mazepa. At first the Russian attempt to ravage the route Charles would take through the Ukraine was foiled by Charles's preparedness; he had brought adequate supplies for just such an exigency. However, the winter of 1708–09 was the worst Europe had known in decades. Charles chose an alternative southern route but got lost on the way. Peter defeated Mazepa and the Russians continued their scorched earth policy.

Charles's exhausted troops arrived at the Russian outpost of Poltava in 1709. The ensuing battle was a disaster. Charles was suffering from a fever due to a bullet wound, his reinforcements were waylaid en route, and his generals disagreed on strategy. One third of his infantry had been destroyed in the Russian bombardment before ever reaching the battlefield. While fifteen thousand Swedish troops survived the fight, it was only to surrender once Charles had fled.

With only 1,300 men, Charles reached the Ottoman empire. He convinced the Ottomans to attack Russia, and was jubilant when the Turkish army surrounded Peter and his army at Pruth, but peace was declared without concessions to Sweden. The Turks, who hated Charles for inciting hostilities, referred to him as Iron Head. In 1713 his headquarters were burned and Charles imprisoned. Augustus regained Poland, Finland was seized by Russia, and Denmark and Prussia controlled the Baltic.

Accompanied by two companions, Charles made a remarkable journey incognito across Europe, arriving in Pomerania in just fifteen days. On returning to Sweden he made significant economic reforms to allow him to regain his lost empire. His new army consisted of eighty thousand men; but Sweden was never to regain its former glory. Charles was struck down by a bullet during the siege of Fredrikshald (Halden) in Norway. Although the bullet may have been a stray, some historians wonder whether it was fired by an associate of his brother-in-law, Frederick of Hesse, who succeeded Charles to the throne. His military ability and bravery became legendary, his wisdom was admired and cited, and he was regarded as an outstanding hero who was defeated by his ambition. ◆

Charles's military ability and bravery became legendary, his wisdom was admired and cited, and he was regarded as an outstanding hero who was defeated by his ambition.

Ch'ien-lung

1711–1799 ● EMPEROR OF CHINA

Ch'ien-lung was the fourth son of Emperor Yung-cheng and a grandson of K'ang-hsi, who established the Manchu dynasty's right to govern. **Primogeniture** was disregarded by the Chinese, so Ch'ien-lung, considered the most intelligent son of Yung-cheng, was chosen at an early age to succeed his father. Ch'ien-lung was a tall, handsome boy who excelled in horsemanship and archery and was an avid hunter, a hobby he pursued until two years before his death. The focus of his education was orthodox Confucianism but he also showed an interest in the arts, particularly poetry. Some 40,000 verses are attributed to Ch'ien-lung, although he probably composed only a fraction of these.

primogeniture: an exclusive right of inheritance belonging to the eldest son.

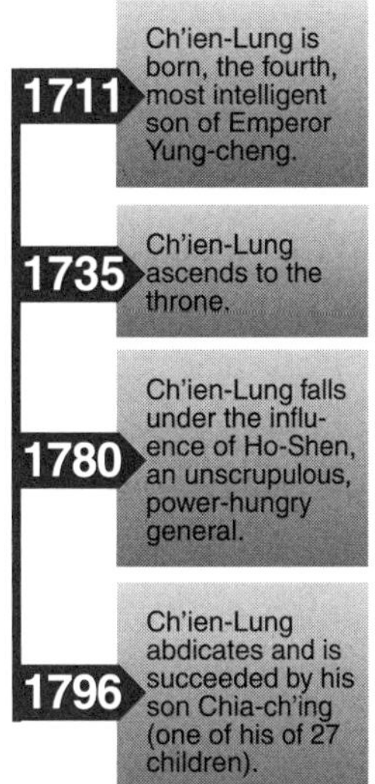

Ch'ien-lung ascended the throne in 1735. He led a temperate court life, spending the mornings dealing with affairs of state and the afternoons reading, composing verse, or painting. His successful military campaigns brought most neighboring countries under China's influence. He added 600,000 square miles to the empire, its greatest territorial extent, while Sinkiang, Tibet, Burma, and Vietnam offered tribute, as did the Gurkhas of Nepal, against whom Ch'ien-lung led his armies over the imposing plateau of Tibet.

However, Ch'ien-lung's campaigns were a burden on the Chinese economy. Toward the middle of his reign he dismissed his most trustworthy advisers in order to govern the empire on his own. No one dared criticize the emperor. He had seventeen sons and ten daughters, but his chosen heir died at the age of seven. Ch'ien-lung sought solace in his second wife, Ula Nara, but an apparent clash with the emperor caused her to leave the palace for a monastery. Ch'ien-lung then turned to a concubine, Hsiang-fei, a prisoner from Central Asia for whom he built a mosque and even an Oriental bazaar to allay her homesickness. Although Hsiang-fei threatened to kill herself if touched, her considerable influence over the emperor disgraced the court. Only when Ch'ien-lung was away from court did the **dowager** empress order Hsiang-fei to commit suicide.

dowager: a widow holding property or a title from her deceased husband.

Ch'ien-lung turned to literature, amassing an official library, the Ssu-ku Ch'uan-shu, of over 36,000 volumes, divided into classics, history, philosophy, and literature. Each book was copied by hand seven times, to be placed in royal libraries for the emperor and select scholars. At the same time, books not appearing in the library's index were hunted down and destroyed. Often their authors were also liable to the most severe punishments. About 2,500 books were proscribed by Ch'ien-lung's literary inquisition; particularly vulnerable were books by people who questioned the corrupt administration. One such author begged Ch'ien-lung to reconsider the appointment of a dissolute official. Angered, Ch'ien-lung asked who taught him to speak in such a manner, to which he replied, Confucius and Mencius. The author was banished and his books banned.

In 1780 Ch'ien-lung fell under the influence of Ho-shen, an unscrupulous, power-hungry general who, in effect, governed the country. Ch'ien-lung overlooked Ho-shen's earlier military failures and promoted him and his lackeys to positions of power. The damage to the Ch'ing dynasty was irreparable.

Ch'ien-lung's reign was marked by extremes. He was a mighty soldier and a fervent patron of the arts who abandoned his early policies for dissolute government by incompetent minions. He allowed foreign missionaries to live in China although they were forbidden to preach, but was reluctant to allow other Europeans to advance trade agreements. The British lord George Macartney visited Ch'ien-lung in Peking, but none of his demands to expand trade links beyond Canton were met. In 1796, Ch'ien-lung abdicated and was succeeded by his son, Chia-ch'ing, but Ch'ien-lung continued to rule in practice until his death. Chia-ch'ing had Ho-shen executed in a futile attempt to correct the damage to the dynasty. ◆

Christina

1626–1689 ● QUEEN OF SWEDEN

Christina's mother, Maria Eleanora of Brandenburg, never forgave her—the heir to the Swedish throne—for being born female (she was a heavy baby with a **caul** and the midwives first announced the baby was a boy) and her father, Gustavus II Adolphus of Sweden, had her educated as a prince. Scorning her femininity, she grew up dressing, swearing, riding, playing, and hunting like a man and always retained a masculine manner and often wore a man's wig. She despised other women (supposedly because of their ignorance), preferring masculine conversation and was one of the wittiest, most learned women of her age. She was nominally queen from age six after Gustavus was killed fighting for Protestantism in the Thirty Years' War (1632) and in her youth Sweden was well governed by a regency led by Count Axel Oxenstierna. After she took the throne in 1644, Christina, who was extremely strong-willed, was constantly at odds with Oxenstierna. A particular point of contention between them was the Thirty Years' War: Oxenstierna supported it militantly while Christina was one of the

caul: the inner fetal membrane of higher vertebrates, especially when covering the head at birth.

prime movers behind the Peace of Westphalia that brought it to an end. Christina was also extremely extravagant and Sweden's finances, already strained from the long war could not support her luxurious court or her grants of crown land to favorites. She eventually had to turn to Oxenstierna to help with Sweden's financial problems.

Sweden may have suffered from Christina's extravagance, but it also benefited from her enlightened rule. She reformed Swedish education, founded colleges, promoted trade and industry, and encouraged science, literature, and the founding of the first Swedish newspaper. However, most of the nobility opposed her policies, continuing in their opposition after she put down their 1651 rebellion and executed its leaders.

An avid scholar, Christina knew nine languages and was particularly interested in philosophy; she invited René Descartes to Sweden to be her teacher. She surrounded herself, and corresponded, with some of the most cultured and knowledgeable minds of the period. The confessor of the Spanish ambassador to Sweden described how she balanced her passion for learning with her conscientiousness toward her duties as Sweden's ruler: "She spends only three or four hours in sleep. When she wakes she spends five hours in reading . . . . She attends her Council regularly . . . . Ambassadors treat only with her, without ever being passed on to secretary or minister." Perhaps it was her rigorous and demanding schedule that undermined her health. Her sexuality has been a subject of debate and she seems to have had lesbian or bisexual proclivities but there is no evidence that any of her many affairs were consummated. When she was seventeen she declared herself against marriage and the thought of childbearing horrified her to the extent that she did not allow pregnant women to approach her.

Seeking a more mystical and ceremonius approach to religion, Christina asked Rome to send Jesuits to discuss Catholic theology with her (1652). Her decision to convert to Catholicism was not an easy one; after all, her father had died for Protestantism. Swedish law, moreover, decreed that only Lutherans could rule Sweden. She decided to convert and was prepared to abdicate her throne, but first entered into lengthy negotiations with the Swedish parliament to secure her future finances and ensure that her choice of a successor (her beloved cousin Charles Gustavus) was accepted. Finally, in June 1654, a moving abdication ceremony took place, Charles was crowned the next day and Christina left Sweden. Six months later, on Christmas Eve, she abjured Lutheranism.

It took Christina eighteen years to make her leisurely, pleasure-filled way from Sweden to Rome, dressed and armed as a knight. She was formally converted to Catholicism in Austria, feted by the Italian towns she passed through, and eagerly welcomed to Rome by the Pope, although he was to become disillusioned with her shocking actions and masculine attitude. She settled in Rome, but had problems with getting her agreed-upon revenue from Sweden. After pawning her jewels, she was helped by an **annuity** from the Pope. Christina also missed being a reigning monarch. Her intrigues of the papal court were no substitute and her attempts to gain a throne failed: her negotiations for Naples's throne fell through during a visit to France when she had one of her retinue put to death for conspiring against her (1657), and her 1668 candidature for the Polish throne was rejected because of her unwillingness to marry. She returned to Sweden twice but was given a cold welcome.

annuity: a sum of money payable yearly or at other regular intervals.

Christina returned to Rome where she spent the last twenty years of her life as a patron of the arts. Her taste in art—reflected in the paintings, statues and art that decorated her apartments (Rome's leading salon)—shaped European culture. She greatly influenced Italian literature, instigated Rome's first opera house, compiled an enormous and valuable collection of books and manuscripts (now in the Vatican library), built an observatory and practiced **alchemy**. A staunch defender of personal freedoms to the end, she also became active in church politics. She was buried in Saint Peter's. ◆

alchemy: a medieval chemical science aimed at turning base metals into gold and discovering a universal cure for disease and means of indefinitely prolonging life.

Cleopatra VII

69–30 B.C.E. ● QUEEN OF EGYPT

Cleopatra's family came from Macedonia and although it had ruled Egypt since the time of Alexander the Great, it had remained Greek in culture, education, and ambitions; Cleopatra was the first to learn the Egyptian language. A native uprising had driven her father, Ptolemy XI, from Egypt in 58 B.C.E., and only Rome's help restored him to his throne. Rome

took an increasing interest in Egyptian affairs, frequently dictated Egyptian policy, and stationed soldiers in Alexandria.

Cleopatra was married to her ten-year-old-brother Ptolemy XII at age seventeen (the marriage was never consummated) and was joint ruler of Egypt at eighteen. Civil war broke out and Cleopatra was banished. When Julius Caesar arrived in Alexandria (48 B.C.E.), he moved into the palace, started putting Egypt's affairs in order, and sent for Cleopatra. She had herself smuggled into Caesar's chambers in some bedding, captivated him with her liveliness and courage, and was returned to her throne. Ptolemy joined the Egyptian army in a rebellion that was defeated by Caesar, but was drowned in the Nile, carried down by the weight of his armor. Caesar then secured Cleopatra's position as Egypt's supreme ruler by marrying her to another brother, twelve-year-old Ptolemy XIII.

> ***"Age cannot wither her, nor custom stale***
> ***Her infinite variety: other women cloy***
> ***The appetites they feed: but she makes hungry***
> ***Where most she satisfies"...***
>
> William Shakespeare, *Antony and Cleopatra*, 1606

Cleopatra and Caesar's relationship stemmed from a mutual desire for each other's assets: Caesar wanted money and Cleopatra wanted power over Rome. Caesar stayed in Alexandria with Cleopatra for nine months until her son Cesarion was born (his paternity is uncertain but Caesar was the presumed father) and placed a golden statue of Cleopatra in his family's temple of Venus. Cleopatra accompanied Caesar back to Rome (47 B.C.E.), and Caesar frequently visited the villa where Cleopatra, Ptolemy, and Cesarion lived. After Caesar's assassination in 44 B.C.E., she returned to Egypt.

Egypt's trade and industry prospered under Cleopatra's competent financial administration. Her political astuteness led her to call herself the daughter of the Egyptian sun god Re, increasing her popularity among the Egyptians. It was her desire to avert Egypt's inevitable subordination to Rome that led to her attempts to gain control over Rome, and it was these ambitous—or desperate—attempts that caused her downfall.

Mark Anthony summoned Cleopatra to answer charges (which were untrue) of aiding Caesar's assassins. Cleopatra came dressed as Venus on a barge laden with gifts, which had the desired effect; Anthony followed Cleopatra to Alexandria, where he spent the winter of 41 B.C.E. indulging in extravagant debauchery until the Parthian invasion of Syria called him away. Cleopatra gave birth to twins.

Anthony made peace with Octavian (the future Emperor Augustus), sealing it with marriage to Octavian's sister, Octavia. However, he then met Cleopatra in Antioch, married her (37 B.C.E.), and gave her the lands that were once part of her family's empire as a wedding gift. Octavian ignored the marriage on the grounds that it was illegal for Roman citizens to have two wives or marry a foreigner, but it created a rift between them.

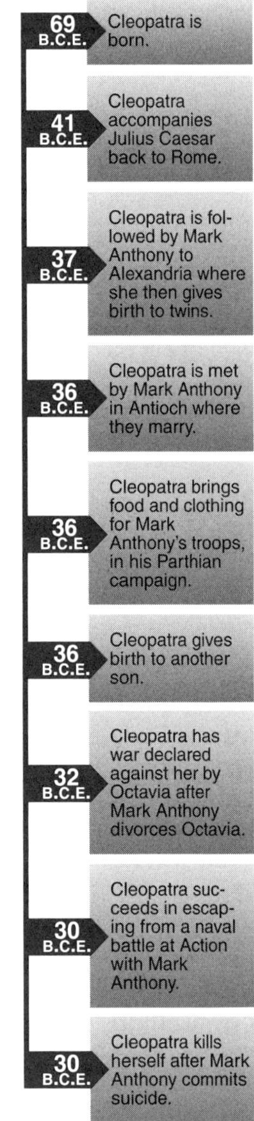

Cleopatra provided Anthony with troops but would not finance his Parthian campaign; she wanted to save Egypt's treasury for fighting Rome. The campaign (36 B.C.E.) was saved from complete disaster by Cleopatra's bringing food and clothing for Anthony's troops after their heroic retreat. Anthony waited in vain for Octavian to send the legions he had promised and Cleopatra won him over to her plans. When Octavia loyally brought the men and supplies Anthony needed, he ordered her back to Rome.

Anthony awarded himself a triumph and scandalized Rome by celebrating it in Alexandria. The triumph was followed by Anthony's declaration that Cleopatra had been Caesar's wife and Cesarion his acknowledged son, which meant disinheriting Octavian as Caesar's heir. Anthony then divided the eastern part of the Roman empire between Cleopatra, their three children (another son was born in 36 B.C.E.), and Cesarion.

Cleopatra financed the attack on Octavian, supplying many of the ships, food, and pay. But she also contributed to its defeat as she was determined to participate in the war, and her presence alienated Anthony's Roman forces, who were not willing to fight for a foreign queen. Stories of Cleopatra's control over Anthony and rumors that she was drugging him spread through Italy.

Anthony's formal divorce of Octavia (32 B.C.E.) cost him many supporters, increased Roman resentment against Cleopatra, and infuriated Octavian, who declared war against Cleopatra. Anthony was defeated in a naval battle at Actium off the Greek coast (30 B.C.E.) and although he succeeded in escaping with Cleopatra, her attempts to shake his apathy were futile. Octavian ordered Cleopatra to disarm, but she shut herself and Egypt's treasury in a mausoleum, threatening to burn it if her son was not crowned. Octavian was stalemated, as he needed the treasury to keep the support of Italy and his troops.

Rumors of Cleopatra's death led Anthony to stab himself. When he learned she was still alive, he asked to be taken to her and died in her arms. Octavian's forces broke into the mausoleum, captured Cleopatra before she could burn the treasury, and imprisoned her in the palace. Octavian killed Cesarion and threatened to kill her other children when she attempted to starve herself to death. Cleopatra tried to seduce Octavian into changing his mind, but when Octavian told her that he planned to annex Egypt and display her in his triumph, Cleopatra decided to commit suicide. Legend has it that she killed herself with the bite of an **asp**, the Egyptian symbol of divine royalty. Octavian granted Cleopatra's request to be buried beside Anthony. Her children were sent to Rome where they were raised by Octavia. ◆

asp: a small venomous snake of Egypt, usually held to be a cobra.

Clovis

C.466–511 ● CHLODWIG, KING OF THE FRANKS

At the death of his father, Childeric I, Clovis (also known as Chlodwig) inherited the realm of the Salian Franks, which extended over part of present-day Belgium, with its capital at Tournai. He united the Frankish tribes under his rule and in 486 attacked Syagrius, the last representative of Roman rule in western Europe, who had established his rule at Soissons and governed northern Gaul. The defeat of Syagrius and the conquest of Soissons enabled Clovis to annex the territory between the North Sea and the River Loire. He founded the Frankish kingdom, establishing his capital at Paris. Continuing his wars eastward, he absorbed the Ripuarian Franks on the Rhine into his realm and began expanding toward Germany. His quarrel with the Burgundians, who threatened his southern boundaries, ended in 492 with his marriage to Clotilda, niece of the Burgundian king Gundobald. Brought up as a Catholic, Clotilda sought to persuade her husband to convert to Christianity.

Clovis's quarrel with the Burgundians ended in 492 with his marriage to Clotilda, niece of the Burgundian king Gundobald.

Clovis allied himself with Theodoric the Great, king of the Ostrogoths, who had conquered Italy; Clovis gave Theodoric his sister as wife. This system of alliances allowed Clovis to extend his rule in Germany, where he defeated the Thuringians and fought against the Alamanni in 496 in a struggle so difficult that his victory was attributed to a divine miracle. Clovis's prayer to the God of Clotilda and his promise to convert to the Christian faith in the case of victory is testimony to the great battle. The victory enabled him to annex the Alamanni realm to his kingdom. His subsequent conversion was the result of a combined effort of persuasion by Clotilda and Remigius, the bishop of Rheims, whom Clotilda had brought to the court. Clovis was the first Germanic king to convert to Catholicism; the other rulers were Arians. He thus won the loyalty and support of the Gallo-Roman population, which was Christian. Moreover, religious unity allowed the emergence of peaceful relations between the conquerors and the conquered and created the conditions for their mutual assimilation, leading to the founding of France and the birth of the French people.

Clovis's achievements climaxed with the war against the Visigoths, who ruled southwestern Gaul. In 507 he defeated them at Vouill and undertook the conquest of Aquitaine and Toulouse, the capital of the Visigoths. The Visigoths were defeated in spite of the support of Theodoric.

Clovis is credited with the establishment of the Salic Law, the compilation of the legal traditions of the Salian Franks. In addition to his military and political achievements, he proved his organizational skills by enforcing rigorous discipline in his army, controlling the distribution of booty and rewarding the army chiefs. He also confiscated public lands and gave them as estates to his followers (the *leudes*), who became the new nobility of his kingdom. He did not, however, expropriate private property and was thus able to integrate the Gallo-Roman aristocracy into the ruling class of the kingdom, although they remained subordinate to the Franks.

After Clovis's death, Clotilda retired to the abbey of Saint Martin of Tours, where she was famed for her piety and good deeds. She later became the subject of many legends.

Clovis and Clotilda were buried in Paris, in the church that she and Clovis had built (now Sainte Geneviève church). ◆

Constantine I

C.274 TO 288–337 ● ROMAN EMPEROR

Constantine I, first Christian Roman emperor and founder of Constantinople, was born in Serbia, and although the month and date of his birth (February 17), is known, as it later became a public holiday, the exact year in

which he was born is uncertain (it has been placed between 274 and 288). His father, Constantius, was a native of southern Serbia and an officer in the Roman army. His mother, Helena, was of humble birth.

Constantine was born into a Roman Empire torn apart by the civil wars of rival emperors and under ever-increasing pressure on its borders from both barbarian invaders and the Persian Empire. Local armies all over the empire proclaimed emperors and battled with rival claimants; emperors who succeeded in reigning for more than five years held special celebrations to mark the occasion. Since many of these rival emperors had once been ordinary soldiers, it was said that every soldier carried the imperial purple in his knapsack; Constantine's father was no exception.

"Therefore, your Worship should know that it has pleased us to remove all conditions whatsoever, which were in the rescripts formerly given to you officially, concerning the Christians and now any one of these who wishes to observe Christian religion may do so freely and openly, without molestation."

Edict of Milan, 313 C.E.

In 284 Diocletian became emperor and in the twenty years of his rule, made administrative reforms that brought order out of chaos. In 285 he instituted a new system of government whereby the empire was ruled by two co-emperors (*augustii*), each of whom had a subordinate emperor (*caesar*). Diocletian appointed Constantius to be caesar in 293, at the same time insuring his loyalty by taking Constantine to live at court and having Constantius divorce Constantine's mother and marry Diocletian's stepdaughter. Constantine was not to see his father again for thirteen years. Constantius proved an able and loyal caesar and in 305 was appointed augustus for the western provinces when Diocletian and his coaugustus, Maximian, abdicated. When Constantius died in York, Britain, in 306 Constantine was proclaimed augustus in his place. Reduced to the rank of caesar shortly thereafter, Constantine gained the support of Maximian, by divorcing his wife and marrying Maximian's daughter.

Although he received little formal education, the years Constantine spent at Diocletian's court were invaluable training for a future emperor. Diocletian was always on the move—inspecting frontiers, reviewing the administration of provinces, suppressing revolts, and dealing with many of the same problems Constantine would later have to face. The seriousness of the Roman Empire's economic and social problems rivaled that of its military problems, but the reforms that Diocletian initiated and Constantine continued (responding to military threats by greatly increasing the bureaucracy and armed forces; ensuring that the army received crucial supplies by making land, trades, and position hereditary) shaped the Roman Empire for centuries to come.

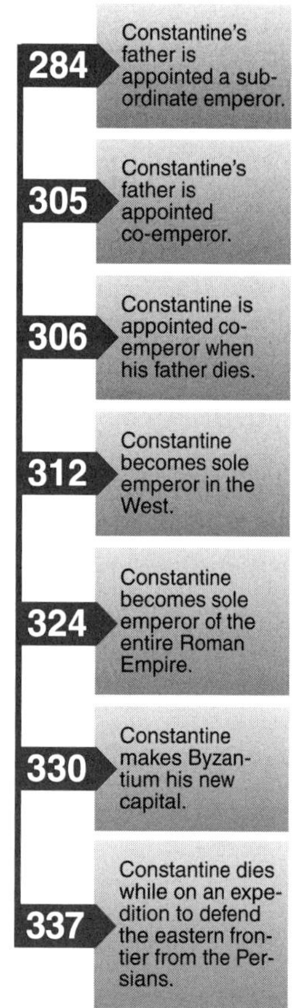

Constantine's feeling that the Christian God was a powerful divinity who must be placated for his own and the empire's continued welfare stemmed from the traditional relationship between the emperor and the multitude of religions in the Roman Empire. One of the emperor's primary tasks had always been maintaining the peace of the gods within the empire. This involved divining and doing what was pleasing to the gods so that they could be worshiped in such a manner as to ensure their continued favor and thus the prosperity and security of the empire.

After Diocletian instituted a persecution of Christians in 303 and then revoked the anti-Christian edicts after becoming seriously ill, Constantine always practiced tolerance toward Christians. In the battles for power among the rival caesars and augustii following Diocletian's abdication in 305, Constantine, according to legend, had a vision in which he saw a cross on the sun before the Battle of the Milvian Bridge (312), against a rival who was anti-Christian. He had the cross emblazoned on all his soldiers' shields and won a victory against all odds. At this point Constantine went beyond mere toleration and began making lavish donations to churches. He wrote letters and edicts on religion, seeing himself as the chosen servant of a divinity who had given him power, and position and victory. The historicity of his Edict of Milan (313), however, which formally made Christianity one of the religions legally recognized within the Roman Empire, is debated by historians.

Beginning in 312 Constantine was sole emperor of the West and in 324 fought and defeated the augustus of the eastern part of the empire, who was anti-Christian, and became the sole ruler of the entire Roman Empire. The following year he summoned and presided over the first general council of the church at Nicaea. In 326 his mother, Helena, visited the Holy Land, identified various sites connected with Jesus, and discovered what was thought to be the cross on which Jesus was crucified; she was beatified after her death in 330. He rebuilt Byzantium as the Christian city of Constantinople and in 330 made it his new capital.

Constantine tried to strengthen the succession of power by giving each of his sons and one nephew the title of caesar, allotting them parts of the empire to govern starting in 317, and sharing the government of the empire between them. While on an expedition in 337 to defend the eastern frontier against the Persians, Constantine died, officially converting to Christianity shortly before his death.

> ***"Being convinced, however, that he needed some more powerful aid than his military forces could afford him, Constantine sought Divine assistance, deeming the possession of arms and a numerous soldiery of secondary importance, but believing the co-operating power of Deity invincible and not to be shaken."***
>
> Eusebius (c. 260–340 C.E.), *Conversion of Constantine*

Constantine's support of Christianity had profound effects on the Roman Empire. An intensely religious paganism had permeated all aspects of life in the empire. Belief in the power of the supernatural and its interest in mankind, expressed through numerous cults, had pervaded all levels of society. The senate, civil service, and army were almost all pagan. Religious tolerance was the norm to which there was one exception, a typical mystery cult with only a few adherents (and those from the unimportant urban middle and lower classes): Christianity. Constantine's sponsorship meant that Christian intolerance of other religions spread to the government. The decorations and wealth of pagan shrines were stripped and given to the new, prestigious Christian churches, leaving the shrines impoverished. Pagans were viewed with disfavor while Christians were promoted. Sunday was proclaimed a weekly holiday and church building was liberally funded, especially at the holy places in Palestine identified by Constantine's mother. He detested and publicly vilified Jews, lavishly subsidizing attempts to convert them to Christianity.

Constantine's personal idiosyncracies played their part in his major failures with both the church and the empire. Susceptible to flattery, he was easily influenced by the nearest dominant personality. Capricious but easily mollified, he would make threats during outbursts of rage that he usually did not fulfill. His inability to enforce discipline also contributed to his failure to reform the civil service, where corruption and extortion were so prevalent that anything could be accomplished with money and nothing could be accomplished without it.

The Byzantine Empire, which preserved the legacy of the Roman Empire for over a thousand years, owed much to Constantine. He increased the use of barbarian troops in the army and his military reforms, which based the empire's defense on a large, centrally stationed, mobile field army that could be sent where needed instead of a system of reinforced frontier posts that required much more manpower, are credited with extending the longevity of the Roman Empire by hundreds of years. He reformed the tax system and stabilized the currency. His support of Christianity led to the decline of paganism and to Christianity's becoming the official religion of the Roman Empire in 380.

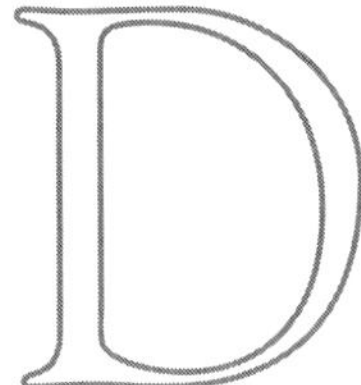

Darius I

550–486 B.C.E. ● KING OF PERSIA

Darius I ruled Persia from 521 to 486 B.C.E. He was one of three kings of the Achaemenid dynasty called Darius, meaning "possessing good things" in Old Persian. The Achaemenid dynasty began with the reign of Cyrus I (645–602 B.C.E.) and ended with the reign of Darius III in 330 B.C.E.

Darius I was the son of Hystaspes, the head of the younger branch of the Achaemenid dynasty. The older branch ended with the death of King Cambyses II, Cyrus the Great's son. According to Darius's own account recorded in the famous Behistun Inscription of 516 B.C.E., he and six other nobles killed the usurper Gaumata the Magian who had pretended to be Bardiya, the brother of King Cambyses. Darius then became king of Persia.

Darius standardized the coinage, weights, and measures of the realm, established a system of roads and a postal service, and opened the land and sea routes.

An outstanding administrator and considered the greatest royal architect of the Achaemenid dynasty, Darius I was also a man of military prowess and foresight able to consolidate an empire torn from within by revolt. After the assassination of Gaumata (or as some modern scholars hold, Bardiya himself), groups claiming to belong to the former ruling families set up their own governments. In the Behistun Inscription, Darius records that he defeated nine rebel leaders in nineteen battles. There were three rebellions in Susiana but the most serious was that in Babylon. In 520 B.C.E. Babylon surrendered, enabling Darius to crush the Medean revolt. Babylon rebelled again in the same year, but by 519 B.C.E. Darius's authority was established over the whole empire.

Darius then embarked on a number of campaigns. His conquests extended to Armenia, the Caucasus, India, the Turanian steppes, and Central Asia. In 513 B.C.E. he took eastern Thrace and crossed the Danube into European Scythia. Under his orders the satraps of Asia Minor took all of Thrace, Macedonia, Lemnos, and Imbros. Persia was thus in control of all the approaches to Greece. The conquest of Greece was strategically important to Darius as well as to Persian rulers after him. No military action was taken by Darius against Greece until 499 B.C.E., when he had to put down an Ionian rebellion backed by Athens and Eretria. In 492 B.C.E. a campaign was undertaken against Athens and Eretria by Darius's son-in-law but it was abandoned because of a storm. In 490 B.C.E. another initiative under Datis, a Mede, destroyed Eretria, but was defeated by Athens. A third campaign was planned, but Darius died in 486 B.C.E. before it could get under way.

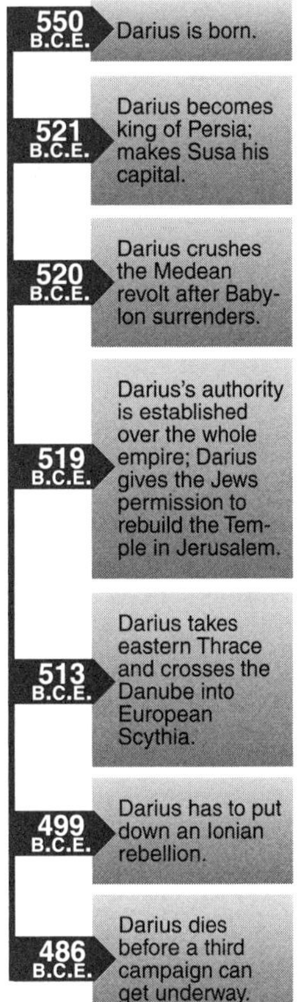

As an administrator Darius organized the empire into satrapies (provinces), completing the work of Cyrus the Great. Each province was subdivided, with governors or satraps of each division. The number of satraps and their districts often changed. Thus, according to the Book of Daniel, "It pleased Darius to set a hundred and twenty princes over the kingdom," while the Book of Esther says that Ahasuerus (perhaps Darius's son, Xerxes I, who ruled 486–465 B.C.E.) "reigned from India even until Ethiopia over a hundred and seven and twenty provinces." The yearly tribute each satrap had to contribute was fixed by Darius. He standardized the coinage, weights, and measures of the realm, established a system of roads and a postal service, and opened land and sea routes. Perhaps the greatest asset in securing the unification of his empire was his religious tolerance.

Zoroastrianism, the belief in one deity but in dual forces of truth and falsehood, was introduced as the state religion of Persia during Darius's reign. According to his inscriptions, Darius may have been a follower of Zoroaster, but this is not certain. What is certain is that he continued the example set by Cyrus the Great of respecting the diverse religious beliefs of the peoples of the empire. In Egypt, where he was held in high esteem, he built one temple, supported and restored others, and gave orders to consult Egyptian priests to codify Egyptian laws. He upheld the rights extended by Cyrus to the Greek temples, and in 519 B.C.E. he gave authority to the Jews to rebuild the Temple in Jerusalem.

In 521 B.C.E. Darius made Susa his capital, restored the walls, and built a hall for holding royal audiences and a residential palace. The foundation inscriptions of the palace record how he brought craftsmen and material from all parts of the empire. In his native Persia he established a new royal residence at Persepolis, Darius initiating a style of architecture that lasted until the end of the Persian empire. ◆

David

C.1037–C.962 B.C.E. ● KING OF ISRAEL

David's reign spanned forty years, seven of them in Hebron as ruler of Judah and thirty-three in Jerusalem as king of all Israel. The sole source of information on David is the Old Testament (1 and 2 Samuel; 1 Kings:1–2), which relates that David was the youngest of the eight sons of Jesse of the tribe of Judah, who lived in Bethlehem. According to the lineage recorded in the Book of Ruth, David was a descendant of Boaz and Ruth the Moabite.

The prologue to the drama of David's activities is the scene in which the prophet Samuel, who has decided that the succession to the throne will not remain in the family of King Saul, is sent to anoint a replacement from among the sons of Jesse; divine guidance leads him to choose the youngest son. According to one biblical account, David was introduced into Saul's royal household as a musician to soothe the king's frequent bouts of depression. According to another, it was his successful encounter with the Philistine giant Goliath, that brought him to the king's attention and led to his advancement in the army and to his marriage with the king's daughter, Michal. His relationship with Jonathan, Saul's son, has become a paradigm of true friendship.

Saul's suspicious, jealous nature turned him against David, whom he sought to kill when he suspected him of wanting to usurp the throne. David fled and, at the head of a group of misfits and malcontents, found refuge in the service of Achish, the Philistine king of Gath. With an eye to gaining support, David also maintained close relations with the elders of Judah. After Saul's death in battle with the Philistines, David and his band moved to Hebron, where the Judahites appointed him their king. Seven years later he became king of all Israel when a new leader was sought after the death of Saul's son Ishbaal; the elders of the other tribes of Israel made a covenant with him. David then turned his energies to overcoming Israel's enemies: first the Philistines on the coastal plain of Palestine then, to the east and north, the Moabites, the Arameans, Ammonites, and Edomites. The defeat of the Arameans saw David extend his rule beyond the tribal boundaries of Israel to the banks of the Euphrates. In addition to the sword, he used economic, diplomatic, and political means to assuage his enemies, developing excellent economic relations with the Phoenician Hiram, king of Tyre.

"Now he was ruddy, and withal of a beautiful countenance, and goodly to look to. And the Lord said, Arise, anoint him: for this is he. Then Samuel took the horn of oil, and anointed him in the midst of his brethren: and the Spirit of the Lord came upon David from that day forward."
King James Bible, 1 Samuel 16:11–13

David's political acumen was put to the test in molding a single nation out of the Twelve Tribes of Israel. One move was to capture Jerusalem—formerly a Jebusite stronghold and hence a neutral area—and make it his capital and center of his well-organized administration. He also turned the city into the religious center of the nation, bringing the Ark of the Covenant there and preparing to build a temple.

While achieving successes on military and political fronts, David did not find domestic peace; having taken wives from different backgrounds he was unable to forge a unified family. Particularly notorious was his plot to kill Uriah the Hittite after he had seduced Uriah's wife, Bathsheba. The two married after Uriah's death, but the adultery was condemned by the prophet Nathan, who foretold the death of the first child of this union. However, Bathsheba remained a powerful figure at court and eventually played a major role in the intrigue that resulted in their son, Solomon, becoming successor.

The system of rule established by David was not unopposed, but the king quashed attempts at revolt, including one headed by his son Absalom. The dynasty founded by David provided the rulers of Judah until the end of the kingdom in 586 B.C.E.

He himself achieved a mythic status in Jewish eyes, and it was held that the Messiah would be of the "seed of David." The New Testament traces the genealogy of Jesus Christ back to him and describes Jesus' birth in Bethlehem, David's birthplace.

Jerusalem, known as the City of David, continues to be venerated by Jews, Christians, and Muslims. As the "sweet singer of Israel," David was regarded in Jewish tradition as the composer of the Book of Psalms, seventy-three of which are specifically attributed to him. ◆

Jean Jacques Dessalines

1758–1806 ● Emperor of Haiti

Jean Jacques Dessalines was emperor of Haiti from 1804 to 1806. In the early hours of an October morning in 1806, a fierce-looking black commander was trying to force his mount through a crowd of mutinous but stunned soldiers. Finally a shot rang out, the commander's horse rolled over, breaking and pinning the rider's leg, and with cries of anguish and curses rolling from the commander's lips, the stunned soldiers knew that their hated victim was mortal after all. They shot him to pieces and dragged his mutilated body from Pont Rouge to Port-au-Prince for public display. There but one person mourned his death—she was Défilée, an insane black woman. The object of her tears and flowers was the emperor, Jean Jacques Dessalines. No man in Haitian history has been more hated by his contemporaries or loved and respected by future generations of his countrymen than Dessalines.

"For our country,
For our forefathers,
United let us march.
Let there be no traitors in our ranks!
Let us be masters of our soil.
United let us march."

"Song of Dessalines," Haitian national anthem, 1904

Born on the Cormiers plantation in northern Saint-Domingue, young Jean Jacques Duclos (later Dessalines, the name of both his owners) experienced many of slavery's horrors. Master Duclos sold his parents and a favorite aunt to neighboring plantation masters, a clear violation of the Code Noir (1685), which mandated that slave families be kept intact. In the late 1780s a free black master named Dessalines acquired the now mature Jean Jacques Duclos. His new master often whipped him, leaving him only pain and a new last name. Small wonder that Dessalines despised whites, mulattoes, and authority by the time of the Haitian revolution.

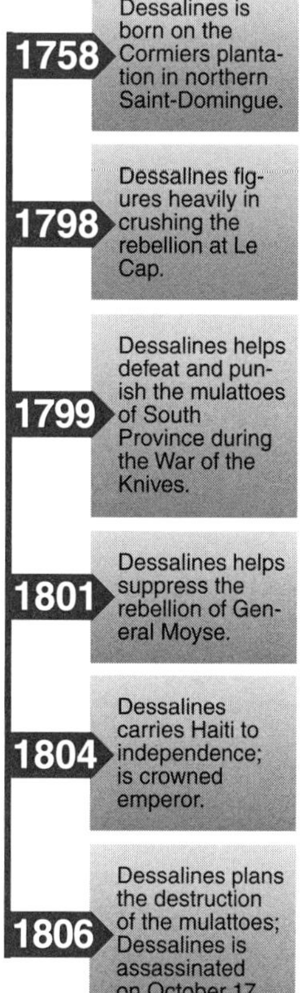

When the revolution began, Dessalines may have been a maroon (slave fugitive), but runaway or not, he soon joined the black rebels. When Dessalines joined the army of Haitian revolutionary leader Toussaint L'Ouverture is unclear, but he became indispensable to the "Black Spartacus" once he did. With a viciousness rare in Toussaint's generals, Dessalines figured heavily in crushing the rebellion of Theodore Hedouville at Le Cap (1798), in defeating and punishing the mulattoes of South Province, led by André Ricaud, during the War of the Knives (1799), in suppressing the rebellion of General Moyse (1801), and in opposing the expedition of French general Charles LeClerc (1802–04). Clearly Dessalines was a gifted field commander, who earned the title of "Tiger."

But Dessalines's brutal manner and greed often tainted these achievements. At one time Dessalines had thirty plantations and an income so large that he refused to join the Moyse rebellion on the grounds that plantation division, one of its demands, threatened his economic interests. When Toussaint sent him to South Province as an occupation governor following the War of the Knives, the Tiger murdered hundreds of mulattoes. He also slaughtered practically the entire white population of Haiti in 1804. And he enforced *fermage* (the system of forced labor and government management on plantations), introduced by Toussaint, with a severity seldom seen in any of the old colonial masters.

Some historians emphasize that Dessalines acted largely on his own. But others, among them Hubert Cole, believe that Dessalines usually acted with Toussaint's knowledge and approval, the War of the Knives providing their best argument. The brutal Dessalines served as a sort of alter ego for the gentle Toussaint. While Toussaint might have found Dessalines useful on the battlefield, he absolutely believed him unfit to rule the emerging black state. Toussaint was right.

Dessalines carried Haiti to independence on January 1, 1804, and himself to the emperorship at his coronation on October 8, 1804. That France might once again attack Haiti was his abiding fear and may have triggered his mass slaughter of all whites in mid 1804. But his furious behavior extended to the mulattoes also. He once quipped that he murdered any mulatto who looked white during the massacres of 1804. Later he mellowed with regard to the mulattoes and remarked that blacks and mulattoes should intermarry and obliterate race lines. But rationality soon gave way to another volcanic eruption of rage in Dessalines. When the mulatto leader Alexandre Pétion refused to marry his daughter, Dessalines once again turned on them, and by the end of 1806 had planned their destruction. The Haitian national historian Thomas Madiou has treated Dessalines's social policies as those of a liberal. But other historians outside Haiti disagree. James Leyburn believes Dessalines brought social disaster on Haiti and fixed the caste system on the new state.

While Toussaint might have found Dessalines useful on the battlefield, he absolutely believed him unfit to rule the emerging black state.

A reckless economic policy finally brought Dessalines down. He challenged mulatto land titles, put most of Haiti's able-bodied men under arms, enforced a harsh labor system, and neglected education. On October 17, 1806, most of Haiti rejoiced over his assassination. ◆

E

Elizabeth I

1533–1603 ● QUEEN OF ENGLAND AND IRELAND

Elizabeth I, the daughter of Henry VIII and Anne Boleyn, was the last Tudor monarch. Raised as a Protestant, she grew up amid violent religious changes that threatened her very survival. Both her mother and her childhood playmate Lady Jane Grey fell victim to political intrigue and were beheaded, while the death of her half brother, Edward VI, at the age of fifteen was followed by the reinstitution of Catholic hegemony in England under her half sister, Mary Tudor. The latter, suspecting Elizabeth of complicity in Protestant intrigues, had her imprisoned for two months in the Tower of London (1554) and confined to residences outside the capital until Mary's death in 1558.

In her early years Elizabeth received the education of a Renaissance prince, mastering Latin, Greek, and several modern languages; she became an accomplished horsewoman, and excelled as a dancer. At the same time, she learned the virtues of patience and caution, the art of dissembling, and the technique of maneuvering people or turning events to her own advantage. Only a few days after the last Protestant martyrs had

"Let tyrants fear; I have always so behaved myself that, under God, I have placed my chiefest strength and safeguard in the loyal hearts and good will of my subjects."
Elizabeth I, 1588

1533 Elizabeth is born to Henry VIII and Anne Boleyn.

1554 Elizabeth is imprisoned for two months by her half sister, Mary Tudor.

1558 Elizabeth is released from confinement upon Mary Tudor's death; Elizabeth succeeds the queen.

1564 Elizabeth approves creation of a national church to include both Catholics and Protestants.

1568 Elizabeth's encouragement of revolt in the Netherlands antagonizes Phillip II.

1586 Elizabeth is the subject of an assassination plot by her cousin Mary, Queen of Scots.

1587 Elizabeth approves Mary's execution.

been burned at the stake, news reached Elizabeth at Hatfield House of the death of "Bloody Mary" (November 17, 1558). Hearing that she had succeeded the childless queen, Elizabeth is said to have quoted Psalm 118: "This is the Lord's doing; it is marvellous in our eyes."

Her coronation three months later was a signal for nationwide rejoicing and displayed Elizabeth's love of pageantry and rich attire, although, like her grandfather Henry VII, she would be known for her tightfisted approach to spending money. One of her first acts was to make Sir William Cecil, Lord Burghley, her principal secretary of state. Like the queen a devoted though moderate Protestant, he was a wily politician, resourceful, diplomatic and, if need be, ruthless; he served her faithfully in various capacities for almost forty years. This was no easy task: while a great conversationalist, remarkably well informed, and kindhearted at times, Elizabeth was also vain, proud, and dictatorial, given to fits of temper, slow to make up her mind and quick to change it, as well as apt to blame others for the outcome of her own decisions. She could swear like a trooper, slap a councillor's face or threaten to make him "shorter by the head"; she once threw a slipper at Sir Francis Walsingham, the head of her secret service, and warned the countess of Nottingham, "God forgive you, but I never can."

An issue that long provoked argument between Elizabeth and her ministers was the desirability of a royal marriage for the sake of providing an heir to the throne. Many eligible foreign suitors were suggested, and the queen dallied with each in turn, but no agreement could ever be reached. "I am already bound unto a husband, which is the kingdom of England," she told her councillors, most probably fearing that a prince consort would diminish her own authority. Yet she did have some favorites at court, notably Robert Dudley, the Earl of Leicester (1532–88), once rumored to be her lover and intended husband, and Leicester's stepson, Robert Devereux, the Earl of Essex (beheaded as a rebel in 1601). Whether by choice or by mischance, Elizabeth remained England's "Virgin Queen."

Throughout her reign, she sought to avoid conflict at home and wasteful campaigns overseas. Disinclined to "make windows into men's souls" and imbued with a hatred of religious fanaticism, Elizabeth approved measures to create a national church broad enough to include loyal Catholics as well as Protestants. This "Anglican compromise," much to the queen's liking, was reached through the Act of Uniformity (1564), which established a Church of England; though doctrinally influenced by Calvinism and prescribing worship in the vernacular, it retained certain Catholic elements in its hierarchy and ritual. Within half a century, however, Anglicanism detached most Catholics from Rome, and England slowly became Protestant.

The tide of events abroad proved unfavorable to Elizabeth's strategy of noninvolvement. Thus, while refusing to support the French Huguenot "rebels," she opposed Spanish efforts to destroy the Reformation and antagonized Philip II by encouraging the revolt of the Netherlands (1568–81). Marauding English sea dogs led by John Hawkins and Francis Drake were another thorn in Philip's side, raiding Spanish colonies in the New World and plundering his treasure-laden galleons. Although Elizabeth protested that these English corsairs were beyond her control, she knighted Drake in 1580 and claimed her own share of the loot. King Philip retaliated by galvanizing foreign hostility toward the English queen and fomenting rebellion among her Catholic subjects.

"I know I have but the body of a weak and feeble woman; but I have the heart of a king, and of a king of England, too; and think foul scorn that Parma or Spain, or any prince of Europe, should dare to invade the borders of my realms: to which, rather than any dishonor should grow by me, I myself will take up arms; I myself will be your general, judge, and rewarder of every one of your virtues in the field."

Elizabeth I, 1588

This mutual emnity and suspicion between England and Spain were exacerbated by the political adventurism of Elizabeth's cousin Mary, Queen of Scots, whose scandalous domestic life led to her becoming an unwelcome refugee in England (1568). As a great-granddaughter of Henry VII, she had an excellent claim to the English throne; as a resolute Catholic, however, she posed a grave threat, and on Cecil's advice Elizabeth had her placed in protective custody. To Roman Catholics abroad—and to some sharing her faith within the realm itself—Mary was the legitimate queen of England. A short-lived rebellion in favor of Mary (1569), followed by Pope Pius V's ineffectual bull deposing Elizabeth three months later (1570), outraged public opinion but failed to harden the Virgin Queen's attitude toward her royal cousin, whom she treated with indulgence. The rebellious duke of Norfolk was executed in 1572 and Jesuits celebrating the newly outlawed Mass were hanged, yet it was not until correspondence implicating Mary in a plot to assassinate Elizabeth came to light (May 1586) that royal assent was finally obtained for Mary's execution in February 1587.

The Spanish monarch's fury was now directed against the **apostate** English and their "doubly accursed heretic queen." While Philip was preparing his "invincible Armada" for an invasion of England, Drake "singed the King of Spain's beard"

apostate: having renounced a religious faith.

with devastating naval attacks on Spanish ports and shipping (April 1587). The armada nevertheless set sail with 17,000 troops aboard on May 30, 1588, prompting Elizabeth to review her land forces at Tilbury, where she was greeted with enthusiasm and then delivered a memorable, rousing speech on August 19, 1588.

By then, Spain's great armada had already been shattered and dispersed (news of its fate being slow to arrive), yet the anticipated danger had the effect of promoting national unity. Saved by its fleet and proud of its warlike queen, England displayed a patriotic self-confidence that bridged religious and social divides.

> ***"We certainly think that if God ever direct our hearts to consideration of marriage we shall never accept or choose any absent husband how powerful and wealthy a Prince soever."***
> Elizabeth I, 1560

Although she could be very difficult in private, Elizabeth gained and retained the affection of her people through her personal charm and sagacity, her image. During the reign of "Good Queen Bess," England replaced Flanders as Europe's center of the wool trade; new markets for English commerce were opened up in distant lands; the East India Company received its first charter (1600), and middle-class prosperity soared. All this foreshadowed the kingdom's emergence as a leading naval and colonial power. There would be far fewer accomplishments under Elizabeth's godson and successor, James I.

The Elizabethan age witnessed a great renewal of English literature, particularly drama, which attained European stature in the works of Ben Jonson, Christopher Marlowe, and William Shakespeare. It was to Elizabeth that Edmund Spenser dedicated his *Faerie Queene* (1590), and it was to honor her also that Sir Walter Raleigh chose the name *Virginia* for England's first colony in North America. ◆

Elizabeth II

APRIL 21, 1926– ● QUEEN OF GREAT BRITAIN

Elizabeth, queen of the United Kingdom of Great Britain and Northern Ireland, was born Elizabeth Alexandra Mary on April 21, 1926, in London, the eldest daughter of Albert, duke of York, and Lady Elizabeth Bowes-Lyon. Princess Elizabeth and her younger sister, Princess Margaret Rose, were educated primarily at home, supervised by their mother and by their governess, Marion Crawford. During

World War II, while the German Luftwaffe was bombing London and other parts of Britain, the princesses Elizabeth and Margaret were moved from London to the comparative safety of Windsor Castle, twenty-one miles west of London, and Balmoral Castle in Scotland. When Elizabeth turned eighteen, as the war was nearing its end, she joined the ambulance service as a subaltern and took an ambulance driving and vehicle maintenance course at Aldershot.

"As a daughter, a mother and a grandmother, I often find myself seeking advice, or being asked for it, in all three capacities. No age group has a monopoly of wisdom, and indeed I think the young can sometimes be wiser than us. But the older I get, the more conscious I become of the difficulties young people have to face as they learn to live in the modern world."
Elizabeth II, 1998

Elizabeth was not directly in line to become queen, and would have lived a very different life had not her uncle King

Edward VIII fallen in love with an American woman named Wallis Warfield Simpson. Edward, who came to the throne in 1936, was a very popular king, but caused a crisis when he announced his intention to marry Wallis Simpson; not only was she an American and not of noble blood, but she was in the process of divorcing her second husband. Edward insisted on his right to marry as he pleased, but the government, headed by Prime Minister Stanley Baldwin, strongly opposed the marriage, and the struggle became a contest between the monarch and the cabinet. Although the king was well liked by his subjects, the public, too, disapproved of his choice. After a stalemate, Edward executed a deed of abdication that ended his 325-day reign and made him the first English king to voluntarily relinquish his throne. Parliament passed a bill of abdication on December 11, 1936, and Edward's younger brother became king. Edward married Wallis Simpson six months later, in France. As eldest child of the new king, Princess Elizabeth became heir to the throne.

The new monarch (born Albert Frederick Arthur George, on December 14, 1895) was crowned King George VI on May 12, 1937; he took the name George in an effort to restore a sense of continuity and stability after the death of his father, George V, the previous year. George VI was an extremely popular king, in part because he and the queen refused to leave London during the Blitz, even though Buckingham Palace was bombed nine times. The king and queen shared the dangers of war with their subjects, and George further boosted the people's morale by visiting bombed areas in Britain, inspecting munitions factories, and touring theaters of war and encouraging the troops, as in his visits to North Africa (1943), Italy (1944), and on the beaches of Normandy just ten days after the D-Day landing of Allied forces in the summer of 1944. The king also devised the George Cross medal for civilian gallantry.

In early 1947 Princess Elizabeth traveled with the king and queen to South Africa. When they returned to London, it was announced that Elizabeth was betrothed to her distant cousin Philip. Born on June 10, 1921, at Corfu, Greece, Philip Mountbatten was a prince of Greece and Denmark (his father was Prince Andrew of Greece and Denmark, 1882–1944); his mother, Princess Alice (1885–1969), was a descendant of Queen Victoria. Prince Philip was raised mainly in Britain, educated at Gordonstoun School, and trained at the Royal Naval

College. He served with the Royal Navy from January 1940 to the end of the war, seeing combat action in the Mediterranean and in the Pacific. He was not, however, a British subject until after the war. On February 28, 1947, Philip renounced his right to the Greek and Danish thrones, and became a British subject. Just before Philip's marriage to Elizabeth, King George designated him a royal highness and named him Baron Greenwich, earl of Merioneth, and duke of Edinburgh—titles he retains to this day.

Princess Elizabeth and Prince Philip married on November 20, 1947, in Westminster Abbey, and made their home at Clarence House in London. Their first child, Prince Charles (Charles Philip Arthur George), was born at Buckingham Palace on November 14, 1948, almost exactly a year after the royal wedding. The queen's other children are Princess Anne (Anne Elizabeth Alice Louise), born August 15, 1950; Prince Andrew (Andrew Albert Christian Edward), born February 19, 1960, and created duke of York in 1986; and Prince Edward (Edward Anthony Richard Louis), born March 10, 1964.

> ***"I have in sincerity pledged myself to your services, as so many of you are pledged to mine. Throughout all my life and with all my heart I shall strive to be worthy of your trust."***
>
> Elizabeth II, coronation address, June 2, 1953

A royal tour of Australia and New Zealand, planned for 1949, had to be postponed indefinitely because of the king's declining health; in the summer of 1951 George's health deteriorated to the point where Princess Elizabeth was called upon to represent him at various state occasions, including the Trooping of the Colour, a public mounting of the garrison guards at Buckingham Palace. In October 1951 Princess Elizabeth and Prince Philip embarked on a very successful tour of Canada and Washington, D.C. They spent Christmas in England, then set out for a tour of Australia and New Zealand, by way of Africa. They were in Kenya when they were told of the king's death; King George VI died in his sleep at Sandringham, his birthplace, on February 6, 1952.

Elizabeth flew immediately back to London, and entered a formal period of mourning that lasted three months. That summer, after moving into Buckingham Palace, Queen Elizabeth, already well instilled with the sense of duty for which her father was famous, began to undertake the regular duties of a sovereign. She carried out her first state opening of parliament on November 4, 1952. Elizabeth's coronation, held at Westminster Abbey on June 2, 1953, was the first to be televised. The splendor and ceremony were a great lift to a nation still staggering from six years of war, and journalists wrote excitedly of a New Elizabethan Age.

Charles at his investiture as Prince of Wales, 1969

The principal concerns early in Elizabeth's reign were, domestically, the nation's need for postwar economic recovery and, internationally, the withdrawal from empire. It was once said that the sun never sets on the British Empire, but after World War II Britain found most of its former possessions breaking loose and becoming republics. One after another—Malaya (1957), Nigeria (1960), Uganda (1962), Jamaica (1962), and Zambia (1964), among others—former colonies were declaring independence. The queen remained head of the British Commonwealth, which included Canada and Australia, but her role was increasingly ceremonial.

Meanwhile, as the Empire diminished and the Commonwealth became less of a unified body, Great Britain was forming stronger ties to Europe. The postwar period saw the rise of many European alliances and economic partnerships, and though these groups offered definite benefits, Britain was not always sure it wanted to join. Sometimes the feeling was mutual; Britain's first two applications to join the European Economic Community were vetoed by France's Charles de Gaulle in 1963 and 1967, before Prime Minister Edward Heath's government finally secured admission in 1972. Plans for a European federation seemed to disturb as many Britons as it attracted, particularly as political and economic integration appeared to threaten national sovereignty. Britain still has not fully joined the European partnership that would necessitate shifting to the "euro" as currency; to do so would overturn over a thousand years' tradition—back to the time of King Alfred—of having the British monarch's image on the back of every coin.

Personal problems have also vexed Queen Elizabeth, almost from the beginning of her reign, and the difficulties have only gotten worse as the British press has grown increasingly intrusive and irreverent. All three of Queen Elizabeth's children's marriages have ended in divorce. Princess Anne's marriage to Captain Mark Phillips was dissolved in 1992; Andrew, the duke of York, divorced Sarah Ferguson in 1995; and the highly publicized marriage of Prince Charles and Princess Diana ended in divorce in 1996, after a separation that was announced in 1993.

Princess Diana, 1988

The year 1992 was particularly cruel to the queen, as she admitted in a speech before the Guildhall in November of that year. In addition to the marital breakdowns and the publication of *Diana: Her True Story*, a tell-all book highly embarrassing to the royal family, a great fire at Windsor Castle devastated the roof of St. George's Hall and reduced the beautiful Waterloo Chamber to a charred shell. In her speech to the Guildhall, she said, "1992 is not a year on which I shall look back with undiluted pleasure. In the words of one of my more sympathetic correspondents, it has turned out to be an ***annus horribilis***." It is a sign of this reserved queen's reluctance to be seen complaining that she used a Latin term to say she had had a "horrible year."

annus horribilus: terrible year.

Meanwhile, a tabloid campaign (largely driven by the same media owner whose network broadcast Diana's interview) resulted in the royal family's agreement to pay tax on their private income. Actually, that idea had been gathering momentum for about two decades. Prime Minister John Major announced to the House of Commons that the queen and the Prince of Wales would pay tax on their private income from 1993, and said that the initiative had come from the queen herself. If the royal family expected any tokens of gratitude from the press, they must have been disappointed; the basic response was that the queen was giving too little, too late.

Though the press has been comparatively easy on the queen herself, she has had to watch as the tabloids of Fleet Street escalated their profits by magnifying in bold front-page stories the minutest embarrassments that leak through the palace walls. Matters weren't helped when in 1994 Prince Charles admitted in a televised interview that he had cheated on Diana, and implied that he had never loved her—at least not as much as his old friend Camilla Parker Bowles. In 1995 Queen Elizabeth received no advance notice when a television station broadcast a confessional interview with Princess Diana that made the House of Windsor look every bit as cold and unfeeling as many had come to suspect it was. Finally the queen wrote letters to Charles and Diana and told them to end the marriage.

By all accounts, the relationship between the queen and Princess Diana had always been strained. When the princess died at the age of thirty-six in a high-speed automobile accident in Paris on the night of August 30, 1997, the world was shocked and grieved, and yet it seemed that even in death the princess was still making life difficult for the queen. The royal family was on vacation at Balmoral Castle in Scotland at the time the news broke. Prince Charles flew at once to Paris to bring his former wife's body back to England, but the queen remained in Balmoral with her grandsons, Prince William and Prince Harry. It is customary when the queen is away from Buckingham Palace for the flagpole to be bare, for that flagpole is only for the royal standard, and the flag is up only when the queen is in residence. The British people in large numbers were offended by the bare flagpole, and felt that the absence of a Union Jack at half-mast was an insult to Diana. For days the royal protocol held firm, and the queen stayed out of sight in Scotland, while tabloid headlines screamed and pleaded, "Where Is Our Queen? Where Is Her Flag?" and "Your People Are Suffering. Speak to Us, Ma'am."

"This week at Balmoral, we have all been trying to help William and Harry come to terms with the devastating loss that they and the rest of us have suffered. No one who knew Diana will ever forget her. Millions of others who never met her, but felt they knew her, will remember her. I for one believe that there are lessons to be drawn from her life and from the extraordinary and moving reaction to her death."

Elizabeth II, speech in response to the death of Diana, September 5, 1997

In the United States the president would have been on television within hours of such a calamitous public event, but the queen remained quiet for many days. On Friday, September 5, nearly a week after Diana's death, the queen returned to London and walked (at a regal distance) among the crowds lining Buckingham Palace, and thanked them for their prayers and flowers. That afternoon she addressed the nation from a room overlooking the crowds outside who had come by the tens of thousands to bring flowers and grieve. "What I say to you now, as your Queen and as a grandmother, I say from the heart. . . . [Diana] was an exceptional and gifted human being. . . . I share in your determination to cherish her memory. This is also an opportunity for me, on behalf of my family, and especially Prince Charles and William and Harry, to thank all of you who have brought flowers, sent messages and paid your respects in so many ways to a remarkable person."

It will take years to see what effect the death of Princess Diana will have on the monarchy, and how people will remember her and Queen Elizabeth II. Many have speculated that the princess's untimely death may have helped jolt the House of Windsor into the twentieth century, and may have loosened some of the rigid protocol that has often made the royal family appear remote and out of touch with the people. Queen Elizabeth, though clearly uncomfortable with the demands of the media age, went a considerable distance to reach out to her subjects and show that she heard them, and cared for them. ◆

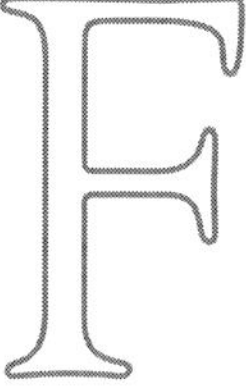

Fahd ibn Abd al-Aziz Al Saud

1921– ● KING OF SAUDI ARABIA

Fahd frequently uses the title Custodian of the Two Holy Places, which reflects his special position in Islam of being responsible for the care of the holy cities of Mecca and Medina and for the conduct of the annual Muslim *hajj* (pilgrimage to Mecca). For nearly forty years, he has played a key part in shaping the policies of Saudi Arabia.

Fahd was born in Riyadh, the eleventh son born to King Abd al-Aziz Al Saud (known in the West as ibn Saud) and the eldest of seven sons of the king's favorite wife, Hassa bint Ahmad Al Sudayri. Fahd and his full brothers form the largest and most cohesive grouping within the Al Saud (House of Saud), the Al Fahd or, in popular Western (not Saudi) usage, the Sudayri Seven. They are thus the dominant faction in a system of government where national politics are essentially family politics. Not only do King Fahd's full brothers hold the two top positions in the key ministries of defense and interior, as well as the important governorship of Riyadh, but his sons and their families have important roles in the domestic and foreign affairs of the kingdom. While their collective ability and energy are impressive, Fahd may be the most intelligent of the sons of Abd al-Aziz next to the late King Faisal.

> ***"I will be father to the young, brother to the elderly. I am but one of you; whatever troubles you, troubles me; whatever pleases you, pleases me."***
>
> King Fahd

Fahd received the traditional Saudi court education, rote memorization of the Koran and mastery of the rudiments of various practical subjects. In middle age, he applied himself to acquiring some knowledge of English, history, and politics.

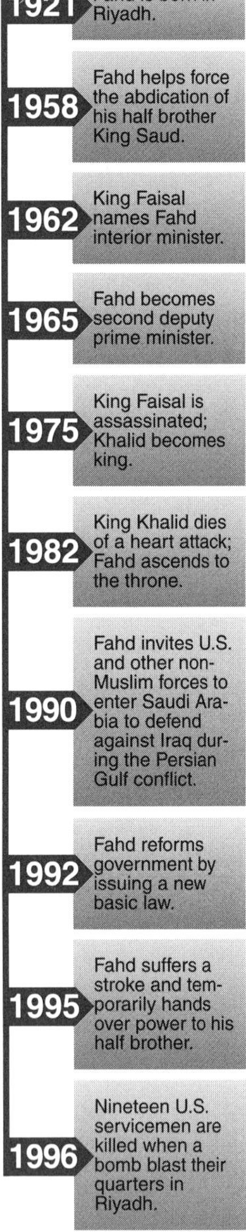

From early adulthood, Fahd's career led rapidly to the exercise of power in key positions. He is the first Saudi king to achieve that position through a career in the bureaucracy. In 1952, just before the death of his father, Fahd had joined the newly established Council of Ministers as the country's first minister of education. In that capacity, he oversaw the creation of a national education system that made possible the enormous expansion of educational opportunities for Saudis at all levels in subsequent decades. In 1958 he helped lead the attempt to force the abdication of his half brother King Saud. When the older half brother Faisal assumed executive powers as prime minister in 1962, he named Fahd interior minister, confirming a close partnership that would continue until King Faisal's death. Fahd was effective in implementing Faisal's reforms and by the early 1970s had emerged as the most influential prince, already a key voice in foreign-policy issues.

In 1965 the royal family had agreed on Fahd's designation as second deputy prime minister, shortly after it had prevailed on the reluctant Prince Khalid ibn Abd al-Aziz to become crown prince. (Thus a smooth succession was assured when an unbalanced nephew assassinated King Faisal on March 25, 1975.) Khalid and Fahd had formed an effective partnership, with contrasting personalities and qualities. Fahd was, in the Saudi context, a progressive and had made his mark as an able administrator, someone who saw clearly the inevitable challenge of modernization that Saudi Arabia faced and the sorts of reforms required if the kingdom and the Al Saud were to meet the challenge successfully. He enjoyed the exercise of power and worked effectively with bureaucrats and technocrats.

Khalid, who had hoped to avoid the burdens of rule, embodied important qualities that Fahd lacked—a genuine religious piety and traditional bedouin simplicity of manner that endowed him with a paternalistic image of great appeal to most Saudis. This helped to maintain Saudi Arabia's stability as its conservative society entered the most rapid phase of its economic and social development. Though King Khalid suffered from heart disease, undergoing open-heart surgery both before and after his accession, he played an active role in all major decisions, and Fahd was always careful to defer to the king in his presence. Together they guided the kingdom through a period of great perils—the U.S.–brokered Camp David Accords between Egypt and Israel, which estranged Saudi Arabia from its principal Arab ally; the Iranian revolution of 1979 that fomented Shiite unrest in Saudi Arabia's eastern province (al-Hasa) and helped trigger a profoundly unsettling attempt at a neoconservative Islamic uprising when militants seized the Great Mosque at Mecca; and the outbreak of the Iran-Iraq War, which threatened to spill over into Saudi Arabia.

> ***"I believe the U.S. can play an important part in solving the [Palestinian] problem if we take into account not only American influence worldwide, but also the strong relationship between America and Israel."***
> King Fahd, 1977

When King Khalid succumbed to a heart attack on June 13, 1982, Fahd's accession was smooth, with his next eldest half brother, Abdullah, immediately confirmed as crown prince and Sultan ibn Abd al-Aziz Al Saud, his next eldest full brother, designated as second deputy prime minister and effectively the next in succession.

Serious challenges have marked Fahd's rule. He became king just as petroleum prices were beginning a downward plunge that would shortly reduce the kingdom's oil revenues more than fivefold. A neoconservative Islamist movement continues to challenge the Islamic legitimacy of the Al Saud. Israel's 1982 invasion of Lebanon, U.S. failures to provide requested weapons systems, and the Iran-Contra revelations of U.S. arms deliveries to Iran for use in its conflict with Iraq appeared to undermine the wisdom of Fahd's close relationship with Washington and weakened his position in the Arab world. Finally, the Iran-Iraq War presented Saudi Arabia with a constant menace.

In facing these challenges, King Fahd has suffered from disabilities that derive from his personality and style of rule.

secularist: one who rejects religion or religious considerations.

Rather than embodying the traditional religious and social values associated with Al Saud leadership, Fahd suffers from identification with Western, secular tastes. Because of his progressive **secularist** image, he is often obliged to defer to the *ulama*—the religious establishment—as in agreeing to impose stricter regulations on the public conduct of Saudis and foreigners. (It was easier for King Faisal to enact far-reaching reforms over the objections of the *ulama*, since his own unassailable piety armed him against their opposition.) Moreover, King Fahd lacks ties to the Arab tribes, still a key constituency in Saudi Arabia, and he generally lacks the common touch that characterized King Khalid's relations with his subjects. Fahd's work habits are noncontinuous; he tends to fluctuate between prolonged inactivity and intense application in dealing with the business of state. Finally, Fahd has an easygoing nature and shies away from confrontation.

"With the blessing and grace of Almighty God and with the assistance of the faithful Saudi people, we shall continue the welfare march of construction and development and maintain the gains which are reflected by comprehensive achievements in various fields."
King Fahd

Despite these drawbacks, Fahd has provided generally effective leadership as king, often surprising those who tend to underestimate him. He has personally supervised an aggressive Saudi oil policy to protect the kingdom's long-term interests. In the Gulf crisis, his decision to invite U.S. and other non-Muslim forces to enter Saudi Arabia in August 1990, over Crown Prince Abdullah's objections, to defend the kingdom against possible invasion by Iraq and then to liberate Kuwait from Iraqi occupation fatally upset the calculations of Iraq's president Saddam Hussein that Fahd would remain passive. On March 1, 1992, Fahd issued a new basic law that included provision for a long-discussed consultative council (*majles*) but going beyond what had been anticipated in the scope of proposed governmental changes, including the opening of the royal succession to the grandsons of ibn Saud.

The basing of U.S. military forces in Saudi Arabia following the Gulf War continues to irritate many Saudis of different political and religious persuasions. The Western presence, although invited by the king, is seen by many as a foreign transgression too close to the holy lands of which the king claims to be the protector. Supposedly on guard against any further incursions by Iraq, the U.S. military is seen as imposing itself on what is a regional, not an international, dispute.

In June 1996 a car bomb exploded outside the Khobar Towers housing complex and National Guard facility in Riyadh, where U.S. trainers instructing the Saudi National Guard were housed. The blast tore away a huge chunk of the building and killed nineteen U.S. servicemen. Iran was suspected of being involved. U.S. investigators have repeatedly expressed frustration with the cautious and slow-moving nature of Saudi "cooperation" in the investigation. Crown Prince Abdullah, the leading man in Saudi Arabia's foreign policy in the second half of the 1990s, has been cultivating warmer relations with Iran (in addition to closer ties with Egypt and Syria), and if indeed Iranians were involved in the bombing, it would not necessarily further Abdullah's Iranian agenda to assist U.S. agents in locating the perpetrators. The Khobar Towers blast followed a similar, though less destructive, bombing in November 1995.

"We shall never sacrifice our values and religion for any materialistic gains. Our aspirations are in response to the aims of our people. With this concept we can face all our difficulties firmly and decisively. We are not only working for today, but looking toward the future."

King Fahd

Although King Fahd has modernized some aspects of the Saudi government, he has shown little interest in allowing social change. Women still must wear veils in public, movies are banned, and alcohol is forbidden. The king has found himself obliged to defer to the *ulama* and to allow the more radical Islamists to speak out, and he must at least appear to favor a conservative social agenda. In November 1990 (only months before the Gulf War), a group of Saudi women staged a demonstration demanding the right to drive cars. Some of the protestors were university professors; they were fired, and their passports revoked for a year, while posters denouncing the women as sexually promiscuous were widely displayed in public by the religious police. The religious police, meanwhile, have seen their funding increased.

Calls for political liberalization—particularly by Salafiyah groups and Shiites—have been answered with evasions, stalling tactics, half measures, and repression. Members of the Council of Senior *Ulama* who showed sympathy with some Salafi demands were replaced by more conservative clerical scholars whom the monarchy could trust to preserve the status quo. Petition signers, critics of the government, and other voices for change have found themselves dismissed from their jobs, blocked from attending universities, or have had their passports confiscated. Some go to prison.

The monarchy is clearly caught between conflicting demands for tightening the society on one hand, and loosening it in a more Western style on the other. Meanwhile, each side receives pressure and reinforcement from the outside world; conservative Islamist groups in neighboring countries do not want the holy lands of Mecca and Medina defiled by "heathen" influences; at the same time, the Saudi government is pressed by human rights organizations—mostly based in the West—to relax its strictures on women and political dissidents. King Fahd, though conservative, is not truly as "hard line" a ruler as he is being pressed to be.

But to what extent is King Fahd still the supreme ruler of Saudi Arabia? In 1995 he suffered a serious stroke and handed over power to his half brother, Crown Prince Abdullah bin Abdel Aziz, for six weeks. The king has never fully recovered from that stroke, and has been hospitalized several times. Since the king's return from the hospital following the stroke, and through his subsequent illnesses, Abdullah has assumed more and more authority in running the kingdom, particularly in foreign affairs and in setting the kingdom's oil policy. He is also the head of the National Guard, which he has led since 1962.

In November 1990 a group of Saudi women staged a demonstration demanding the right to drive cars.

While the king has a reputation among his people as a Western-style former playboy who is not sufficiently devout, Abdullah is an austere, pious traditionalist with strong ties to the Arab world, and has the respect of the kingdom's powerful tribes and religious leaders. Although Vice President Al Gore paid his respects to King Fahd in a May 1998 visit to the Asalama Palace, the session was brief; the real business took place at another palace where the vice president had a working dinner with Crown Prince Abdullah.

Abdullah is widely seen by Western diplomats as a safe bet for basic continuity and good relations, but he is regarded as less likely than Fahd automatically to take a pro-Western position in policy matters. It is not definite, only presumed, that Abdullah will succeed Fahd. He is seventy-five, and even if he is the next king, he must soon be thinking about his own successor. How Abdullah and succeeding kings will manage the social and political tensions pulling at Saudi Arabia will determine not only the fate of that nation but of its monarchy. ◆

Faisal I ibn Husayn

1889–1933 ● KING OF IRAQ

The third son of Sharif Husayn of the Hijaz, Faisal was from a prestigious, wealthy family (Hashimite) that traced its lineage back to the Prophet Muhammad. He spent his early boyhood among the bedouin in Arabia, was educated by private tutors, and at age six, moved to Istanbul, capital

of the Ottoman empire, where he lived during his father's exile until 1908. Faisal completed his education in Istanbul, becoming multilingual and well versed in court etiquette and politics. Life in cosmopolitan Istanbul and his later service as representative from Jidda in the Ottoman parliament, where he was an early spokesman for Arab interests, provided valuable political experience that served Faisal well in his later negotiations with the European powers.

In January 1915 Faisal was sent by his father to Istanbul to determine the political situation of the Hijaz and to contact secret Arab societies in Damascus, Syria, to ascertain if there was support for an Arab uprising against the Ottoman Turks. At first, signs were positive; but at a second meeting in Damascus in January 1916, after these groups had been disbanded by Cernal Pasa, the few remaining nationalists indicated via the Damascus Protocol that Husayn should initiate a revolt for Arab independence. Husayn incorporated these ideas in his correspondence with the British. Faisal was less sanguine about British support than was his brother, Abdullah ibn Husayn, but Ottoman Turkish moves to strengthen their hold on Medina made action more imminent. (The Turks were fighting on the side of the Central powers—Austria-Hungary and Germany—and against the Allies, including Britain and France, in World War I.)

Faisal's note to Cernal Pasa advocated an Arab *ummah* (community). His statement and the cutting of the railroad lines between Damascus and Medina launched the Arab revolt on June 10, 1916. Concern in Cairo that the Arab troops in Arabia needed military training led to the dispatch of the British colonel Thomas Edward Lawrence, who by December 1916 had joined Faisal and suggested to the British that the emir become the field commander of the Hijaz. The suggestion was taken, and, though unable to take Medina, Faisal's troops later occupied Aqaba on July 6, 1917, a victory that provided the Arabs credibility with the British. Faisal was deputized a British general under the command of General Edmund

bedouin: a nomadic Arab of the Arabian, Syrian, or north African deserts.

Allenby, commander-in-chief of the Egyptian Expeditionary Force. Faisal's troops, some 1,000 **bedouin** supplemented by approximately 2,500 Ottoman ex-prisoners of war, proceeded to harass the Ottoman Turkish army as the British moved to take Gaza, Beersheba, and Jerusalem.

On September 25, 1918, Allenby ordered the advance on Damascus. As party to the Sykes-Picot Agreement, Britain attempted to assign organized administration of the city both to the French and to the Arabs, but in the confusion of the British advance and the Ottoman retreat, the Damascus Arabs hoisted their own flag before Faisal and his army had time to reach Damascus. With the aid of Faisal's supporter, Nuri al-Said, pro-Faisal officials controlled the city and were later confirmed by the French. Lawrence asserted that Faisal's men had slipped into the city on September 30–October 1 and had liberated it in advance of the British and Australian troops.

At the Versailles conference in 1919, Faisal was caught between British–French international diplomacy and events in the Middle East that were taking their own course. As the Arab representative to Versailles, Faisal pressed claims for Syrian independence, but under British sponsorship. Discussions with American proponents of Zionism and with Zionist leader Chaim Weizmann elicited Faisal's support for Jewish immigration to Palestine, culminating in the Faisal-Weizmann Agreement signed on January 3, 1919. To the published document, Faisal added a handwritten addendum that Arab support for Jewish aspirations would be conditional upon the achievement of Arab independence. Faisal continued to support Jewish immigration within the context of his later pan-Arab federation programs.

In May Faisal called for a general congress to be held in Damascus to endorse his position at Versailles. Convened in June, the meeting was dominated by the prewar Arab nationalist clubs—the primarily Iraqi al-Ahd, the Palestinian Arab Club (al-Nadi al-Arabi), which tried to persuade Faisal to relinquish his support for Zionism, and the al-Fatat (Youth)-dominated Istiqlal party. The congress called for an independent Syria that also would include Lebanon, Jordan, and Palestine. Backed by the British, who wished to exclude the French from the Middle East, Faisal received a grudging acquiescence for an Arab regime from the politically weakened French president, Georges Clemenceau.

Still in session in March 1920, the congress declared Syria (including Lebanon and Palestine) an independent kingdom ruled by Faisal as constitutional monarch. Some Arabs in Palestine proclaimed Palestine a part of Syria, and Basra and Baghdad were declared independent by a group of Arabs in Iraq who wished to be ruled by Faisal's brother, Abdullah. In spite of the international repercussions, Faisal accepted the Syrian draft and allowed Arab nationalists to harass French troops in Syria while he began to negotiate with the forces of Kemalism in Anatolia who had proclaimed an independent Turkey. As the British withdrew their support from the Arabs in Syria, and a new government in Paris followed a more vigorous policy in Syria, the French ordered their high commissioner in Syria, General Henri-Joseph-Eugène Gouraud, to confront Faisal. Occupying Damascus on July 26, 1920, the French forced Faisal into exile the following day and proclaimed Syria to be under French rule.

A shift in British priorities affected policy after 1920, influenced by an Arab revolt in Iraq against the British occupation and the policies of Winston Churchill, newly appointed colonial secretary, which included leaving Syria to the French and installing Hashimites elsewhere as local rulers who would "reign but not govern" in order to save the expense of full-scale occupation. At the Cairo Conference in March 1921, Churchill and his aides proceeded to redraw the map of the Middle East and to plan the installation of Faisal as king of a newly created Iraq.

The British looked to Faisal as a **malleable** vehicle for their Mesopotamian/Iraqi policy, which was to secure the area and its oil for themselves. He was deemed suitable to both the Sunni and Shiite Iraqis because of his Hashemite lineage and his Arab nationalist credentials as leader of the Arab revolt. Any local candidates, such as Sayyid Talib of Basra, were duly eliminated. The British contrived a **plebiscite** in July 1921 to authorize Faisal's candidacy. In August 1921 Faisal arrived in Iraq to a lukewarm reception and was proclaimed king.

malleable: capable of being influenced by outside forces.

plebiscite: a vote by which the people of an entire country express an opinion for or against a choice of government or ruler.

The leader of the Arab revolt brought with him to Iraq a **coterie** of Iraqi (former Ottoman) Arab nationalist army officers who had supported him in Syria and who now took top positions in the new Iraqi administration. Jafar al-Askari became minister of defense; perennial cabinet minister Nuri al-Said became chief of staff of the new Iraqi army; and Ottoman educator Sati al-Husri instituted an Arab nationalist curriculum in Iraqi schools. Faisal's tenure in Iraq was a tightrope walk between nationalism and cordial relations with Britain, without whose financial and military support and advisers he could not rule. Always maintaining his own goals, while remembering the

coterie: an intimate group of persons with a unifying common interest or purpose.

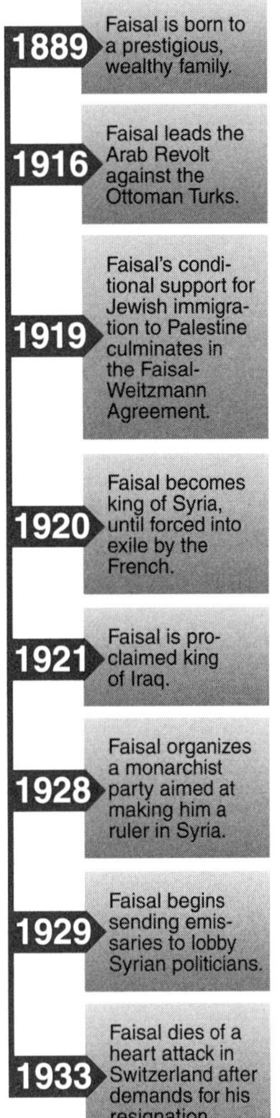

bitter Syrian experience, Faisal worked from 1921 until his death in 1933 to create a modernized, unified country with a centralized infrastructure, to achieve immediate political independence from Britain, and to continue his dream of uniting Arab areas of the Middle East into a pan-Arab union under Hashemite aegis. From the beginning, the British regretted their choice, as Faisal proved to be less docile than they had anticipated.

Throughout the 1920s Faisal was preoccupied with the fact that Iraq was a British mandate and not an independent state. Faced with local nationalist opposition to himself and to the British presence in the country, he used his considerable personal charisma to garner the support of urban nationalists and tribal leaders in Shia areas. Comfortable both in traditional dress meeting with bedouin and in Western-style clothes playing bridge with British officials in Baghdad, Faisal negotiated for independence. He also understood the necessity for British political and military support to ensure the territorial integrity of the new state until Iraq was able to build up its own army and defend its interests against the Persians, Saudis, and Turks, from whom Britain managed to secure Mosul for Iraq.

During treaty negotiations in 1922, delayed by his appendicitis attack, and again in 1927, the king encouraged the anti-British nationalist opposition, all the while advocating moderation by both sides. The result was an agreement signed in 1930 that gave Britain control of Iraqi foreign policy and finances but also resulted, in 1932, in Iraq's nominal independence and admission to the League of Nations.

The Iraqi constitution gave Faisal the power to suspend parliament, call for new elections, and confirm all laws. During his tenure, the king attempted to forge a united Iraq with a nationalist focus instead of the patchwork of disparate religious and ethnic groups. Once independence was assured, Faisal used his prestige and his position as king of an independent Arab state to engage in foreign policy.

Faisal never abandoned his interest in Syria. In contact with the French in Syria over the possibility that a Hashemite such as Abdullah or Ali (especially after the latter lost his throne in Arabia to the Saudis) might be installed there as he was in Iraq, Faisal was also active in local Syrian politics. In 1928 he organized a monarchist party aimed at making him ruler both in Iraq and in Syria. To Faisal, Iraqi independence in 1932 would be but the first step toward an Arab union to include not only Syria and Palestine, but possibly Arabia as well. From 1929 until Syrian elections in 1932, Faisal sent emissaries to lobby Syrian politicians, conducted an intense propaganda campaign to promote his interests, and used the Islamic Congress that met in Jerusalem in 1931 to advance his cause. Plans were made for another congress to meet in Baghdad in 1933, despite British opposition to Faisal's pan-Arab plans. The defeat of his cause in the Syrian elections, anti-Saudi revolts in the Hijaz, and his untimely death put Hashemite unity attempts on hold.

To Faisal, Iraqi independence in 1932 would be but the first step toward an Arab union to include not only Syria and Palestine, but possibly Arabia as well.

In June 1933 Faisal left for London on a prearranged state visit, leaving an anti-British government in power in Baghdad. He then spent the summer in Switzerland for reasons of health. When word reached him of the crisis with the Assyrian minority in Iraq, Faisal pleaded for moderation. But the exploits of the new Iraqi army that resulted in hundreds of Assyrian civilian deaths were popular in Baghdad, where there were demands for Faisal's resignation. On September 7, 1933, Faisal died of a heart attack in Geneva. He was succeeded by his son, Ghazi ibn Faisal. ◆

Faisal ibn Abd al-Aziz Al Saud

C.1904–1975 ● KING OF SAUDI ARABIA

Faisal was the third son of Abd al-Aziz Al Saud (known in the West as ibn Saud), born in Riyadh, Saudi Arabia, probably in 1904 or 1905, though some accounts place his birth on April 9, 1906, to coincide with one of his father's important early victories. With no full brothers and no half brothers close to him in age, Faisal grew up in relative isolation. He left the royal court at an early age to study under his maternal grandfather, a prominent religious scholar, which served to reinforce that isolation.

Faisal assumed military, political, and diplomatic responsibilities at a young age. He led Saudi forces in the Asir campaign of 1920 and by 1926 was his father's viceroy in charge of the recently conquered province of Hijaz. This included

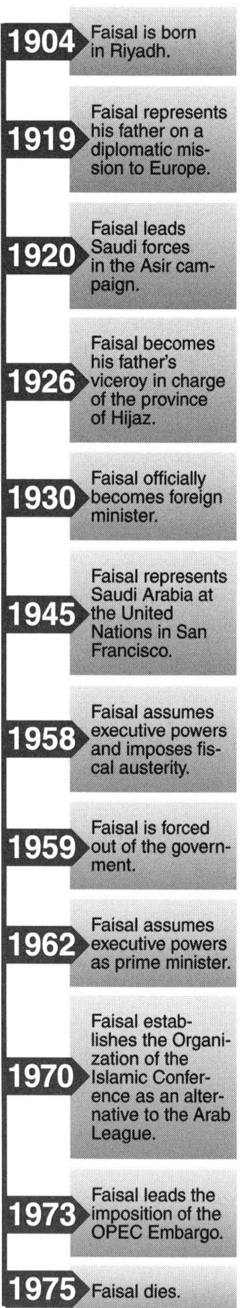

responsibility for the Muslim holy cities of Mecca and Medina and the annual *hajj* (pilgrimage). He early developed a special, broadly informed expertise in the area of foreign affairs; this began in 1919 when he represented his father on a diplomatic mission to Europe, the first of the Al Saud family to do so. In 1930 Faisal officially became foreign minister, retaining that position until his death in 1975, with only a brief interruption, thus making him the longest serving foreign minister in the twentieth century.

Faisal's natural intelligence and his success on important state assignments, such as representing Saudi Arabia at the creation of the United Nations in San Francisco in 1945 clearly marked him as the ablest of the sons of ibn Saud. Yet in 1933 ibn Saud had the family recognize Faisal's elder brother Saud, the crown prince, as successor despite Saud's obvious lack of intellectual gifts or meaningful preparation for rule. Faisal had doubtless hoped, perhaps expected, that his demonstrated abilities would have secured him the succession, consistent with the well-established Arabian custom of choosing the ablest near relative of the deceased as the new shaykh or emir. Ibn Saud evidently sought to avoid intrafamily rivalries that had fatally weakened the Al Saud during his own father's generation. Though Faisal came to feel contempt for his incompetent elder brother, he insisted in family councils on a scrupulous adherence to the oath of allegiance (*bay'a*) to Saud that he had led the family in swearing. To do otherwise would, in his view, have established a dangerous precedent in undermining the family's rule.

King Saud's reign, 1953–64, brought nearly constant crisis, with a pattern of events in which the Al Saud called Faisal to assume responsibility for the government, although Saud subsequently reasserted his claim to power. In early 1958 the kingdom was financially bankrupt from Saud's profligacy and at risk because of his ill-conceived challenge to Egypt's president Gamal Abdel Nasser and radical Arab nationalism. Faisal then assumed executive powers, imposing for the first time fiscal austerity with real limits on princes' pensions and a true budget. He came to a modus vivendi with Nasser, with whom he had earlier been careful to cultivate tolerable relations, though ideologically they were poles apart. By 1959 Saud had forced Faisal out of the government and allied himself with a group of reformist half brothers, the Free Princes, whose embarrassing public split with the rest of the Al Saud and declaration of solidarity with Nasser helped to place the kingdom in real peril.

In 1962 Faisal once again assumed executive powers as prime minister, doing so as a republican coup was about to overthrow the traditional **imamate** in Yemen and Saudi Air Force officers were preparing to defect to Cairo (Egypt). Faisal revamped the Council of Ministers and established the team of princes that continued to lead Saudi Arabia during the 1990s. This included the progressive and ambitious Fahd and Sultan ibn Abd al-Aziz Al Saud. They comprise part of the largest and most powerful grouping of full brothers in the family, those born to the favorite wife of ibn Saud, Hassa bint Ahmad Al Sudayri. Fahd at forty-one was both interior minister and, in a new departure, was designated second deputy prime minister behind Prince Khalid, while thirty-eight-year-old Sultan ibn Abd al-Aziz Al Saud became defense minister. To counterbalance them, Faisal selected the traditionalist Abdullah, who, in contrast both to the king and the Al Sudayri family enjoyed close ties with the Arab tribes, a constituency whose support was critical to the monarchy. Faisal himself, with his genuine piety and austere morality well established (after sowing a few youthful wild oats), secured the support of the crucial religious establishment. Faisal's care in creating and maintaining balance in the government was key to preserving stability. Thus, when Saud's final attempt to recover his powers led the senior princes, backed by a *fatwa* (ruling) from the *ulama* (religious establishment), to force his abdication in 1964, the government had been put in place that would endure with few changes through King Faisal's own eleven-year rule and then Khalid's seven years as king.

imamate: the office held by, or region or country ruled over by an imam, or Muslim leader.

The creation of an efficient, stable government in place of the circle of cronies and inexperienced sons on which Saud had heavily relied was typical of the reforms that Faisal enacted.

The creation of an efficient, stable government in place of the circle of cronies or inexperienced sons on whom Saud had heavily relied was typical of the reforms that Faisal enacted. They were meant not to open up the political system in a modern, democratic sense but to enable it to confront the challenges of the twentieth century, so as to preserve the kingdom's traditional values. Thus, Sultan, Fahd, and King Faisal's brother-in-law Kamal Adham, head of the state intelligence service, were given full rein to build up the military and internal security establishments. Bright young technocrat commoners—like Ahmad Zaki Yamani, who long served as petroleum minister, and Ghazi al-Qosaibi, for many years minister of industry and electricity—began to play significant roles, though without political power, as the bureaucracy began a rapid expansion. Modern public instruction at all levels underwent massive expansion, with girls admitted for the first time, reflecting the king's realization of the necessity of an educated population. The press and radio broadcasting experienced rapid expansion and, against strong conservative opposition, Faisal introduced television—he saw the need to diffuse information rapidly in a modern state and viewed the print and broadcast media as means of promoting national unification.

The press and radio broadcasting experienced rapid expansion and, against strong conservative opposition, Faisal introduced television.

Faisal met external dangers to the kingdom with reliance on restored prestige and stability at home and on bold initiatives when required. Financial assistance to Yemeni royalists helped to checkmate the radical threat in that quarter, and Nasser's defeat in the Arab–Israel War of 1967 greatly strengthened Faisal's hand in dealing with the Arab nationalist challenge. As oil revenues mounted toward the end of his reign, "Riyal diplomacy" helped to moderate the behavior of radical recipients of largesse and to strengthen conservative regimes. The new wealth gave substance to Faisal's attempt to promote an international policy based on the conservative values of Islam. In 1970 he took the lead in establishing the Organization of the Islamic Conference as an intended alternative to the Arab League (the League of Arab States). Ultimately, however, Faisal knew that Saudi Arabia's security against external threats—principally the Soviet Union, its regional allies, and proxies—could come only from the United States. This dependence placed Saudi Arabia in the painful dilemma of being intimately linked to the principal supporter of Israel. The dilemma became an acute crisis in U.S.–Saudi relations when Faisal led the imposition of the 1973–74 OPEC (Organization of Petroleum Exporting Countries) embargo after President Richard M. Nixon's decision to resupply massively Israel's armed forces during the Arab–Israel War of 1973. It was typical of Faisal's pragmatic realism that within months of that crisis the United States and Saudi governments had signed agreements, especially the Joint Commission on Economic Cooperation, that created unprecedented links between the two countries.

realpolitik: politics based on practical and material factors rather than on theoretical or ethical objectives.

In his statecraft, Faisal balanced a fundamental commitment to traditional values with an informed acceptance of the means of creating a strong modern state. He combined a rigorous Islamic view of the world with a sophisticated **realpolitik**, and he devoted himself unswervingly to the survival of Saudi Arabia. It is likely that, next to his father, Faisal will be remembered as the greatest of the twentieth-century Saudi rulers. ◆

Farouk

1920–1965 ● King of Egypt

Farouk, the son of King Fuad I (r. 1922–36) and Queen Nazli, and the grandson of Khedive Ismail ibn Ibrahim (r. 1863–79), was born in Cairo, on February 11, 1920. Privately tutored until the age of fifteen, Farouk intended to enter a British public school. He was, however, unable to gain admission to Eton and the Royal Military College at Woolwich, but he went to England anyway to pursue his studies. At the Royal Military College he took afternoon classes as an unenrolled student. His formal education was cut short by the death of his father, King Fuad, on April 28, 1936. Returning to Egypt, he ascended the throne as a minor and ruled with the assistance of a Regency Council until July 1937.

Upon first coming to power, he enjoyed much local popularity. Young, handsome, and seemingly progressive, he was thought to be an ideal person to foster parliamentary democracy in Egypt. In truth, however, he engaged in the same anticonstitutional practices that had so marked his father's tenure of power. During his reign he constantly plotted against the Wafd, Egypt's majority political party, contended with Britain over monarchical privilege, and intrigued to enhance the sway of the monarchy over the Egyptian parliament. In 1937, shortly after coming to the throne, he removed the Wafd from office. The Wafd had just concluded the Anglo–Egyptian Treaty of 1936, which increased Egypt's autonomy but fell far short of realizing the long-cherished goal of complete independence.

> ***"In a few years, there will be only five kings in the world—the King of England and the four kings in a pack of cards."***
> Farouk I, quoted in *Life* magazine, 1950

1920 Farouk is born in Cairo on February 11.

1936 Farouk's formal education is cut short by the death of his father, King Fuad.

1936 Farouk ascends to the throne as a minor, ruling with the help of a Regency Council until 1937.

1952 Farouk is exiled by the new rulers.

1953 Farouk's infant son, who has succeeds to the throne, is dethroned when Egypt abolishes the monarchy and becomes a republic.

1965 Farouk dies of a heart attack in a nightclub in Rome.

With the onset of World War II, Farouk's clashes with the British intensified. The monarch supported a series of minority ministries, many of which were, in British eyes, insufficiently committed to the Allied war cause. Political tensions came to a head in early 1942 while Germany military forces under the command of General Erwin Rommel were advancing in the western desert toward Alexandria. The British demanded a pro-British Wafdist ministry. When Farouk delayed, the British ambassador, Miles Lampson, on February 4, 1942, surrounded Abdin Palace with tanks and compelled the monarch, under threat of forced abdication, to install the Wafd in office. That day was a defining moment in Egypt's twentieth-century history. It undermined the legitimacy of parliamentary democracy and prepared the way for the military coup of 1952.

The immediate postwar years in Egypt were full of political violence and official corruption. In 1948 the Egyptian army suffered a humiliating defeat in the Arab-Israel War as the state of Israel came into being. During this period, groups opposed to parliamentary government increased their following throughout the country, most notably the Muslim Brotherhood, the communists, and the socialists. Within the army an elite of idealistic, young officers organized themselves in the Free Officers movement. Increasingly, King Farouk came to symbolize all that was wrong with the old order. Outrageously wealthy, he flaunted his wealth in a country wracked by poverty. His penchant for gambling and carousing with women offended many. Learning of the growing opposition to his rule inside the military, he tried to move on his enemies before they turned on him. He did not succeed. On July 23, 1952, the Free Officers, led by Gamal Abdel Nasser, seized power. Three days later, on July 26, 1952, the new rulers exiled the king. Sailing from Alexandria harbor on the royal yacht *Mahrussa*, he was accompanied into exile by his family, gold ingots, and more than two hundred pieces of luggage. His deposition in 1952 effectively brought an end to the rule over Egypt of the family of Muhammad Ali, who had come to Egypt as a military leader in the midst of Napoléon Bonaparte's invasion and had installed himself as Egypt's ruler in 1805. Farouk's infant son, Ahmad Fuad, succeeded briefly to the throne, but in June 1953 Egypt abolished the monarchy and became a republic. Farouk continued to lead a dissolute life while residing in Rome. On March 18, 1965, he succumbed to a heart attack in a nightclub. ◆

Ferdinand I

1503–1564 ● Holy Roman Emperor

Ferdinand I was born in Spain, the son of Philip duke of Burgundy and grandson of Holy Roman Emperor Maximilian I. His mother was Joan the Mad, daughter of King Ferdinand II and Queen Isabella. Considered heir to the Spanish throne, Ferdinand was raised in that country, but the throne was inherited by his older brother, Charles (Charles V), who was crowned Holy Roman Emperor in 1520. In the succeeding years, he and Ferdinand divided the empire between themselves and Ferdinand was granted the Habsburg duchies in Austria, Württemburgh, Alsace, and Breisgau. He was also appointed head of the government during Charles's frequent absences.

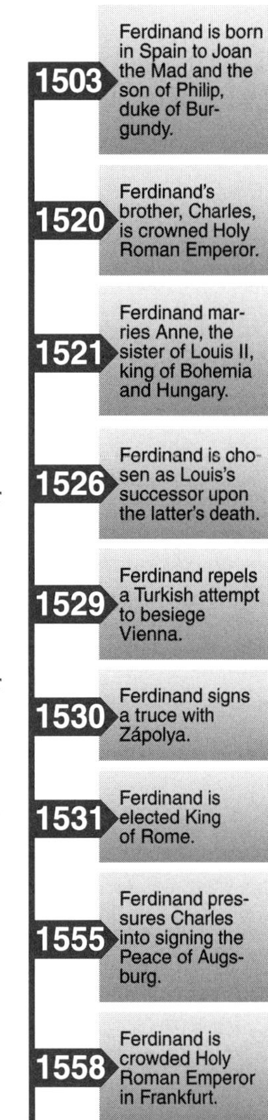

Since Charles had a son, it was unlikely that Ferdinand would succeed to the throne. In the following years, however, Ferdinand broadened his power base. He was a competent administrator of his realms, although he was unable to subdue Austrian regionalism. In 1521 he married Anne, the sister of Louis II, king of Bohemia and Hungary, and they had two sons and eleven daughters. Louis II was childless and upon his death in 1526, Ferdinand was chosen as his successor. Ferdinand was unable to govern his new kingdom adequately. Approximately half the country was under Turkish occupation, while much of the remainder was occupied by János Zápolya, a rival claimant to the throne. In 1529 Ferdinand repelled a Turkish attempt to besiege Vienna; the following year, he signed a truce with Zápolya.

Like his brother Charles, Ferdinand was hostile to the newly founded Protestant religion, but he also recognized the importance of the Protestant princes of northern Germany as allies against the invading Turks. In turn, these princes endorsed Ferdinand as heir to the empire, rather than Charles's own son, Philip. Official sanction for Ferdinand came in 1531, when he was elected king of Rome, the title assumed by imperial successors.

With his authority acknowledged, Ferdinand pressured Charles into signing the Peace of Augsburg in 1555. The treaty recognized Lutheranism (but no other Protestant sect) as a co-official religion with Catholicism in the empire. Princes were given the right to decide which religion their subjects must follow, and all those who declined to conform were required to emigrate. In only a few principalities with a traditionally mixed population were both religions allowed to coexist. Although the Peace of Augsburg favored Catholicism, and declared that the emperor must be of that faith—Ferdinand's own son, Maximilian II, was forced to renounce Protestantism before succeeding to the throne—it was sharply condemned by the Catholic clergy and eventually led to the Thirty Years' War. But Ferdinand had won the admiration of the influential German princes and was chosen king of the German Territories the year the treaty was signed. The next year, Charles abdicated in his favor, and Ferdinand was crowned in Frankfurt in 1558.

Although his reign was brief, Ferdinand had ensured the rise of Protestantism as a legitimate religion in Europe and had absorbed Bohemia and Hungary into the empire. ◆

Ferdinand II

1578–1637 ● HOLY ROMAN EMPEROR

The Jesuits sought to prepare Ferdinand to rule in his father's realm in the spirit of the Counter-Reformation.

Born in Graz, Austria, Ferdinand II was the son of Archduke Charles, ruler of inner Austria, grandson of Ferdinand I, and brother of Emperor Maximilian II. He received a traditional religious education at the University of Ingolstadt, where he was influenced by the Jesuits; throughout his life he maintained a particular fondness for religious literature. He also acquired a knowledge of languages and was fluent in German, French, and Spanish. The Jesuits sought to prepare Ferdinand to rule his father's realm in the spirit of the Counter-Reformation. Upon succeeding his father in 1596 the otherwise good-natured prince adhered to his religious upbringing by embarking on a ruthless persecution of Protestants. Churches were shut, and adherents were given the choice of either reverting to Catholicism or emigrating.

When he was a child, it seemed unlikely that Ferdinand would ascend the imperial throne, but Maximilian's sons,

Rudolf II and Matthias, were childless. The Habsburg dynasty in Spain favored Ferdinand to inherit the throne in return for future territorial concessions in Alsace and Italy. A secret agreement was reached between Ferdinand and the Spanish Habsburgs in 1615; in 1617 he was elected king of Bohemia, and the next year king of Hungary. In 1619 Ferdinand was chosen to succeed Matthias as Holy Roman Emperor.

Bohemia opposed Ferdinand's accession to the throne; the largely Protestant province recalled his harsh measures against their coreligionists and feared similar treatment. When Bohemia elected Frederick V of the Palatinate as king, Ferdinand mustered the support of Bavaria and the Catholic League to suppress the Bohemian insurrection in what became the Thirty Years' War. Bohemia was crushed in the Battle of the White Mountain (1620), and Spain took advantage of the confusion to enter the Palatinate. Within a short time, Protestant northern Europe, led by Sweden, was embroiled in a bitter conflict with Catholic middle Europe. The initial outcome of the war was largely in Ferdinand's favor. His forces, led by General Albrecht von Wallenstein, conquered Silesia and Moravia. In 1629 Ferdinand enacted the Edict of Restitution, in which all former church lands were restored.

Ferdinand was a temperate monarch who maintained a frugal court. With his favorites, however, his generosity was often excessive. The nobles were particularly alarmed at the favor shown Wallenstein. The general was raised to the highest status in the nobility, with virtual independence in his new realm. At the same time, he was suspected of negotiating with the enemy (he had, in fact, met with France's Cardinal Richelieu) to support them against the empire. The nobles persuaded Ferdinand to dismiss Wallenstein in 1630, but eighteen months later the emperor was forced to recall him to confront the Swedes. The first battle against Sweden was a resounding victory for Ferdinand's army, but the outcome was not decisive. Wallenstein faced Sweden again in 1632 in one of the fiercest battles of the war at Lützen. Both sides suffered tremendous casualties—the Swedish king Gustavus Adolphus was killed—but Wallenstein was finally defeated. Ferdinand forced him to resign, and probably had a hand in his assassination in 1634.

Wallenstein was replaced by Ferdinand's son, Prince Ferdinand, who, despite a further victory over Sweden, urged the emperor to sign the Peace of Prague (1635), revoking the Edict of Restitution and assuring religious freedom for local princes. France entered the war shortly after, but Ferdinand was not to witness the outcome. He died in 1637 and was succeeded by his son Ferdinand III. ◆

Ferdinand II

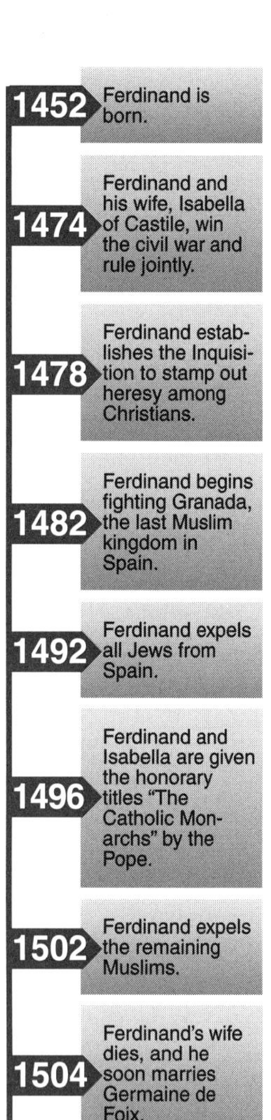

1452–1516 ● KING OF ARAGON

The king most admired by Niccolò Machiavelli, Ferdinand II was the son of John II of Aragon. His father personally supervised his education, stressing both humanism and statesmanship, and ensured that he learned from personal experience as well as carefully selected teachers. He was nine when his father named him heir apparent and sixteen when he became king of Sicily in an attempt to make him a more acceptable husband for his cousin Isabella, heiress of the prestigious kingdom of Castile. At seventeen he married Isabella over the objections of her brother, the king of Castile, forging the papal bull necessary to legalize the marriage of cousins when the pope refused to sign it. (A genuine bull was obtained from another pope after they were already married.)

When the king of Castile died in 1474 a civil war broke out over his successors: Ferdinand and Isabella, or his daughter Juana and Alfonso V of Portugal. Ferdinand and Isabella won and ruled jointly, although each of their now-united kingdoms continued to be governed through its own institutions. In Castile, for instance, while official decrees were cosigned by both rulers, Isabella remained in charge of internal administration. Castile never really accepted or trusted Ferdinand, only tolerating him for Isabella's sake.

Ferdinand's goal was a strong united Spain and to achieve this he used any means at his disposal: trickery, diplomacy, war, religion. He traveled from kingdom to kingdom, bringing order out of anarchy and powerful nobles under the control of an even more powerful monarchy. As a result of Ferdinand's efforts, his young grandson inherited the strongest kingdom in Europe.

Ferdinand firmly believed that religious uniformity would make a united Spain both stronger and easier to rule. Christian Spaniards regarded church and state as one and the same and gave both their fierce support. They also supported Ferdinand's establishment of the Inquisition in 1478, and with its aim of stamping out all heresy among Christians, especially the greatly resented New Christians (Jews and Muslims who had been converted to Catholicism by force, under threat to their properties and lives, who still clung to their old ways and religions). The Inquisition, Ferdinand's favorite tool in his campaign to unify Spain, was extremely profitable as the crown had the right to confiscate the property of the condemned. From 1482 to 1492 Ferdinand fought against Granada, the last Muslim kingdom in Spain. In 1492 all Jews were expelled from Spain and in 1496 the Pope gave Ferdinand and Isabella the honorary titles "The Catholic Monarchs." In 1502 the remaining Muslims were expelled, and Spain became, in theory at least, uniformly Christian.

The newly united kingdom became involved in Italian affairs in 1494 when Pope Julius II asked Ferdinand for help in expelling French forces from Italy. This led to a struggle between France and Spain for control of Italy that would last for over fifty years before Spain was finally victorious. Christopher Columbus's voyages and the pope's carefully manipulated division of the New World between Spain and Portugal (then more powerful), "gave" most of it to Spain. This led to Spain's eventual conquest of the peoples, lands, and riches of the New World.

Isabella died in 1504 and Ferdinand mourned her, but soon married Germaine de Foix, the niece of the king of France, in an attempt to keep the crown of Castile. He lost it in 1506 when his son-in-law, Philip, the husband of his only surviving child, the mentally afflicted Juana, claimed Castile. Philip was welcomed by a kingdom alienated by Ferdinand's quick remarriage.

Ferdinand stayed in his kingdom of Aragon until Philip died three months later, returning to Castile to become regent for Juana. Without Isabella's moderating influence, his rule for the next ten years was vindictively totalitarian and he continued his expansionary policies.

Finally Ferdinand began to age and became suspicious of those around him; he died at sixty-four in the forty-second year of his reign and was buried beside Isabella. During his reign he united the kingdoms of Spain, established the administrative and legal basis for a united Spain and a strong Spanish monarchy, expanded Spain's holdings in Europe, and discovered and claimed a rich new continent. He also sowed the seeds for the eventual destruction of Spain's economy by inaugurating an inquisition and expelling the Jews and Moors. ◆

"For as much of you, Christopher Columbus, are going by our command, with some of our vessels and men, to discover and subdue some Islands and Continent in the ocean, and it is hoped that by God's assistance, some of the said Islands and Continent in the ocean will be discovered and conquered by your means and conduct, therefore it is but just and reasonable, that since you expose yourself to such danger to serve us, you should be rewarded for it."

Privileges and Prerogatives of Ferdinand and Isabella to Christopher Columbus, April 30, 1492

Frederick I

c.1123–1190 ● Holy Roman Emperor

"An emperor is subject to no one but God and Justice."
Frederick I, quoted by J. W. Zincgref in *Apophthegmamta*, 1626

As duke of Swabia, Frederick I (Barbarossa) was a member of the influential Hohenstaufen dynasty, led by his uncle, Holy Roman Emperor Conrad III. The Hohenstaufens, also known by the name of their ancestral castle Waibling, were challenged by the rival Welf family of Bavaria (the prolonged feud eventually spilled over to Italy, where the names were altered into Ghibellino and Guelfo), who claimed the imperial throne for themselves. Fearing that his own sons would prove unable to withstand the Welfs, Conrad chose Frederick as his successor. Frederick was both imposing and intelligent; he sported a bushy red beard (*barba rossa* in Latin), and always looked as if he was about to laugh. Furthermore, Frederick's mother was a Welf and Conrad hoped that he would be acceptable to both parties as a compromise. Frederick succeeded Conrad in 1152. For two years he appeased his Welf kinsmen by granting them substantial territory in return for recognition of his ultimate suzerainty. Although no private wars were permitted for personal aggrandizement and the slightest infraction of the agreement was ruthlessly punished, Frederick's measures temporarily mollified the Welfs. Germany was at peace, allowing Frederick to focus his attention on troubled Italy.

The southern half of the empire was plagued with republican and regional sentiment undermining the emperor's ultimate authority. In Rome, Arnold of Brescia, a religious reformer and disciple of Peter Abelard, had overthrown Pope Eugene III and established a commune. Rome's self-proclaimed independence was imitated by other Italian cities, particularly those of the northern Lombard region. Frederick concluded a pact with the papal aspirant Adrian IV enabling him to recapture Rome and execute Arnold. Once established as Pope, Adrian was allowed virtual autonomy in return for recognition of Frederick's ultimate sovereignty. Adrian crowned Frederick as Holy Roman Emperor in 1155, but the two soon had a falling-out over Frederick's insistence on his prerogative to reject papal nomination of clergy. Soon after Frederick returned to Germany, Italy reasserted its independence.

Frederick returned to Italy in 1158, this time sparing no measure to dispel any challenge to his authority. Rebellious cities were subject to cruel sieges in which prisoners were often catapulted against the walls. Once defeated, towns were razed and their inhabitants slaughtered. Frederick then lost support even among the clergy he had appointed. Upon the death of Adrian in 1195 the majority of the college of cardinals rejected Frederick's candidate in favor of Alexander III, who enlisted British and French support against the emperor and his lackey, the antipope Victor IV. Following Victor's death in 1164 even the minority of cardinals preferred to transfer their allegiance to Alexander rather than support the new candidate, Paschal III. The German nobility grew uneasy over Frederick's break with the established papacy—Frederick's proposed canonization of Charlemagne did little to alleviate the situation—forcing Frederick to defeat Alexander. Rome was conquered in 1167 and Alexander barely escaped to France.

Rome was not the only troubled region of Frederick's Italian realms. That same year the northern cities proclaimed their independence as the Lombard League. Frederick was preparing to face this new challenge when a plague decimated his armies in Rome. The emperor was forced to make a harrowing retreat to Germany, much of the way through hostile Lombard territory.

His vulnerability was eagerly exploited by the German Welfs. Led by Henry the Lion, the Welfs reached agreement with Denmark, allowing them to extend their realms beyond the Elbe River along the southern Baltic seacoast. Henry also strengthened his ancestral territories by establishing fortified towns, among them Munich, in strategic locations. With his forces depleted, Frederick resorted to diplomacy and bribery to frustrate Henry's ambitions. A corrupt uncle of Henry's was persuaded to sell much of the new Welf territories to Frederick, thereby confirming him as German overlord. Overly confident, Frederick made the premature decision to return to Italy to defeat the Lombard League.

The German setback in the ensuing Battle of Legnano (1176) was disastrous. Frederick's own shield and personal standard were captured by the rebel Italians. Fearing that another such defeat would signal the end of his empire, Frederick adopted the diplomatic methods that had served so well against Henry the Lion. After concluding a six-year truce with the Lombards, he agreed to a reconciliation with Pope Alexander. Frederick entered Rome as a penitent; when Alexander approached, he prostrated himself before him. Alexander was moved by Frederick's tears. He lifted him from the ground and

According to legend, Frederick is still alive; he sits, sleeping, in a secret chamber in Kyffhauser Castle, his bushy red beard twisted twice around the table before him.

embraced him before leading him into church to sign a formal reconciliation.

In 1183 the Treaty of Constance replaced the truce with the Lombards. Frederick recognized their autonomy in return for their recognition of his sovereignty. The empire, once centered around the person of the emperor, had evolved of necessity into a federation of autonomous principalities. Unity had been achieved at the price of imperial power. Frederick's authority, however, could not be slighted. The princes and barons remained his lieges in a newly emerged feudal state. Rivals like Henry were forced to flee; their lands were redistributed among Frederick's loyal retainers such as the Wittelsbachs, who ruled Bavaria until 1918. Peace in his expanded empire fostered a cultural renaissance unparalleled in the medieval period.

Seeking challenges abroad, Frederick led 20,000 men on a crusade against Saladin. He never reached the Holy Land; while attempting to cross the Saleph River in Cilicia, Frederick Barbarossa drowned. Today his place is firmly established in the pantheon of German heroes. According to some legends he is still alive. He sits, sleeping, in a secret chamber in Kyffhauser Castle, his bushy red beard twisted twice around the table before him. Only when it completes its third revolution will Frederick awaken to fight the last battle before the Day of Judgment. ◆

Frederick II

1194–1250 ● HOLY ROMAN EMPEROR AND KING OF SICILY

Frederick II was born the day after his father, Emperor Henry VI, was crowned king of Sicily. Henry schemed to alter the laws of succession in the Holy Roman Empire so that Frederick could succeed him, but his premature death prevented this. Only three years old, Frederick became king of Sicily, with his mother acting as regent. Before her death the following year, she appointed Pope Innocent III as Frederick's guardian and regent of the kingdom of Sicily. Frederick was declared of age in 1208; the following year he married Constance of Aragon, ten years his senior. Constance was genuinely fond of the orphan prince, and in 1211, the couple had a son, Henry.

Sicily's importance as a maritime trading center tempted Emperor Otto IV to conquer the country in 1210. Pope Innocent III regarded this as a challenge to papal authority and urged the German princes to depose Otto in favor of Frederick, who, in return, renounced the Sicilian throne in favor of Henry. Frederick accepted and traveled to Germany to assume the imperial throne, avoiding the harassment of troops still loyal to Otto. To ensure his accession, he concluded a pact with Philip II of France. In the Battle of Bouvines (1214), Philip defeated Otto and captured his standard, the golden eagle, symbolic of the transfer of power to Frederick.

"We wish that in all parts of the Kingdom many will become wise and knowledgeable, by having access to a fountain of knowledge, and a seminary of doctrine, so that they, made proficient by study and observation, will serve divine justice, and will become useful to us, for the administration of Justice and of the laws which we urge everyone to obey."
Frederick II, *Licterae Generales*, 1224

However, Frederick also earned the indignation of the new pope, Honorius III, by appointing Henry king of Germany. Hailed throughout Europe as a new Charlemagne, Frederick sought papal approval for his reign by having Honorius crown him emperor in Rome, and agreed to govern Sicily as a dominion independent of the empire. Following his coronation, he returned to Sicily to develop his native realm. Although severe with Christian heretics, he was more favorable toward his Muslim and Jewish minorities. However, the leaders of a Saracen revolt were treated mercilessly; as one prostrated himself before the emperor, Frederick split him in half with the spur of his boot. The Muslim masses were resettled in Apulia, where they enjoyed considerable autonomy. Under Frederick's patronage, non-Christian minorities enhanced the intellectual life of Sicily. In 1224 he inaugurated the University of Naples, which he required all civil servants to attend. This school, staffed by Thomas Aquinas among others, became a leading academic institution. Important trade routes were secured by the conquest of Djerba off the Tunisian coast. At the same time, Frederick was opposed by both the Lombard League of northern Italy for interfering in its internal affairs and by the new pope, Gregory IX.

Gregory attempted to curb Frederick by persuading him to fulfill his coronation vow to liberate the Holy Land. By marrying the daughter of the **titular** king of Jerusalem, Frederick attempted to have himself declared king, but an epidemic frustrated his immediate departure on a crusade. Gregory responded by excommunicating Frederick in 1227. The following year Frederick reached the Holy Land and found that the ruler of Egypt, challenged by his brother in Syria, was willing to negotiate control of Jerusalem, Bethlehem, and Nazareth in return for military support against Damascus. Frederick's acceptance

titular: having the title belonging to an office without the duties, functions, or responsibilities.

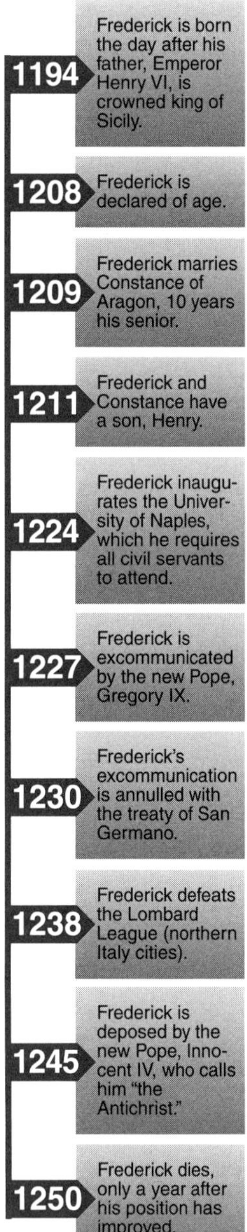

resulted in his peaceful acquisition of the holy sites. Bloated by his success, Frederick now considered himself a messiah. Despite his excommunication, he crowned himself king of Jerusalem in the Church of the Holy Sepulcher.

The pope saw Frederick's absence as an opportune time to invade Sicily, but Frederick quickly returned to regain his realm. Peace was finally concluded at the Treaty of San Germano (1230), in which Frederick's excommunication was annulled.

Henry had represented his father in Germany throughout his father's decade-long absence. After conceding demands by local princes for autonomy, he agreed to lead a rebellion against his father. Frederick crushed this new challenge and replaced Henry with his second son, Conrad IV. Henry was imprisoned, never to see his father again; Frederick attempted a reconciliation prior to his death, but Henry misinterpreted his father's intention and committed suicide.

With Germany subdued, Frederick could now suppress the rebellious Lombard League. They were defeated in the Battle of Cortuenova in 1238, but Frederick's demand for unconditional surrender was rejected by the Milanese and tensions continued until his death. The Pope again excommunicated Frederick for his supposed claim that Moses, Christ, and Muhammad were impostors. Believing that the Romans preferred him to the pretentiously wealthy papacy, Frederick prepared to conquer Rome. However, he underestimated the local population's loyalty to the papal institution. His imprisonment of over one hundred cardinals, bishops, and other church leaders further diminished his popularity. His siege of Rome was only lifted upon hearing of Pope Gregory's death.

The new Pope, Innocent IV, was no less hostile to Frederick and officially deposed him in 1245, calling him the Antichrist. Plans to travel to the Pope in Lyons were stymied by a revolt in central Italy, the declared neutrality of the German princes in the conflict, and the capture and imprisonment of his son Enzio, king of Sardinia, by the Bolognese. Only by 1249 did Frederick's position improve, but his sudden death the following year left his empire vulnerable.

Although his final years were marked by decline, Frederick's popularity among his subjects never wavered. His uncompromising stand against the church, hated for its wealth and power, led many to believe that the church, not Frederick, was the true Antichrist; Frederick was seen by many as a messianic figure come to restore Christendom. For some time after his death, it was believed he would return from hiding to deliver the final blow against the enemies of the true church, as represented by the Pope in Rome. ◆

Frederick II

1712–1786 ● FREDERICK THE GREAT, KING OF PRUSSIA

Frederick II was the third son of Frederick William I of Prussia but after the death of his elder brothers in childhood, he became heir to the throne. His father was a rigid authoritarian who imposed spartan discipline on all his children, particularly Frederick. From his mother, however, Frederick acquired a love of the arts. Throughout his life he spoke French, considering German to be a barbaric language, and spent considerable time playing the flute and composing verse. His father opposed these pastimes, preferring that Frederick devote himself to statecraft. Violent rows ensued in which Frederick was caned or obliged to kiss his father's boots. His animosity toward his father finally led Frederick to contemplate an escape with a close friend, Lieutenant Hans Hermann von Katte, to his uncle, George II of Britain, but his father learned about this attempt and had the two youths arrested. A military tribunal sentenced Katte to two years imprisonment for desertion, but was unwilling to try Frederick because of his status. Frederick William, however, sought sterner measures against the two, and Frederick was forced to watch from his cell as Katte was beheaded. Although Frederick anticipated a similar fate, his father revoked the sentence and gradually reinstated him. In return, Frederick was compelled to serve in the civil administration to learn the skills demanded of an heir to the throne.

"Princes, sovereigns, and king have not been given supreme authority in order to live in luxurious self-indulgence and debauchery. They have not been elevated by their fellow-men to enable them to strut about and to insult with their pride the simple-mannered, the poor and the suffering."

Frederick II, *Essay on the Forms of Government*

After several years Frederick retired to a country estate, where his artistic inclinations thrived. Through correspondence, he cultivated a meaningful friendship with Voltaire and other leading intellectuals. In 1733 he married Elizabeth Christina, daughter of the duke of Brunswick-Bevern, but the marriage lasted just three weeks before the couple separated. Frederick had no significant romantic affairs throughout his life, leading to speculation that he was homosexual.

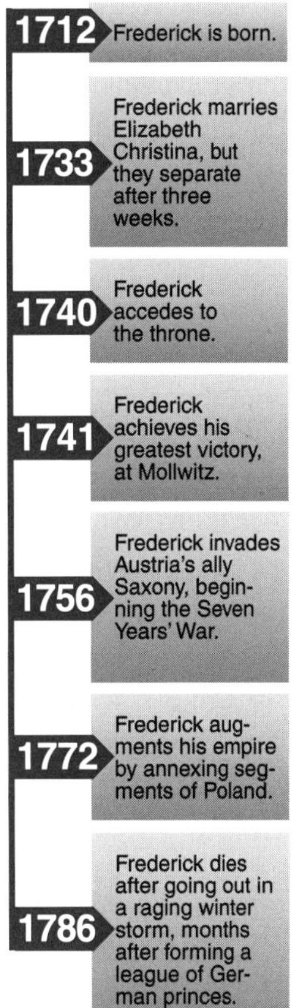

When Frederick acceded to the throne in 1740, it was assumed that Prussia would enter an enlightened period under the guidance of a philosopher king. Artists and scientists were encouraged to settle in Berlin to revive the Royal Academy, long neglected by Frederick William, and Frederick himself published a work, *Antimachiavel,* just prior to his accession, in which he defined the monarch's role as that of a servant of the people. At the same time, his primary objective was personal aggrandizement. He enacted laws abolishing torture, censorship, and religious discrimination, but these reforms were generally not enforced.

Having developed a fascination with the military similar to his father's, Frederick sought an opportunity to demonstrate his prowess. Such an opportunity soon arose: The Holy Roman Emperor Charles VI died, leaving his young daughter, Maria Theresa, to inherit the throne of Austria. The European powers sought to exploit the situation by carving the empire up among themselves. Frederick hoped to annex the wealthy region of Silesia, to which Prussia had historical claims. His surprise invasion of that region sparked the War of the Austrian Succession. The planned invasion was a well-kept secret to all but a few trusted advisers. The evening before, as Prussian troops mustered on the Silesian border, Frederick sponsored a ball with his estranged queen.

The invasion of Silesia was an exceptional success—the region was overrun in just seven weeks. Frederick's greatest victory was at Mollwitz in 1741; having little experience in warfare, however, Frederick fled the battlefield, believing defeat inevitable. Not until ten hours after the Austrians were defeated did Frederick learn of his victory. In 1742 Frederick signed the Treaty of Breslau with Maria Theresa. Austria recognized Prussia's claims to Silesia in return for Prussian recognition of Maria Theresa's husband as Holy Roman Emperor. The treaty, although beneficial to Prussia, tarnished Frederick's reputation. By signing a separate peace with Austria, Frederick had neglected his ally France.

Despite the treaty, Austria did not forego its claims to Silesia. A secret coalition of Austria, England, Holland, and several smaller states threatened invasion to check the rising Prussian military might. Frederick recognized the danger to his throne and responded by invading Bohemia in 1744. He succeeded in capturing Prague, but the Austrian army was able to counter any further offensives. At the same time, France invaded Bavaria and Frederick withdrew from Bohemia to concentrate on securing Silesia. After further pointless battles, peace was finally concluded in the Treaty of Dresden (1745). Austria again recognized Frederick's claims to Silesia.

The following ten years were relatively quiet. Frederick devoted considerable effort to improving his military infrastructure. The Treaty of Dresden earned him the title "the Great," and recognition of Prussia as a major European power, but tensions in Europe had not ceased. Austria still yearned to gain Silesia.

France found it expedient to ally itself with Austria to counter Prussia. Russia, too, feared Prussian expansion on the Polish frontier, and Sweden, anticipating an eventual Prussian reverse, wanted a share of the spoils. Only England, for whom France was the sole competitor in the New World, sided with Frederick. Always an advocate of offensive actions to preempt attack, Frederick invaded Austria's ally Saxony in 1756, taking the entire army captive and thereby beginning the Seven Years' War. This war, which had little impact on European power politics, was among the bloodiest the continent had seen. It was marked by rapid reversals and events steered by luck more than military might.

"The sovereign is the representative of his State. He and his people form a single body. Ruler and ruled can be happy only if they are firmly united. The sovereign stands to his people in the same relation in which the head stands to the body. He must use his eyes and his brain for the whole community, and act on its behalf to the common advantage."

Frederick II, *Essay on the Forms of Government*

Frederick was an aged, broken man by the war's end; he continued to wear his tattered army uniform until his death. For the next quarter century he embarked on a reconstruction program which assured Prussian ascendancy in Europe. He also developed a unified legal system, the *Codex Fredericianus*, promising fair trials for citizens of all ranks. At the same time, he retained the class system, believing the aristocracy to be a better breed than the peasantry and middle class. All middle-class officers were discharged for possessing "unrefined manners." Although Frederick now disavowed war, his empire was augmented by the annexation of significant segments of Poland following that country's partition in 1772. In 1777 Joseph II of Austria marched into Bavaria. Frederick again led his troops into battle, but after a series of bloodless maneuvers both monarchs retreated.

In 1786, just months before his death, he succeeded in forming a league of German princes, a forerunner of the idea of German unity. Some months later, he went out to inspect his troops despite a raging winter storm. Already an old man, he fell ill and died. Later, German nationalists idolized Frederick as the man most responsible for forging Prussia into a major world power. Adolf Hitler was a fervent admirer of Frederick, to whom he compared himself, and a portrait of Frederick was one of his most treasured possessions. ◆

Frederick William

1620–1688 ● King of Prussia

elector: any of the German princes entitled to take part in the choosing of the Holy Roman Emperor.

Frederick, known as the Great **Elector**, was the eldest son of the Hohenzollern elector George William and Elizabeth Charlotte of the Palatinate. Due to the Thirty Years' War, he left Berlin to study in Kustrin and in 1634 went to the Netherlands, where he attended the University of Leiden. While studying mathematics, Latin, history, and military science he developed a strong admiration for Dutch culture and throughout his life carried this love for the Netherlands as an imposing maritime and commercial power.

George William's rule of Brandenburg was masterminded by Count Adam von Schwarzenberg. Frederick despised him and his attempts to control his father, and even accused the elector's councilor of poisoning him when he came down with the measles. Distrust, paranoia, and enforced inactivity depressed Frederick when he moved to live in Königsberg, Prussia, where he remained until his father's death in 1640.

At the time of Frederick's accession to power in Brandenburg, its fortunes were at an all-time low, with some 50 percent of the population as well as crucial territories being lost in the Thirty Years' War. His father had allowed the nobility, known as the "Estates," to pursue its own interests and to assert power over the central government. Relying upon his mother's political prowess, he reduced Schwarzenberg's power and created a plan to rebuild the army, at the same time negotiating with Sweden, which had taken over Brandenburg territory.

A two-year armistice between Brandenburg and Sweden, concluded in 1641, underlined Frederick's political and military impotence, with Sweden retaining Brandenburg territory. As a Polish duke, Frederick turned to King Wtadstaw IV in order to gain the duchy of Prussia, where he was invested with power later the same year. From an economic point of view, Prussia was more important than Brandenburg because there he could tax directly in order to rebuild the army. In 1646 Frederick married Louise Henriette of Orange, daughter of Frederick Henry of Orange. However, this did not secure Dutch support for the army that Frederick had been building since 1644.

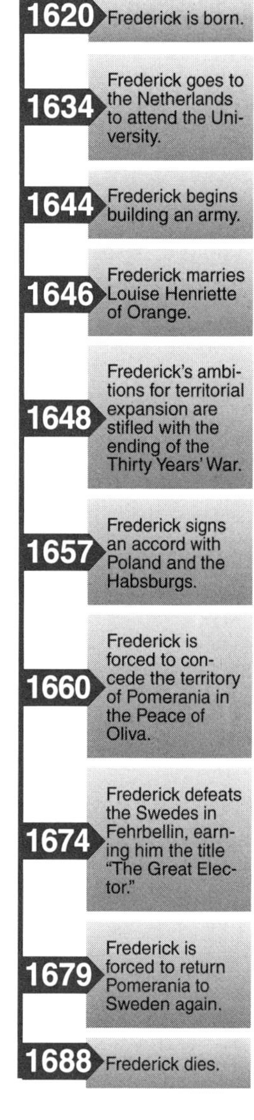

Frederick's ambitions for territorial expansion were stifled in 1648, when the Treaty of Westphalia, officially ending the Thirty Years' War, left him with important lands linking him to his west German territories, but without the prize he hoped for—all of Pomerania. France was on the rise and the Swedes blocked the elector's route to the Baltic Sea. Nonetheless, he retained grandiose plans for the rise of Brandenburg-Prussia as a great commercial and maritime power like the Netherlands.

After a peaceful interlude, the First Northern War (1655–60) broke out between Poland and Sweden. As a vassal of the Polish king, Frederick was obliged to help, but in 1656, through the treaties of Konigsberg and Marienburg, he allied himself with the Swedes. The Brandenburg army's first victory, in the Battle of Warsaw, gave Frederick full sovereignty over the duchy of Prussia. Turning his back on Sweden, he now signed an accord with Poland and the Habsburgs in 1657. The shift in alliances upset Sweden and hostilities broke out. Standing at the head of a 30,000-strong army, Frederick expelled the Swedes from Schleswig-Holstein, gaining the much-desired territory of Pomerania. However, the French, as Sweden's allies, amassed an enormous army and forced Frederick to concede the territory in the Peace of Oliva in 1660.

For twenty years, Frederick had ruled in conjunction with some of his closest advisers. Now, after Oliva, he was to become one of the strongest proponents in Europe of princely **absolutism**. His sense of mission was strengthened by the fact that he was a Calvinist who felt he had to prove himself as a ruler. His scattered possessions lacked physical unity so he used strict economic administration in order to achieve political consolidation. He also utilized terror through the execution of his main opponents in order to demonstrate the strength of the central state over the Estates.

absolutism: a political theory that absolute power should be vested in one or more rulers.

By heavy taxing and subsidies from Austria, Spain, France, and the Netherlands, Frederick laid the foundation of a powerful bureaucracy that was dependent upon him. His foreign policy consisted of maintaining the balance of power in Europe, and he often opted to ally himself with weaker powers in order to preserve the status quo.

Frederick William's sense of mission was strengthened by the fact that he was a Calvinist who felt he had to prove himself as a ruler.

Frederick's support of the Spanish Netherlands against the French proved a complete failure, prompting him to join an alliance with Austria, Spain, and Denmark. In 1674 the Swedes invaded Brandenburg and within two weeks Frederick's army was back in Brandenburg, where he defeated the Swedes at Fehrbellin; a poem of the time honoring the victory called him "The Great Elector." Now he saw his chance to gain Pomerania once and for all. The war lasted for five more years with the Great Elector achieving his goal, but once again he was forced by the French to return Pomerania to Sweden (Treaty of Saint-Germain, 1679).

Instead of fighting France, Frederick felt that entering an alliance could gain him what he had sought for so long. The secret pact, established in 1679, lasted as long as Frederick thought he would regain Pomerania. However, France's only interest was obtaining lands along the German border. The alliance was severed and Frederick changed allegiances for the last time in 1685, turning again to his first love, the Netherlands.

While Frederick did not make Brandenburg-Prussia into a major European power, he established a well-organized government that had a respectable army and a functioning economy. He also founded the Berlin royal library, reorganized the universities, opened canals, and developed the city of Berlin. The institutions and administration he founded would become the backbone of the powerful Prussian state developed by his successors. ◆

Fuad

1868–1936 ● KING OF EGYPT

Fuad was born in Giza, Egypt, on March 26, 1868, the youngest child of Khedive Ismail Pasha, who ruled Egypt from 1863 until 1879. Fuad left Egypt for Constantinople (now Istanbul) in 1879 at the time of his father's exile. Subsequently, he studied at Geneva, Turin, and the Italian Military Academy, returning to Egypt in 1892. His eligibility for the Egyptian throne was enhanced when the British deposed Abbas Hilmi II as **khedive** of Egypt in 1914 at the beginning of World War I. At the time of Abbas's removal, Britain severed the

khedive: a ruler of Egypt from 1867 to 1914, governing as a viceroy of the sultan of Turkey.

juridical ties that bound Egypt to the Ottoman empire, proclaimed a protectorate over the country, and named Fuad's elder brother, Husayn Kamil, as the first sultan of Egypt. When Husayn Kamil died on October 9, 1917, Fuad succeeded him to the throne.

Fuad reigned in Egypt from 1917 until his death in 1936. He aspired to be a powerful ruler and did much to enlarge the powers of the monarchy. Following the conclusion of the war, Egypt's elite, including Sultan Fuad, pressed the British to end the protectorate and to increase the political autonomy of their country. Britain's failure to respond to these overtures set off a powerful protest movement, led by Sad Zaghlul and his new political party, the Wafd. The political turmoil led to Britain's unilateral proclamation of Egypt's independence on February 28, 1922, subject to the exclusion of a wide range of powers reserved to the British. In the wake of the altered political status of the country, Fuad became king of Egypt on March 15, 1922. In 1923 an appointed committee drafted a new constitution for the country. Through the intervention of Fuad and the British, the constitution gave far-reaching authority to the monarch. Under its provisions, the crown had the power to designate the prime minister, dissolve the parliament, and postpone sessions of parliament. Additionally, the king controlled charitable and educational institutions and decided upon diplomatic appointments and military commissions.

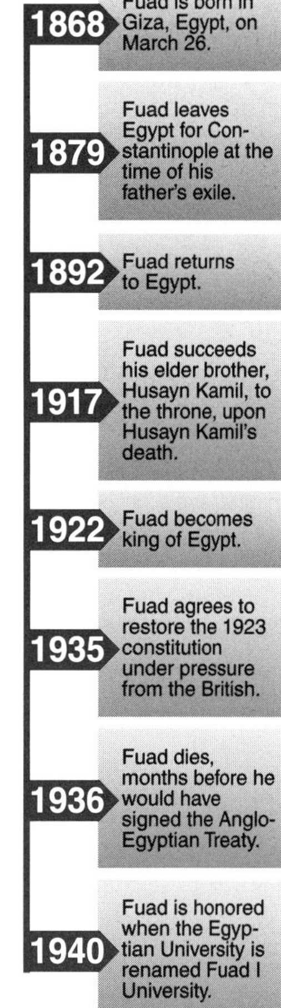

Armed with its formal, albeit restricted, political independence and a new, sophisticated constitution, Egypt embarked upon an experiment in liberal democracy. Unfortunately, civilian parliamentary government, which lasted until the military ousted the politicians from office in 1952, tended to degenerate into a three-cornered struggle among Egypt's most popular party, the Wafd, the palace, and the British. During these years, the Wafd invariably won any fair electoral contest, but was kept from office through the political manipulations of the palace and the British. Monarchical power reached its apex between 1930 and 1935, after Fuad removed the Wafd from office and appointed Ismail Sidqi as prime minister. Immediately upon assuming power, Sidqi replaced the 1923 constitution with a new one and enacted a new, more restrictive electoral law. Both changes enhanced royal authority. Jealous of the power that Sidqi wielded, Fuad removed him from office in 1933 and ruled Egypt through a set of palace appointees. In 1935, under pressure from the British and responding to fears of an impending world war, Fuad agreed to restore the 1923 constitution and to hold new elections. Predictably, the Wafd won the 1936 elections. Fuad died on April 28, 1936, just months before the signing of the Anglo-Egyptian Treaty, which gave greater political autonomy to Egypt.

autocrat: a person ruling with unlimited authority.

Although he was an **autocrat** and did much to impede the development of parliamentary democracy, Fuad was a noteworthy patron of Egyptian education. He played a role in reviving the Egyptian University, which had been founded in 1908 but had languished until Fuad and others gave it their support. It was named Fuad I University in 1940 and became today's Cairo University in 1954. ◆

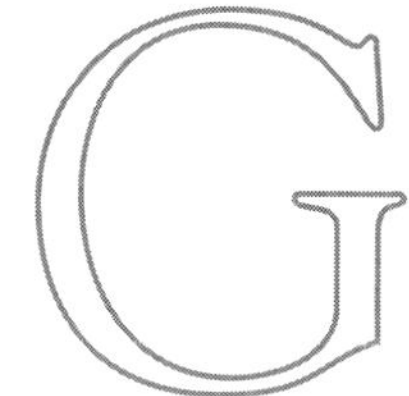

Galawdewos

1522?–1559 ● EMPEROR OF ETHIOPIA

Galawdewos, the son of Lebna Dengel, was emperor of Ethiopia from 1540 to 1559. In the latter years of Lebna Dengel's reign, Ethiopia was almost completely overrun by the jihad (holy war) of Ahmad Grañ (Ahmad ibn Ibrahim al-Ghazi), the **imam** of Adal, who by 1540 had set up his capital north of Lake Tana and had become the effective ruler of the country. The arrival of a Portuguese expedition led by Cristovão da Gama in 1541 helped save the situation, though da Gama was defeated and executed by Grañ. The remainder of the Portuguese joined forces with Galawdewos; together they defeated and killed Grañ in February 1543 at Woguera.

imam: a leader claiming descent from Muhammad and exercising spiritual and temporal leadership over a Muslim region.

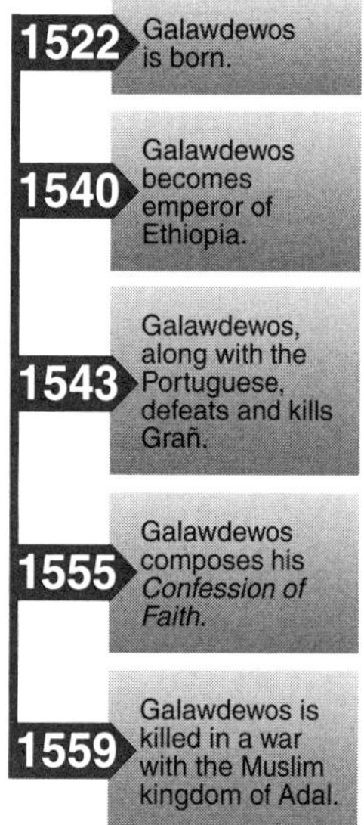

Galawdewos then had to rebuild the devastated country. Grateful as he was to the Portuguese, he had no intention of altering his religious allegiance to please them and was embarrassed by the arrival of Jesuits who hoped to persuade him to accept the authority of Rome. In reply he composed his *Confession of Faith* in 1555, a remarkably temperate assertion both of the traditional doctrine of the Ethiopian Orthodox Church and of the practical issues at stake: the celebration of the Sabbath, the rite of circumcision, and the eating of pork. The Jesuits recognized his outstanding qualities in both theological debate and diplomacy. In 1559 Galawdewos was killed in a war with the Muslim kingdom of Adal. He appears as one of the most attractive, intelligent, and humane in Ethiopia's long line of rulers. ◆

Genghis Khan

1167–1227 ● MONGOL EMPEROR

Genghis Khan united and ruled half of the world as he knew it. A man of immovable will, violent energy, and enormous mental ability, he was merciless toward enemies but lenient and generous with his followers. Although he himself was superstitious, he knew well how to use superstition as a weapon. Above all he was obsessed by the love of power.

Genghis Khan was born to the Mongol chief Yesugai and his beautiful wife, Houlun, who had been snatched from her newly betrothed husband as they were traveling home together. On the day of his son's birth to Houlun, Yesugai returned home with a captive Tartar chief named Temujin. He marked the occasion by naming the newborn boy after his prisoner.

Murder, rape, theft, and clan feuding were a normal part of life for the Mongols, and children grew up quickly.

Hunters and nomads, the Mongols gave pride of place at the fire and first choice of food to the warriors. Women and elders came next, leaving the children to fight for warmth and scraps of food. Murder, rape, theft, and clan feuding were a normal part of life, and children grew up quickly. When Temujin was thirteen, he was betrothed to the nine-year-old Bortai and left in the tent of his future bride, as was customary. Temujin never saw his father again; on the way home Yesugai was fatally poisoned, leaving his firstborn to rule as tribal chief.

Most of Yesugai's former followers deserted the tribe. His mother exhorted Temujin to avenge his father's death and regain the old chief's glory. Because his father's former kinsmen saw Temujin as an enemy, they sought his life, and thieves almost stole the eight horses upon which the family's livelihood depended. Temujin prevailed, however, and at the age of seventeen set out to claim Bortai and assume the responsibilities of leadership. His first success was the renewal of an old alliance with his father's former friend Togrul, cemented with the offering of Bortai's dowry—a sable coat—as a gift. Success, however, was followed by defeat, for the Merkit tribe, from whom Houlun had been stolen, now took revenge by kidnapping Temujin's new wife. Invoking his friendship with Togrul, Temujin managed to regain Bortai, but it was never clear whether the son she bore nine months later was his or his enemy's.

Temujin eventually regained the power his father had lost, and his followers renamed him Chingis (Genghis), which in

Chinese means "son of heaven" and "perfect warrior" and may also be derived from the Mongol word for "strong." At this point Genghis was primarily known for keeping order in his tribe, but by 1206, when he was fifty years old, he had come to dominate his subjects and his hostile neighbors by a combination of military genius, superior organization, and treachery. He had conquered most of Mongolia, and his name had been amended to Genghis Khan (Turkish *Khan*, "lord").

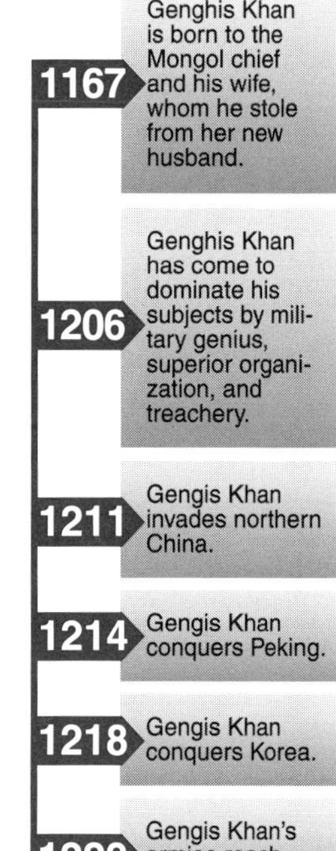

Fired by his passion for conquest, Genghis Khan began to look beyond the Mongol boundaries. In 1211 he refused to pay tribute to the Chinese emperor, scaled the Great Wall and invaded northern China. Peking (Beijing) fell in 1214, followed by Korea in 1218. His Mongol armies then turned west with relentless fury, looting, massacring, and leaving destruction in their wake. They conquered what is now Iraq, Iran, and the Asian parts of what was later the Soviet Union. Invading parts of India and sweeping through Turkestan, Khan's armies drove the Turks out, preventing the establishment of a Turkish empire in central Asia. In 1222 they reached Russia, expanding an empire that now reached from the China Sea to the Dnieper and from the Persian Gulf almost to the Arctic Ocean.

Uneducated though he was, Genghis Khan demonstrated a remarkable military genius paralleled by an amazing talent for statesmanship. Like his armies, his entire regime was characterized by superb organization and discipline. In Mongolia he had created the Mongol feudal state out of the anarchy of a deteriorating clan system, drawing up a code of law, the *yasak*, to govern it. There were laws on punishment for sexual offenses and rulings on spying and interference, presumably intended to stamp out clan feuds. The *yasak* codified customs of desert hospitality, hygiene, and religious practice, and established codes of behavior and organization for the army.

Genghis Khan organized his empire and united it with great roads, encouraging the growth of trade and providing security. It was claimed that one could travel from one end of the empire to the other without fear of danger. Paradoxically, by destroying everything in his path, he had created the conditions for peace and culture. By founding his empire, he opened up Asia to Europe and made possible a world market and international exchange of ideas. After his death his empire was divided among his four sons, and four of his grandsons—among them Kublai Khan—became great Mongol leaders in turn. ◆

George III

1738–1820 ◆ King of England

"Knavery seems to be so much the striking feature of its inhabitants that it may not in the end be an evil that they will become aliens to this kingdom."
George III, describing America, 1782

Born in London to Frederick Louis, prince of Wales, and his wife, Augusta of Saxe-Gotha, George III became heir to the throne at the age of twelve upon the death of his father. George's early years were dominated by the influence of his formidable mother who sought to isolate him from potential moral dangers in the decadent court society around her.

George was not a quick student and did not learn to read until he was eleven. A child of strong emotions, his determination was second to none but this was undermined by feelings of inadequacy. He needed a hero to look up to and found one in his tutor John Stuart, the earl of Bute, a talented and ambitious politician who soon won George's total confidence.

George acceded to the throne in 1760 and continued to rely on Bute for support and instruction. Bute persuaded the king to put aside all ideas of marrying the young lady he had set his heart on, Lady Sarah Lennox. Apart from the association of her family with Bute's political opponents, she was not of suitable royal stock. George was easily convinced to adopt the safe course and find a Protestant German princess as his queen.

In 1761 he married Princess Charlotte Sophia of Mecklenberg-Strelitz. Although George married out of his sense of duty, the marriage was a success, lasting fifty years, with the king's faithfulness to his wife a striking exception to the other monarchs of the house of Hanover. The royal couple had fourteen children between 1762 and 1783.

Duty to his country was a concept deeply embedded in him from his earliest years. Whereas his two predecessors had considered themselves Germans first and English second, King George III declared in his first speech from the throne, "Born and educated in this country, I glory in the name of Britain." He told his subjects, "I do not pretend to any superior abilities, but will give place to no one in meaning to preserve the freedom, happiness and glory of my dominions and all their inhabitants."

His first decade of rule was a difficult period of unstable governments and financial crisis resulting from the Seven Years' War (1756–63). Although he lacked experience, he handled the shifting alliances of lords and gentlemen well and by the mid-1760s had dispensed with his dependence on Bute and widened his circle of advisers.

> ***"I can never suppose this country so far lost to all ideas of self-importance as to be willing to grant America independence; if that could ever be adopted I shall despair of this country being ever preserved from a state of inferiority and consequently falling into a very low class among the European states."***
> George III, 1780

King George set for himself a spartan and vigorous routine. Rising at six each morning he worked for an hour or more before taking breakfast and saying his morning prayers. Most of his day was occupied with state business and meals were sparse and eaten hurriedly. During the 1790s, when the wars of the French Revolution caused a rise in bread prices, the king ordered that only brown bread be served at his palace in Windsor. But there were also relaxations, for George was fond of riding and hunting and, along with the queen, he delighted in theater, preferring pantomime and comedies, not tragedies. George was an enthusiastic book collector, favoring books that were educational rather than amusing. In a famous encounter with the writer Samuel Johnson, George engaged Johnson in literary conversation; Johnson commented afterwards, "They may talk of the King as they will, but he is the finest gentleman I have ever seen."

King George took an active interest in agriculture and did much to popularize the new advances in farming methods, earning the popular nickname of "Farmer George." Under the name of Ralph Robinson he contributed two articles to the *Annals of Agriculture*. Scientific progress also attracted the king's attention. He was fascinated by advances in astronomy and contributed £2,947 toward the cost of William Herschel's forty-foot telescope, which was, at the time, the biggest in the world. When he went to view Herschel's telescope with the archbishop of Canterbury, they walked through the huge tube. The archbishop had difficulty keeping his balance and the king extended a helping hand quipping, "Come my lord bishop, I will show you the way to heaven."

The king's ability as a ruler was affected by his innate conservatism and obstinately held prejudices. This was illustrated during the American War of Independence, prolonged several years by George's view of the revolt in terms of a child rebelling against a parent. He put his views forward at the start in the following terms: "The die is now cast, the colonies must either

British Empire

The British Empire was a network of possessions around the world that were subordinate to the British government for varying periods of time between the early seventeenth and the twentieth centuries. The empire developed from the British search for trade, resources, markets, and strategic military bases. The empire of the seventeenth and eighteenth centuries, often known as the first British Empire, was built up primarily by commercial companies and individuals who established settlements on the east coast of North America, the Caribbean, India, and southeast Asia. By defeating France in the Seven Years' War (1756–63), Britain also acquired Canada. The British crown allowed a great deal of local self-government in these early colonies, concerning itself primarily with establishing and enforcing mercantilist regulations governing the empire's trade.

During the American Revolution (1776–83), thirteen British colonies won their independence and became the United States. This was a major loss to Britain and is considered the end of the first empire, but Britain quickly built up a second empire. The British settlement of Australia began in 1788. Britain acquired Trinidad and Ceylon in 1802. In 1806 Britain obtained the Cape of Good Hope at the southern tip of Africa, and Singapore became a British possession in 1819. Britain began enlarging its area of control in India in the early nineteenth century. New Zealand became an official possession in 1840. Britain gained control of Hong Kong during the mid 1800s. In the 1880s and 1890s Britain seized large areas of Africa.

The British Empire peaked around World War I, when it included about one-fifth of the earth's surface and one-quarter of the world's people. In 1931 the British Parliament established the Commonwealth of Nations, a group of self-governing nation–states bound only by a common allegiance to the British crown. Canada, Australia, New Zealand, and South Africa—all former dependencies settled by large numbers of Britons and other Europeans—became the first members, along with Britain. Exhausted financially by World War II and facing the growth of nationalism among the native populations of its colonies, Britain began granting independence to its former possessions. In the late 1940s most of its Asian dependencies were freed. In the late 1950s and the 1960s most of the African and West Indian colonies won their liberation. Many of the former possessions joined the Commonwealth of Nations.

submit or triumph. I do not wish to come to severe measures, but we must not retreat; by coolness and an unremitted pursuit of the measures that have been adopted I trust they will come to submit." With the war ultimately lost and the king's prestige damaged, he showed magnanimity when he greeted John Adams, the first U.S. minister to England, on the friendliest of terms, saying he wished to be "the first to meet the friendship of the United States as an independent power."

The second half of George's rule was marked by increasing family conflict with sons whose personalities were in direct contrast to that of their staid and frugal father. Two future kings, princes George and William, were particular thorns in his side. their displays of extravagance and womanizing contradicted the strict upbringing and devotion to public duty he had sought to imbue in them.

The king also suffered increasingly from mental illness resulting from a metabolic disorder thought to have been prophyria. He recovered from a severe attack in 1788, when his eyes looked like black currants and foam poured from his mouth. Popular legend has him dismounting from his carriage to shake hands with an oak tree in Windsor Park, mistaking the tree for King Frederick the Great. Certainly it is recorded how at one cabinet meeting he concluded each sentence with the word "peacock," to the utter consternation of his ministers.

By 1805 the king was blind and from 1811 his state of mental imbalance necessitated the appointment of his eldest son George as regent. George III, when he was not fastened in a straitjacket or tied to his bed by his ignorant doctors, wandered around his palace playing on his harpsichord, convinced he was talking to angels. ◆

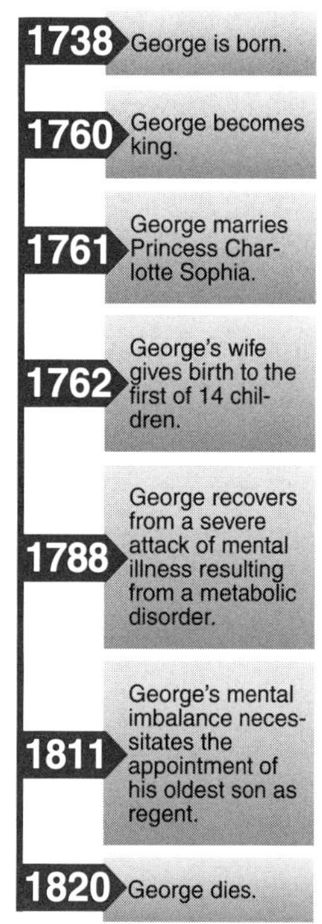

Gustavus II Adolphus

1594–1632 ● King of Sweden

Gustavus II Adolphus transformed Sweden into one of Europe's great powers. He succeeded his father, Charles IX, who had used his brief but unpopular reign to reform Sweden's government, promote industry and commerce, suppress the aristocracy, and make war. Although he had attended the Diet since he was nine, received ambassadors since he was thirteen, ruled a province, and had fought in battle, the nobility, organized as the Estates, would only crown sixteen-year-old Gustavus king if he signed a charter granting them important constitutional concessions subjugating the monarchy to them, to which he agreed.

Gustavus inherited Charles's wars: a dynastic struggle with Poland, a war with Denmark—then one of Europe's strongest states—for control of trade between the North and Baltic seas,

and a war with Russia to keep its vacant throne out of Polish hands (the Polish conflict continued to flare up intermittently for almost sixty years). The war with Denmark was clearly a lost cause, and Gustavus ended it in 1613 by promising Denmark a huge indemnity which cost Sweden years of heavy taxation and left a lingering bitterness against the Danes. After a Romanov became czar of Russia, Sweden fought to keep Russia out of the Baltic (1613–17). Eventually Sweden annexed enough territory to cut Russia off from the Baltic, thereby stopping Russia from becoming a major European power for another eighty years.

Gustavus also concerned himself with much-needed internal reforms. He enjoyed the support of the nobility, which responded to his willingness to observe the spirit of the charter (if not all of its clauses) with a readiness to sacrifice some of their privileges and serve in Sweden's administration as well as its army. He also had the able assistance of his chancellor, Count Axel Oxenstierna, whose phlegmatic personality balanced Gustavus's fiery temperament. Together they promoted commerce, established schools and universities, relieved the poor, developed the mining industry, modernized the army, and reorganized the bureaucracy, giving Sweden the most modern and efficient central administration in Europe.

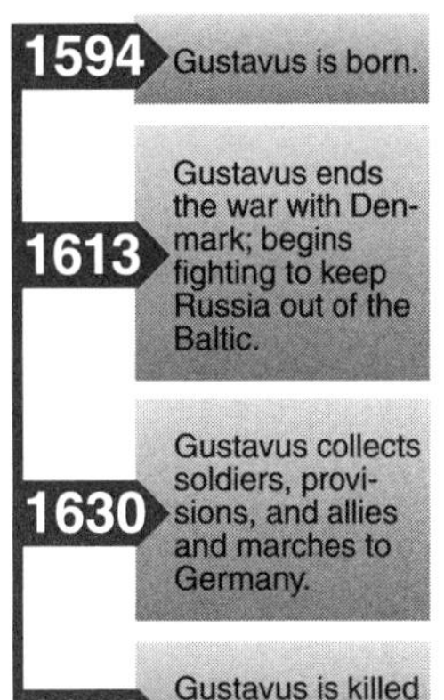

The Thirty Years' War—a struggle for political and religious domination between Protestant and Catholic powers—was devastating Europe. The major Catholic military force belonged to the Austrian Habsburg Empire, which fought the Protestant northern German kingdoms, the Netherlands, and Denmark. Catholic France, believing that it was more important to check Austria's growing power than to fight Protestantism, formed an alliance against Austria, which Sweden joined, but rivalry among its members soon caused its breakup. Austria conquered Denmark in 1626 and formed an alliance with Poland.

Gustavus believed that "all wars in Europe hang together," and was concerned that Sweden's defeat by an Austro-Polish alliance could turn the Baltic into an Austrian-controlled sea. After the Swedish Diet agreed to support and finance his entry into the war, he collected soldiers, provisions, and allies and marched to Germany in 1630.

The main reason for Gustavus's entry into the Thirty Years' War was his desire to strengthen and save Sweden, but he was also a sincere fighter for Protestantism; his soldiers attended prayer meetings twice a day, heard a sermon on Sunday, and were barred from bringing prostitutes into their camp. Gustavus led his troops into battle personally and fought ferociously, scorning the use of armor; under his command the Protestant forces enjoyed their first victories of the war. He allowed the areas he conquered religious freedom, organized Swedish-type administrations, and proposed the formation of a Protestant League under his direction as the best hope for Protestant security. Jealously resentful, some of the German Protestant princes refused to join the league, thus delaying Germany's unification by two hundred years.

Gustavus was killed in battle at Lützen, after becoming separated from his men while leading a cavalry charge. Oxenstierna became regent for Gustavus's four-year-old daughter, Christina. ◆

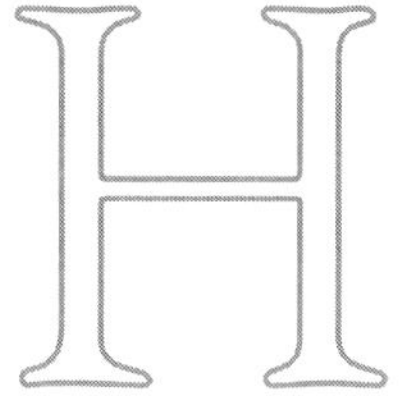

Hadrian

76–138 ● Roman Emperor

The cousin of the emperor Trajan, Hadrian (Publius Aelius Hadrianus) was born to an Italian family long settled in Spain. His father died when he was ten and Trajan became his guardian, marrying him off at sixteen to his grandniece, Vivia Sabina. She, in turn, accompanied him on many of his wanderings, occupying herself with founding a Little Senate of Women that decided matters of feminine dress, jewelry, etiquette, and rank, and tolerating his passion for his young Greek page. They had no children.

Hadrian was forty-one years old and the commander of Rome's armies in Syria when he became emperor following Trajan's death in 117. Tall, strong, and elegant, with a full beard (which made beards fashionable for the duration of his reign) he also loved the company of philosophers and scholars. He himself was a musician, architect, the author of several books, and a patron of the arts, preferring Greek to Roman culture.

Among his first acts as emperor was the reversal of Trajan's expansionist policy, to which Hadrian had expressed opposition during Trajan's lifetime, by withdrawing Rome's forces beyond the Euphrates, which then became the empire's new eastern boundary. There was opposition to this policy but it did not last long: the four generals who had led Trajan's forces believed that Hadrian's switch from an offensive to a defensive policy was cowardly and the beginning of the end of the empire; they were

"Hadrian had also a most agreeable style of conversation, even towards persons of decidedly humble rank. He hated those who seemed to envy him this natural pleasure, under pretext of causing 'the Majesty of the Throne' to be respected."
Aelius Spartianus, *Life of Hadrian*

executed by the Senate on a charge of conspiring to overthrow the government.

Hadrian devoted himself to the task of reorganizing the empire and carrying out administrative, military, and legal reforms. He supervised every aspect of government, increased the administrative bureaucracy and regulations, and greatly increased tax receipts without raising taxes by appointing an attorney for the treasury to guard against cheating. Eventually his government was so well trained that it continued to function while he toured the empire for years at a time.

> ***"In poetry and in letters Hadrian was greatly interested. In arithmetic, geometry, and painting he was very expert. Of his knowledge of flute-playing and singing he even boasted openly. He ran to excess in the gratification of his desires, and wrote much verse about the subjects of his passion. He composed love-poems too. He was also a connoisseur of arms, had a thorough knowledge of warfare, and knew how to use gladiatorial weapons."***
>
> Aelius Spartianus, *Life of Hadrian*

Determined to follow a policy of peace, Hadrian felt that the only way to do so was to strengthen Rome militarily so that weakness would not make it a tempting target for its enemies. To this end border defenses, weapons, and supplies were thoroughly inspected and improved, while new, severe regulations improved military discipline and soldiers' legal and economic status.

The codification of Roman law initiated by Hadrian has influenced Western law up to the present day. He commissioned a corps of jurists to codify existing Roman law into a superseding Perpetual Edict. Roman law traditionally protected the person and property of citizens; Hadrian's reforms extended that protection.

Hadrian spent years visiting every province in the empire. His travels had a twofold purpose. Firstly, he was an indefatigable traveler, eager to view the many peoples and sights in his empire. Secondly, he did not view the provinces as sources of wealth to be drained off to Rome but as integral parts of the empire. He saw it as the emperor's duty to inspect the provinces to determine their needs and how the resources of the empire could best be used to meet them. The supreme authority wherever he went, Hadrian heard petitions and complaints, judged, punished, and rewarded. Cities devastated by earthquake were rebuilt and new cities and roads sprang up. He erected public buildings with imperial funds. In Athens his extensive building program renovated the city while solving its unemployment problem. In Britain he ordered the building of Hadrian's Wall, a seventy-four mile long defensive measure. He beautified Rome with new buildings and renovations (such as the Pantheon), of which many were of his own design, while none bore his insignia. The empire was never so prosperous as during Hadrian's rule.

Having rebuilt many cities during his travels, Hadrian ordered the rebuilding of Jerusalem as the Roman colony of Aelia Capitolina, with a temple to Jupiter on the Temple Mount. That order, and one prohibiting circumcision, resulted in the Bar Kokhba rebellion of 132–135, in which Jewish forces recaptured Jerusalem and destroyed an entire legion. It was a bitterly fought, brutally suppressed war which Hadrian won only by sending in legions from all over the empire. Although it ended victoriously for Rome, Roman casualties were so heavy that Hadrian omitted the customary phrase "I and my army are well" from his report to the Senate.

In 135 Hadrian fell sick with a painful wasting disease. Foreseeing his own death, he adopted Titus Aurelius Antoninus as his successor. Maddened by pain, he accused some of his closest friends of being part of a conspiracy to kill him and had several put to death. Later, crushed by ever increasing pain, he tried desperately but unsuccessfully to kill himself or to get someone to kill him. ◆

Haile Selassie I

1892–1975 ◆ EMPEROR OF ETHIOPIA

Ras (prince) Tafari was the son of Makonnen, king of Shoa, a cousin and vassal of Menelik II, emperor of Ethiopia. According to Ethiopian tradition, the family was descended from King Solomon and the queen of Sheba through their supposed son, Menelik I. Although he was not expected to succeed to the throne of Ethiopia, the diminutive, pale-skinned Ras Tafari was a great favorite of Menelik II. He was appointed *dejazmatch* (keeper of the door) in Menelik's court when he was only fourteen years old, and at eighteen succeeded his father as governor of Harar. The next year he married Wayzaro Menen, a great-granddaughter of Menelik.

Menelik II was succeeded by his grandson, Lij Yasu, in 1913. Lij Yasu's father was a Muslim who was forcibly converted to Christianity, and Lij Yasu himself flirted with Islam, to the chagrin of the predominantly Christian population of Ethiopia. Ras Tafari therefore led a coup that deposed Lij Yasu in 1916. Menelik's daughter

Zauditu assumed the throne, with Ras Tafari serving as regent. He was a popular leader who continued Menelik's policy of modernization, building schools and encouraging outstanding students to further their education abroad. His greatest success was obtaining the international recognition accorded his country upon joining the League of Nations in 1923. The next year, slavery was abolished in Ethiopia, and many additional reforms were instituted after his state visit to Europe, the first by an Ethiopian head of state. In 1928, Ras Tafari assumed the title of *Negus* (king).

"Apart from the Kingdom of the Lord there is not on this earth any nation that is superior to any other. Should it happen that a strong Government finds it may with impunity destroy a weak people, then the hour strikes for that weak people to appeal to the League of Nations to give its judgment in all freedom. God and history will remember your judgment."
Haile Selassie, appeal to the League of Nations, 1936

Upon Zauditu's death in 1930, Ras Tafari was proclaimed Conquering Lion of the Tribe of Judah, Elect of God and King of the Kings of Ethiopia. At his coronation ceremony in Saint George's Cathedral in Addis Ababa, he assumed the name Haile Selassie (Power of the Trinity). The early years of Haile Selassie's reign were characterized by sweeping reforms. He gave Ethiopia its first written constitution, institutionalized taxation, created the Bank of Ethiopia, and formed a parliament, a secretive institution whose infrequent sessions were subject to the whims of the emperor. Nonetheless, local forces favoring rapid modernization saw this as a great step forward.

Despite the changes at home, world events were taking their toll on Ethiopian development. Italy received British support for a sphere of influence in Ethiopia. Despite his pleas at the League of Nations, Haile Selassie was powerless to prevent Italian incursions into his territory. A clash between Italian and Ethiopian troops over a water hole in the Ogaden Desert resulted in an arms embargo by France and Britain against Ethiopia, while Italy used the dispute as a pretense to escalate tensions. Italian troops, led by Marshal Emilio de Bono and later, Marshal Pietro Badoglio, invaded Ethiopia in 1935. Two hundred and fifty thousand Ethiopian soldiers were killed attempting to repulse the onslaught of the better-armed Italian troops. On May 2, 1935, the royal family fled, and three days later Addis Ababa fell.

Haile Selassie spent the following six years in exile in Europe attempting to muster support for his beleaguered country. Reports reached him of atrocities committed and concentration camps built to subjugate his people. In the five years of Italian occupation, 760,300 Ethiopians are said to have been killed. In 1936, Haile Selassie again turned to the League of Nations in an impassioned speech, begging the member states to help liberate Ethiopia. This plea by a frail, homeless emperor from an obscure land was considered by many to be the finest speech ever made to the League, but the world governments, on the brink of World War II, were unwilling to risk the fragile peace of Europe for a remote African kingdom. Haile Selassie retired to London, where he remained until 1940.

Only after the outbreak of World War II did Britain and France recognize the strategic importance of Ethiopia to world shipping and trade. Haile Selassie traveled to Khartoum in 1940 to take part in the liberation of Ethiopia; an army of Ethiopian exiles was established in the Sudan and in 1941 British and Ethiopian forces drove out the Italians. Haile Selassie returned to Addis Ababa in 1941.

"Our people of Ethiopia, you know how grim life is to people robbed of their government, independence and their motherland. The time has now come when each and every one of us should protect and serve our beloved country, Ethiopia, with more zeal and vigour."
Haile Selassie, 1940

Once back on his throne, he continued his policy of modernization. The Italian territory of Eritrea was annexed in 1950, to the chagrin of its predominantly Muslim population. In 1955 he granted a new constitution, ceding considerable powers to parliament and even allowing for elections. Despite these reforms, the pace of modernization was considered too slow by some and a failed coup attempt was made in 1960.

Haile Selassie took an active role in world and particularly pan-African politics; the Organization of African Unity was founded in Addis Ababa in 1963. However, the final years of his reign were marked by harsh famine and corruption in the army. The aging emperor was rapidly growing inarticulate and senile; although he was deposed by the military in 1974 and placed under house arrest, Haile Selassie failed to grasp the events taking place and believed that he was still in power. It was claimed that he died in his sleep in 1975.

For many Africans, Haile Selassie represented the suffering of embattled Africa, torn by colonialism and exploitation. He is often regarded as a symbol of Africa's yearning for freedom. One Jamaican-based religious group of pan-African nationalists, the Rastafarians (after Ras Tafari), believe that Haile Selassie was the personification of Christ returned to redeem Africa. ◆

Hamad ibn Khalifa Al Thani

1950– ● EMIR OF QATAR

Shaykh Hamad became the emir of Qatar on June 27, 1995, when he ousted his father in a bloodless palace coup. The eldest son of his predecessor, Shaykh Khalifa, Hamad was born in Doha in 1950. He graduated from the Royal

Military College in Sandhurst, England, in 1971, and in 1977 he was named heir apparent and defense minister by his father. In 1992 he took control of the day-to-day governing of Qatar when his father allowed him to appoint a cabinet of his own choice. In his first cabinet, appointed in July 1995, he retained for himself the positions of defense minister and commander of the Qatari armed forces and, in addition, appointed himself prime minister, a position previously held by his father.

Hamad ruled in the same style that his Al Thani forebears had in the days when they were tribal chiefs (shaykhs) in the desert, raising camels and fishing the gulf waters. But wealth from petroleum exports begun in 1949 had hurled the desert kingdom into the modern economic and political world. Hamad recognized the need for Qatar to change, but he proceeded cautiously, keeping Qatar's wealth and power in Al Thani hands. Hamad made his brother Abdallah bin Khalifa Al Thani prime minister and another brother, Muhammad bin Khalifa Al Thani, deputy prime minister. The emir appointed all cabinet members, and he selected his third son, Jassim bin Hamad bin Khalifa Al Thani, as crown prince in 1996.

One of his first efforts as emir was to recover several billion dollars from his father. In the mid 1970s Shaykh Khalifa's government had taken ownership of the nation's petroleum industry. Over the years, Khalifa transferred large amounts of oil revenue from Qatar's treasury directly into his own accounts. Hamad fought for nearly a year and a half—in and out of courts—to recover much of the money.

Hamad soon began surprising regional leaders with progressive moves. He announced an end to censorship of Qatari newspapers and set up a satellite television station that became the Middle East's most outspoken media outlet. He also announced his intention of creating a constitutional monarchy. On March 8, 1999, Hamad made a dramatic step toward political reform by holding the first election of any Persian Gulf nation in which all adult citizens—including women—could both vote and run for election. The vote was for a council on municipal affairs, which would simply make recommendations on minor matters such as road maintenance and food safety. Six women and 221 men ran for a twenty-nine-seat council, which was seen as a transitional body toward a full parliament.

Although they won no seats on the council, Qatar's women celebrated the vote as a victory, representing their increased numbers in the workplace and universities. In the 1990s the number of Qatari women in government jobs rose by more than 60 percent. Women made up 44 percent of registered voters. One of the emir's wives, Sheikha Mouza bint Nasser al-Misnad, was a major supporter of women's rights. Mouza was credited with influencing her husband's 1996 act of naming a woman as undersecretary of the ministry of education, the highest position ever held by a Qatari woman. Mouza is the second of the emir's three wives, each of whom has seven children. Mouza's son is the crown prince.

In the 1990s, the production of petroleum accounted for 95 percent of Qatar's income. Hamad worked to develop other sources of income as his nation entered the twenty-first century. ◆

Hammurabi

REIGNED C.1792–1750 B.C.E. ● BABYLONIAN KING

The sixth king of the first Babylonian dynasty Hammurabi was descended from nomadic Amorite tribesmen. Upon ascending the throne, he continued the expansionist policies of his father, Sin-muballit, asserting Babylonian hegemony over the Euphrates basin. Chief among his rivals was Rim-Sin, king of Larsa, who had invaded Isin, a neutral buffer town separating the two kingdoms. In a war against Rim-Sin, Hammurabi freed Isin and captured Uruk (biblical Erech).

"The king who ruleth among the kings of the cities am I. My words are well considered; there is no wisdom like unto mine."

Code of Hammurabi

Having secured his southern border, Hammurabi proceeded to strengthen his realm. As was customary, each year of Hammurabi's reign was named after the most notable event to take place. This practice allows modern archeologists to reconstruct fourteen tranquil years during which Hammurabi fortified his northern frontier, where powerful city-states such as Asshur, Elam, and Eshnunna were no less threatening than Larsa. He also developed the economic and religious infrastructure of his state. Temples and administrative buildings were restored and rebuilt, and irrigation canals were dug to improve agricultural productivity. It is probable that the well-known Code of Hammurabi, important to scholars studying the development of a secular legal system, was codified at this time.

Three large black steles (stone slabs) containing the Code of Hammurabi were discovered by French archeologists in Susa in 1901–02. This was the first known legal system predating the Bible and many parallels were identified with later biblical law, as well as significant differences. Future discoveries would show that both Hammurabi's Code and the biblical laws had even earlier predecessors, but it remains the earliest complete legal code so far discovered.

"If anyone bring an accusation against a man, and the accused go to the river and leap into the river, if he sink in the river his accuser shall take possession of his house. But if the river prove that the accused is not guilty, and he escape unhurt, then he who had brought the accusation shall be put to death, while he who leaped into the river shall take possession of the house that had belonged to his accuser."

Code of Hammurabi

The Code's 282 laws are indicative of the evolution of power from religious to lay courts. They contain only five prohibitions, other laws being conditional statements ("if a man . . . he shall be . . .") and legislation regulating day-to-day affairs, including the fees for a variety of professions. It assumes the existence of a caste system of patricians and slaves. The basis of the law is *talio* (retaliation): the punishment of the accused attempts to parallel the damage caused. Therefore, if a builder's faulty construction of a home results in the death of the inhabitant's daughter, the builder's daughter would be put to death; hitting one's father is punishable by amputation of the hand, etc. Also included is trial by ordeal, particularly for people accused of sorcery or adultery. The suspect was thrown into the Euphrates; survival denotes innocence, drowning is proof of guilt. Legislation also protected the individual. Falsely accusing one's wife of adultery is punishable by branding, while malpractice in selling beer is punished by drowning.

In 1763 B.C.E. Rim-Sin again threatened Hammurabi in the south. Hammurabi, based upstream, simply dammed the river, starving Rim-Sin before suddenly bursting the dam, resulting in devastating floods. He repeated this technique in his war against Zimrilin, king of Mari, two years later. Hammurabi went on to conquer the important city of Sumer near the Persian Gulf and lands to the east of the Euphrates.

Hammurabi was succeeded by his son Samsuiluna. Years of warfare had prevented him from establishing an efficient bureaucracy to govern his realm and the country rapidly disintegrated. Although his empire could hardly compare with the later Babylonian and Assyrian empires, it was an important step in the evolution of city-states into regional states. Unlike his predecessors, Hammurabi did not plan his posthumous deification, which, like his legal system, was important in establishing the role of a secular monarch independent of the priesthood. Previously, scholars identified Hammurabi with the biblical Amraphel, king of Shinar, who defeated Sodom and carried off Lot, but this claim is not supported now. ◆

Hans-Adam II

1945– ● PRINCE OF LIECHTENSTEIN

Prince Hans-Adam II of Liechtenstein was born on February 14, 1945, the eldest son of Prince Franz Josef II von und zu Liechtenstein and Princess Gina. The name Hans-Adam is derived from Prince Johann Adam Andreas of Liechtenstein (1657–1712), who founded the state through his purchases of the lordship of Schellenberg in 1699 and the county of Vaduz in 1712. (Vaduz is the capital of Liechtenstein.) Prince Hans-Adam II is the first ruling prince to have actually grown up in Liechtenstein.

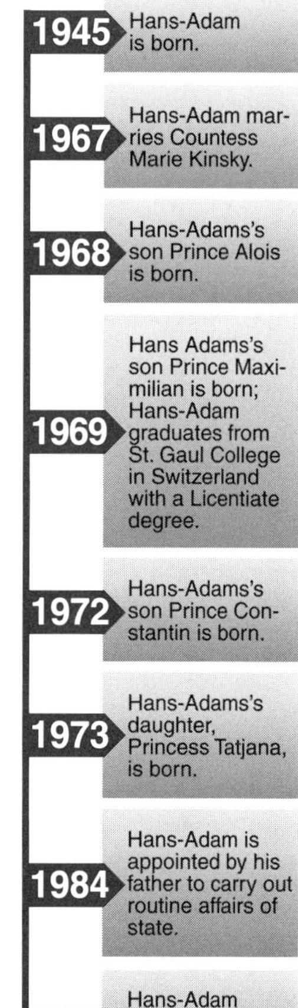

The Grand Duchy of Liechtenstein, founded in 1719, has a population of about 32,000 and is the last surviving constituent of the Holy Roman Empire. A hereditary constitutional monarchy about the size of Washington, D.C., the principality is a small pocket along the Rhine between Austria and Switzerland, and its foreign policy is handled by Switzerland. Liechtenstein is a corporate haven, with about 25,000 corporations with headquarters there, at least in name, and it has one of the highest per-capita gross national product in Europe.

The current dynasty ruling over Liechtenstein was established in 1699. Prince Franz Josef II took the throne in 1938, and yielded his executive powers to his son, Hans-Adam, in 1984. Hans-Adam II has been the prince of Liechtenstein since November 1989.

Hans-Adam spent his early childhood with his brothers and sisters at Vaduz Castle, attended the primary school in Vaduz-Ebenholz along with other children in the capital city, and was a member of the Vaduz scouts. Like his father before him, Prince Hans-Adam attended the famous Schottengymnasium in Vienna, Austria, where he studied from 1956 to 1960. He finished his secondary schooling at Zuoz, Switzerland, where he received both Swiss and German certificates in 1965. Immediately after secondary school, the prince worked for a short time at a bank in London. Though his first language is German, the prince also speaks English and French.

In the fall of 1965 Prince Hans-Adam enrolled at St. Gall College in Switzerland, where he studied business and economics. He graduated in 1969 with a Licentiate degree. On July 30,

1967, Hans-Adam married Countess Marie Kinsky of Wchinitz and Tettau, born in Prague on April 14, 1940. Marie has a degree in applied art, and studied English in Great Britain and lived for a while in Paris to learn French.

After completing his studies at St. Gall, Hans-Adam began managing the property and finances of the House of Liechtenstein, also known as the princely assets. His father was sufficiently satisfied with Hans-Adam's management that in 1972 Prince Franz Josef II issued a general power of attorney entrusting the hereditary prince with the management and administration of the entire assets. In 1984 Franz Josef appointed Hans-Adam as his representative to carry out all the routine affairs of state. Five years later, on November 13, 1989, Prince Franz Josef II died at the age of eighty-three, at which time Prince Hans-Adam II took the throne.

Prince Hans-Adam and Princess Marie have four children: hereditary prince Alois (b. June 11, 1968), Prince Maximilian (b. May 16, 1969), Prince Constantin (b. March 15, 1972), and Princess Tatjana (b. April 10, 1973).◆

Harald V

1937– ● King of Norway

King Harald V of Norway was born on February 21, 1937, at Skaugum, the estate that is the home of the royal family, in Asker, just outside Oslo. Because Norway was ruled by Sweden for many years (until 1905), the birth of Prince Harald to Prince Olav and Princess Märtha marked the first time in 567 years that a prince of Norway had been born in that country.

In 1905 the Storting, Norway's national assembly, declared a dissolution of the union with Sweden after a nearly unanimous public **plebiscite** on the question, and in a second vote approved a monarchy. The Storting chose as king Prince Charles, the second son of Frederick VIII of Denmark, and he took the name Haakon VII, a respected royal name in Norwegian history. Haakon married Princess Maud, a daughter of King Edward VII of England, and ruled Norway till 1957. Their

plebiscite: a vote by which the people of an entire country express an opinion for or against a choice of government or ruler.

King Harald V and Queen Sonja of Norway.

eldest son was Olav (or Olaf), born in 1903. Olav married Princess Märtha of Sweden in 1929 (d. 1954), and Harald was their eldest son.

Crown Prince Harald's first few years were tranquil, but German dictator Adolf Hitler's aggressions ensured that there would be no peace in Europe. Norway had sought to remain neutral in World War II, but in the early hours of April 9, 1940, German troops invaded. Because the royal family was one of the German forces' primary targets, they were compelled to flee in great haste; the family and the government escaped Oslo by train just hours before the German forces arrived. Norwegian officials tried to resist the German occupation, but capitulated in June, and the Nazi forces remained until the end of the war five years later. While Haakon and his cabinet set up a government-in-exile in London, Crown Prince Olav (Harald's father) took an active role in the Norwegian resistance movement (eventually becoming supreme commander of the Norwegian forces in 1944). Crown Princess Märtha took Prince Harald and his two sisters, the princesses Ragnhild and Astrid, to the United States, where they lived outside Washington, D.C., until the liberation of Norway in May 1945.

Crown Prince Harald's early years were tranquil, but German dictator Adolf Hitler's aggressions ensured that there would be no peace in Europe.

After the liberation, Prince Harald attended Smestad Primary School, a Norwegian state school. His education there was

like that of any other Norwegian child, except for the security police standing guard out in the corridor. From a very early age, the prince was active in sports. At ten, he began training as a regatta sailor, and had his own boat, which he sailed to victory during summer regattas in the Oslo Fjord. Harald continued his studies at Oslo Katedralskole; he took his upper secondary school (= high school) diploma in science in 1955, and that autumn he began studies at the University of Oslo.

After college, Harald began his military education, first attending the Cavalry Officers' Candidate School at Trandum (1956–57), and then the Military Academy, where he graduated in 1959. As King Harald, he is a general in the army and air force, and an admiral in the navy.

Harald was made crown prince in 1957. King Haakon VII died on September 21, 1957, and Crown Prince Harald sat beside his father, Olav V, in the Council of State on September 27; he was now officially his father's deputy.

After completing his compulsory military service as an officer, in 1960 Crown Prince Harald went to Oxford, where he studied political science, history, and economics at Balliol College, where his father had studied in the 1930s. That same year, the crown prince made his first major official journey abroad, visiting the United States for the fiftieth anniversary of the American Scandinavian Foundation. He proved himself an able ambassador for Norwegian interests, particularly for his nation's shipping industry, which had rebounded well, though half of its fleet was sunk during World War II.

In 1968 King Olav V announced that Harald wished to marry Sonja Haraldsen, whom the crown prince had known for nine years. The announcement ignited a heated debate on the future of the monarchy, for Sonja Haraldsen was a commoner. King Olav consulted with the government, the president of the Storting, and leaders of the various parliamentary groups within the Storting, and made the decision that the couple could proceed with their plans to marry. The idea of the crown prince's marrying this particular commoner was received enthusiastically by a strong majority of the Norwegian people, an indication of the royal family's overall good standing with the public and of Sonja Haraldsen's own popularity among the people.

The couple was engaged on March 19, 1968, and the royal wedding took place on August 29 that year. Queen Sonja was born on July 4, 1937, and grew up in Oslo. She studied dressmaking and fashion design in Lausanne, Switzerland, and received a B.A. degree from the University of Oslo, where she studied French, English, and art history. The queen has been especially involved in humanitarian work: in 1982 she was awarded the Nansen Medal by the United Nations High Commissioner for Refugees, and she served as vice president of the Norwegian Red Cross from 1987 to 1990.

After the royal wedding, the crown prince and crown princess traveled together and separately on various official journeys to all parts of Norway and around the world, including visits to the United States, China, Latin America, Australia, India, and Thailand.

When Harald V took his oath of allegiance to the constitution in the Storting, his wife, Sonja, accompanied him, marking the first time in sixty-nine years that a queen had entered the national assembly.

When King Olav fell ill in 1990, Crown Prince Harald became regent and presided over the Council of State and handled other official duties. Olav V, king of Norway since 1957, died in January 1991. On January 21 King Harald V took his oath of allegiance to the constitution in the Storting. Queen Sonja accompanied him, marking the first time in sixty-nine years that a queen had entered the national assembly. By his own request, King Harald was consecrated (ordained to office) on June 23, 1991, in the Nidaros Cathedral in Trondheim.

For the 1994 Winter Olympic Games held in Lillehammer, Norway, King Harald was honorary chairman of the Lillehammer Olympic Organizing Committee and a member of its general assembly, and Queen Sonja was pleased to serve as honorary chairman of the Olympic Committee's cultural committee. The king was no stranger to Olympic competition, having represented Norway several times on its sailing team. He won the Gold Cup Races in 1968 and took first place in the Kiel Week Races in 1972. In the summer of 1987 he won the world championship with his new yacht, the one-ton *Fram X*, a fiftieth-birthday present from the Norwegian business community.

The royal family resides at Skaugum, near Oslo, which covers 325 acres and is run as a farm with livestock and cultivated fields. King Harald and Queen Sonja have two children. Princess Märtha Louise was born on September 22, 1971, and Crown Prince Haakon, born on July 20, 1973. Both children studied at the Smestad Primary School and at the Kristelig Gymnasium; Princess Märtha Louise graduated in 1990 and Crown Prince Haakon in 1992. ◆

Hassan II

1929–1999 ● KING OF MOROCCO

Hassan II was the son of Muhammed V, king of Morocco. As Crown Prince Mulay Hassan, he graduated from the University of Bordeaux in France. In 1961, when his father died unexpectedly, the thirty-two-year-old playboy prince came to power. The heir of the Alawite dynasty, which has governed Morocco since the sixteenth century, Mulay Hassan had been well prepared by his father—as early as World War II—to assume the throne. He had also attended the 1942 meeting between Muhammed V and U.S. president Franklin D. Roosevelt.

Since the French had entered North Africa in the eighteenth and nineteenth centuries to end the Corsairs and Barbary piracy in the Mediterranean, they had established a policy of colonialism and protectorates. Hassan had therefore been trained in both Arabic and French and had studied law and economics at the university; he was at ease in both cultures. He was also acutely aware of the ideas and changes that might come to Morocco from outside. Since his adolescence, he was known to favor nationalism, as did many Moroccans of his age. He was said to have some influence on his father, who was more cautious and less brilliant than Hassan. When in 1948 a conflict arose with France's resident general—which had to do with the signing of legal texts presented by French colonial authorities—Hassan was among those who favored a break with France. The consequence was Muhammad V's exile to the French-controlled islands of Corsica and Madagascar. Supporting his father, Hassan participated in the negotiations through intermediaries to reestablish the previous links with the French government and effect Muhammed V's return, which was accomplished in 1955.

In contrast with Muhammed V, who was careful not to offend the parties who had joined the struggle for independence—especially the Istiqlal party—Hassan wanted to preserve the autonomy of the monarchy. Designated chief of staff of the Royal Armed Forces, Hassan appeared as the main guarantor of his peoples' destiny. He gathered around himself the former Moroccan officers who had served in the French army, and he ended rebellions in al-Rif, Tafilalt, and Beni-Mellal, which had been provoked by various **dissident** movements. He also reduced the size of the Liberation Army, born of the Moroccan resistance, since it was almost autonomous in the south; it pretended to be fighting the French and Spanish colonial powers but could easily have offered armed and organized support to any given opposition.

dissident: disagreeing, especially with an established religious or political system or belief.

France and Spain recognized Morocco's independence in 1956; by 1958 Hassan's forces prevailed throughout the country and dissidents were no longer a threat to the monarchy. Thus Muhammed V was able to incorporate the various splinter groups of the former nationalist movement within the government. Hassan was sometimes irritated by his father's caution, and he tried to convince him to take back direct control. A change began in May 1960, with Hassan appointed prime minister. When his father died in March 1961, Hassan II had both the experience and the means to put his theories into practice.

Hassan was sometimes irritated by the caution of his father, King Muhammad V, and he tried to convince him to take back direct control.

The independence of Algeria (July 5, 1962) appeared to be a potential threat to Hassan II's monarchy. It bordered Morocco to the east and south, and Algeria's National Liberation Front (Front de Libération National; FLN) was known to support the Moroccan left (socialists) against the monarchy. Hassan sought a new legitimacy by mobilizing universal suffrage, which was largely supported by the rural populace. The December 1962 referendum guaranteed Hassan's success with 80 percent approval of his new constitution.

The results of the March 1963 election did not, however, give him similar support. The old Istiqlal had lost its governmental majority and the king's followers were not able to form a political coalition quickly enough. Most of the ministers were defeated and it seemed that the parliament could not easily be governed despite a promonarchy majority. In the meantime, the danger posed by Algeria had faded away. The October 1963 border war and rivalry related to Tindouf had revived in Morocco a strong nationalist feeling, which resulted in support for the monarchy.

Hassan II dismissed the parliament in 1965 and relied mainly on his army for legitimacy. He protected those in the military who had served French and Spanish colonialism, although some of the young officers were not as loyal or as committed as he expected. Tempted by populist idealism, some succeeded in convincing former officers of the French colonial army (who controlled the military organization) to join their project. In July 1971, in Skhirat, General Medbah and General Muhammad Oufkir, among others, faced death after their rebellion failed.

Paradoxically, Hassan would succeed in restoring faith in his monarchy in 1975, when a dispute with Spain (at the time of Spanish dictator Francisco Franco's death) led to the defense of Morocco's position in the former Spanish colony of Western Sahara. A local nationalistic movement, the Polisario, supported mainly by Algeria and Libya, emerged to challenge Morocco. Both Algeria and Libya saw opportunities in the situation—Algeria, especially, under President Houari Boumédienne, wanted to demonstrate its control over the Maghreb before the new European Community. Bolstered by petroleum revenues, the growing power of Algeria had the effect of reuniting Morocco under Hassan.

Although Hassan had plans for political pluralism, albeit controlled by the monarchy, his army had been reequipped for possible conflict with Algeria; since they did not want to engage in this fight, they attempted another coup. General Ahmed Dlimi was to be their leader, but the plot was discovered by the home secretary and Dlimi disappeared in an "accident." In the long run, Morocco was to benefit from its tactical building of the "wall" (fortified sand barriers in Western Sahara), and Algeria succeeded in having seventy-five countries recognize the POLISARIO and make it a member of the Organization for African Unity (OAU).

Hassan managed Moroccan nationalism very cautiously to establish national unity. He found external financial resources by getting Western countries as well as the Arab oil monarchies to support his military efforts and to launch economic development based on a private sector far larger than those of neighboring countries. For that reason, as the Pahlavi dynasty in Iran did (before the Islamist Iranian revolution of 1979), Hassan's monarchy became a major economic actor through the All North Africa association (Omnium Nord-Africain; ONA), not only to find resources but to prevent other North African countries from obtaining power and becoming politically influential. Since Morocco had no oil, Hassan encouraged and often provided an example of an economic–development policy based on modern agriculture (launching a program to irrigate 2.47 million acres [1 million ha]); he also encouraged small and medium-sized manufacturing industries.

In 1984 Hassan signed a treaty of unity with Libya after Libya withdrew its support for the POLISARIO in the Western Sahara and Morocco agreed to refrain from sending troops to aid the French in Chad. In 1986 Libya **abrogated** the treaty when Hassan became the second North African leader to meet with an Israeli leader during Prime Minister Shimon Peres's visit to Morocco.

abrogate: to abolish; to nullify.

In 1988 international factors continued to prevail over those within Morocco. After Tunisian president Habib Bourguiba had been replaced by General Zayn al-Abidine ben Ali in November 1987, a process of realignment occurred among the North African countries. A consequence was the reintegration of Morocco, first at a meeting in Algiers (August 1988), then when the Union of the Maghreb (Union du Maghreb; UMA) treaty was signed in Marrakech, Morocco (March 1989). The treaty marked the end of the Algerian/Moroccan rivalry related to the Western Sahara, but, at the same time, deprived Morocco of a strong factor for internal unity.

The UMA had another hidden aim: to constitute a united front against the growing Islamist political movements in North Africa (an effort to establish Islamic religious regimes). Tunisia appeared the weak link at that time, and it needed support. Political changes nevertheless occurred in Algeria, and their effects were important for Morocco. After the October 1988 riots in Algiers, President Chadli Benjedid controlled the situation by creating a **pluralistic** political system, open to Islamists, which led to competitive elections. That strategy gave an attractive look to Algerian pluralism in relation to the established Moroccan political system, where the same actors repeated their opposition to the existing power through the years. Algeria was no longer seen as a danger by the people but as an example at a time when the annexation of Kuwait by Iraq (1990) became a military crisis and thus reduced the possibilities of action.

pluralistic: having to do with the state of society in which members of diverse ethnic or religious groups maintain their own cultures and interests within a common civilization.

In Morocco the riots that took place in provincial cities by the end of 1990, the important demonstrations in the capital city at the beginning of 1991, and the reports of deserters leaving the Moroccan army to go to Iraq (by way of Algeria), indicated the gap between Hassan's cautious choice—sending a limited contingent to help the UN coalition forces to defend an oil monarchy—and Moroccan public opinion that favored Iraq's president Saddam Hussein. The Gulf War made visible the differing factions in Morocco.

The Gulf War also left Morocco's economy weaker than before. Riots in Fez in 1991 left a hundred dead and hundreds more injured during a general strike against low wages and poor employment prospects. Moroccan society was divided about whom to support in the war; mass demonstrations were staged in support of Saddam Hussein while the Moroccan military was helping wage Operation Desert Storm.

King Hassan II became the premier mediator in inter-Arab affairs, and Morocco has hosted more Arab and Islamic summits than any other Arab nation.

The government's standing was threatened in 1992 by Muslim fundamentalist demands for greater representation. The king offered parliamentary elections in 1993, but the elections made no real difference. Abderrahmane El Youssoufi, an opposition leader who has since been appointed head of the government, protested the 1993 elections as "manipulated" and temporarily left the country for exile in France.

Amid these domestic disturbances, Hassan remained active and influential (sometimes behind the scenes) in the Arab world and in Middle East affairs. After the death of Jordan's King Hussein in February 1999, he became the region's most accomplished mediator, particularly regarding Arab-Israeli relations—and at the end of the twentieth century he was the region's longest ruling leader. Hassan kept a busy schedule of meetings with foreign heads of state—including meetings with President Clinton in Washington, Chinese vice premier Qian Qichen, and Egyptian president Hosni Mubarak.

King Hassan II was the premier mediator in inter-Arab affairs, and during his reign Morocco hosted more Arab and Islamic summits than any other Arab nation. In October 1994 he hosted the Middle East and North African Economic Summit, a gathering designed to promote the economic aspects of the peace process, and he chaired the Islamic Conference Organization's Jerusalem Committee. His most dramatic diplomatic gesture was his public hosting of Israeli prime minister Shimon Peres for talks in 1986. Hassan also chaired or presided over summit meetings of the Arab Maghreb Union (principally Morocco, Algeria, and Tunisia) and other gatherings of Arab leaders. Hassan II was similar to the late King Hussein of Jordan in his efforts to promote peace in the Middle East and in his readiness to meet and negotiate with Israeli officials; the king's negotiating skills and hospitality for summits have established Morocco as a key player in mediating Arab-Israeli affairs.

Hassan demonstrated similar openness in permitting relations between Jews in Morocco and Israel, and allowing Israelis to visit Morocco. He appreciated (and perhaps to some extent idealized) the old Arab-Jewish relations that existed in Morocco before the foundation of the state of Israel, but he also understood that strong ties with Moroccan Jewish emigrés in Israel and France could only strengthen his country's political, economic, and cultural stability. Showing his endorsement of the September 1993 Oslo agreement between Israel and the Palestine Liberation Organization, Hassan invited Israel's prime Minister Yitzhak Rabin and foreign minister Shimon Peres to visit Casablanca on their return from signing the agreement. A year later Morocco and Israel officially established diplomatic relations. After Rabin was assassinated in November 1995, Hassan did not attend the funeral, but he did send Prime Minister Fillali.

In 1996 King Hassan proposed a two-tier parliament with the intention of extending democracy and giving more of a voice to the outlying regions. The idea was carried overwhelmingly in a referendum late that year. An upper house of parliament, which has the power to topple the government, was formed in December 1997.

Just as King Hassan did not attend Yitzhak Rabin's funeral in 1995, he did not go to Amman in February 1999 for the funeral of Jordan's King Hussein.

In February 1998 King Hassan appointed opposition leader Abderrahmane El Youssoufi to serve as prime minister. The November 1997 general election resulted in more noticeable change than the disappointing half attempt in 1993: this time the votes were roughly split among three parties, but the party with the largest bloc of votes was the Socialist Union of People's Forces, of which Youssoufi was first secretary. Youssoufi, seventy-three at the time of his appointment, is an attorney and a longtime opposition leader who was exiled from Morocco in 1965, but was granted amnesty by the king in 1980. He is a well-known and respected figure in Moroccan politics and is expected to be a strong force for increasing freedom and democracy. In March 1998, for the first time, the king appointed an opposition government—a coalition of seven political parties—led by Youssoufi.

Just as King Hassan did not attend Yitzhak Rabin's funeral in November 1995, he did not go to Amman in February 1999 for the funeral of Jordan's King Hussein. Instead, Morocco was represented by Hassan's son Crown Prince Sidi Mohammed, whom he had been grooming as his heir. In addition to the crown prince, born on September 21, 1963, King Hassan had three daughters and one son: the princesses Lalla Meriem (b. August 26, 1962), Lalla Asma (b. September 29, 1965), and Lalla Hasna (b. November 19, 1967), and Prince Moulay Rachid (b. June 20, 1970). Hassan died in July 1999 of a heart attack. He was succeeded by his son Sidi Mohammed, who became King Mohammed VI. ◆

Hassanal Bolkiah

1946– ● SULTAN OF BRUNEI

The Sultan of Brunei became synonymous with extreme wealth when he was named the world's richest man in the 1980s. Sultan Haji Hassanal Bolkiah Mu'izzaddin Waddaulah gained fame for extreme spending, as he and his family squandered billions of dollars on airplanes, cars, gold and jewels, hotels, yachts, and personal entertainment.

The discovery of oil in 1929 off the coast of Brunei changed the nation forever.

Most people hearing of the sultan's legendary wealth could not even find Brunei on a world map. Brunei is a small nation, about the size of Delaware, nestled into the larger country of Malaysia on the island of Borneo in Southeast Asia. Hot and humid Brunei is lushly forested, with many swamps and a 100-mile coast on the South China Sea. Three-quarters of Brunei's people are ethnic Malays who belong to the Muslim religion. Close to half the people live in rural areas where they have farmed, fished, and traded for centuries.

The first sultan ruled in the 1200s. Brunei's location made it a powerful trading center of the region. Some of this traffic involved the many pirates who skillfully navigated the seas in small boats from which they could hijack large ships. The first Europeans to reach Brunei were members of Portuguese Ferdinand Magellan's expedition in 1521. During the 1600s and 1700s, many European nations traveled to the Southeast Asian islands, and in the early 1800s, Great Britain took over Brunei. By then, Brunei had lost much of its power and land.

The discovery of oil in 1929 off the coast of Brunei changed the nation forever, shooting its wealth as high as $50 billion. When studies in the late 1960s showed that Brunei's oil reserves would dry up in about fifty years, the sultan began investing his billions all over the world. Brunei soon pulled away from Britain, reaching full independence on January 1, 1984.

Sultan Haji Hassanal Bolkiah Mu'izzaddin Waddaulah is the twenty-ninth ruler of Brunei. He was born in 1946 and installed as crown prince in 1961. In 1966 he went to England to study at the Royal Military Academy at Sandhurst. In 1967 his father, Sultan Omar Ali Saifuddin, gave up the throne to his son. The sultan serves as Brunei's prime minister and minister of defense. Several family members and a council of advisors, appointed by the sultan, help him rule his nearly 320,000 subjects. A constitution written in 1959 was suspended in 1962, and there have been no elections since then, making Brunei an absolute monarchy.

The people of Brunei tolerate this lack of democracy mainly because the nation's oil wealth has created a high average standard of living. All citizens receive free schooling and medical care as well as food and housing allowances. There is little unemployment, especially since the government employs about 50 percent of the nation's workers.

Hassanal Bolkiah has four sons and six daughters by two wives. He married his first cousin when they were both sixteen years old. She is Queen Saleha. He later fell in love with a stewardess on Royal Brunei Airlines, and she became his second wife, Queen Mariam. She is regarded as the favorite wife and fulfills most official wifely duties. Queen Mariam lives in a palace built for her at a reported cost of $120 million.

Three years after Brunei became independent of Great Britain, the sultan topped *Fortune* magazine's famous list of the world's richest people. The sultan built himself a 1,788-room palace, one-third of a mile long. Builders used sixteen acres of Italian marble in it, and furniture buyers spent more than $13 million on furniture and fittings. The bathroom sinks are covered in 14-karat gold, and there are fifty crystal chandeliers in a dining room that seats 4,000. Strands of diamonds dangle from branches of trees lining the hallways. The sultan owns several rare paintings and bought a Renoir for $70 million, a world record in the 1980s. His palace grounds have seven mansions, pools, tennis courts, a sports complex, and air-conditioned stables for 200 polo ponies. The sultan and his brothers have been said to own seventeen aircraft, 2,000 luxury cars, and two 152-foot yachts. When the sultan turned fifty, he threw himself a $17-million party that featured three concerts by pop singer Michael Jackson.

The bathroom sinks are covered in 14–karat gold, there are fifty crystal chandeliers in the dining room, and strands of diamonds dangle from branches of trees lining the hallway.

However, events in the mid and late 1990s raised serious questions about the kingdom's financial future. In 1997 a former

By the late 1990s billions of dollars had disappeared under the management of Prince Jefri, who was serving as Brunei's finance minister.

American beauty queen sued the sultan's brother Prince Muda Jefri Bolkiah, charging that his agents had lured her to Brunei promising her a job but expecting her to join a bevy of women Prince Jefri kept as entertainers. The brothers eluded the charges due to their official status.

By the late 1990s billions of dollars seemed to have disappeared under the management of Prince Jefri, who had served as Brunei's finance minister. This caused a feud between Prince Jefri, the sultan, and their other brother, Prince Muda Mohamed Bolkiah. Jefri had invested in huge projects, many of which failed, and accountants and lawyers worked to assess the damage in 1999. The near bankruptcy of Jefri's investment organization combined with Brunei's approaching decline in oil reserves has made Brunei's economic future look much less dazzling. ◆

Henry IV

1553–1610 ● King of France

"I want there to be no peasant in my realm so poor that he will not have a chicken in his pot every Sunday."
Henry IV of France, attributed

The son of Antoine de Bourbon and Jeanne d'Albret, queen of Navarre, Henry IV was brought up by his mother as a Protestant and at the age of sixteen took part in the Wars of Religion (a series of civil wars in France with foreign intervention) on the Huguenot side. Becoming king of Navarre when his mother died in 1572, he married Marguerite de Valois, the daughter of Catherine de Médicis and sister of the king of France, Charles IX. The arrival of many Huguenots to Paris to celebrate the marriage led, a week later, to the Saint Bartholomew massacre (August 23–24), in which Henry himself was forced to convert to Roman Catholicism to save his life. In 1576, however, he regained his freedom and rejoined the Protestants, establishing himself at their head. In 1584 the death of the duke of Anjou, brother of Henry III, made Henry of Navarre the heir-presumptive to the crown of France. However, his claim was rejected by the Holy League, the organization of the Roman Catholic party in France formed to combat the Huguenots, and headed by Henry, duke of Guise. In 1580 the seventh War of Religion, known as the Lovers' War, opened with the slaughter of Catholics in Cahors, a town claimed by Henry of Navarre as part of the dowry of his wife. Although Henry of Navarre defeated the royal army at Coutras during the eighth war, the so-called War of the Three Henrys (1585–87), his prospects of acceding to the throne were as slim as ever. But in 1588 Henry III broke with the Holy League, and finding himself without support against a popular insurrection of militant Roman Catholics in Paris, the king fled to Henry of Navarre's camp and the following year, before he was murdered, the king pronounced Henry his legitimate heir. However, the Holy League, aided by Philip II of Spain, continued to oppose the new king, and it was not until 1593 that Henry, realizing that he could not remain a Protestant and rule a predominantly Roman Catholic nation, decided to convert, declaring that "Paris is well worth a Mass." In 1594 he was crowned at Chartres and took possession of the capital; in 1596 the opposition of the League came to an end.

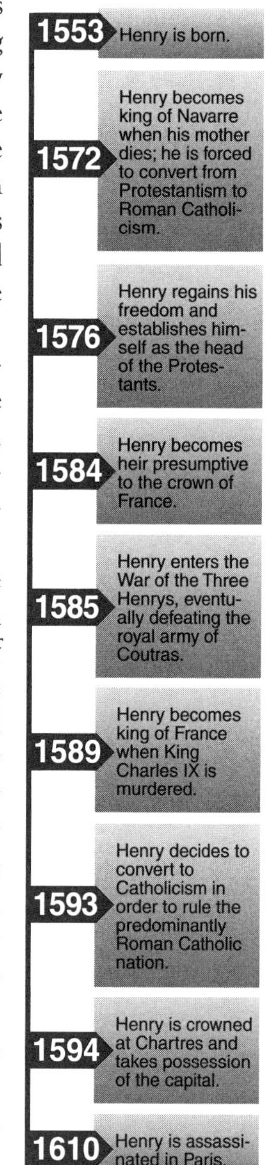

Among his domestic policies Henry's most important measure was the Edict of Nantes (1598), which put an end to the Wars of Religion and settled the status of the Protestants, according them religious freedom with certain limitations (freedom of worship with the exception of Paris) and laid the foundation for religious coexistence in France.

During his reign much was done to heal the wounds of the previous fifty years, with the help of well-chosen counselors. In particular, his finance minister Maximilien de Béthune, duke of Sully, did much to rehabilitate France's economy. However, his new tax, the Paulette, made French officeholders into a closed caste: In return for an annual tax, offices were made hereditary and could be passed on or sold at will. The judicial machinery was brought under control, the financial basis of the monarchy reformed, and agriculture and industry were encouraged; the silk industry was introduced, and the manufacture of cloth, glassware, and tapestries encouraged. The army was also reorganized and strongholds were fortified. French architects began to adorn Paris with splendid monuments and palaces (the Tuileries, Place Royale, Pont Neuf, the Hôtel de Ville). France's system of canals dates from this reign.

In foreign policy, Henry terminated the conflict with Spain (1598) and maintained generally friendly relations with England, the Italian states, the United Provinces of Holland, and the Ottoman empire. Henry was instrumental in the truce between Spain and the Netherlands (1609). He believed that the peace of Europe was threatened by the ambition of the Habsburgs, declaring that the greatness of the Habsburg Empire meant the ruin of peace in Europe.

Henry was known for his easygoing manners and his many love affairs. The most famous was with Gabrielle d'Estrées, who wielded a strong influence over the king, made him adopt Catholicism, and bore him three children; and with Henriette de Balzac d'Entragues, whose three children he legitimized. He is remembered as Henry the Great for his political achievements and for his concern for the poor, wishing that every laborer have a *poule au pot* (a chicken in his pot) on Sunday. By his second wife, Marie de Médicis, whom he married in 1600, he had six children.

Henry IV was assassinated in Paris by François Ravaillac, a Catholic fanatic, thus ending his plan to mobilize an international military coalition against Spain and Austria, and his intention of forming a European confederation.◆

Henry IV

1050–1106 ● KING OF GERMANY AND HOLY ROMAN EMPEROR

In 1062 a group of nobles led by Archbishop Anno of Cologne kidnapped the boy king, intending to rule in his name.

Henry IV, the son of Henry III and Agnes of Poitou, became king at age six. Agnes served as regent during Henry's minority; her inability to maintain control permitted the German nobility to pursue their own personal political ambitions in a country plagued by civil war and conflict. In 1062 a group of nobles led by archbishop Anno of Cologne kidnapped the boy king, intending to rule in his name. Conflict among the new regents thrust the leaderless German kingdom into complete disarray.

Henry began to consolidate control over Germany in 1066. Due to the deterioration of the kingdom under his mother, he was forced to establish his own power, independent of German nobles and clergymen. Upon winning the loyalty of the nobles of the Rhine, Henry concentrated on the restoration of his power in the northern region, Saxony; the ensuing wars in Saxony, which continued intermittently between 1073 and 1088, strongly influenced the struggle for domination between the German king and the papacy. Open rebellion broke out in east Saxony in the summer of 1073. With the Pope's blessing, Henry led a combined military force from the duchies in the south and defeated the rebel forces at the river Unstrut in 1075.

In order to offset the power of hereditary nobles, German kings usually depended upon the selection and control of loyal bishops who oversaw administrative functions within their sees. After his victory over the Saxons, Henry invested a new nominee with the sees of Milan, which were crucial to maintaining his power in Lombardy. Pope Gregory VII, however, contested Henry's power of investiture, and excommunicated him in 1076, declaring him deposed.

Seizing upon the papal excommunication, opponents of the king claimed that he would lose his kingdom if he did not regain the pope's favor within a year and a day of his excommunication. In anticipation of the diet to be called at Augsburg in February 1077, Henry slipped out of Germany to meet the Pope at a castle in Canossa, Italy on the eve of Christmas 1076 in order to receive absolution from him. Standing outside the castle gates, barefoot in the snow. Henry repented for three days in what was to be an important political victory for the Pope, reasserting the church's role in sustaining the German monarchy.

The rebel German nobility, however, deposed Henry and elected Duke Rudolf of Swabia as anti-king. Henry still had strong support among many German bishops and in most of Lombardy, Burgundy, Bavaria and Franconia. He invaded Saxony and divided the Saxon forces. In light of this substantial diplomatic victory, Henry once again broke ranks with the Pope, and was once again excommunicated. This time, however, Henry, seen as a martyr, had the power to contest Gregory's tyrannical decision.

Members of a council at Brixen deposed Gregory and installed archbishop Guibert of Ravenna as anti-Pope Clement III. With the death of the anti-king, Rudolf, in battle against Henry in 1080, Gregory turned to the invading Normans and their leader, Robert Guiscard, for support. Meanwhile Henry invaded Rome in 1081; he was crowned Holy Roman Emperor by Clement III. However his victory was short-lived: the Normans destroyed the city on returning from their campaign against the Byzantines in Apulia and Henry was forced to flee.

After Gregory's death, Henry strengthened his power in Germany. He reasserted his authority over the church, in opposition to Pope Urban II, and had his son, Conrad, crowned as king of Germany in 1087.

The emperor's power and prestige diminished when Urban consolidated his own strength. In spite of the threat of a renewed rebellion in Germany, Henry set off to invade Italy once again. However, when rebellion did indeed break out in Germany, Conrad supported it, believing that Henry's policies endangered the monarchy. Conrad died fighting his father in 1101; secular opposition was quelled, but the rest of Henry's life would be plagued by familial treachery and strife.

Henry's second son (the future Henry V) was crowned king of Germany in his brother Conrad's stead in 1098, but in 1104 he too rebelled against his father. Henry was captured by his son in 1105 and was forced to give up his empire, escaping to Cologne. He died the following year while building up an army to confront his son in battle. He came to be seen as a tragic national hero who opposed the Roman papacy in order to maintain a strong Germany.◆

Henry V

1387–1422 ● KING OF ENGLAND

Henry V was king of England from 1413 to 1422. He was born in Monmouth, Wales. His father, Henry of Bolingbroke, of the House of Lancaster, seized the English throne in a coup in 1399, becoming King Henry IV.

As royal prince, Henry took command of the successful campaign to put down the rebellion of Owen Glendower in Wales. Victory came with the capture of Aberystwyth in 1407 and Harlech in 1408. Relations with his father were strained by Henry's demand for a larger role in government but a reconciliation was effected before Henry IV's death in 1413.

> ***"We few, we happy few, we band of brothers;***
> ***For he to-day that sheds his blood with me***
> ***Shall be my brother"...***
>
> William Shakespeare, *The Life of King Henry V*, 1599

Upon assuming the kingship Henry V turned his back on the wildness of his youth and devoted his energies to the strengthening of his kingdom. Two uprisings were easily put down and he could turn his full attention to recovering lands held by his ancestors in France and to extending his dominion further. War also provided a distraction for the nobility from domestic quarrels.

His first expedition to France in 1415 almost ended in disaster. His army succeeded in capturing the port of Harfleur but was decimated by an outbreak of dysentery. Henry took his depleted forces to Agincourt in the direction of Calais, and

where a pursuing French army of some forty thousand caught up with his force of six thousand. Henry's men were positioned in a way that forced the French to approach along a narrow front. He inspired his soldiers to make a courageous stand and the English archers, skilled in the use of the longbow, wrought havoc in the French ranks. It was a famous victory in the Hundred Years' War and helped establish England as a major European power.

Henry returned to France in 1417 and, exploiting deep divisions in the enemy camp, captured Normandy and forced the French to accept him as the legitimate heir to the French throne and to agree to his marriage with Catherine of Valois, daughter of the mentally ill French king, Charles VI. The Treaty of Troyes was a triumph for Henry the soldier king, but it was gained at the cost of neglecting the government of England, which Henry failed to place firmly under his control.

The treaty with France might have afforded Henry more time to enjoy other pursuits. He was fond of hunting but was also a musician of talent and loved to have minstrels accompany him on his expeditions. He was also literate, an advantage over his predecessors, favoring tales of chivalry. After the conclusion of the Treaty of Troyes, however, rather than grant himself a respite from war, he continued his pursuit of military glory. He did not live to enjoy the fruits of victory as his health had been weakened on the battlefield and he died of fever, still at war with France.◆

Henry VI

1165–1197 ● King of Germany and Holy Roman Emperor

A member of the Hohenstaufen family, Henry VI was the second son of Frederick Barbarossa. He was crowned king of Germany in 1169 but did not become the sole ruler of the German kingdom until his father's death while on a crusade in 1190. Henry sought to consolidate his own power in Germany, Italy, and the Mediterranean through political maneuvering.

In 1186 Henry married Constance of Sicily. In 1190 he traveled to Rome where he was crowned emperor by Pope Clement III. He immediately set out to purchase the support of cities in northern Italy. When he returned to Rome, the new Pope, Celestine II, would not honor the coronation; only after a treaty was signed between the powerful German army and the Romans did the Pope crown Henry.

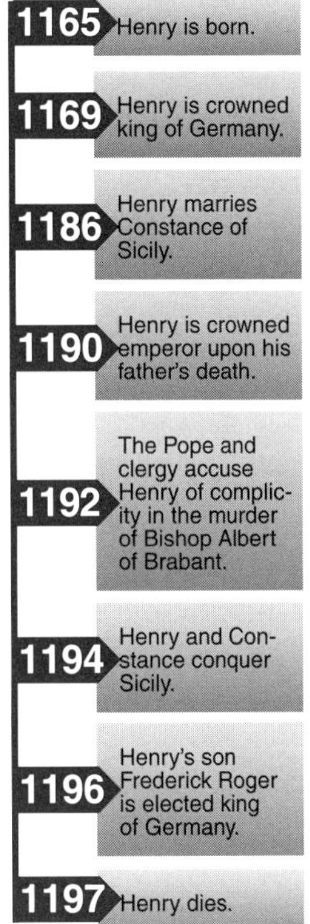

The new Holy Roman Emperor met his first challenge when Queen Constance became the legal heiress to the throne of Sicily following the death of William II. Neither the Sicilians nor the papacy wanted the Germans to unite Sicily with the German kingdom. The Pope conspired against Henry by supporting the election of Tancred, Count of Lecce and the illegitimate son of Constance's brother, as king in Sicily. Henry, preparing to besiege Sicily, was accused by the Pope and the clergy of compliance in the murder of Bishop Albert of Brabant by German knights in 1192, and returned to Germany in order to defend himself.

At this time, the English ruler, Richard I (The Lionhearted), returning from a crusade in the Holy Land, was captured by his enemy the duke of Austria, who summarily handed him over to Henry in 1193. Richard, an ally of the Welfs in Germany and Tancred in Sicily, made a deal for his release that would defuse the imminent rebellion against Henry. He was released on terms favorable to the German monarchy: 150,000 marks' ransom, vassalage of England to the Holy Roman Empire, reconciliation of the Welfs to the empire, and the abandonment of Tancred.

With nothing now standing in their way, Henry and Constance conquered Sicily, where she assumed the throne in 1194. A few days later, the empress gave birth to Frederick Roger, who was elected king of Germany in 1196 despite Henry's attempts to establish a hereditary monarchy. During his brief rule Henry expanded the empire to its widest boundaries. However, the instability of his alliances and incomplete reconciliation with the papacy left him without a sound political foundation. Thus, by the time of his death he found himself incapable of surmounting the growing opposition of his vassals and a politically powerful pope.◆

Henry VII

1457–1509 ● King of England

Henry VII, king of England 1485–1509, was the founder of the Tudor dynasty. Henry Tudor was born in Pembroke, Wales; through the House of Lancaster he had an ancestral claim to the English throne, although not as strong as that of other contenders. His mother, Margaret Beaufort, was only thirteen when he was born; his father, Edmund Tudor, had died a few months earlier and the boy was raised by his uncle, the earl of Pembroke. In 1471 the forces of the House of York brought Edward IV to the throne and Henry took refuge in Britanny. The murder of Henry VI and the death of his son in battle left Henry the leading Lancastrian claimant to the throne.

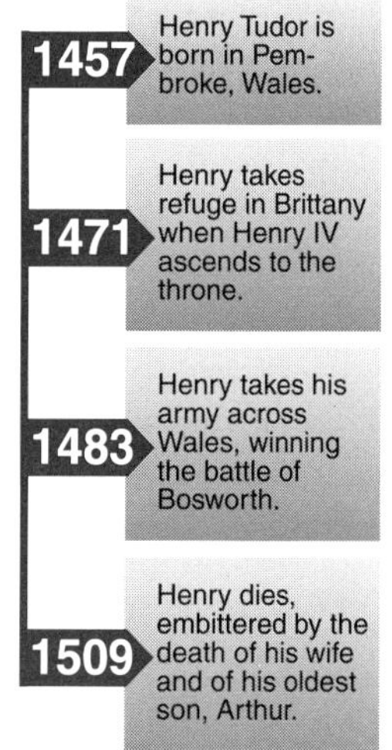

Edward IV's death in 1483 prompted a seizure of power by his brother, Richard III. The Yorkist party was divided and this gave Henry his opportunity. Landing on the coast of Wales with a small force of mercenaries he marched north and took his army across Wales, defeating Richard's superior forces at the battle of Bosworth. It was a ferocious battle and Richard fought his way to within yards of Henry before he was killed.

Henry married Richard's niece, Elizabeth of York, in accordance with an oath he had made at Rennes Cathedral. This was a strategic alliance that grew into a marriage of deep affection. It also succeeded in ending the War of the Roses, symbolized by the red and white Tudor rose combining the signs of Lancaster and York.

Almost to the end of his reign, Henry was rightfully fearful of coups. One of the best known of these was led by Lambert Simnel, who pretended to be Richard, son of Edward IV. Simnel, a baker's son taught by a priest to impersonate the royal duke, was crowned King Edward VI in Ireland. Henry took mercy upon him after his defeat and found him work in the royal kitchen, appropriate to his background.

A man of religious feelings, Henry was keen to limit bloodshed through mercy to domestic opponents and peaceful policies in Europe. Convenient marital alliances with the French and Scottish royal families also strengthened his position but his last years were embittered by the early death of his eldest son, Arthur, and shortly afterward, of his wife. Heavy taxation caused discontent among the nobles but his dynasty was by this time firmly established and the foundation was laid for a century of relative stability and prosperity in England. ◆

Henry VIII

1491–1547 ● KING OF ENGLAND

Henry VIII (Henry Tudor) was the second son of King Henry VII and Queen Elizabeth of York. His father disliked him and, although he granted Henry many impressive titles, denied him any power. Prince Henry was left to wile away his days in sport while his elder brother, Arthur, was groomed for the throne. The death of Arthur in 1502 placed Henry first in line for the succession, and he became king following his father's death in March 1509.

Educated under the direction of the poet John Skelton, Henry had acquired fluency in Latin and French and an excellent grounding in court etiquette. He enjoyed the company of leading intellectuals, including Thomas More and Desidarius Erasmus, and delighted in music, composing a number of impressive musical pieces.

Henry developed into a fine sportsman and hunter. Six feet four inches tall and with fine features, he represented the ideal of the young Renaissance prince. One visitor from abroad wrote of him: "His majesty is the handsomest potentate I have ever set eyes on—above the usual height, with a fine calf to his leg, his complexion very fair and light, with auburn hair, and a round face so beautiful it would become a pretty woman."

Henry's accession was welcomed among the cultural elite, and the ordinary people were pleased that one of his first acts was to order the execution of two of his father's leading ministers, Dudley and Empson, who had been associated with the high taxation of Henry VII's reign. Henry VIII also won popularity with the success of his armies against the French and the Scots, traditional enemies whose defeat the English relished.

Despite inexperience in government, the young monarch displayed from the first a shrewdness and ruthlessness in the exercise of power that was to mark his reign. The daily routine of correspondence and government meetings held little interest for him, but the ultimate authority remained firmly in his hands, albeit exercised through ministers—if all went well he could take the credit and in the event of disaster there were suitable scapegoats.

"I am very sorry to know and hear how unreverently that most precious jewel, the Word of God, is disputed, rhymed, sung, and jangled in every ale-house and tavern, contrary to the true meaning and doctrine of the same."

Henry VIII, speech to Parliament, 1545

Henry benefited from the services of a succession of statesmen of competence and international prominence, including Archbishop Thomas Wolsey, Thomas More, and Thomas Cromwell. He utilized their political skills as long as he believed they served his interests. As soon as they were suspected of plotting against him or not working zealously enough to promote his cause (and the distinction he drew was a fine one), he had no scruples about parting them first from their high offices and eventually from their heads.

Henry's appearance had the color and fashionable glamour that demonstrated to all who saw him the English king's wealth and power. In 1515, for example, the Venetian ambassador was impressed by Henry's gold collar with a diamond the size of a walnut. King Henry's famous meeting with the king of France, Francis I, at the Field of the Cloth of Gold in 1520, was a stunning display of royal grandeur—huge palaces of stone, brick, and wood rapidly constructed and their walls lined with expensive gold cloth, a lavishly decorated chapel, and a store of three thousand barrels of the best wine. Henry himself excelled in the jousting tournament and chivalrously let the French king's shield be given the place of honor.

Acting on the request of his father, on becoming king in 1509 Henry married Catherine of Aragon, the wife of his deceased brother, Arthur. It was an alliance with great strategic advantages, linking England with countries that could form a front against the traditional enemy, France. Moreover, Henry for years had loved Catherine, calling himself "Sir Loyal Heart." When she bore him a son in 1511, he was ecstatic and the city of London celebrated with pageants and bonfires. The child, however, lived only seven weeks; from a succession of pregnancies, Catherine's sole child to survive was a girl, the future Queen Mary. Henry found comfort with his mistress, Elizabeth

Blount, one of Catherine's ladies-in-waiting. She bore him a son in 1519 and he was named Henry Fitzroy. Later his father made him duke of Richmond and considered making him his legitimate heir, but Fitzroy died at seventeen.

In the mid-1520s Henry fell in love with Anne Boleyn, a woman of noble birth but no great beauty. There was one obstacle to the king's passion—Anne's refusal to be his mistress. His marriage with Catherine had to be dissolved and Henry decided the Pope must be persuaded (or threatened) into taking the necessary steps. At the time, Henry was in papal favor for his fierce attack on the Lutheran heresy in a book he had written in 1521. As a token of esteem he had been awarded the title "Defender of the Faith," still today proudly displayed by English sovereigns in their formal title. Nevertheless, granting Henry's request was not such a simple matter, for his queen was not only related to the Spanish royal family but was a relative of the powerful Holy Roman Emperor, who represented the secular power of the Catholic church in Europe.

In the mid-1520s Henry VIII fell in love with Anne Boleyn, a woman of noble birth but no great beauty.

Henry enlisted the help of leading theologians, including Wolsey and Thomas Cranmer. He hoped to prove that the marriage was invalid due to the relationship between his wife and his brother; the judicious use of bribes won him considerable support. In the background there remained the threat of making a break from the church of Rome since the exercise of papal power had long been viewed as impinging on English sovereignty and the corruption of the church in England had brought it into disrepute.

The divorce case against Queen Catherine continued for seven years but during that time Henry prevailed upon Anne to become his mistress, separating from Catherine in 1531. In 1533 Anne was pregnant; should this be the long-awaited male heir, their marriage had to be speedily legitimized. The two were secretly married and the break with Rome put into effect. A separate English church was established, with Cranmer as archbishop of Canterbury and Henry as supreme head. At last Henry got his divorce and Anne Boleyn was declared his legitimate wife. The child, however, was a girl, the future Queen Elizabeth I.

Henry remained concerned for the succession and when he met Jane Seymour in 1535, Anne became an obstacle. She was arrested and charged with adultery; while she awaited her fate in the Tower of London, Henry enjoyed himself at a succession of lively parties. Archbishop Cranmer granted him a divorce and Anne was executed. His marriage to Jane Seymour at last produced a son who survived infancy, the future King Edward VI, but his mother died soon after the birth. Anne of Cleves, Catherine Howard, and Catherine Parr became in succession his last three wives. The first he married for state reasons but never cared for, the second he had beheaded for adultery, and the last outlived him. The break with papal authority opened up to Henry an attractive way of augmenting his power base by dissolving the monasteries, at the time among the major landowners in England and unpopular for the rapacious manner in which they had dealt with their tenants and the immoral behavior imputed to the monks. Dissolution gave Henry access to huge funds and to lands he could apportion out to the nobility and squires. Religious conviction does not seem to have been the major factor; he successively switched his favor between the Catholic and Protestant camps and persecuted both ruthlessly to his own advantage.

"I see and hear daily that you of the clergy preach one against another, teach one contrary to another, inveigh one against another without charity or discretion. Some be too stiff in their old mumpsimus, others be too busy and curious in their new sumpsimus."
Henry VIII, speech to Parliament, 1545

In Henry's last years he could no longer walk or even lift his huge frame, which overeating had burdened with a fifty-four-inch waistline. Although physical powers failed him, he retained his grip on government as well as a good measure of popularity.

Among the achievements of Henry's reign were the Protestantization of his realm, accomplished without widespread violence, the upgrading of parliamentary rule, and the building up of the English navy, which was to play such a crucial role in the reign of his daughter Queen Elizabeth I. ◆

Heraclius

C.575–641 ● BYZANTINE EMPEROR

Heraclius was born into an empire of contrasts: between great wealth and dire poverty, between religious piety and brutal corruption. Invasion was responded to by refusing to serve in the military. A centurion, Phocas, had butchered the emperor Maurice and his entire family in 602, and subsequently led the empire to defeat in every battle he fought against the Persians. Constantinople's aristocracy pleaded with the governor of Africa to come to their aid and save the empire. He sent his son, Heraclius, in his stead.

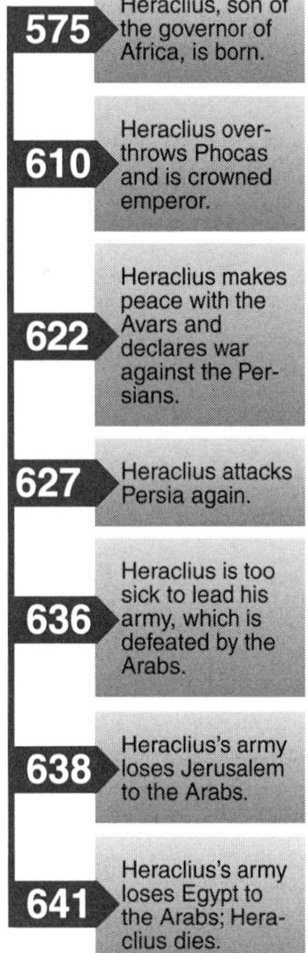

Heraclius faced tremendous problems after overthrowing Phocas and being crowned emperor in 610. The bureaucracy that had run the empire more or less efficiently for hundreds of years had disintegrated; the treasury was empty and the trade that had once flowed through Constantinople had been disrupted by war and revolution. Repeated defeats had devastated the army's personnel and morale, and the empire's citizens had become unsettled by religious persecutions, high taxes, and fear.

Heraclius's administrative reforms departmentalized the bureaucracy, made Greek rather than Latin the empire's official language, and initiated the military district system, which placed provinces under the rule of military governors and gave land to peasants in return for military service, and to soldiers in lieu of pay. It eventually led to the revival of agriculture and the replacement of unreliable mercenary forces with peasant soldiers. Heraclius's attempt to unify his empire by resolving religious conflict was less successful; his doctrine of monothelitism—that Jesus had one will but two natures—was not accepted.

After the conquest of Syria, Palestine, Egypt, Libya, and Asia Minor by Khosrow II, all that was left of the Byzantine Empire was a fragment of southern Europe and Africa, a few ports in Asia, its navy, and a besieged Constantinople that was left desperate and hungry by the loss of Egyptian grain. The patriarch of Constantinople agreed to lend Heraclius money (at interest) to finance the recapture of Jerusalem, and in 622 Heraclius made peace with the Avars and declared war against the Persians. He set out with his army from Constantinople dressed as a penitent, carrying a sacred image of the Virgin Mary and accompanied by psalm singers. A brilliant military tactician who personally led his men into battle, Heraclius succeeded in pushing the Persians out of Anatolia before attacking Persia through Armenia. The Persians advanced to the Bosphorus, where they planned a joint attack on Constantinople with the Avars, but Heraclius forestalled them by sinking the Avar fleet. He attacked Persia again in 627, and Khosrow fled in the face of the defeat of one Persian army after another. He was deposed, imprisoned, and put to death by his son in 628.

The unusual mercy that Heraclius had shown to the areas he conquered by not enslaving or massacring the population or prisoners of war helped him to make peace quickly with Khosrow's son. He asked only for the return of the True Cross, which had been stolen from Jerusalem, and the people and lands

Khosrow had captured. Heraclius personally restored the Cross to Jerusalem and returned to Constantinople in triumph.

Heraclius was old and ill when Arabs poured out of Arabia, unified and inflamed by the new religion of Islam. Persia and the Byzantine empire were defenseless before them, having fought themselves into mutual exhaustion and ruin. The Arabs defeated Heraclius's army (which Heraclius was too sick to lead personally) in 636, captured Jerusalem in 638, and Egypt in 641. However, the Byzantine Empire did not fall, but continued to hold out against the Muslims until 1453, and much of the credit for its ability to do so belongs to Heraclius's administrative and military reforms. ◆

Herod the Great

C. 73–4 B.C.E. ● KING OF JUDEA

Herod the Great was the first of a dynasty of rulers over the Roman-occupied region of Palestine around the time of Jesus Christ. Most of what is known about the Herodian age and family comes through the writings of Flavius Josephus, a Jewish historian. Herod's father, Antipater, was an Idumæan, a people brought under Roman subjection and obliged to live as Jews. Herod was considered a half Jew by some and a Jew by others. Antipater had helped the Romans in the Orient, and the favor of Rome brought the Herodian family into great prominence and power.

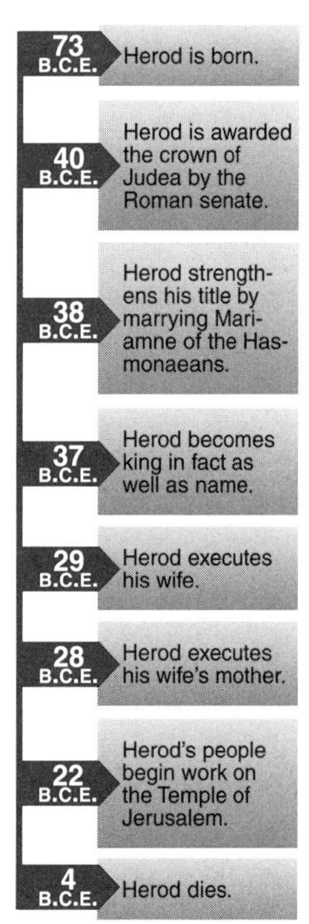

Herod was born about 73 B.C.E. and became governor of Galilee at about age twenty-five. Herod earned the favor of many important Roman rulers above him, and in 40 B.C.E. the Roman senate awarded him the crown of Judea. The Romans, under Mark Anthony, beheaded Judean king Antigonus in 37 B.C.E. and from that date Herod became king in fact as well as in name. He strengthened his title by marrying Mariamne in 38 B.C.E., entering into matrimonial alliance with the Hasmonaeans, also called the Maccabees, a family of Jewish patriots and rulers who were popular among the Jews.

Herod built great cities and temples in honor of the emperor and the gods. He erected theaters, amphitheaters, and hippodromes for games. The greatest work of his reign was the Temple of Jerusalem, begun about 22 B.C.E. The splendor of Herod's reign contrasted strongly with the horrors of his home. During the first period of his reign, he secured his position by removing rivals of the Hasmonaen line. He executed Mariamne's grandfather, Hyrcanus, and her brother, Aristobulus, who was only seventeen years old but had been made a high priest. Their offense was that they were very popular. Herod also executed Mariamne in 29 B.C.E. and her mother, Alexandra, in 28 B.C.E.

Herod had ten wives, by whom he had many children. He put to death even his own sons Aristobulus and Alexander, whom another son, Antipater, had accused of plotting against their father's life. Antipater was himself convicted of having prepared poison for his father and was put to death. Five days after receiving a letter from Rome authorizing him to kill his son, Herod himself died. The king had sought relief from a serious illness in the hot springs of Callirrhoe, east of the Dead Sea. As his end drew near, he gave orders to have the prominent men of the country imprisoned in the stadium at Jericho and slaughtered as soon as he had passed away. This brutal command was not carried out, but rather the Jews celebrated the day of Herod's death. Archelaus, his heir, buried him with great pomp near Bethlehem.

"Then Herod, when he saw that he was mocked of the wise men, was exceeding wroth, and sent forth, and slew all the children that were in Bethlehem, and in all the coasts thereof, from two years old and under, according to the time which he had diligently inquired of the wise men."
King James Bible, Matthew 2:16

The death of Herod is important in its relation to the birth of Jesus. According to the dates provided by Josephus, Herod died 4 B.C.E. But according to the book of Matthew, in the New Testament of the Bible, Christ was born before Herod's death, though how long before is not clear. Josephus does not mention what Christians often call the Slaughter of the Innocents, which is related in Matthew. According to Matthew, when Jesus was born in Bethlehem, Judea, Wise Men of the East came to Jerusalem asking about the new king of the Jews, whom they had come to worship. Herod heard of this and was troubled. He questioned his advisors, who told him that prophecies said a ruler would be born in Bethlehem and would govern the people of Israel. Herod summoned the Wise Men to find out what they knew. He instructed them to continue to Bethlehem and to report back to him afterward. He claimed he also wanted to worship the child.

After seeing the child, the Wise Men received a warning in dreams not to return to Herod. An angel also appeared in a dream to Joseph, the father of Jesus, to flee because Herod sought to kill the child. Joseph and Mary, Jesus' mother, fled to Egypt until after the death of Herod. According to Matthew, Herod learned that the Wise Men had eluded him, and he flew into a rage. He sent out soldiers to kill "all the male children in Bethlehem and in all that region who were two years old or under, according to the time which he had ascertained from the wise men."

Although other reports do not verify that of Matthew, some historians say that may be because Herod's cruelties were so many that this one paled in comparison, or that the number of children slain may have been few.

After Herod died, three of his sons inherited his kingdom. One of them, Herod Antipas, ruled over the regions of Galilee and Perea. He imitated his father in cruelty, killing people he viewed as a threat to the throne. One of these people was John the Baptist, who had become a popular figure in the region. John was, according to the New Testament, the cousin of Jesus. At about age thirty, he began preaching along the Jordan River to prepare people for the coming of the Messiah. John preached against Herod Antipas for marrying Herodias, the wife of his brother. Herod imprisoned John for this, according to the book of Luke. The book of Matthew says that Herod feared executing John because people revered him as a prophet. However, on Herod's birthday, Salome, the daughter of Herodias, danced for him, and when he granted her a reward for her dance she said, "Give me the head of John the Baptist on a platter." Herod granted her wish and had John beheaded. When she received John's head, Salome presented it as a trophy to her mother. ◆

On Herod's birthday, Salome danced for him, and when he granted her a reward for her dance she said, "Give me the head of John the Baptist on a platter."

Hirohito

1901–1989 ● EMPEROR OF JAPAN

Hirohito's family had been emperors in Japan since the seventh century B.C.E. However, from the twelfth century onward, Japan's real rulers had been the shoguns (warlords). Hirohito's grandfather, Emperor Meiji, wrested power from the shoguns and, responding to Admiral Matthew Perry's naval expedition of 1853, started modernizing his country and opened up to trade with the West. By the time Hirohito was born, Japan had abolished feudalism, established a parliament, adopted a constitution, modernized its navy, and industrialized. In 1905, with its victory over Russia, it became a major power.

Emperor Hirohito in coronation robes, 1928.

1901	Hirohito is born, heir to Japan's Chrysanthemum Throne.
1926	Hirohito becomes emperor of Japan upon the death of his father, Taisho.
1931	Hirohito opposes the army's activities in Manchuria.
1941	Japan bombs Pearl Harbor during World War II.
1945	Hirohito surrenders after atomic bombs hit Hiroshima and Nagasaki.
1989	Hirohito dies.

Heir to Japan's Chrysanthemum Throne from birth, Hirohito's life was considered too precious to be exposed to the intrigues of the court. He was separated from his mother when only three months old and sent to a foster home for safekeeping. At age three he was taken to the palace of his father, Crown Prince Taisho, but still only saw his mother once a week and his father even more rarely. A guardian, conscious that he was shaping a future emperor, supervised Hirohito's education and surrounded him with protective and disciplinary restraints. By seven, Hirohito had learned to hide his feelings and was conscious of his responsible position.

According to legend, Japanese emperors were the descendants of a Shinto goddess and were themselves revered as gods. Hirohito began to doubt his family's divine origin as he grew older but was persuaded to keep his feelings private so that Japan might not be denied the unifying symbol of a divine emperor. In return he was allowed to pursue his interest in natural history and to study marine biology: in a small boat at sea he could collect the biological specimens that fascinated him unaccompanied by a retinue of officials.

Meiji died in 1912 and Taisho proved a self-indulgent, dissipated, mentally unstable fop. His advisers were not displeased that Taisho's lack of interest made him disinclined to interfere with them, but they were upset when Hirohito, as prince regent, wanted to become a constitutional monarch. Hirohito envied the comparative freedom and informality enjoyed by Britain's royal family, whom he had visited during his 1921 tour of England and the Continent. Japan's powerful military clique and secret societies were appalled; their unquestioned power derived from their role as the instruments of a divine emperor: a nondivine, constitutional monarchy would be open to public scrutiny and actions could be challenged. Determined to end Hirohito's tentative bids for independence, they pressured his advisers to rebuke him for trying to free himself from some of the stifling Japanese protocol and create a new image by such devices as throwing a party, waving his hand to acknowledge cheers, and smiling in public. Chastened, Hirohito conformed, although he continued to eat an English breakfast of bacon and eggs each morning.

Hirohito was sixteen when his marriage with the Princess Nagako was arranged and twenty-three when it was solemnized. In 1926 he became emperor of Japan upon the death of his father.

Military fanatics were gaining control of Japan through threats and assassination. Disliking their growing influence, Hirohito opposed the army's activities in Manchuria in 1931. He requested that a new prime minister be selected "who has no fascist leanings . . . who is moderate in thought and who is not militaristic," and expressed misgivings about withdrawing from the League of Nations in 1933. Fanatical young officers mutinied against their more conservative superiors in 1936 and plotted Hirohito's assassination. Bursting into Hirohito's study, the would-be assassin was challenged by an outraged Hirohito: "How dare you come in here? Do you not know that I am your emperor?" The assailant, taught from childhood to revere the emperor as a god, bowed himself out, and committed suicide. The mutineers obeyed Hirohito's orders to surrender and on Hirohito's insistence, were severely punished for their crimes.

Hirohito was able to assert his will in a crisis but his nature was gentle and reserved rather than dominating. He reverted to being a figurehead immured in the royal palace. When the military seized control of Japan, they kept Hirohito uninformed of their activities, disregarded his stated opposition to Japan's alliance with Germany, brought Japan into World War II (ignoring his desire for peace), and evoked his name in every patriotic speech and proclamation exhorting the Japanese people to greater efforts.

In May 1945 Germany surrendered and Tokyo was in ruins. The Potsdam Conference called for Japan's unconditional surrender; the atomic bombs were dropped on Hiroshima and Nagasaki, yet the Japanese cabinet still could not decide whether Japan should surrender or fight to the bitter end. In desperation, it decided to take the unprecedented step of asking the emperor to decide Japan's fate. He chose to surrender: "I have given serious thought to the situation prevailing at home and abroad, and I have concluded that continuing the war can only mean destruction for the nation and a prolongation of bloodshed and cruelty in the world." The radio broadcast he made informing the Japanese people of his decision to surrender marked the first time that they had heard his voice.

"Moreover, the enemy has begun to employ a new and most cruel bomb, the power of which to do damage is indeed incalculable, taking the toll of many innocent lives. Should we continue to fight, it would not only result in an ultimate collapse and obliteration of the Japanese nation, but also it would lead to the total extinction of human civilization."

Hirohito, announcing Japan's surrender, August 15, 1945

"We declared war on America and Britain out of our sincere desire to ensure Japan's self-preservation and the stabilization of East Asia, it being far from our thought either to infringe upon the sovereignty of other nations or to embark upon territorial aggrandizement."
Hirohito, 1945

Hirohito was not accused of being a war criminal (even after he accepted responsibility, as emperor, for Japan's wartime actions), but there were still attempts to cut the emperor down to size. Six thousand palace servants were dismissed (in their stead, more than twenty thousand Japanese volunteers a year came to help clean the palace) and the imperial family was given the same rations as other Japanese. Forced by the American occupation forces to deny his divinity in a New Year message and to go out to meet his people face to face, Hirohito became more popular than ever before.

Hirohito's role in postwar Japan was mostly ceremonial and involved attending state functions and various events around Japan. He resumed his beloved research in marine biology and became a recognized authority, writing six books on the subject. The name Showa (Enlightened Peace), given his reign at its start, seemed increasingly prophetic with the growth of Japan's postwar economic power. ◆

Hussein ibn Talal

1935–1999 ● King of Jordan

His Royal Majesty King Hussein ibn Talal was the great-grandson of Husayn ibn Ali (Sharif) of Mecca and the grandson of King Abdullah ibn Husayn, the founder of the Jordanian kingdom (then Transjordan, 1921). It was created out of the collapse of the Ottoman empire at the end of World War I. Because of the schizophrenia suffered by Hussein's father, Talal, the leadership recognized that Prince Hussein would be the next to assume the throne. Accordingly, Emir Abdullah started instructing the young prince in statecraft at an early age. Hussein became monarch in August 1952, at the age of seventeen, but only after reaching his majority in 1953 did he formally begin his rule.

"God help us from those who believe that they are the sole possessors of truth. How we manage at times to agree willingly to become prisoners within our own minds and souls of beliefs and ideas on which we can never be flexible."
Hussein I, 1998

Despite the family's lack of worldly goods—they could not even buy him a bicycle—Hussein enjoyed a broad but abbreviated education. In Amman, he successively attended a religious school and Kulliyat al-Matran (the Bishop's School); this instruction was supplemented by special tutorials in Arabic and Islam. For his middle preparatory years, he was enrolled in the prestigious Victoria College in Alexandria, Egypt, where he

broadened his world view. During this period, the Middle East and Jordan were experiencing momentous events. In 1948, when Prince Hussein was thirteen, Israel was created, and the Arab armies attacked, fighting until 1949. They were defeated, but Transjordan gained possession of the West Bank and absorbed a major wave of Palestinian refugees. In 1950, when Prince Hussein was fifteen, the West Bank and Transjordan (also known as the East Bank) were formally joined to create the Hashemite Kingdom of Jordan.

In 1951 this succession of events began directly to affect the young prince; on July 20 King Abdullah was assassinated. While his father, Talal, temporarily ascended the throne, Prince Hussein was moved to England to join his cousin, Crown Prince Faysal of Iraq, at Harrow, an elite school for future leaders of Britain and the British empire. On August 11, 1952, King Talal was constitutionally removed from the Jordanian throne due to illness, and the crown was passed to his eldest son, Prince Hussein. Since he had not yet reached his majority, the young King Hussein was transferred to Sandhurst, the British military academy, while a regent ruled in Amman. In May 1953 King Hussein returned to Jordan and assumed the throne.

King Hussein married four times. His first wife was Sharifa Dina, a distant and older cousin from Cairo. They married in 1954; because of incompatibility they divorced eighteen months later. In 1961 King Hussein married the daughter of a British military attaché, Princess Muna, but this union also ended in divorce, in 1972. In the following year the king married a third time, to Alia Tuqan, the daughter of a prominent Nablus, West Bank, family. In 1977 Queen Alia died in a helicopter crash. In 1978 the king married Lisa Halaby, who became Queen Noor, the daughter of Najeeb Halaby, an Arab-American former chairman of Pan American Airways. The king had by his marriages seven daughters and five sons.

> *"Peace cannot be achieved unless we are equals and based on mutual respect and true desire for its establishment so that the future generations can benefit from it. It is not a matter of bargaining over small matters. The issue at hand is far bigger, and its dangers are real."*
>
> Hussein I, 1995

King Hussein enjoyed and projected a set of attributes that were crucial to his legitimacy in the minds of the Jordanian people. First, because with T. E. Lawrence (of Arabia) they led the

Arab revolt against the Ottoman empire, the Hashemites have a unique claim on the origins of Arab nationalism. From his speeches and actions, is was clear that the king had a strong feeling for and sense of duty toward the larger Arab nation. His vision, though, was not one of a grand political unity. Rather, he thought that it was incumbent on the Arab states and peoples to cooperate with one another in terms of cultural, social, economic, and strategic matters, which in turn would make the whole Arab nation more than the sum of its parts.

Second, King Hussein was a scion of the family of the Prophet Muhammad. Accordingly, the king had a special relationship to Islam, which he and those around him frequently invoked. This in turn had meaning for more traditional and religious Jordanians. In the age of popular fundamentalism, this legacy was at times an asset that other Arab leaders, King Hassan II of Morocco excepted, have not possessed.

Third, the king and his brother, Crown Prince Hassan, were perceived as genuinely interested in and, more important, capable of delivering socioeconomic development. During the four decades of the king's rule, Jordan was transformed from a very underdeveloped small state to one that enjoyed many features of a middle-income country, including broad availability of drinking water, electricity, and health care, virtually universal education, a sophisticated communications infrastructure, industrialization, and major agricultural projects.

Fourth, Jordanians enjoy a relatively high degree of personal freedom and security, especially when they compare their lot to some of their neighbors, particularly Iraq, Saudi Arabia, Syria, and the Israeli-administered territories. As long as citizens are not a threat to the state or causing disorder, they can go about life without undue interference. There are limits, however. King Hussein's regime frequently and severely restricted political freedom. After an absence since 1970, parliament was recalled in the mid 1980s. In 1989 free elections were held accompanied by vibrant debates and a relatively free press, but very considerable power and authority remained with the king.

Fifth, King Hussein's very ability and success at staying on the throne despite adversity and regime challenges created respect. The king was personable, spoke eloquent Arabic, had strength of character and physical courage, and had an attractive family with many children. Jordanians also enjoyed seeing the head of their small state dealing as an equal with the leaders of the Middle East and the world.

King Hussein's rule may be divided into three major historical periods. The first twenty years were marked by crises and threats to the throne originating from inside and outside the country: street riots stimulated by radical Arab nationalism, challenges from his own prime minister in 1956 and 1957, destabilization by larger and stronger Arab states, and the devastating loss of the West Bank to Israel in the Arab-Israel War of June 1967. Soon after, in 1970, the Palestinian guerrilla organizations challenged Jordan in a bloody civil war. Nonetheless, while relying on his loyal military to survive, the king helped put in place the bases for development.

The second phase, starting after the Arab–Israel War of October 1973, is distinguished by quieter internal political conditions, more rapid development fueled by funds (direct grants, loans, individual remittances) derived from the petroleum boom in neighboring states, and improved relations with most of Jordan's Arab neighbors. It was a relatively less radical, regional atmosphere. Despite his problems with the Palestinians and his frequently strained relations with the Palestine Liberation Organization (PLO), the king came to be a respected leader in most Arab capitals. Indeed, he hosted two Arab summits—in 1980 and 1987—in Jordan.

"As for the process of democratization, which we have adopted as a way of life, we want it to be an example for others to follow, and a point of pride for this noble nation. We must be committed to its substance and spirit in every dispute, because freedom entails the responsibility to stop before the higher national good."
Hussein I, 1996

The third phase is dominated by the end of the Cold War and the alteration of regional relationships. In a sense, King Hussein's decision to disengage Jordan politically and administratively from the West Bank, in response to the pressures from the Palestinian Intifada (uprising) of 1987, was a precursor to these changes. More important was the withdrawal of the Soviet Union as an active player in the region (1989–90), the United States' dominance in areas of its perceived interests, and the resulting polarization of the Arab world, so that the 1990–91 Gulf crisis and war left Jordan (at the time allied with Saddam Hussein's Iraq) and a few other poor Arab states politically, economically, and regionally isolated. Nevertheless, King Hussein continued with the democratization process in Jordan. Most notably, under a mandate from the king, leaders from all political streams wrote a national charter, which defines the general principles for political life in the country. A special general congress made up of 2,000 representatives ratified the document June 9, 1991.

A long-term trend in the king's rule was his moderation and centrism. As a corollary, he did not seek out enemies; he did not try to make enemies or hold grudges against people. Thus after times of internal threat to the regime, he did not execute the challengers. Some were sent to prison or exiled, but in time many were brought back and given positions of some authority. Nor did the king follow radical or overly conservative social, economic, or cultural policies.

The king's relations with the Arab world followed a similar pattern. As the leader of a small state, and in accordance with his perception of Arab nationalism, he attempted to maintain positive relations with the other Arab states. From another viewpoint, King Hussein followed a strategic policy for the survival of his country as he consistently attempted to maintain acceptable ties with some of the strong Arab states; this policy did not always meet with success as, for example, during the post–Gulf War period. Finally, he sought positive relations with the West, with both the United States and European nations. Consequently, in September 1993, he signed the peace accords with Israel.

"Let us always remember that our homeland needs people who would tackle its problems and concerns in a rational and realistic fashion as well as in a creative and balanced way, and not those who would take it to the level of dreams and unrealistic imagination in a world of illusions and sloganism."
Hussein I, address on the eve of the General Elections, 1989

In July 1992 King Hussein was found to have cancer, and underwent surgery at the Mayo Clinic in Rochester, Minnesota. As Hussein said shortly before the signing the peace accord with Israel, this health scare—and the enthusiastic welcome he received upon his return to Jordan (more than a million lined the roads between the Amman airport and the capital)—intensified his resolve to make peace and to leave his people with a more secure future.

In November 1993 King Hussein and Israeli foreign minister Shimon Peres (with the approval of Prime Minister Yitzhak Rabin) met secretly in Amman to sign an agreement on economic relations and other cooperative measures. In July 1994, when Hussein and Rabin signed a declaration on the White House lawn, Israel and Jordan formally ended the state of war that had existed between the two countries for nearly half a century. The agreement was solidified in a signing ceremony at Wadi Arava, a strip of desert between Jordan and Israel, on October 26, 1994, attended by President Clinton and other dignitaries. Before the ceremony the king said, "This is without a doubt my proudest accomplishment: leaving my people a legacy of peace."

When Yitzhak Rabin was assassinated a year later in November 1995, Hussein was deeply grieved, and traveled openly to Jerusalem for the first time since Jordan lost the city to Israel in the 1967 war. Hussein wept openly at the funeral, spoke of the slain prime minister as his "brother," and said, "It is peace that has been assassinated."

The Israelis' affection for this king who was once an enemy, whom many regarded warmly as a "mensch in a kaffiyeh," was captured in an unforgettable image when King Hussein paid a condolence visit to the families of Israeli victims of a deranged Jordanian gunman—a scene of mourning that was replayed repeatedly on Israeli television after Hussein's death. With tears in his eyes, the king knelt to hug members of the victims' families. The mother of one victim recalled, "The king said one sentence I'll never forget: 'I promise you peace.' "

"Every Arab citizen has the right to enjoy freedom. His rights must be respected. He must have the opportunity to participate in shaping his present and his future. He must feel safe for himself, his honor, and his dignity."
Hussein I, 1996

Rabin's successor, Benjamin Netanyahu, offered in word and deed little assurance that Hussein and Rabin's hopes for peace would proceed smoothly. The king initially tried to calm Arab alarm about the new prime minister's commitment to peace, but Netanyahu's public comments and his steady expansion of Jewish settlements in the West Bank and housing projects in East Jerusalem caused King Hussein to grow disenchanted with Netanyahu's reliability. It was difficult for Hussein to sustain public support for a "peace process" that his neighbor seemed to honor more in the breach than in the observance, while to Jordanians it appeared that their country was making all the concessions. By early 1998 many in Jordan were openly dismissing "the King's peace"; it had done them no good that they could see, while their economy was turning weaker. But regardless of his private misgivings, Hussein refused to break with Netanyahu for fear of losing the fragile goodwill that had been slowly cultivated—and of frightening away the foreign investors so important to Jordan's economy.

In July 1998 King Hussein told his brother, Crown Prince Hassan, that recent tests at the Mayo Clinic indicated that he probably had cancer of the lymph glands—usually fatal. In the final months of his life, during an eight-month-long struggle with non-Hodgkins lymphoma, King Hussein pondered and planned to secure a succession that would ensure stability. Though the world didn't know it yet, he was unhappy with the thought of his brother, Hassan, being the next king of Jordan. In fact, family discord in Amman was keeping him awake at night.

It was after undergoing four chemotherapy treatments at the Mayo Clinic that Hussein dragged himself to the Wye Plantation in Maryland in October 1998 to urge Israeli and Palestinian negotiators to take a step forward to the next phase of the peace accord. (The king's appearance was a sure sign that the talks were foundering; the fact that President Clinton, after exerting his diplomatic and persuasive powers through many hours over several days, still needed to call in the king—this was obviously a last-resort measure that the president surely would have avoided except in desperation.) In an impromptu speech at the signing ceremony, King Hussein said, "If I had an ounce of strength, I would have done my utmost to be there and to help in any way I can."

"Peace which results from negotiations is permanent because it is the outcome of mutual understanding and accommodation between the parties to the conflict, but without sacrificing rights or deviating from the principle of international legitimacy. For peace to be permanent it must be balanced and not governed by a disparity between the materially strong and weak. It must be founded on the basis of right and justice and the common good of those who conclude it."
Hussein I, 1991

The king's remarks, one of his last public statements, summarize well his wisdom and responsibility: "There has been enough destruction, enough death, enough waste, and it's time that together we occupy a place beyond ourselves, our peoples, that is worthy of them and of their sons, the descendants of the children of Abraham. . . . We have no right to dictate through irresponsible action or narrow-mindedness the future of our children or their children's children."

Two weeks before his death, in a stunning reversal, he bypassed his brother, Prince Hassan, fifty-one, who had been in line for the throne since 1965, and named his own son Abdullah as crown prince. He wrote a long letter to Hassan explaining his decision, charging Hassan with spreading rumors and not supporting Hussein's wish to have his own sons succeed Hassan as king. Hussein also thanked his brother for his "sincere efforts," and for his loyal acceptance of the king's decision. Up to the last days of his life, King Hussein ibn Talal was the undisputed ruler of Jordan.

When he died on February 7, 1999, it seemed that King Hussein was the most beloved and respected monarch who ever ruled. It is certain that he was sincerely mourned by millions, not least by former enemies, who worried about stability in the Middle East now that his moderating influence was gone.

In announcing his father's death (his first televised address to the nation), King Abdullah II said, "We will preserve the course that Hussein set. . . . Hussein was a father, a brother, to each of you, the same as he was my father. . . . Today you are my brothers and sisters, and with you I find sympathy and condolences under God."

The attendance at King Hussein's funeral service, though limited by Muslim tradition to admitting only male representatives, was nevertheless like a who's who of world dignitaries. Among the leaders from the Middle East were Hosni Mubarak, Yasir Arafat, Benjamin Netanyahu, and Hafez Assad. Others paying their respects were President Clinton and former presidents Bush, Carter, and Ford; Britain's Prince Charles and Tony

Blair; and Russia's Boris Yeltsin. Dozens of other countries sent their highest officials. "It was as if Hussein were hugging them all," President Clinton said of the event, "countries that are at each other's throats, meeting in peace and friendship, under the sanctity of the umbrella of this great man." ◆

I

Abd al-Aziz ibn Saud

1880–1953 ● King of Saudi Arabia

Abd al-Aziz ibn Abd ar-Rahaman ibn Faysal ibn Turki Abd Allah ibn Muhammed Al Saud, warrior-statesman, united the tribes and emirates of the Arabian Peninsula into the kingdom of Saudi Arabia. Ibn Saud was a Wahhabi Muslim of the Saudi dynasty, a tribe whose roots can be traced to the mid-1700s. His ancestor Muhammad Abd al Wahhab was chased from his village by relatives after his conversion to strict Hanbali Sunni Islam. He and his protector Muhammad ibn Saud teamed up and converted nearby Arab tribes. Known as the Saudi dynasty, and teaching what became called the Wahhabi doctrine, they and their followers extended their influence throughout much of northern Arabia, taking control of the holy cities of Mecca and Medina in the early nineteenth century; they eventually lost power to the Ottoman-backed Rashid clan.

At the time, Saudi Arabia had no modern government framework, and no division was made between the king's personal fortune and state wealth, which was kept in wooden chests in the palace.

Ibn Saud was born in Riyadh but his family was driven out of the city ten years later by the Rashids and took refuge near the Rub' al-Qali, the Empty Quarter, of the Arabian Peninsula. There, among poor bedouin tribes, ibn Saud learned to ride and shoot expertly, and became accustomed to dealing with tribal Arabs. In 1902 he and a band of loyal Wahhabi tribesman retook Riyadh from the Rashids, thus beginning thirty years of conquests that would unify the peninsula under his rule.

In 1906, after subduing the Rashid clan, ibn Saud defeated tribes in the central and eastern parts of the peninsula. During

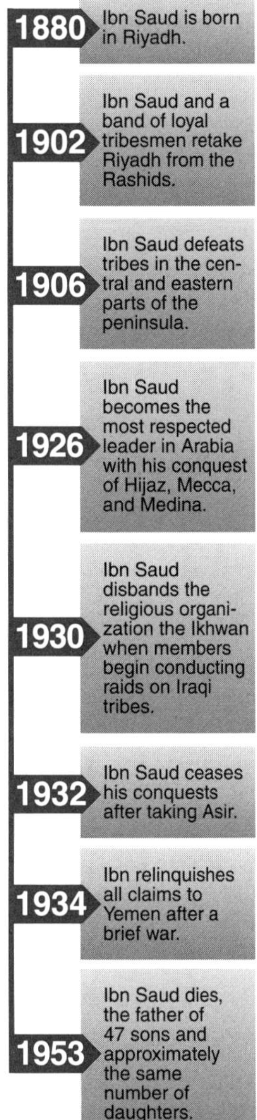

World War I the British made a treaty with him recognizing him as ruler of an independent Najd and Hassa, and were content with his benevolent neutrality. His conquests attracted foreign notice when he took the Hijaz and the holy cities of Mecca and Medina in 1926, thereby becoming the most respected leader in Arabia, ibn Saud strictly adhered to the teachings of Wahhabi Islam and enforced them among his troops, using religious beliefs to temper the bedouin tribesmen's love of battle and loot.

In addition to his martial skills, ibn Saud used marriage as a way of cementing tribes' loyalty, marrying daughters of newly subdued tribes. To remain within the Koran's limit of four wives, ibn Saud frequently divorced his wives after a brief marriage and sent them, laden with gifts, back to their guardians.

A decisive factor in ibn Saud's ability to unify Arabia was his formation of the religious organization the Ikhwan (the Brothers), which required bedouins to give up their nomadic lifestyle in favor of an agricultural one. This made the men easier to control, more willing to heed Wahhabi religious teachings, and more easily disciplined when they were needed for military service. Without the Ikhwan, it is doubtful that ibn Saud would have been able to unite Arabia within one generation. However he disbanded the Ikhwan in 1930 when members began conducting raids on Iraqi tribes. After conquering Asir in 1932 and creating the kingdom of Saudi Arabia, ibn Saud ceased his conquests. He also, after a brief war in 1934, relinquished all claims to Yemen, a wise move since the residents of Yemen were Zaydi Shi'ites and would have bitterly resisted conquest by Wahhabi Sunni Muslims. By the 1940s ibn Saud was widely regarded as the Arabs' elder statesman.

Until the late 1930s, the Saudi kingdom was desperately poor, relying on trade in dates and camels, and the revenue brought in by the approximately one hundred and fifty thousand tourists who visited the holy cities on the annual hajj (pilgrimage). It was believed that Arabia had mineral wealth and oil, but the harsh climate, fierce bedouin tribes, and religious fanaticism discouraged foreign prospectors until the American Charles Crane and his partner, Karl Twitchell, began prospecting for oil in 1931.

Crane and Twitchell found nothing, but two years later Twitchell returned as an employee of Standard Oil of California, which had obtained exploration rights in eastern Arabia. For a $300,000 loan, an annual rent of $30,000 and a small royalty, ibn Saud gave the Americans a sixty-year concession to search for and export oil. Within five years, crude oil was being exported and refineries were being built; a "little America" had sprung up in Dharan, where the American oil workers lived, complete with lawns, swimming pools, and a commissary that sold American food.

At the time, Saudi Arabia had no modern government framework, and no division was made between the king's personal fortune and state wealth, which was kept in wooden chests in the palace; no state bank existed. Each of King ibn Saud's subjects could approach him personally to air grievances. Wahhabi Islam was strictly enforced, with religious leaders going from house to house to ensure that Muslims prayed five times daily. Justice was administered according to the Koran—thieves' hands were chopped off, murderers beheaded. Alcohol, tobacco, Western clothes, movies, and dancing were forbidden.

Eventually the royal family became corrupted by the tremendous oil wealth and the aging, lame, half-blind king was unable to understand the change or comprehend modern economics.

In this atmosphere, the effect of the "little America" of the oil workers was revolutionary. It was, for nearly all Saudis, their first exposure to the Western world, although ibn Saud himself had learned the value of technology in helping him to maintain his power; he owned a car, and introduced the telegraph and telephone into Saudi Arabia.

Ibn Saud had forty-seven sons by twenty-two different women, and approximately the same number of daughters. They were required to marry into one of a few well-respected families. Each member of the royal family had his own palace, a state income, and held some public office. Eventually the royal family became corrupted by the tremendous oil wealth and the aging, lame, half-blind king was unable to understand the change or comprehend modern economics. When he died, his eldest son, Saud, took over and quickly ran up $300 million of debt before being deposed and replaced by King Faisal. ◆

Isa ibn Sulman al-Khalifa

1933–1999 ● RULER OF BAHRAIN

Isa became ruler of Bahrain on December 16, 1961, upon the death of his father. He had served as president of the Manama municipal council, supervising the creation of a free-trading area at the capital's port, following the anti-British disturbances during the mid-1950s. He was designated heir

Emir Isa al-Khalifa of Bahrain meets with U.S. president George Bush in Washington in 1991.

apparent in January 1958 and accompanied his father on an official visit to Saudi Arabia in February, which produced a treaty confirming the marine borders of both countries.

Shaykh Isa assumed greater responsibly for Bahrain's internal and external affairs during the next two years, as his father suffered a series of debilitating heart attacks. Isa also took charge of the Khalifa family council, enabling him to decide how oil revenues should be divided among the members and supporters of the clan. He was thus well positioned to accede to the rulership following his father's death in November 1961.

"He left us a well-developed, flourishing, and secure nation. He turned Bahrain into an oasis of civilization and prosperity and a landmark of knowledge and progress."

Emir Shaykh Hamad, on the death of his father, 1999

As it became clear during the late 1960s that the smaller Arab states in the Persian/Arabian Gulf region would be incapable of forming a political union in the wake of Britain's withdrawal from the area, Shaykh Isa began establishing an autonomous government apparatus for Bahrain: he declared it an independent state on August 14, 1971, and took the title of emir, at the same time decreeing that elections would be held for a constitutional assembly in 1972, over the objections of several senior members of the ruling family. He approved the constitution in June of 1973 and presided over subsequent parliamentary elections. When his brother, the prime minister, submitted the cabinet's resignation in 1975—in the face of growing criticism of the regime's domestic and foreign policies on the part of its parliament—Isa dissolved the assembly and reinstated the cabinet as the legislative body. He generally epitomizes the pragmatic wing of the al-Khalifa, consistently supporting the gradual introduction of new technology and social services, while at the same time conciliating the family's more conservative shaykhs.

Bahrain's production and processing of oil accounted for about 60 percent of its export and government revenues, and the nation's economy rose and fell with oil prices in the late 1980s and the 1990s. Seeing that Bahrain's oil was limited, Shaykh Isa worked to make Bahrain a major banking and financial center of the Middle East. Many international companies made Bahrain their Middle East headquarters.

Isa continued to rule as his al-Khalifah clan had since the late 1700s—with complete authority. While the prosperous and powerful al-Khalifa were Sunni Muslims, a majority of Bahrain's 600,000 people were less-prosperous Shiite Muslims. After Iran's Shiite revolution of 1979, Bahrain's Shiites grew restless. In the 1980, Bahrainian officials reportedly suppressed several Iranian-inspired revolutionary plots in the emirate. In 1994 and 1995, Shiites protested their lack of political power. Isa negotiated with Shiite leaders, but the talks dissolved with no resolution. In 1996 Isa ordered the arrest of dozens of Shiite leaders charged with rioting and sabotage. The Shiite campaign for political reform had left up to forty people dead by the late 1990s. Few Bahrainians openly discussed politics, as they feared retaliation.

Bahrain joined the thirty-nine-nation alliance led by the United Nations that defeated Iraq in the Persian Gulf War of 1991. Isa committed troops to the conflict and hosted a large U.S. naval presence. He also allowed the use of Bahraini airfields by British and American warplanes. After the Gulf War, Isa traveled to Washington to sign a security pact with the United States.

On March 6, 1999, Shaykh Isa suddenly died of a heart attack at age sixty-five after thirty-eight years as emir. Isa collapsed minutes after a morning meeting with visiting U.S. defense secretary William Cohen. The emir was buried within hours in keeping with Muslim custom. Thousands of Bahrainis showered his twelve-mile funeral route with flowers and a three-month period of mourning followed. Isa was reportedly survived by his wife, five sons, and four daughters. Some sources reported that Isa had dozens of wives—though never more than four at a time, in keeping with the Muslim religion. Bahrain's cabinet met within hours of Isa's death to recognize his son

Shaykh Hamad bin Isa al-Khalifa, forty-nine, as emir. Hamad, the crown prince since 1964, already held the title of commander-in-chief of Bahrain's armed forces and had been involved in the daily governing of the country.

Analysts expected Hamad to follow his father's model of traditional Arab leadership, based on tribal solidarity between the ruler and his subjects. While this system permitted access to their leader, allowing subjects to air grievances and request financial assistance, it did not allow for political change or democratic action. But exiled dissidents expressed their hope that Shaykh Hamad would open the government up to greater democracy and popular participation.◆

Isabella I

1451–1504 ● QUEEN OF CASTILE

Isabella I was the daughter of John II of Castile and his second wife, Isabella of Portugal. John died when Isabella was three and she was brought up away from court by her mother, whose extreme piety had a great influence on Isabella's character. John's successor, Isabella's half brother Henry, was known as "Henry the Impotent" because of his wastefulness, incompetence, and childlessness. Dissatisfied nobles searched for a competent heir, so Henry brought Isabella to court at thirteen to watch over her. Henry did claim to have a daughter, Juana, but the nobles doubted that Henry the Impotent was really her father and forced Henry to acknowledge Isabella as his heiress when she was seventeen.

Isabella had a number of suitors but chose at eighteen to marry her cousin Ferdinand, king of Sicily and heir to the kingdom of Aragon. The nobles helped to contrive the match over her brother's disapproval; a Jewish lawyer loaned them enough money to get married. Henry's death precipitated a war of succession against Juana and her husband, which Ferdinand won in 1476.

Ferdinand and Isabella made an extremely effective team. Though officially joint rulers of their kingdoms, Castile's internal administration remained in Isabella's hands. With Ferdinand's cooperation she restored order in Castile, subduing powerful nobles, ending highway robbery, and reforming the legal system. Interested in education, she studied Latin, encouraged scholars, and patronized the arts. Publicly extravagant and privately frugal, she spent her spare time making embroideries for churches.

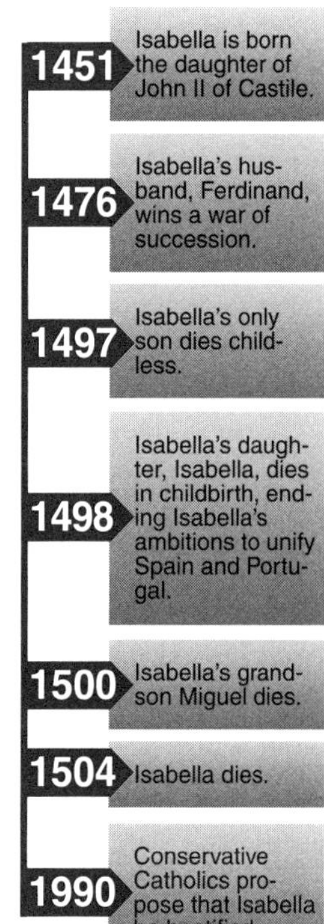

Entitled "the Catholic" by the pope, Isabella demonstrated extreme piety and selected the sternest, most intolerant priests as her confessors and spiritual guides. She tried to reform the morals of both clergy and laity and even criticized the immorality of some popes. She refused to accept several papal appointers to positions in Spain on the grounds that their moral standards were not high enough and that such appointments infringed on royal rights. Intensely interested in the war against Granada (the last Muslim kingdom in Spain), she courageously kept her court with the besieging army for years and was personally responsible for improving military supply lines and establishing a military hospital. The lure of potential new souls for Christianity led her to overcome Ferdinand's lack of interest and send Christopher Columbus off on his voyages of discovery. Loyal to her friends and tender to her children, she was cruel to heretics. Although loved by her Christian subjects for her warmth and kindness, she was responsible for instituting the Inquisition and expelling both Jews and Muslims from Spain.

Isabella suffered much from the tragedies of her private life. Ferdinand was frequently unfaithful, seven of her ten children died young or were stillborn, and her only son died childless in 1497. Her ambitions to unify Spain and Portugal ended when the queen of Portugal, her own daughter Isabella, died in childbirth in 1498 and, further, with the death of her grandson Miguel in 1500. Her only surviving child, Juana, went mad. In 1990 conservative Catholic circles proposed that she be **beatified** during 1992, the five hundreth anniversary of Columbus's voyage. The proposal was contested within the church, which thought that aspects of her zeal—such as her devotion to the **Inquisition** and cruel attitude to Muslims and Jews—made the suggestion untimely, and it was shelved. ◆

beatify: to authorize the title "Blessed" and limited public religious honor.

Inquisition: a former Roman Catholic tribunal for the discovery and punishment of heresy.

Agustin de Iturbide

1783–1824 ● EMPEROR OF MEXICO

Agustin de Iturbide was born in the Mexican town of Valladolid (now Morelia). He joined the Spanish colonial army when only fourteen years old and quickly rose through the ranks. He supported the colonial power against independence-minded rebels and was responsible for the capture of Jose María Morelos, a prominent leader of the independence movement.

"The distinction of castes is abolished, which was made by the Spanish law, excluding them from the rights of citizenship. All the inhabitants of the country are citizens, and equal, and the door of advancement is open to virtue and merit."

Plan of Iguala, 1821

Fearing the collapse of Ferdinand VII's regime in 1820, Mexican conservatives sided with the independence movement in a bid to ensure the continuation of favorable local policies. Iturbide was chosen to lead them. At first the liberals, suspicious of Iturbide's abrupt turnabout, were reluctant to meet with him, but eventually, liberal rebel leader Vicente Guerrero agreed to coordinate policy between the two movements. Early contacts with the liberals were doomed by Iturbide's insistence on dictating a conservative agenda for independence, but in 1821 the two produced the Plan of Iguala, a compromise allowing the divided factions to join forces against Spain. The plan contained three guarantees: independence agreed upon by both parties; recognition of the official status of the Roman Catholic church (a gesture to the conservatives); and racial equality for all Mexicans (a gesture to the liberals). Another thorny issue was the nature of the future government; the conservatives were avowed monarchists, while the liberals were republicans. The final compromise envisioned a constitutional monarchy with Ferdinand or another European prince as head of state.

The already demoralized Spanish troops were easily defeated by the combined liberal and conservative forces. On August 24, 1821, Viceroy Juan de Donoju initiated the signing of the Treaty of Córdoba recognizing the Plan of Iguala as the basis for immediate Mexican independence. The Treaty of Córdoba, however, contained one significant deviation from the Plan of Iguala, initiated at Iturbide's behest. A new clause was inserted stating that should no European prince be willing to accept the kingship, that role would be assumed by a native Mexican.

Iturbide joined a five-man junta appointed to govern Mexico until a king was chosen. Already the conservative favorite for the role, his supporters ensured his preeminence over other junta members by having him appointed commander in chief of the Mexican army with the pompous title *Generalissimo de Tierra y Mar* (Commander of Land and Sea). Knowing that his support among the liberals, who had not abandoned the idea of a republican government, was abating, Iturbide began campaigning on his own behalf as the most suitable candidate for king. A massive demonstration was organized to march from the Congress buildings to his own home demanding his acceptance of the throne. As the mob stood chanting his name in the street, Iturbide appeared on the balcony and proclaimed his acceptance. He told the crowd that he sought no self-aggrandizement, but would not venture to insult them by rejecting their offer. He then joined the mob and led them back to Congress, where he was voted emperor although the necessary quorum for congressional proceedings was lacking. That afternoon, Iturbide was sworn in as Emperor Agustin I.

"This kingdom of America shall be recognized as a sovereign and independent nation; and shall, in future, be called the Mexican Empire."
Treaty of Cordoba, 1821

Agustin I reigned only ten months, but in that short time he managed to ruin the Mexican economy, already in shambles after twenty years of civil war. Congress ignored pressing economic and social issues to deliberate on matters of imperial etiquette and protocol. Among the issues discussed were whether the motto on the new currency should be in Latin or Spanish; whether newly appointed nobles should be required to kiss the emperor's hand at the coronation, and whether the coronation should be preceded by a three-day national fast (determined as impractical to enforce). The coronation ceremony itself was modeled on that of Napoleon.

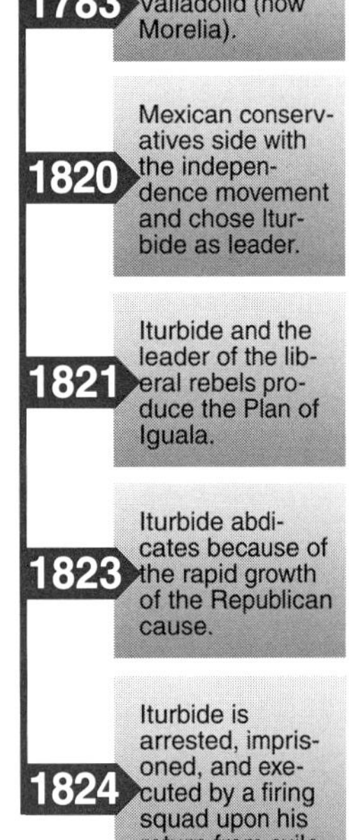

Iturbide's despotic regime lost all support when he dissolved congress in favor of his own absolute rule. Former revolutionary comrades, including Guerrero and Antonio López de Santa Anna, plotted in Vera Cruz to oust Iturbide and proclaimed a republican government in that city. The rapid growth of the republican cause led to Iturbide's abdication in February, 1823. He was forced into exile in Italy, but was provided with a sizable pension in recognition of his contribution to Mexican independence.

Noting from exile how the republican revolution exacerbated rather than resolved Mexico's problems, Iturbide plotted to regain his throne. He returned to Mexico but was arrested, imprisoned, and executed by a firing squad. Mexico remained a republic until Maximilian assumed the throne in 1863. ◆

Ivan III

1440–1505 ● Grand Prince of Moscow

Born in Moscow, Ivan III Vasilyevich (Ivan the Great) was to become a pawn in the civil war between his father, Grand Prince Vasily II of Moscow, and members of his father's family who sought the predominance of Novgorod, Moscow's rival as guardian of Orthodox Christianity. When Vasily's fortunes were at an ebb (he was arrested and blinded), his supporters spirited Ivan, age six, out of Moscow; they then betrayed Vasily by giving Ivan up to Vasily's enemies. On Vasily's return to power, he cemented a political alliance with Tver by having his son, still six years old, betrothed to the daughter of that city's grand prince.

From 1446 until his father's death in 1462, Ivan was groomed for the throne. At the age of twelve he married the princess to whom he had been betrothed and took command, at least in name, of a troop sent out by Vasily to the far north to eliminate the last of his enemies. At eighteen Ivan distinguished himself against the Tatars in the south of Russia. On his father's death he became grand prince, and the next five years passed relatively quietly.

In 1467 Ivan's wife died. Having only one son from this alliance and wishing to secure the succession, he decided to remarry. After a long period of indecision, in 1472 he married the niece of the last Byzantine emperor and ward of Cardinal Bessarion of Rome, Zoë Paleologus. During these years, having succeeded in annexing both Novgorod and Tver by a mixture of Machiavellian religious intrigue and straightforward fighting, he had sent out parties of explorers to the new regions that had come under his power, especially in the northeast as far as the Arctic.

Zoë, whose name had been changed to Sophia upon her marriage, escaped from the Kremlin in 1480, the year in which Ivan's two younger brothers rebelled against him and the Tatars invaded his territory. Ivan, using bribery and intrigue, had tried to avoid outright battle, but in 1480 he was forced to face the Tatars, who had crossed the Don and reached the Oka, menacing Moscow. He waited for weeks before ordering his army to retreat to Moscow; this battleless campaign of 1480 was later seen as marking the end of Tatar oppression of Russia. It was in fact typical of Ivan's policy and the means by which Moscow slowly and relatively bloodlessly absorbed its neighbors and possible rivals.

When Ivan's heir, his son by his first wife, died in 1490, the problem of succession became more serious. He hesitated until 1497, unable to decide between Dmitri, his nephew or Vasily, his own eldest son by Sophia. His decision was made harder by his need to cement relations with Moldavia, his ally in the ongoing conflict with Lithuania; Dmitri's mother was the daughter of Moldavia's ruler. In 1497 Ivan chose Dmitri, who was then fourteen years of age, and had him crowned grand prince in 1498 after uncovering a plot against him concocted by Sophia and Vasily, then nineteen.

In 1500 Vasily defected to the Lithuanians, and after two years of indecision, Ivan deposed Dmitri and had him imprisoned, nominating Vasily as his heir instead. Despite the various successes and innovations that marked his reign, including the introduction of compulsory military service to be rewarded with a grant of land, on his death three years later Ivan left many political, ecclesiastical, and territorial problems unsolved. ◆

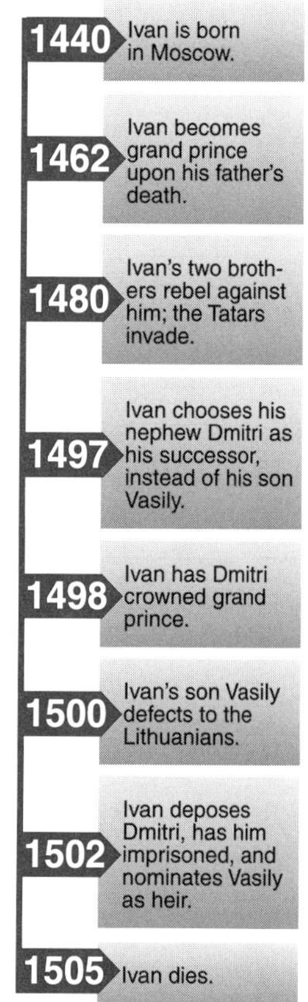

Ivan IV

1530–1584 ● CZAR OF RUSSIA

Ivan IV Vasilyevich, better known as Ivan the Terrible, completed the formation of the Russian Empire. Born in Moscow, he was three years old when his father died and he was proclaimed grand prince. His mother, Princess Yelena Glinskaya, ruled as his regent until 1538, when she too died, possibly having been poisoned. The target of much intrigue at court, he spent most of his time studying religious works under a tutor, the monk Sylvester, author of the *Domostroi*, a book setting out rules covering every aspect of Russian domestic life. Ivan was possessed of a cruel streak that led him to take advantage of his autocratic powers, ordering the execution or punishment of anyone he considered to have committed lèse-majesté against his person. At the age of thirteen he had the leader of one of the court factions executed; he imprisoned the noble who had assisted his mother during the period of her regency, and sent the man's sister, who had been his nurse, to a nunnery. One of the few people who had an influence on him was the metropolitan Makary, who was instrumental in saving some, although not all, of the courtiers the young Ivan wished to punish, and who later served as regent when Ivan was absent from Moscow during his campaigns against the Tatars.

> ***"When we reached the age of fifteen, we, inspired by God, undertook to rule our own realm and, with the aid of almighty God, we ruled our realm in peace and undisturbed, according to our will. But it happened then that, on account of our sins, a fire having spread, by God's will, the royal city of Moscow was consumed."***
> Ivan IV, 1564

In 1547 Ivan was crowned czar, ending *boyar* (aristocratic) rule. Shortly afterward he married, on Makary's advice, after selecting his bride, Anastasiya Romanovnan, a member of the Romanov family, from hundreds brought to Moscow for this purpose in a Cinderella-like episode. During this period Makary prevailed upon Ivan to work toward shaping the conglomeration of cities and territories that made up his domain into a state based on religious ideals. Ecclesiastic assemblies in 1547 and 1549 ratified Ivan's church reforms. A new legal code was drawn up, and a national assembly consisting of representatives of local administrations convened in 1549. Together with a faction of court favorites known as the "chosen council," the assembly served Ivan in an advisory capacity.

In 1552 Ivan achieved the final subjugation of the Kazan Tatars and in 1556 that of the Astrakhan Tatars, the latter without bloodshed. In the years between these two successes, despite—or perhaps in part due to—the reforms he had introduced, internal tension ran high. In 1553 Ivan, sick at the time with a fever contracted during his Kazan campaign, succeeded in having his son Dmitri, then a child, named as heir to the throne after a struggle that split the court, which was divided between Ivan himself and his cousin Vladimir. On gaining the upper hand, Ivan took no immediate steps against his rival, but Vladimir was to die in 1569 by Ivan's hand.

In 1565 Ivan divided his realm into two. Due to the lack of documentation from this period his reasons for taking this step are not clear, although they were probably connected to his mistrust of his advisors and military functionaries. He himself administered an extensive personal territory known as the *oprichnina*, or "widow's share," backed up by a brotherhood of 1,000 black-garbed men known as *oprichniki*, his personal troop who helped him institute a reign of terror. The other territory was administered by the various councils of boyars, and this arrangement continued until 1572 when the people of Moscow, tired of the chaos it caused, petitioned Ivan to return.

In 1556, two years after subduing the Tatars, Ivan had set out to solve a problem that would tax Russia until the time of Peter the Great. Seeking an outlet to the sea, he embarked on the useless, costly Livonian War with Poland and Sweden which was to continue for twenty-four years. In 1581, a year before the war ended, Ivan quarreled with his heir (Ivan, not Dmitri, who had died) and killed him in a fit of rage, thus bringing to an end his own dynasty. His remorse, which may have contributed to his death, led him to buy prayers for his son, as well as for over 3,000 men he had had executed, mainly during his *oprichnina,* when his cruelty had apparently had no restraint. He was also apparently married seven times, doing away with his wives when he felt necessary by murder or consignment to a nunnery.

Although he was an autocrat with an overriding belief in the divine right of kings, and a tyrant with an uncontrollable, paranoid temper, Ivan was also a devout Orthodox Christian. He loved music and wrote at least two hymns. An educated man who read widely, he introduced the printing press into Russia. Under his direction, Makary completed an encyclopedia that included world as well as Russian history. Ivan expanded Russian art and built a lavish cathedral in the Kremlin (legend has it that Ivan had the architects blinded when the work was finished so that they would never build anything more beautiful).

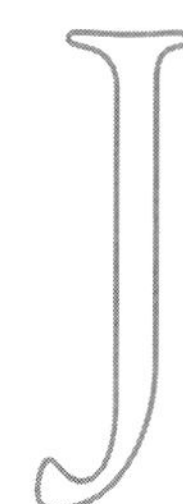

Jabir Ahmad Al Sabah

1926– ● EMIR OF KUWAIT

Emir Jabir belongs to the Jabir branch, one of the two branches of the al-Sabah family that has ruled Kuwait since the middle of the eighteenth century. The other branch is al-Salim. Jabir and Salim were the two sons of Emir Mubarak "the Great," who ruled Kuwait from 1896 to 1915. Jabir ruled from 1913 to 1917, and his son Ahmad ruled from 1921 to 1950. Ahmad's son Jabir Ahmad ascended to power on December 13, 1977. Mubarak's other son, Salim, ruled Kuwait from 1917 to 1921, and two of his sons also ruled—Abd Allah from 1950 to 1965 and Sabah from 1965 to 1977. Abd Allah's son Sa'd is the current prime minister and crown prince, and he is expected to be the next ruler of Kuwait.

Many significant developments occurred in Kuwait during Jabir's rule. In the late1970s and early 1980s he promoted democratization and free speech and encouraged a free press.

Many significant developments occurred in Kuwait during Jabir's rule. On the positive side, in the late 1970s Kuwait became a financial giant, both regionally and internationally. In the late 1970s and early 1980s he promoted democratization and free speech and assembly, resurrected the National Assembly in 1981 after its dissolution in 1976, and encouraged a free press. However, in response to the rise in terrorism in Kuwait in the mid-1980s, Jabir dissolved the National Assembly in 1986, muzzled the press, and suspended the constitution. Also, in 1982 Kuwait experienced the crash of the unofficial stock market, the Suq Al-Manakh; the effects were felt in Kuwait throughout the 1980s.

During the Iran–Iraq War (1980–89), Kuwait, under Jabir's rule, walked a tightrope between the two combatants; it supported

Iraq financially but was careful not to anger Iran excessively. Toward the end of the war, Kuwait felt seriously threatened by Iran, and Kuwaiti shipping began to be attacked by Iranian naval vessels and armed patrol boats. Kuwait sought U.S. help in protecting its oil tankers and other vessels. The U.S. Navy and Coast Guard provided protection by placing the U.S. flag on Kuwaiti ships. This reflagging operation brought the United States almost into a direct military confrontation with Iran.

Following the Iran–Iraq War Kuwait became embroiled in a dispute with Iraq over several issues: the loans that Kuwait extended to Iraq during the war; the Iraq-Kuwait boundary; the Bubiyan and al-Warbah islands and access to the sea; the Rumaylan oil field; and the oil quota and pricing policies. Iraq refused to pay back the loans, claiming it fought the war against Iran on behalf of Kuwait and the rest of the Gulf **shaykhdoms**. Also, Iraq accused Kuwait of pumping more oil than the approved Organization of Petroleum Exporting Countries (OPEC) quota agreement in order to keep the prices low. Furthermore, Iraq accused Kuwait of "stealing" more oil than its share from the neutral zone. Iraq argued that Kuwait's activities were unacceptable and would not be allowed to continue. Attempts at reconciliation through Saudi Arabia in the late spring and early summer of 1900 failed; on August 2, 1990, Iraq invaded Kuwait.

Hours after the invasion, Jabir and most of his family and government fled the country to Saudi Arabia, where he set up a government in exile. He and his government returned to Kuwait after liberation, in March 1991. Jabir was criticized severely by many Kuwaitis, especially those who stayed in the country during its occupation by Iraq, for fleeing Kuwait so quickly and without any resistance. Leaders of the Kuwaiti resistance movement also criticized Kuwait's armed forces for their **precipitous** collapse in the face of the Iraqi invasion.

sheikhdom: a region under the rule of an Arab chief.

precipitous: unexpected; showing undue haste.

Emir Jabir and Crown Prince Sa'd attempted to nullify the criticism by promising a return to democracy after liberation. This promise was made by the ruler and the crown prince at the Kuwaiti people's conference held in Jidda, Saudi Arabia, in October 1990. Upon his return to Kuwait, Jabir announced that national elections would be held in October 1992.

After the war Kuwait faced immediate problems of obtaining food, fresh water, and electricity. In addition, hundreds of oil wells had been set on fire by retreating Iraqis. These fires took a great deal of effort to extinguish and caused tremendous environmental damage. Animosity grew between Kuwaitis and

Palestinian residents, whom Kuwaitis accused of having collaborated with Iraqi occupation forces. Palestinians had made up Kuwait's largest group of foreign residents, but after the war most Palestinians left Kuwait. Kuwait paid $16.5 billion to the United States to cover its share of war expenses.

As promised, Jabir allowed national elections in October 1992, and Kuwaitis elected a new fifty-member National Assembly. Groups opposed to the emir won a majority in the elections, but these groups disagreed with one another on major issues. Jabir also reinstated Kuwait's constitution.

In October 1994 Iraqi troops gathered along Kuwait's border, and the United Nations demanded their immediate withdrawal. Finally, on November 10, 1994, Iraqi president Saddam Hussein officially recognized Kuwait's sovereignty and its borders.

In early 1998 the United States prepared to take military action against Iraq if Hussein failed to cooperate with U.N. weapons inspectors searching Iraq for evidence of nuclear, chemical, or biological weapons. Kuwaiti officials hoped that a U.S.-led bombing campaign could topple Iraq's regime, either by killing Hussein or by setting off a popular uprising or coup. Jabir gave permission for U.S. warplanes to fly bombing missions against Iraq from Jabir Air Base in southern Kuwait.

United Nations efforts to rid Iraq of its weapons of mass destruction failed, and the United States and Britain began a series of air strikes in mid-December 1998. Iraq threatened retaliation against Kuwait in February 1999 if Kuwait did not stop allowing the United States and Britain to use its military bases. Attacks and counterattacks continued between the Western forces and Iraq into the spring of 1999, but the situation seemed to be a stalemate. ◆

James I (James VI)

1566–1625 ● KING OF SCOTLAND AND ENGLAND

James I was king of Scotland as James VI and of England as James I from 1603. James VI became king of Scotland when only eighteen months old, after his mother, Mary Stuart, queen of Scots, was deposed over her alleged role in the assassination of her husband and James's father, Henry Stewart, Lord Darnley. Much of Scotland's animosity toward

Divine Right of Kings

A doctrine that supported royal absolutism, the divine right of kings reached its most influential and extreme form in seventeenth-century England under the Stuart kings (r. 1603–49 and 1660–89) and in seventeenth- and eighteenth-century France under Louis XIV (r. 1643–1715). The doctrine held that monarchs received their authority from God, not from the people or their legislatures. If kings did wrong, they were to be punished by God, not by humans, who must practice complete obedience to their rulers. The increasing influence of divine right theory coincided with the growth of powerful, centralized nation-states.

King James I of England (r. 1603–25), the first Stuart monarch, expressed the divine right starkly when he asserted that kings were above the law. Under King Charles II (r. 1660–85), the English court promoted the publication of *Patriarcha* (1680), by Robert Filmer, which became a famous defense of divine right. On the other hand, English philosopher John Locke, in his *First Treatise on Civil Government* (1689), contended that government was established by a compact of the people, and that monarchs were ultimately accountable to them.

When King James II (r. 1685–88), the last Stuart king, was overthrown in the Glorious Revolution of 1688–89, the days of divine right monarchy were over in England, and Locke's theory of government prevailed. The French Revolution, which began in 1789, was the death knell of divine right in France.

Mary was the result of her fervent Catholicism. In contrast, James received an austere Calvinist education, stressing subjects' rights as against the powers of the monarchy. James repudiated this doctrine in *The Trew Law of Free Monarchies* and *Basilikon Doron*, expounding his philosophy of the divine right of kings.

"And as ye see it manifest that the King is overlord of the whole land, so is he master over every person that inhabiteth the same, having power over the life and death of every one of them."
James I, 1598

With James's early reign plagued by civil war, his safety was of concern. He was constantly surrounded by armed troops, generating a phobia of weapons throughout his life. The danger was, however, real; three regents met violent deaths between 1600 and 1602.

In 1579 James, whose sexual preference was for members of his own sex, fell in love with Esmé Stuart d'Aubigny, a relative raised in Roman Catholic France. As James began assuming royal authority, Stuart d'Aubigny was named duke of Lennox. Another favorite was Captain James Stewart, later earl of Arran. Lennox's involvement in a plot to restore Mary led to a Protestant coup in which James was captured and imprisoned by the earl of Gowrie for ten months. Lennox was banished from Scotland, but with Arran's help James escaped to assert his rule.

James recognized the necessity to accommodate all factions to avoid insurrection. Arran was deposed as James began centralizing authority in his own hands as the self-proclaimed "Universal King." At the same time, he coveted the English throne of Elizabeth I, who was without heir. Elizabeth never officially recognized James as her heir, but granted him a sizeable pension in return for peace between the two countries. James, in turn, did much to placate her; even the death sentence passed against his mother was answered with only a mild threat. In 1589 James married Anne of Denmark, who bore him three children to survive infancy: Henry, Charles (later Charles I), and Elizabeth. Having heirs increased his eligibility to succeed Elizabeth, and James corresponded with English secretary of state Robert Cecil to that effect. When Elizabeth died in 1603, James was summoned to the English throne. Before leaving Scotland, he promised his subjects to return regularly—in fact, he did so only once.

Poets described his dramatic journey south from the bleak Scottish highlands to the fertile plains of England. En route he was greeted by cheering crowds unaware of James's intention to implement the divine right of kings. This animated reception soured rapidly, however, upon James's entry into London, then in the throes of a plague. His coronation was delayed, but James immediately assumed his new throne with ardor. He convened a synod to define the role of the church under his reign, and alienated both Catholics and Puritans with caustic witticisms and his claim to be the supreme religious authority. Presbyterian Scotland was also perturbed by his assertion, "No bishops, no king," by which he professed the need for an established episcopacy. Many disgruntled Puritans eventually left for the New World, as the Pilgrims did in 1620, but James did concede to their request for a new English translation of the Bible, the Authorized, or King James, Version, completed in 1611.

> ***"The state of monarchy is the supremest thing upon earth: for kings are not only God's lieutenants upon earth and sit upon God's throne, but even by God himself they are called gods."***
>
> James I, 1610

English Catholics proved more militant. The queen herself was a devout Roman Catholic who refused Anglican communion at the coronation. In 1605 Guy Fawkes was caught attempting to blow up the House of Parliament. Under torture he revealed the names of other eminent Roman Catholics plotting to overthrow James. Roman Catholic historians later claimed that the Gunpowder Plot was actually fabricated by James and Cecil (now earl of Salisbury) to discredit the Catholic gentry.

James's popularity also waned with Parliament because of his insistence that full authority be delegated to his privy council, a collection of favorites, several of them lovers. Some were promoted to the nobility, among them: James Carr, earl of Somerset; George Villiers, later duke of Buckingham; and the Spanish ambassador, the count of Gondomar, responsible for the death of Sir Walter Raleigh. James summoned Parliament only once during his reign, in 1614. Known as the Addled Parliament, it refused to sanction his self-styled title, King of Great Britain (it was only in 1707 that England and Scotland were formally united). Sir Edward Coke, England's first chief justice, asserted Parliament's independence and denied James's claim to be head of the judiciary.

> ***"I will not be content that my power be disputed upon; but I shall ever be willing to make the reason appear of all my doings, and rule my actions according to my laws."***
> James I, 1610

Under such celebrities as Ben Jonson and William Shakespeare, England continued the literary renaissance begun under Elizabeth. James was an intellectual who wrote verse as well as studies on witchcraft, politics, and religion. However, the common folk despised the king with the thick Scottish accent who had squandered England's wealth gambling and bestowing **exorbitant** gifts on favorites. It was suggested he be granted a state salary, but compromise over an acceptable sum was never reached. Instead, he took to selling honors; all propertied men were expected to pay thirty pounds to obtain a knighthood, or compensation should they decline. The country anticipated the succession of Henry, but his premature death placed the inept Charles in line to the throne.

exorbitant: exceeding appropriate limits; excessive.

By the time of his death in 1625, the flamboyant James had alienated both his English and Scottish subjects, allowing Parliament to assert its ascendancy. ◆

Jean

1921– ● GRAND DUKE OF LUXEMBOURG

Grand Duke Jean of Luxembourg, duke of Nassau, prince of Bourbon Parma, was born in the Castle of Berg in Luxembourg on January 5, 1921. He was the eldest son of Grand Duchess Charlotte and Félix, prince of Luxembourg, prince of Bourbon-Parma. Jean's godfather was Pope Benedict XV. He has been grand duke of Luxembourg since 1964, when Grand Duchess Charlotte formally abdicated, though he had been her representative as head of state since 1961. Grand Duchess Charlotte died in 1985.

Most of Jean's childhood was spent at the Chateau de Colmar-Berg. He received his primary and secondary education in Luxembourg, and he went to England to study at Ampleforth College in Yorkshire from 1934 to 1938. He returned to the Grand Ducal Palace in Luxembourg and from 1938 to 1940 he completed his studies under private tutorship by various professors.

In Luxembourg, a constitutional monarchy, the hereditary prince comes of age at eighteen, so on January 5, 1939, Jean assumed the titles of Hereditary Grand Duke of Luxembourg, Hereditary Prince of Nassau, and Prince of Bourbon Parma.

War, and threats of worse war, were already shaking Europe. When Germany invaded neutral Luxembourg on May 10, 1940 the Grand Ducal family and the government fled to neighboring France. The French government provided them with a chateau near Paris, but as the Nazis moved in on Paris, the Luxembourgers fled to another chateau in the south of France, and finally through Spain to take refuge in Portugal. The British royal family invited the grand duchess to London, and she and her cabinet set up a government-in-exile there.

In Luxembourg, the hereditary prince comes of age at eighteen, so on January 5, 1939, Jean assumed the titles of Hereditary Grand Duke of Luxembourg, Hereditary Prince of Nassau, and Prince of Bourbon Parma.

President Franklin D. Roosevelt sent a U.S. warship to Lisbon, Portugal, which took Prince Félix and the Grand Ducal children to safety. From the United States they went to Canada, where Jean studied law and political science at the University of Quebec. He also made radio broadcasts from New York to appeal to the American people to assist the oppressed peoples of Europe. On August 19, 1942, President Roosevelt invited Grand Duchess Charlotte, Prince Félix, and Hereditary Grand Duke Jean to a dinner at the White House. A short time later, Félix and Jean flew to Great Britain to enroll in the Allied Forces. Jean trained with the Irish Guards regiment, then took officer's training under instructors from the Royal Military College at Sandhurst. He was eventually promoted to lieutenant.

Meanwhile, in London, Jean was also president of the Luxembourg Society and president of the Luxembourg Relief Fund

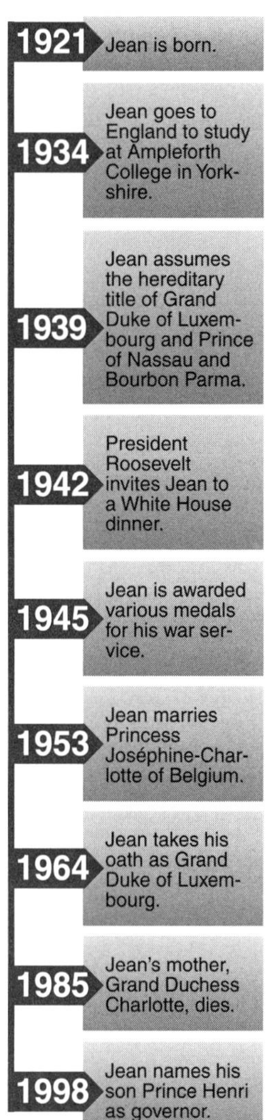

abdication: renunciation of a throne or high office.

in Britain. At the British Broadcasting Corporation (BBC) he broadcast further morale-building messages to the people of Luxembourg. Little Luxembourg, a country the size of Rhode Island, valiantly resisted Nazi rule; in a plebiscite in October 1941 only 3 percent of Luxembourgers favored joining the Third Reich, even though they were being showered with Nazi propaganda about the better world promised by Adolf Hitler. For his war service, Jean was awarded the 1939–45 War Medal, the 1939–45 Star, and the France and Germany Star.

On April 9, 1953, in the Cathedral of Luxembourg, Hereditary Grand Duke Jean married Princess Joséphine-Charlotte of Belgium. The Papal Nuncio, Monsignor Fernando Cento, conducted the ceremony, and gave the Papal blessing to the Grand Ducal couple.

From 1951 to 1961 the hereditary grand duke was a member of the Luxembourg State Council, guiding his nation's legal and political life. On April 28, 1961, Grand Duchess Charlotte appointed him her "lieutenant-representant," a position that gave legal effect to the delegation of Grand Ducal powers.

On November 12, 1964, after forty-five years on the throne, Grand Duchess Charlotte signed a declaration of **abdication** in favor of her son. On the same day, in a solemn ceremony in the Chamber of Deputies, Jean took his oath as Grand Duke of Luxembourg. A great celebration throughout Luxembourg was soon followed by Grand Duke Jean and Grand Duchess Joséphine-Charlotte's tour of the main towns of the grand duchy.

Luxembourg, traditionally a neutral nation, abandoned its "perpetual neutrality" through a constitutional revision in 1948. It was a founding member of both the United Nations (1945) and the North Atlantic Treaty Organization (NATO) in 1949. Luxembourg was also a founding member of the European Economic Community (EEC) in 1956, and joined with Belgium and the Netherlands in an economic union, signed in 1958 (effective 1960), known as the Benelux Economic Union. Luxembourg is home to many international banking firms, an industry that accounts for over half of its gross national product. A recent problem faced by the grand duchy has been its aging, shrinking population, with a resulting strain on social services and dependence on foreign workers.

In March 1998 Grand Duke Jean named his son Prince Henri as governor, the first formal step toward passing the crown on to the next grand duke. ◆

João VI

1767–1826 ● KING OF PORTUGAL

João was the second son of Queen Maria I and Pedro III of Portugal who became heir to the crown when his elder brother José died in 1788. In 1785 João married Carlota Joaquina, the daughter of the Spanish king Carlos V. When Queen Maria became mentally ill, João took the government in his hands in 1792 and was officially declared regent in 1799. With the invasion of Portugal by Napoleon Bonaparte's troops in 1807, he embarked with the royal family and his court for Brazil. After a short stay in Bahia, João chose Rio de Janeiro as the seat of his government.

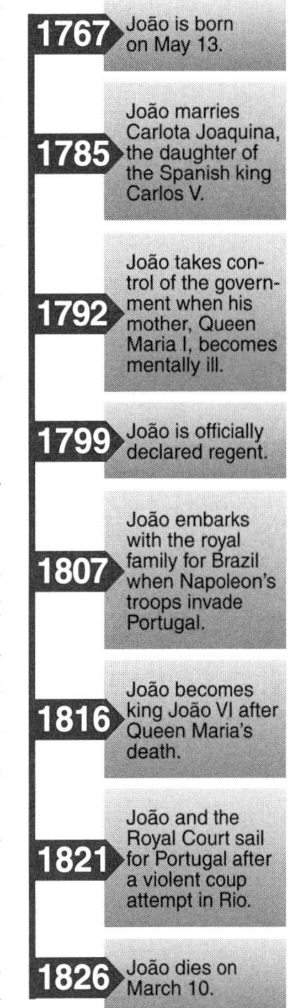

Among his first reforms was the opening of the Brazilian ports to international trade, which changed the colony considerably. The capital became crowded with civil servants, aristocrats, and foreigners, a **demographic** and cultural change for which the police intendant general, Paulo Fernandes Viana, sought to prepare the urban space. The regent and the royal family were housed in a *chácara* (farm) in São Cristóvão that had belonged to a rich merchant. The Portuguese elite took refuge in the beautiful neighborhoods, where they built the noble houses to which they were accustomed in Portugal. The downtown shops and warehouses occupied by Portuguese and foreign merchants began to display European goods and fashions. Court life contributed to the development of a luxury trade, and the lifestyle changed in many aspects: housing, furniture, transportation, fashions.

Dom João soon adjusted to the Brazilian environment and enjoyed the musical events in church and in the palace. Every day he received his subjects in a ceremony called *beija-mão*, and on special occasions he favored them with a promotion in military rank, an honor in the Order of Christ, or a public office in some part of the Brazilian territory. When Napoleon Bonaparte was defeated in Europe (1815), Dom João and the royal family were supposed to return immediately to Portugal, but the regent preferred to stay in Brazil. On March 9, 1816, after Queen Maria's death, he became King João VI.

The Pernambucan revolution of 1817 was the result of the struggle between **absolutism** and **liberalism** that began after the fall of Napoleon. The conspiracy was put down, but in Portugal

demographic: relating to population.

absolutism: the political theory that absolute power should be vested in one or more rulers.

liberalism: a political philosophy based on belief in progress and the protection of political and civil liberties.

the king's continued absence was a major grievance. In 1820 the commander-in-chief of the Portuguese army, the English officer William Carr Beresford (1768–1854), left for Brazil in order to warn the king of the **imminence** of revolution in Portugal and the urgent need for his return. João VI was not a man of quick decisions. He always listened to his ministers, and since they held differing views about monarchy, the constitution, and the cortes, the king delayed his return.

imminence: the state of being ready to take place.

After many ministerial discussions, the opinion prevailed that the king should return to Portugal, leaving his elder son, Pedro, in Brazil. João VI and the court finally sailed on April 26, 1821, after the city of Rio de Janeiro had been the stage of a violent coup attempt and the persecution of those who defended the immediate adoption of the Spanish Constitution of 1812—an unpleasant event for which the king was not directly responsible. Rather, they were the result of Pedro's personal interference and of his fear of a more democratic form of constitutional government. The years before João VI's death in 1826 in Portugal were troubled by the absolutist movement conducted by his younger son Miguel (1802–66) in 1823 and 1824. ◆

John I

1167–1216 ● KING OF ENGLAND

"No freemen shall be taken or imprisoned or outlawed or exiled or in any way destroyed, nor will we go upon him nor send upon him, except by the lawful judgment of his peers or by the law of the land."
Magna Carta, Article 39, 1215

John was born in Oxford on December 24, 1167, the youngest son of King Henry II (1154–89) and Eleanor of Aquitaine. In 1177 Henry named him lord of Ireland and sent him there in 1185 to consolidate English conquests between Dublin and Cork and set up a government. John did not succeed in either task and was recalled by his father. Henry died in 1189 and was succeeded by John's brother Richard I (known as Richard the Lionhearted).

Richard had little interest in governing England; he spent almost his entire ten-year reign defending his possessions on the European continent against Philip II of France (r. 1179–1223), known as Philip Augustus, and participating in the unsuccessful Third Crusade to recapture Jerusalem from the Muslims. When Richard was held for ransom by the Holy Roman Emperor on his way back from the crusade in 1192, John plotted against him, making futile attempts to seize the crown. Richard returned to England briefly in 1194 and forgave John; since Richard had no children, John became king on his brother's death in 1199.

John's reign can be divided into three periods. From 1199 to 1205 he fought for his French possessions against Philip Augustus. From 1205 to 1213 he was preoccupied with a struggle against Pope Innocent III (r. 1198–1216). From 1213 to 1216 John fought with the feudal nobility, a conflict that led to the Magna Carta, or Great Charter.

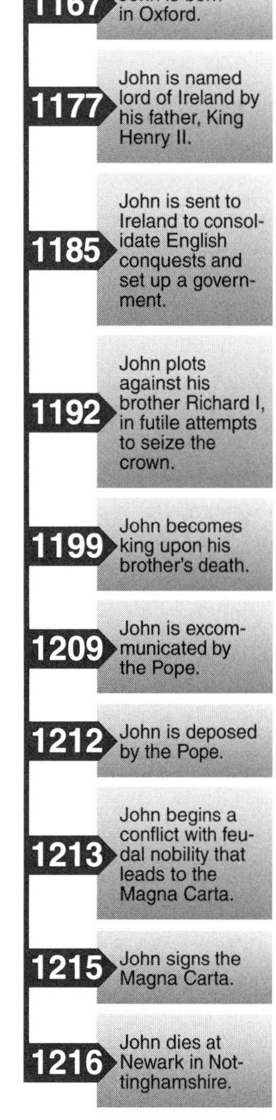

John's French possessions were not part of the kingdom of England; rather, they were held by John under various feudal titles inherited from Richard. In 1200 Philip, distracted by a conflict with the papacy, recognized John as the legitimate heir to the French lands. But in 1202, after a French court ruled that John had forfeited his titles by violating his obligations to one of his vassals in France, Philip initiated war against John. By the end of 1205 John had lost most of his possessions across the Channel, including Normandy, Anjou, Maine, Brittany, Touraine, and part of Poitou.

For the English as a whole, these losses meant a relief from the heavy taxes that had been levied for the defense of the French lands. But the military defeats diminished John's prestige. Also, since many of the barons lost their French possessions as a consequence of John's setbacks, they subsequently devoted more attention to their English holdings and therefore made greater efforts to restrict the power of the English monarchy.

In 1205 John rejected Pope Innocent's nominee for archbishop of Canterbury, Stephen Langton. John was merely exercising the traditional right of the monarch to control the appointment of bishops. But Innocent was aggressively dedicated to increasing the power of the **papacy**, and he retaliated in 1208 by laying England under an interdict, which meant that English churches were barred from conducting public functions. When John refused to give in, Innocent **excommunicated** him in 1209.

At first John managed to maintain the support of the nation. But he undermined his domestic backing through heavy taxation and the injustices he committed against the barons and other classes as he aggrandized his wealth and power. In 1212 Innocent deposed John, and reports circulated that Philip

papacy: the office of Pope.

excommunicate: to exclude from the rights of the church.

"Wherefore we will and firmly order that the English Church be free, and that the men in our kingdom have and hold all the aforesaid liberties, rights, and concessions, well and peaceably, freely and quietly, fully and wholly, for themselves and their heirs, of us and our heirs, in all respects and in all places forever, as is aforesaid."
Magna Carta, Article 63, 1215

vassal: a person under the protection of a feudal lord; a feudal tenant.

Augustus would invade England to implement the Pope's decree. Fearing that the barons would not back him, John gave in to Innocent in 1213, accepting Langton as archbishop and declaring his vassalage to the pope.

In 1214 John, hoping to regain his possessions on the Continent, joined a military alliance of Philip Augustus's enemies. Many barons believed that John would not succeed, and they resented a heavy tax imposed on them for a continental military expedition. They were also more interested in reforming royal government than in military adventures across the Channel. The campaign against Philip Augustus failed miserably, and when John returned to England late in 1214, he faced angry and rebellious barons. They began a civil war early in 1215 and won support among the clergy and the population in general.

Caught in a corner, John met the barons at Runnymede and on June 15, 1215, signed a document subsequently called the Magna Carta. The charter revived the idea of the feudal contract, in which both the king and his **vassals** were bound to fulfill their obligations, so for the most part its focus was upon guaranteeing the nobility its traditional rights within the feudal system. But in the long run the Magna Carta had a much greater significance. It established the principle that the monarch is not above the law. Also, the freedoms granted to the nobility in the document were eventually extended to all classes. The document is considered one of the great building blocks of English constitutional government.

Soon after John signed the Magna Carta, civil war broke out again. John was winning the conflict against the barons when he died at Newark in Nottinghamshire on the night of October 18–19, 1216. ◆

Joseph II

1741–1790 ● HOLY ROMAN EMPEROR

Joseph was the fourth child and eldest son of Maria Theresa and the Holy Roman Emperor Francis I. He was an "enlightened" despot who was at once a militarist and absolutist as much as he was a liberal humanitarian. Cold and calculating, he personally claimed that "a great king did not need to be loved, he only needed to be right." Maintaining that the empire required transformation, he introduced unpopular reforms to that end. His attempt to modernize and unify the ethnically diverse Habsburg Empire ultimately met with failure.

As a child, Joseph was difficult and reserved, concentrating endlessly on his studies. His marriage to Isabella of Parma in 1760 brought considerable, albeit short-lived, joy into his life: three years later his wife died of smallpox. His second wife, Maria Josepha of Bavaria, also died of smallpox in 1767, two years after their marriage. His father died in 1765, and Joseph was then elected Holy Roman Emperor and coruler, with his mother, of the Habsburg lands.

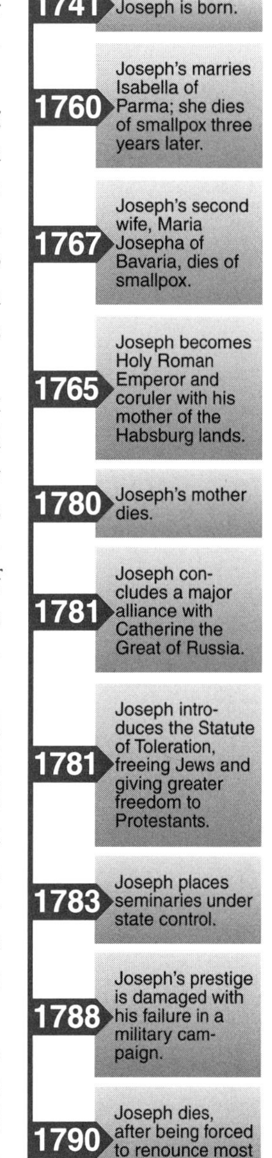

Dressing simply, usually in military uniform, Joseph was not interested in the ceremonial pomp of royal power. He perceived himself as the leader of a secular state, not the head of a divinely sanctioned empire. As an austere and dutiful statesman, he was committed to bureaucratic efficiency and meticulous organization. In 1768 he wrote to his brother Leopold, grand duke of Tuscany: "Love of country, the welfare of the Monarchy, that is genuinely the only passion I feel, and I would undertake anything for its sake."

Until the death of his mother in 1780, Joseph concentrated his attention on foreign affairs, aiming to strengthen imperial power. His attempts to rejuvenate his kingdom were thwarted by the aristocracy supported by Austria's chief enemy, Frederick II (Frederick the Great) of Prussia. A nominal alliance with France gained him leverage, and he temporarily solved the conflict of interest between Prussia, Russia, and Austria at the expense of Poland. The civil war in Poland (1772) provided for its partition, with Joseph acquiring Galicia and Bukovina.

The death of Maria Theresa gave Joseph absolute power in both the domestic and foreign spheres. In 1781 he concluded a significant alliance with Catherine the Great of Russia. Freed from worry about the east, the Austrians broke their treaty with the Dutch and pressed for the opening of the Scheldt River to benefit the Austrian Netherlands, giving them a route to the sea. The Dutch, however, protested, forcing Joseph to retract.

Joseph's first complete failure in foreign policy was his bid to exchange the Austrian Netherlands for Bavaria. Prussia protested and marched into Bohemia, a domain of the Habsburg Empire. Concurrently, Frederick the Great was persuading numerous German princes in the League of Princes to oppose

Joseph's power. In response, Joseph was forced to strengthen his alliance with Russia, and was propelled into the Russo-Turkish war of 1787 as a result. The campaign of 1788 was a disaster and Joseph's military prestige was damaged: open rebellion broke out in the Austrian Netherlands, and sporadic unrest in other parts of the empire.

Joseph's domestic policy called for increased centralization and despotic absolutism. Continuing his mother's policies, he sought to base his rule in a sound bureaucratic apparatus. In 1782 he concentrated his entire administration in two main offices in Vienna and Budapest. He imposed a system of districts according to population density, without regard to ethnic diversity, and attacked "regional peculiarities" by making German the official language of law and commerce throughout his lands; the link between Germanization and centralization was now forged.

In the economy and the area of civil law, Joseph sought to resolve problems that existed between the landowners and the peasants. **Serfdom** was abolished in the edicts of 1781 and 1782, restricting **patrimonial** justice and giving the peasants the right to move, marry, and change occupations. In return, they had to obey the state, pay taxes, and serve in the army. In compensation to the landed nobility, Joseph promoted mercantilist economic policies through free trade and moderate protectionism.

serfdom: the community of members of a servile feudal class subject to the will of their lord.

patrimonial: having to do with an estate inherited from one's father or ancestor.

Joseph's secularization of the empire caused the most unrest, leading to a breach in relations with the Roman Catholic church. He felt it was necessary to reform the church within his domain because it diminished the state's ability to rule absolutely. First, he introduced the Statute of Toleration (1781), which emancipated the Jews and gave greater freedom to Protestants. Then, he dissolved monastic orders and closed seven hundred monasteries. He went on to restrict the issuance of papal bulls, reorganized various dioceses, and placed seminaries under state control in 1783. Finally, he consolidated the educational system, limiting the church's role.

Foreign setbacks and domestic problems threatened to split the Habsburg Empire apart. The landed nobility in places like Hungary, Germany, and the Austrian Netherlands, remained strong enough to oppose reforms that were not to their liking. Lying on his death bed, Joseph was forced to renounce most of his reforms. In his policies, as in other **despotic** systems of the Enlightenment, new forms of freedom went hand in hand with new forms of restraint. ◆

despotic: of or relating to a ruler with absolute power and authority.

Juan Carlos

1938– ● KING OF SPAIN

King Juan Carlos of Spain (in full, Juan Carlos Alfonso Victor María de Borbón y Borbón) was born on January 5, 1938, in Rome, rather than in Spain, because his family was in exile. His grandfather, Alfonso XIII, had left Spain on April 14, 1931, after being deposed in a municipal election that revealed the monarchy's unpopularity and marked the beginning of the second republic. Alfonso was still in exile when he died ten years later. He was the last king of Spain from 1931 until his grandson Juan Carlos took the throne on November 22, 1975, two days after the death of General Francisco Franco. Shortly before his death in Rome, Alfonso XIII had renounced his rights to the throne in favor of his third son (the present king's father), Juan Carlos Teresa Silverio Alfonso de Borbón y Battenberg, Count de Barcelona (1913–93), popularly known as Don Juan. Don Juan married María de las Mercedes de Borbón y Orleans, and their first son was Juan Carlos.

"Let no one believe that his cause will be forgotten; let no one expect an advantage by a privilege."
Juan Carlos, 1975

Alfonso's marriage in 1906 to Princess Victoria Eugénie of Battenberg, granddaughter of Britain's Queen Victoria, introduced hemophilia into his family. Alfonso's first and fourth sons both died, and his second son, Jaime, renounced his right to the throne for medical reasons. His third son, Juan Carlos (Don Juan), was free of the disease.

When Alfonso abdicated in favor of Don Juan in 1941, Juan Carlos became next in line to the throne after his father. General Francisco Franco, the ruler following the traumatic Spanish Civil War (1936–39), had monarchist sympathies and was agreeable to a restoration of the monarchy in Spain, but only after his own death, and only if the future kings would accept the principles of his regime. This meant, in effect, that Don Juan must accept that he himself would not reign. In 1947 Franco passed a law of succession that

declared Spain a kingdom, with himself the regent until a king should be chosen; this meant that Franco was holding the Borbón family in waiting, but at a distance. More than twenty years later, in 1969, Franco formally named Juan Carlos as his successor—but again, not effective until the end of Franco's life.

Franco had personally overseen the planning of the prince's education and training. Juan Carlos had begun his first studies in 1946, at age eight, at the College Ville Saint Jean in Freiburg, Switzerland. Franco and Don Juan met twice (once aboard a yacht) to plan Juan Carlos's academic career. The prince came from Rome to Madrid in 1948 to study in Spain. At the second interview in 1954 it was decided that Prince Juan Carlos would be trained at the three military academies at Saragossa, Marín, and Cartagena, and in two of the colleges at the Central University of Madrid.

In 1961 Juan Carlos married Princess Sofía (b. 1938) of Greece, the daughter of Paul I (1901–64) and Federica (1917–64). Soon afterward, Franco designated Juan Carlos as his successor to take the throne upon his death.

On January 7, 1969, after many years of saying that his father's claim to the throne preceded his own, Juan Carlos said publicly for the first time that he would accept the throne if offered. On July 22 Franco presented to the Spanish *Cortes* (national assembly) a law designating Juan Carlos as the future king of Spain.

When Franco died in November 1975, the Cortes proclaimed Juan Carlos king, and a difficult transition toward democracy and national integration began. In his first official speech, the king affirmed his intention of ruling over all the Spanish, and returning their liberties. Juan Carlos set out on a series of trips throughout the kingdom and to foreign nations, and everywhere he went he repeated his commitment to democratization and integration of Spain.

It quickly became clear that the reforms the king wished to bring about were not going to move forward under the government of Carlos Arias Navarro, and soon Navarro was dismissed. The minister to help create the changes necessary for democracy was Adolfo Suárez, who came with the recommendation of Torcuato Fernández Miranda, the president of the Cortes. Suárez succeeded in carrying out the transition the king desired, including a bicameral legislature with both houses to be elected by the people. Remarkably, even the Cortes holdovers from the Franco period supported the changes, effectively voting themselves out of office. The king's reforms were ratified by a referendum in December 1976, and almost immediately the political parties Franco had outlawed were legalized. Elections in July 1977—the first since 1936—were a triumph for Suárez, and with a newly created centrist party, the Unión Central Democrática (UCD), he began the creation of a new state.

The new Constitution of 1978, passed by agreement among various political factions, satisfied the king's requirement that the transition be consensual, a cooperation that would satisfy most everyone. Juan Carlos had assumed **sovereignty** in 1975 in order to direct the nation's transition to a representative government, and now, having attained this aim, he transferred the sovereignty back to the people.

sovereignty: freedom from external control.

The Constitution of 1978 configured Spain as a state of autonomous regions, an arrangement similar to a federal system. In 1980 Catalonia and the Basque country were granted home rule following strong **plebiscite** victories. Since the time of Franco, a Basque organization, Basque Homeland and Freedom (in the Basque language, Euzkadi ta Askatasuna [ETA]), has insisted on total independence, and has continued to agitate violently for a separate Basque nation, to which the government cannot agree. Terrorist bombings, assassinations, and state crackdowns on the Basque separatists seem to be an unending source of trouble for the king and the government.

plebiscite: a vote by which the people of an entire country express an opinion for or against a choice of government or ruler.

The king's reforms were ratified by a referendum in 1976, and almost immediately the political parties Franco had outlawed were legalized.

Spain joined the Council of Europe in 1977, the North Atlantic Treaty Organization (NATO) in 1982, and the European Union in 1986. Under Prime Minister Felipe González Marquéz of the Socialist Workers party, Spain's gross domestic product grew by an average of almost 5 percent per year between 1986 and 1990, and business investment increased by about 10 percent a year. In 1992 world attention was brought to Spain with the Summer Olympics in Barcelona and the Universal Exposition in Seville.

Economic growth slowed in the early nineties, and unemployment rose to 22 percent. The elections in May 1996 brought the Popular Party and its leader, José Maria Aznar, to power. (The Popular Party was supported by the Basque and Catalan nationalists, though it was not officially affiliated with them.) In recent years Spain's economy has turned around and regained its former strength, though its unemployment remains the highest in the European Union.

King Juan Carlos has from time to time been beset by threats of coups, though none has seriously threatened his rule.

In February 1981 the ultrarightist lieutenant colonel Antonio Tejero and conspirators attacked the Cortes and held parliamentarians hostage, though the attempt was foiled and the members of the Cortes were released unharmed. Following the coup attempt, massive popular demonstrations proclaimed support for the government and the king.

King Juan Carlos has made many international trips to Latin America, the United States, the former Soviet Union, much of Africa, the Middle East, and Britain. He and Queen Sofía joined King Hussein and Queen Noor to celebrate the late Jordanian monarch's sixtieth birthday in 1995, a visit that included a trip to the renovated historic village of Taybet Zaman near Petra.

Crown Prince Felipe (b. 1968), the príncipe de Asturias, swore his oath in the Cortes when he reached his majority in 1986, and that same year, King Juan Carlos and Queen Sofía celebrated their silver wedding anniversary amid a great national celebration. Besides Crown Prince Felipe, King Juan Carlos and Queen Sofía have two daughters, the **infantas** Elena (b. 1963) and Cristina (b. 1965). ◆

infanta: the daughter of a Spanish or Portuguese monarch.

Justinian I

483–565 C.E. ● BYZANTINE EMPEROR

Although Justinian was born into an Illyrian peasant family, his illiterate uncle, Justin, was a senator who brought Justinian to Constantinople and provided him with a good education. Justin usurped the throne of Emperor Anastasius after his death and enjoyed the prerogatives of his position, leaving the management of the empire to Justinian. When Justin died in 527, Justinian became emperor. For the entire thirty-eight years of his reign, he was sensitive to the weakness of his claim to the throne and encouraged the concept of the divine right of kings, demanding whoever came into his presence to kneel and kiss his toes or the hem of his robe.

Justinian sought to create an updated, uniform code of law for the entire Roman Empire.

The historian Procopius, intimately acquainted with Justinian, wrote a biased book describing him: "insincere, crafty, hypocritical, dissembling his anger, double-dealing, clever, a perfect artist in acting out an opinion which he pretended to hold, and even able to produce tears . . . to the need of the moment. . . . He was a fickle friend, a truceless enemy, an ardent devotee of assassination and robbery." This might have been true, but he was also abstemious, amiable, accessible, generous, hard-working, eager to learn, merciful, and religious.

Justinian was deeply attached to Theodora, daughter of a bear master, whom he made first his mistress, then his wife, and finally empress. He granted her power equal to his own which she sometimes exercised in opposition to him. She was capable of both murder and mercy and her love of worldly pleasures moderated Justinian's monkish ways. A controversial version of Theodora's early life holds that she was a prostitute. This story may have stemmed from the fact that, as empress, she founded a convent of repentance for reformed prostitutes, banned brothel keepers from Constantinople, and became a strict moralist in her old age.

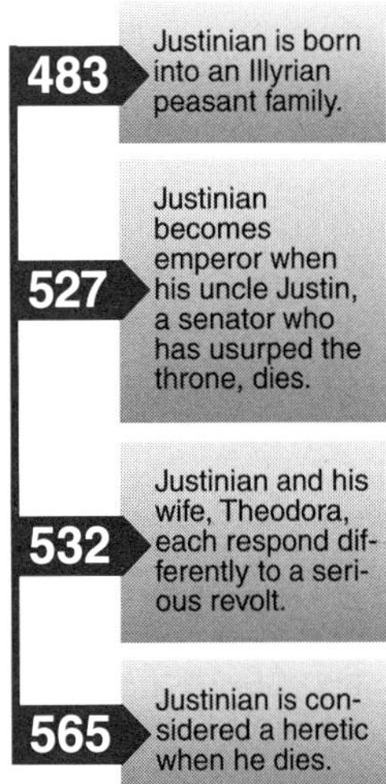

The response of Justinian and Theodora to the serious revolt they faced in 532 reveals much about their characters and their relationship. Justinian responded to the murderous, burning and looting mobs rampaging through the streets by hiding and trying to flee. Theodora called on the army, which mercilessly quashed the rebellion. Justinian then showed mercy to the rebels and their families.

Justinian's passion for unity shaped his reign. Militarily, he wanted to drive out the barbarians and restore one rule within the Roman Empire's old borders. He also wanted to end religious divisions, particularly the disagreements between the Eastern and Western churches. He sought to create an updated, uniform code of law for the entire Roman Empire, to replace the existing, often conflicting, jumble of laws from the multitude of nations within the empire.

The military achievements of Justinian's reign were due to his generals, notably Belisarius and Narses. His own contributions to his wars were diplomatic—he never fought in an actual battle. He would forge an alliance with potential foes, allowing him to concentrate his forces on one war at a time. The end of one war would mean the creation of a new alliance so he could freely attack his old ally. Despite a serious lack of both funds and soldiers, Justinian succeeded in doubling his territory. North Africa was to remain Roman until the Arab conquest and Italy was so devastated from eighteen years of war that it did not recover until the Renaissance. The empire would prove incapable of defending its expanded territory, and within a hundred years the rest of Justinian's conquests were lost and the Roman Empire was smaller than when his reign began.

He was responsible for an ambitious building program, the jewel of which was the Constantinople church of Saint Sophia (Hagia Sophia). To finance his projects he exacted heavy taxation and if the people rose up in protest, they were savagely massacred.

heresy: adherence to a religious opinion contrary to church dogma.

Justinian's legal reform, the Code of Justinian, was essentially rigid and conservative. It decreed severe punishment for **heresy** and sexual deviation, the inalienability of church property, the supreme authority of the emperor, and legalized serfdom. Justinian wanted to forbid divorce but was persuaded that that would increase the number of poisonings, so divorce laws remained quite liberal. The code was too severe to be widely enforceable, but it remained the law of the Byzantine Empire until its end and became a cornerstone of the Western legal system.

Justinian's efforts to resolve certain theological controversies failed. He was devastated by Theodora's death when he was sixty-five. He lost all interest in government after that and immersed himself in theology. Justinian ruled for seventeen more years, but rarely dealt with any of the series of disasters ranging from earthquake to an invasion of the Huns that plagued his empire. His theological studies took some strange turns, and he was considered a heretic when he died at eighty-three. ◆

Kamehameha I

1758?–1819 ● King of Hawaii

The islands of Hawaii were originally settled nearly two thousand years ago, when oceangoing canoes from the vicinity of Tahiti first pulled ashore. For most of their history, the islands were not united under a single ruler. Instead, they were governed under a loose network of *ali'i nui* (hereditary chiefs). It was not until the coming of Kamehameha I, also called Kamehameha the Great, that the eight islands were gathered together into a unified kingdom. And in the process this great ruler also founded a dynasty.

Kamehameha's rule, from 1796 to 1819, was a period of uninterrupted peace.

The first and greatest of Hawaii's kings, Kamehameha I was born to Keoua Kupuapaikalaninui, chief of the Kohala district of the island of Hawaii, and to chieftess Kekuiapoiwa of Kona. The exact date of his birth is uncertain but, as befits the legend of the founder of a ruling dynasty, traditional lore tells of the appearance of a "bright star" in the sky at about the time that he was born. This "star" may well have been Halley's Comet, first seen by astronomers in 1758.

At about the time of Kamehameha's birth, a *kahuna* (holy man) is said to have prophesied that this child would grow to become a "killer of chiefs," inciting fear among the powerful leaders of all the islands. As the time approached for the birth of her child, Kekuiapoiwa went to the royal birthing place in secrecy, for fear that nervous rivals among the chiefs would kill her infant. When Kamehameha I was delivered, his mother

Leis drape a statue of King Kamehameha I in Honolulu.

entrusted him to the care of a loyal servant, Nae'ole. Nae'ole hid the newborn away in the mountains of Kapaau, where he grew to manhood.

Few details are known about Kamehameha's childhood. He first enters the European historical record in 1778. When the famous explorer Captain Cook made an unsuccessful attempt to land at the island of Maui, his party was turned away by a contingent of native Hawaiians. One of the ship's company, Lieutenant James King, was so impressed by the regal bearing of one young native—none other than Kamehameha I himself—that he made special note of the meeting in his diary.

Kamehameha's obscurity was not to last much longer. In the mid-eighteenth century one of Hawaii's powerful traditional chiefs was Kalaniopuu, who ruled over the southern portion of the island. When Kalaniopuu died in 1782, his designated successor was his son, Kiwaloa, but his lands and authority were divided among many factions. At about this same time, Kamehameha I became leader of the northern portion of the island. With the support of many of the local *ali'i*, Kamehameha I challenged Kiwaloa for the throne. He would spend nine long years in battle against Kiwaloa before finally securing his rule, first over the whole of the island of Hawaii, then over all the other islands as well.

Kamehameha's rule, from 1796 to 1819, was a period of uninterrupted peace. During this time Kamehameha I welcomed commerce with European ships plying the fur and sandalwood trades in the Pacific. As Hawaii's importance in this trade grew, it earned ever-increasing attention from American and European economic interests. With the introduction of plantation crops, the islands began to attract greater numbers of foreign settlers.

Throughout this time, King Kamehameha I pursued a foreign policy that actively encouraged strong economic relations with America and Europe. But while Kamehameha I was willing to accommodate trade treaties and economic development, he was adamant about Hawaii's sovereignty—he did not permit foreigners to participate in island politics. He had no desire to see his nation annexed or its autonomy compromised.

During his rule Kamehameha I followed traditional practice by making several political marriages intended to secure alliances with the other powerful island families. Only one wife, however, could provide him with his heir and successor. This was Keopuolani—the "sacred wife" born to the same royal family as Kamehameha I himself. Her eldest son, Liholio, was born in 1799.

As was customary in Hawaii at the time, Kamehameha's heir, Liholio, was taken from his mother to be raised by another of the king's wives. This surrogate mother was Queen Kaahumanu. When Kamehameha I died in 1819, Liholio assumed the throne and adopted the dynastic name, becoming Kamehameha II, but Queen Kaahumanu exerted great influence over his rule from the start.

In the year following the death of Kamehameha I, the first Christian missionaries—a group from Boston—arrived on Hawaii. Among their first converts was Queen Kaahumanu. Although Kamehameha II did not himself convert, the queen's enthusiasm for the new religion encouraged its spread throughout the islands. Through her influence, Kamehameha II ended the traditional judicial system of *kapu,* in which the priests determined guilt and punishment. Further, Kamehameha II abolished local temples, effectively ending the divine authority of the kingship with this single act. At about the same time as the arrival of the missionaries, whaling was introduced in the islands, adding yet another attraction for American and European business interests. As the islands grew in economic importance, so also grew the number of foreigners, particularly Americans, who came to settle on Hawaiian lands.

Kamehameha II did not rule long. In 1824 he traveled to London with his wife and entourage. There his favorite wife contracted measles—a disease for which the Hawaiians had no immunity. She died, and her heartbroken husband shortly followed her to the grave.

Next in line for the throne was Kauikeaouli, Liholio's ten-year-old brother, born in 1813. As he was still too young to rule, Queen Kaahumanu served as regent. Through carefully chosen political marriages, she deflected rival claimants to the throne, keeping it in the Kamehameha line. She also influenced her young royal charge to convert to Christianity, making him the first of Hawaii's rulers to be wholly educated by the missionary schools.

Kauikeaouli took full rulership and became Kamehameha III upon the death of Queen Kaahumanu in 1836. The influence of his missionary education soon made itself plain. In 1840 he introduced a constitution that established a representative legislature, elected by all male citizens of the islands. Three years later, Hawaii gained recognition as an independent nation from America and the major powers of Europe. Unfortunately, the seeds of Hawaii's loss of that independence had already been sown. The new constitution, drafted under the **tutelage** of predominantly American settlers, laid the groundwork for the privatization of land, access to which up to now had been controlled by the chiefs. At the same time, the first sugar mills were introduced to the islands—bringing yet another economic attraction to replace the waning sandalwood trade and whaling industry. In the 1840s American business interests in the islands made their first attempt at annexing the kingdom to the United States. It was unsuccessful, but spoke of things to come.

tutelage: guardianship.

When Kamehameha III died in 1854, his nephew Alexander (Liholiho's son), who was born about 1820, stepped up to the throne and adopted the dynastic title of Kamehameha IV. During his brief rule he sought to reverse the trend of missionizing that his uncle had encouraged, and attempted to forestall political **annexation** by the United States by encouraging trade and diplomacy.

annexation: incorporation of a country or other territory within the domain of another.

By this time, however, the diseases introduced by Europeans and other non-Hawaiians (primarily Asians brought in to work on the plantations) had devastated the **indigenous** population, so that the king found himself ruling over an increasingly diverse population, of which native Hawaiians comprised a rapidly shrinking proportion. When he died in 1863—rumor has it of poisoning—there was no direct heir to the throne (his only son had succumbed to brain fever at the age of four).

indigenous: having originated in a particular region; native.

Instead, his brother Lot Kapuaiwa Kamehameha, born in 1830, succeeded him to the throne, becoming the last of the Kamehameha kings.

As Kamehameha V, Lot ruled only nine years. During his brief regency, he did away with the constitution of 1840 in an effort to return traditional powers to the royal family. In addition, he actively pursued a policy of expanding Hawaii's trade relations and began what would become a dangerous, and finally devastating trend of increasing the role of foreigners in internal affairs.

By the time of his death, Kamehameha V had not married and had produced no heir. The last of Kamehameha I's direct descendants, Princess Bernice Pauahi, refused to become queen, so the Hawaiian legislature was forced to choose the new ruler. They chose Lunalilo, of a **peripheral** branch of the royal family. He ruled for just one year, before he died of what was then called consumption (tuberculosis), to be replaced by David Kalakaua, in 1873. ◆

peripheral: the outward bounds of something.

Khalid ibn Abd al-Aziz Al Saud

1912–1982 ● King of Saudi Arabia

Khalid was born in Riyadh, the seventh son of King Abd al-Aziz Al Saud (known as ibn Saud the West), the founder of modern Saudi Arabia. Khalid's only full brother was Muhammad ibn Abd al-Aziz Al Saud two years his elder. It is ironic that Khalid, a modest and retiring man surrounded by brothers ambitious to exercise power, was fated to be king during seven of the most turbulent and dangerous years of his country's history.

Khalid's moral reputation was spotless, his tastes were simple, and his piety was genuine while lacking any fanatical edge.

Khalid received the prescribed education for a royal Saudi prince of his day—rote memorization of the Quran (Koran) and limited study of several practical subjects, together with first-hand observation of court politics. He did not pursue an overtly political career but, from early adulthood, played an important part in family councils and by his thirties had become part of the small circle of princes that would guide Saudi Arabia's affairs. Of all his brothers, he was, perhaps, the closest to the aloof Faisal. When only nineteen, he acted as viceroy in Hijaz during Faisal's absences, accompanied Faisal to the United

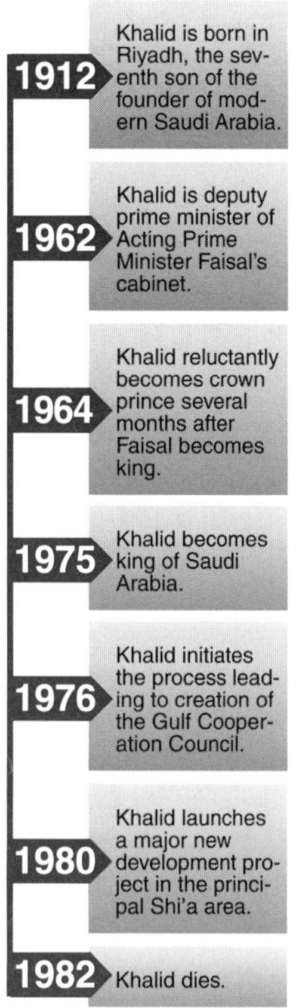

States in 1943, and was deputy prime minister in the cabinet that Faisal, acting as the Saudi prime minister, appointed in October 1962. Following Faisal's accession as king in November 1964, the senior princes and he pressed the reluctant Khalid to become crown prince. After several months of resistance, Khalid yielded to their pressure.

The selection was a wise one that served the country well when King Faisal was assassinated ten years later. Khalid was demonstrably neutral in the politics of the Al Saud family and represented to many family members a desirable check to putting excessive power in the hands of Fahd, crown prince under Khalid, and his full brother Sultan ibn Abd al-Aziz Al Saud, next but one in the succession. More important, his qualities of character were perfectly matched to the needs of the kingdom. Khalid's moral reputation was spotless, his tastes were simple, and his piety was genuine while lacking any fanatical edge. He exhibited none of the arrogance associated with many of the Al Saud and in contrast to several, especially his brother Muhammad, he possessed an equable temperament. Thus he frequently acted as an effective **conciliator** and **mediator**, a vital role in a society where all significant decisions are reached by consensus. Moreover, his obvious attachment to traditional bedouin values strengthened the Al Saud's links to the still important tribal element in Saudi society, and his old-fashioned fatherly manner connected the ruling family more firmly to the population for whom he was a comforting presence.

conciliator: one who gains goodwill by pleasing acts.

mediator: a go-between or diplomat.

All this proved critically important during a reign that encompassed Saudi Arabia's most rapid phase of economic and social development, the outbreak of the Lebanese civil war, the Camp David Accords between Egypt and Israel, the Iranian revolution, the seizure of the Grand Mosque in Mecca by Sunni Muslim ultraconservatives attempting to overthrow the Al Saud, the Soviet occupation of Afghanistan, and the outbreak of the Iran–Iraq war. All these events had represented severe threats to the kingdom. In the West, Khalid's retiring nature was mistakenly interpreted to suggest indecisiveness or passivity. In fact, although Fahd saw to the day-to-day conduct of affairs—an arrangement that suited both Khalid's inclinations and his delicate health—Khalid's authority was never in doubt. It was Khalid who acknowledged the legitimacy of some complaints that those who seized the Grand Mosque had raised and sought to address them. Following the 1979–80 disturbances among the long mistreated Shiites of the eastern province (al-

Hasa), he launched a major new development project in the principal Shia area and made a personal visit, the first time a reigning Saudi monarch had done so. His 1976 tour of the other conservative Gulf Arab states to discuss common security concerns initiated the process that led to creation of the Gulf Cooperation Council in 1981. Khalid's so-called interim rule eased Saudi Arabia through a critical period and paved the way to a smooth succession by King Fahd upon his death in June 1982. ◆

Kublai Khan

1216–1294 ● MONGOL EMPEROR

Kublai Kahn was born in the year that his grandfather, Genghis Khan, took Peking (Beijing). His connection with China took a more tangible form when he was granted lands there in 1236. The inhabitants fled but were induced to return when they realized that the young Mongol was implementing agrarian policies in the area, not the traditional nomadic policies of his forefathers. From 1251 to 1259 he led military campaigns in southern China and in 1260 succeeded his brother as head of the empire founded by Genghis Khan.

> ***"In Xanadu did Kubla Khan***
> ***A stately pleasure-dome decree:***
> ***Where Alph, the sacred river, ran***
> ***Through caverns measureless to man***
> ***Down to a sunless sea."***
>
> Samuel Taylor Coleridge, "Kubla Kahn," 1816

Kublai was elected supreme leader of the Mongols by a *khuriltai* (convention) of Mongol leaders in K'ai Ping, in northern China. This choice of location was to cast a shadow of illegitimacy over his reign since the *khuriltai* had traditionally been held in the Mongol homelands, and opposition to him was bitter. In the first year of Kublai's reign, his brother Arigh Boke was elected supreme ruler of the Mongols at a *khuriltai* convened in Karakorum, the Mongol capital. After several clashes, Arigh Boke surrendered in 1264, and was pardoned. However, those Mongol nobles who had supported him, especially Kaidu (who eventually became the de facto ruler of the Mongol homelands), remained hostile to Kublai's rule, considering it a dilution of the glorious Mongol nomadic tradition.

Since adaptation to agrarian and urban policies was seen by Kublai as the key to effective administration in China, his response to such accusations took the form of an aggressive foreign policy, aimed both at the Southern Sung dynasty, which ruled in the south of China, and at China's Indo-Chinese and

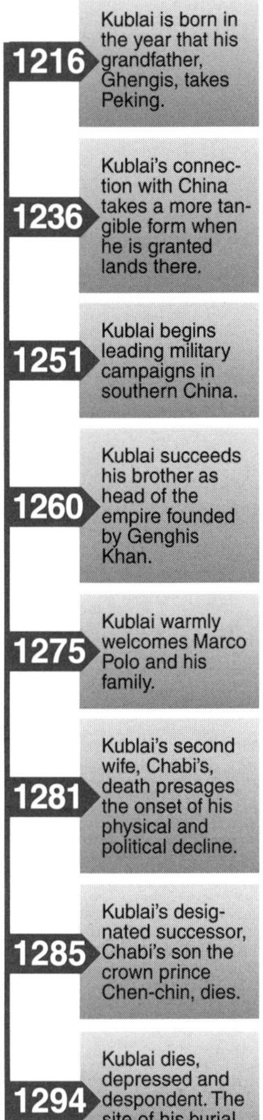

Japanese neighbors. In addition, Kublai abandoned the Mongol capital of Karakorum, and replaced it with Beijing, called T'aitu by the Mongols. The Turks called the town Khan-Balik, Marco Polo and the Italians called it Kanbalu or Cambulac, and Samuel Taylor Coleridge made Kublai's capital famous as Xanadu, site of the pleasure dome in his poem "Kubla Khan."

Early on in his rule, Kublai achieved a diplomatic coup in Korea—which had been conquered in 1258 by the previous Khaghan, his brother Mongke—by marrying his daughter to the Korean crown prince. Kublai's sobriety and thriftiness in his early years was manifested in his distaste for the Korean craftsmen who used pure gold in decorations on ceramics, a practice he declared to be unnecessary and wasteful.

Kublai's successes in China in terms of administration of a large and diverse area were remarkable. He gathered about him an extensive court, relying heavily on the advice of his Chinese advisers in the management of Chinese affairs, although senior administrative positions were open only to Mongols and foreigners. His main deviation from Chinese practice was in the abolition of the civil service examinations. In addition, he divided the population into four main groups: Mongols, other foreigners, northern Chinese, and southern Chinese. There was clear racial segregation, and the Chinese were forbidden to learn the Mongol language, to marry Mongols, or to carry arms.

Several new government institutions were established, including a secretariat to deal with most civilian matters, a privy council responsible for the supervision of military affairs, and a censorate, essential for the inspection of and reporting on all major officials and thus for the control of Kublai's huge domain.

A countrywide system of three types of paper currency was instituted, one based on silk and the other two backed by a silver reserve. The system of transport was greatly improved, tree-lined avenues were built, and postal stations established to facilitate delivery of mail. Merchants were among those who benefited greatly from the Mongol regime: Marco Polo and members of his family reached Kublai's court in 1275 in search of trade and were warmly welcomed. In line with Kublai's policy of giving foreigners key positions in the administration of China, Marco Polo acted as governor of Yangchow, near Nanking, for three years. He writes of the support given to merchants and artisans, to physicians, astronomers, geographers, and mapmakers. Theater blossomed under Kublai's rule, and colloquial language was encouraged, which strengthened the development of the novel.

Kublai's elaborate court was enhanced by his second wife, Chabi, who exerted great influence on imperial decision making. It was she who persuaded him to leave the assault on the Southern Sung until after he had dealt with the threat posed by Arigh Boke's counterclaim to supremacy over the Mongols, a decision that strengthened Kublai's position in subsequent campaigns. Chabi was inventive, resourceful, and **frugal**. Ever practical, she designed hats with a rim to be worn against sunshine, and a sleeveless garment for Mongol soldiers to wear in combat. She saw herself as a Chinese empress and encouraged her husband in his emulation of Tang Tai-Tsung, the great seventh-century emperor of the Tang dynasty. Her death in 1281 presaged the onset of Kublai's physical and political decline.

frugal: sparing.

Despite the efficient administration of the country and the Pax Mongolica, which enabled merchants to trade freely throughout Asia and Eastern Europe, the Chinese hated their foreign masters and resented their exclusion from the army and from high-ranking positions in the civil service.

In Japan, Kublai suffered a resounding defeat. Several delegations urging the Japanese to bring tribute to the Mongol court were ignored, and Kublai's ambassadors were often executed. Expeditionary forces were repelled by bad weather and by effective Japanese defenses in 1274 and 1281. The seizure of Champa's capital in 1283, the invasion of Tonkin (which was halted at Hanoi in 1285), and the defeat of the king of Annam in 1288 drained Kublai's finances, supplies, and manpower.

Theater blossomed under Kublai's rule, and colloquial language was encouraged, which strengthened the development of the novel.

Kublai, aided by the famous general Bayan, was more successful in his campaigns against the Southern Sung. The fall of Hangchow in 1276 signified the end of the Sung dynasty, and the last Sung emperor, aged nine, drowned near Canton in 1279. However, despite Kublai's economic support for the south following the conquest, Chinese scholar-officials refused to cooperate with him.

Following the death of his wife, Kublai's health deteriorated. He became obese, drank to excess, and suffered from gout, which he tried to alleviate by wearing special slippers made of fish skins. He was in financial difficulties, which, according to Chinese sources, were due to his three chief ministers during that period, each of whom was eventually dismissed or executed. Anti-Muslim edicts were enacted after Muslim merchants refused to eat meat that had not been ritually slaughtered that was served at a banquet hosted by Kublai. This added to the atmosphere of civil unrest. His designated successor, Chabi's son the Crown Prince Chen-chin, died in 1285. Depressed and despondent, Kublai died in his eightieth year. The exact site of his burial is unknown. The Mongol regime in China collapsed some seventy years after his death. ◆

Lebna Dengel

1496–1540 ● KING OF ABYSSINIA

Lebna Dengel succeeded to the throne of ancient Abyssinia (later called Ethiopia) in 1508 at the age of twelve. At the age of thirteen or fourteen he added to his title of king the further titles of King of the Sea and Friend of God, Pillar of Faith. A devout Christian, he believed that he alone was able to save and protect God's creatures. His sympathies always lay with the Church of Rome. With his throne established on justice and mercy, Lebna Dengel devoted himself to the study of the Scriptures and religious works, and to conversations with holy men.

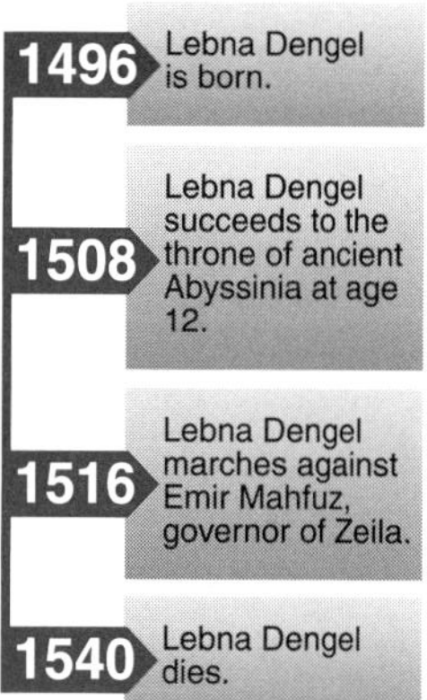

Lebna Dengel inherited the far-flung, crumbling empire built by his grandfather Baeda-Maryam (r. 1468–78), an empire that was further weakened by recently conquered feudal lords in the outlying provinces who were reasserting their regional authority. Lebna Dengel's kingdom extended from the port city of Mitsiwa on the west coast of the Red Sea south to Lake Langana and west to Abay Winz (the Blue Nile) and Lake Tana. On the east the kingdom was bounded by the lowlands of the Danakil, the Adal sultanate, and the southern Muslim states of Hayda and Ifat.

In 1516 Lebna Dengel marched against Emir Mahfuz, governor of Zeila, whose army of Muslim Adalites was making incursions against the Christian highlands. In a spectacular military victory, the Adalites were routed and Mahfuz slain. Lebna Dengel then invaded Adal, burned towns, destroyed fortresses, and laid waste the sultan's castle in Zankar.

With his throne established on justice and mercy, Lebna Dengel devoted himself to the study of the Scriptures and religious works, and to conversations with holy men.

The Portuguese mission to Abyssinia in 1520, which ended the isolation of the country from the European Christian world, referred to Lebna Dengel reverently as the legendary Prester John of the Indies, though he was not a priest. In 1527, the year after the Portuguese mission left Abyssinia, the invasions of the Christian highlands by the Muslims from the sultanate of Adal began. Sultan Abi Bakr transferred his capital to Harar, where his most forceful military commander, Imam Ahmad ibn Ibrahim al-Ghazi, nicknamed Grañ, "the left-handed," launched a jihad against the Christian kingdom. Grañ's invasion inundated nearly the entire territory of traditional Abyssinia, burning churches and monasteries and forcibly converting large numbers of Christians. Shoa province was conquered in 1531; Amhara and Lasta in 1533. Later to fall were Begemdir and Gojjam. With most of his empire fallen to Grañ, Lebna Dengel sought the active support of Portugal and other Christian powers but died before such assistance came. It was under the reign of his son Galawdewos that Portuguese forces ended the Muslim occupation of the Christian highlands in 1543. ◆

Letsie III

1963– ● KING OF LESOTHO

"The people here love their king. Their respect for him goes right across all sections of the community. He is a real unifying force."

Ron Cadribo, resident of Lesotho, CNN *World News Report*, October 31, 1997

Letsie David Bereng Seeiso, or King Letsie III, is the leader of Lesotho, a beautiful mountainous country surrounded on all sides by South Africa. Lesotho is small and has few natural resources other than water. Most of the nation's people live in small villages where they raise food crops and livestock.

In the early 1800s many attacks by such leaders as Shaka, a Zulu chief, scattered ethnic groups in southeastern Africa. A chief named Moshoeshoe (pronounced moe-SHWAY-shway) united several tribes and clans, and in 1824, led them to a safe mountain called Thaba Bosiu (Mountain of Night). He soon had about 21,000 followers. They became the Basotho people and eventually formed Basutoland.

In the 1830s white settlers from the Cape Colony began to invade Moshoeshoe's territory, and the Basotho fought them

numerous times. In 1868 Moshoeshoe asked Great Britain for help, so the British made Basutoland a protectorate. Moshoeshoe died in 1870, and the next year the Cape Colony annexed Basutoland. However, Great Britain resumed control in 1883.

Throughout Africa of the 1950s and 1960s, nations threw off their European colonizers, and Basutoland was no exception. In 1960 the nation established its own elected legislative council. Then Basutoland took a major step towards independence by writing a constitution and putting it into effect in the mid 1960s. The constitution established a constitutional monarchy with a two-part legislature. The first general elections under the constitution were held in 1965, and Chief Joseph Leabua Jonathan became prime minister.

On October 4, 1966, Basutoland officially became Lesotho, an independent nation. The nation's top chief, Oxford-educated Constantine Bereng Seeiso, became King Moshoeshoe II. However, in 1970, when the opposition seemed to be winning national elections, Jonathan voided the elections and declared a state of emergency. He suspended the constitution and parliament and exiled Moshoeshoe for several months.

Many hoped Letsie's ascendancy to the throne would bring an era of peace.

Further turmoil occurred in 1986, when Jonathan was overthrown and executive powers were formally vested in King Moshoeshoe. A military council took control, though, and Moshoeshoe was exiled in 1990 and officially dethroned. At this point, the military leadership temporarily enthroned Moshoeshoe's reluctant son, Prince Letsie David Bereng Seeiso, as Letsie III. In 1993 Lesotho ended this period of military rule when a new leader was sworn in as prime minister. Lesotho adopted a new constitution, in which the king was given no executive or legislative authority. Executive power went to the prime minister. Legislative power went to a national assembly, consisting of sixty-five elected members, and a senate, made up of traditional chiefs and nominated representatives.

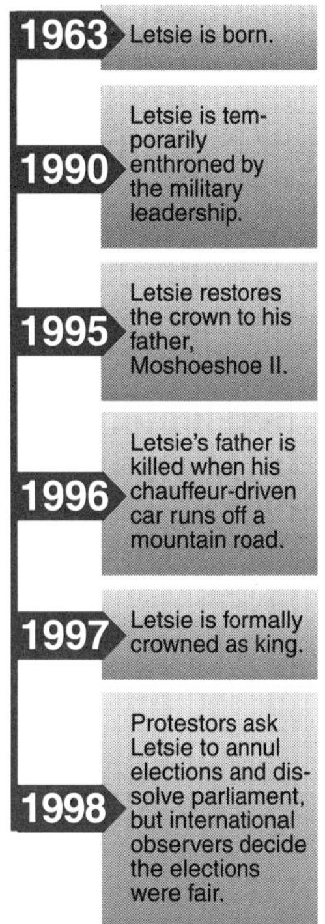

In 1995 King Letsie restored the crown to his father, Moshoeshoe II. However, on January 15, 1996, Moshoeshoe II, age fifty-seven, was killed when his chauffeur-driven car ran off a mountain road. He had been returning to the capital city of Maseru from inspecting his cattle herds. The people of Lesotho, along with such African leaders as Nelson Mandela, mourned their king of thirty-six years as he was buried on the plateau of Thaba Bosiu, considered the spiritual center of Lesotho.

On October 31, 1997, Prince Charles of Great Britain and several African leaders looked on as Letsie III was formally crowned king of Lesotho. More than 20,000 people cheered in Maseru's sports stadium when Letsie, age thirty-four, put on the traditional calfskin headband and a leopard-skin robe. A Basotho tribal chief then placed a long, gray feather in the new king's hair. Many hoped Letsie's ascendancy to the throne would bring an era of peace.

However, in 1998, Lesotho experienced more political struggle. After parliamentary elections of May 23, protesters claimed that the ruling party had rigged elections in which it won seventy-nine out of eighty seats. A ten-day protest vigil by thousands of people at the royal palace ended with a shoot-out. Shops in Maseru closed, and food was scarce. Protesters demanded that Letsie III dissolve parliament and annul the elections. In August, an international team of experts arrived to determine if King Letsie III should order a new election. All 150 international observers decided that the elections had been free and fair. In September, South Africa sent troops into Lesotho to end a military mutiny. Altogether, sixty people died in fighting around Maseru. In October Lesotho officials and opposition leaders agreed on a structure to hold the kingdom together until new elections could be held in 2000. South Africa agreed to withdraw half of its 3,500 troops.

The troubles coincided with Lesotho's worst period of hardship in years. The country's top export had been laborers sent to South Africa, where most worked in mines. This income declined as the gold industry cut back on imported labor. Lesotho placed great hopes in a project called the Lesotho Highlands River Project, conceived in 1986. The proposed dam would divert water from rivers in Lesotho to South Africa. The dam was expected to create many jobs for Lesotho's people and expand the economy, especially from the creation of electricity for Lesotho and payments from South Africa for water. The project was officially inaugurated on January 22, 1998. ◆

Liliuokalani

1838–1917 ● QUEEN OF HAWAII

Born into the Hawaiian royal family and tracing descent from a cousin of King Kamehameha I, Liliuokalani was the last of Hawaii's monarchs. She ruled the islands from 1891 until January 1893—the date she was forced to surrender her throne to American settlers at gunpoint.

Both of Liliuokalani's parents had served as councillors to King Kamehameha III. She grew up in the household of her aunt and uncle, Konia and Abner Paki—her aunt was a direct descendant of Kamehameha I. Young Liliuokalani was educated at the American missionary-run Royal School. Although she was briefly engaged to Prince Lunalilo (1833–74), who later became king of Hawaii, she married John Owen Dominis, the son of an American sea captain, in 1862.

Liliuokalani's ascent to the throne followed the death of her brother, King David Kalakaua, who had succeeded her erstwhile fiancé as Hawaii's ruler from 1874 to 1891. Her reign was heavily influenced by the actions of the two monarchs who preceded her to the throne—actions that led directly to the end of Hawaii's independence.

Lunalilo was the first of Hawaii's elected rulers not directly descended from Kamehameha the Great. He attained the throne in 1873 when Princess Bernice, the last living descendant of Kamehameha I, refused to become queen and Princess Ruth (half sister of Kamehameha V) removed herself from consideration. Lunalilo was not a strong leader and he suffered from consumption (now known as tuberculosis). As a result, he left much of the business of running the government to his cabinet, in which American businessmen had a disproportionate influence. These men were already actively seeking U.S. annexation of the islands.

Notwithstanding his brief engagement to Liliuokalani, Lunalilo never married,

Hawaiian king Kalakaua in 1881.

so when he died within a year of taking the throne the legislature once again was forced to step in and designate a successor. They chose David Kalakaua.

Civil turmoil greeted King Kalakaua's coronation. Although he was of royal blood, he was not directly descended from King Kamehameha I. Many wished instead to see Dowager Queen Emma, widow of Kamehameha IV, placed on the throne, but powerful American interests within the legislature secured his election. Upon his selection, rioting ensued—British marines had to be called in to quell the unrest.

After this inauspicious start, King Kalakaua concentrated on building up the sugar trade with the United States. This lucrative trade attracted powerful economic interests to the islands and increased the already quite large number of foreign settlers. At the same time, Kalakaua sought to strengthen the power of the Hawaiian monarchy, reducing the role of foreigners in Hawaii's government, by revising the Hawaiian constitution. Kalakaua's goal ran counter to the interests of the foreign businessmen who had established prosperous plantations and processing plants on the islands. In 1887 they struck back by

Iolani Palace

Iolani Palace, in downtown Honolulu, Hawaii, was the residence of the last king and queen of Hawaii. King Kalakaua began to build the palace (whose name means "royal or heavenly hawk") in the 1870s, sparing no expense. Many of its furnishings were made in Boston and shipped to Hawaii, and modern amenities such as electricity and telephones were installed. Before Iolani Palace was constructed, a temple and a smaller palace (destroyed by termites) had occupied the site. King Kalakaua moved into Iolani Palace in 1882. His sister Liliuokalani succeeded to the throne when Kalakaua died in 1891. When Hawaii's monarchy was overthrown by a handful of American and European businessmen in 1893, Liliuokalani was imprisoned in Iolani Palace for eight months. The palace served as the capitol of the post-monarchal Hawaiian government until the mid twentieth century. After Hawaii became a state in 1959, construction began on a new capitol building. Ten years later Iolani Palace became a historical museum, with restoration work carried out by an organization called Friends of Iolani Palace, which operates the museum.

forming the Hawaiian League, a secret organization comprised of American and European planters and colonists. With the assistance of the Honolulu Rifles, a militia organized within the European enclave, they forced Kalakaua to approve what is now known as the "Bayonet Constitution" in 1887.

This constitution extended the vote to American and European residents for the first time—and in so doing effectively disenfranchised the indigenous population, whose numbers had

"There is little question that the United States could become a successful rival of the European nations in the race for conquest, and could create a vast military and naval power, if such is its ambition. But is such an ambition laudable? Is such a departure from its established principles patriotic or politic?"

Queen Liliuokalani, 1898

enclave: a distinct territorial, cultural, or social unit enclosed within a foreign territory.

been disastrously reduced over the years through exposure to European diseases for which they had no immunities. The new constitution also forced the monarch into the role of "rubber stamp," requiring that he sign into law all bills presented by the legislature. Kalakaua thus became a figurehead, and took to spending his time on long trips away from the islands as he pursued an expensive European lifestyle.

When King Kalakaua died in 1891 of kidney disease, his sister Liliuokalani assumed the throne. She was no stranger to the duties of royal office, having served as regent during her brother's frequent absences. But she inherited a vastly diminished monarchy, subject to the demands of the plantation and trading interests of the American settlers.

To a woman of her pride and courage, this was an unacceptable state of affairs, and from the outset she sought to reinstate the pre-1877 powers of the monarchy. Relations with the American **enclave** were strained at best. When, forced by the provisions of the Bayonet Constitution, she signed into law a bill that favored the Chinese population by permitting the import and sale of opium, the Americans were outraged.

American settlers, under the leadership of John L. Stevens, then a U.S. minister to Hawaii, organized to overthrow this impudent queen. In 1893 the economically powerful American colonists called upon the U.S. Marines to support a revolt. Queen Liliuokalani was forced to step down from the throne, and a provisional government led by Sanford Dole, a wealthy plantation owner, occupied the government buildings in Honolulu. President Cleveland's own envoy confirmed the illegality of the settlers' actions, and the president himself went before Congress to condemn their treatment of the queen. Nonetheless, the American colonists refused to relinquish control of the islands, and in 1894 they declared the formation of the Republic of Hawaii, naming Dole as president. The new republic called for the United States to annex the islands, but President Cleveland refused their demands, once again deeming them illegal.

Through all of this upheaval, Liliuokalani was not without supporters. One man, Robert Wilcox, organized a faction of royalists among the native Hawaiian population who sought to restore her to her throne. This man, who had led an unsuccessful revolt against the initial passage of the Bayonet Constitution back in 1889, had become a hero to the indigenous people of the islands. In 1895 he used his prestige to lead an armed insurrection against the American usurpers. The rebellion lasted for ten days, during which time weapons were found buried in the queen's own garden. She was arrested, as were all the others who participated in the uprising.

Dole and his government ultimately freed the royalist rebels in 1896, and the queen a year later, but by this time there was no returning to monarchy for Hawaii and its people. Queen Liliuokalani appealed once again to President Cleveland, but although he confessed himself ashamed of the entire affair, he could provide no help. Within three years of the uprising, Hawaii was formally annexed, and became a United States territory in 1900. Upon her release from house arrest in 1897, Liliuokalani remained in Hawaii as a private citizen. In that year she composed the famous song "Aloha Oe" as a commemoration of and farewell to the Hawaii she had once ruled and always loved. She died of a stroke in her home in Honolulu in 1917. ◆

Louis XI

1423–1483 ● King of France

The son of Charles VII and Mary of Anjou, Louis XI had an austere upbringing and was married in 1436 against his wishes to Margaret of Scotland. When he was seventeen he joined the Praguerie, a movement of the nobility directed against the king and, in 1446, was exiled by his father, whom he never saw again, to Dauphiné. There Louis strengthened his position as a semi-independent ruler. After his wife died he married Charlotte of Savoy in 1452, who gave him five daughters and a son. In 1456, when his father approached Dauphiné with his army, Louis took shelter at the court of Philip the Good of Burgundy, with whom he remained until he succeeded his father in 1461.

> ***"I will not censure him, or say I ever saw a better prince; for though he oppressed his subjects himself, he would never see them injured by anybody else."***
> *The Memoirs of Philip de Commines,* an official of Louis XI, c. 1500

As king, Louis pursued from the start a policy designed to strengthen the monarchy in alliance with the urban middle classes. Of his father's councillors he retained those of lowly origins who were known for their antifeudal attitudes. His policies estranged him from his former protector Philip the Good, and provoked the formation of the League of the Public Weal, a movement among the higher feudal French nobility supported mainly by Burgundian forces, who opposed Louis. The League

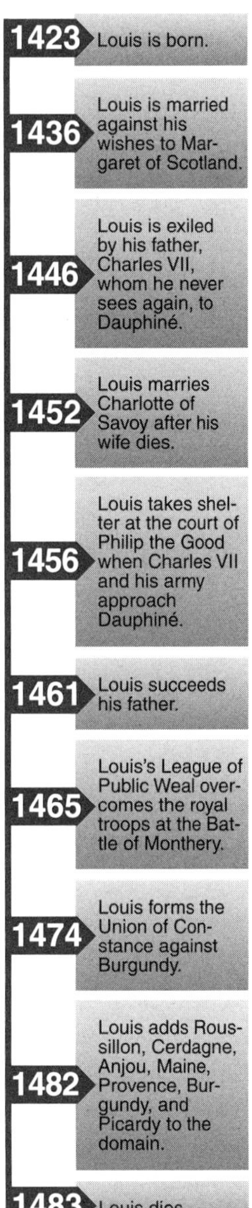

overcame the royal troops at the Battle of Montlhery (1465) and besieged Paris.

The king had to make concessions to the rebels but soon regained much of his losses. However, he found himself confronting the powerful alliance of England and Charles the Bold, duke of Burgundy. Louis scored the first victories. Then, in a meeting between the king and Charles the Bold (1468), the duke accused Louis of encouraging sedition among his subjects in Flanders, kept him captive, and released him only after he had signed a humiliating treaty. Louis responded by intensifying his repressive measures against the high nobility and by aiding the Lancastrians against Edward IV of England (1470). Not until two years later, when his own brother's death weakened the internal coalition against him, was Louis able to make real progress. He then forced the duke of Brittany to make peace and crushed the powerful house of Armagnac. In the meantime he continued successfully to wage war in the south, as a result of which the Pyrenees became France's southern boundary.

The struggle against Charles the Bold took longer and necessitated cooperation with foreign allies. In 1474 Louis formed the Union of Constance against Burgundy, with the Swiss and Sigismund of Austria. On his side, Charles called for help from Edward IV, who invaded France, but Louis met the king of England and bought him off with a substantial sum of money and the promise of an annual pension. The Swiss defeated the duke of Burgundy, who finally met his death at Nancy in 1477. Rid of his strongest adversary, Louis continued his successful repression of the recalcitrant French nobles and pursued his goal of suppressing feudalism and achieving the unity of France. He added to the royal domain Roussillon, Cerdagne, Anjou, Maine, and Provence, and took over Burgundy and Picardy (1482).

Louis XI was the true architect of the centralized French monarchy. He made the *taille*, a property tax paid by all except the nobles and the clergy, the main source of government revenue, to which were added the *gabelle*, the salt tax, and other indirect taxes. He expanded the economy by introducing the silk industry to Lyons, and encouraged the production of textiles in the north of France. Traveling constantly around the kingdom, he ran the government while being in direct contact with his people. He was, however, resistant to any restraint on his personal authority and was continually at odds with the *parlement* of Paris. A brilliant diplomat, a compulsive talker, and totally unscrupulous, Louis practiced a brand of **Machiavellianism** that was tempered by religious piety. He built shrines, endowed many churches, prayed often, and went on pilgrimages, but this behavior may have been designed to keep the support of the church.

Machiavellianism: the view that politics is amoral and that any means however unscrupulous can be used in achieving power.

Louis XI is described as a tireless worker, though physically weak and ugly, with a long hooked nose. He dressed simply and was recognized by his old felt hat. Yet the "Spider," as he was nicknamed, was the greatest European monarch of his time. ◆

Louis XIV

1638–1715 ● KING OF FRANCE

Known as the Sun King and as the Great Monarch, Louis XIV was the builder of Versailles and his reign marked the climax of monarchical absolutism in France. He was born in Saint-Germain-en-Laye and was nicknamed le Dieudonné, "the gift of God," because the marriage of his father, Louis XIII, and Anne of Austria had been barren for more than twenty years and many had given up hope of an heir to the Bourbon throne.

He was only four years old when his father died. His mother served as regent, but it was her adviser Cardinal Mazarin who really ruled. In 1648, when Louis was nine years old, the nobles and the Paris *parlement* (law court) rebelled against the crown, beginning the civil war known as the Fronde (1648–53). His experiences during these turbulent years taught Louis that divine authority was not enough to rule a kingdom, but that he also needed a powerful army. As a result, his reign was marked by a distrust of the Paris *parlement*, the nobility, and his capital city. In 1653 Mazarin proved victorious over the rebels and continued in his task of creating a strong administration and teaching Louis the art of statehood. Although Louis had now been proclaimed of age, he did not dare to dispute Mazarin's right to govern.

In 1660 Louis married his cousin, the Spanish infanta Marie-Thérèse. For this political alliance he sacrificed his true love for Marie Mancini, the niece of Mazarin. This attempt to ratify peace between Spain and France later gave France a legal claim to a portion of the Spanish inheritance, Louis claiming that the dowry, in consideration of which Marie-Thérèse had renounced her rights to the Spanish inheritance, had never been paid. This marriage was Mazarin's last act of state, for he died the following year.

> ***"Considering how advantageous it would be to this realm to reestablish its foreign and domestic commerce . . . we have resolved to establish a council particularly devoted to commerce, to be held every fortnight in our presence, in which all the interests of merchants and the means conducive to the revival of commerce shall be considered and determined upon, as well as all that which concerns manufacturers."***
>
> Louis XIV, 1664

Louis now declared his intention to assume all responsibility for governing the kingdom. His statement "L'etat, c'est moi" ("I am the state") aptly personifies his reign, for without his permission nothing could be signed, "not even a passport."

In taking power into his own hands Louis profited by inheriting experienced ministers from Mazarin. Jean-Baptiste Colbert developed industry and commerce on mercantilist principles and opened up colonial trade. The war minister, the Marquis de Louvois, built up the army and the navy. With their assistance Louis laid the foundations for absolute monarchism. In 1665 he ordered the *parlement* to register royal edicts without discussion. A police system was created in Paris and *intendants* (executive agents) were established permanently in the provinces.

In his foreign policy, Louis sought to achieve ultimate power and control. When Philip IV of Spain died in 1665, Louis used his marriage as an excuse for the War of Devolution (1667–68), as a result of which he received part of Flanders, although the Dutch then established the Triple Alliance (England, Holland, and Sweden) to oppose him. In 1672 Louis attacked the Dutch, which resulted in his annexation of Franche-Comté but brought on financial problems. Louis now abandoned war for diplomacy and sought legal grounds to lay claim to various cities, which he then annexed. He seized the German town of Strasbourg in 1681, securing it by treaty three years later. Europe now feared him and he was faced with a broad **coalition** when he attacked the Holy Roman Empire in 1688. This war ended in the Treaty of Rijswijk (1697), through which Louis forfeited most of the territories he had gained since 1679, except for Strasbourg. His last war, the War of Spanish Succession (1701–14), had to be fought in the Netherlands and in Italy, and Louis suffered a series of defeats. It left France in

coalition: a temporary alliance of distinct parties or states for joint action.

debt and deprived of colonies, but Louis's grandson did obtain the Spanish throne. Louis, however, had brought France to the verge of ruin.

Louis's other attempts at achieving glorification of the crown involved the building of a lavish palace on a swamp at Versailles. As well as adding to his own sense of importance, this served as a means to remove the court and administration from the politically unstable capital. In addition, Louis used the creation of a magnificent new court as the means to distract the court nobles by luring them into a hedonistic lifestyle, thus ensuring that they could not be plotting against him elsewhere. His reign was an era of great culture: the period of Jean Racine, Pierre Corneille, and Jean-Baptiste Moliere. However, the heavy taxation he imposed for his luxury and ostentation almost bankrupted France.

In his personal life the king had a series of mistresses, among them Louise de la Vallierè and Madame de Montespan, the wife of the prince of Monaco. The queen died in 1683, leaving behind only one living child (out of six), the grand **dauphin**, born in 1661. With her beauty vanishing and rumors of witchcraft and poisoning affecting her reputation at court, Madame de Montespan was replaced by Madame de Maintenon, the former governess of the Montespan children, as the object of Louis's affections. After the death of the queen, Louis secretly married her and under her influence adopted a more pious lifestyle. However, with advancing years and the result of overindulgence, Louis's health began to suffer and between 1684 and 1686 he had three operations.

With the onset of failing health combined with his newfound sense of piety, Louis turned his attention to religious affairs. Although at the outset he was tolerant of dissent, he now wished to impose religious uniformity. His persecution of the Huguenots led to the revocation of the Edict of Nantes in 1685, causing the emigration of half a million Protestants from France. Many of them were merchants and skilled artisans and their departure further crippled the economy. His actions also alienated the Protestant powers, eventually costing France its supremacy.

Louis died at the age of seventy-seven and his body was taken to the abbey church of Saint-Denis. The grand dauphin and his son, the duke of Burgundy, had already died (1711 and 1712, respectively), and the latter's only surviving son, Louis's five-year-old great-grandson, was not expected to live (but

dauphin: the eldest son of a king of France.

recovered, to succeed him as Louis XV). Louis had distrusted his nephew, the duke of Orléans, and had wanted to leave the task of governing to his son by Madame de Montespan. Toward this end Louis had written a will detailing his intentions, but after his death the will was annuled by the Paris *parlement*, anxious to regain powers lost during Louis's reign. In a famous scene the dying king bade farewell to the future Louis XV and warned him, "Do not imitate my wars and my love of building." ◆

Louis XVI

1754–1793 ● KING OF FRANCE

> ***"A king should die on his feet."***
> Louis XVI, on his deathbed, attributed

Louis XVI was the third son of the dauphin Louis and his consort Maria Josepha of Saxony, grandson and successor of Louis XV. In 1770 he married Marie Antoinette, an Austrian archduchess and daughter of Maria Theresa and the emperor Francis I. In 1774 Louis acceded to the throne totally devoid of the personal qualities necessary to govern France at a time of social and political turmoil. Lacking in self-confidence, shy and awkward, he was easily subject to the political agenda of his court intimates.

Faced with an ineffective king, reforms introduced by the finance controller, Anne-Robert-Jacques Turgot, were easily resisted by the court alliance. In 1787, unable to ward off bankruptcy, the king convoked the Assembly of Notables to ask their consent to tax the privileged classes. A few minor reforms were accepted but the assembly refused to consent to taxation, referring the matter to the Estates-General (the representative assembly of the three "estates": the nobility, the clergy, and the people). In 1789 Louis finally summoned the Estates-General, but his resistance to the combined meeting of the estates resulted in the third estate proclaiming itself a national assembly. Undeterred, Louis ordered the estates to assemble but to vote as separate bodies, but on June 27, 1789, he was forced to capitulate and allow the estates to sit together and vote as individuals. Suspicious of the French guards, he sent troops to Paris in the hope of suppressing any pro-assembly sentiments. This action combined with the dismissal of his finance minister, Jacques Necker, was seen as an attempt by the king to subvert the assembly and prompted the storming of the Bastille on

July 14, 1789. Faced with such violent opposition Louis was forced to withdraw his royal troops, retain Necker, and accept the new national red, white, and blue cockade, symbol of the revolutionaries.

Despite outward appearances to the contrary, and encouraged by his wife and court intimates, Louis continued to oppose the revolutionaries. In August he refused to approve the abolition of feudal rights and as a result of his persistent refusal to accept **populist** demands, a mob marched on Versailles on October 6, 1789, and forced the royal family to return to Paris where they were confined in the Tuileries palace.

Louis's fate was finally sealed when in June 1791 the royal family attempted to escape. Disguised as a servant of his children's governess, Louis was detected and apprehended by the mayor of Varennes and an innkeeper from a neighboring village. The attempted escape was seen as proof of Louis's **treasonable** contacts with émigré circles and he was forced to accept the constitution of 1791.

Following his return, Louis concentrated his efforts on the intervention of foreign powers. During this period, he was in constant communication with Austria and Prussia, imploring them to intervene on his behalf. In 1792 the outbreak of the war with Austria, combined with the duke of Brunswick's threat to destroy Paris if the royal family were harmed, enraged the revolutionaries and on August 10 the Tuileries was captured by the people of Paris and the provincial militia. The royal family was imprisoned, the king's powers suspended, and on September 21 the first French republic was proclaimed.

In November documents discovered in an iron chest in the Tuileries after the fall of the king proved his correspondence with the émigrés and his desire to subvert the constitution. Louis was indicted on December 11, charged with plotting against the nation, with paying troops raised by the émigrés abroad, and with attempting to overthrow the constitution. Once he appeared before his judges, the members of the Convention, his conviction for the high political crimes of which he was accused was assured. His stubborn refusal to recognize the authority of the evidence against him created a bad impression. The chief plea of his leading defense counsel, that the king was inviolate under the terms of the constitution of 1791, proved useless. A unanimous verdict of guilty was returned against the king and he was condemned, 387 votes to 334. As twenty-six of the majority had been in favor of an amendment for suspending

populist: relating to the belief in the rights and virtues of the common people.

treasonable: relating to the offense of attempting to overthrow the government or to kill or injure the sovereign.

guillotine: to behead by means of a machine with a heavy blade that slides down in vertical guides.

the death sentence, a fresh vote was taken on the deferment of execution and the final decision to execute Louis was taken by a majority of seventy. On January 21, 1793, he was **guillotined** in what had formerly been the Place Louis XV, now renamed the Place de la Revolution. Marie Antoinette suffered the same fate in October.

As France's final monarch preceding the revolution of 1789, Louis XVI proved incapable of responding to the demands of his position. With his easygoing temperament and slow-witted approach, he was easily manipulated by the court reactionaries. This complete subservience caused him to adopt a policy of sheer inaction, the consequences of which sealed his fate. ◆

Mahmud II

1785–1839 ● Ottoman Sultan

Mahmud, youngest of twelve sons of Sultan Abdülhamit I, ascended the throne on July 28, 1808, through a chain of accidental events. An armed coup led by the provincial ruler Mustafa Bayrakdar was intended to restore the deposed Sultan Selim III (1789–1807). During the military operation, however, Selim was killed, Mustafa was deposed, and Mahmud, the only legitimate candidate of the Ottoman dynasty, was declared sultan. Until he ascended the throne, Mahmud had spent his life in seclusion.

During the first months of Mahmud's reign, real power was wielded by Bayrakdar, who had himself appointed grand vizier. In mid-November 1808, Bayrakdar's government was overthrown by the janissaries of Constantinople (now Istanbul), who then set up a reign of terror and once again began to interfere in state affairs. The anarchy that had prevailed in the capital since the fall of Selim III in May 1807 left the political elite hopelessly divided and demoralized. Mahmud, demonstrating strong leadership and dedication to traditional values, gradually assembled a coalition of religious and political leaders desiring the reestablishment of

orderly government. Throughout his reign he endeavored to strengthen the court's position by subordinating all other political forces.

War with Russia, which had begun in 1806, was concluded with the Treaty of Bucharest (May 28, 1812), by which the Ottomans ceded Bessarabia to Russia. Meanwhile, Mahmud had initiated a policy designed to restore central authority over the provinces, and when the war ended this became his primary concern. By 1820 he had reasserted Constantinople's control over most of the provincial centers in Anatolia as well as Thrace, Macedonia, and the Danube districts. Local rulers were replaced by governors appointed from Constantinople.

The Serbs had twice risen in rebellion (1804–13, 1815). Under Russian pressure, Mahmud agreed to grant them complete autonomy (1829). In February 1822, after almost two years of warfare, the government defeated and executed the rebellious Tepedelenli Ali Pasha, the most powerful *a yan* (local ruler) in Albania and Greece. This drawn-out conflict aided the Greeks, who rose up in arms in March 1821. The Ottoman forces subdued the Greek uprising in Macedonia and Thessaly but could not advance into the Peloponnesus, and a stalemate ensued. Mahmud appealed to Muhammad Ali, the governor of Egypt, for assistance, promising to cede to him the governorships of Crete and the Peloponnesus in return for his services. In February 1825 Egypt's newly formed, European-style army landed in Greece. The Ottomans renewed their attacks, and by April 1826, with the fall of the key fortress of Missolonghi, the Greek position became desperate.

Since early in his reign Mahmud had been cautiously introducing significant improvements in the military, especially in the artillery and the navy. In the spring of 1826, with his authority restored at the capital and in many provinces, and with the Greek uprising appearing close to extinction, Mahmud decided that the time had come for more comprehensive reforms. The first project was reorganizing part of the janissary corps as an elite unit of active soldiers called Eskinciyan. Mahmud enlisted the support of the religious and bureaucratic elites as well as the janissary officers themselves. Nevertheless, on the night of June 14 the janissaries rose up in arms. Mahmud mustered loyal troops, and on June 15 the rebellion was crushed with considerable bloodshed. Two days later an imperial decree abolished the janissary corps.

It is difficult to exaggerate the impact that the suppression of the janissaries had on Ottoman society and in Europe. In an effort to gain universal approval, the regime called the incident "the Beneficial Affair" (Vaka-i Hayriye). The Eskinciyan project was abandoned in favor of a more ambitious plan calling for the formation of an entirely new army organized and trained on Western models. The new force was named the Trained Victorious Troops of Muhammad (Muallem Asakir-i Mansure-yi Muhammadiye; Mansure, for short).

Since early in his reign Mahmud had been cautiously introducing significant improvements in the military, especially in the artillery and the navy.

Meanwhile, the plight of the Greeks elicited European intervention. Britain, Russia, and France offered mediation. When the Ottomans objected, the three powers sent their fleets to Greece, where on October 20, 1827, inside the harbor of Navarino, they destroyed an Ottoman Egyptian fleet. This was followed in May 1828 by a Russian offensive. The Russian army captured Adrianople (now Edirne) on August 20, 1829, and threatened to advance on Constantinople. The war was concluded by the Treaty of Adrianople (September 14, 1829). The Ottomans ceded to Russia the Danube delta in Europe and the province of Akhaltsikhe (Ahisha) in Asia. In addition they were required to pay Russia a sizable indemnity and to recognize the autonomy of Serbia, Moldavia, Wallachia, and Greece under Russian protection. Later, in negotiations among the European powers, it was determined that Greece should become an independent monarchy. In July 1832 Mahmud accepted these terms.

Military defeat and the apparent failure of the government's attempts to reform the army rekindled unrest and rebellion in far-flung provinces, especially in Bosnia, Albania, eastern Anatolia, and Baghdad. The government was generally successful in suppressing these uprisings by employing the new disciplined troops, who proved effective as an instrument of coercion and centralization.

Meanwhile, Muhammad Ali sought compensation for his losses in Greece and demanded that Mahmud **cede** to him the governorship of Syria. When this was rejected, Egypt's army invaded Syria (October 1831), defeated three Ottoman armies, marched into Anatolia, occupied Kütahya (February 2, 1833), and was in a position to march on Constantinople. Mahmud sought help from the great powers, but only Russia dispatched a naval force to defend Constantinople (February 1833). This induced Britain and France to offer mediation, resulting in

cede: to yield or grant, typically by treaty.

the Peace of Kütahya (April 8), which conferred on Muhammad Ali the governorship of Syria and the province of Adana. Meanwhile, Russia's paramountcy in Constantinople was underscored by the Treaty of Hünkâr-Iskelesi (July 8), a Russian–Ottoman defensive alliance. The treaty alarmed other powers, especially Britain, which decided to help the Ottomans free themselves of their dependence on Russia.

During Mahmud's reign, the Ottoman empire continued to weaken in relation to the West. Its dependence on Europe increased, and it continued to suffer military humiliation and territorial losses.

Despite military disasters and political setbacks, during the 1830s Mahmud proceeded with his reform measures. He continued to focus on centralization of government and greater efficiency in its work. In 1835 he reconstituted the entire administration into three independent branches: the civil bureaucracy (*kalemiye*), the religious–judicial hierarchy (*ilmiye*), and the military (*seyfiye*). Their respective heads—the grand vizier, the *seyhülislam*, and the *ser asker*—were considered equal and were responsible directly to the sultan. The aggrandizement of the court, now the seat of all power, was mainly at the expense of the grand **vizier's** office. Traditionally the grand vizier was considered the sultan's absolute deputy (*vekil-i mutlak*) and, as such, the head of the entire government. To underscore the reduction of his authority, in 1838 the grand vizier's title was officially changed to chief deputy, or prime minister (*bas vekil*). At the same time his chief assistants were given the title of minister (*nazir*, later *vekil*). Consultative councils were established to supervise military and civil matters and to propose new legislation. The highest of these, the Supreme Council for Judicial Ordinances (Meclis-i Vala-yi Ahkam-i Adliye), established in 1838, acted as an advisory council to the sultan.

vizier: a high executive officer of the Ottoman empire.

The military, which during Mahmud's last years was allocated about 70 percent of the state's revenues, continued to be the focal point of reform. Most significant was the gradual extension of the authority of the commander in chief (*ser asker*) of the Mansure corps over other services and branches. His headquarters (*bab-i ser asker*) gradually came to combine the roles of a ministry of war and general staff, and was in charge of all land forces. The navy continued to operate independently under the grand admiral, whose administration comprised a separate ministry.

In May 1835 an Ottoman expeditionary force occupied Tripoli in Africa, claiming it back for the sultan. In the following years, Ottoman fleets appeared several times before Tunis, but were turned back by the French navy. The continued occupation of Syria by Muhammad Ali could not be tolerated by the autocratic Mahmud. In the spring of 1839, believing that his army had sufficiently recovered and that a general uprising in Syria against Egypt's rule was imminent, Mahmud precipitated another crisis. On June 24 the Egyptians decisively routed the Ottoman army at Nizip. Mahmud died on July 1, probably before learning of his army's defeat.

During Mahmud's reign, the Ottoman empire continued to weaken in relation to the West. Its dependence on Europe increased, and it continued to suffer military humiliation and territorial losses. Yet within the reduced confines of his realm, Mahmud's achievements were considerable. He resurrected the sultan's office, and reformed and rejuvenated the central government. He arrested the disintegration of the state and initiated a process of consolidation. In spite of his intensive reform activities, Mahmud was inherently dedicated to traditional values. He did not attempt to alter the basic fabric of Ottoman society, but rather to strengthen it through modern means. He generally succeeded in integrating the old elites into the new institutions. This was in keeping with his strong attachment to the ideal of justice in the traditional Ottoman sense. The sobriquet he selected for himself, Adli (the Just or Lawful), is an indication of the cast of his mind. Though he may not have intended it, Mahmud's reforms produced basic change and launched Ottoman society on the course of modernization in a final and irrevocable manner. ◆

Though he may not have intended it, Mahmud's reforms produced basic change and launched Ottoman society on the course of modernization.

Mansa Musa

14TH CENTURY ● EMPEROR OF MALI

Mansa Musa was emperor of Mali in western Africa from ca. 1312 to 1337. Mansa Musa was the most famous of the Malinke sovereigns, under whom the empire reached its maximum size. He owes his fame to the pilgrimage he made to the holy places of Islam in 1325.

Ascending the throne after his predecessor, Abobakar II, died in a maritime expedition in the Atlantic Ocean, Mansa Musa endeavored to consolidate the borders of the empire. He was assisted in this by a brilliant general, Saran Mandian.

A prince educated in Arabic, he resumed the tradition followed by Malian sovereigns of making a pilgrimage to Mecca. He prepared painstakingly for the journey and, following tradition, required the towns and provinces to make a contribution. He left Niani with a large retinue, taking with him a great quantity of gold drawn from the treasure accumulated by several generations of sovereigns.

Mansa Musa dazzled the inhabitants and the court of Cairo upon his arrival in 1324. According to a historian of the time, he came on horseback superbly clothed, with over ten thousand subjects of his empire, and distributed gorgeous gifts magnificent to behold. The Malian sovereign and his companions distributed so much gold in Cairo that the price of that precious metal dropped. This added to his fame; several decades after his trip to Cairo, chroniclers were still writing about the splendor and the generosity of the Malians.

Mansa Musa returned home from the holy places with an architect, the famous Ishaq El Teudjin, who constructed for him several buildings. Among these were the Gao mosque; the Djinguereber, which is the well-known Timbuktu mosque; and a palace, named the Madougou, in the same city. In Niani itself the Arab architect built a mosque and a remarkable "audience room," a square room topped by a dome and decorated with arabesques of bright colors. Of these monuments, all built with earthen bricks, none survives except the Djinguereber in Timbuktu.

A patron sovereign, Mansa Musa attracted poets and other people of letters to his court. He built several libraries and supported education in the Qu'ran.

Under his reign Mali reached its greatest size. The empire extended from Teghazza in the Saharan plain in the north to the Guineo-Ivorian forest in the south; from Banjul in the west to Azelik (in present Niger) in the east. At the end of the fourteenth century, a portrait of Mansa Musa holding a large nugget of gold in his hands appeared on the first European maps showing the kingdoms and peoples of Africa.

Despite his fame, however, Mansa Musa is not favorably remembered in Mandinka oral traditions. He is reproached for squandering the gold of the Crown and thus weakening the empire. Yet his work is long lasting. All Malian cities bear his mark. To him are owed their monuments of hard-packed earth spiked with wood, a style so characteristic of Sudanese architecture. ◆

Manuel I

1469–1521 ● King of Portugal

Born in Alcochete, Manuel was the youngest child of Prince Fernando, second duke of Viseu and first duke of Beja, master of the Orders of Christ and Santiago, and Dona Beatriz, daughter of Prince João. Both parents of Manuel were grandchildren of King João I (reigned 1385–1433), and Prince Fernando was the younger brother of King Afonso V (r. 1438–81). One of Manuel's sisters, Leonor, was married to King João II (r. 1481–95). Another sister, Isabel, was married to Dom Fernando, third duke of Bragança, who was executed for treason in 1483. An older brother of Manuel was Dom Diogo, fourth duke of Viseu and third of Beja, master of the Order of Christ, who was stabbed to death in 1484 by King João II for conspiring against the monarch. Manuel, who was only fifteen years old at the time of Diogo's death, had earlier been adopted by King João II, his cousin and brother-in-law, and was allowed to succeed his deceased brother as duke of Viseu and Beja and master of the Order of Christ. In July 1491 João II's only legitimate child, Crown Prince Afonso, who had married Princess Isabel, daughter of the Catholic monarchs Ferdinand of Aragon and Isabella I of Castile, was fatally injured in a horseback-riding accident. Although João II had an illegitimate son, Dom Jorge, who by 1492 had become master of the Orders of Santiago and Avis, the monarch was pressured to name Manuel as heir to the throne and did so in his last will and testament.

The most controversial action of Manuel's reign was the forced conversion to Christianity of all Jews living in Portugal.

When João II died in 1495, Manuel was acclaimed king of Portugal on October 25. In 1496 King Manuel recalled the Bragenças to Portugal from exile in Castile and restored that family's properties and titles, which earlier had been confiscated by the crown. In 1498 Manuel named his nephew, Dom Jaime, fourth duke of Bragança, heir presumptive to the Portuguese throne. The previous year, in hopes of unifying the Iberian Peninsula under Portuguese rule, Manuel married Isabel, the widow of Prince Afonso. Isabel, who had become crown princess of Aragon and Castile because of the death of her brother Juan, died in childbirth in 1498. Manuel and Isabel's son, Miguel, heir to the thrones of Portugal, Castile, and Aragon, died in 1500. King Manuel then married Isabel's younger sister, Maria. Among their many children were future

King João III (r. 1521–57); Princess Isabel (who married Emperor Charles V in 1526); Cardinal-King Henrique (r. 1578–80), who was also Grand Inquisitor of Portugal; Prince Luis (father of the illegitimate Dom Antõnio, prior of Crato, pretender to the Portuguese throne in 1580); and Prince Duarte (father of Dona Catarina, sixth duchess of Bragança and grandmother of King João IV, the first of Portugal's Bragança monarchs). In 1518, following Queen Maria's death the previous year, King Manuel married Leonor, oldest sister of Charles V and Catherine of Austria (future wife of Manuel's son, King João III).

The most controversial action of Manuel's reign was the forced conversion to Christianity of all Jews living in Portugal. At the prodding of Princess Isabel and her parents, Manuel issued an edict in December 1496, giving all Jews in Portugal from January to October of 1497 to convert to Christianity or to leave Portugal. Contrary to what is frequently written, relatively few Jews were expelled or allowed to depart from Portugal since Manuel did all in his power to prevent them from leaving the country. With few exceptions, Jews in Portugal either voluntarily accepted Christianity or were forcibly baptized. Among the crown's incentives to conversion was the taking of all children under fourteen years of age from Jewish parents who would not convert and giving them to Christians throughout Portugal to raise. By the end of 1497 the process of forced conversion was completed. In 1498 Manuel issued an edict allowing twenty years' grace regarding the sincerity of the conversions. An additional sixteen years was later granted. The result of this forced conversion was a new group in Portuguese society called "New Christians," who later were hounded by the Inquisition and subjected to "purity of blood" statutes until 1773, when King José I (r. 1750–77), at the urging of the Marques de Pombal, abolished these distinctions.

During his reign Manuel I presided over numerous financial, legislative, and administrative reforms, including an updated codification of Portuguese law. The monarch replaced the Ordenaçoes Afonsinos of his uncle with the Ordenaçoes Manuelinas, which began to be printed in 1512. A new corrected edition was published in 1521, the year of Manuel's death. Manuel's reign is probably most famous for the great overseas discoveries he sponsored. On July 8, 1497, he sent Vasco da Gama and four ships to find a sea route to India. This aim was achieved with da Gama's arrival in Calicut on May 20, 1498. By the end of August of 1499, two of da Gama's ships had arrived back in Portugal. On

March 9, 1500, a follow-up expedition of thirteen ships, headed by Pedro Álvares Cabral, left Lisbon. On April 22, Monte Pascoal in Brazil was sighted, and on May 2, Cabral continued to India, but not before sending his supply ship back to Portugal with news of his discovery. In 1501 Manuel sent three ships under the command of Gonçalo Coelho to explore the eastern coast of Brazil. Upon Coelho's return the following year, Manuel leased out Brazil for three years to a **consortium** headed by Fernão de Loronha. However, Manuel was more interested in North Africa, East Africa, and Asia than in America, and concentrated his energies on those regions. ◆

consortium: association; society.

Marcus Aurelius

121–180 ● Emperor of Rome

Aurelius was raised by his rich grandfather after his father's death when he was three months old. Well educated (he had seventeen tutors), he grew to love philosophy, while his ascetic ways (e.g., sleeping on straw strewn over the floor) almost ruined his already weak health. Administrative offices tempered his philosophic and religious beliefs with realism. Yet acceptance of other people's seamy sides did not lower his expectations of himself: "self-government, and not to be led aside by anything; cheerfulness in all circumstances, and a just admixture of gentleness and dignity, and to do appointed tasks without complaining."

Emperor Hadrian, a frequent visitor to Aurelius's grandfather, took a fancy to Aurelius and recommended to his adopted successor, Antoninus Pius, that he in turn adopt Aurelius (seventeen years old) and a certain Lucius Aelius Verus (eleven years old) as his successors. Antoninus became Aurelius's mentor and had a tremendous influence on him (as emperor, Aurelius would live simply and unostentatiously, occupied with official duties and the study of philosophy—like Antoninus). Lucius, meanwhile, spent his time pursuing pleasure. In 146 Antoninus adopted Aurelius as his sole heir and kept him privy to his counsels and actions.

Aurelius became emperor upon Antoninus's death in 161 and immediately made Lucius his coruler and son-in-law, fulfilling Hadrian's wishes despite Lucius's demonstrated unfitness.

"Thou must now at last perceive of what universe thou art a part, and of what administrator of the universe thy existence is an efflux, and that a limit of time is fixed for thee, which if thou dost not use for clearing away the clouds from thy mind, it will go and thou wilt go, and it will never return."

Marcus Aurelius, *Meditations of Marcus Aurelius Antoninus*, 167

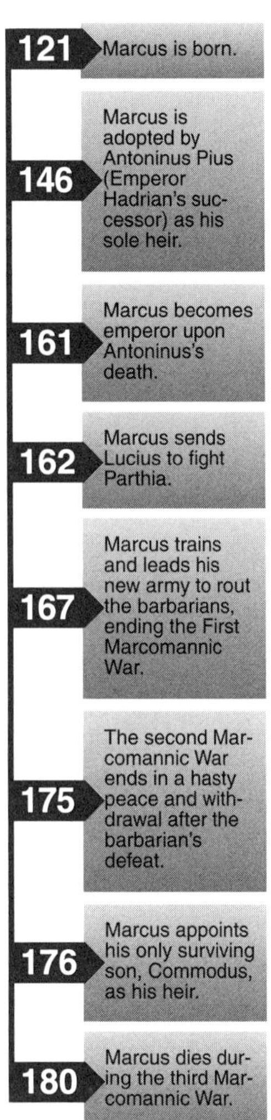

Lucius abandoned himself to hedonism and left Aurelius to run the empire.

As emperor, Aurelius tried to realize his "idea of the state in which there is the same law for all, a polity of equal rights and freedom of speech, and the idea of a kingly government that most of all respects the freedom of the governed." He respected the rights of the senators and made himself into a public servant. He spent large sums of public money on gifts, games, and the corn dole, while waiving unpaid taxes and tribute. He extended Hadrian's legal reforms administratively (more court days and shorter trials) and socially (legislating protection for the weak against the strong, wards against dishonest guardians, debtors against creditors, provinces against governors).

Barbarians and rebels interpreted Aurelius's reputation as a peaceful, kindly philosopher-king as weakness. In 162 revolt broke out in Britain, barbarians invaded the North, and Parthia declared war. Aurelius sent capable generals to deal with the revolt and invasion, but sent Lucius to fight Parthia. In Antioch, Lucius made love rather than war while Parthia overran Syria. Aurelius sent a plan of action with which Lucius's second-in-command defeated Parthia.

Lucius's troops returned to Rome, bringing plague as well as victory. Infection spread everywhere they went; Syria, Mesopotamia, Asia Minor, Egypt, Greece, Italy, and Gaul were devastated. Corpses lay in heaps. So many died that famine followed plague as farms lay empty and transportation of goods was disrupted.

Attracted by Rome's weakness, northern barbarians invaded en masse in 167, laying waste to northern Italy. Rome's plague-decimated legions met defeat when sent against the invaders. Aurelius took charge of the war, financing it by auctioning off objects from his palaces. He enlisted anyone, even slaves and barbarians. He trained and led his new army to rout the barbarians skillfully, ending the First Marcomannic War (167–68). Then he fortified the border and returned to Rome to rest, his frail body overstrained.

Rumor credited Aurelius's pretty, lively wife, Faustina (daughter of Antoninus Pius), with many lovers. True or not, Aurelius treated her with affection and respect, promoted her rumored lovers to high offices, and **deified** her when she died. Of their four children, one girl died young, one married Lucius, and one of their twin boys died at birth. The much doted-upon surviving son, Commodus, rejected both morals and education,

deify: to take as an object of worship.

preferring gladiator sports and cruelty to philosophy. Aurelius chose to ignore his son's true nature; hoping that Commodus's promotion to high office would have a salutary effect resulted in his appointing Commodus as his heir in 176. He justified his decision with the belief that Commodus would be less harmful to Rome as emperor than as a potential insurgent in a civil war.

Aurelius spent the rest of his life fighting the barbarians (his famous book *Meditations*, a distillation of Stoic thought, was written on campaign). He planned to extend the empire to the Carpathian Mountains, a more defendable border against the barbarians. However, the Second Marcomannic War (169–75) ended in a hasty peace and withdrawal after the barbarians' defeat because of the rise of a rival emperor in Egypt. Aurelius died in 180 during the Third Marcomannic War. Commodus had promised to continue fighting until he reached the mountains; instead he immediately made peace with the barbarians and returned to Rome to enjoy himself. ◆

"Since it is possible that thou mayest depart from life this very moment, regulate every act and thought accordingly."

Marcus Aurelius, *Meditations of Marcus Aurelius Antoninus*, 167

Margrethe II

1940– ● QUEEN OF DENMARK

Queen Margrethe II of Denmark is the latest monarch in the oldest royal family in the world, and the first official queen to rule this Scandinavian country. Tracing her heritage to the Viking rulers of the tenth century, since 1972 Margrethe II has served as sovereign of Denmark's fourteen counties, as well as Greenland and the Faroe Islands, from her capital at Christiansborg Castle in Copenhagen.

Margrethe Alexandrine Torhildur Ingrid, later Queen Margrethe II, was born on April 16, 1940, a day her subjects celebrate annually with a national holiday. Eldest daughter of King Frederik IX and Queen Ingrid, she succeeded her father on January 15, 1972, the day after his death. By that time, the thirty-one-year-old had been trained to take the reins of the country by her father. Frederik IX organized special study programs for his daughter to learn about the inner workings of Danish government and society. In addition, Margrethe II studied history, political science, economics, and languages—all subjects essential for a head of state—at universities from Copenhagen to Paris and London.

By the time she was crowned queen, Margrethe II had already laid the groundwork for a distinguished career as a creative artist. Equally comfortable with painting, illustration, textiles, and theater design, she illustrated J. R. R. Tolkien's *Lord of the Rings* in a 1977 edition. She also designed a critically acclaimed set for the popular ballet *Et Folke Sagn* at the Danish Royal Theatre. Along with her husband, Prince Henrik, she has translated several Swedish and French classic texts into Danish.

Margrethe's husband, Prince Henrik (born Henri-Marie-Jean-André, count of Laborde de Monpezat), is a former diplomat from southwestern France. The couple met at the French embassy in London and married on June 10, 1967. Prince Henrik changed his nationality, religion, and language to take the challenging new position alongside Queen Margrethe II.

"Something or other has happened. Things have begun to hang together better. It seems as if my position as Queen and the side of me that likes art and expressing itself artistically are beginning to fuse together."
Queen Margrethe, *The Mermaid Lounge*, publication of the Consulate General of Denmark, 1998

Crown Prince Frederik, born to Queen Margrethe and Prince Henrik on May 26, 1968, is heir to the Danish throne. The unmarried prince has spent his teenage and adult years seriously preparing for his future duties as king, including earning political science degrees from Arhus University and Harvard University. He has also trained with the Danish mission to the United Nations. Prince Joachim, born on June 7, 1969, has studied agriculture to prepare himself to administer the vast Schackenborg Estate that he inherited in southern Jutland. The younger prince has also trained as an army officer, and is married to the former Alexandra Manley, now Princess Alexandra.

Although the constitutional monarchy that characterizes the Danish government today was established in 1849, Denmark has been an independent country since the tenth century. For more than a thousand years, the Danish royal house has flourished. From the earliest rulers of the tenth century to today's constitutional monarchs, nearly all the kings and queens have been related to one another in some way. Margrethe II traces her ancestry back to the first Viking king, Gorm the Old, who died in 940.

In this long line of fifty-two monarchs, Margrethe II occupies a unique position as the first official queen to rule Denmark. Her predecessor and namesake, Margrethe I (1353 to 1412), ruled as regent on behalf of her son, Oluf. It was only in 1953 that the constitution was amended to allow women to assume the throne. Among the monarch's duties are appointing the country's prime minister and the cabinet, as well as its Supreme Court justices, who serve for life. The queen holds weekly meetings with the country's prime minister and foreign minister to keep abreast of current events. She hosts foreign officials and makes state visits to other countries.

Margrethe II has been immensely popular with the Danish people, who view her as a modern queen in sync with both royal tradition and a changing society. Like most contemporary monarchs, she does not express political views, but the queen is known for her stimulating annual addresses to the Danish people about the state of the country, presenting thought-provoking ethical and moral questions. She regularly makes herself available for interviews with the press, where she comments on her creative projects and offers her perspectives on contemporary Danish culture and society. It is perhaps the ability of this monarchy to adapt to the changing times that the Danish royal family has persevered through a millennium with remarkable resilience. ◆

Maria Theresa

1717–1780 ● Queen of Hungary and Bohemia

When his only son died, Holy Roman Emperor Charles VI promulgated the so-called Pragmatic Sanction, which asserted the right of female issue to succeed to Habsburg domains, thus clearing the way for his daughter Maria Theresa to become his heir. In 1736 Maria Theresa married Francis Stephen, duke of Lorraine, who gave up his ancestral duchy in exchange for the grand duchy of Saxony. The union was a love match and the couple had sixteen children, ten of whom survived to maturity.

On her accession to the throne in 1740, Maria Theresa faced the invasion of her territory by land-hungry neighboring states, who chose to reverse their **acquiescence** in the terms of the Pragmatic Sanction. Her naive courage in weathering the eight-year War of Austrian Succession won her many supporters

acquiescence: the act of accepting or submitting passively.

in her previously factious Hungarian estates, and in 1745 she succeeded in installing Francis Stephen as Emperor Francis I, while the 1748 Treaty of Aix-la-Chapelle ratified her rights of succession. However, she suffered the loss of her most wealthy and populous region, Silesia, to Frederick the Great of Prussia.

Surrounded by potentially or actually hostile states, Maria Theresa decided that the establishment and maintenance of an effective standing army was essential to the security of her kingdom. Friedrich Wilhelm Haugwitz, the first in a series of gifted advisers, recommended that in order to raise the money required to fund such a force she institute wide-ranging fiscal changes designed to reduce the power of her dominion estates to control the purse strings of the empire. As a result, she abolished the tax exemptions of the great landowners.

Administering the new tax system meant introducing complementary social reforms and increasing central government intervention in the running of the empire. Maria Theresa had little formal education herself, but she had the common sense to understand that an effective system of higher education was necessary if the state was to produce men competent to staff the expanded bureaucracy and judiciary necessitated by her reforms. She pioneered the introduction of textbooks to secondary schools, and the linking of the University of Vienna medical school with the embryonic public health service, while establishing the sovereign's right to veto the election of deans by the university faculties.

"In a little while, her Majesty entered followed by the three princesses. My husband and myself each sank upon the left knee and kissed the noblest, the most beautiful hand that has ever wielded a scepter."

Luise Gottsched, describing her meeting with the empress in 1749

While Maria Theresa's reforms led to some real improvements in the welfare of the empire's citizens, these were largely incidental to her main purpose, which was the creation of an Austria rich and strong enough to resist foreign aggression. Like most rulers of her time, she had no sense of duty to maintaining the welfare of the population at large. Thus it was only when peasant riots in Bohemia threatened the stability of her domains that she limited the use of forced labor. Similarly, she introduced compulsory primary education in an effort to strengthen the human resources available to the state rather than because of any desire to enrich the lives of her subjects. A curious mixture of pragmatism and piety, Maria Theresa was a strictly observant Catholic and intolerant of religious dissent; nonetheless, reasons of state prompted her to allow control of education to be taken out of the hands of the Jesuits whom she revered.

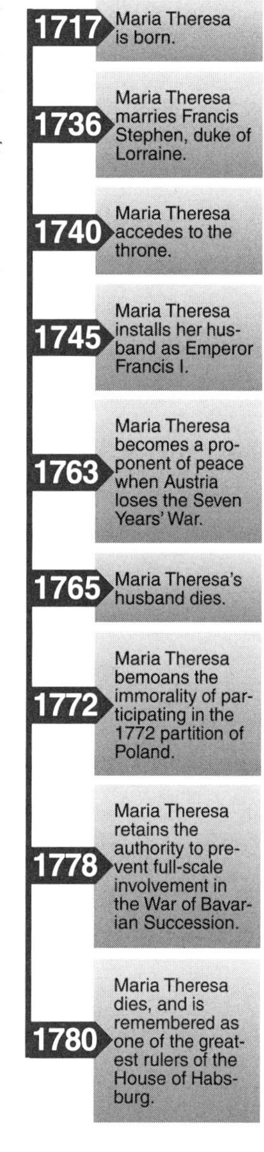

In an attempt to respond to the growth of Prussia's power in the European arena, and in the hope of winning back Silesia, Maria Theresa initiated a radical political realignment by jettisoning Austria's traditional ally, England, in favor of agreements with France and Russia. However, when Austria still emerged on the losing side of the Seven Years' War (1756–63), she quickly became a proponent of peace, realizing that her debt-ridden exchequer could not finance another major conflict.

Maria Theresa was devastated by Francis I's death in 1765, but found some solace in renewed legislative activity. Her government evolved a new public-debt policy, oversaw the settlement of unpopulated areas of Hungary, and drafted a unified penal code to supersede the plethora of local systems.

While she had reason to look on her reforms with satisfaction, her own family life gave Maria Theresa less reason for pride. She personally supervised the education of her children but was generally disappointed with the results, being particularly alarmed by her willful eldest son, Joseph (later the emperor Joseph II), who was fascinated by the new philosophy of the Enlightenment. Four of her daughters were married to princes of the House of Bourbon, thus cementing the Franco-Austrian alliance; Maria Theresa railed against their **frippery** and warned them of the dire consequences that might follow from such behavior (in light of the fate of one of them, Marie Antoinette, who married the future Louis XVI and was eventually guillotined, her fears seem to have been prophetic).

frippery: ostentation.

As Joseph took an increasingly active role in government, Maria Theresa often found herself in opposition to his policies. She bemoaned the immorality of participating in the 1772 partition of Poland—when Austria, Russia, and Prussia resolved their differences at Poland's expense by dividing its territory among them—and was hurt when her attitude was taken as hypocritical in many of the courts of Europe. She still retained the authority to prevent full-scale involvement in the 1778–79 War of Bavarian Succession, but her last years were spent in increasing isolation in her palace at Schönbrunn. Despite her disappointments, the successes of her reign meant she was remembered as one of the greatest rulers of the House of Habsburg. ◆

Marie Antoinette

1755–1793 ● QUEEN OF FRANCE

Marie Antoinette, the daughter of Maria Theresa, archduchess of Austria, and Francis I, Holy Roman Emperor, was born on November 2, 1755. With such a pedigree, it was only to be expected that she would be obliged to make an arranged marriage designed to further the political needs of the empire. In 1770 that obligation came due: she was wed to a reluctant Louis XVI, dauphin (crown prince) of France, to cement an alliance between the two countries.

From the moment of her marriage, the fourteen-year-old newlywed was not well received by the French people. Her Austrian heritage was viewed with hostility among the people and within the court. Her upbringing, in the more informal (by French standards) Austrian court, also ill-prepared her for her new responsibilities, from holding audiences with courtiers, ministers, and the public, to attending dinners of state, and—most important—to providing an heir to the royal dynasty. Marie Antoinette failed on all counts.

Her groom, a year older than she, was uninterested, unattractive, and unable, for the first seven years of their marriage, to fulfill his part of the royal duty—a childhood illness had left him unable to father a child. And although he was loved by the people, he was not well trained in statecraft. Louis retreated from his responsibilities by spending much of his time hunting, and the young Marie, disappointed in her husband and in her role within the court, reacted by diverting herself with the company of a fashionable but dissolute crowd of pleasure seekers.

When Louis XV died in 1774, the new queen's scandalous private behavior made her vulnerable to gossip spread by malicious members of the court who were maneuvering to further their own political agendas. She was called the "Austrian Whore" for her dalliances with prominent men in her circle. Jealous courtiers published pamphlets detailing her indiscretions, including one that purported to be her confessional diary. She was also referred to as "Madame Deficit"—in condemnation of her addiction to gambling and lavish spending.

Perhaps her most outspoken enemy at court was the Duc D'Orleans, who wanted to put forward his own son as claimant to the throne (his son did, in fact, eventually claim the throne in 1814, with the fall of Napoleon and the restoration of the French monarchy). But it was not only the nobility who charged the queen with scandalous behavior. She was routinely castigated in the popular press, which printed lurid tales of her debauchery.

But Marie Antoinette's frivolous living did not last long. Upon attaining the throne, Louis XVI's obligation to father a child assumed even greater importance so, three years into his reign, he submitted to corrective surgery to reverse the damage that his childhood illness had caused. Shortly after that, Marie Antoinette gave birth to a daughter, Marie-Therese Charlotte, the first of her four children. Soon after, she would give birth to Louis-Joseph (who died in childhood), Louis-Charles (who became Louis XVII), and Marie-Sophie, who died in infancy. With motherhood, the young queen settled into her maternal responsibilities, but the damage to her reputation was, by this time, irreversible.

In the year 1775, when Louis XVI had just begun to rule, the American Revolution had just begun. Many of France's aristocracy, including the king, supported the Americans in their war; the king sent secret assistance during the first three years, and provided open support for the remainder of the war. But Marie Antoinette was less inclined to support the colonial upstarts, perhaps perceiving the threat to the institution of monarchy that it embodied.

If that was her fear, she soon would be proved correct. The American Revolution ushered in an era of antiroyalist sentiment in France, which was only **exacerbated** by the indecisiveness of the king and the unpopularity of the queen. Still weighed down

> ***"On Tuesday I had a fête which I shall never forget all my life. We made our entrance into Paris. As for honors, we received all that we could possibly imagine; but they, though very well in their way, were not what touched me most. What was really affecting was the tenderness and earnestness of the poor people, who, in spite of the taxes with which they are overwhelmed, were transported with joy at seeing us."***
>
> Marie Antoinette, letter to her mother, 1773

exacerbate: to make more severe.

by the scandals of her youth, Marie Antoinette became a focus of revolutionary fury—a fury that was inflamed by continual denunciations of her behavior in the popular press. By 1787 public discontent was so intense that a scheduled unveiling of her portrait had to be canceled—for fear it would touch off violent demonstrations.

It was during this period of serious public unrest that Marie Antoinette is said to have proclaimed of the starving peasantry "let them eat cake." This is almost certainly another instance of the inflammatory—and unfounded—accusations put forward by the popular press, but by this point reasonable discourse was nowhere to be found. In 1789 revolution was upon the land: a mob of women (and men in women's dress—believing that the royal troops would not fire upon women) stormed Versailles, demanding her blood. It was only the intercession of Lafayette—considered a hero to the French populace for his role in the American Revolution—that saved her. He joined her on the palace steps and kissed her hand, by this gesture turning aside the wrath of the mob. But the situation was clearly intolerable, and the royal family was taken to the Tuilleries, where they were imprisoned.

> ***"I cannot describe to you, my dear mamma, the transports of joy and affection which every one exhibited towards us. Before we withdrew we kissed our hands to the people, which gave them great pleasure. What a happy thing it is for persons in our rank to gain the love of a whole nation so cheaply. Yet there is nothing so precious; I felt it thoroughly, and shall never forget it."***
>
> Marie Antoinette, letter to her mother, 1773

Held under house arrest, the king and queen were powerless to do much in their own behalf. One Axel Ferson, an old friend—and rumored lover—of the queen, attempted to arrange an escape for the royal family. Traveling at night in a large slow coach driven by Ferson, they made for the border, but were recognized en route and turned back by the mob.

Meanwhile, the situation in France was rapidly deteriorating. Lafayette's attempts to mediate between the nobility and the revolutionaries earned him the disfavor of both. The king, as indecisive and apathetic as ever, was of little help, so it fell to Marie Antoinette to attempt to negotiate for the royal family's safety. She also sought help from abroad, turning to her family in Austria for support. But when Austria and Prussia declared war on France, this plan backfired, as Marie Antoinette and Louis XVI were accused of passing military secrets to the enemy.

In 1792 the monarchy was abolished by the revolutionary council and the royal family were imprisoned. Louis XVI was tried by the revolutionary court, convicted, and executed by guillotine on January 21, 1793. Marie Antoinette remained imprisoned with her children, awaiting their fate.

Louis XIV's brother, who had escaped from France when revolution first threatened, declared the dauphin, Louis-

Charles, to be the new king of France. This prompted the jailers to separate Marie Antoinette from her children and take her to a new prison, the Conciergerie, where she lingered until her trial in October. (Her son, Louis Charles, remained imprisoned until his death of tuberculosis in 1795—though any number of claimants to his name, and his throne, have appeared over the years. Her daughter Marie-Therese Charlotte eventually emerged from her cell and was sent to live with relatives in Austria. She became the Duchesse d'Angouleme and was influential during the subsequent reigns of Louis XVIII and Charles X. She died sometime after 1851.)

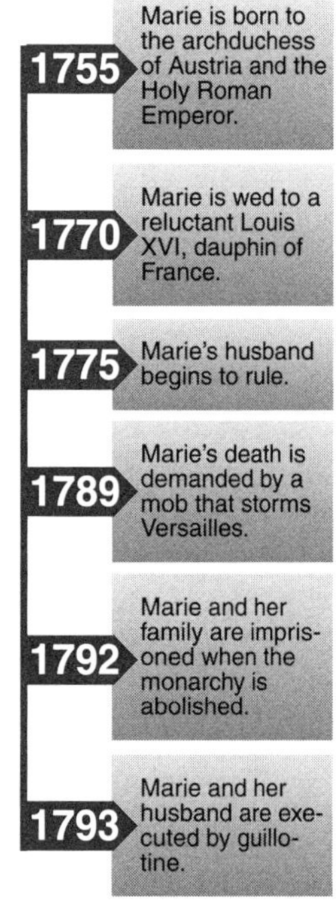

When Marie Antoinette was brought to the courtroom for judgment, she was stripped of her royal title—she was now referred to as the "Widow Capet." Standing before her judges, she learned that she had been condemned beforehand and that, like her husband, she was to face the guillotine. On October 16, 1793, Marie Antoinette was driven through the crowds of Paris in an open cart to the place of execution, where she met her death before the accusing mob calmly and with dignity. ◆

Mary I

1516–1558 ● QUEEN OF ENGLAND AND IRELAND

Born to Henry VIII and his first wife, Catherine of Aragon, Mary initially enjoyed a warm relationship with both parents, her father proclaiming her princess of Wales in 1523; but when Catherine fell out of favor with Henry after failing to produce a male heir, so did her daughter. Mary was further estranged from her parents owing to the influence of Anne Boleyn, whom the king married in 1532. Henry's claim that his previous marriage had been invalid implied that Mary was illegitimate, and so without rights to succession.

Later that year, when Anne gave birth to the future queen Elizabeth I, Mary was ordered to dismantle her household and take up residence with Elizabeth's entourage; but when called upon to abandon her title, she refused. Anne Boleyn conducted a vehement persecution of Mary, who fell victim to bouts of hysterical illness. She retained a deep affection for her mother, despite being denied any contact with her from 1532 onward, and was deeply distressed at her death in 1536.

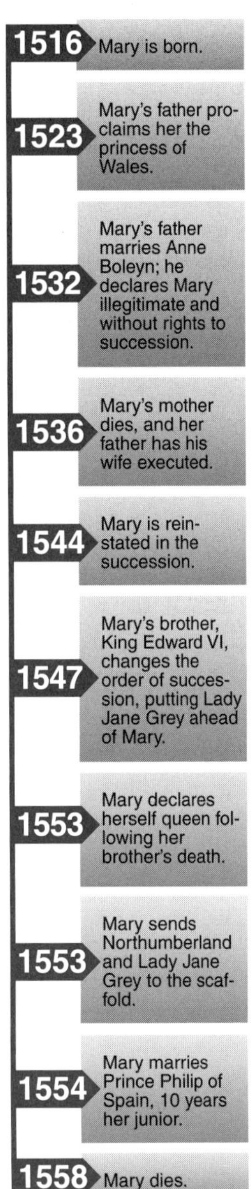

Anne Boleyn was executed later that year, and Mary enjoyed far better relationships with her father's subsequent wives, and also grew very fond of her brother, Edward.

Mary, despite her own devout Catholicism, finally gave in to her father's pressure and signed an act of submission, acknowledging Henry as Supreme Head of the Church of England, renouncing the authority of the Pope, and acknowledging Henry's marriage to her mother as having been unlawful. She was thereafter reconciled with her father and was reinstated in the succession in 1544.

Generous by nature, Mary enjoyed bestowing gifts upon friends and regularly gave alms to the poor. She was not very interested in learning or the arts but, like her father, had a passion for gambling.

Edward VI succeeded Henry in 1547 and, under the influence of his protectors, tried to induce Mary and her household to adopt Protestant rites. Mary refused and as Edward's health failed, John Dudley, duke of Northumberland, who was, in effect, ruling the kingdom, arranged a marriage between his own son and Lady Jane Grey, a royal claimant. Edward was persuaded to change the order of succession, so that precedence was given to Lady Jane Grey. In July 1553 Mary, en route to visit her dying brother at Northumberland's request, got wind of the latter's plans to capture her, and took flight to Sawston Hall. She left in disguise, narrowly escaping an arson attack on the building by a group of her opponents.

Mary proclaimed herself queen on July 9, and, in response to her pleas, vast numbers rallied to defend her from Northumberland's advancing forces. She entered London victoriously in August, and was crowned the following month, sending Northumberland—and later Lady Jane Grey—to the scaffold.

Following her accession, Mary was primarily concerned with finding a husband, in order to reestablish and perpetuate the Catholic line. She accepted a marriage proposal from Prince Philip of Spain (Philip II), a man ten years her junior, but fear of a Catholic restoration, and, more pertinently, a Spanish marriage, provoked plans for popular rebellion that, in most parts of the land, failed to ignite. In Kent, however, Sir Thomas Wyatt and his men crossed the Thames and advanced on the capital. Against the advice of her ministers, the queen rode into the city and called upon her subjects to resist the insurgents. Wyatt and his followers were subsequently crushed, and Elizabeth was arrested for suspected **complicity**, and held in

complicity: association or participation in a wrongful act.

the Tower of London, saved from the executioner's axe by Wyatt's admissions, after prolonged questioning.

Philip received a cool reception upon his arrival in England in 1554, and the couple, who shared no common language, were duly wedded. Mary lost no time in embarking upon a program of complete Catholic restoration, naively assuming that this was what most of her subjects desired. Eminent Protestants, including one quarter of the country's clergymen, were deprived of their living, some being sent to prison, and several bishops were deprived of their sees. Parliament would not, however, pass a bill punishing people failing to attend church services.

Reginald Pole, a staunch Catholic, who had been living in exile in Padua for the past twenty years, returned to England in 1554, with the task of restoring Catholicism by overseeing the abolition of all **ecclesiastical** legislation passed in England since 1529, so that the nation could be reconciled to papal authority. Mary renounced the title of Supreme Head of the church, but Parliament managed to evade the highly explosive issue of the return of lands confiscated from **papal** dominion under Henry VIII.

ecclesiastical: of or relating to a church.

papal: of or relating to a pope.

From 1555 until the end of Mary's reign, nearly three hundred Protestants—including the outstanding churchmen Latimer, Ridley, and Thomas Cranmer, the archbishop of Canterbury—were executed, a legacy that has earned the English queen the epithet "Bloody Mary."

Although Mary succeeded in bringing France and Spain to negotiate peace, Philip's invasion of the Papal States the following year led to a renewal of war. Mary wished to remain neutral, but pressure from her husband, along with provocation from France, compelled her to join forces with Spain and declare war in June 1557. The English navy was successful in removing all French shipping from the Channel, and English troops prevented an invasion by the Scots, who were allied to France; but a temporary halt in hostilities allowed the French to replenish their forces, and launch a surprise attack on Calais, the loss of which dealt a severe blow to English morale. With the war proving ever more costly, and Protestants continuing to burn in intolerable numbers, the queen once more fell ill, while Philip abandoned her for a lover in Brussels. Mary, who had had several false pregnancies in the past, developed a swelling in her belly, and yet again believed that she was with child. She made a will bequeathing the throne to her offspring, but finally accepted the truth, acceding to a request from Philip, delivered by one of his council, to acknowledge Elizabeth as heir. Popular legend related that she died with the words "Philip" and "Calais" etched on her heart. ◆

Mary Stuart

1542–1587 ● QUEEN OF SCOTLAND

The only surviving child of King James V of Scotland and Mary of Guise, Mary was heir to the Scottish throne and, as the great-granddaughter of Henry VII of England, could lay claim to that throne also.

When news arrived that his wife had given birth to a baby girl, James V, already in a state of despair at his battle losses to the English, cried out (in reference to the Stuart dynasty): "Adieu, farewell, it came with a lass, it will pass with a lass." Within a few days he was dead, leaving the six-day-old Mary Stuart as queen, the earl of Arran acting as regent.

On hearing of the Scottish king's death, Henry VIII of England temporarily ceased hostilities and was eager to see an eventual marriage between his own son, Edward, and Mary, thus uniting the two kingdoms under English rule. Two treaties relating to this union were drawn up, but fear that Henry VIII might attempt to kidnap the baby queen prompted Mary of Guise to head north with her child to the relative safety of Stirling castle, where Mary Stuart was crowned at the age of nine months. Meanwhile the Scottish parliament denounced the treaties and an enraged Henry VIII launched a fullscale attack on his northern neighbors.

While Mary was growing into a clever, charming, and energetic child, her troubled kingdom floundered under unrelenting attacks from the English. In despair, the Scots looked to France for help. The French king, Henry II, offered support in return for a marriage alliance between Francis, his sickly son, and Mary. The Scots agreed and in August 1548, Mary, age six, set sail for France accompanied by a small entourage, but without her mother. The French court was charmed by the beautiful child queen, Henry II describing her as "the most perfect child that I have ever seen." Despite the great distance between them, Mary of Guise took great interest in her daughter's upbringing and Mary Stuart was raised a devout Catholic, remaining so until her death.

In 1558 Mary, age sixteen, and Francis, a year younger, were married, and the following year Francis ascended the French throne. The death of her mother in 1559 threw Mary into a state of grief, accompanied by physical collapse. Six months later she lost her husband also, and grieved deeply for him. Now that she was only dowager queen of France, the influence she had been able to exert in Scotland through the French crown and through her Guise relations' direction of French foreign policy, was no longer secure. Amidst an array of propositions to remarry, Mary, age eighteen, decided to return to her native Scotland to rule.

She arrived in Scotland in 1561, welcomed by subjects who approved of their young and beautiful ruler. From the outset, Mary showed remarkable tolerance toward her mainly Protestant subjects, but, a Roman Catholic herself, was persistently maligned by John Knox, the Presbyterian leader. Under her influence, the royal court at Holyrood Palace, Edinburgh, soon became a center of learning, peopled by painters, musicians, and poets. Mary herself loved music and poetry and was a graceful dancer. From time to time she enjoyed dressing in men's attire to wander in the streets of Edinburgh incognito.

Mary finally married her handsome but self-centered English cousin, Henry Stewart, Lord Darnley, in 1566, but her passion for him soon cooled, and Darnley, along with several other nobles, began to resent the favor Mary showed her Italian secretary and confidant, David Rizzio, also a Catholic. Darnley, encouraged to believe that his wife was Rizzio's lover, became party to his bloody murder, which was committed in front of the pregnant queen. Mary was now aware of the possibility of Darnley making an attempt on her own life.

Mary gave birth to a son (the future James VI of Scotland and James I of England) in 1566 and sent him to Stirling castle to be brought up by relatives. Apart from a few brief visits with her son during his infancy, Mary was never to see him again.

The queen's intention to divorce Darnley was preempted by his murder in 1567, committed by several lords including James Hepburn, earl of Bothwell. The queen's marriage to Bothwell three months later incensed her subjects, and she was suspected of having been party to Darnley's murder, especially after the appearance of the incriminating Casket Letters, claimed to have been written by the queen to Bothwell, but whose authenticity has never been proved.

"As an absolute Queen, I cannot submit to orders, nor can I submit to the laws of the land without injury to myself, the King my son and all other sovereign princes. . . . For myself I do not recognize the laws of England nor do I know or understand them as I have often asserted. I am alone without counsel, or anyone to speak on my behalf."
Mary's reply to commissioners at Fotheringhay, 1586

Three weeks after their wedding Bothwell took Mary from Holyrood to the castle of Borthwick, which was soon surrounded by insurgents. Bothwell fled the country, leaving Mary in the hands of rebel lords who held her captive in the castle of Lochleven in the middle of the vast lake of that name (1567). Mary was forced to abdicate and in July of that year, James VI, aged thirteen months, was crowned king, and Mary's half brother, James, the earl of Moray, proclaimed regent.

After more than ten months in captivity, Mary managed to escape and made her way to England. Far from being welcomed there, Elizabeth I decided to hold her captive, fearful that the Scottish queen might try to overthrow her. Mary had been publicly blamed for Darnley's death and this provided the excuse for her prolonged confinement. For the next eighteen years Mary was held prisoner, transferred from castle to castle, her health failing, her youth and beauty ravaged. Despite Mary's constant pleas, virtually all communication with her son was prohibited, while James VI was brought up to believe that his mother had murdered his father so that she could marry her lover. In Europe, Mary gradually came to symbolize the martyrdom that Roman Catholics underwent in England.

When, in 1586, Mary was found guilty of conspiracy in a plot to murder Elizabeth and take the English throne from her, she was sentenced to death. As her death warrant was read to her, Mary replied calmly, "I thank you for such welcome news. You will do me great good in withdrawing me from this world out of which I am very glad to go." She was beheaded in February 1587. ◆

Maximilian

1832–1867 ● EMPEROR OF MEXICO

Maximilian was emperor of Mexico from 1864 to 1867. Born in the Schönbrunn Palace in Vienna, Maximilian was the younger brother of Emperor Francis Joseph. He served as Austrian governor of Lombardy and Vene-

tia from February 1857 until April 1859, when his liberal policies caused a breach with the Vienna authorities. In July 1857 he married Charlotte (known in Mexico as Carlota), daughter of Leopold I of the Belgians, who had earlier declined the Greek throne and the offer of a Mexican crown on the grounds that financial support had been lacking. Carlota, however, fervently believed in the Mexican imperial idea.

Rather than a politician, Maximilian was a romantic who wanted to do something for humanity. Before Napoleon III's suggestion of the Mexican crown, he had traveled the Mediterranean, and by the end of 1859 had also visited Madeira and Brazil. Francis Joseph, reluctant to be drawn into the Mexican scheme, left the matter of the crown to Maximilian, who verbally accepted the offer on October 3, 1863. Following Maximilian's acceptance, Napoleon, in the secret convention of Miramar, agreed to maintain an army of 20,000 men in Mexico until 1867 and the Foreign Legion until 1873, while in exchange, Mexico would cover the entire cost as well as pay back its past debts. In September–October 1863, he was apparently studying Lucas Alaman's *Historia de México*, a pro-monarchy tract. On April 10, 1864, Maximilian formally accepted the crown offered to him by a delegation of Mexican monarchists. Four days later he and Carlota set sail, by way of Rome, where they received the blessing of Pope Pius IX, reaching Mexico City on June 12, after a Te Deum celebrated at the shrine of Our Lady of Guadalupe by Archbishop Labastida. Maximilian had no intention of restoring the position of the church to that held before the Reform Laws, an attitude that led to intense conflict with the bishops and the papal nuncio. He ignored the Pope's request to suspend liberal measures, which he himself had ratified, and issued imperial decrees confirming purchases of ecclesiastical properties (December 28, 1864) and continuing sales—though providing for division of rural properties (February 26, 1865).

Maximilian also was determined to free himself of the French and disliked Marshal François Bazaine, the French commander in chief in Mexico, who had abandoned the attempt to

create a Mexican army late in 1864. The French army encountered fierce guerrilla resistance across Mexico. At the same time, Maximilian made the serious mistake of sending Miguel Miramón and Leonardo Márquez, the best conservative generals, on missions in Europe.

Maximilian's council of state and cabinet consisted in the main of moderates, since there existed little basis of support for the empire among conservatives and the clergy. The emperor's competition for the middle ground was undermined further by Napoleon III's determination from late 1866 to evacuate all French forces. After Miramón's return to France in November, Maximilian for the first time became dependent on the conservatives for his survival. He had in the meantime withdrawn to Orizaba for one month to ponder the question of abdication and indulge his passion for catching butterflies. Meanwhile, Carlota went to France to appeal to Napoleon III to save the empire by committing more funds. She reached Paris in August 1866, but to no avail.

Maximilian's decision to remain on the throne was made public on November 30, 1866. A junta of notables voted on January 1, 1867, in Mexico City to uphold the empire by one vote, in spite of Bazaine's reservations concerning the empire's military position. Maximilian refused to abandon Mexico City with the last French troops and departed for the interior to take personal command of his army. He was captured by forces loyal to President Benito Juárez and was summarily tried and executed at Querétaro on June 19, 1867. The case against him rested on Juárez's decree of January 25, 1862, for the execution of all collaborators, and the death sentence, which Juárez refused to commute, was determined by the imperial decree of October 3, 1865, which had established the death penalty for all members of rebel bands or bandit groups. Juárez refused all appeals for clemency and delayed sending the corpse to Europe. ◆

Maximilian I

1459–1519 ● Holy Roman Emperor

Maximilian was the eldest son of the emperor Frederick III and Eleanor of Portugal. In 1477 he married Mary, the daughter of Charles the Bold, duke of Burgundy.

He acquired considerable tracts of land in Flanders and on the eastern border of France. As a result, the French, under Louis XI, invaded, but were defeated at the battle of Guinegate in 1479. With the death of his wife in 1482 he had to assert his right to retain power by defeating the armies of the Netherlands States General who challenged his rule.

With the Treaty of Arras (1482) Louis recognized Maximilian as the regent of Flanders until his young son, Philip, could assume control. The possession of the Netherlands would later become so well established that they remained loyal to the Habsburgs for nearly three hundred years. Maximilian was crowned king of the Romans (heir to his father) in 1486. He went on to forge an alliance with Spain, England, and Brittany in order to continue his war against France and insurgent Flemish towns. During a campaign in the Netherlands he was captured and imprisoned by the burghers of Bruges. As a result, his father had to collect an army and release his son personally.

At the diet of Frankfurt in 1486 Maximilian perceived the dangers of a disunited Germany facing powerful military neighbors, among which were France, Spain, and the Ottoman empire. In order to consolidate power, he sought imperial reforms that were in his own interest. His plan included the cessation of private wars, improvement of imperial justice, establishment of an imperial army paid for by imperial tax, and allowing the Estates (local representative assemblies) to share power. The reforms faced opposition from local rulers, who contested a centralized form of government that would compete with them for power within their own domains. Maximilian's inability to gauge the political environment was to make his reign a frustrating one, with many disappointments and failures.

In 1490 Maximilian married by proxy the duchess Anne of Brittany in an anti-French move. This came at a time when he had recently reestablished his family's control in Austria and was busy asserting his claim to the throne in Hungary. Charles VIII of France subsequently rejected the hand of Margaret, Maximilian's eldest daughter, and succeeded in making Anne of Brittany break her alliance with Maximilian and become his wife in 1491. While tensions with France heightened, Vladislav II of Bohemia was elected to the Hungarian throne. Despite inadequate resources, Maximilian attacked and, through the Treaty of Pressburg (1491), assured that if there were no male heir to the throne in Hungary, it would pass to the Habsburgs.

The Peace of Senlis in 1493 confirmed German control of the Low Countries and increased Maximilian's popularity on the eve of his succession to the sole rulership of the kingdom with the death of his father. In the summer of that year the Germans drove the Turks from the southeastern borders of their country, and Maximilian married Bianca Maria Sforza of Milan in order to contest control of Italy with the French. However, the French invaded Italy in 1494, forcing the Germans to join the Holy League with the pope, Spain, Venice, and Milan. The alliance with Ferdinand of Spain led to a double marriage between Maximilian's children Philip (now duke of the Netherlands) and Margaret, and Juana and Juan of Spain. This alliance would help to establish Habsburg control over half of Europe.

"By the Lombards I am betrayed. By the Germans deserted. But I will not let myself again be bound hand and foot as at Worms."
Maximilian, 1498

At the meeting of the Reichstag at Worms in 1495, the German princes weakened Maximilian's centralizing policies and limited his power. The subsequent defeat of the Holy League's forces and the German king's unsuccessful bid to consolidate his own authority crippled Germany. In a speech at Freiburg in 1498, following the death of Charles VIII and the succession of Louis of Orleans to the throne in France, Maximilian claimed that "By the Lombards I am betrayed. By the Germans deserted. But I will not let myself again be bound hand and foot as at Worms. . . . I must and will make war. . . . This must I say, even should I have to throw the crown at my feet and stamp upon it."

In 1499 the Germans were defeated by the Swiss confederation in a war that the king did not want and which forced him to grant Switzerland de facto independence. At the same time, the French moved further into Italy, while in 1500 the princes of Germany created a supreme council to diminish the king's power.

Maximilian strengthened his position by coming to an agreement with France and securing funds from various south German business firms. With the revival in his fortunes, he campaigned, in 1506, to assure his succession to the Hungarian crown in spite of Vladislav's male heir. He now felt the time was right to be crowned officially by the pope as Holy Roman Emperor. However, he was kept out of Italy by the Venetians and his campaign against them failed miserably. The roads to Rome were blocked, and he was forced to content himself with the title of "Emperor-elect" bestowed on him in Trent in 1508 with the consent of Pope Julius II. He was never formally crowned and decided to wage an unpopular war of revenge on the Italian peninsula. Joining the League of Cambrai, with his daughter (now regent of the Netherlands), Spain, and the Pope, he unsuccessfully renewed his fight against Venice. His attempt at conquering Venice being futile, he betrayed his agreement with the French and pursued their expulsion from Italy.

Maximilian was never successful in establishing German control in Italy, while Germany itself was plagued with private wars and anarchy. He continued to pursue his plans for peripheral expansion (into Poland, Bohemia, and Hungary) to the benefit of the Habsburg family, all the while neglecting the ambitions of a unified Germany. He died a poor and broken man who did not live to see how the Habsburg family's possessions would, indeed, spread from the Iberian peninsula to the plains of Hungary and Bohemia.

Personally, Maximilian was charming, congenial, and talented, with a passion for athletics, the hunt, and the arts, of which he was a great patron. He was the author of two **chivalric allegories** in verse, and planned to write his autobiography in Latin. His many admirers dubbed him "the last of the knights." ◆

chivalric: relating to medieval knighthood.

allegory: the expression by means of symbolic fictional figures and actions of truths about human existence.

Menelik II

1844–1913 ● Emperor of Ethiopia

Menelik II was the founder of the modern Ethiopian state. Menelik was the son of King Haile Malakot of Shoa, a vassal of the emperor of Ethiopia. Menelik's grandfather, Sahla Selassie, was the first emperor of Ethiopia. Nothing is known about his mother and it is possible that he was illegitimate. Haile Malakot died when Menelik was only a boy; much of his youth was spent under the shadow of the emperor Theodore, who regarded Menelik as a rival claimant to the throne and curbed his movements. Upon Theodore's death Menelik made a bid for the imperial throne but was defeated by John IV, whom he later recognized as emperor. In return, John granted Menelik the southern part of the empire and named him his heir. John was killed in battle in 1889; Menelik, not only the emperor's named heir but, as a result of his extensive

conquests, the most powerful individual in Ethiopia, assumed the throne.

The greatest problem facing Menelik's reign was European colonialism in the horn of Africa. The British occupied the Sudan and the Italians were making inroads on the coast. Shortly before assuming the throne Menelik signed the treaty of Uccialli, thereby recognizing Italian control of Eritrea. Since Menelik's expansionist policy centered on the Muslim and pagan areas of the south, the northern territories, although containing Ethiopia's only outlet to the sea, were not considered as vital in importance as European recognition of his kingdom. Yet despite his concessions, a mistranslation of the treaty led to a conflict with the Italians. They understood the treaty to recognize their ultimate sovereignty over all of Ethiopia; Menelik assumed it to include only the area surrounding the port of Asmara. The dispute broke into full-scale war in 1896. At the Battle of Adowa Menelik's army of seventy thousand troops defeated seventeen thousand Italian soldiers, killing over twelve thousand. Following Italy's defeat, a new accord was signed recognizing Ethiopian sovereignty. Nonetheless, the Italians kept Eritrea.

His empire secure, Menelik was free to embark on sweeping reforms aimed at bringing Ethiopia up to the level of those European countries whose colonies surrounded her. The French were commissioned to build a railroad connecting the new capital of Addis Ababa with the port of Djibouti. Although Menelik maintained absolute power, he created a panel of ministerial advisers to counsel him on affairs of state. New ministries included justice, commerce, and foreign affairs, indicative of Menelik's objective of bringing Ethiopia into the family of nations. Laws were also passed banning slavery, but these were largely ignored.

Throughout his reign Menelik was influenced by his empress, Taitu. A young woman of remarkable beauty, Taitu had several influential husbands. Her sway over the emperor was such that she retained the title of empress although she bore him no heir. As she aged Taitu lost much of her beauty, but she remained popular with the people because of her devotion to the empire. In one battle against insurgents, she herself led a successful cavalry charge; at the battle of Adowa, she prostrated herself before the troops and had a large stone placed on her back. Remaining in this position, she prayed until the battle was concluded.

In the last years of his reign, Menelik became increasingly feeble and suffered from frequent memory lapses. Since no heir had been named, leading contenders schemed vigorously to succeed him. Rival claimants included Ras Mekonnen, father of Haile Selassie, and Menelik's daughter Zauditu (Taitu's choice). The succession was finally awarded to Lij Yasu, a grandson of Menelik and the son of a southern king who had opposed Menelik's ascension to the throne after the death of John IV. Menelik died after five years of illness. ◆

Mohammad Reza Pahlavi

1919–1980 ● SHAH OF IRAN

Mohammed Reza was born in Tehran on October 26, 1919, to Brigadier Reza Khan (later Reza Shah Pahlavi). He was designated crown prince in April 1926 and graduated from a special primary military school in Tehran in 1931, from Le Rosey secondary school in Switzerland in 1936, and from Tehran Military College in 1938. In 1939 he married Princess Fawzia, the sister of King Farouk of Egypt; they had a daughter, Shahnaz, in 1940 and were divorced in 1948. In 1950 he married Soraya Esfandiari Bakhtiari; this marriage, too, ended in divorce in 1958 because she was not able to produce a male heir. In 1959 he married Farah Diba, who gave birth to Crown Prince Reza in 1961, and three other children thereafter.

Mohammad Reza Shah's thirty-seven-year reign can be divided into five distinct phases: from the 1941 occupation of Iran by the Allied forces to the 1953 coup d'état; the postcoup period (1953–59); the period of political strife (1960–63); the period of the shah's increasingly **autocratic** rule (1963–76); and the period of revolutionary crisis that ultimately led to the collapse of the Pahlavi dynasty (1977–79).

autocratic: of or relating to the government in which one person possesses unlimited power.

Mohammad Reza acceded to the throne on September 17, 1941, after Russian and British troops invaded Iran on August 25, forcing Reza Shah to abdicate. A major crisis in the early years of his reign came in 1945 when the Soviet Union refused to withdraw its forces from northern Iran. Through a combination of international pressures and internal maneuverings by Prime Minister Ahmad Quavam, the Russian force finally left Iran in late 1946, and the pro-Soviet republics of Azerbaijan and Kurdistan collapsed. For much of this period, the shah was forced to conform to the will of the *majles* (parliament), which

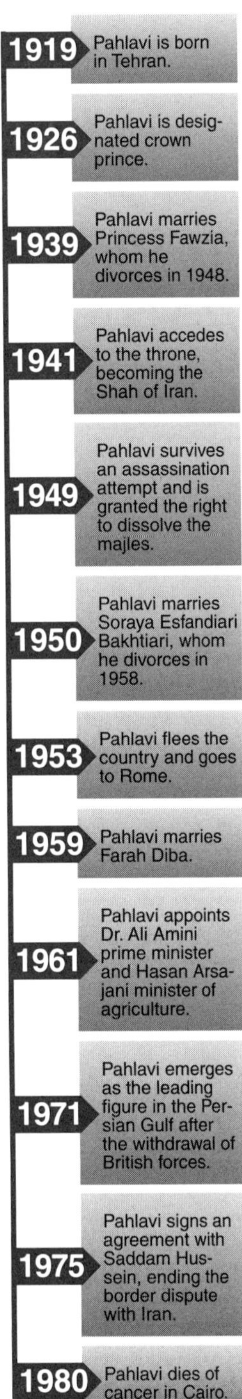

as a political institution dominated both the young monarch and the cabinet. Following an assassination attempt on February 4, 1949, a Constitutional Assembly was convened on April 21; it granted him the right to dissolve the *majles*. In March 1951 the British-dominated Anglo–Iranian Oil Company was nationalized by an act of the *majles* under the initiative of Mohammad Mossadegh, the leader of the National Front, who subsequently became prime minister. Although 1951 to 1953 were "the worst years" of the shah's reign, he did not take any initiative to dismiss Mossadegh until he was urged to do so by Prime Minister Winston Churchill and President Dwight Eisenhower, who also urged him to appoint General Fazlollah Zahedi as prime minister. When Mossadegh refused to accept the shah's dismissal order on August 16, the shah fled the country and went to Rome. On August 19, 1953, he was reinstated to power in a coup conceived by MI-6 (British Military Intelligence) and carried out by the Central Intelligence Agency. The leading *ulama*, the old-guard politicians, the propertied classes, and a core of army generals supported the shah and the coup.

The period 1953 to 1959 began with the repression of members of the intelligentsia who had supported either the National Front or the pro-Soviet Tudeh party, and saw a gradual increase of the shah's power vis-à-vis the old-guard politicians, the propertied classes, and the *ulama*. In this period, the government signed an agreement with a consortium of major Western oil companies in August 1954, joined the Baghdad Pact (later the Central Treaty Organization, CENTO) in October 1955, established an effective intelligence agency (Savak) in 1957, and launched the 1954–62 development plan.

The period from 1960 to 1963 began with a reactivation of opposition groups and increasing pressures from the administration of John F. Kennedy for reforms. In May 1961 the shah appointed Dr. Ali Amini as prime minister and Hasan Arsanjani as minister of agriculture; the latter became the architect of land reform. The shah, who could not tolerate an independent-minded prime minister, dismissed Amini in July 1962 and asked Amir Asadollah Alam, his closest confidant, to form a new cabinet and continue the reform. The land reform program, which was the centerpiece of the shah's White Revolution, and women's suffrage met with strong resistance from the *ulama*, who joined the opposition forces and instigated urban riots on June 5, 1963, to protest Ayatollah Ruhollah Khomeini's imprisonment. The shah was indecisive in responding to the situation, but Alam took command and gave the shoot-to-kill order to the security forces; over one hundred were killed, and resistance of religious groups was crushed. This event marked the suppression of all opposition forces and the beginning of increasingly autocratic rule by the shah.

In the period 1973 to 1976 the shah emerged as the sole policymaker; he allocated oil revenues among various agencies and projects and directly supervised the armed forces and security organizations, foreign policy and oil negotiations, nuclear power plants, and huge development projects. In this period, Iran's gross domestic product grew in real terms by an average annual rate of around 10 percent. Meantime, public services substantially expanded and modernized, and the enrollment at all educational levels increased rapidly. The shah also dramatically expanded the military and security forces and equipped them with advanced weapon systems. In the early 1970s he played a key leadership role in the Organization of Petroleum Exporting Countries (OPEC) and helped the organization to raise the price of oil sharply. Meanwhile, he emerged as the leading figure in the Persian Gulf after the withdrawal of British forces in 1971. Furthermore, he signed an agreement with the Iraqi leader Saddam Hussein in 1975, ending the two countries' border disputes. By the mid-1970s the shah managed to establish close ties not only with the United States, Western Europe, and Muslim countries but also with the communist bloc countries, South Africa, and Israel.

The many diplomatic and economic achievements of the shah led to ostentatious displays of royal **hubris**. For example, in October 1971 he celebrated the 2,500th anniversary of the foundation of the Persian empire by Cyrus the Great and formed, in March 1975, a one-party system. Both acts were resented by the **intelligentsia** and middle classes. He also replaced powerful, independent-minded politicians with more accommodating and submissive aides, a strategy that cost him dearly at times of international and domestic crisis. Concurrently, the shah's White Revolution had undermined the traditional foundation of his authority—the *ulama*, the bazaar merchants, and the landowning classes. They were replaced by the entrepreneurs, the young Western-educated bureaucratic elites, and new middle classes who had developed uneasy relations with the shah. The intelligentsia resented the lack of political freedom and violations of human rights, the rigged elections, corruption, and close ties with the United States.

hubris: exaggerated pride or self-confidence.

intelligentsia: intellectuals who form an artistic, social, or political elite.

The old religious groups and the bazaar merchants and artisans resented the un-Islamic Western lifestyle promoted by the shah's modernization policies. The entrepreneurial and political elites were discontented with the shah's autocratic rule, and with the lack of their own political power and autonomous organizational base. Under these circumstances the nucleus of an anti-shah revolutionary coalition was formed by a large group of liberal and radical intelligentsia, and a small group of militant *ulama* and their important followers in the bazaar.

> ***"Those who imagine that some force other than Islam could shatter the great barrier of tyranny are mistaken. As for those who oppose us because of their opposition to Islam, we must cure them by means of guidance, if it is at all possible; otherwise, we will destroy these agents of foreign powers with the same fist that destroyed the Shah's regime."***
> Ayatollah Khomeini, 1979

The opportunity for the opposition to challenge the shah came after the victory of Jimmy Carter in the U.S. presidential race of November 1976 and the ensuing active support given by his administration to the cause of human rights. When the political upheavals began (1977), the shah's weak and indecisive character contributed to the collapse of the Pahlavi regime and the rise of the Islamic Republic under the leadership of Ayatollah Khomeini, a charismatic figure with a strong will to power. Despite the mass-based nature of the Iranian Revolution, however, not all sectors of the population opposed the shah. The peasantry, for example, constituting over half of the population at the time, continued to support him, though passively. Even labor and the majority of public-sector employees and the middle and lower-middle classes did not join the uprising until the last phases of the revolution, when the shah's regime was on the verge of collapse. After a series of mass demonstrations, mass strikes, and clashes between the shah's security forces and opposition groups in the latter half of 1978, the shah left the country in January 1979; he died of cancer in Cairo on July 27, 1980.

For the shah the ideal model of the imperial persona was the Persian image of the "benevolent autocrat," as exemplified by great Persian monarchs, including his father, Reza Shah. Although this model implied that he should be determined, self-confident, and brave, in reality he was gentle, timid, and indecisive. The shah's inherently fragile character became evident particularly during periods of instability and crisis, whereas his "benevolent autocrat" tendencies came up during periods of stability and success. Furthermore, he was not immune to conspiracy theories. He therefore often saw the secret hands of foreign powers, specifically those of the British, behind virtually every international and domestic incident. He believed, for example, that the Anglophobic Mohammad Mossadegh and the xenophobic Ayatollah Khomeini were British agents. Referring to an Anglo–Russian conspiracy, the shah attributed the Islamic revolution to the "unholy alliance of Red and Black." Belief in conspiracy theories further intensified his inherent vulnerability during periods of crisis. As a result, in the critical periods of 1941 to 1953 and 1960 to 1963 Mohammad Reza showed considerable indecisiveness. On the other hand, in the postcoup period (1953–59) he began to show more determination, and in the stable period of 1963–76, he emerged as a "benevolent autocrat," who devoted himself, in his own way, to the welfare of his people. Finally, during the period of revolutionary crisis (1977–79), the shah, for the third time during his reign, turned indecisive, once again embraced conspiracy theories, and displayed a mood of withdrawal—traits and reactions that may have contributed significantly to his downfall. ◆

Moshoeshoe

1786–1870 ● King of the Sotho and Founder of the Basotho Nation

Moshoeshoe was born Lepoqo in the village of Menkhoaneng. His parents were Mokhachane (Libenyane), a minor Koena chief, and Kholu, daughter of Ntsukunyane, a neighboring Fokeng chief. From an early age, Moshoeshoe aspired to be a great chief. However, he was a very impatient, hot-tempered youth who killed followers for offenses as trivial as slowness in carrying out his orders. He sought advice from Mohlomi, a doctor, sage, and Koena kinsman, on how to become a successful leader. Mohlomi advised Moshoeshoe to be humane and just, to form alliances by marrying into different lineages, and to fight only if peaceful means failed. Mohlomi's advice and Moshoeshoe's own realization that peace, not war, would earn him more followers changed him into a mature, dignified personality. From 1830 to 1870 he was able to grasp and deal with the complex changes resulting from the interaction of black and white populations. His approach to these developments earned him the respect of contemporary African rulers, colonial officials, and European commentators.

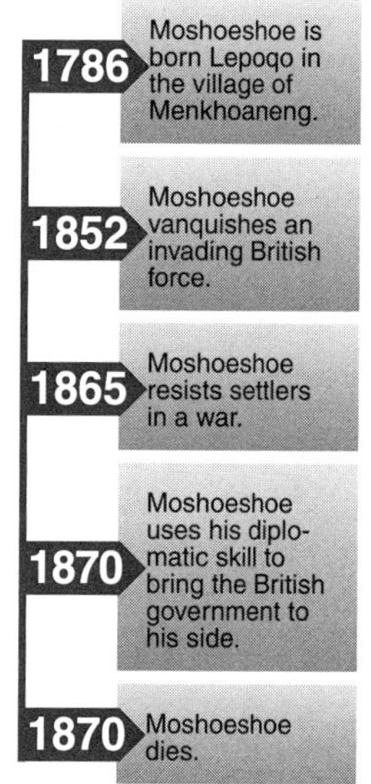

The greatest challenges facing Moshoeshoe during his reign were European settlers' attempts to conquer Basotho and seize their land. Forced by economic and political pressures at home,

Britain, the dominant political power in the region, took sides with the settlers. Despite the modernity and sophistication of the British and the settlers' weaponry, Moshoeshoe vanquished an invading British force in 1852, while in two wars in 1858 and 1865 to 1867 the settlers failed to defeat him. Such was his diplomatic skill that by 1868 he was able to pry the British government's loyalty from the settlers' side and bring it firmly onto his side—an act that saved war-weary Basotho from total conquest by the settlers. By doing so Moshoeshoe achieved his lifelong dream to make an ally of Britain and secure for Basotho the protection of the only superpower then existing. It is therefore not an exaggeration to say that the existence of an independent Lesotho today is a result of his statesmanship. ◆

Motecuhzoma I

C.1397–1468/69 ● AZTEC EMPEROR

Motecuhzoma I (also spelled Montezuma) was Aztec emperor of what is now Mexico from 1440 to 1468. The elder Motecuhzoma (He Becomes Angry Like a Lord) was the fifth Mexica ruler, or *tlatoani*, and the first who can be called an emperor: his conquests extended Aztec rule beyond the Valley of Mexico and ensured a luxurious tribute supply. He was the son of Huitzilihuitl, the second *tlatoani*, and Miahuaxihuitl, a Cuauhnahuac (Cuernavaca) princess; the legend of his birth reflects Huitzilihuitl's temporary control over Cuauhnahuac, later reestablished by Motecuhzoma. Miahuaxochitl's sorcerer father set scorpions and other vermin to guard her. Huitzilihuitl attached a precious greenstone to an arrow he shot over the wall; when Miahuaxihuitl swallowed the stone Motecuhzoma was conceived. The name Ilhuicamina, "He Shoots Arrows at the Sky," by which he was probably known during his lifetime, may have suggested the tale.

According to native histories, Motecuhzoma sent envoys to the mythical origin places of the Mexica and their deity Huitzilopochtli. With his half brother Tlacaelel, he codified Aztec law and instituted the Flowery Wars, periodic skirmishes that provided sacrificial victims. The worst crisis of Motecuhzoma's reign was the famine of 1450–54, which emptied the imperial granaries and forced people to flee to the humid lowlands; intensification of agriculture helped to prevent further famines. ◆

1440 Motecuhzoma becomes Aztec emperor.

1450 Motecuhzoma's reign's worst crisis is a four-year famine that begins this year.

Motecuhzoma II

C.1466–1520 ● AZTEC EMPEROR

Motecuhzoma II (also spelled Montezuma) was the ninth Aztec emperor of what is now Mexico (c. 1502–20). Motecuhzoma Xocoyotl (or Motecuhzoma the Younger, often designated Motecuhzoma II) was described by an early chronicler as "a man of medium stature, with a certain gravity and royal majesty, which showed clearly who he was even to those who did not know him" (Cervantes de Salazar). Also described as deeply religious, very aware of his status as head of the Mexica ruling hierarchy, and rigid and elitist in his application of law and custom, Motecuhzoma was leader of the Mexica and their empire when, bent on conquest and colonization, Hernán Cortés led an army of Spaniards into the Aztec capital of Tenochtitlán (present day Mexico City) in 1519.

Motecuhzoma II has long been depicted as superstitious, weak, and vacillating in contrast to the "determined" and "bold" Cortés. This picture is overdrawn and does not accurately portray the multiple, though ultimately ineffective, ways that Motecuhzoma II sought to protect his people and empire in the face of an enemy far different than any he had faced before.

He was chosen as his uncle Ahuitzotl's successor in about 1502. Almost every Mexica *tlatoani* (or supreme ruler) had enlarged the territorial holdings of the empire. Motecuhzoma II did so, though he did not gain as much territory as his immediate predecessor. His conquests followed the general geographic patterns of Ahuitzotl's conquests and lay largely to the east and south of the Valley of Mexico, concentrating especially on central and southern Oaxaca and northern Puebla and adjoining areas of latter-day Veracruz. He ignored areas lying to the west

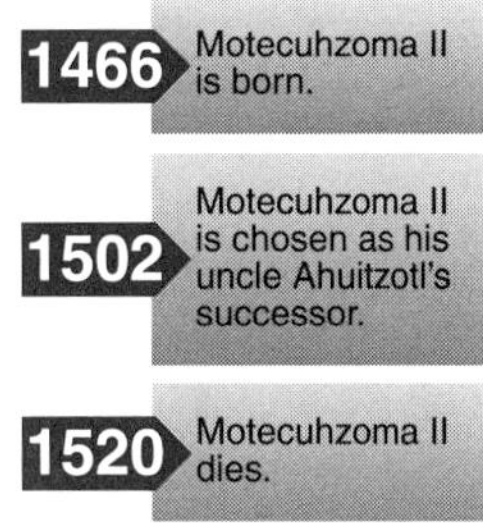

and north of central Mexico, and left the southern regions of the empire still only loosely tied. Continuing warfare with Tlaxcala—and the inability of the Tenochca Mexica and their allies to subdue it—created a political wedge that the Spanish were later able to use to their advantage during the Conquest.

While Motecuhzoma II is reported to have believed that Cortés was the returning deity Quetzalcoatl, it is unlikely that Motecuhzoma or his advisers still thought this when the Spaniards reached Tenochtitlán. Motecuhzoma tried to discourage the Spaniards from their inland march in search of the center of his empire. Unfortunately, one of Motecuhzoma's means of discouraging them was to send gifts such as gold, which only further excited Spanish interest. As the Spaniards moved closer to Tenochtitlán, the Mexica leader attempted to have them captured but to no avail.

When Motecuhzoma II and Cortés finally met, Motecuhzoma again tried to discourage Spanish interest in his empire. But in his much quoted address to Cortés, he acknowledged Spanish military skill and apparently stated that the Mexica would obey the Spanish. Inexplicably, Motecuhzoma allowed himself to be taken captive by Cortés and some of his soldiers. Although Motecuhzoma II sought to form an alliance with Pánfilo de Narváez while imprisoned, he had lost control of events and died in 1520. The Spanish sources generally state that he was stoned by other Mexica and died from his wounds. There is disagreement among Indian sources, though some, such as Chimalpahin, state that the Spaniards killed him. It was left to his successors, Cuitlahua (Cuitlahuac) and Cuauhtemoc, to mount a military opposition, which ultimately failed. ◆

Mswati II

C.1820–1865 ● KING OF SWAZILAND

Mswati II was a Swazi king under whom Swaziland was unified as a nation. Mswati II was the first son, and hence the heir, of King Sobhuza I, the founder of Lobamba City (known today as Old Lobamba). Assuming the kingship in 1839, he gained fame throughout southern Africa as a great soldier, second only to King Shaka of the Zulu. He modeled his own armies after the efficient Zulu forces, recruiting non-Swazi fighters, including Sothos and Ngunis, to fight for him. In part due to the coeval decline of the Zulu empire, Mswati was successful in his raids of nearby Zulu territories as well as his domination of other surrounding terrain. His kingdom came to be known as Swaziland, after a European corruption of his name, "Swazi."

Also exerting his influence through diplomacy, Mswati avoided conflict with bordering states and sent his soldiers to settle disputes among neighboring chiefs. He signed a nonbelligerence treaty with the Afrikaner boertrekkers who then occupied the Transvaal and openly defended his own kingdom against European influences. Mswati died in Hhohho in 1868. His son, Mbandzeni, succeeded him and, through a series of grazing and mineral concessions to Europeans, began to lose control of Swaziland; the kingdom became a British High Commission Territory in 1906. ◆

Mswati III

1968– ● KING OF SWAZILAND

King Mswati III is the ruler of the Kingdom of Swaziland, a small nation almost surrounded by South Africa, except for an eastern border with Mozambique. Swaziland's environment includes mountains, grassy midlands, and low plains near sea level. Among the nation's greatest assets are four major rivers that provide irrigation and hydroelectric power.

In the late 1400s Swazi people migrated from central east Africa seeking better grazing land and settled in what is now Mozambique on the Indian Ocean. In 1750 King Ngwane III led the Swazis inland, away from the danger of sailors and explorers. They created Lobamba, now a city that is considered the heart of the Swazi people. The Swazi survived skirmishes with warrior Zulus during the mid 1800s, but when Europeans found gold in the area during the 1880s, the Swazis were

1968 Mswati is born.

1986 Mswati, one of his father's more than 100 sons, becomes king.

1993 Mswati allows a parliamentary election in which a majority of the assembly is directly elected.

1995 Mswati celebrates his birthday with 5,550 guests.

1996 Mswati appoints a prime minister.

1997 Mswati spends two weeks in a retreat while the public demands democracy.

1998 Mswati selects his sixth wife from several hundred maidens who dance before him.

unprepared. They signed over their land without realizing it. In 1894 the British and the Boers (Dutch farmers in South Africa) placed Swaziland under the administration of South Africa. Swazi men were forced by unfair taxes to work in South African mines, beginning a long-term dependence on South Africa. After the British defeated the Boers, Britain took over Swaziland. The British exploited Swazi labor and forced the people to give up tribal customs.

The Swazi monarchy survived European domination, and in 1921 Sobhuza II became king. He was college educated because his mother, Queen Labotsibeni, wanted him to have the same powers as whites. Sobhuza worked to regain ownership of his people's land. As other African nations gained their independence, the Swazis pushed for theirs. In 1967 Swaziland elected its first parliament. The nation attained full independence on September 6, 1968, with King Sobhuza II as head of state. Dissatisfied with a British model of government, Sobhuza suspended the new constitution in 1973 and revived a tradition of tribal councils. He issued a new constitution in 1978 that kept power in his hands and banned political parties. After sixty years of rule, Sobhuza died in 1982 at the age of eighty-three.

Succession to the Swazi throne is unique. The heir must be chosen from among the king's sons, but the king has many wives, some publicly unknown. Sobhuza was thought to have more than 70 wives and more than 100 sons. The choice of king begins when the royal council chooses a queen mother from among the wives. Her role is important, because she will rule along with her son.

After a brief reign by Sobhuza's eldest wife, Queen Mother Dzeliwe, the royal council announced its choice of Makhosetive, son of Queen Ntombi. In 1986 eighteen-year-old Crown Prince Makhosetive became King Mswati III. His crowning took place in traditional secrecy, but he then appeared before the Swazi people wearing the royal garb: red feathers in his hair, leopard-skin garments, a shield of cowhide, and a special stick. Mswati soon dissolved the royal council to acquire power for himself. Criticism of the government grew by the early 1990s among organized political parties, which were illegal under the constitution. Mswati allowed a parliamentary election in 1993, in which a majority of the National Assembly was directly elected for the first time. In 1996 Mswati appointed a prime minister.

Another unique feature of Swazi royalty is how the king selects his wives. An annual week of celebration culminates in the Reed Dance. In this ceremony, several hundred Swazi maidens dance before the monarch, wearing nothing but small beaded skirts and body paint. The king watches the young women dance and chant and makes his selection. His first wife, called the ritual wife, bears no children and maintains an elder status. In September 1998 Mswati III selected his sixth bride at the Reed Dance.

Mswati rules absolutely. Swazi royalists argue that preserving ancient ways has maintained peace. Critics reply that Mswati owns half a dozen palaces and an assortment of expensive cars, while a third of Swazi workers are unemployed. In 1995 the king's birthday party included 5,550 guests who feasted on meat while many Swazis went hungry due to a drought. Taxpayer money supports the many wives and children of both Mswati and his father, Sobhuza.

Swazi royalists argue that preserving ancient ways has maintained peace. Critics reply that Mswati owns half a dozen palaces and an assortment of expensive cars, while a third of Swazi workers are unemployed.

In 1997 public discontent boiled over in a monthlong strike by unions demanding democracy. Mswati spent two weeks of that time in an annual mystical ceremony to renew his powers of kingship. Few Swazis voted in the 1998 election, since a lack of political parties or public debate made voting pointless.

Swazi women have begun to criticize such policies as Mswati supporting mandatory virginity tests for unmarried women and his wives advocating submission for Swazi women. Widows cannot vote or enter parliament. In spite of all these conflicts, most Swazi people seem to revere Mswati. Reformers, though, want his role to change from an absolute to a constitutional monarch. ◆

Mubarak al-Sabah

1896–1915 ● KING OF KUWAIT

Mubarak al-Sabah, often called "Mubarak the Great," has been called the most forceful ruler of Kuwait. He is the only ruler in Kuwait's history to achieve his position as the result of a coup; he killed one of his brothers, Muhammad, the then ruler, and one of his sons killed another of Mubarak's brothers, Muhammad's close adviser Jarrah. Apologists excuse these actions by pointing to Muhammad's pro-Turkish proclivities. Critics agree that Mubarak prevented the absorption of Kuwait into the Ottoman empire but note that he did this not by keeping Kuwait independent but by making it a British client. The result of Mubarak's several secret treaties with Britain was to relinquish Kuwait's autonomy in foreign policy. This amounted to a larger concession of sovereignty than had been made to the Ottomans by Mubarak's predecessor. More important for the political development of Kuwait in the twentieth century, however, was Mubarak's use of British economic and military resources to attenuate the power of local notables, a process that was continued by his successors, who relied on oil revenues to insulate themselves from popular checks on their power.

Kuwait's economy thrived during Mubarak's reign. However, his domestic power rested on his close relationship to the bedouin tribes rather than to the urban merchants. Even after he became ruler, Mubarak spent time camping with the bedouins in the desert. Unlike the tradition established by most previous emirs of Kuwait, however, Mubarak publicly enjoyed a lavish lifestyle. His income from taxes, British payments and annuities, and family investments (including date gardens located in Iraq) enabled Mubarak to live well and to employ armed guards to protect himself from his subjects. Resentment of his high taxes and military levies provoked several leading pearl merchants to leave Kuwait for Bahrain in 1910. A delegation from the ruler that carried Mubarak's promise to **rescind** the burdensome taxes encouraged only some to return.

rescind: to take away; remove.

Mubarak's military campaigns against the al-Rashid shaykhs of the Jabal Shammar were aimed at allies of the exiled relatives of Muhammad and Jarrah. In September 1902 British warships were sent against a force commanded by two of Mubarak's nephews who were seeking revenge for their fathers' deaths. But Mubarak's military adventures were also problematic for the British, who wanted to maintain their alliance with the Ottomans. Nevertheless, they continued to support him, and in 1905 the Turks abandoned their efforts to incorporate Kuwait into the vilayet of Basra.

Mubarak had confidence in the British as Kuwait's ultimate protectors against the Turks. But British **rapprochement** with the Sublime Porte prior to the outbreak of World War I produced the Anglo–Turkish Convention of 1913. This declared Kuwait to be a *kaza* (autonomous province) of the Ottoman empire and recognized Turkey's right to have a political representative in Kuwait. Mubarak was shocked by what he saw as a betrayal of his interests. However, the convention never went

rapprochement: establishment of cordial relations.

into effect. On November 3, 1914, it was repudiated, and two centuries of diplomatic ties between Kuwait and the Ottomans were broken. One year later Mubarak died. True to their promise to a leader who had become a staunch ally, the British planned to honor another of their pledges to Mubarak: that they would ensure that the next ruler of Kuwait would be his designated heir rather than a descendant of the brothers he had killed in 1896. In the event, no external intervention was necessary. Subsequent rulers of Kuwait have also been direct descendants of Mubarak. ◆

Muhammed V

1910–1961 ● KING OF MOROCCO

Sidi Muhammed Ben Yusuf was the third son of Mulay Yusuf, a colorless prince and brother of the sultan of Morocco, Mulay Hafid. Muhammed was born in Fez in 1910, at the beginning of the protectorate period; it seemed unlikely he would reign. Two years later, the French nominated his father to succeed the sultan, whom they had deposed because he refused to rule as they wanted. Muhammed V came to power after his father's death in 1927, because French authorities considered him to be more flexible and less ambitious than his brothers. However, he used his popularity and his skills in international diplomacy to involve himself in a struggle, at first unequal, with the protectorate's authorities.

After the Berber *dahir* in 1930, which relieved Berber tribes from submitting to *Sharia* (Islamic law), Muhammed became more sensitive to Moroccan nationalism, which was just beginning to awaken. Without breaking off from the protectorate, he supported demonstrations by young traditional and modern intellectuals, such as Allal al-Fasi, Hassan El Ouezzani, and Ahmed Balafrej, which, in 1944, gave birth to the Istiqlal (Independence) party. World War II presented the opportunity to convince the protectorate to move toward a cooperative regime more faithful to the spirit of the original agreement between France and Morocco.

Muhammed opposed the French attempt to protect Moroccan Jews from persecution while he helped rebuild military forces to fight again with the Allies. The 1942 Casablanca

1910 Muhammed is born in Fez, the third son of a colorless prince.

1927 Muhammed becomes sultan and king of Morocco after his father's death.

1930 Muhammed becomes more sensitive to Moroccan nationalism.

1942 Muhammed opposes France's attempt to protect Moroccan Jews from persecution.

1953 Muhammed is deposed and exiled to Madagascar.

1955 Muhammed regains his throne and becomes a spokesman for nationalism.

1960 Muhammed takes the reins of power by naming Mulay Hassan prime minister.

1961 Muhammed dies suddenly after surgery.

meeting with U.S. president Franklin D. Roosevelt and Britain's prime minister Winston S. Churchill strengthened his resistance. From then on, he utilized a strategy of promoting gradual change to regain the sovereignty his country had lost in 1912. He approached French authorities directly to avoid the obstacles set up by both settlers and French civil servants, who opposed any change. But he did not succeed despite his good relationship with General Charles de Gaulle. At the local level, opposition to the French became more and more violent and led to the sultan's deposition and exile in Madagascar on August 20, 1953.

But France could not depose Muhammed in 1953 in the same way it deposed his uncle Mulay Hafid in 1912. The international environment was unfavorable to France; French public opinion accepted unwillingly the proconsuls' plots; and, above all, Muhammed was the symbol of a very deep opposition movement, which mobilized Moroccan cities as well as the countryside. The nation could no longer be governed, and the French administration collapsed within two years in the face of the uprisings. Muhammed was called back to preserve the French economic and military presence, which otherwise could have been swept out by nationalistic currents far more radical than those represented by the king and the Moroccan bourgeoisie.

Once he regained his throne, in November 1955, Muhammed took on the role of spokesman for nationalism. He let the Istiqlal party exert power without, however, becoming a prisoner of the nationalist movement. He continued to defend the monarchy's privileges. Muhammed kept his country out of the confrontation between France and the Algerian Front de Libération Nationale (FLN), which he supported. But, profoundly hurt by the 1956 hijacking of a Moroccan plane with FLN leaders on board, he then attempted to play an intermediary role in the Algerian conflict, hoping, in vain, that de Gaulle's return to power in 1958 would facilitate his reconciliation with France. The king would die without witnessing success. But, he was careful not to jeopardize his country's position within a new Maghrib that, already, some perceived as dominated by a revolutionary Algeria, the main heiress of the former colonial power.

Having succeeded in reestablishing his country's independence on the international stage, Muhammed also consolidated the position of the monarchy within an institutional system, which was shaken by the 1953–55 crisis. Some among the nationalists welcomed a king who reigned without governing. But Muhammed did not share that philosophy for himself or his son, Prince Mulay Hassan, his heir, whom he had gradually introduced to power since the end of World War II.

The support he gained by fighting with the Istiqlal against the protectorate helped him keep his authority over an important part of the nationalist movement. In that struggle, the monarchy recovered its powers that the Treaty of Fes (1912) had alienated and, added to that, the administrative means set up by the protectorate. The military and police forces were placed under monarchical authority, but other administrative sectors depended upon a government dominated by the Istiqlal. Without the help of the monarchy, it was not possible to ensure either the control of the resistance movement or the settlement of rural uprisings. A pluralist text related to public freedom rights allowed, in April 1958, the legalization of new political parties and soon favored the split of the Istiqlal party, with a right wing remaining close to the king and a left wing following a moderate line. In May 1960 Muhammad took the reins of power by naming Mulay Hassan prime minister. The prince had been, at the beginning of independence, chief of staff in the Royal Armed Forces.

Chosen because of his apparent docility, Muhammed V proved, in the long run, to be a cautious opponent, capable of appreciating modernizing actions.

As Algeria's independence approached, the more anxious Muhammed became to grant his country a constitution and to organize its democratization under the monarchy's control. He died suddenly in March 1961 after surgery and left the country to the authority of his son, Hassan II.

During this thirty-two-year reign, Muhammed V listened to his country and took part in its evolution, which allowed it to recover its independence and to project itself into modernity. Chosen because of his apparent docility, he proved, in the long run, to be a cautious opponent, capable of appreciating the modernizing actions of such French resident generals as General Auguste Nogues or Eric Labonne. They reciprocated by respecting his dignity. In extreme circumstances, he displayed firmness and intuitively anticipated the reactions of common Moroccan people. As far as the rivalry with the nationalist movement, which gradually replaced the common fight against the protectorate, is concerned, he knew how to take advantage of time, how to safeguard his best cards; he went on being attentive to the rural world and sometimes contributed to undermining the credit modern leaders were already losing. Thus, four years after his return, he regained all the power without having to share it. While favoring Algeria's independence, he feared Nasserist or Marxist influences, which could have come from that neighboring country and be exerted upon Morocco.

A man of tradition, Muhammed V was the symbol both of independence and modernity. That symbol continues to stamp the monarchy's image and to give Morocco a strong identity highly differentiated from that of its neighbor countries. ◆

Mutsuhito

1852–1912 ● EMPEROR OF JAPAN

During Mutsuhito's forty-five-year rule, Japan emerged from two hundred and fifty years of cultural and economic isolation to become a major world power. Mutsuhito was a hardworking, austere, and sincere ruler who ordered the sweeping reforms that would modernize Japanese society under one central government in a remarkably short period of time.

The second son of Emperor Komei, Mutsuhito took the throne at the age of fourteen, upon his father's death. The following year he was formally enthroned and, in a Shinto ceremony, selected a slip of paper that bore the Chinese characters "bright" and "rule": taken together these read "Meiji," which was the name (which may be translated as "enlightened rule") subsequently used to designate his reign. Mutsuhito, unlike his father, was dedicated to Japan's modernization. In order to achieve this task he first sought to consolidate his power under one central government. For this it was necessary to subjugate the Tokugawa shogunate, which had long ruled the country. When the emperor established three ministerial posts, Yoshinobu Tokugawa, leader of the **shogunate**, led his forces against the loyalists in the Battle of Fushimi-Toba (1868). His defeat, and the unwavering commitment of the subsequently assembled council to the restoration of imperial power, marked the beginning of the era known as the Meiji Restoration.

shogunate: the dominion of a military governor ruling Japan until the Revolution of 1867–68.

Later in 1868 Mutsuhito took the "Charter Oath of Five Principles," which launched the country on its course of westernization. The charter claimed that a council chamber would be established, that all classes would achieve their "just aspirations," that wisdom would be sought throughout the world, and that strange customs of the past would be discarded. The shoguns, having surrendered to the emperor, gave him their capital, Edo. Mutsuhito's move to Edo and his proclamation that it would be the capital of all Japan, under the name Tokyo, was a sign of the triumph of the forces of modernization.

From his new residence in Tokyo, the emperor passed the laws that ushered Japan into the modern era. In 1871 the country was divided into prefectures and the feudal system was officially abolished. The imperial army was expanded and the first railroad was built between Tokyo and Yokohama. A new educational system was implemented in 1872, Japan adopted the Gregorian calendar, and a senate was instituted in 1875. In 1877 the government successfully faced its first test of power when the Satsuma Rebellion broke out: retaliating against Mutsuhito's attempts to do away with them, the ancient order of the Samurai led a forty-thousand-man army into battle against imperial forces numbering sixty thousand, but were defeated.

In 1881 Mutsuhito promised a constitution within ten years. By 1885 a cabinet system had been established to replace the previous oligarchical system, with the constitution being promulgated in 1889; the following year a national assembly was instituted. The constitution declared that the emperor was "sacred and inviolable" and that legislative power would be exercised in conjunction with the national assembly. However, the emperor was to maintain absolute command of the army and navy, and retained the sole right to declare war, make peace, and confer all ranks and titles.

Under Mutsuhito's control of the armed forces, Japan gained territory and commanded respect abroad. The emperor played a crucial role in Japan's victories in the Sino-Japanese War (1894–95) and the Russo-Japanese War (1904–05).

After the Anglo-Japanese Alliance of 1902, the British prince, Arthur of Connaught, visited Japan and conferred upon the emperor the Order of the Garter, making him the first Oriental monarch ever to receive this decoration. As a result of Japan's victories in war, Mutsuhito acquired the beginnings of an empire. The annexation of Korea to the Japanese empire in 1910 was a significant accomplishment for a country which had emerged from feudalism less than fifty years earlier. ◆

1852 Mutsuhito is born.

1868 Mutsuhito takes the "Charter Oath of Five Principles," launching Japan on its course of westernization.

1871 Mutsuhito sees Japan divided into prefectures, and the feudal system is officially abolished.

1877 Mutsuhito's ancient order of the Samurai is defeated by imperial forces.

1881 Mutsuhito promises a constitution within 10 years.

1894 Mutsuhito plays a crucial role in Japan's victories in the Sino-Japanese War.

1902 Mutsuhito is the first Oriental monarch ever to receive the Order of the Garter.

1904 Mutsuhito is a key factor in Japan's victories in the Russo-Japanese War.

1910 Mutsuhito annexes Korea to the Japanese empire, a significant accomplishment.

1912 Mutsuhito dies.

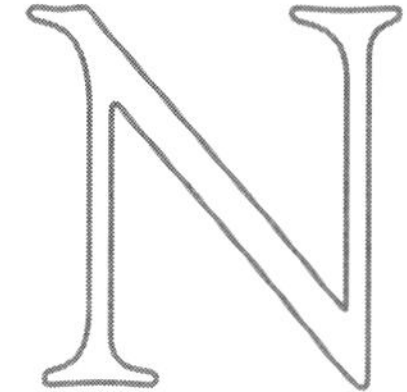

Napoleon I

1769–1821 ● EMPEROR OF FRANCE

Napoleon Bonaparte was born in Corsica, an island in the Mediterranean Sea, but his father, a small landowner who originally supported Pasquale di Paoli's fight for Corsican independence, became pro-French in return for French recognition of his claims to nobility. This made Napoleon eligible, at ten, for acceptance into French military academies for aristocrats, where his schoolmates' scorn for his poverty, Corsican origins, and unfamiliarity with French (Italian was his native tongue) made him an ardent Corsican patriot.

When his father died, leaving his family in desperate financial straits, Napoleon became the real head of the household, supporting them with his salary after entering the army at sixteen, when he became a second lieutenant and was assigned to the artillery. Peacetime garrison duty was undemanding and he spent much of his time with his family in Corsica, immersing himself in books about political philosophy.

The French Revolution in 1789 ended Paoli's exile from Corsica, but he was only interested in an independent

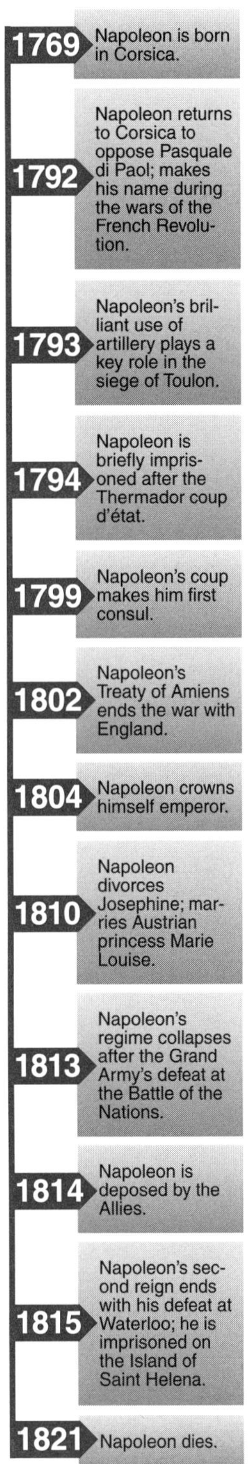

Corsica and had no use for republican principles or Napoleon. In 1792 Napoleon returned to Corsica to oppose him openly. Napoleon lost his army commission because of his prolonged absence, and he and his family had to flee to France when his attempt to seize Ajaccio failed.

A known supporter of the revolution, Napoleon made his name during the wars of the French Revolution (1792–1802); his brilliant use of artillery played a key role in the 1793 siege of Toulon. The Thermidor coup d'état, which ended the Reign of Terror saw a temporary decline in his fortunes; he was even imprisoned briefly in 1794. The ability and expediency with which he suppressed the mobs that threatened the Thermidoreans' corrupt rule, however, made him a favorite of the dictatorship's leader, Paul François de Barras. When Napoleon married Barras's widowed former mistress—the lazy, unfaithful, but kind opportunist Josephine de Beauhamais, with whom he was passionately in love—Barras gave him command of France's Italian campaign as a wedding present.

Napoleon's Italian campaign was a resounding success even though he had no previous experience in large-scale military operations. He reveled in being greeted as a liberator by an Italian population rejoicing at the defeat of their Austrian masters. He negotiated a peace treaty and founded a new Italian Republic on his own initiative (massive shipments of booty reconciled the French government to his independence). He also made sure his family shared in his victory: his brother Joseph became rich supplying Napoleon's army.

Despite the debacle of his 1798–99 Egyptian expedition against the British, which aimed at blocking Britain's lucrative India trade but ended with Napoleon abandoning his troops and escaping back to France, France's bourgeoisie welcomed the 1799 coup that made Napoleon First Consul, feeling that only he was strong enough to bring France peace and stability. In 1801 his second Italian campaign forced the Austrians to make peace and his concordat with the papacy gave the blessing of the church to his rule, while the 1802 Treaty of Amiens ended the war with England. Highly intelligent and hardworking, Napoleon instigated much-needed administrative reforms, established the Bank of France, centralized civil administration, reorganized education, reformed the legal system, completing the codification of civil law (the Napoleonic Code), stabilized the currency, and founded a bureaucracy. He also imposed strict censorship, and 90 percent of political newspapers ceased publication.

Chateau of Fontainebleau

The Chateau (castle) of Fontainebleau, about 40 miles from Paris, France, was originally a royal hunting lodge built in the twelfth century. Around 1527 King Francois I brought in the best French and Italian architects and artists of the time, and rebuilt the lodge into an elaborate palace. French monarchs continued to live in the chateau, redesigning and enlarging it, until the late 1700s. Following the French Revolution, Napoleon I resided in a small wing on the first floor of Fontainebleau. He redecorated the wing into an imperial suite, although his bedroom resembled a military barracks, with an iron bed and a desk. Napoleon signed his abdication there in 1814. During World War II Fontainebleau was taken over as a German military headquarters. After it was liberated near the end of the war, it served as an Allied Forces headquarters. Today the chateau is the Museé National du Chateau de Fontainebleau, a national museum. Beautiful gardens and a forest of more than 40,000 acres surround it. An estimated 11 million visitors tour the grounds every year and view a large art collection housed in the chateau.

In 1802 Napoleon became "consul for life" with the right to choose his successor; he crowned himself emperor in 1804. Meanwhile, Britain ended the uneasy peace between the two countries by declaring war in 1803. The British naval victory at Trafalgar in 1805 reasserted British control of the seas and ended Napoleon's hopes of invading England. However the stunning French victory over Austria at Austerlitz (1805) convinced

"Peoples of Italy, the French army comes to break your chains; the French people is the friend of all peoples; approach it with confidence; your property, your religion, and your customs will be respected. We are waging war as generous enemies, and we wish only to crush the tyrants who enslave you."
Napoleon I, 1796

guerrilla: one who engages in irregular warfare especially as a member of an independent unit.

Europe of the invincibility of Napoleon's army and of the need to accede to his wishes. By 1808 he controlled the Continent, having defeated its armies with his combination of military genius, phenomenal luck, and swift decisiveness. He reshaped the political map of Europe by installing puppet rulers (often members of his own family) and implementing republican governmental frameworks in conquered territories; in theory, Europe remained closed to British trade.

It little concerned Napoleon that this control and blockade existed more on paper than in reality. What did bother him was that his empire—his bid for immortality—had no heir. His love for Josephine had long since faded into mutual infidelity but he appreciated the benefits derived from her popularity and skills as a hostess. She was barren, however, so Napoleon divorced her and married the Austrian princess Marie Louise in 1810. France rejoiced with him at the birth of his only legitimate child.

Napoleon's insatiable ambition led him to look for more battles to fight and more lands to bring under his control. France was war-weary, tired of the unending conscriptions. Deserters and draft evaders abounded, while the sale of government bonds dropped with news of renewed hostilities. Napoleon was indifferent to the needs of his soldiers for food, clothing, pay, and medical attention, regarding them as so much cannon fodder. Defeat began to shatter the myth of his invincibility. Spain was the first to stand up to him and he became involved there in a long **guerrilla** war, in which the Spanish were supported by British troops. Then the Austrians rose against him, followed by the Russians.

Napoleon's defeats were distinguished by military blunders, misfortune, and indecisiveness in battle; inadequate supplies and/or supply lines; disdain for the wishes of allies (including relatives or subordinates he had rewarded with a throne); emphasis on the collecting, guarding, and transporting of booty rather than military matters; abandonment (on four separate occasions) of his defeated army to escape back to France.

Napoleon's Grand Army was depleted by his disastrous invasion of Russia in 1812. The Russians pulled back beyond Moscow, destroying everything as they retreated, and when Napoleon in desperation sought to withdraw, his army was destroyed by the Cossacks and the wintry conditions. His regime collapsed after the Grand Army's defeat at the Battle of the Nations (1813), and he was deposed by the Allies in 1814. He was granted the island of Elba in the Mediterranean as a principality, given a lavish annual income, and allowed to keep the title of emperor, but a Bourbon king, Louis XVIII, mounted the French throne.

The new Bourbon rule was much more liberal than Napoleon's, but it delegitimized the Revolution. Resentment of this was behind France's enthusiastic acceptance of Napoleon's return after ten months' exile in Elba. The army went over to him without a fight, the Bourbon king fled, and once again Napoleon was in control of the country. However, the France he ruled was once again a republic, not an empire, and he chafed under the strict limitations placed on his powers. A new anti-Napoleon international coalition was determined to overthrow him, and he was eager to fight it, convinced that victory in battle would restore his absolute rule. Instead, his second reign ended after one hundred days with his defeat at Waterloo in 1815. He abdicated and was taken, at the age of forty-six, to the South Atlantic island of Saint Helena where he stayed, a British prisoner for the rest of his life.

"I have sacrificed all of my interests to those of the country. I go, but you, my friends, will continue to serve France. Her happiness was my only thought. It will still be the object of my wishes."

Napoleon I, farewell to his troops, April 20, 1814

One of history's great figures and a military and organizational genius, Napoleon emerged at the beginning of his career with a message of hope and liberation, spurred by the noble ideals of the French Revolution. However, these were discarded under the urge for power that led him to unbridled expansionism and caused Europe to unite against him, eventually achieving his downfall. Inside France, he introduced much-needed reforms that determined the nature of modern France and long outlived him, with the Napoleonic Code inspiring lawmakers in many lands. In the words of Johann Wolfgang Goethe, "He went forth to seek Virtue, but since she was not to be found, he got Power." Of small stature but charismatic personality, he has never ceased to fascinate. ◆

Napoleon III

1808–1873 ● EMPEROR OF FRANCE

Charles-Louis Napoleon Bonaparte, the son of Napoleon I's brother Louis and stepdaughter Hortense, lived his whole life in Napoleon's shadow. Born during his father's brief reign as king of Holland, he was the first Bonaparte to be a prince from birth. His father lost his throne when his

determination to be more than Holland's puppet king displeased Napoleon. The restored Bourbon regime banished all Bonapartes from France in 1815 and Louis-Napoleon's mother, Hortense (estranged from her husband), spent years traveling Europe seeking a country that would withstand French pressure and grant her refuge. She was finally allowed to settle in Bavaria (where her brother was the king's son-in-law).

Louis-Napoleon's character was shaped by his Bavarian childhood, and he became much more German than French, speaking French with a German accent all his life. Other childhood influences were his sternly republican private tutor, his extremely religious (after the loss of her lover) mother, and prolonged visits to his Bonaparte relations, who instilled in him an admiration for Napoleon's genius.

The 1830 insurrections that flared through Europe (toppling the Bourbons from the French throne and replacing them with the Orléans) threw Italy into turmoil. Vitally interested in the dream of a united Italian nation, Louis-Napoleon participated in the abortive Romagna rebellion and only Hortense's daring ingenuity and the help of the future Pope Pius IX saved him when it failed.

Louis-Napoleon became the Bonapartist pretender for the French throne after Napoleon I's only legitimate son died in 1832, and embarked on an extensive public relations campaign to restore credibility to Bonapartism. His 1832 pamphlet asserting that France could only combine glory and liberty under an emperor, publicized both his name and his cause (he was an accomplished political writer); complimentary copies of his knowledgeable Artillery Manual were sent to members of the French military, establishing courteous relations with them.

Louis-Napoleon's farcical attempts to stage coups by winning over the French army (in Strasbourg in 1836, and in Boulogne in 1840) were unsuccessful; he was not sufficiently dashing or stylish to capture soldiers' imagination and loyalty. Exiled to America after Strasbourg, he might have sunk into obscurity if the French king, Louis-Philippe, had not imprisoned him in the Castle of Ham when he returned to Switzerland to be with his dying mother, thereby winning him international sympathy and publicity; after six months he escaped to England in 1846.

Louis-Napoleon went to Paris at the outbreak of the Revolution of 1848, but the provisional government sent him back to England. However, his name and his disassociation from the failed attempts of the various French factions to gain control of the government and maintain order led to his election to the constituent assembly a few months later. He returned to Paris and prepared to run for the presidency, supported by the Catholic-royalist Party of Order, which considered him a harmless nonentity it could use.

Louis-Napoleon was a modern politician in terms of his regard for public opinion, use of propaganda, and his election campaigns. His campaign for the presidency of France was masterly: evoking the Napoleonic legend, he promised to bring back the days of national glory while keeping the peace, and give the **bourgeoisie** order and prosperity while helping the poor. His victory was overwhelming, winning the support of the vast majority of the French people, and when the assembly voted against amending the constitution to enable him to run for president a second time, he overthrew the government in a bloody **coup d'état**, brought in a new constitution, restored the empire, and became Napoleon III.

bourgeoisie: a social order dominated by the middle class.

coup d'état: the violent overthrow of an existing government.

As emperor, he seldom used the police and military to suppress rioting and civil disorder, not because he had any compunction about so doing but because, except for a brief period in 1851–52 and again after an 1858 assassination attempt by an Italian radical, there was no need. Political meetings were prohibited throughout most of his reign because they contributed to factional strife, but he instituted almost universal suffrage and men of every political persuasion participated in his government. The arts flourished; in the Second Empire there was freedom of speech, press, and ideas—but not of action.

Describing himself as a socialist, Napoleon III used his government to enhance French prosperity and the welfare of the French people, promoting industry and agriculture, improving the transport infrastructure, and establishing credit institutions and mutual assistance societies. His concern for the welfare of the poor expressed itself in a variety of ways, from lowering the price of bread to constructing hygienic houses for laborers.

Louis-Napoleon married the Spanish countess Eugènie de Montijo in 1853, and they had one son. Eugènie was beautiful, fashionable, capricious, virtuous, and haughty—but not very wise or intelligent. She was devoted to her son, worked hard at being empress, conducting a brilliant court, and sought power to compensate for the pain of her husband's many infidelities. Feeling guilty and physically weak (he was incapacitated by repeated bladderstone attacks after 1860), Louis-Napoleon let

Eugènie have power. Staunchly Catholic and determined to preserve her son's inheritance, her influence on France's foreign policy was catastrophic. She encouraged the preservation of the pope's rule over Rome, France's disastrous part in Archduke Maximilian's attempt to create a Mexican empire, and the territorial pretensions that led to France's defeat at the hands of Prussia and the consequent end of the empire in 1870.

Louis-Napoleon's interest in innovative military technology (modern artillery, armored warships, and military use of captive balloons) evidenced his interest and promotion of modern technology in general. He had mixed motives for his foreign military involvements—he firmly believed in the national right to self-determination and the use of international arbitration to solve Europe's problems, but to keep the support of French Catholics he helped restore the Pope to Rome in 1849, withdrew his support of Piedmont in its war against Austria in 1859, and even preserved the Pope's rule over Rome with French troops between 1860 and 1870.

The French army was badly in need of reform, but Louis-Napoleon's attempts to achieve this aroused enormous opposition, since the French did not want to admit that their army could not conquer Europe, while the bourgeoisie did not want to be subject to a general draft. Sick and weak, Louis-Napoleon could not control the territorial ambitions that led the country headlong into the Franco-Prussian War and his empire's fall in 1871. He went to live in England, where he continued to study technical and social problems, publish articles defending his politics, and suffer from bladderstones. He died between operations two years later. ◆

Nebuchadnezzar

C.630–562 B.C.E. ● CHALDEAN KING

The eldest son of Nabopolassar, the founder of the Chaldean (Neo-Babylonian) Empire, his name is from the Akkadian Nabukudurri-Usur, "O Nabu, protect my boundary-stone," the "boundary-stone" referred to being the line of kingly succession. While his father had disclaimed royal descent, Nebuchadnezzar sought to further legitimize his rule by claiming the third-millennium B.C.E. ruler Naram-Sin as his

Hanging Gardens of Babylon

According to tradition, the magnificent Hanging Gardens of the ancient city of Babylon (in present-day Iraq, 30 miles south of Baghdad) consisted of a sequence of terraces rising from the shore of the Euphrates River that were linked by stairs of marble and lavishly planted with trees, shrubbery, and flowers. The gardens were reportedly watered by pumps drawing water from the Euphrates.

The construction of the Hanging Gardens has been attributed to either an Assyrian queen around 800 B.C.E. or, more often, to Nebuchadnezzar, Chaldean king of Babylon, two centuries later. Some sources claim that Nebuchadnezzar built the Hanging Gardens for the benefit of one of his wives, to remind her of the hilly terrain of her native Medea (in the northwest of today's Iran). Most of our information about the Hanging Gardens comes from ancient Greek writers who did not themselves see the gardens but based their accounts on descriptions offered by Greek travelers to Babylon. There is no mention of the Hanging Gardens in cuneiform tablets, and archaeologists have not found remains that can definitively be attributed to the gardens.

However, the foundation of the royal palace complex in Babylon and some remains of its structures have been discovered. One archaeologist has pointed to an area at the northeastern end of the complex with unusual constructions as a possible location of the Hanging Gardens. Some archaeologists have cited remains in the southern area of the complex, but others say this site is too far from the Euphrates to have housed the Hanging Gardens.

ancestor. The true facts of his career are liberally spiced with legend: the only available sources of information about him are a number of cuneiform inscriptions and the later writings of Jewish and classical authors.

Nabopolassar ensured that his son had a reverence for the gods of his kingdom instilled in him from an early age; one of Nebuchadnezzar's first tasks was working as a laborer in the restoration of the temple of Marduk, the national god of Babylonia. He was also trained from an early age in the arts of war and kingship, becoming a military administrator by 610 B.C.E. and taking command of an army in the mountains north of Assyria in 607 B.C.E. After the empire's armies were defeated by the Egyptians in 606 B.C.E., he took his father's place as military commander-in-chief and demonstrated brilliant generalship in routing the Egyptian forces at Carchemish and Hamath, victories that signaled the beginning of the end of Egypt's power in West Asia. Shortly thereafter his father died, but so firm was Nebuchadnezzar's grip on power that he was able to return to campaigning just three weeks after ascending the throne.

"When he, the Lord god my maker made me, the god Merodach, he deposited my germ in my mother's (womb): then being conceived I was made."

Inscription of Nebuchadnezzar

Nebuchadnezzar pursued an expansionist territorial policy throughout his reign, engaging in regular military expeditions. His 604 B.C.E. expedition in Syria and Palestine led to the submission of local states including Judah, but his gains were reversed when his heavy losses in clashes with the Egyptians in 601 B.C.E. triggered defections among his vassal states. He then retreated to Babylonia to rebuild his forces, only returning to campaigning in 598 B.C.E. By 597 B.C.E. Jerusalem had fallen to him, and he deported its king, Jehoiachin, to Babylonia. When Zedekiah, his appointed successor to Jehoiachin, rebelled, Nebuchadnezzar besieged and then destroyed Jerusalem (586 B.C.E.), carrying many Jews into captivity in what the Old Testament refers to as the Babylonian Exile. Despite his sack of the holy city, the biblical prophets Jeremiah and Ezekiel regarded him as an appointed instrument of God. Subsequent campaigns saw him capture Tyre, after a thirteen-year siege, in 573 B.C.E., and attempt an invasion of Egypt in 568 B.C.E.

His military accomplishments notwithstanding, Nebuchadnezzar was proudest of being "the one who set into the mouth of the people reverence for the great gods." He achieved this by completing the rebuilding of Babylon in a manner commensurate with its status as the religious center of the empire, and scorned those of his predecessors who had built palaces elsewhere. He extended the fortifications begun by his father, built canals, a moat, and an outer defensive wall, and embellished the principal temples.

A thoughtful and loving spouse, Nebuchadnezzar tried to ease the homesickness of his Median wife by creating a system of terraces, watercourses, and exotic trees to simulate the hills of her native land. These Hanging Gardens of Babylon were classified by the Greeks as one of the seven wonders of the ancient world. Even more visually striking was the ninety-meter-high ziggurat, a series of tiers and stairways.

Nebuchadnezzar is an important figure in the Old Testament, where he is represented as a majestic, just, but troubled ruler, who is moved to recognize the god of the Jews as a result of repeated evidence of his might. However, the tale of his seven years of madness following the prophecy of Daniel that "thy dwelling shall be with the beasts of the field, and they shall make thee to eat grass as oxen" is apparently apocryphal, the result of an exaggerated recounting of events that actually took place under a later ruler, Nabonidus, who quit Babylon to live for a decade in the deserts of Arabia.

At his death, Nebuchadnezzar was able to bequeath to his son and successor, Amel-Marduk, an empire bigger than that of any Assyrian or Babylonian predecessor. ◆

Nero

37–68 C.E. ● EMPEROR OF ROME

Nero's mother, Agrippina, was an ambitious, ruthless woman. Married and widowed three times, she got her son, Nero, from her first marriage, great wealth from her second, and a crown from her third. She played on the extreme susceptibility to women of her uncle, Emperor Claudius, to become his fifth wife. Claudius was unfortunate in his choice of wives: one died, two he divorced, one he had killed, and the last one, Agrippina, murdered him.

Marriage to Claudius did not satisfy Agrippina's ambitions. She wanted Claudius to adopt Nero as his heir over the rival claims of Claudius's own son, Britannicus. Nero was eleven when his mother married Claudius and sixteen before she succeeded in persuading Claudius to adopt him and marry him to Claudius's daughter, Octavia (aged thirteen). Meanwhile Agrippina had become powerful and feared, using the weapons of exile and death, and the power of the Praetorian Guards headed by her friend Burrus. Claudius finally realized what Agrippina was doing and threatened to end her power and name Britannicus as his heir. Agrippina killed him before he could make good his threats and Nero became emperor at seventeen (54 C.E.). The new emperor accepted the crown but had little interest in government. What he loved was sports (gymnastics, chariot racing, and so on), and what he really wanted to be was a great artist. He set about learning music, art, drama, and poetry and surrounded himself with artists and musicians, holding private competitions with them to see whose work was best. He took their compliments and his successes in these contests at face value, choosing to ignore the idea that the punishments meted out to anyone who beat him might have prevented his work from being judged on merit alone.

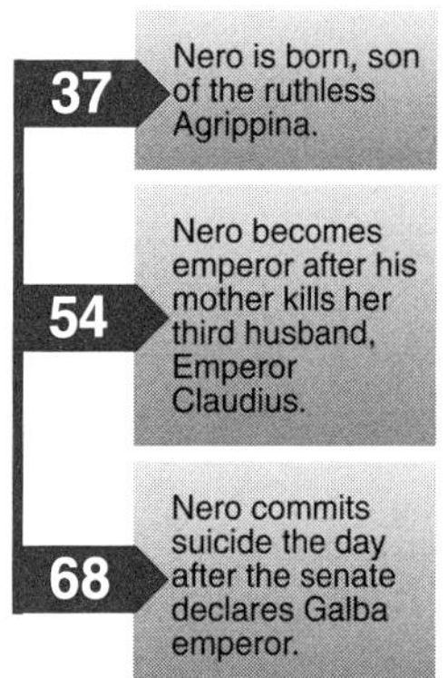

At first Agrippina administered the empire for Nero, but the philosopher Seneca (Nero's old tutor) and Burrus persuaded Nero that they should replace her. Furious, Agrippina threatened Nero by announcing that Britannicus was the real heir, whereupon Nero had Britannicus poisoned and Agrippina retired to her villa.

Seneca and Burrus encouraged Nero to occupy himself with indulging his appetites to prevent his interference in governmental matters. As a result Nero ran wild while Rome thrived under Seneca's wise guidance; frontiers were well guarded, corruption and oppressive taxes were reduced, sea travel was made safe, the empire expanded, and peace made. The young emperor recognized no moral or temporal authority other than his own immediate desires. He wandered the streets of Rome from brothel to tavern, committing robbery, murder, and mayhem. Poppaea Sabina, a married woman, agreed to become his wife if he divorced Octavia. At twenty-two he murdered his mother for opposing the divorce. Three years later he divorced Octavia and married Poppaea, then exiled and murdered Octavia.

His excesses drained the treasury. To replenish it he stripped temples and confiscated the estates of those who "plotted" against him or did not leave him enough in their wills. Degenerate, uncontrollable—Burrus was dead and Seneca dismissed—Nero declared himself a god.

Nero dreamt of redesigning and rebuilding a Rome too crowded for the palace he wanted to build. According to legend he ordered the famous fire that destroyed most of Rome while he played on his lyre. He did in fact, respond to the emergency with strenuous efforts to control the fire and alleviate suffering, while he blamed the Christians for setting it. Then he had the pleasure of rebuilding the improved Rome of his dreams—at the cost of thousands of lives and many priceless buildings, manuscripts, and works of art.

In his twenty-eighth year he began giving public performances as a musician, singer, and actor. His performances increased his popularity with a populace flattered at an emperor's begging for their applause. Large crowds that gathered did not stop him from ensuring a captive audience by forbidding anyone leaving alive before he finished performing—even women in labor. His wife, Poppaea, died that year, pregnant with his longed-for heir. Rumors of Nero's responsibility for her death did not prevent his eulogizing her or finding, castrating, and marrying a boy who resembled her. The discovery of a plot to overthrow him led to many deaths (including Seneca's) and exiling many others.

Nero spent the next year in Greece, participating in the Games as both athlete and performer. Carefully obeying all the rules, he "won" every contest he entered (including the chariot race he did not complete), rewarding Greece with an exemption from paying tribute and his opponents with Roman citizenship.

In 68 Gaul rebelled against Nero and was soon joined by the Roman army in Spain, headed by Galba, which marched against Rome. Threatened with the defection of the Praetorian Guard, the Senate declared Galba emperor and Nero fled—to commit suicide a day later. ◆

Nicholas II

1868–1918 ● CZAR OF RUSSIA

The son of Czar Alexander III, Nicholas II was born in Tsarskoye Selo outside the Russian imperial capital of Saint Petersburg. He received the standard education accorded to the Russian heir to the throne, including foreign languages, diplomacy, and his favorite subject, military science. One tutor, an Englishman named Charles Heath, taught him English and imbued him with the love of sports that would remain with him throughout his life. In addition to receiving military training Nicholas developed a fondness of military pomp and ceremony; he was always attracted by uniforms and loved parades. His most influential tutor, however, was Konstantin Pobedonostov, an ultranationalist reactionary and bigot who remonstrated with Nicholas against reform, particularly after the assassination of Nicholas's reform-minded grandfather, Alexander II, when Nicholas was thirteen years old.

After completing his education, Nicholas toured the Middle East and Far East but his journey was cut short following an assassination attempt in Japan. Nicholas never forgave the Japanese people for the attempt on his life, which left him with a scar.

Alexander III died suddenly in 1894 and Nicholas, then twenty-six, ascended the throne. Despite his friendly features, he often appeared shy and even sad. He looked very much like his cousin George V of England and was sometimes mistaken for him. Although he was an obdurate autocrat, Nicholas was often plagued by doubt as to the wisdom of his decisions as czar.

Russian czar Nicholas II (center) with Czarina Alexandria (standing right) and their children.

He was weak-willed and allowed himself to be dictated to by his mother, the empress dowager Maria Fyodorovna, and later by his wife, the czarina Alexandra. Although there was much excitement and an air of expectation at his coronation (three thousand people were crushed to death at his coronation festivities), Nicholas's subjects soon came to pity the czar and even regarded him with contempt. Nicholas himself commented on his ascension, "I am not prepared to be a czar. I never wanted to be one. I know nothing of the business of ruling. What is going to happen to me—to all of Russia?" Nicholas's words were ominous. At his coronation the Imperial Chain fell from his chest to the ground, an omen perceived by the people as suggestive of upheavals to take place during his reign.

Immediately after his ascension to the throne, Nicholas married Princess Alix of Hesse-Darmstadt, a minor German princess who was a granddaughter of Queen Victoria. Princess Alix or, as she became known, the czarina Alexandra, was a strong-willed woman who manipulated her husband. She bore Nicholas four daughters: Marie, Olga, Tatiana, and Anastasia, before she finally produced in 1904 an heir to the throne, Alexei, a sickly child who suffered from a rare form of hemophilia. The royal family sought the aid of Rasputin, a mystic monk and faith healer who seemed able to relieve the boy's suffering. Rasputin soon wielded a remarkable influence over the empress and through her, over the czar.

The Winter Palace of the Czars

The Winter Palace in St. Petersburg, Russia, served as the winter home of Russian rulers for over 150 years. Czarina Elizabeth began its construction in 1754, but the first to live in the palace was Czar Peter III, who moved in with his mistress. His wife, Catherine the Great, later removed Peter from the throne. She established a huge art collection in the adjoining Hermitage building, but would not allow the public to view it. A fire in 1837 destroyed the palace, although the adjoining Hermitage was saved. A replica of the original palace was built immediately. In 1905 the Russian Revolution was launched when soldiers fired on a crowd of workers demonstrating peacefully near the palace. Nicholas II, the last czar, fled the palace because of the unrest. After he was forced from power during the October Revolution in 1917, the Provisional Government used the Winter Palace as its headquarters. Today the Winter Palace is part of Russia's State Hermitage Museum, which houses an art collection of almost 3,000,000 items.

Nicholas sincerely tried to govern Russia well. He was a dedicated autocrat who claimed that "certain people . . . have let themselves be carried away by the senseless dream of participation by elected regional representatives in internal government. Let all know that in devoting all my strength on behalf of the welfare of my people, I shall defend the principles of autocracy as unswervingly as my deceased father." He dreamed of a

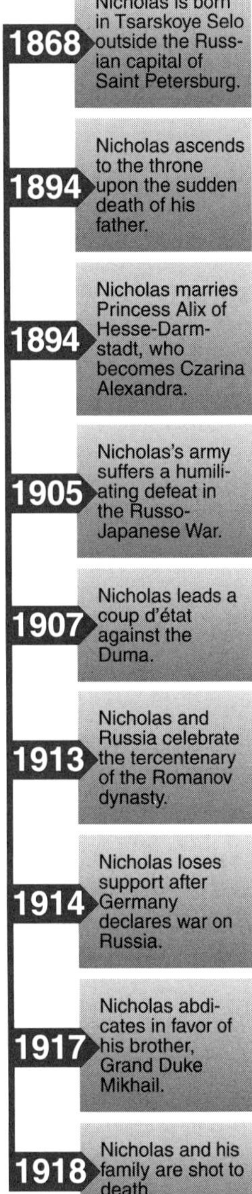

Russian superpower and was urged by Kaiser Wilhelm II of Germany, as well as by his own military and economic advisors, to assert Russian influence in China and Korea. No one believed that Japan would respond to Russian inroads in that region but the Russians misread the mood of Japan; the Russo-Japanese War of 1904–05 ended in a humiliating defeat for Russia.

Revolution was fomenting throughout Russia. In January 1905 a group of citizens led a peaceful march on the Winter Palace in Saint Petersburg to present a petition for democratic reform. The palace guards opened fire, injuring and killing hundreds. Although Nicholas was away at the time of the massacre, he was blamed. His position became increasingly precarious as several attempts were made on his life and on the lives of leading government officials. To ensure the safety of the royal family, two identical trains were built to carry the imperial household from destination to destination. It was hoped that the uncertainty as to which train actually held the royal family would thwart would-be assassins.

Nicholas was forced to respond to growing pressures for democratization. In 1905, under the influence of Prime Minister Serge de Wine, Nicholas issued the October Manifesto, promising civil liberties and democratic elections to a national body of representatives, the Duma. Nicholas retained the power to dissolve the Duma, and did so twice.

Although some authorities have argued that Nicholas did not comprehend the scope of reforms promised by the October Manifesto, others claim that he simply did not agree to any reforms that would limit his authority as autocrat, a title Nicholas insisted on keeping. In 1907 Nicholas led a coup d'état against the Duma and installed a more compliant body of representatives. This third Duma enacted a more conservative electoral law, disenfranchising many of the voters. With his authority assured. Nicholas then withdrew from politics to his family. In 1909 he made a state visit to England; in 1912 Kaiser Wilhelm II of Germany visited Russia. In 1913, amid great pomp, Nicholas and Russia celebrated the tercentenary of the accession of the Romanov dynasty.

Nicholas regarded himself as a protector of the smaller Balkan States. He tried to prevent the outbreak of World War I but when the Balkans were threatened by Turkey's territorial ambitions, particularly in the Dardanelles, Nicholas saw the need to maintain Russia's warm water port and decreed a general mobilization. Forty-eight hours later, on August 1, 1914,

Germany declared war on Russia. At first the war received wide popular support but increasing defeats and four million Russian deaths destroyed any remaining support for the war and the czar. Nicholas was under pressure from strikes and from protests in the Duma to form a Government of National Confidence but urged on by Alexandra, he used the opportunity to turn against Rasputin's enemies in the government. Rasputin's influence had reached the point that it was whispered that he, rather than Nicholas, was the true ruler of Russia. Alexandra herself was a stern autocrat who wrote to her husband that "responsible government . . . would be the ruin of everything," and Nicholas responded in a letter signed, "Your poor, little, weak-willed hubby." He fired the commander of his armies, his uncle Grand Duke Nikolai Nikolayevich, and assumed command himself. His absence from the capital allowed Alexandra and Rasputin to assume total authority over the country. Even Rasputin's assassination in December 1916 by a group of aristocrats who saw him as the greatest threat to the monarchy could not stem the growing tide of opinion opposed to a monarch totally removed from the people. Unemployment was rampant, the cost of living rose 300 percent, and food was scarce. Nicholas was shocked by the February revolution in 1917. He attempted to make his way from army headquarters to the capital, only to find his way blocked. Finally, on March 15, 1917, he abdicated in favor of his brother, Grand Duke Mikhail. Immediately after signing away his crown, Nicholas returned to the book he was reading, *Julius Caesar*. Mikhail himself renounced the crown the next day and a provisional government was formed.

"In these decisive days in the life of Russia we have thought that we owed to our people the close union and organization of all its forces for the realization of a rapid victory; for which reason, in agreement with the Imperial Duma, we have recognized that it is for the good of the country that we should abdicate the Crown of the Russian State and lay down the Supreme Power."

Czar Nicholas II, March 15, 1917

The Romanov family was kept under house arrest in their palace at Tsarskoye Selo. Nicholas tore up the lawns and planted a vegetable garden, content with the calmer turn his life had taken. Although many revolutionaries called for the czar's execution, Alexander Kerensky, leader of the provisional government, refused to hand over Nicholas. With the arrival of Vladimir Lenin and Leon Trotsky in Russia, Kerensky sent the czar to Tobolsk, Siberia, for his safety.

The royal family was installed in the governor's mansion but with the rise of the Bolsheviks to power following the October Revolution, the palace soon became a prison. Eight months later, the family was moved to Ekaterinburg in the Urals. The Bolsheviks feared Menshevik and royalist threats to save the royal family. Some time on July 16–17, 1918, the royal family was awakened from sleep and brought to a dark room, where a death sentence was passed against them. Nicholas rose to protest as his judges pulled revolvers from under their coats and shot the royal family to death. Their bodies were burned and thrown in a mine shaft; only the slightest remains identified the bodies as those of the royal family.

Since the circumstances of the murder of the Russian royal family remained obscure (no one would take credit for ordering their execution), several individuals have claimed to be surviving members of the Romanov family. Nicholas was reportedly seen in London in the 1920s. Nicholas's youngest daughter, Anastasia, was reported to have survived the massacre and over the years several women have claimed to be Anastasia, but the evidence shows that the entire family was indeed shot. Nicholas and his family have been made saints of the Russian Orthodox Church. ◆

Noor

1951– ● QUEEN OF JORDAN

Queen Noor al-Hussein was born Lisa Najeeb Halaby on August 23, 1951, to a prominent Christian Arab-American family and raised primarily in Washington, D.C. Her father, Najeeb E. Halaby, was a Texan descended from a Syrian family. Halaby headed the Federal Aviation Administration in the Kennedy administration, and then became chairman and chief executive officer of Pan American World Airways.

Halaby attended schools in Los Angeles, Washington, D.C., New York City, and at Concord Academy in Massachusetts before entering Princeton University in its first coeducational freshman class in 1970. At Princeton she was a cheerleader and studied architecture and urban planning. She received a B.A. degree in architecture and urban planning in 1974, and joined several international urban planning and design projects in the United States, Australia, Iran, and Jordan. In 1976 she traveled throughout the Middle East researching aviation-training facilities in preparation for a master plan for an Arab Air University to be established in Jordan. She later joined Royal Jordanian Airlines as director of planning and design projects.

Halaby met King Hussein, and, as she said in an interview with *Vanity Fair* in 1991, "We courted on motorcycles. It was the only way we could get off by ourselves." The queen later caused a stir when she and the king posed on one of his Harley-Davidsons for a magazine cover photograph; it was one thing for the king, but an Arab woman should know better. She took the name Noor al-Hussein (Arabic for Light of Hussein) when she converted to Islam and married King Hussein on June 15, 1978. (King Hussein's first two marriages ended in divorce; his third wife, Queen Alia, was killed in a helicopter accident in 1977.) Queen Noor gladly became a warm stepmother to the king's two children with Queen Alia, Prince Ali and Princess Haya.

Already an accomplished professional, Queen Noor was well prepared to use her new position to join her husband in promoting peace, and in establishing foundations to further her strong interests in international exchanges, health care for women and children, women's rights, and environmental protection. In 1979 the queen established the Royal Endowment for Culture and Education, which conducts research on Jordan's employment needs and provides scholarships for students—women in particular—in fields deemed vital to Jordan's economic and cultural development. She convened the first Arab Children's Congress in 1980 to bring together children from around the Arab world for two-week educational programs designed to foster cultural solidarity.

> ***"Whether as individuals or states, Jordanian or American, or any of two hundred other nationalities, our separate efforts can meet and reinforce one another, as we work for parallel goals of human progress."***
> Queen Noor, 1998

In 1985 the Noor Al Hussein Foundation (NHF) was established to bring under one "umbrella organization" the administration of the queen's various development initiatives. The NHF has worked with the Jordanian government, the United Nations, and other international organizations to promote social development projects, particularly in the Middle East and developing nations, that are closely linked with each country's economic priorities.

The queen is also a patron of the World Conservation Union (the world's oldest international conservation organization) and is president of the United World Colleges, a network of ten equal-opportunity international colleges around the world that offer programs designed to foster cross-cultural understanding and, it is hoped, more peaceful international relations.

Although the queen was well liked and admired, she had some difficulties in winning the trust of some Jordanians, for even though she is of Arab descent, she was born a Christian in the United States. In addition, some found her too ambitious and outspoken to be a good role model for Arab women. Her tireless efforts to promote world peace and foster good relations among Arab nations was fine, some said, but her activities on behalf of women's rights and education they could do without.

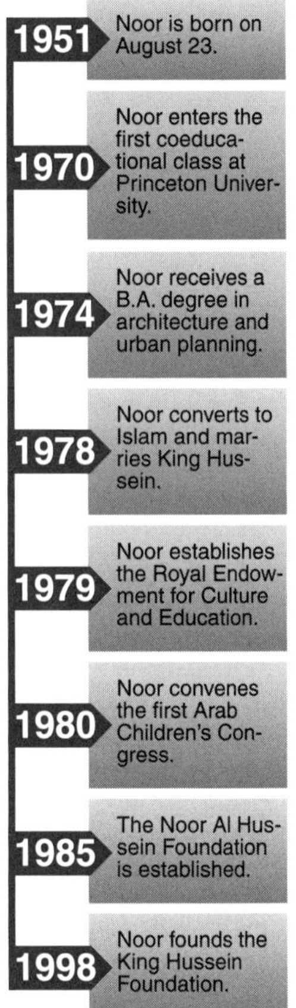

The eight-month illness of King Hussein, however, caused a warming toward the queen even among many of those who might have preferred a more traditional, preferably Palestinian partner for the king. Queen Noor was with him constantly, at the palace Bab al Salaam (Door of Peace) and at the Mayo Clinic in Rochester, Minnesota. While the king was undergoing surgery and treatments for non-Hodgkins lymphoma, a type of cancer, the queen lived with him at the clinic, and they would keep up with national affairs by e-mail. While the king lay dying, kept alive by a respirator, the queen went outdoors to console the crowds gathering around King Hussein Hospital. Many were touched by her coming to thank them and comfort them, when she was about to be a widow.

When King Hussein died on February 7, 1999, one of the most impressive gatherings of world leaders in recent memory came to pay their respects, but Queen Noor and the other women in the family were prohibited by Muslim custom from joining the men at the funeral ceremony. President Clinton, a close friend, called her "a daughter of America and a queen of Jordan," who had "made two nations very proud."

Even though the new king, Abdullah II, is not her son, Queen Noor is expected to remain a strong and inspiring presence in Jordan. Abdullah's first act in office (reportedly in accordance with King Hussein's request) was to name Noor's oldest son, Prince Hamzeh, as crown prince. Abdullah has named his wife, Rania, "Her Majesty the great Queen," but palace officials said the title would not reduce the standing of the late king's widow. Queen Noor shared the title of queen with Hussein's mother, Queen Zein, until she died in 1994. Shortly after the king's death, Queen Noor founded a King

Hussein Foundation through which she hopes to further the goals of international understanding that she shared with her late husband, and perhaps to offer a humanitarian prize. As she said in an interview shortly after the king's death, "On a spiritual level, I feel we are still making the journey together." ◆

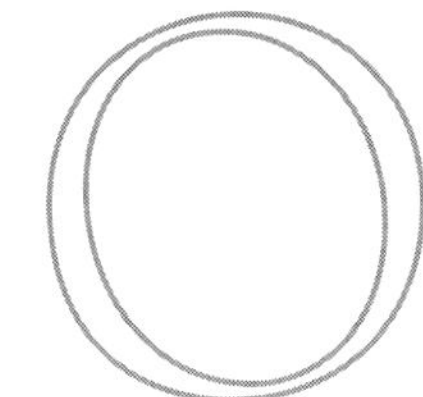

Osman I

1258–1326 ● OTTOMAN EMPEROR

Much of what is known about Osman is shrouded by legends perpetrated by later Ottoman historiographers to confer a stately lineage on the imperial family. They claim that Osman's father, Ertugrul, led four hundred nomadic Seljuk horsemen through Anatolia where they encountered Sultan Aladdin of Konya besieged by Mongols. His men favored siding with the Mongols, but Ertugrul admonished them that justice demanded they support the weaker Aladdin. The Mongols were defeated, and Ertugrul was rewarded with Eskishehir and Sugut, where Osman was born. When Osman succeeded Ertugrul, Aladdin granted him a banner and drum, traditional symbols of sovereignty.

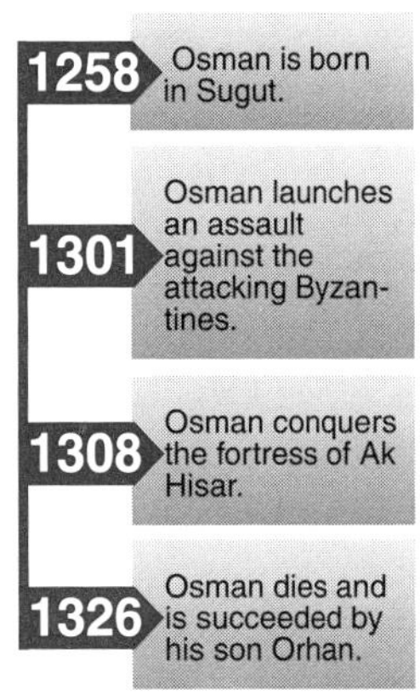

Osman was originally a pagan, but while residing at a Muslim's house, he noticed how his host cherished a well-worn Koran. When told that the book contained the word of God, Osman studied it throughout the night until, just before dawn, he began to doze. God appeared to him in a dream and said, "Since you have honored my word, so too your descendants will be honored forever." Inspired by his vision, Osman converted to Islam, which he studied with the *kadi* (Muslim religious judge) Edebali. He fell in love with Edebali's daughter Malkatun, but the *kadi* was hesitant about giving her to Osman. After two years of courtship, Osman had another dream. In it, a full moon rose from the sheikh's breast and entered his own. A tree then grew from his loins, bearing branches that shaded the world. He

Ottoman Empire

The Ottoman empire was a Turkish Muslim state that originated about 1300 when Osman I, after whom the empire is named, established the independence of his warrior principality in northwestern Anatolia from the collapsing Seljuk Turk state. In the fourteenth century, Osman's successors conquered almost all of Anatolia and captured much of southeastern Europe, including Gallipoli, Thrace, Macedonia, Bulgaria, and Serbia. From early on, the Ottoman empire was an absolutist state in which total allegiance to the sultan was mandatory.

The Ottomans were temporarily halted by Timur, a Tatar leader who defeated Sultan Bayezid I at the Battle of Ankara in 1402. During the mid fifteenth century, however, the Ottoman emperors regained lost territory and conquered Constantinople, the capital of the Byzantine empire. By defeating the Mameluks, Selim I (r. 1512–20) brought Syria, Palestine, the Arabian Peninsula, Egypt, and Algeria into the empire. His son, Süleyman I (r. 1520–66), conquered Hungary, Tripoli, and Mesopotamia. The reign of Süleyman I is considered to be the high point of the Ottoman empire. The empire began to decline in the late sixteenth century due to the growing power of the elite *deyshirme* class, made up of forcefully converted Christians who were placed in high government and military posts. Their conflicts with the older Turko-Muslim elite led to factionalism in the imperial court. That and imperial corruption resulted in inefficiency and other forms of misrule. As central authority weakened, many localities became autonomous entities.

Decay of the empire accelerated in the eighteenth and nineteenth centuries as technological progress and economic development in Europe went unanswered in the land of the Ottomans. Attempts by Selim III (r. 1789–1807) to reform the government failed. The growth of nationalism in southeastern Europe during the nineteenth century, capped by the Balkan Wars (1912–13), stripped the sultanate of virtually all of its territory west of the Bosporus Straits. Defeat in World War I, followed by the establishment of a Turkish republic in 1922, put a finish to the empire.

then saw four mountain ranges: the Balkans, the Caucasus, the Atlas, and the Taurus, watered by four rivers: the Tigris, the Euphrates, the Nile, and the Danube. The land contained noble cities in which the cry to prayer mingled with the singing of nightingales. Suddenly, the leaves of the tree became swords, pointing to Constantinople. The city was a diamond ring, mounted between two emeralds and two sapphires. Just as Osman was about to put the ring on his finger, he woke up. Edebali interpreted the dream as meaning that from the union of Osman with Malkatun, a great empire would emerge and so allowed them to marry.

Osman was an imposing figure, who radiated a natural sense of superiority to his subjects. As a neophyte, he had a well-developed sense of Islamic justice but insisted on peaceful relations with his Christian neighbors, many of whom later embraced Islam. In return, he adopted their administrative and mercantile practices, and did little to harass the cities of Nicaea, Nicomedia, and Bursa, blocking his way to Constantinople. The Byzantine emperor, however, was wary of Osman's mounting strength and unsuccessfully endeavored to enlist Mongol assistance in constraining him. Only after the Byzantines attacked Osman in 1301 was he persuaded to launch his own assault. In 1308 he conquered the fortress of Ak Hisar, controlling the descent of the Sakarya River to the Black Sea, enabling him to sever the land route between Bursa, Nicaea, and Nicomedia. Determining that Bursa was the weakest link in the defense of Constantinople, he lay siege to the city. For seven years, the local governor Evenros waited for troops from Constantinople to relieve him. Finally, as Osman lay dying, Evenros surrendered the city and converted to Islam. At his death, Osman left just a salt cellar, a spoon, a robe, and a number of sheep. He was succeeded by his son Orhan. In later Ottoman (a word derived form "Osman") tradition, new emperors were girded with Osman's sword and blessed, "May he be as good as Osman." ◆

Otto I

912–973 ● King of Germany

The son of King Henry I, Otto, a strong and practical leader, sought to bring order and justice to the newly developed German Reich. His vassal dukes feared him more than they loved him. In spite of a failed rebellion led by his half brother and supported by his younger brother, Henry, Otto continued to rely on family alliances in order to control his kingdom. However, loyalty and trust within the duchies quickly began to deteriorate under the corrupt feudal system.

Hereditary feudalism posed a serious threat to Otto's monarchy. In response, he began to appoint trusted, celibate church officials who could not distribute fiefs among their relations. The monarchy's alliance with the church became crucial to Otto's own consolidation of power; the mores of Christianity and German security were used to justify the ensuing wars against the Slavs in the east.

Holy Roman Empire

The Holy Roman Empire was a political state created during the Middle Ages as a Christianized version of the ancient Roman empire that was meant to incorporate all of western Christendom. The empire was to be the secular complement to the Roman Catholic church, the two working together to defend and disseminate the true faith. It was agreed in theory that the Pope, who crowned the emperor, would be the most powerful.

Theory and reality diverged, however. Some historians trace the Holy Roman Empire (which was not called that until the twelfth century) back to the crowning in 800 C.E. of Charlemagne as emperor by Pope Leo III. Charlemagne's territories did indeed include most of the old Roman empire in Europe. But from the crowning in 962 of Otto I of Germany by Pope John XII, the imperial title was held by German princes whose area of authority was largely limited to the German states and northern Italy. Therefore, the empire by no mean incorporated all western Christians.

Furthermore, relations between emperors and popes varied from era to era. Otto and his successors were strong emperors who propped up a weak papacy. In the mid eleventh century, Henry III even influenced elections of the Pope. But imperial authority began to be challenged in the late eleventh century, when Popes Gregory VII and Urban II insisted on papal independence. Until the early twelfth century, the emperors became the German king by inheritance and then were crowned emperor by the Pope; subsequently, they were chosen king by their fellow German princes. Emperors Otto IV (r. 1209–15) and Frederick II (r. 1220–50) of the German House of Hohenstaufen made strong challenges to the papacy, but subsequently the authority of the emperors declined sharply in Italy and even in the German states. The Reformation of the sixteenth century divided Germany into Catholic and Protestant principalities, further diminishing the possibility of a strong, united, Christian empire. The end of the Holy Roman Empire came after Napoleon defeated Habsburg Austria in his wars of conquest at the turn of the nineteenth century. Francis II, the last emperor, gave up the crown in 1806.

After subduing the Slavs through the conquest of Bohemia in 950, and increasing his political influence among weak kings in France, Otto invaded Italy in 951. His bid to restore the empire of Charlemagne appeared feasible as he tried to control a route to the East while reinforcing his alliance with the church through closer relations with the papacy in Rome.

Otto assumed the Lombard crown in Pavia, where he married his second wife, Adelaide. In the midst of his military campaign to establish control over the Italian peninsula, his son Liudolf, from his first wife, led a revolt in Germany. However, the rebel forces were weakened by the Magyar invasion of Bavaria in 954. Liudolf and the rebelling dukes submitted their armies to Otto, who defeated the Magyars in the Battle of the Lechfeld, near Augsburg, in 955.

Otto's consolidation of power in Germany was complete with the crowning of his son Otto II as king of Germany in 962. Otto once again invaded Italy, conquered the Papal State and was crowned Holy Roman Emperor by Pope John XII in 968, recreating the Empire of the West, which had existed under Charlemagne. A few days after the coronation, a treaty, the *Privilegium Ottonianum*, defined the roles of the emperor and the Pope in an empire that was to be the central ruling power of Europe for centuries. Problems, however, arose in Rome, where Pope John XII was unwilling to cede control over the Papal States to Otto. Otto deposed him and nominated Leo VIII as pope. After Leo VIII's death in 965, his successor, John XIII, was expelled by the Romans. Otto marched into Italy for the third time, to reestablish his control over the region and reinstate John XIII as Pope.

The appointment of John XIII and the creation of new Latin archbishoprics in the south brought Otto's empire into conflict with the Byzantine empire of the East. Otto attempted to exacerbate the conflict through military confrontation but eventually initiated negotiations with the Byzantine emperor Nicephorus Phocas. The resulting marriage of Otto II with the Byzantine princess Theophano (daughter of Romanus II) in 972, reinforced the Holy Roman Emperor's sovereignty over a reunited Europe. Otto I spent six years in Italy before returning to Germany, where he died.

Otto's reign as Holy Roman Emperor revived and reunited the Western world after its near collapse following the demise of the Carolingian empire. While the resurrected empire was not quite as spectacular as that of Charlemagne, it was more firmly based on contemporary social and cultural forces, which stimulated literature, language, and art in a more civilized Europe. ◆

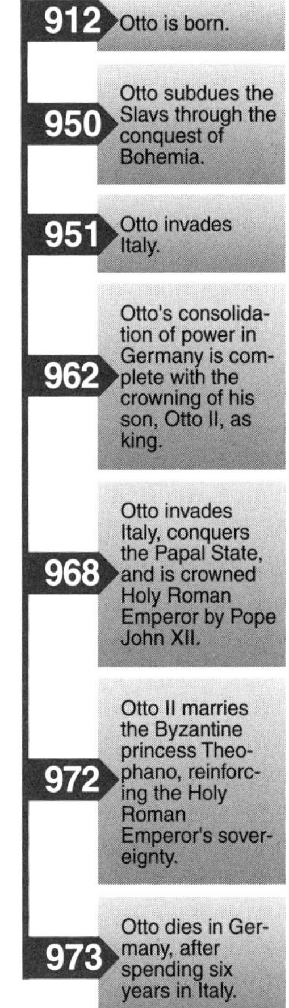

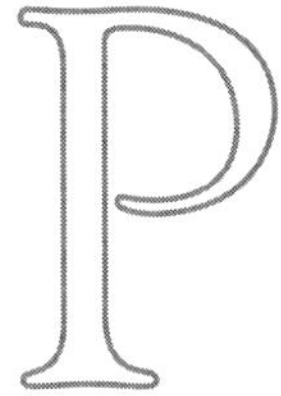

Pachacuti

c.1391–c.1473 ● Inca Emperor

Pachacuti (also spelled Pachacuteq) was Inca emperor from about 1438 to about 1471. Pachacuti is regarded as the greatest of the Inca emperors. His name has been translated from the Quechua variously as "Cataclysm," "Earthquake," or literally "You Shake the Earth." Pachacuti ascended the throne after defending the Inca capital of Cuzco against the Chanca invasion and overthrowing his father, Viracocha Inca, in 1438. He then founded the Inca state and initiated its first great expansion. With his son Topa Inca, Pachacuti conquered a huge territory from Lake Titicaca on the modern Peru–Bolivia border in the south to the city of Quito in modern Ecuador to the north. Among his other achievements were the design and rebuilding of the imperial capital of Cuzco and the construction of Sacsahuaman and other classic Inca monuments including Ollantaytambo and Machu Picchu. Pachacuti is credited with inventing the bureaucratic structure of the Inca state, codifying Inca law, reorganizing and codifying the Inca religion, and developing the institution called the *panaca,* which provided households for the royal mummies. He transformed the Incas from a predatory chiefdom into a highly centralized and **stratified** state administering a **redistributive** economy through a monopoly of force and **codified** law. ◆

stratified: divided or arranged into classes or social levels.

redistributive: spreading to other areas.

codified: systematized.

Machu Picchu

Machu Picchu (pronounced Mah choo Pee choo) was the royal estate of the Inca emperor Pachacuti. Its ruins are located about fifty-four miles northwest of the city of Cuzco at approximately 9,000 feet above sea level, in the cloud forest of the rugged mountain region on the eastern watershed of the Peruvian Andes. Machu Picchu is believed to have been abandoned at the time of the Spanish conquest in the early 1500s. It lay in obscurity until American explorer Hiram Bingham visited the site in 1911 and recognized it as a major Inca monument. Scholars have long debated the function of Machu Picchu. Bingham believed it to be the last capital of Vilcabamba, an Inca state established after the Spanish conquest. Recent research, however, indicates that the site was built about a century before the conquest, and probably served as a residence of the Inca royal family. Machu Picchu's importance, aside from its beauty and aesthetic qualities, lies in the fact that the Spanish never discovered it. It is therefore one of only a very few examples of an imperial Inca installation that was not altered or affected by the European invasion.

Pedro I

1798–1834 ● EMPEROR OF BRAZIL

Born in Queluz palace, Portugal, Prince Pedro de Bragança e Borbón was nine years old when he fled with the Portuguese royal family to Brazil to escape an invading

French army. The Braganças settled in Rio de Janeiro in 1808 and Pedro spent the next thirteen years in and around that city. Though he was the elder son and heir of the Portuguese regent, later King João VI (r. 1816–26), Pedro received little formal education and spent much of his youth hunting, horse racing, bullfighting, brawling, and tavern hopping—often in the company of the Falstaffian Francisco Gomes da Silva, a native of Portugal commonly known as the *Chalaça* (Joker). Intellectually, the prince was most influenced by the count dos Arcos, former viceroy of Brazil and a proponent of enlightened despotism, and by his tutor and confessor, the liberal Friar António de Arrábida. In his quieter moments, especially after his marriage in 1817 to Princess Leopoldina de Habsburg, Pedro read extensively in political philosophy.

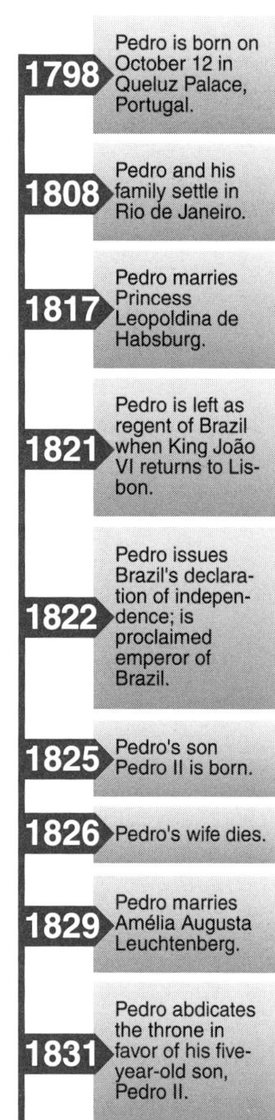

In February 1821 Pedro persuaded his father to accept publicly in Rio the constitutionalist principles proclaimed by the revolutionary regime in Portugal. Two months later Pedro played a major role in suppressing a movement led by Portuguese-born radicals to set up a revolutionary government in Rio. In April 1821, when King João VI obeyed a summons from the Portuguese Cortes to return to Lisbon, he left Pedro in Rio as regent of Brazil with the advice not to resist Brazilian independence should it seem inevitable but to take control of the separatist movement and make himself king of the new nation.

As regent of Brazil, Pedro disregarded orders from the Cortes that he dismantle his government in Rio and embark for Europe. Fearing the return of Brazil to colonial status if Pedro left, various city and town councils in southern Brazil petitioned him to stay. In Rio in January 1822, Pedro publicly declared "Fico" (I am staying). Following his announcement, Pedro installed a new ministry headed by the Brazilian savant José Bonifácio de Andrada e Silva, and events marched swiftly toward Brazil's declaration of independence, which Pedro issued near São Paulo on September 7, 1822. With the support of José Bonifácio and the major municipalities of the south, Pedro was proclaimed emperor of Brazil in Rio in October 1822.

Overcoming token opposition from the Portuguese garrison in Rio and fierce resistance from Portuguese army and navy units in Bahia province, Pedro's forces extended the emperor's control over virtually all of Portuguese America by the end of 1823. That same year a dispute arose between the emperor and his chief minister over the latter's persecution of his political enemies, which led to José Bonifácio's resignation from the government. A confrontation between the emperor and a constitutional convention he had summoned ended when Pedro forcibly dissolved the assembly and exiled José Bonifácio. Pedro then produced his own constitution, which he promulgated in March 1824. While in some respects more authoritarian than a draft the convention was considering, Pedro's constitution also was more liberal in providing religious toleration and **enumerating** civil rights.

enumerating: specifying one after another; listing.

The promulgation of Pedro's constitution sparked a major revolt in northeastern Brazil, which imperial forces suppressed in 1824. In the south, however, Pedro's army and navy were unable to prevent the loss of the empire's Cisplatine province (present-day Uruguay), which was invaded by forces from Buenos Aires in 1825.

The loss of Uruguay (conceded in 1828), the emperor's hostility toward slavery and his attempts to end the African slave trade, his employment of European mercenaries in the Brazilian armed forces, his involvement in Portuguese dynastic affairs, his unconcealed marital infidelities, and his uncouth Portuguese companions contributed to Pedro's growing unpopularity among influential Brazilians. Reconciliation with José Bonifácio and marriage to the admirable Amélia Augusta Leuchtenberg in 1829 (Leopoldina had died in 1826) slowed but did not halt the erosion of his support. In the midst of **nativist** riots in Rio, Pedro refused to make ministerial changes demanded by the mob and, on April 7, 1831, he abdicated the Brazilian throne in favor of his five-year-old son Pedro II.

nativist: having to do with the policy of favoring indigenous inhabitants as opposed to immigrants.

Pedro returned to Europe and concentrated on removing his reactionary brother Miguel from the Portuguese throne and replacing him with his own daughter, Maria. Shortly after achieving these goals, Pedro died of tuberculosis in Queluz on September 24, 1834. ◆

Pedro II

1825–1891 ● EMPEROR OF BRAZIL

A central figure in Brazil's development as a nation state, Pedro II was a man of complex personality and considerable abilities. His actions first consolidated and ultimately undermined the monarchical regime. Born in Rio de

Janeiro, the son and heir to the emperor Pedro I and the empress Leopoldina, Pedro II was set apart by both ancestry and nurture. Related to almost all the monarchies of Europe, he grew up surrounded by a rigid etiquette and omnipresent deference inherited from the royal court at Lisbon. His destined task was to command, the role of all others to obey. His formal education gave him a love of knowledge and instilled a sense of self-restraint and a devotion to service.

Pedro II's early years were disturbed and psychologically cramping. His mother died before his first birthday, and he lost his father, his beloved stepmother, and his eldest sister when they sailed for Europe following Pedro I's abdication in his favor on April 7, 1831. As guardian of Pedro II from 1831 to 1833, José Bonifácio de Andrada failed to protect his ward's physical and emotional health. An epileptic attack in August 1833 nearly proved fatal. Pedro II's health and conditions of life did improve markedly after José Bonifácio's dismissal, but the psychological pressures remained. Pedro II's approaching adolescence and his intellectual **precocity** made him credible as a possible savior for Brazil, which was mired in crisis in the late 1830s. Deference and adulation fed his sense of indispensability and intensified his isolation from ordinary life. He offered no resistance to the political campaign that prematurely declared him of age, at fourteen years and seven months, on July 23, 1840.

precocity: exceptionally early development.

The trappings of authority did not, Pedro II soon discovered, denote real power. Courtiers and politicians cooperated to manipulate his views, exploit his prerogatives, and determine his life, as he realized in October 1843 when the bride chosen for him, Teresa Cristina, proved to be plain and not an intellectual. Coldness, arbitrariness, and brevity of speech increasingly characterized Pedro II's public conduct. In 1845 the birth of a son (to be followed by three more children) and a long tour through the far south of Brazil provided the catalyst that brought maturity and unleashed his capacities as a ruler. By 1850 Pedro II had ended the power of court factions, learned

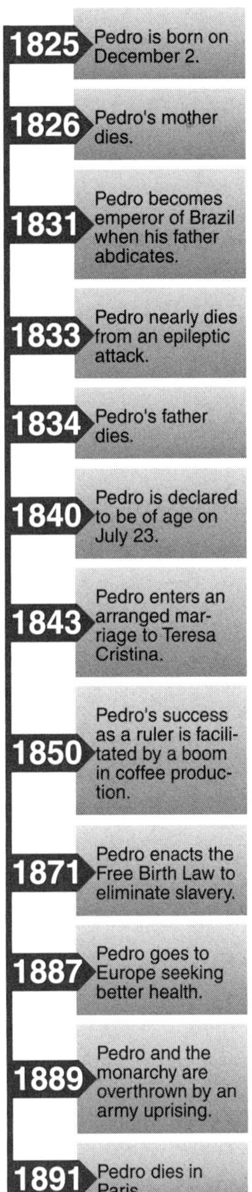

the efficient management of public affairs, and established his public image as a beneficent, highly cultured, and dedicated sovereign. His success as ruler was facilitated both by a boom in coffee production and by an eclipse of radicalism and republicanism following the Praieira revolt of 1848–50.

During the 1850s and 1860s Pedro II embodied, as monarch, the only legitimate source of authority. He exemplified the European civilization that Brazilians desired for their nation. His talents as ruler were formidable: inexhaustible energy, remarkable memory for faces and facts, iron control of speech and action, firmness in purpose, freedom from petty resentments, acute sense of tactics, and utter indifference to the trappings of power. Politicians came and went. He alone remained entrenched at the center of affairs, ultimately determining both the political agenda and the personal characteristics requisite for political success.

Pedro II's skill as ruler played a part in securing long-term political stability for Brazil. He worked tirelessly to promote the development of the nation's infrastructure. Two particular achievements must be mentioned. He pursued the War of the Triple Alliance for five years until Paraguayan president Francisco Solano López was eliminated in 1870. Initiating in 1865 a campaign to force the eventual elimination of slavery, Pedro II brought it to fruition in 1871 with the enactment of the free birth law.

After 1871 new factors—a shift in the intellectual climate toward republicanism, greater confidence among Brazilians in their capacity to rule themselves, and growing resentment against a highly centralized administration—undermined the regime's legitimacy. Pedro II's innate conservatism in thought and behavior, his staleness in mind and body induced by three decades of rule, and his unwillingness to surrender any part of his powers inhibited him from meeting this challenge. He held no intellectual belief in monarchy as such. Both his sons had died in childhood and, much as he loved Isabel as a daughter, he did not perceive her as a credible successor. He therefore felt no duty to assure her future as monarch, an obligation that would have restricted his freedom of action. His antediluvian court, shabby palaces, and distaste for ceremony destroyed the emotional appeal of monarchy.

The growth in the size and complexity of government made Pedro II's insistence on personally supervising every detail of public business a clog on effective administration. His love of knowledge and concern for culture appeared increasingly as superficial, amateurish, and antiquated. His dominance of public life and elimination of all competing centers of power produced a vacuum at the heart of the system. Among younger Brazilians his monopoly of power bred feelings of impotence and futility and a resentment against his tutelage.

Among younger Brazilians Pedro II's monopoly on power bred feeling of impotence and futility and a resentment against his tutelage.

From the middle of the 1880s diabetes increasingly deprived Pedro II of the qualities that had made him so effective as a ruler. Still respected and even loved, he had ceased to be indispensable or even present in the country. During his prolonged absence in Europe in search of better health (1887–88), Isabel used her powers as regent to secure the immediate abolition without compensation of slavery (May 13, 1888). The disposal of one long-established institution could only suggest similar treatment for another that, for many Brazilians, had become an anachronism.

The army uprising that overthrew the monarchy on November 15, 1889, was as unexpected as it was decisive. Pedro II had no wish nor the ability to contest his dethronement and banishment to Europe. He conducted himself during exile with unwavering dignity, pursuing, as far as ill health would permit, his quest for knowledge. He died in Paris. ◆

Peter I

1672–1725 ● CZAR OF RUSSIA

Peter I, also known as Peter the Great, was czar of Russia. His father, Czar Alexei, died before his fourth birthday and was succeeded by Peter's sickly half brother, Fedor. A few years later Fedor died without issue and Peter, at the age of ten, became czar together with his half brother Ivan (1682). However, his half sister Sophia, backed by a revolution of the palace guard (the Streltsy), took power and ruled as regent. Peter and his mother left Moscow for the countryside where he enjoyed much more freedom than was usually allowed members of the royal family. He amused himself planning military maneuvers with boys of his own age, eventually forming regiments of six hunded youths. He spent time learning the crafts of carpentry, masonry, printing, and smithery. He also developed a passionate love of boats. This unorthodox education served as the base for his later effort to force Russia into the contemporary post-Renaissance world.

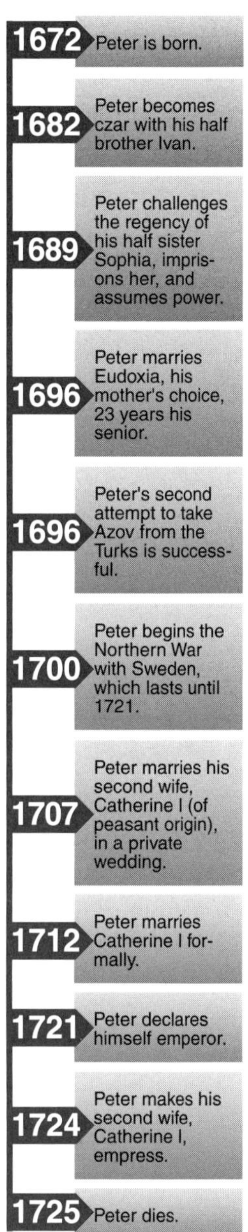

Toward the end of 1689 Peter challenged Sophia's regency, aided, and to some extent encouraged, by the failure of her second Crimea campaign, and backed by the Streltsy troops, loyal to him as the anointed czar. He assumed power (Ivan, a figurehead, died in 1696) and sent Sophia to the Novodevichy monastery outside Moscow where she spent the rest of her life in luxurious imprisonment. Some of her supporters were executed. Peter himself showed sadistic traits and enjoyed watching people being tortured. At the beginning of 1689 he married Eudoxia, his mother's choice, twenty-three years his senior, who bore him two sons.

Peter now set out to achieve the Westernization of Russia and expand his borders toward the Baltic and the Black seas, Russia possessing at the time only one seaport on the White Sea. In Moscow there was a small settlement of foreigners, almost a ghetto, known as the "German Suburb." They were not all Germans, but were almost all of wider education and experience than the Russians they lived among, a fact which attracted Peter to their company. Together with Russian friends, they formed a convivial group that remained in existence with Peter at its head until his death. Their orgies and buffoonery, including drunken celebrations held on religious festivals, scandalized many and led church dignitaries to see Peter as the antichrist, especially after the reforms he was later to force on them.

In 1696 Peter made his second and successful attempt (the first had ended in a costly retreat) to take Azov from the Turks, founding a navy in the process. After his victory, he sent twenty-eight Russians, most from the nobility, to Venice and twelve others to Holland and England to learn the crafts of navigation and shipbuilding. He also sent a "Great Embassy" (1697–98) to travel in Western Europe, accompanying it himself incognito, and spent four months in Amsterdam as a ship's carpenter. He visited England and lived for three months in the writer John Evelyn's house in Deptford; after the Russians left, Evelyn was horrified to see the damage they had done (he received £350.0s.9d in compensation from the English authorities).

Peter visited Dresden and Vienna, but his grand tour was cut short by a letter bringing him news of a military revolt—four Streltsy regiments were marching on Moscow. Halfway home he received news that the revolt had been put down, but decided not to resume his tour.

Almost his first action on returning to Moscow was to shave the beards of the boyars who came to greet him. Peter believed that their beards made Russians ridiculous in the eyes of the West. Eventually he was to tax those who did not want to shave (except for clergy and peasants); the church was shocked by what it saw as a godless act. Later that same winter (1698) he cut off the boyars' traditional wide sleeves, and later still decreed the compulsory changing of Russian for Western-style clothes. Not long after his return Peter sent his wife, Eudoxia, to whom he had never been close, to a convent, putting his sister in charge of his son Alexei, then nearly nine years of age.

He set in motion a series of startling reforms, some designed to displace the church. A partial list includes universal taxation and the emancipation of women from their lowly status and the *terem* (the Russian equivalent of a harem); he abolished the Moscow patriarchate and established a holy synod in its stead, with himself at its head; he reformed the calendar and the alphabet, at least for nonchurch purposes (the Bible and other church writings were still printed in the church Slavonic alphabet). He built hospitals and founded a new upper class of civil and military administrators. He encouraged trade by minting a new Russian currency to replace the foreign coins in circulation. While he was beginning his reforms, he had the rebellious Streltsy troops sadistically tortured and executed.

With his victory in the Battle of Poltava (1709) during the Northern War with Sweden (1700–21), Peter gained access to the Baltic Sea. In the midst of the war he built the city of Saint Petersburg, "a window on Europe," where the river Neva flows into the Gulf of Finland. Constructed on swampland, far north enough to have a summer of very short nights, the city became his capital in preference to Moscow despite its damp, unhealthy climate (*neva* is Finnish for "swamp"). He peopled the city in the same way he had Westernized Russian dress: by force.

Peter's attempts to prepare Alexei, the surviving son of his first marriage, for his future role proved frustrating for both father and son. Alexei, a weak character, fled from Russia and eluded Peter for several months. He was found by Peter's envoys and brought back to Russia. Humiliated by his son's public defection and fearing that Alexei might serve, unwittingly, as a focus of discontent within Russia, Peter first made Alexei sign away his rights to the throne; later, fearing a plot, he questioned his son about his "fellow conspirators." (One of the most famous

"He is a man of very hot temper, soon inflamed and very brutal in his passion. He raises his natural heat by drinking much brandy, which he rectifies himself with great application. He is subject to convulsive motions all over his body, and his head seems to be affected with these. He wants not capacity, and has a larger measure of knowledge than might be expected from his education, which was very indifferent. A want of judgment, with an instability of temper, appear in him too often and too evidently."

Bishop Burnet, *Peter the Great*, 1698

"He was a lover of company, and a man of much humor and pleasantry, exceedingly facetious and of vast natural parts. He had no letters; he could only read and write, but had a great regard for learning and was at much pains to introduce it into the country."

General Alexander Gordon, *History of Peter the Great*, 1718

of nineteenth century Russian paintings, by Nikolai Gai, depicts Peter's interrogation of his son.) A number of courtiers, including senators, military officials, Eudoxia herself, and Alexei's tutor, were arrested and imprisoned, exiled, or executed. As the "evidence" grew, Alexei was arrested and two courts, civil and ecclesiastical, were convened. Alexei was tortured and sentenced to death; however, he died on the following day before Peter had ratified the sentence. The cause of death is not known.

Peter declared himself emperor ("Father of the Fatherland, Peter the Great, Emperor of All Russia") in 1721 and in 1724 he made his second wife, Catherine I, a woman of peasant origin and dubious early history, empress. They were formally married in 1712, a private wedding having been performed in 1707. They had twelve children, of whom only two daughters survived.

Peter was a strange and enigmatic character. His capacity for self-discipline and hard physical work was as great as his capacity for pleasure, and his demands of himself were as ruthless as his demands on others. He suffered from convulsions, the exact nature and cause of which were never diagnosed. ◆

Philip II

1527–1598 ● King of Spain

Philip was the only son of Charles V, who as Holy Roman Emperor ruled over more territory than any of his predecessors. In 1543 Philip married his cousin Maria of Portugal, who died in 1545 while giving birth to Don Carlos. Upon his second marriage to Mary I of England in 1554, he received the kingdoms of Naples and Sicily, followed by the Netherlands in 1555. He became king of Spain and its overseas dominions in 1556, when his father abdicated in his favor.

Philip's marriage to Mary served as a pretext for England's entering the conflict between Spain and France on the Spanish side in 1557. In the same year Spain won an important victory over the French at San Quentin, and in honour of San Lorenzo, on whose feast day the battle was won, Philip commissioned the building of El Escorial palace north of Madrid, where he conducted and orchestrated affairs of state. Suspicious of his court intimates, Philip refused to delegate even the simplest of administrative tasks, which resulted in bureaucratic stagnation and bickering between rival court factions. In 1558 Mary died leaving no heir and a year later Philip signed the peace treaty of Cateau-Cambresis that ended the war with France and sealed his marriage to Elizabeth of Valois, daughter of Henry II of France, with whom he had two daughters. Elizabeth died in 1568, and in 1570 Philip was married for the fourth and last time, this time to his cousin Anne of Austria; their son was to become his successor as Philip III (Don Carlos, whom he hated, having died in prison).

Philip became increasingly obsessed by a grandiose plan to defeat Protestantism and to continue the work of unification. Spain was enjoying a golden age, with accomplishments in literature and painting, and Philip believed that it could and should become the moral voice of Catholicism. In his quest for political hegemony, resistance was quashed by force: the suppression of rebellion of the Moriscos (1568–70) was an attempt to secure religious unity in Spain; the conquest of Portugal in 1580, an attempt to increase Spanish dominion. However throughout the latter part of his reign, Philip was confronted with rebellion from the Netherlands, which only ended when the Seven United Provinces achieved independence in 1579. He also faced a revolt by the Aragonese in 1591–92.

English and French support of the Dutch rebellion and constant attacks by England on Spanish shipping vessels led to Philip's building and equipping of the Spanish armada. However, his plan to invade England in 1588 failed and his "invincible" armada was crushed, with less than half of the 130 ships reaching home. In 1590, continuing his campaign to restore the power of the Roman Catholic church, Philip sent troops and funds to France to aid the Catholic League in its fight against the Protestant ruler, Henry of Navarre (Henry IV). After failing in his attempt to seize the throne in the name of his daughter, Isabella Clara Eugenia, Philip was forced to accept the accession of Henry of Navarre to the French throne, but had the consolation that Henry had become a Catholic.

On Philip's death, the debts of the Spanish government were estimated at around one hundred million ducats, and interest payments on this sum alone constituted almost two-thirds of all Spanish revenues; the Spanish government never recovered from the excessive spending during his reign and faced bankruptcy throughout the seventeenth century. Philip had remained indifferent to these problems, concerned only with his political and religious quest. His dreams were not totally unfulfilled and—despite his losses with respect to England, Scotland, and Holland—he had managed to maintain Spanish rule in Belgium, beat off the Ottoman challenge to the east at the battle of Lepanto (1571), and add Portugal to the Catholic crown. Furthermore, he had strengthened the position of the Catholic church in what he saw as its fight against the rising tide of Protestantism. ◆

Pu Yi

1906–1967 ● EMPEROR OF CHINA

Pu Yi was the last emperor of China. His abdication from the throne in 1912 terminated 267 years of rule by the Ching dynasty, an empire established by the Manchu people of what is now the region called Manchuria in northeastern China. It also brought to an end 4,000 years of dynastic rule in China. Pu Yi, known in the West by his chosen English name, Henry Pu Yi, survived an extraordinary series of political and social changes that transformed him from the most powerful person in China to a humble worker.

Pu Yi was born on February 7, 1906, to Prince and Princess Chun. He was named heir to the throne at the age of two by the empress dowager, Tzu Hsi, a distant relative who ruled China. The dowager was an imposing figure who was greatly feared by many. Pu Yi's uncle, Emperor Kuang Hsu, had been held in captivity by the empress for years. The emperor died on November 14, 1908, and the empress died soon after. On December 2, 1908, Pu Yi was enthroned as emperor. His father served as regent, but real administrative power lay in the hands of an empress dowager, Lung Yu, who had been appointed by Tzu Hsi. As emperor, he saw little of the rest of his family.

In 1911 and 1912 a republican revolution led by Sun Yat-sen overthrew the imperial throne, and General Yuan Shi-kai, a longtime ally of the old dowager, forced the abdication of Pu Yi on February 12, 1912. Yuan Shi-kai then became president of the new republic. Pu Yi was allowed to remain with a reduced staff in the Forbidden City, the imperial palace in Beijing, until 1924. After his abdication, Pu Yi was still treated like the emperor by his attendants, and he continued to lead an isolated existence. His days were mostly filled with schoolwork. Over time, he grew haughty and developed a taste for cruelty. Pu Yi became known for his hard heart and nasty temper, and he flogged members of his staff almost daily.

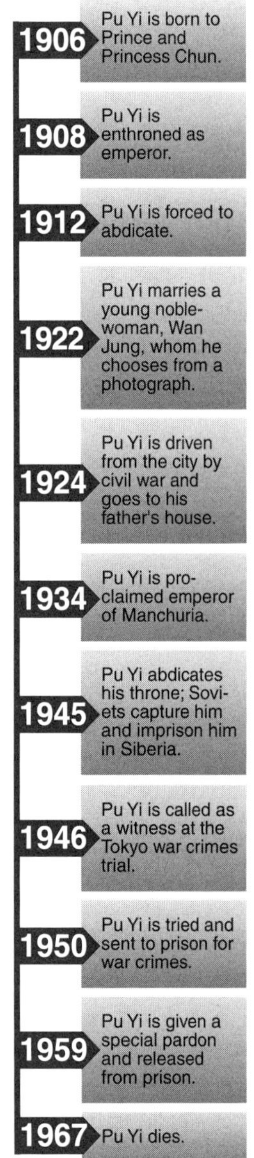

In 1922 Pu Yi married a young noblewoman named Wan Jung. He gave her the English name Elizabeth. Pu Yi chose Wan Jung from among women he had seen in several photographs that were presented to him by his family and staff. Throughout his life, he also had a number of secondary wives, a common custom among nobility in China, but he treated none of them well. Wan Jung remained with Pu Yi for many years, though he paid her little attention. Eventually, she became an opium addict.

In 1924 civil war and advancing armies drove Pu Yi from the Forbidden City, and he went to his father's house. Out of concern for his life, Pu Yi later fled with his staff to the official residence of the Japanese foreign representatives in Tientsin in early 1925. His family arrived later. While in Tientsin, a plot was hatched to install Pu Yi as a Japanese puppet emperor in his people's native homeland, Manchuria. Japanese forces invaded Manchuria in 1931, and Pi Yi, his attendants, and family secretly moved there later that year. In 1934 Pu Yi was proclaimed emperor of Manchuria. He held that title for fourteen years, though he was not allowed to play any part in politics, and his days were long and dull.

After the defeat of the Japanese in World War II in 1945, Pu Yi abdicated his throne and attempted to escape Manchuria for Japan via a small airplane, leaving many of his family members behind. But Soviet soldiers captured him and took him to Siberia for detention. Pu Yi's life in detention was relatively comfortable. He had radios, books, and games to play. He had three meals a day and a Russian tea in the afternoon. Doctors attended to his health, and a few family members in detention continued to wait on him. Pu Yi was detained in Siberia for five years.

In 1946 Pu Yi was called as a witness at the Tokyo war crimes trial. There, he testified that he had been a tool of the Japanese military and not an instrument of Manchurian self-determination. That year, his wife died in the Long White Mountains in China.

While in prison, Pu Yi had to learn, for the first time in his life, how to do simple things for himself, such as wash his clothes and make his bed.

In 1950 the Soviets handed Pu Yi and his household over to the Chinese authorities for trial as a war criminal. He was sent to a military prison in Fushun and later to Harbin for rehabilitation into Communist Chinese society. While in prison, he was separated from his family, and he had to learn, for the first time in his life, how to do simple things for himself, such as wash his clothes and make his bed. In 1959 he was given a special pardon and released from prison.

After his release, Pu Yi went to live in Beijing, where he worked in a mechanical repair shop and later as literary and historical worker for the national archives. With a team of assistant writers, he produced his autobiography, *From Emperor to Citizen*, in the 1960s. He married his last wife, Lu Shu-hsien, in 1962. Pu Yi died in 1967. Lu Shu-hsien died in 1997 at the age of seventy-two. ◆

Qabus ibn Sa'id

1940– • SULTAN OF OMAN

Qabus ibn Sa'id was born in Salala, in the southern Omani province of Dhufar, on November 18, 1940. His father was Sultan Sa'id ibn Taymur Al Bu Sa'id, while his mother came from the Bayt Ma'shani tribe of the Dhufari mountains. In 1958 Qabus was sent to England for schooling, and he subsequently attended the Royal Military Academy at Sandhurst. Attached to the British Army of the Rhine for seven months, he then spent a short period studying local government in the English Midlands. A world tour in 1964 was followed by years of enforced inactivity back in Salala, studying Islamic law under the watchful eye of his father, who had not been to his capital at Musqat since 1958.

"My first act will be immediate abolition of all the unnecessary restrictions on your lives and activities. My people, I will proceed as quickly as possible to transform our life into a prosperous one with a bright future. Every one of you must play his part towards this goal. Our country in the past was famous and strong."

Qabas, upon his succession to the throne, 1970

The late 1950s saw increasing unrest in Oman, due to Sultan Sa'id's apparent refusal to spend his new oil revenues and because of the Dhufar Rebellion against the sultan's paternalistic rule. By mid-1970 the situation had worsened and Qabus joined forces with his friends in Salala and British and Omani backers in Musqat to organize a coup d'état against his father on July 23, 1970.

In contrast to his father, Qabus threw the country open to development and welcomed back the thousands of Omanis working abroad. Within a week of his accession, the country's first true Council of Ministers was formed with Qabus's uncle, Tariq ibn Taymur Al Bu Sa'id, as prime minister. Two weeks after the coup, Sultan Qabus arrived in Musqat for the first time

and took charge of the new government. Unfortunately, differences between the two men forced Tariq's resignation in 1971; Qabus has served as his own prime minister since then.

Qabus was one of the few Arab leaders not to break off relations with Egypt following the Camp David Accords.

From the beginning of his reign, Qabus faced two primary challenges: economically transforming one of the world's most underdeveloped countries and dealing with the serious rebellion in Dhufar. In the early 1970s development activity concentrated on providing education, health care, water, and electricity to the people and creating a modern infrastructure. By 1976 sufficient groundwork had been laid for implementing the country's first five-year development plan. At the same time, the course of the Dhufar rebellion was reversed with British, Jordanian, and Iranian assistance and through an intensive "hearts and minds" campaign, and the sultan was able to declare the war over in December 1975.

Qabus clearly stands at the apex of the political system of Oman. Decision making tends to bypass the Council of Ministers and flow directly up to the sultan. He has steered the country to a moderate path in international affairs, establishing diplomatic relations with China and the former Soviet Union while maintaining close political and security links with Britain and the United States. Qabus was one of the few Arab leaders not to break off relations with Egypt following the Camp David Accords. The sultan was careful to keep channels open to both sides during the Iran-Iraq War and permitted Western powers to use Omani facilities during the 1990–91 hostilities against Iraq.

When those hostilities flared into the Persian Gulf War in 1991, Oman joined the thirty-nine-nation coalition, led by the United Nations, that defeated Iraq. The war highlighted shifting alliances among Arab states, as most sided with the United Nations. In 1981 Oman had joined neighboring nations to form the Gulf Cooperation Council (GCC). Those links strengthened after the Iraqi invasion of Kuwait. Oman also acted as a contact between Iran and its Arab neighbors. Oman and Iran shared responsibility for allowing oil tankers to pass safely through the Strait of Hormuz, and in late 1998 Iran established a military friendship committee with Oman.

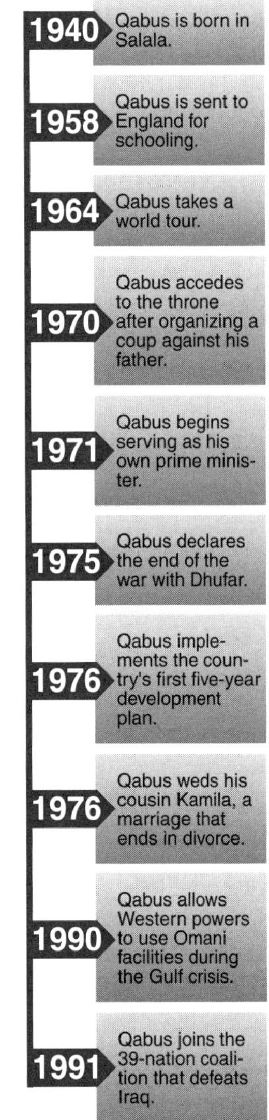

By the late 1990s Oman's economy remained tied to the rise and fall of world petroleum prices. Oman was the world's nineteenth largest producer of oil, which it had begun exporting in 1967. Petroleum earnings reached 75 percent of Oman's export and government revenues. Unlike some other Middle East nations, though, Oman's oil reserves were limited and expected to be depleted by 2020 or 2050.

Qabus addressed the vulnerability produced by Oman's dependency on such a limited natural resource, and he increased funding for the development of renewable resources that could provide long-term economic growth, such as agriculture, fishing, tourism, and production of consumer goods. The nation's financial plan also included creation of a major shipment facility at the port city of Salalah and sales of liquefied natural gas. The mining industry was also revived; with plans to extract deposits of gold, copper, and silver.

Qabus recognized that bringing his nation into the twenty-first century economically required allowing greater participation of his subjects in government. He opened up the political process somewhat by establishing the Consultative Council in 1991. This fifty-five-member body, appointed by the sultan, advises the government. The sultan appointed several women to the council. When Omani officials arrested several members of the activist Muslim Brotherhood in 1994, Qabus pardoned them, but analysts pointed to citizens' anxieties about the economy as the root of political protest. Omanis had become dependent on social welfare and state-owned industry, with public services that were among the best in the developing world. But some feared for their future in a post-oil economy. Qabus acknowledged Oman's need to privatize industries to increase profits and efficiency.

Qabus entered the twentieth century as a widely respected monarch, known for his courage and political skill in both domestic and foreign affairs. He was admired among regional leaders for completely transforming Oman from an undeveloped desert hinterland to a cosmopolitan nation with one of the most successful Arab economies. Admirers credited Qabus for achieving this while retaining conservative political values.

Qabus has no direct heirs. A marriage arranged by his father to the daughter of an important tribal shaykh was never finalized. A marriage in 1976 to his cousin Kamila, a daughter of Tariq, ended in divorce. ◆

Rainier III

1923– • PRINCE OF MONACO

Prince Rainier III became one of the most celebrated royal figures in the world when on April 18, 1956, he married the American film star Grace Kelly. Prince Rainier is a descendant on his father's (Count Pierre de Polignac) side of a prominent house of French nobility. The house of Polignac dates back to the 1050s, and, by some reckonings, to the year 860. But it was through his mother, Princess Charlotte, that Rainier was a descendant of the ancient Grimaldi family that has ruled Monaco for seven hundred years. (Prince Rainier and his children and several thousand Monégasques celebrated the seven-hundredth year of Grimaldi rulership in January 1997.)

About the size of New York's Central Park, Monaco has a population of 30,000, of whom only 5,000 are citizens.

Monaco, a principality politically allied with and protected by France, is a tiny enclave on the Riviera, along the Côte d'Azur (gold coast) of the Mediterranean Sea, east of Nice, France. About the size of New York City's Central Park, or London's Hyde Park, Monaco has a population of 30,000, of whom only 5,000 are citizens, or Monégasques. Although the Grimaldi family has ruled since 1297, Monaco has been a possession of Spain (from 1542), France (from 1641), and Sardinia (from 1815). Its modern status as a principality dates from 1861.

Prince Rainier was born Rainier-Louis-Henri-Maxence-Bertrand Grimaldi on May 31, 1923, in the Palace de Princier, the first Grimaldi heir to be a Monégasque since Honoré IV was born in 1758. Rainier was the second child of Princess Charlotte and Prince Pierre de Polignac; an older sister, Antoinette,

Prince Rainier III of Monaco in 1956 with his fiancée, actress Grace Kelly, who later became Princess Grace.

was born in 1921. De Polignac was not loved by the Grimaldis; Charlotte was not happy with him, and her father, Prince Louis II, despised him. Once Rainier was born and the male heir thereby supplied, the family appears to have had no further use for de Polignac.

Prince Rainier and Princess Antoinette grew up mostly outside of Monaco, with their mother and grandfather Louis, who had little interest in his principality and spent only about three months a year in Monaco. The rest of the time the family stayed in Paris or Marchais. With Louis's encouragement, Charlotte and de Polignac separated and filed for divorce. Once the divorce was final, Louis issued an order that prohibited de Polignac from entering Monaco; he was to be physically thrown out if he set foot in the principality again.

One right that de Polignac had secured in the divorce was that of deciding his son's education. Up to the age of ten, Rainier had been educated entirely by private tutors. Although his grandfather would naturally have preferred a French school, de Polignac sent Rainier to a private English school near Oxford called Summer Fields, known as the "nursery for Eton." Rainier was unhappy there, and terribly homesick, though he did excel on the boxing team and won a school title for his weight. After the school holidays in 1935 he refused to go back, threatening to run away. He was sent to another English school called Stowe School, but as the only foreigner among five hundred, and the only hereditary prince, he again found the conditions intolerable. Rainier made the headlines in newspapers in England and France when he ran away from Stowe School.

A bitter custody battle between grandfather Louis and de Polignac over Antoinette resulted in both children being removed from de Polignac's influence. After Easter 1936 Rainier was sent to Le Rosey in Switzerland, where he was happy. Le Rosey was nicknamed "the school of kings" because many future monarchs attended it, and it is said to resemble a luxury hotel more than a school.

Prince Rainier III with his daughter Princess Stephanie in 1984.

Rainier graduated from Le Rosey in 1939, and at the age of sixteen began university studies at Montpellier University in August of that year. He enrolled in general studies with an emphasis on French history, though he had no particular leanings toward any one subject. Outside the classroom, however, he enjoyed tennis and golf, and loved animals. Rainier graduated from Montpellier with a B.A. degree in June 1943, and promptly moved to Paris to be closer to an actress he had met in Monaco named Gisèle Pascal, and also for additional studies at the École Libre des Sciences Politiques.

The Second World War was going on at this time, and even royal families were not exempted from its effects. Rainier was formally made direct heir to the throne on June 2, 1944, a few days after his twenty-first birthday. (At the same time, his mother, Princess Charlotte, renounced her rights to the succession.) In July Prince Rainier enlisted in the Free French Army as a foreign volunteer, and saw action in the Alsatian campaign against the Germans. He was cited for bravery under fire, and was awarded the Croix de Guerre, the Bronze Star, and the Cross of the Legion of Honor, military division. Rainier also served as a liaison to the Texas Rangers at Strasbourg and with the rank of colonel, was transferred to Berlin in the Economic Section of the French Military Mission. He was decommissioned from the French Army in January 1947, and returned to Monaco.

Rainier's grandfather Louis became fatally ill in April 1949, and delegated power to the grandson. Louis died on May 9, 1949, less than a month before Rainier's twenty-sixth birthday.

One of the new prince's first acts was to lift the ban that had long excluded his father from Monaco. Although he had been most unhappy with Pierre de Polignac's choices of schools, Rainier had secretly kept in touch with his father through correspondence, and they had a good relationship. Rainier arranged a luxurious accommodation for his father at the Hôtel de Paris and, hoping to restore his father's reputation in the principality, established a prestigious annual literary prize, the Prince Pierre Prize in Literature, to be given each year to a distinguished European author selected by a committee appointed by Prince Rainier.

The prince met the American film actress Grace Kelly when she was on the Riviera for the Cannes Film Festival in 1955. He began courting her, discreetly, and visited her on the set of *The Swan*, a film about an American girl whose mother is determined to marry her to a prince. On January 5, 1956, it was announced that Prince Rainier would marry Grace Kelly (born Grace Patricia Kelly in Philadelphia on November 12, 1929). At first, many in Monaco were displeased at the prospect of having another film star as their princess. (Late in his life, Louis II had displeased almost everyone in Monaco, especially his own family, by marrying an actress who came to be known, and detested, as Princesse Ghislaine. Louis had willed her half his estate, and the ensuing court battle, eventually settled to the Grimaldi family's satisfaction, was a great embarrassment to everyone involved.) Further, many Monégasques were uncomfortable with the idea of having an American as their princess.

The marriage, on April 18, 1956, was an international sensation. MGM had the rights to film the wedding, in exchange for letting Grace Kelly out of her remaining contract; one of the conditions of the marriage was that she would have to quit her film career. Rainier persuaded her to abandon moviemaking with the argument that she would have one of the world's premier roles—Her Serene Highness, Princesse de Monaco—and that she would never have to worry about being out of the public eye.

Prince Rainier and Princess Grace had three children: Her Serene Highness Princess Caroline, born in Monaco on January 23, 1957; H.S.H. Prince Albert, Heir to the Throne, Marquis of Baux, born in Monaco on March 14, 1958; and H.S.H. Princess

Stephanie, born in Monaco on February 1, 1965. Princess Grace died on September 14, 1982, as a result of an automobile accident the previous day.

From the time of his accession to the throne in 1949, Prince Rainier has been actively involved in the development of Monaco's industry, tourism, scientific research, and culture, as well as its sports. He has also taken a strong interest in adding to Monaco's territory through land **reclamation**; since the end of World War II, pushed by a real estate boom, Monaco has added about 20 percent to its territory through reclaiming some lands from the sea.

reclamation: the act of regaining possession of.

One of the prince's greatest challenges has been to broaden the principality's economy so that it would not rely entirely on the casino. This change was needed both for reasons of economic security and to erase Monaco's image of being a tax haven and playground for the rich and famous (or, in the words of the author Somerset Maugham, "a sunny place for shady people"). Gambling once provided 95 percent of the principality's income; the Société des Bains de Mer (or Seabath Company), which operates the casinos and major hotels, had its maximum contribution to state revenues set at 4 percent, and this cap impelled the desired **diversification** of the economy. There are now over a hundred light industries located in Monaco. ◆

diversification: the act of producing variety.

Ramses II

DIED 1237 B.C.E. ● PHARAOH OF EGYPT

Third king of the nineteenth dynasty of Egypt, Ramses reigned from 1304 to 1237 B.C.E. His wide-ranging military exploits brought Egypt to the height of its imperial power, and his battles were made known throughout the empire, inscribed on the walls of the numerous temples he built. This military prowess, together with his massive building projects and the prosperity that accompanied his reign, made him a legendary figure and a model for Egyptian kings who followed. It is thought by scholars that Ramses was ruler of Egypt during the end of the enslavement of the Jews and their Exodus.

Ramses II's grandfather, Ramses I, was the first of his family to rule Egypt, having ascended to the throne after being the previous king's general and vizier, while his father, Seti I, ruled

from 1318 to 1304 B.C.E., struggling for dominance in the region against the Hittites, who had become the most powerful nation in Asia; he also fended off a threat from the Libyans and reasserted control over the rebellious territories of Palestine and Syria. When his son, the future Ramses II, was still very young, Seti I made him crown prince, and at the age of ten he became coregent with all the accoutrements of royalty, including a palace and a harem. His military rank of captain was largely symbolic at this time, perhaps an attempt to ensure his accession to the throne over an older brother whose presence is blotted from the records. The young prince, nevertheless, did accompany his father during his military exploits, and by the time he assumed power he was an experienced soldier and commander.

Ramses's dwelling place, called Per-Ramesse and located in the eastern delta, was actually a new city which became famous for its magnificence. Ramses incorporated into the four quarters of his new domicile the recently arrived gods of Asia: the north was presided over by Buto, the royal cobra goddess, the south by Seth, Amon was located in the west, and Astarte, the Syrian goddess, ruled in the east. The incorporation into Egypt of such Asian gods was a common practice at this time, and Ramses's behavior attests to his participation in local beliefs.

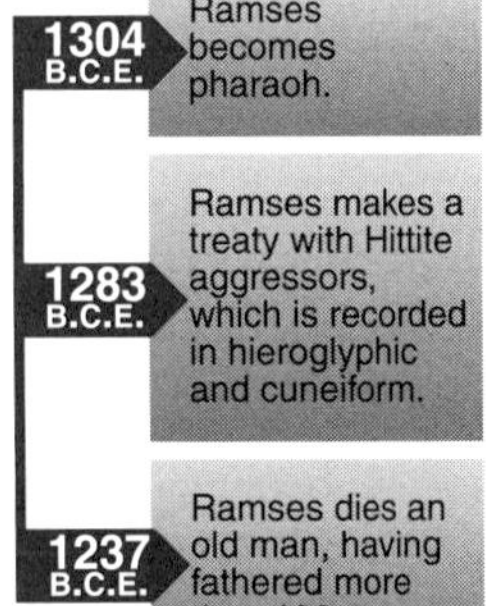

The period of Ramses II's rule was marked by vast changes in the Mediterranean world: new peoples of the region, notably the Greeks and later the Romans, were slowly establishing themselves as powers. Thus Ramses, in the first years of his reign, had to battle to drive off invaders from the sea, a Mediterranean people known as the Sherden. In the fourth year of his reign, he began a series of ambitious military campaigns designed to reassert Egyptian hegemony over Asia. He drove his troops through Palestine and Lebanon, subduing Syria and establishing a base for an attack against the Hittite nation at their fortress city of Kadesh. One year later he mounted the attack, splitting his army and sending a small force to take the seaport of Simyra. Before they could attack Kadesh, Ramses's forces were ambushed by the Hittites and all but a small royal guard fled. If not for the timely appearance of the second force marching to rejoin the main army, Ramses's forces would probably have been wiped out. As it was, the narrow escape from the Hittite ambush was the extent of Ramses's success. Although Ramses's own temple inscriptions publicized the pharaoh's personal courage in a "heroic victory," Hittite accounts reveal that he was defeated in the battle and retreated to Damascus.

This failure to take Kadesh lessened fear of Egypt among its client states to the north, and as a result Ramses was forced, once again, to put down rebellions in Palestine and Syria. In the sixth or seventh year of his reign, he reconquered Palestine and three years later he won victories over the Hittites, capturing Katna and Tunip. He found he could not control these regions against Hittite aggression from a distance and after sixteen years of war, a treaty with Egypt's foremost competitor was made in 1283 B.C.E., recorded in hieroglyphic and cuneiform. The treaty called for each side to respect the other's holdings in Palestine and Syria, with Egypt claiming Phoenicia for itself. Both nations also entered a defensive agreement in the event that a third nation attack these regions. The two powers were further united when Ramses married the Hittite king's eldest daughter, and possibly a second daughter as well.

Ramses also warred against the smaller kingdoms of Edom, Moab, and Negeb as well as defending the Nile delta from the attacks of the Libyans. Although his military ability has sometimes been questioned, the prosperity of his kingdom and his popularity among his people despite the frequency with which he waged war suggests that he must have been a force to reckon with.

In addition to his military exploits, Ramses left his mark with a vast number of monuments and temples. His most famous legacies are the two temples carved in the sandstone cliffs at Abu Simbel. The enormous statues of the pharaoh overlooking the Nile were moved to higher ground when the Aswan dam was built during the 1960s. Another extant monument, the Great Hypostyle Hall at Karnak, was attributed to Ramses, but it is possible he only adorned it with his own inscriptions and reliefs.

Of Ramses's many wives, his most beloved appears to have been Nefretari, his first queen, to whom he dedicated one of the temples at Abu Simbel. In addition to his many wives, the pharaoh had a harem, and all told more than one hundred sons were born to him, who themselves constituted a special class

"From behind, his voice cried out, I have hastened to you, Ramses Miamun, Behold! I stand with you, Behold! tis I am he, Own father thine, the great god Ra, the sun. Lo! mine hand with thine shall fight, And mine arm is strong above The hundreds of ten thousands, who against you do unite, Of victory am I lord, and the brave heart do I love, I have found in you a spirit that is right, And my soul it does rejoice in your valor and your might."

Temple inscription commemorating the military prowess of Ramses II, early 1300s B.C.E.

within Egyptian society. Ramses lived his life in opulence and ease, king of the greatest power of the ancient world. When he died, his twelve oldest sons were already dead and he was succeeded by Mer-ne-Ptah, his thirteenth son. The well-preserved mummy of Ramses II, in a mausoleum in Cairo, confirms that he died as an old man. ◆

Richard I

1157–1199 ● KING OF ENGLAND

1157 Richard is born in Oxford.

1173 Richard joins in a rebellion against his father, Henry II, instigated by his mother and older brother.

1188 Richard's father declines to recognize him as the rightful heir.

1189 Richard becomes king of England upon his father's death.

1191 Richard's marries Berengaria of Navarre for political expediency.

1191 King Phillip accuses Richard of trying to keep Cyprus for himself despite their agreement to share conquests.

1192 Richard concludes a peace treaty with Saladin.

1199 Richard is killed by a stray arrow during the siege of a castle in Limoges.

The third son of Henry II and Eleanor of Aquitaine, Richard (known as Richard the Lionhearted or Coeur de Lion) was born in Oxford. While still a child, he was granted the dukedom of Aquitaine, land Henry II had acquired on marriage. Richard ruled over his lands with a severity that brought him respect yet also aroused the resentment of the powerful barons he subjugated.

In 1173 Richard joined in a rebellion against his father instigated by his mother and elder brother, Henry. Richard supposedly said of his family origins: "We came from the Devil, and to the Devil we will return." Not long after peace was restored with his father, Richard was fighting his brother Henry. Denied any estate of his own, Henry was envious of his brothers and when the barons of Aquitaine rebelled against Richard's harsh rule, he supported them. Henry died suddenly and the rebellion ended, leaving Richard with the claim to his father's kingdom.

Henry II refused to concede the power Richard believed he had the right to demand and when they met in 1188, with King Philip Augustus of France, Henry II declined to recognize Richard as the rightful heir. Richard then switched allegiance to his father's enemy, the king of France, and during the war that followed, Henry died in 1189 and Richard became king of England and Normandy. His coronation was marred by a massacre of Jews who wished to attend the ceremony, and the violence spread to York. Richard took steps to stop the attacks, for the Jews were a valuable source of funds and regarded as the king's private property.

Richard was tall and well proportioned, with blond hair and blue eyes. He proved himself a fearless soldier and possessed a keen understanding of issues and a gift for conversation. At the same time he was arrogant, devoid of compassion, and sunk in a debauched lifestyle sharply in contrast with the heroic image of "lion heart." He was as tyrannical to his own family as he was rapacious to his subjects. His marriage to Berengaria of Navarre in 1191 was assauged solely for its political expediency, for Richard was a homosexual.

Richard's interest in his new kingdom was largely financial, to obtain the funds he needed for an Anglo-French crusade to capture Jerusalem. Richard made victorious progress eastward, capturing Messina and Cyprus despite continual disputes with his French ally. The day after the capture of Acre in 1191, the two kings again quarreled as the French ruler, King Philip, accused Richard of trying to keep Cyprus for himself despite an agreement they had made to share their conquests. Richard replied: "The victory over the infidels in the Holy Land was indeed a joint endeavor but the conquest of Cyprus is no business of yours as I carried it off alone." After they captured Acre, Philip fell ill and returned to France, leaving Richard in charge. He was responsible for the massacre of twenty-seven hundred Muslim survivors of the garrison at Acre by having their throats cut. He moved his army down the coast and defeated Saladin's armies at the Battle of Arsuf. Richard was then able to enter Jaffa, which he fortified to give himself a strong base on the coast. His reputation was now at its highest and, as a result of his behavior on the battlefield, he was seen as the incarnation of the demon of war. However, by delaying in Jaffa, he gave Saladin the opportunity to reorganize and when he moved on his real goal, Jerusalem, his attacks were beaten off. Richard was only able to see the city from a distance but never entered it.

In 1192 Richard concluded a peace treaty with Saladin whereby the coastal cities were left in the hands of the Christians and the interior of the country remained with the Muslims; pilgrims were permitted to visit the holy sites. Richard then set off to return to England. Bad weather forced his boat to call at Corfu. Fearing that he might be taken prisoner by the hostile Byzantines, he disguised himself as a Templar knight and traveled on a pirate boat headed for the north Adriatic. The boat was wrecked and, maintaining his disguise, he journeyed through the territories of his bitter enemy, Leopold, duke of Austria. Resting at an inn near Vienna, he was recognized and led before the duke, who imprisoned him. Three months later he was handed over to another enemy, the emperor Henry VI. He languished in prison for a year and was only released when

"Whoever slays a man on shipboard shall be bound to the dead man and thrown into the sea. But if he shall slay him on land, he shall be bound to the dead man and buried in the earth. If any one, moreover, shall be convicted through lawful witnesses of having drawn a knife to strike another, or of having struck him so as to draw blood, he shall lose his hand."

Laws of Richard I Concerning Crusaders Who Were to Go by Sea, 1189

his loyal subjects raised the huge ransom demanded after he gave the emperor an oath of vassaldom.

On his return, he found that his lands in England had been exposed to the intrigue of his brother John Lackland (the future King John). Richard's return to take over from John forms the background to the Robin Hood legend. Before long, Richard went to France where he spent the rest of his life at war with King Philip, defending his inheritance. A stray arrow shot by an archer during the siege of a castle in Limoges killed him. ◆

Rwabugiri

1840?–1895 ● KING OF RWANDA

Rwabugiri was king of Rwanda from about 1865 to 1895. Kigeri Rwabugiri is renowned as the great warrior-king of Rwanda of the late nineteenth century. But his reign was equally as important for structural transformations within Rwanda as for his external wars.

Rwabugiri came to power as the result of a complicated set of events that amounted to an internal coup. Having acceded by power, Rwabugiri ruled by force. Within the state he appointed administrative authorities (including Hutu and Twa) dependent on his favor as a counterweight to powerful Tutsi political lineages; he thus consolidated power at the central court and increased the arbitrary power of the monarch.

Booty and reward from Rwabugiri's military campaigns made possible the expansion of power at the central court.

Nonetheless in song and memory, Rwabugiri is best remembered for his external military campaigns, especially in areas west and north of Rwanda. In fact, the booty and rewards resulting from those campaigns (cattle, women, and political position) made possible the expansion of power at the central court. Yet despite the vast area attacked, relatively few regions were permanently annexed; one must distinguish the full incorporation of conquered regions (the geographical expansion of Rwanda) from military occupation (often of brief duration) and simple raids.

Rwabugiri's death marked not only the end of an era of energetic expansion and the consolidation of royal power, but also an end to Rwanda's status as an independent monarchy. Shortly after Rwabugiri's death many of Rwanda's greatest military heroes perished in two battles fought against troops associated with the Congo Free State. The court thereafter followed a policy of collaboration with the European intruders, a policy that, though not without tension and political manipulation on both sides, served the objectives of both the Rwandan elites and the colonial powers. ◆

Salahuddin

1926– ● KING OF MALAYSIA

The king of Malaysia, called the *yang di-pertuan agong*, serves largely as a ceremonial leader in a nation that is a constitutional monarchy. While that role is not unusual among nations, the method by which Malaysia's king comes to his position is quite unique. Nine of Malaysia's thirteen states have hereditary rulers called sultans, and every five years these sultans elect one from among themselves to serve as king for the next five years.

On February 26, 1999, the sultans elected Sultan Salahuddin Abdul Aziz Shah to be the eleventh king of Malaysia. His term began on April 26, when he officially became His Majesty the Yang di-Pertuan Agong Sultan Salahuddin Abdul Aziz Shah. He replaced the seventy-seven-year-old Tuanku Ja'afar ibni Al-Marhum Tuanku Abdul Rahman, whose five-year term expired on April 25. Salahuddin Abdul Aziz Shah, seventy-three, was the sultan of Selangor, a Malaysian state. Sultan Salahuddin was born on March 8, 1926, and became the eighth sultan of Selangor when he was crowned and installed in that position on June 28, 1961.

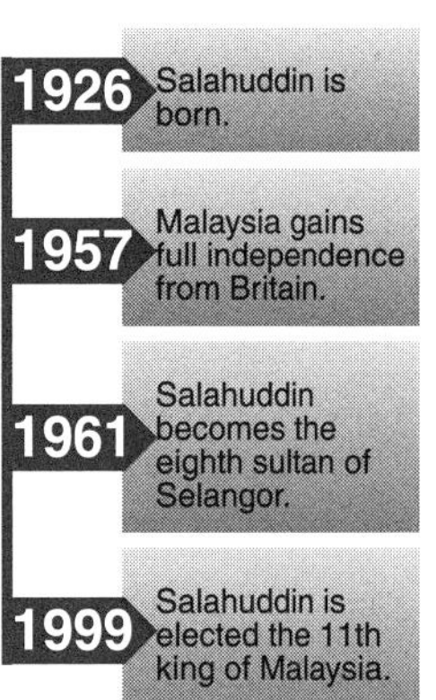

The term *yang di-pertuan agong* translates as the "supreme head" or "paramount ruler." Every act of Malaysia's government is said to flow from his authority, but his official acts mainly stem from the directions of parliament and the cabinet. The king appoints the prime minister, but upon the direction of parliament. The king has the right to refuse to dissolve parliament, though, even against the advice of the prime minister. The king appoints the judges of the federal court and the high courts on the advice of the prime minister, in accordance with procedures prescribed in the Malaysian constitution. The king can bestow orders of chivalry or give other honors or recognition.

The *yang di-pertuan agong* also has power to grant pardons and reprieves for offences that have been tried by court-martial and any offence committed in the federal territories of Kuala Lumpur—Malaysia's capital—and Labuan. Sultans of individual states have power to grant certain pardons and reprieves in those states. The king also has certain powers to grant pardons concerning offences against the Muslim religion.

Malaysia has a diverse population, with about 21 million people in the late 1990s. About 50 percent of the people are Malays, 50 percent Chinese, and 10 percent Asian Indian. Located in southeast Asia, Malaysia is made up of a peninsula extending south from Thailand and one-third of the island of Borneo, bordering Indonesia, Brunei, and the South China Sea. Malaysia is a tropical country that extends from swampy coastal areas to the peak of Mount Kinabalu.

Malaysia has one of the strongest economies in southeast Asia, stemming from a convergence of many potent political, economic, and social forces.

Malaysia has one of the strongest economies in southeast Asia, stemming from a convergence of many potent political, economic, and social forces over the past two centuries. During the 1800s and early 1900s the British gained control of much of Malaysia. In 1896 several regions organized into the Federated Malay States. The sultans of these regions gave up much of their power to a central British government, headed by a Resident-General, based in Kuala Lumpur. As they entrusted the British with administrative and financial duties, the sultans maintained authority over religious and local matters in their regions. The sultans ruled with pomp and became loyal supporters of Britain, adopting English education and style. Several other Malay states resisted the British, but were brought under British control by 1909.

The world's automobile boom fueled the development of a rubber plantation economy in Malaysia. The British colonials lived prosperously and comfortably as the rubber industry grew rapidly. They cleverly ruled as much as possible through native leaders, including the Malay sultans. By 1920 Malaysia produced more than 53 percent of the world's rubber. However, Japan invaded Malaysia in 1937, changing the nation forever. After the Japanese lost World War II, the British returned to rule Malaysia. But the war had changed the balance of power.

Asian nations were ousting their colonial rulers, and Malaysian people sought freedom too. Chinese Communists and other rebels fought the British in Malaysia, and the nation gained full independence from Britain in 1957. ◆

Sargon II

DIED 705 B.C.E. ● KING OF ASSYRIA

The name Sargon, known through the Bible, is the Hebrew rendering of Sharru-kin, "the righteous king." He succeeded his presumed father (actually more probably his brother), Tiglath-Pileser III, in 722 B.C.E.; his elder brother, who was next in line for the throne, may have died or been deposed.

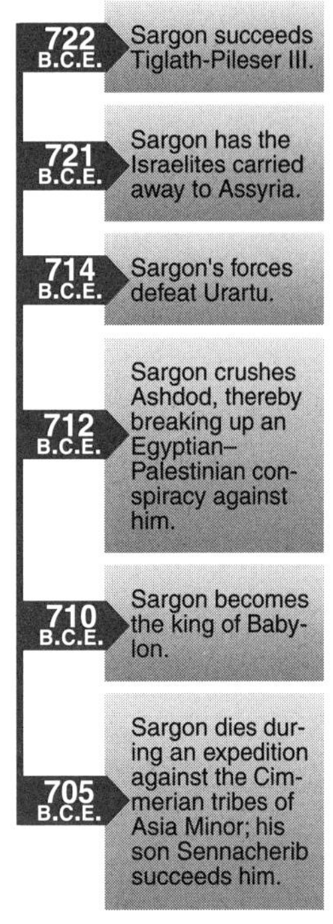

Primary documentary sources of evidence about Sargon's reign are sparse, consisting of a few cuneiform inscriptions, but in conjunction with references in the Old Testament they provide some idea of his achievements. Confronted by a succession of rebellions that constantly broke out in various parts of his empire, he nonetheless managed to consolidate the conquests of his predecessor. The year after his accession was marked by the successful conclusion of the campaign which had been set into motion by Tiglath-Pileser, to destroy the northern kingdom of Israel. The Old Testament relates (2 Kings 17) how Sargon had the Israelites carried away to Assyria, an action which attests to his policy of transporting peoples from conquered regions to distant parts of the empire to prevent a subsequent reemergence of nationalist sentiment.

The defeat of Hamath and Damascus in 720 B.C.E. signaled the subduing of the major previously-unconquered states of Syria, while in 714 B.C.E. Sargon's forces succeeded in defeating those of Urartu (modern-day Armenia) and breaking the power of that rival kingdom. In 712 B.C.E. Sargon crushed Ashdod, thereby breaking up an Egyptian–Palestinian conspiracy against him; the latter part of his reign was marked by such insurrections, which were incited and masterminded by the Chaldean tribal chieftain Merodach-Baladan with the support of Hezekiah in Judah. Sargon eventually triumphed against his opponents, becoming king of Babylon in 710 B.C.E., but Merodach-Baladan managed to escape into exile and, after Sargon's death, returned to plague his son, Sennacherib.

Sargon's rule was a time of great artistic and cultural accomplishments. He built a splendid new capital for his empire, the city of Dur Sharukin (modern Khorsabad, Iraq), which contained a magnificent palace adorned with remarkable stone **reliefs**, some of which are now on display in the Louvre Museum, Paris. One of the most outstanding relics of his rule is a poetically resonant record of his invasion of Urartu. Most probably commissioned and approved by Sargon, it consists of a dramatic reconstruction of the campaign and includes an arresting description of the might of his armies as they would have appeared to the anxious enemy soldiers viewing their approach from afar. The style and finesse of the composition testify to the levels of literary excellence which were achieved through the king's patronage, and suggest that the Assyrian court was a place of great sophistication.

reliefs: sculpture or sculptural forms that are distinguished from a surrounding plane surface.

Sargon died as he had lived, campaigning to preserve and strengthen his domain; he met his end during an expedition against the Cimmerian tribes of Asia Minor, to be succeeded by Sennacherib. ◆

Saul

11TH CENTURY B.C.E. ● KING OF ISRAEL

Saul was the first king of ancient Israel, reigning from about 1020 B.C.E. to 1000 B.C.E. His story comes from the Old Testament of the Bible and is recounted in the book 1 Samuel. According to the Bible, after the Israelites spent forty years in the wilderness with Moses, they entered Canaan, their homeland from before the exile in Egypt. For the next 200 years, the Israelites fought the Canaanites, the Philistines, and other peoples as they struggled to reinstate themselves in Canaan. The period between the Israelite conquest of Canaan and the time of Samuel is called the period of the Judges and is recorded in the book of Judges. The judges served as judicial and military leaders who united the Israelites, loosely organized as twelve tribes, during crises.

Saul was the son of a landowner named Kish of the tribe of Benjamin. His name is first mentioned in relation to the prophet Samuel, the last judge of Israel and the first prophet after Moses. As Samuel grew old, he passed on the administration of the civic and religious matters of Israel to his sons. However, the sons proved unreliable. The Israelites petitioned Samuel to select a king to rule over them, especially as they were under threat of warfare with the Philistines. Samuel resisted their request, reminding the people that the Hebrew God, Yahweh, was to be their only monarch. But Yahweh instructed Samuel to comply with the demands of the people.

The narrative in 1 Samuel relates a series of fateful incidents that led to the choice of Saul as king. Saul was searching for two of his father's lost she-donkeys when he consulted Samuel the "seer" in order to find his donkeys. Meanwhile, Yahweh had told Samuel, "I will send to you a man from the land of Benjamin." Upon meeting Saul, "a handsome man in the prime of life," Samuel welcomed him to a feast. The prophet reveals to Saul that Yahweh wants him to lead His chosen people, and he anoints Saul king.

A short time later, after Saul has returned to work his land, he is called forth to fight the Ammonites, who have besieged the city of Jabesh-gilead. Saul assembles thousands of men, leading them to defeat the Ammonites and liberate the city of Jabesh-gilead. This victory establishes Saul as the clear leader of his people. Saul later engaged his men in war with the Philistines and the Amalekites. After one victory, he is instructed to await the arrival of Samuel to make a sacrifice to Yahweh. Samuel is delayed, so Saul goes forth with the sacrifice, which angers God. The prophet Samuel admonished Saul for assuming the priestly function. In another instance, after defeating the Amalekites, Saul disobeyed God again. He had been instructed to "utterly destroy all that they have; do not spare them, but kill both man and woman, infant and suckling, ox and sheep, camel and ass." Instead, Saul allowed his men to keep the best of the livestock for themselves.

Yahweh tells Samuel that he is sorry he made Saul king. Samuel informs Saul that Yahweh will remove the kingdom from him, telling him, "Since you have rejected the word of Yahweh, he has rejected you as king." Saul is filled with remorse and begs, "I have sinned. . . . Now, I pray you, forgive my sin." Samuel forgives Saul, but Yahweh does not. Yahweh tells Samuel that he is ready to chose a new king and arranges for Samuel to anoint David, son of Jesse, as Israel's next king. David will be a king "after God's own heart," and, though

"So Saul took the kingdom over Israel, and fought against all his enemies on every side, against Moab, and against the children of Ammon, and against Edom, and against the kings of Zobah, and against the Philistines: and whithersoever he turned himself, he vexed them."

King James Bible, 1 Samuel 14:47

merely a shepherd boy, he is taken into Saul's household. Saul loves David at first and often calls upon David to play the harp for him, to soothe his bouts of ill-temper. But Saul becomes consumed by jealousy of David's status as the beloved of Yahweh and attacks him on several occasions, causing David to flee.

"And all the people went to Gilgal; and there they made Saul king before the Lord in Gilgal; and there they sacrificed sacrifices of peace offerings before the Lord; and there Saul and all the men of Israel rejoiced greatly."
King James Bible, 1 Samuel 11:15

On the eve of a new invasion by the Philistines, Saul is filled with fear, having been forsaken by Yahweh. Samuel is dead, so Saul disguises himself and seeks the guidance of a medium in Endor. She calls forth the spirit of Samuel, who predicts Saul's fate at the hands of the Philistines. Saul and his forces are overcome by the Philistines, and three of Saul's sons are killed in the battle. Fearing that he may fall into the hands of the enemy, Saul begs his armor bearer to take his life. The soldier refuses from fear, so Saul ends his own life by falling on his sword. The victorious Philistines cut off his head and display it as a trophy in various towns of their country, while Saul's body and those of his sons are hung on the walls of the town of Bethsan. Loyal subjects of Saul come in the night to remove the bodies and give them a reverent burial.

The Bible mentions Ahinoam as the wife of Saul, and two daughters, Merab and Michal. His several sons included Jonathan, who befriended David and died with Saul. Another son, Isboseth, attempted to continue the dynasty of his father, but was assassinated by two captains of his own army. This removed any obstacle to the accession of David to the throne.

David unified the Israelites and founded the kingdom of Israel. Under David and his successor, his son Solomon, the power and size of the kingdom expanded greatly. David captured the city of Jerusalem from a people called the Jebusites and made it his capital. Solomon built a magnificent temple in Jerusalem. The New Testament books of Matthew and Luke trace the lineage of Jesus Christ back to David, among others. ◆

Selim III

1761–1808 ● OTTOMAN SULTAN

The son of Mustafa III, Selim was allowed by his uncle Abdülhamit I an unusually free and liberal upbringing, on the assumption that he would succeed to the throne. Wars against Russia during the reigns of his father and uncle convinced Selim of the need to modernize the Ottoman army, and while still a prince he sought advice and assistance from King Louis XVI of France for this purpose.

When Selim succeeded his uncle in April 1789, the Ottoman empire was again at war with Russia and Austria. Selim's first act, in May, was to convene a special assembly of leading statesmen to discuss the empire's military and financial problems, and to request detailed reports on how to proceed with reforms. The resulting New Order program accelerated and formalized the piecemeal military and educational Europeanization started earlier. A new army corps was formed, with a separate financial bureau to administer earmarked revenues to support the effort. Schools to train officers for the army and navy in the European manner were given new **impetus**. Another extension of a process begun earlier was in diplomatic relations with European powers. Ambassadors had been sent to leading capitals to gather information on European politics and international relations, and to study recent military and technological advances; in 1792 the Ottoman government established permanent embassies in London, Paris, Berlin, Vienna, and St. Petersburg so that the empire could be better informed about European relations and present its concerns directly.

impetus: stimulation or encouragement resulting in increased activity.

With Europe increasingly preoccupied with French Revolutionary wars, Selim turned his attention to internal political problems, using his new troops to suppress provincial notables who controlled large areas of the empire's territories. They had some initial success, but from 1797 the empire was embroiled in the European war when France took an active interest in the eastern Mediterranean, culminating in Napoleon's invasion of Egypt in 1798. The Ottoman empire was thus forced to accept support from Britain and Russia against its traditional ally France. After Britain's navy and Selim's army turned Napoleon back from Palestine, France left Egypt in 1801, and Britain followed soon thereafter. Nevertheless, full Ottoman control could not be restored; the vice commander of the New Order army in Egypt, Muhammad Ali, eventually gained power.

Though a Europeanizing reformer, Selim was educated in the classical Islamic-Ottoman culture.

In Arabia, Wahhabi doctrine had taken hold, and its Saudi champion rejected Selim's position as caliph of the Sunni Muslim community. In the Balkans, Russia's influence was growing, both in the Danubian principalities and in Serbia, where a revolt began in 1804. Since France's threat to the Ottoman territories had been lifted, Britain had assumed an active role in the eastern Mediterranean. After Napoleon's victories in central Europe, Selim, wishing to balance the influences of Britain and Russia, attempted to revive the alliance with France, but Russia's advance into Moldavia and Wallachia in October 1806 and Britain's naval activity near Istanbul in January 1807 prevented it.

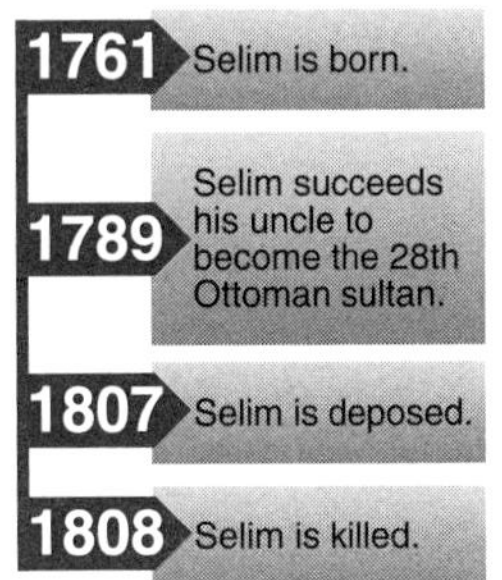

Beset by foreign engagements not of his choosing; unable to establish authority in the provinces, where political, religious, and ethnic uprisings challenged his rule; and alienating large segments of Istanbul's population by what seemed to be an overhasty attempt to Europeanize while European powers dominated the empire's policies, Selim was deposed in May 1807 after a popular insurrection supported by palace attendants and out-of-favor officials. A year later, when provincial forces loyal to Selim marched on the capital, he was killed to prevent a countercoup.

Though a Europeanizing reformer, Selim was educated in the classical Islamic-Ottoman culture. He was a distinguished poet and a talented composer. He tried to regenerate the power of his empire through a European-style army, but in his political behavior he was a typical sultan. He helped develop policy and direction, but left government in the hands of viziers. To keep factionalism in check, he changed viziers and other statesmen frequently. His greatest misfortune was that his empire no longer could set its own course and go at its own pace. In the last decade of his rule, Selim found himself responding to foreign threats from rapidly shifting directions, desperately trying to keep in check external and internal forces that proved to be beyond his control. ◆

Shah Jahan

1592–1666 ● Emperor of India

The penultimate ruler among the six great Moghuls, Muslim leaders who ruled India between 1527 (Babur's conquest) and 1707 (when the death of Aurangzeb was followed by the empire's rapid disintegration), Shah Jahan is primarily remembered for the Taj Mahal, the exquisite mausoleum built as a final resting place for his beloved wife Mumtaz Mahal. However, this was only one of the many magnificent

Taj Mahal

Although many people think that India's Taj Mahal is a castle, it actually is the tomb of Emperor Shah Jahan and his favorite wife, Mumtaz Mahal (Chosen One of the Palace). After she died in 1631, while giving birth to their fourteenth child, Shah Jahan ordered the construction of a huge mausoleum in her honor near the city of Agra. The Taj Mahal was designed by famous Islamic architect Ustad Isa. Thousands of workers labored for 22 years building it, at a reported cost of almost 40 million rupees. The Taj Mahal is built of white marble and rests on a square red sandstone platform surrounded by symmetrically placed turrets. A huge garden with four reflecting pools adjoins the mausoleum, and both the interior and exterior of the building are inlaid with designs and calligraphy made from precious gems. One of Shah Jahan's sons later toppled him from the throne, and the shah spent eight years imprisoned in a nearby fort, where he could see the Taj Mahal from his cell. After he died, his own casket—the only asymmetric object in the entire complex—was placed next to his wife's. Today the Taj Mahal is one of the most popular tourist attractions in India.

buildings constructed during his thirty-one-year reign, which saw the creation of some of the most vivid and permanent reminders of Moghul glory.

Third son of the emperor Jehangir and grandson of Akbar, Khurram gained the title of Shah Jahan for his services to his father in the military campaign of 1617. The heir apparent after

his elder brother's assassination, he was in revolt against his father from 1624 but succeeded him in 1628 after ruthlessly having his male collateral relatives killed. His reign saw the culmination of Moghul rule in India, and the splendor of his court was well known. However, although Shan Jahan was able to sustain the empire he inherited, even expanding it to the northwest, he did so at the price of delegating a degree of power to his sons, which subsequently cost him his throne.

The favorite of his three wives, Mumtaz Mahal, whom he married in 1612, was the niece of an equally remarkable woman: one of Jehangir's wives, Nur Jahan, who had been the real power behind the imperial throne. Despite the fact that raisons d'etat contributed to the expediency of the match, the couple were deeply in love; Shah Jahan was heartbroken when Mumataz died bearing their fourteenth child in 1631.

The building of the Taj, the white marble monument on the bank of the river Jumna in the Moghul capital of Agra, began in 1632 and was not completed until 1653. A total of twenty thousand workers from all over India and central Asia were involved in its construction, while experts were brought in from as far away as western Europe. The supervising architect was Ustad Isa, from Shiraz in Persia; Ismail Khan Rumi, from Constantinople, constructed the soaring marble dome. The ornamentation throughout the structure is of unsurpassed excellence, and here the Indian art of pietra dura—decorating marble with an inlay of semiprecious stones—reached its zenith.

A number of other superb architectural ventures were undertaken in Shah Jahan's time: the Red Fort and Jami Masjid (the largest mosque in India and religious center of the empire) in Delhi being, with the additions to Agra Fort and the great mosque in Agra, the most famous. The structures succeed admirably in evoking the sentiment recorded in the Red Fort's Hall of Public Audience: "If there be a Heaven on earth / It is this, it is this, it is this."

Shah Jahan's extravagant plans, which included the building of a replica of the Taj in black marble opposite the original, to house his own grave, were brought to an abrupt end when he was overthrown by his son Aurangzeb in 1658. He lived out his last years imprisoned in Agra Fort, within sight of his own breathtaking monument to his beloved Mumtaz, next to whom he was buried. ◆

Shih Huang Ti

C.259–210 B.C.E. ● EMPEROR OF CHINA

Shih Huang Ti (also spelled Shi Huangdi) was the founder of the Ch'in dynasty and the first emperor to unite China. Cheng was prince of Ch'in in western China, one of several independent and warring states that made up China. Little is known about his early life, although he was probably educated in the Legalist rather than Confucianist tradition. It has been suggested that he was the son of Lu Pu-wei, a wealthy silk merchant who turned to politics, although it is more likely that Lu was his advisor.

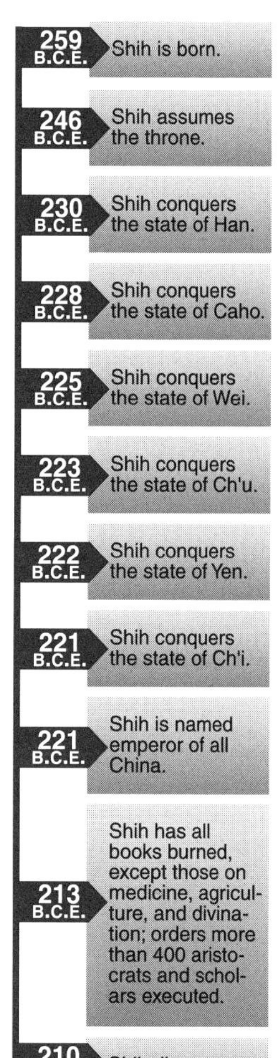

Cheng assumed the throne of Ch'in in 246 B.C.E. Upon reaching maturity he set out on a series of campaigns intended to bring the other Chinese states under his jurisdiction. Although no one had before succeeded in uniting the kingdoms, Cheng was at an advantage in that he was the first to use iron weapons. Among the states conquered by Cheng were Han (230), Chao (228), Wei (225), Ch'u (223), Yen (222), and Ch'i (221). Within just seven years, he had conquered all of China, earning the epithet, "Tiger of Ch'in." In 221 B.C.E. Cheng was named emperor of all China and assumed the name Shih Huang Ti, which means "First August Emperor."

Shih Huang Ti was not merely a conqueror. Under the guidance of his minister Li Ssu, he instituted important reforms aimed at the political and social unification of his realm. He created a unified system of measurements, a much-simplified unified writing system, and a single currency similar to the one still used today. The former states were dissolved and the country was divided into thirty-six and then forty-two prefectures. Shih Huang Ti was also a great builder. Apart from a series of roads and canals intended to facilitate travel in the vast state, he completed the Great Wall in the north to protect the kingdom from nomadic herdsmen, the Hsiung-nu, who threatened invasion. Once the wall had been finished, Shi Huang Ti sent troops against the Hsiung-nu. In other expeditions he reached as far south as Vietnam and as far north as Korea.

Despite his military and political successes, Shih Huang Ti was an unpopular monarch who seemed intent upon depriving his citizens of their most basic rights. His vast building projects

The Army of Terra-cotta Warriors

Emperor Shih Huang Ti, who died in 210 B.C.E., was buried in a large tomb near the city of Xian in central China. In 1976, almost two thousand years after Shih Huang Ti's death, farmers digging a well near the tomb discovered a vast underground chamber housing an army of life-sized terra-cotta warriors. The chamber was subsequently excavated, revealing more than 6,000 soldiers and horses facing east in rectangular battle formation, apparently guarding the dead emperor. The soldiers wear a number of different uniforms and the facial features of each one are different. Most of the warriors originally held real swords, spears, and shields, many of which have survived. Some archaeologists think that thousands more warriors may remain buried, awaiting discovery and excavation, in the region of Shih Huang Ti's tomb.

required great amounts of tax money and forced labor; people could not protect themselves—the bearing of arms was forbidden. Weapons were confiscated, melted down, and cast into twelve enormous statues in the capital, Hsien-yang. The nobility despised the emperor for depriving them of their ancestral estates. To assure their loyalty Shih Huang Ti ordered all noble families to relocate to the capital and its environs. One hundred and twenty thousand families took part in this transfer of populations.

Perhaps the most dramatic act of Shih Huang Ti's reign was the "burning of the books." Legalism was declared the sole acceptable school of thought in the kingdom; Confucianism, Taoism, and other schools were ruthlessly suppressed. To enforce this suppression, all books, except those on medicine, agriculture, and divination, were burned in 213. This act of barbarism was followed by the execution of more than 400 aristocrats and scholars perceived as being a threat to the regime.

Shih Huang Ti died in 210 B.C.E. He was succeeded by his son, who took the name Shi-erh Huang Ti, or Second August Emperor. His son's reign was brief, however. Although the people were enraged by his father's decrees, they dared not rebel for fear of him, but Shih-erh Huang Ti's weak rule led to open rebellion within a year of his ascension and the Ch'in dynasty collapsed in 206 B.C.E. Despite its brevity and unpopularity, it paved the way for future dynasties to promote Chinese unification as a goal. Many believe that the name "China" is derived from Shih Huang Ti's Ch'in dynasty. ◆

Norodom Sihanouk

1922– ● KING OF CAMBODIA

Norodom Sihanouk is king of Cambodia, a country slightly smaller than Oklahoma, bordering Vietnam, Laos, and Thailand in Southeast Asia. Sihanouk was born in Phnom Penh, Cambodia's capital. His mother's father, Sisowath Monivong, reigned as king from 1927 to 1941. His father, Norodom Suramarit, was a grandson of King Norodom (r. 1860–1904). Sihanouk, the only child of this unhappy marriage, was educated privately and at a French high school in Saigon, from which he was summoned, before his graduation, to be king. For the rest of World War II, he was closely supervised by French advisers, except for the period from March to October 1945, when the Japanese imprisoned French authorities throughout Indochina and encouraged Sihanouk to declare Cambodia's independence.

When the French returned at the end of 1945, Sihanouk, although attracted to the idea of eventual independence, decided to welcome them. During the years 1946–53, he quarreled frequently

with the nationalist members of Cambodia's elite, who wanted independence on their terms, rather than on terms acceptable to the French. In 1953, to outflank this group (and to counter Communist-led guerrilla opposition to the French) Sihanouk dramatically embarked on a "Crusade for Independence," threatening to abdicate if the French persisted in political and economic control. The French caved in and granted Cambodia's independence at the end of 1953. This decision was ratified in 1954 at the Geneva Conference.

In 1955 King Sihanouk abandoned the throne, had his father named as king, and set out on a full-time political career. His main objective was to smash Cambodia's political parties, and he did so by founding his own political movement, the Sangkum Reastr Niyum, which remained the dominant political force in Cambodia for the next fifteen years. Indeed, the years 1955–70 can justifiably be called the Sihanouk years. The prince, under various titles, including prime minister and chief of state, dominated Cambodian political life and the conduct of foreign affairs. In 1956, for example, he opted for a neutralist foreign policy, which enabled him to obtain economic aid from the Communist bloc as well as from Western powers. The United States' disapproval of his policies and U.S. involvement in anti-Sihanouk plots led the prince to sever diplomatic relations with the United States in 1965. For the next five years, as fighting intensified in Vietnam and Laos, he attempted to maintain a neutral course, but opposition to his rule increased on both left and right.

A full-scale civil war directed against Communist-led Cambodian guerrillas (the so-called Khmer Rouge) broke out in 1968. By this time, Sihanouk's own behavior had become increasingly erratic. He spent much of his time directing and starring in popular films that dramatized Cambodia's past. His support among government workers in the capital and among younger members of the Cambodian elite began to diminish.

In March 1970 he was overthrown by his own government while he was traveling abroad. The new regime, led by Lon Nol, named itself the Khmer Republic and plunged into an alliance with the United States and warfare against Communist forces inside the country. Sihanouk himself, taking refuge in Beijing, where he had long enjoyed the patronage of Zhou Enlai, almost immediately became the titular head of a government in exile. Real power was in the hands of the clandestine Communist Party of Kampuchea (CPK) directed by Saloth Sar, soon to be known as Pol Pot—the people who had been trying to overthrow Sihanouk since 1968 and probably before.

In April 1975 CPK forces triumphed over those of the Khmer Republic. With victory, the CPK set in motion a series of economic and political measures that were, by the end of 1978, to tear Cambodia apart. In early 1976 Sihanouk was brought back to Phnom Penh, forced to resign as chief of state, and placed under house arrest. The regime in power named itself Democratic Kampuchea. When Vietnamese forces invaded Cambodia at the end of 1978 (following two years of warfare), Sihanouk was flown to Beijing and the United Nations to plead Democratic Kampuchea's case. Before very long, once Democratic Kampuchea had been deposed, Sihanouk was expressing anticommunist ideas and setting himself up as an acceptable alternative to the pro-Vietnamese Communist government now ensconced in Phnom Penh. In 1981 he agreed to form a coalition government in exile alongside the leaders of Democratic Kampuchea and a Cambodian elder statesman, Son Sann, who had served as his prime minister in the 1960s. Sihanouk was able to gain credibility among governments unfriendly to Vietnam. The coalition succeeded in holding Democratic Kampuchea's seat at the United Nations.

"The King is the guarantor of the national independence, sovereignty, and territorial integrity of the Kingdom of Cambodia, the protector of rights and freedom for all citizens, and the guarantor of international treaties."

Article 8, the constitution of Cambodia, adopted 1993

By the mid 1980s several factors tended to reduce Sihanouk's popularity among Cambodians. Some opposition came from older people, who recalled his erratic performance as chief of state in the closing years of his regime. Still more stemmed from his marriage of convenience with the CPK and from his failure to dissociate himself from the surviving leaders of Democratic Kampuchea. He nevertheless remained a central figure in Cambodian politics throughout the decade. In October 1991 the opposing Cambodian factions signed a peace treaty in Paris. The United Nations set up transitional government with Sihanouk as head of state. In May 1993 Cambodian voters elected a new parliament. Later that year the parliament approved a new constitution that established Cambodia as a multiparty liberal democracy under a constitutional monarchy with Norodom Sihanouk as king. As head of state, King Sihanouk has the power to appoint the country's prime ministers, who head the government. ◆

Sobhuza I

1780?–1839 ● KING OF SWAZILAND

Sobhuza I (Sobhuza waNdvungunye Dlamini) fashioned the Swazi kingship out of disparate Nguni-speaking clans in southern Swaziland. His father, Ndvungunye, by the turn of the nineteenth century had made the Dlamini the dominant clan among numerous contesting clans in what is now southern Swaziland. To establish the kingship, Sobhuza brought the important clans together under his hegemony (quite tenuous at first). Sobhuza incorporated some families under the Dlamini by force; others he incorporated by various diplomatic means of persuasion and enticement, including marriage alliances, positions of status, and choice lands. He then campaigned northward with the dual objectives of escaping the powerful and aggressive Ndwandwe to the south and occupying the fertile and defensible heartland of the country. Sobhuza defeated or incorporated various clans he found in central Swaziland, then refashioned his strengthened kingdom along regimental lines. By the time of his death Sobhuza had successfully fended off powerful Ndwandwe and Zulu attacks from the south, captured Sotho land and cattle far northward into the Transvaal, and was attempting to consolidate his kingdom through diplomacy with missionaries.

Sobhuza II (Sobhuza waBhunu Dlamini, 1899–1982), whose original name was Nkhotfotjeni, was a direct descendant of Sobhuza I through the male line. Nkhotfotjeni was given the name Sobhuza II upon being designated heir to the throne in 1900. Crowned in 1921, he inherited an enfeebled monarchy, which he proceeded to restore brilliantly over the following two generations using a number of stratagems: invoking tradition and ritual; assiduously courting an array of powerful allies, black and white; and playing British colonials, European settlers, and domestic rivals against each other to achieve his own ends. Consequently, at independence in 1968 his control over the levers of power was unmatched by any other postcolonial monarchy in all of sub-Saharan Africa. Sobhuza consolidated his rule in 1973 by scrapping Swaziland's Westminster-style constitution and ruling without official opposition, yet with a high degree of popularity, until his death as the result of a long-standing illness, probably leukemia. ◆

Solomon

TENTH CENTURY B.C.E. ● KING OF THE ISRAELITES

Solomon was the fourth son of King David, third king of Israel, builder of the First Temple in Jerusalem, and in Jewish tradition the wisest of all men. Most of the biographical material on Solomon is found in the Old Testament in 2 Samuel, 1 Kings 1–11, and 2 Chronicles 1–9. His mother was Bathsheba; he acceded to the throne three years before his father's death and reigned for thirty-seven years after it.

Called Solomon by his father, he was named Jedidiah (literally, "friend of God") by Nathan the prophet (2 Samuel 12:24–25), who was instrumental in ensuring Solomon's nomination as his father's successor (1 Kings 1–2), even though he was among the younger of David's sons.

Solomon inherited from his father a substantial kingdom, stretching beyond the borders of Israelite settlement, "from the river [the Euphrates] to the land of the Philistines and to the border of Egypt." Except for Aram-Damascus in the north, he maintained his hold on all of it. Moreover, he added Hamath (modern Hama, Syria) and Tadmor (Palmyra, an oasis 150 miles northeast of Damascus).

Solomon's first acts upon taking the throne were zealous dealings with his opponents: Adonijah, his brother who declared himself king; Joab, David's commander in chief and supporter of Adonijah; and Shimi ben Gera, who had taunted and cursed David; all of whom Solomon had executed. He banished Abiathar the priest to Anathoth, relieving him of his priestly duties. The image of Solomon as his father's ruthless avenger is somewhat at odds with his depiction as pursuer of peace found in 1 Chronicles 22:5–9, where his name ("Shelomo" in Hebrew) is linked to the Hebrew word for peace, *shalom*.

On the whole his reign was quiet and his direction of his kingdom orderly. The names of his administrative staff and their job descriptions are given in 1 Kings 4:2–6, with the range of duties listed including that of priest, secretaries, household manager, and tax overseer. Solomon apportioned Israel into twelve administrative units, each headed by an appointee, to provide for the needs of the king's household and food one month a year. Two of the unit heads were married to Solomon's daughters.

"And God gave Solomon wisdom and understanding exceeding much, and largeness of heart, even as the sand that is on the sea shore. And Solomon's wisdom excelled the wisdom of all the children of the east country, and all the wisdom of Egypt."

King James Bible, 1 Kings 4:29–30

Solomon's love for non-Israelite women is specifically noted (1 Kings 11:1). He had a total of seven hundred wives and three hundred concubines. A special wedding gift accompanying the daughter of the Egyptian pharaoh was the Canaanite city of Gezer. The Bible finds that rather than serving as cement for political or military alliances, these matches drew Solomon away from the ways of the Lord and attributes the subsequent split in his kingdom to this behavior.

"And all King Solomon's drinking vessels were of gold, and all the vessels of the house of the forest of Lebanon were of pure gold; none were of silver: it was nothing accounted of in the days of Solomon."

King James Bible, 1 Kings 10:21

To maintain his kingdom Solomon depended on military might—infantry, extensive cavalry, and chariots—aimed at control and protection of trade routes and established Israelite colonies where needed to accomplish this. The thrust of his empire was commercial and he worked along with rulers such as King Hiram of Tyre. The queen of Sheba went to Jerusalem from her south Arabian kingdom, probably to expand trade relations (although later legend spoke of other relations, with the royal house of Ethiopia claiming descent from their union).

The most significant result of Solomon's construction efforts was the Temple in Jerusalem, which took seven years to build, and "there was neither hammer nor axe nor any tool of iron heard in the house while it was in building." Hiram of Tyre provided timber, and gold, receiving land and foodstuffs in return. Among other structures built by Solomon in Jerusalem were his palace, which took thirteen years to complete, and a city wall. He also established garrison cities and built fortresses throughout the empire.

Solomon's reputation for wisdom is based on biblical and extra-biblical material. In response to God's asking him in a dream "What shall I give thee?" Solomon requested a discerning heart. The biblical story of his judgment in the case of two women, each of whom claims to be the mother of the same child, gives perhaps the most famous illustration of this wisdom (1 Kings 3:16–28). Biblical books traditionally ascribed to him are Proverbs, the Song of Songs (also known as the Song of Solomon), and Ecclesiastes. Later works attributed to him are the Odes of Solomon, and the Psalms of Solomon.

Although Solomon's reign saw developments in the economy, agriculture, and administration of the empire, the cost to the nation in taxes and work outweighed the benefits as far as most people were concerned, and they were deeply dissatisfied. After his death, ten tribes rejected the rule of Rehoboam, his successor, and created their own kingdom of Israel. The remaining territory became Rehoboam's **truncated** kingdom of Judah. ◆

truncated: made smaller by cutting away a portion.

Sujin

LATE 3RD TO EARLY 4TH CENTURY ● EMPEROR OF JAPAN

Sujin was the tenth emperor of Japan, according to early chronicles. Most of Sujin's predecessors are mentioned only briefly in the chronicles, with no significant achievements credited to their reigns. He, however, is described as having played an active role in the formative period of the Japanese nation. For this reason, some historians regard him as the real founder of the Japanese state.

In the earliest years of Sujin's rule, political instability prevailed. To restore peace, Sujin assembled eighty thousand deities and sought guidance from them: "At this time the Gods inspired Shinto priestess Yamato-totohi-momoso-hime to say as follows: 'Why is the Emperor grieved at the disordered state of the country? If he duly did us reverent worship it would assuredly become pacified of itself.' " The emperor worshiped as he was told, but without any effect. Then, having bathed and practiced abstinence and purified the interior of the hall, he prayed. That night he had a dream. A man of noble appearance told him, "If thou wilt cause me to be worshiped by my child, Ōtata-neko, then will there be peace at once." Delighted, the emperor did so, and peace returned to the country.

A man of noble appearance told the Sujin, "If thou wilt cause me to be worshiped by my child Otata-neko, then will there be peace at once."

After that, Sujin sent four shoguns, including a shogun named Ōbiko, in four directions to conquer the local chiefs who refused to submit to him. Until recently, historians doubted that such an expedition had actually occurred, but a sword inscribed with the name Ōbiko and the date 471 C.E. has been discovered at a tomb near Tokyo that corroborates the account in the chronicles. According to this inscription, Ōbiko was regarded as the ancestor of the local chiefs. As the chronicles often refer to intermarriages between a central government official and the daughter of a local chief frequently resulting in children, the validity of the statement in the sword inscription is supported. There was an expedition, probably in the late third or early fourth century, and it brought the eastern region, including what is now Tokyo, under the control of the Yamato rulers of central Honshu, the largest of the four islands to constitute Japan.

During his reign Sujin first consolidated his control over the territory he had inherited from his predecessors by appeasing the local deities, and then expanded the kingdom. For this reason, he is given the name August Founder of the Country. ◆

Süleyman the Magnificent

c.1494–1566 ● Ottoman Emperor

Süleyman the Magnificent was one of the Ottoman empire's most famous sultans, presiding over the era of the empire's greatest expansion. He was called Süleyman the Magnificent in Europe; within the empire he was referred to as Süleyman the Lawgiver, because in addition to leading troops in thirteen wars, Süleyman improved the empire's code of justice. He filled in loopholes in the existing code of law, and executed corrupt officials—including a son-in-law—a first in Turkish history. He also constructed numerous **mosques**, schools, and hospitals that rivaled the masterpieces of some of Europe's master builders. His wall still stands around the Old City of Jerusalem.

mosques: buildings used for public worship by Muslims.

Süleyman came to power at the age of twenty-six in 1520, succeeding his father, Selim I. An only son, Süleyman was spared from fratricide (a ruler often killed his brothers and nephews). His father had sent him to study government in provincial capitals for ten years, so he had been well prepared to rule. He removed incompetent officials and instituted far-reaching internal reforms. During his youth, Süleyman had made a close friend of a Christian slave boy, Ibrahim, who held high office in his government.

The custom of his time provided for the sultan to have an enormous harem of slave girls. The first four to bear sons were elevated to the status of a sultana but, nevertheless, remained slaves. The highest ranking woman in the harem was the mother of the sultan. Süleyman's harem numbered three hundred women. He fell deeply in love with the second sultana, a Russian girl called Roxelana, and after the birth of their son, remained faithful to her. She convinced him to marry her, freeing her from slavery. A sultan had not taken a wife in six centuries, ever since the wife of a sultan had been captured and humiliated by her captors. The wedding was celebrated with a week of lavish feasting throughout Constantinople.

When Süleyman came to power, he had a standing army of fifty thousand troops, which he personally led into battle. Their first campaign was to take Belgrade. They then moved on to Rhodes and were successful, but the battle cost nearly one hundred thousand lives (1523). Süleyman retired from the battlefield for three years, during which time his relationship with Ibrahim grew much closer. They spent much time together and sometimes even slept in the same quarters. This aroused jealousy and anger among other officials, and in Roxelana, who had also begun taking an active role in government, advising her husband and listening in on parliament meetings. Ibrahim, who developed a taste for luxury and led an ostentatious life, married the sultan's sister.

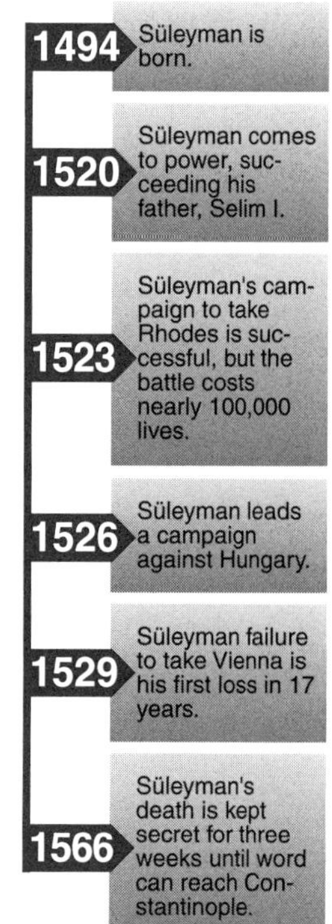

Süleyman's next campaign, in 1526, was against Hungary. At this time, the empire stretched across the Middle East, comprising parts of Europe, Asia, and Africa and included the cities of Carthage, Alexandria, Jerusalem, Damascus, Nice, Athens, and Belgrade. The navy ruled the Mediterranean, under the command of Barbarossa, a pirate whom Süleyman had bribed to serve the empire. After Hungary was subdued, Süleyman turned to besiege Vienna (1529). Unseasonably heavy rains slowed the transport of Süleyman's heavy guns to the front and, although the Turks vastly outnumbered the defending Viennese, Süleyman's army was defeated, his first failure in seventeen years.

Returning to Constantinople, Süleyman slipped into a life of luxury and idleness while Ibrahim took over more and more power. When Ibrahim began boasting that it was really he who ruled the empire, Roxelana became incensed. She began a campaign against him, supported by his many enemies among the officers. Finally, she persuaded Süleyman that Ibrahim intended to usurp his power completely and the sultan arranged to have his longtime friend strangled as he slept.

Ibrahim's first three successors came and went quickly, but the fourth became friendly with Roxelana and married her daughter. Together, they plotted against Mustafa, the sultan's eldest son and heir apparent. Roxelana wanted her son, Selim, to succeed Süleyman in power, but as the eldest son, Mustafa, stood next in line. Furthermore, Mustafa was an intelligent and well-liked young man who was popular among the officers. As with Ibrahim, although this time with entirely fabricated "evidence," Roxelana managed to convince Süleyman that Mustafa was plotting against him. Süleyman arranged to have his beloved son strangled, and he is reported to have watched the murder from behind a curtain and emerged afterward showing no trace of emotion.

Süleyman arranged to have his beloved son strangled, and he is reported to have watched the murder from behind a curtain.

Five weeks after assuring her son's place in line for the throne, Roxelana died. Meanwhile, Süleyman's health had also begun to fail and he suffered stomach problems and occasional fainting spells. He stopped attending parliament meetings and began promoting favorites and relatives, the start of the corruption that was to plague the next several rulers, until it finally brought about the end of the empire.

Süleyman died in his tent on the battlefield during another campaign in Hungary. His death was kept secret for three weeks, until Selim could reach Constantinople, the sultan's physician having been murdered so he would not let the secret out. ◆

Sundjata Keita

C.1205–1255 ● FOUNDER OF THE MANDINKA EMPIRE (MALI)

Sundjata (also spelled Sundiata) Keita was the founder of the Mandinka empire, also known as the empire of Mali in western Africa, which he ruled from about 1235 to 1255. Born in Dakajala, the second son of Maghan Kon Fatta, king of Manding, Sundjata had an unhappy childhood. When he was only seven years old, his father died and his elder half brother, Dankaran-Tuma, ascended the throne. Sundjata, now persecuted, went into exile with his mother, sisters, and younger brother.

The Manding kingdom, situated on the High Niger, encompassed the Boure, a province rich in gold.

The Manding kingdom, situated on the High Niger, encompassed the Boure, a province rich in gold. Its king was a vassal to the emperor of Ghana. Yet the Ghana empire was torn apart by civil war and in decline. Sumanguru Kante, the king of Susu and the chief of the blacksmiths (a powerful caste), subjugated Ghana and imposed his domination on Manding. Unable to defend his kingdom, Dankaran-Tuma relinquished the throne and fled. The king of Susu then brought a reign of terror to Manding and suppressed several revolts by the Mandinka and the Malinke.

These groups dispatched a secret mission to find Sundjata, who was known to have taken refuge somewhere in eastern Manding. He was found at the court of Mema, where King Mema Farin Tounkaran had entrusted him with important responsibilities. The king gave him an army and Sundjata and his family took the road back to their native country. When it became known that Sundjata had come, the Malinke revolted against Sumanguru's authority. Then began a fierce battle between the Malinke and the Susu; the decisive skirmish took place in 1235 at Krina on the banks of the Niger River. The Susu were utterly routed, Sumanguru fled, and Sundjata completely destroyed the city of the Susu.

United, the Malinke led the way to victory after victory under the banner of their young king, assisted by two brilliant lieutenants, Tiramakhan Traore and Fakoli Kourouma. They imposed their domination on all the kingdoms of the **savanna** and built up a vast kingdom extending from Timbuktu on the Niger to Banjul on the Atlantic Ocean. This kingdom, the Mali empire, was the largest and most famous of African empires in the Middle Ages.

savanna: a treeless plain.

Sundjata reigned from 1235 to 1255. The war of the liberation of the Malinke from the yoke of Sumanguru is the subject of the Mandinka epic, which Mandinka oral tradition has transmitted through the griots (bards) from generation to generation even at the end of the twentieth century.

In addition to being a brilliant military leader, Sundjata proved a skilled administrator and lawmaker. The great empire under his power comprised kingdoms and several tribes. A flexible administration gave these groups a great deal of autonomy, with each community allowed to keep its own traditions and customs. The empire was divided into two military regions. The roads and trails in the empire were completely secure.

Sundjata's work as lawmaker was considerable. He established the laws and laid down the rules that have become the customs governing the lives of the Malinke people even today. For instance, modern marriage customs go back to the time of Sundjata. He created a system of alliance both among Malinke clans and between Malinke clans and others. For example, among the Malinke, the **patronymics** Conde and Traore correspond to N'Diaye and Diop, respectively. That is to say, if a Malinke of the Conde or Traore clan wants to establish himself in the Wolof country, that is, Senegal, he takes the name N'Diaye or Diop in order to be accepted as such in the clan. A similar system of correspondence was established between the Malinke and Fulani (Fulbe) patronymics.

patronymics: names derived from that of the father or a paternal ancestor.

In the Malinke oral tradition, Sundjata Keita is the man of many names and prestigious titles. He is called Nare Maghan

Konate (the King of the Konate tribe, from which the Keita dynasty arose), Marijata (Lord Lion), Maghan Sundjata (Sundjata the King), and Sogo Sogo Simbon Salaba (Master Hunter with the Venerable Bearing).

After his victory at Krina, Sundjata converted to Islam and established his capital at Niani on the Sankarani River, tributary to the Niger. Some excavations made at this site have revealed stone foundations of dwellings and public buildings dating back to the time of Sundjata. ◆

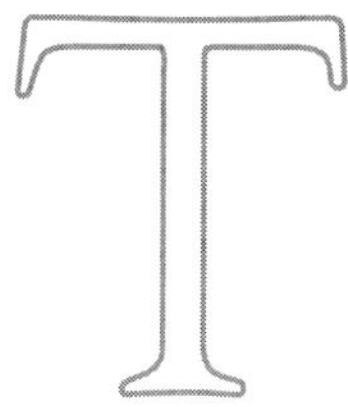

Talal ibn Abdullah

1909–1972 ● KING OF JORDAN

King Talal is the tragic figure of Jordanian politics. He sacrificed his health and happiness by assuming the duties of king at a critical period of transition in Jordan's history. When King Abdullah ibn Husayn was assassinated on July 20, 1951, a group of Jordanian royalists, who were to resemble an **oligarchy** over the next two years, were deeply conscious of the fact that King Abdullah had chosen his grandson, Prince Hussein ibn Talal, as his successor and had begun grooming him for the task. But Hussein was too young. Crown Prince Talal was suffering from acute depression and paranoia yet had improved considerably under medical treatment in Switzerland. He could have led an almost normal life had he been kept in an anxiety-free environment. But the only way to ensure the legitimacy of transition to Hussein was for Talal to become king. The alternatives were either to crown Prince Naif, the regent and Talal's half brother, or to accede to some form of union with Iraq, in which case a member of the Iraqi branch of the Hashimite dynasty would succeed to the Jordanian throne. Neither alternative was considered **palatable**. From this perspective, Talal was to be an interim figure, yet he was significantly more than that.

oligarchy: form of government in which all power is held by a few people.

palatable: agreeable or acceptable.

At the time of Abdullah's assassination, Prime Minister Samir Rifai convened an emergency cabinet meeting. It was decided that the veteran prime minister Tawfiq Abd al-Huda should be entrusted with the formation of a new cabinet under the regent's commission. On September 5, 1951, the cabinet

proclaimed Talal king, and the newly elected parliament confirmed Talal on the throne on receipt of a medical report by Minister of Health Jamil Tutunji. Prince Naif, the regent, flew to Switzerland to escort his brother home.

The most notable legacy of King Talal's brief reign was to turn Jordan into what was the truest democracy in the Arab world at the time in view of the separation of powers and the ability of parliament to act as a check on the actions of government, a function that the Lebanese parliament, for instance, did not exercise. Under Talal's instructions, Abd al-Huda won a vote of confidence in parliament on September 24, 1951. This was unprecedented in the constitutional history of Jordan. A new constitution was promulgated, declaring the people the source of all power. Citizens were guaranteed individual liberty and equality before the law. The constitution was approved by the lower house on November 7, 1951, passed the upper house on December 29, and was signed by King Talal on January 1, 1952. It enshrined the freedom of opinion, the right to hold public meetings and form political parties and trade unions, the freedom of conscience and worship, compulsory free education, as well as the right to own property. It was these liberties that were to make possible the phenomenon of Sulayman al-Nabulsi a few years later.

The new constitution made the cabinet collectively and individually responsible to parliament. Ministers could be impeached. The king could dissolve parliament, but new elections had to be held within four months, otherwise the old parliament would be reinstated. According to Article 93, parliament could override the king's veto over legislation by a two-thirds majority. Parliament was empowered to ratify treaties and could assemble without being called to do so by the king.

The fly in the ointment was that in the event of an emergency, on the decision of the cabinet, the king could declare martial law by decree.

Perhaps the biggest factor responsible for this liberal constitution was King Talal himself, though other conditions were ripe. There was a need to satisfy the Palestinians, who had more liberal traditions and who had recently been incorporated into the union, and the cabinet was wary of an authoritarian king, given the circumstances. King Talal became immensely popular.

On the foreign policy front, he invited Abd al-Huda to declare on September 18, 1951, that Jordan was not seeking union with Iraq. In December 1951 he visited Saudi Arabia and made clear his desire for good relations with the house of Saud.

He was skeptical of Western alliances, and in January 1952 King Talal led Jordan into acceptance of the Arab Collective Security Pact.

Yet barely within eight months of ascending the throne, the tribulations of office were having a visible effect on the king. His psychological troubles had returned and his weight had dwindled to a mere ninety pounds. He left the country in May 1952 to vacation in Europe, leaving behind a Regency Council. Within a week, the cabinet transformed that body into a Crown Council, which exercised the powers of head of state for the rest of Talal's reign. On August 11, 1952, parliament deposed him and proclaimed Prince Hussein king. King Talal accepted gracefully. The duties of king were assumed by a Regency Council until Hussein came of age, the same Regency Council the king had established earlier, headed by Ibrahim Hashim. Abd al-Huda remained in the office of prime minister. Paradoxically under the circumstances, he exercised more power than any other prime minister in the history of Jordan.

"The tragedy of King Talal seemed to be rendered more poignant by the fact that, apart from his insanity, he appeared so ideally fit to be king."
John Bagot Glubb, *A Soldier with the Arabs*

Meanwhile, the press in Israel and rival Arab countries accused the Jordanian government, in complicity with the British, of inventing the king's illness to be rid of him.

King Talal moved to Egypt for a while, then he took up residence in Turkey for the rest of his days. He was given a hero's funeral when he died twenty years later. He was the first king of Jordan to graduate from the Royal Military College at Sandhurst, an English school, and had absorbed a real taste for democracy. Sir John Bagot Glubb recalls in his memoirs, *A Soldier with the Arabs*: "The tragedy of King Talal seemed to be rendered more poignant by the fact that, apart from his insanity, he appeared so ideally fit to be king. . . . He was of acute intelligence, outstanding personal charm, faultless private morals, and inspired by a deeply conscious wish to serve his country and his people, with no selfish motives." ◆

Téwodros

C.1820–1868 ● EMPEROR OF ETHIOPIA

Téwodros, called the "king of kings," was emperor of Ethiopia from 1855 to 1868. Born around 1820 to noble parents, Téwodros was originally named Kasa. He was

apocalyptic: wildly unrestrained; grandiose.

fiefdom: the feudal domain over which a lord has rights and exercises control.

vernacular: the normal spoken form of a language.

educated at monasteries and began his independent career in the early 1840s as a *shefta,* or bandit. In 1852 he launched a campaign that, three years later, brought him to his coronation, when he took the **apocalyptic** regnal name Téwodros. Téwodros promised to revive the monarchy and reunite the country, which, since the 1770s, had collapsed into a cluster of warring **fiefdoms**. His initial successes foundered on entrenched local interests. His hopes of introducing Western technology were foiled by the disinterest of the British, to whom he turned for help. The British failure to acknowledge a letter of friendship, written in 1862, led Téwodros to imprison their consul and a number of other foreigners. The result was a British expedition to the emperor's fortress of Maqdala and Téwodros's death by suicide on April 13, 1868. The first of Ethiopia's modern rulers, Téwodros began the process of national reunification and pioneered the use of the modern **vernacular**, Amharic, over the classical literary language, Ge'ez. He remains a popular figure in poetry and prose, of particular appeal to the young and the radical. ◆

Theodoric the Great

C.454–526 ● OSTROGOTH KING

Theodoric was from the royal Ostrogoth family of Amoli, the fourteenth generation of the line. He was born near present-day Vienna two years after the death of Attila the Hun and a subsequent victory by the Ostrogoths that restored them to independence from Hun enslavement.

Soon afterward, Theodoric's father, Theodemir, in an attempt to improve the conditions of his people, entered into an alliance with Leo, emperor of the Eastern Roman Empire. To ensure Theodemir's compliance, Leo took the ruler's son, Theodoric, as ransom. Thus from the age of eight, Theodoric lived in Constantinople, held captive in amenable surroundings and given a traditional Roman education by the most capable teachers. When he was eighteen he returned to his people, whom Emperor Leo was treating as liberally and generously as possible so as to avoid trouble with any of the barbarian tribes.

During this time, Theodemir led the Ostrogoths in battle and they were able to establish themselves in Pannonia (present-day western Hungary). Nevertheless, the Ostrogoth people lacked food and clothing. Eager to get what they needed for survival, they approached Constantinople and the Byzantine court. Leo, fearing for the capital's safety, granted Theodemir control over the lower Danube in an effort to appease him. It was at this time that Theodoric replaced his father as tribal leader. Meanwhile, Zeno replaced Leo as emperor, and he and Theodoric came to work together cooperatively, although the latter was known for his occasional pillaging rampages.

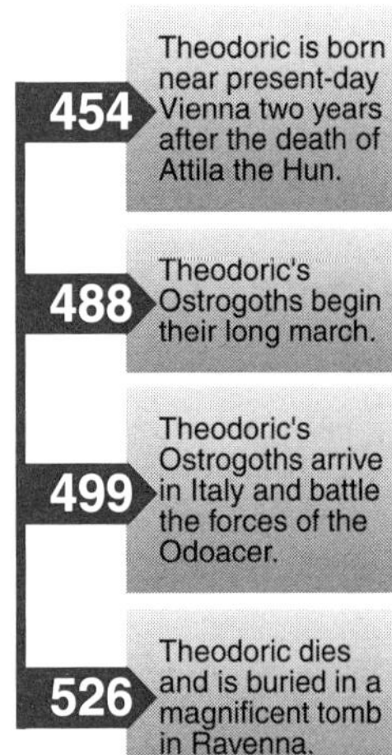

The Ostrogoths' inability to make their fertile lands produce adequately meant that they remained a threatening presence; Theodoric himself was kept in opulence by the Roman emperor, but he refused to forget the miserable conditions of his people in a land they were ill-adapted to occupy. Realizing his power to threaten the stability of the empire, he proposed a plan of mutual benefit to his people and the emperor, offering to take his entire people, numbering over one hundred thousand, across to Italy to conquer the center of the former western Roman empire. Zeno agreed, calculating that this would finally remove the Ostrogoth threat.

In 488 the order was given and the Ostrogoths began their long march. They arrived in Italy in mid 489, engaging in battle the forces of the barbarian ruler Odoacer. Odoacer's forces were eventually vanquished, but the barbarian king retreated to the impregnable citadel of Ravenna, where he succeeded in fending off Theodoric's army for another three years; only treachery enabled the latter's forces to enter the fortress and kill Odoacer, his family, and eventually his followers throughout Italy.

Having achieved total victory, Theodoric divided the spoils of war, parceling out one third of the territories to his soldiers. Although he had confiscated large tracts of Roman land, he now tried to ensure the peaceful coexistence of the two peoples by keeping his nation separate from the former inhabitants who had been already been Romanized. Theodoric maintained his people's distinct language, customs, and religion, while the Romans were permitted to live undisturbed under the remnant of the Empire's civil service and to worship according to their Catholic traditions; the Ostrogoths adhered to Aryan Christianity.

Theodoric shed the skins and furs of traditional Ostrogoth leadership and donned the purple robes of the empire. His thirty-three-year reign was remarkably peaceful, both because of his statesmanship and due to the fear of him. He was buried in a magnificent tomb in Ravenna that remains intact to this day. ◆

Thutmose III

15TH CENTURY B.C.E. ● PHARAOH OF EGYPT

Thutmose III was pharaoh of Egypt from about 1490 to 36 B.C.E. He was the son of Thutmose II and a concubine and ascended the throne only because Thutmose's wife, Hatshepsut, failed to produce any male progeny. In order to confirm his rights to the throne, he was wed to Hatshepsut's daughter, half sister Meryte.

regent: one who governs a kingdom in the minority, absence, or disability of the sovereign.

Thutmose inherited his father's throne at a young age, with Hatshepsut acting as **regent**. Hatshepsut was, however, an ambitious woman who declared herself pharaoh and ruled as such for twenty years; legends that she was of divine descent insured her grasp on power. Contemporary statues show her in full royal regalia, including an artificial beard she apparently wore to disguise her sex.

Hatshepsut died when Thutmose was twenty-two years old; there is reason to believe that he was responsible for her sudden death. All documents and inscriptions pertaining to Hatshepsut's reign were destroyed and her advisor Senenmut was overthrown. His authority safeguarded, Thutmose chose to continue the Asian conquests begun by his father. He appointed two viziers, one in Thebes, the other in Memphis, to govern the kingdom in his absence, and set off for Asia.

suzerainty: the dominion of a feudal lord; overlordship.

At that time Palestine and Syria were divided into many small city-states governed by minor princes under nominal Egyptian **suzerainty**. Only southern Palestine remained loyal to Egypt; the Hyksos (invaders who had taken possession of Egypt) had formed a coalition of 330 northern princes to overthrow Egyptian rule. Thutmose led his armies to Megiddo, an important center of the coalition in northern Palestine, to subdue the city and break the coalition's resolve. When his officers suggested that Thutmose take a roundabout route to the city, leaving his armies less vulnerable to attack, he rejected their advice as cowardice. Thutmose reached Megiddo without encountering any resistance; the allied princes chose to make their stand outside the city's walls. The ensuing battle was an outstanding victory for Thutmose; he crushed the coalition forces, leaving the few remaining survivors to seek sanctuary within the city walls. Rather than attack the well-fortified town, however,

Thutmose laid siege to it for seven months. With the fall of Megiddo, Thutmose was free to sweep through Syria toward the Euphrates.

Opposition crumbled before the advancing Egyptian forces and Thutmose overran Kadesh, Aleppo, Katna, and Carchemish. He crossed the Euphrates in cedarwood boats carried from Lebanon and set up a boundary **stela** on its far bank, next to the stela placed there by his father years before.

stela: a carved or inscribed stone slab or pillar used for commemorative purposes.

Having achieved his goal in the north, Thutmose began the journey home. Upon receiving news that the king of Kadesh had revolted, he encircled that city with his chariots; the king sent out a mare in heat, hoping to distract the Egyptian horses. Thutmose's general Amenemhab promptly cut off the mare's head and disembowelled the beast, calming the horses and allowing for an attack. Amenemhab further distinguished himself during an elephant hunt; when one of the animals charged Thutmose, Amenemhab rushed to the elephant and cut off its trunk.

Thutmose was a brilliant strategist who often preferred a ruse to brute strength. During the siege of Jaffa, the local king was invited to the Egyptian camp. The Egyptian general offered to show him Thutmose's famed war club, only to batter the king with it. Two hundred Egyptian soldiers were then hidden in baskets while five hundred others hid their arms under their cloaks. Soldiers were led to the city walls to report that the Egyptians had surrendered and were bringing two hundred baskets carried by five hundred Egyptian prisoners as booty. The queen opened the gates to receive the treasure when, to her surprise, the Egyptians removed their cloaks, jumped from the baskets, and captured the city.

Thutmose also made conquests in Nubia but it is assumed that he did not personally participate in these conflicts. He created an effective bureaucracy of commissioners and high commissioners to govern his realm, guaranteeing future payments of tribute. The bounty he brought Egypt led to Thutmose's reign being referred to as Egypt's golden age. In his final years Thutmose shared the throne briefly with his son Amenhotep.

Complete lists of the cities conquered by Thutmose can still be seen at the Temple of Karnak. Three lists contain the cities' names surrounded by an ellipse and an engraving of a captured prince with his arms bound, paying tribute to Thutmose. ◆

Tiberius

42 B.C.E.–37 C.E. ● EMPEROR OF ROME

When Tiberius was four years old the Emperor Augustus fell in love with Tiberius's pregnant mother, Livia, and married her after persuading her husband to release her. Livia became the power behind the throne, exerting great influence over Augustus.

Livia brought two sons to her marriage with Augustus: Drusus, whom Augustus loved and adopted, and Tiberius, serious even as a child, whom Augustus eventually respected but never loved. Tiberius was well educated, then sent off early to war, the custom for boys in Augustus's household. Following Augustus's policy of extending the empire on every frontier, Tiberius and Drusus commanded armies for the next ten years until 9 B.C.E., when Drusus sustained a deadly injury when he was thrown from his horse while fighting German tribes. Tiberius loved his brother deeply; he rode from Gaul to be present at his death, then brought Drusus's body back to Rome for burial before returning to the battlefield.

That same year Augustus forced Tiberius to divorce his pregnant wife and marry Augustus's twice-widowed daughter, Julia, to end the gossip caused by Julia's numerous lovers. Tiberius tried to be a good husband, enduring Julia's many love affairs in the hope that Augustus would adopt him as his successor. When it became clear that Augustus preferred his own grandchildren, Tiberius resigned and went to live in Rhodes as a private citizen. Julia continued to go from lover to lover until Augustus banished her to a barren island, where she died sixteen years later, still imprisoned.

Augustus was left without a successor (his grandsons had died) and rebellion was brewing in several provinces. Seeing no other choice, in 2 C.E. he reluctantly summoned Tiberius, adopted him as his son and coruler, and sent him to the revolts. An extremely capable general who won by strategy, not by squandering his soldiers in bloodbaths, Tiberius ended the disturbances.

Tiberius returned to a Rome that accepted him as coruler even while it hated him for his austerity and his tightfisted monetary policies. Augustus's reign had yielded a long period of peace and prosperity; Egyptian treasure and prosperous Roman trade had created a luxurious society in which poetry, literature, art, and the pursuit of pleasure flourished while the populace was mollified with games and doles of corn. Tiberius the stoic, who idealized the old Roman virtues, had no place in this epicurean society.

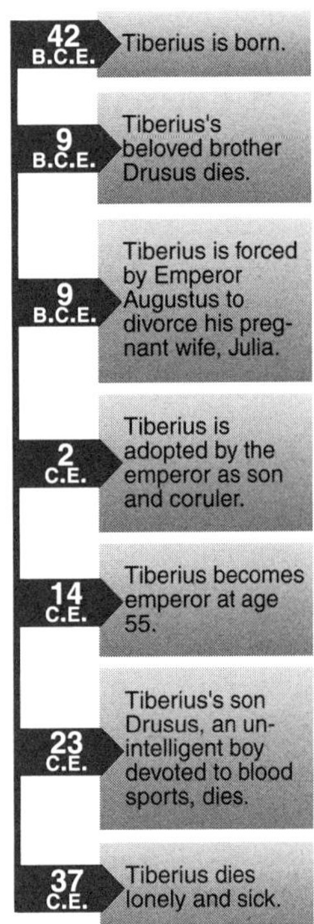

Livia, his mother, felt that Tiberius owed his throne to her and that he therefore ruled only as her representative. She insisted on cosigning official documents during the first years of his reign, then wanted to rule alone, until Tiberius could no longer live with her and built a separate palace. He refused even to attend her funeral.

Tiberius was fifty-five when he became emperor in 14 C.E. A careful, conscientious ruler, his diligence ensured efficient government, but nothing he did pleased Rome. Without increasing taxes he repaired and built public buildings, distributed charity to stricken families and regions, and greatly increased the treasury; but the poor were upset because he gave them bread, not circuses. He kept the empire at peace and was slandered by those with imperialistic designs or an eye to plunder. He tried to restore the Republic and the power of a degenerate Senate that wanted honors and wealth, not responsibility. Believing in and protecting freedom of speech, he was the victim of gossip and lampoons.

His troubles made Tiberius gloomy and withdrawn. Sejanus, the prefect of the Praetorian Guards, took advantage of this by preventing anyone from seeing Tiberius without his approval and presence. Sejanus acquired more and more power, first by recommending people for office, then by selling the offices to the highest bidder, and finally by exiling his enemies.

Tiberius's son, named Drusus after his father's beloved brother, was an unintelligent youth much devoted to blood sports who died in 23 C.E. Overcome with disappointment and bitterness, Tiberius moved to Capri at age sixty-seven. He continued to carefully rule the Empire through Sejanus. Especially in his latter years he was cruel and depraved and the Roman historians recorded many of his monstrous acts. Increasing fear of Sejanus, his Praetorian Guard, and even Tiberius, made the

Senate obey Tiberius's communications as royal commands, further diminishing the Senate's authority. Sejanus's "rule" only came to an end when his plot to kill Tiberius was discovered, whereupon he was executed. Old, lonely, and sick, Tiberius himself died seven years later. ◆

Trajan

53–117 ● EMPEROR OF ROME

Praetorian Guard: Roman imperial bodyguard.

Trajan succeeded the emperor Nerva, whose brief rule had aroused the resentment of the **Praetorian Guard**. Besieged and humiliated, Nerva looked for a successor able to control both the Guards and discontented frontier commanders in revolt. He chose Trajan, a respected and honored general in charge of Rome's armies in Cologne, adopted him as his son and died several months later in 98. Trajan continued his work on the frontier, summoning the rebellious frontier leaders to him one by one. They never returned.

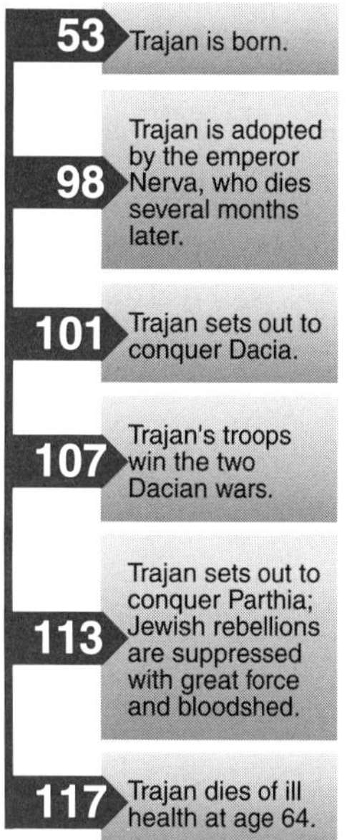

Trajan, originally from Spain, was a soldier by profession and by nature. He was forty when he became emperor of a Rome weakened by moral decay. Sexual freedom had replaced political freedom. The poor lived off corn doled out to keep them quiet and passive, while the rich wallowed in decadent luxuries, unwilling to assume civic responsibilities. Senators wanted prestige without responsibility. Foreigners poured into Rome, making overcrowding a serious problem at the same time that family limitation practices combined with plague and malaria to seriously reduce the native population. Peasant families, dispossessed by the expansion of large estates, migrated to the city to live off the dole.

Trajan arrived in Rome two years after being appointed emperor. In typically modest manner, he walked through the streets of Rome toward the Senate. His wife, Plotina, by her very appearance an example of earlier strict Roman family virtues, walked by his side. He promised the Senate that he would not threaten but respect it and be its servant, not its master. He kept that promise and found that he could wield almost absolute power if he observed the forms of deferring to the Senate.

A conscientious administrator, he required an equal devotion from senators who wished to enjoy his favor. The rich began to work at the tasks of government. To encourage the birth of more children, Trajan expanded the corn dole so that both children and parents received their own doles, and extended the *alimentia* established by Nerva (a monthly state subsidy for each child of Italian peasant families). He helped the peasants keep their lands by establishing a state fund of low-interest loans; his careful financial management of the Empire, starting with the personal example of his household, placed its economy on a sound basis.

Rome had been paying Dacia (roughly equivalent to modern Romania) tribute in return for peace for fifteen years and Trajan refused to pay anymore; in 101 he set out to conquer Dacia. The two Dacian wars (101–2 and 105–7) resulted in the annexation of Dacia and eventually the creation in Rome of the still-standing Column of Trajan, carved with realistic reliefs commemorating incidents in the Dacian wars in a spiral style, each scene melting into the next. Roman culture was based upon that of Greece, but the realistic style of these carvings was far more expressive of the Roman character than was the classical Greek style.

War booty and Dacia's gold mines enabled Trajan to build extensively without raising taxes, countering demobilization unemployment. Trajan built or improved aqueducts, harbors, bridges, roads, canals, tunnels, and public buildings and aided disaster-stricken cities. His first priority was Rome, then Italy, and finally the provinces, which he saw as a source of wealth to be milked for Rome. Rome provided the provinces with order, economic security, and protection against their enemies in return for providing Rome with specific goods and taxes that were no more burdensome than those they had paid to their own preconquest rulers.

Essentially a man of war, Trajan experienced six years of peace and administrative duties as quite enough. In 113 he set out on a campaign of imperial conquest against Parthia, sweeping through Armenia, Assyria, and Mesopotamia to the Indian Ocean, creating new provinces as he went. Massive Jewish-led rebellions broke out and were put down with great force and bloodshed. Unable to consolidate his conquests because of ill health, he died at the age of sixty-four.

The new emperor, Hadrian, was Trajan's nephew, but incompatibility between Trajan's straightforward nature and Hadrian's complex personality prevented Trajan from adopting Hadrian as his heir; Hadrian's appointment as Trajan's successor was contrived by Plotina after Trajan's death. ◆

"The Christians are not to be hunted out. If brought before you, and the offense is proved, they are to be punished, but with this reservation—if any one denies he is a Christian, and makes it clear he is not, by offering prayer to our gods, then he is to be pardoned on his recantation, no matter how suspicious his past."

Trajan, letter to Pliny the Younger, governor of Bithynia, 112 C.E.

Tupou IV

1918– • King of Tonga

Taufa'ahau Tupou IV is king of Tonga, a South Pacific country comprising about 170 small volcanic and coral islands, only thirty-six of which are inhabited. During the 1840s a powerful tribal chief, Taufa'ahau, ended warfare between the inhabitants of the various islands and united them into the a single nation. In 1845 Taufa'ahau was crowned King George Tupou I, the country's first monarch. Tonga adopted a constitution in 1875, officially establishing the monarchy as its form of government. Taufa'ahau Tupou IV, a direct descendant of Tonga's first king, was born Siaosi Taufa'ahau Tupoulahi, the eldest son of Queen Salote Tupou III and Prince Tungi Mailefihi. A highly skilled athlete and musician, Taufa'ahau attended Newington College, Sydney, Australia, and earned a B.A. and L.L.B. at Sydney University, becoming the first Tongan king to earn a university degree. He served his country as minister of education (1943), minister of health (1944), and premier (1949). Upon the queen's death in 1965, he became king; his lavish coronation, covered by *National Geographic*, was held on July 4, 1967.

Tupou's long tenure has been marked by two themes—his independent spirit and the climate of political change in his nation. A physically immense man, he began a successful diet and exercise regimen in the late 1980s, losing 200 pounds and inspiring his adoring subjects to follow him in what would become a nationwide health and fitness craze. He is widely praised for his progressive stances on the development of transportation and communication; he has also helped establish wildlife preserves in his country, for which he received a conservationist award from the Seacology Foundation in 1996.

Tupou IV's ideas have not always been embraced, however. For example, his invitation to American states to use

Tonga as a dumping ground for their used tires—they would be burned to generate electricity—was ridiculed by critics who argued that the largely agrarian country had no need for such a high volume of electricity; similar criticisms greeted his suggestions for the building of a nuclear power plant.

Moreover, Tupou IV has not encouraged political change with the enthusiasm reformers would like. The Tongan government includes a twelve-seat cabinet (all chosen by the king) and an eighteen-seat parliament (half of whom are chosen by the king). Efforts in the mid and late 1990s to decentralize power—for example, to allow cabinet members to be appointed from representatives popularly elected to the Tongan parliament—were rebuffed by the king. Such resistance to change has only fueled critics' perceptions of widespread corruption in Tongan politics. One especially embarrassing event was the government's decision—at first secret—to raise money by selling Tongan passports to anyone who could pay $50,000; the takers of this offer tended to be those who might need quick political asylum—including, most notably, the wife of deposed Philippine president Fernando Marcos, Imelda Marcos. While reform-minded leaders such as Akilisi Pohiva, political party head and newspaper publisher, have advocated greater democracy and accountability in Tonga, Tupou IV's inaction in the face of government lawsuits designed to squelch the freedom of the press has also generated widespread criticism.

Tupou IV is married to Halaevalu Mata'aho, the queen. They have four children—a daughter and three sons. The eldest son, Prince Tupouto'a, is expected to succeed his father as king. ◆

1918	Tupou is born.
1943	Tupou becomes minister of education.
1944	Tupou becomes minister of health.
1949	Tupou becomes premier.
1965	Tupou becomes king upon the queen's death.
1967	Tupou is crowned king of Tonga.
1996	Tupou receives an award from the Seacology Foundation for helping to establish wildlife preserves.

Tutankhamen

1343? B.C.E.–1325? B.C.E. ● PHARAOH OF EGYPT

Young pharaoh Tutankhamen reigned only briefly, but in death he gave the modern world an exquisite view into the world of ancient Egypt. Archeologists uncovered Tutankhamen's tomb, one of the richest discoveries in the history of archeology, in 1922. His tomb lay in Egypt's Valley of the Kings, an area that secretly housed the tombs of many ancient kings. Tutankhamen's tomb and its contents were in

exceptional condition and have provided abundant material for scholars of many disciplines.

Ancient Egyptians considered their kings divine and revered them more as divinities than for their individual personalities. This partly explains why little is known of Tutankhamen, who was born around 1343 B.C.E. and belonged to a period that historians call the New Kingdom, which lasted from 1570 B.C.E. to about 1085 B.C.E. Tutankhamen became king at about age nine. Some scholars believe he was a son-in-law of King Akhenaton, an important ruler who had come to the throne in 1367 B.C.E. Some scholars believe that King Akhenaton was Tutankhamen's father. Others believe that Tutankhamen and Akhenaton were brothers.

Akhenaton had caused a great shift in Egypt by worshiping the sun god Aton and decreeing that Aton was to replace Amon and all other gods except Re, or Ra, the sun god. His move angered many Egyptians, who preferred their old gods and rejected Aton. These people included powerful priests who were followers of Amon. Tutankhamen reversed Akhenaton's decree when he became king. Tutankhamen's original name was Tutankhaton, which meant "the living image of Aton," or "the life of Aton is pleasing." By changing his name to remove the "aton," Tutankhamen restored the old religion.

Tutankhamen received assistance in ruling from his vizier (minister of state) named Ay. It is believed that Ay succeeded as king when Tutankhamen died about 1325 B.C.E. at the age of eighteen or nineteen from causes that are not known to scholars. A top Egyptian general, Horemheb, followed Ay as king. Horemheb and his successors destroyed or removed monuments that had been built by Tutankhamen or in his honor.

Fortunately, the tomb of Tutankhamen was not destroyed, and it lay nearly untouched for over 3,000 years until British archaeologists Howard Carter and Lord Carnarvon made their astonishing discovery in 1922. Tutankhamen's tomb was the last of thirty-four tombs of New Kingdom rulers to be found in the Valley of the Kings, a barren desert area on the west bank of the Nile River opposite the modern town of Luxor. The site, hidden by high cliffs, may have been chosen to prevent theft of treasures from the tombs. Even at that, Tutankhamen's tomb remained the only one that had not been completely looted in ancient times, and it had been robbed twice.

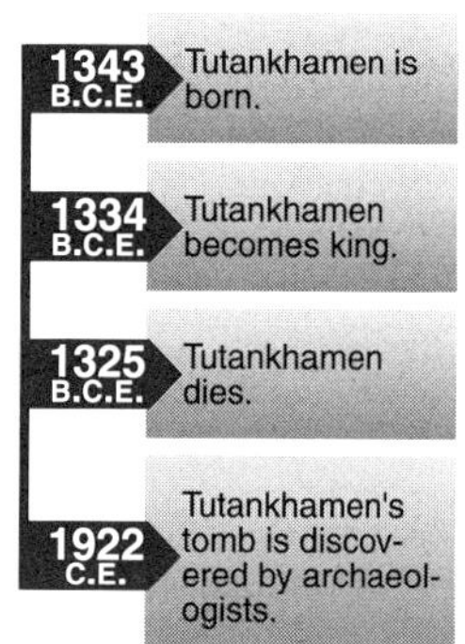

Modern explorers had discovered the first of the tombs in 1817. Most of them were carved deep into rock, and they each had several rooms and a similar layout. **Hieroglyphic** texts, magical scenes, and symbolic images had been carved and painted over many of the walls of the tombs, telling the stories of ancient Egypt.

Carter had been searching for Tutankhamen's tomb nearly ten years before he realized that debris from another dig, the nearby tomb of King Ramses VI, had hidden the entrance to Tutankhamen's tomb. After finding the entrance, Carter and his companions ventured down sixteen steps, through a doorway, and along a forty-five-foot passageway. They then entered a second door, which brought them into a four-room area. An antechamber was filled with objects, including two life-sized statues guarding the entrance to the burial chamber. The burial chamber held Tutankhamen, whose mummified body lay within a series of cases and gold coffins. Beyond the burial chamber was a room that came to be called the treasury room. More than 5,000 objects were found throughout all four rooms.

hieroglyphic: the picture script of the ancient Egyptians.

Ancient Egyptians viewed the afterlife as an extension of their natural world, and in that belief they paid great attention to how they buried their dead. They developed complex **mortuary** practices based on the importance of ensuring survival in body and spirit, because they believed their dead would be resurrected in the afterlife. They mummified the dead so they could be resurrected. Skillful embalmers used salts, resins, and wax to preserve the corpses. Egyptians also provided an eternal supply of sustenance for the spirits of the dead, leaving food and drink in the tomb. They even carved and painted lists and images of certain items on tomb walls, which were magically to provide substitutes for actual food and drink. They sometimes created images of servants producing food and clothing for the dead and bearing gifts to the tomb.

mortuary: of or relating to the burial of the dead.

Of all the objects furnished for the deceased, the coffin was the most important, designed to protect the mummy inside. Magical decorations and inscriptions were made on the coffin to help the deceased move to the afterlife. Kings were given extra care to survive into the afterlife. Tutankhamen's mummy and coffin were exceedingly elaborate. His body was wrapped in many yards of linen cloth, within which were found 143 extremely valuable objects, including jeweled necklaces and bracelets, gold sandals, toe and finger rings, and a gold handled dagger with an iron blade.

Tutankhamen's head and shoulders were covered by a lifelike mask made of gold inlaid with the precious stones lapis lazuli and carnelian. The mask has become famous worldwide as an icon of ancient Egypt. The brilliant sculpted gold face shows a refined nose and full mouth. Dark, bold lines create wide outlined eyes and strong eyebrows. A pointed, braided beard juts out from the chin. The gold headdress fans out about the head and shoulders with dark horizontal stripes on it. Heads of a cobra and an eagle emerge from above the forehead. The mask is part of the full coffin that encases Tutankhamen, which is made of gold, stones, and glass. It is wide at the shoulders and tapers toward the feet, with the shape of arms crossed at the chest. One hand holds a scepter and the other a staff.

Ancient Egyptians viewed the afterlife as an extension of their natural world, and in that belief, they paid great attention to how they buried their dead.

Egyptian dead also had their favorite possessions as well as useful items buried with them to be used in the afterlife. Among the items discovered in Tutankhamen's tomb were luxurious chests and thrones. One magnificent throne made of gold, silver, and stone featured sculpted lion heads on the armrests. The back of the throne depicts an affectionate Tutankhamen with his queen, Ankhesenamun, both garbed in clothing of the era. A headrest, shaped like a small animal with legs, is sculpted from ivory. Other items included beds, linens, clothing, and earrings. The archeologists also found many hunting items, including chariots, bows and arrows, swords, daggers, and shields. They found statues of Tutankhamen and other Egyptian gods, figures of animals, models of ships, and storage jars of precious oils. The handle of a fan pictured Tutankhamen hunting. Several objects show scenes of Tutankhamen fighting in battle, but experts think these scenes picture fictional events.

In the 1700s and 1800s many Europeans viewed mummies as curiosities and brought many back to Europe as souvenirs. Consequently, one of the world's most comprehensive collections of Egyptian coffins is in the British Museum in London. In 1935 the Egyptian government established a special department to stop the **plundering** of the nation's archaeological sites and to arrange the exhibition of the collected artifacts owned by the government. This led to today's Egyptian Museum in Cairo. Most of the items found in Tutankhamen's tomb are now displayed in the Egyptian Museum. ◆

plundering: taking goods wrongfully or by force.

Tz'u-hsi

1835–1908 ● Empress Dowager of China

Tz'u-hsi (also spelled Cixi or Tse-hsi) was the mother of the Chinese emperor, the power behind the Chinese throne. Beginning her career as a low-ranking concubine of the Hsien-feng emperor, Tz'u-hsi contrived, by dint of ruthless determination, to become the most powerful woman in the China of her day and de facto ruler of the empire for over forty years.

She initially rose in status and authority in her capacity as mother of the emperor's only son, whom she bore in 1856. Increased foreign demands for diplomatic and trading rights marked this as a particularly turbulent period domestically: when, in 1860, British and French armies moved on Peking (Beijing) in retaliation for the emperor's refusal to allow foreign diplomats into the Forbidden City, members of the court fled to Jehol, where the emperor died.

After an accommodation had been reached with Britain and France, the court returned to Peking and Tz'u-hsi's son, aged only five, now became the T'ung-chih emperor. A regency council of eight older officials took charge of state affairs, but Tz'u-hsi, in alliance with Hsien-feng's former senior consort, Tz'u-an, swiftly usurped their authority; Hsien-feng's brother, Prince Kung, helped them in their intriguing and became prince counselor. This triumvirate was responsible for quelling the Taipang and Nien rebellions, which had raged since the early 1850s.

China was forced to concede to many of the demands for modernization and socioeconomic liberalization made upon it by trade-hungry Western powers: between 1864 and 1889 it was opened to Christian missionaries and its internal transport infrastructure was upgraded with the aid of Western know-how. From 1863 Sir Robert Hart built up a maritime customs service that came to generate a

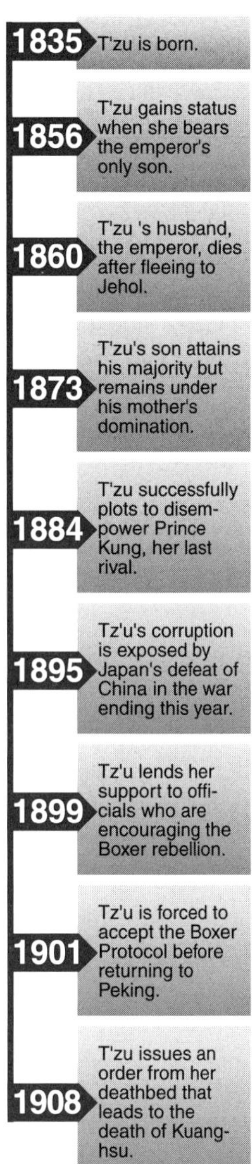

significant proportion of the Chinese government's revenues. Kung promoted the establishment of schools for the study of foreign languages, Western-style weapons arsenals, and a Chinese foreign service. In 1876 the Chafoo convention opened up a further ten Chinese ports to foreign traders. Many Chinese were vehemently against Western interference in their affairs and the changes initiated at the foreigners' behest, and Tz'u-hsi came to align herself with these opponents of reform, who included many members of the traditional military and government hierarchies.

T'ung-chih attained his majority in 1873, but remained under the domination of Tz'u-hsi. She forcefully disrupted his personal life and may also have been responsible for encouraging the **debauched** excesses which contributed to his early death. With the backing of the army, she then overturned the traditional laws of succession and had her three-year-old nephew, Kuang-hsu, named as the new heir to the throne, thus ensuring that she and Tz'u-an retained their positions as regents. Tz'u-an died in 1881 and three years later Tz'u-hsi successfully plotted to disempower Kung and sabotage his reform program; she was now without rival. Marrying Kuang-hsu to one of her nieces in an effort to maintain her hold on him, she nominally relinquished her control of government and retired to her palace in northwest Peking. Charming, intelligent, persuasive, and authoritative, she continued to manipulate court affairs, while diverting funds destined for the much-needed modernization of the Chinese navy into her own hands.

The shortcomings of the corrupt and **anachronistic** system that Tz'u-hsi had patronized were exposed by the defeat of China by Japan in the 1894–95 war, which came as a devastating shock to a nation that had considered itself the unquestioned regional superpower. In 1898 Kuang-hsu, influenced by a coterie of foreign-educated student radicals led by Chang Chih-tung and K'ang Yu-wei, initiated a number of radical proposals designed to renovate and modernize government and eliminate corruption. During the period subsequently called the one hundred Days of Reforms, he struck hard at the vital interests of civil and military officials by abolishing sinecures and the Green Banner provincial armies and introducing a budget system. The offended interest groups turned to Tz'u-hsi, who used the military to institute a coup, reversed the reforms, imprisoned, executed, or banished the reformers, and had the emperor confined to the palace.

debauched: extremely indulged in sensuality.

anachronistic: being from a former age that is incongruous in the present.

The following year Tz'u-hsi, a fierce traditionalist, lent her support to officials who were encouraging the Boxers (militia forces organized in Shantung and southern Chihli provinces) in their rebellion against foreign intervention in China. These rebellions took the form of persecution of visible representatives of the foreign powers, such as missionaries. Some 100 foreigners were killed during the hostilities, which culminated in 1900 with the murder of the German minister Baron Klemens von Ketteler and the siege of the foreign legations in Peking. The siege was lifted by a coalition of foreign troops who captured the capital and suppressed the uprising. Tz'u-hsi fled and was forced to accept the humiliatingly apologetic Boxer Protocol of 1901 before being allowed to return to Peking. Thereafter she implemented many of the reforms she had previously rejected, but still refused to allow Kuang-hsi to participate in government and, from her deathbed, issued the order that led to his death from poisoning a day before her own decease. ◆

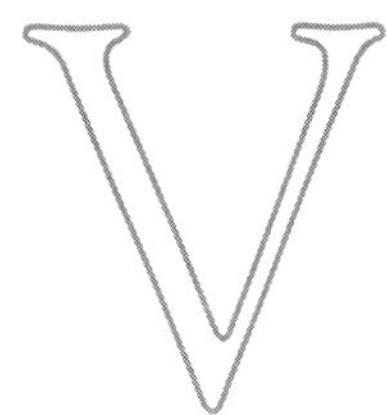

Victor Emmanuel II

1820–1878 ● KING OF ITALY

Victor Emmanuel II was born in Turin to Charles Albert, king of Sardinia, from the Savoy family line, and Maria Teresa of Tuscany. He grew up primarily in Piedmont, where he acquired his love of the countryside and disdain for city life. A rude and boorish man, he was ill at ease with high society.

At the age of twenty-two he married Maria Adelaide, the daughter of Archduke Rainier of Habsburg, and she bore him five children. Despite his marriage, he was a notorious womanizer with many mistresses, including his favorite, Rosina, who bore him three children. A popular waggish saying in Turin claimed that "no sovereign has been more successful in becoming the father of his subjects." When duty forced him to attend state dinners, which he dreaded, he would not eat at all, but would leave as early as possible for dinner with Rosina or another mistress.

A popular waggish saying in Turin claimed that "no sovereign has been more successful in becoming the father of his subjects."

From 1848 to 1849 Victor Emmanuel fought in his father's losing cause against the Austrians and developed a liking for battle. He considered himself a great and courageous warrior, but most others thought him merely a braggart who loved to tell stories of the supposed dangers he had overcome. After the defeat at Novara, his father abdicated and Victor Emmanuel acceded to the throne of Sardinia as one of Europe's highest paid constitutional monarchs. However, his liberal regime brought him great popularity while he personally led the Piedmontese armies in the crucial battles of Magenta and Solferino.

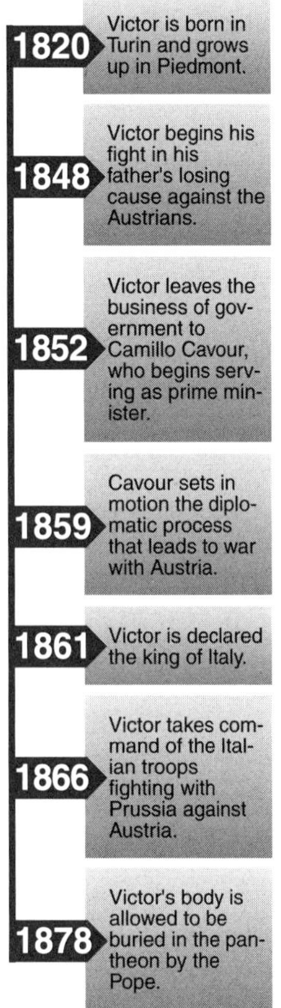

A poorly educated and lazy man, he signed laws without reading them and generally left the business of government to his prime minister, especially Camillo Cavour, who served in that post from 1852 until his death in 1861. Nonetheless, it was the king who was the symbol of the Risorgimento, the movement for Italian unification. Cavour, to the delight of the bloodthirsty Victor Emmanuel, sent troops to fight in the Crimean War with England and France and this set in motion the diplomatic processes which led to the 1859 war against Austria.

With the help of tremendous French forces, Austria was forced to cede the territory of Lombardy to Victor Emmanuel II and Modena, Parma, Romagna, and Tuscany soon followed. Meanwhile, in southern Italy, the great nationalist general, Giuseppe Garibaldi, won stunning victories in Sicily and Naples. Garibaldi turned southern Italy over to Victor Emmanuel, whose reign was confirmed overwhelmingly by plebiscite, and, in 1861, was declared the first king of Italy, ruling the peninsula except for Rome, Venice, Trieste, and Trent.

In 1866 Victor Emmanuel was once again on the battlefield, taking personal command of the Italian troops fighting with Prussia against Austria. Though his campaigns were dismal failures, Prussia was victorious and the province of Venice was given to him as war spoils. When the French withdrew from Rome in 1870 this too was added to the Italian kingdom.

He spent his final years much as he had spent the previous ones, with his mistresses and his hunting. He hunted wild boar in Tuscany, ibex and chamois in the Alps, birds throughout Italy, and bears in the Abruzzi. Often he killed hundreds, even thousands of animals in a day, with hordes of gamekeepers hired to drive the game within his shooting range. One friend estimated that Victor Emmanuel II spent a third of his life hunting.

Despite the Pope's enmity for the captor of Rome, he allowed the body of Victor Emmanuel to be buried in the Pantheon. ◆

Victoria

1819–1901 ● QUEEN OF ENGLAND

Victoria was queen of the United Kingdom of Great Britain and Ireland and its longest-reigning monarch, whose reign became known as the "Victorian Age."

Victoria was the only child of the duke and duchess of Kent and fifth in line to the throne, but deaths and the lack of other legitimate heirs led to her becoming next in line while still a child.

Her father died when she was eight months old and she had a lonely and insecure upbringing under the watchful eye of her mother and the comptroller of her household, the ambitious Sir John Conroy. The duchess was receptive to his scheme to isolate and protect Victoria from the rest of the royal family, whom the duchess strongly disliked, but Victoria resented this policy and the desolate childhood that resulted.

However, there were some happy times, with outings to the theater and opera and rare visits from her German cousins, the only boys with whom she was allowed to fraternize. Her negative childhood experiences embittered Victoria's relations with her mother but also contributed to her strong independent spirit. Nonetheless although she was capable of taking care of herself, the need for the comfort and counsel of men she could trust became a constant theme in her life.

"Great events make me quiet and calm; it is only trifles that irritate my nerves."
Queen Victoria, 1830

Upon the death of her uncle William IV in 1837, Victoria was proclaimed queen. She was just eighteen, of plain appearance and only about 4 feet 10 inches tall. The position she inherited was daunting and it was fortunate she had capable politicians such as William Melbourne and Henry Palmerston to guide her. She became so dependent on Lord Melbourne that she could not bear the thought of his being out of office; her partiality evoked the anger of his Tory rivals.

The happiest years of Victoria's life began with her marriage to her first cousin Prince Albert of Coburg in 1840. This handsome and highly intellectual German prince gave the impression of being cold and austere but to the queen he was her "angel," a devoted husband and idol. At first many resented the alliance; Albert's German attitudes and mannerisms aroused traditional English bigotry. But his competence at palace administration and involvement in public charities and works, not least the fabulous 1851 Great Exhibition, gained him popularity.

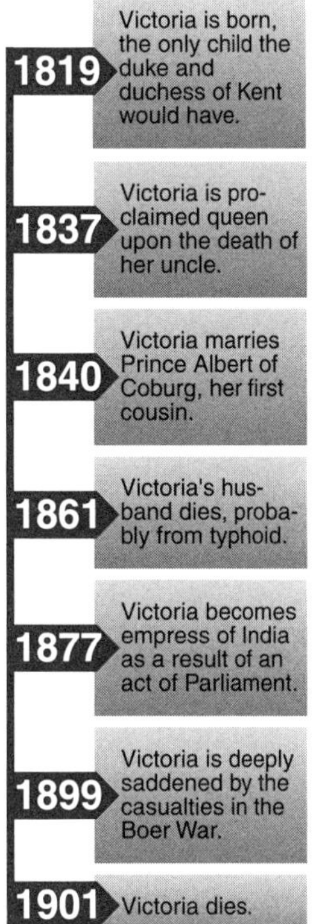

Victoria and Albert had nine children (although she felt that women who were always pregnant were "disgusting—more like a rabbit or a guinea pig than anything else") and made every effort to be devoted parents. Both had been raised in one-parent families, which heightened their desire to provide their own children with a secure and happy childhood. In great measure they succeeded, but at a cost. The queen was determined that her sons would be formed in Albert's image, leading to continual conflict with her fun-loving son Edward, prince of Wales. Edward's sheltered youth made him easy prey for his fellow recruits in army camp in 1861; they smuggled a notorious prostitute into his bed and the resulting scandal contributed, the queen believed, to Albert's death at the age of forty-two in 1861. It is more probable that he died from typhoid transmitted through the primitive plumbing system at Windsor Castle.

Albert's death left Victoria close to a mental breakdown. His room was preserved as he left it, and twice each day his clothes were laid out and soap and towel changed. Victoria dressed mainly in black for the rest of her life and, always shy of public engagements, now had a good excuse to avoid them, much to the frustration of her ministers. She did not attend meetings of the privy council, but sat in the next room with the door open. Her retirement was accepted by the public at first but after several years satirical notices were fixed to Buckingham Palace railings, advertising its sale due to "the late occupants' declining business."

Victoria felt more at ease away from London in the Scottish Highlands; fondly remembered excursions with Albert created nostalgic appeal and she was attracted by the plain-speaking, naturally dignified Highlanders. She developed a strong attachment to her footman John Brown, by royal decree "The Queen's Highland Servant"; over the next eighteen years Brown became friend and comforter as much as footman. But his outspoken manner made enemies at court, contributing further to Victoria's unpopularity with the public at large.

During the 1870s the queen emerged from self-imposed isolation, with the prime minister, Benjamin Disraeli, whom she called "Dizzy," playing a crucial role. He knew the right mixture of sympathy and flattery to win her heart, unlike his rival, the Liberal party leader, William Gladstone, who spoke to her, she said, as if he were addressing a public meeting. Disraeli guessed Victoria's ambition to be an empress and in 1877 shepherded through Parliament the act making her empress of India. In turn, she supported Disraeli's policies. In 1878, when he favored moves to stop Russian expansionism, Victoria remarked to her daughter, "Oh if only the Queen were a man, she would like to go and give those Russians such a beating." When Disraeli lay dying in 1881 the queen continually telegraphed for news.

Victoria displayed amazing stamina until her last year, although by this time she had to be wheeled around in a chair and her eyesight was poor. She continued to stay up late working on government papers, took a keen interest in British and international politics, and was deeply saddened by casualties in the Boer War (1899–1902). She knitted scarves for her soldiers and had one hundred thousand tins of chocolate sent out to them. She was also kept busy by her constantly growing family. Her children and grandchildren linked her by marriage with most of the ruling dynasties of Europe. The Golden (1887) and Diamond (1897) Jubilees bore witness to the might of her empire and the affection of her subjects. When she died there was a feeling of national loss, as much for the passing of an era as for the loss of a formidable old lady. ◆

"I am every day more convinced that we women, if we are to be good women, feminine and amiable and domestic, are not fitted to reign; at least it is **contre gré** ***that they drive themselves to the work which it entails."***

Victoria, letter to Leopold I of Belgium, 1852

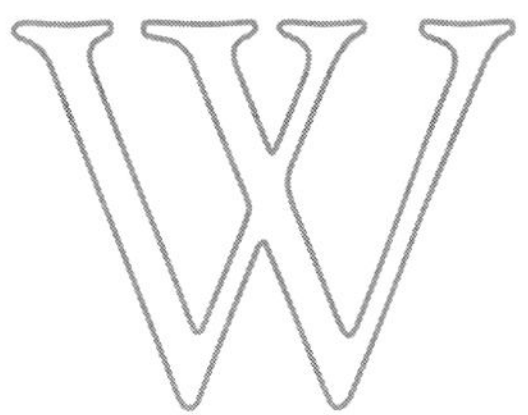

Jigme Singye Wangchuck

1955– ● SULTAN OF BHUTAN

King Jigme Singye Wangchuck rules the small Kingdom of Bhutan, called Druk-yal, Land of the Thunder Dragon, by its people. The king is known as the Druk Gyalpo, Precious Ruler of the Dragon People. Bhutan is often called the Hidden Holy Land, as it was ruled for centuries by Buddhist clergy and isolated by its rugged terrain. Bhutan lies in southern central Asia, in the eastern Himalaya Mountains. It is bordered on the north and northwest by Tibet and on the east, south, and southwest by India.

King Wangchuck felt the pressure of leading the Himalayas' last Buddhist monarchy and one of the two remaining absolute monarchies in Asia.

Fires and an earthquake in the 1800s destroyed many documents of Bhutan's history, so scholars must reconstruct information from various sources. It is believed that princes from India ruled Bhutan until the 800s, when they were replaced by local kings, ancestors of Bhutan's dominant ethnic group, the Bhotia. During the 1600s, a ruler who combined both spiritual and religious leadership established a central authority in Bhutan. Followers of Buddhism brought their religion into Bhutan and by the 1700s had built many *dzongs*, fortified monasteries that served as temples and seats of government.

Beginning in the late 1770s, Bhutan was in conflict with the British East India Company, which was expanding from India. A 1910 treaty agreed that the British would not interfere in Bhutan's internal affairs if the British were allowed to direct Bhutan's foreign relations. For this, Bhutan received an annual

King Jigme Singye Wangchuck of Bhutan (center, standing) with elected officials in 1991.

subsidy. After India gained independence from Britain, India maintained that bargain through a 1949 treaty. This treaty continues to help both India and Bhutan maintain a united front against the Chinese border.

In 1907 Ugyen Wangchuck, a regional governor, gained national power and became Bhutan's first hereditary monarch. His successors were Jigme Wangchuck (crowned 1926), Jigme Dorji Wangchuck (1952), and Jigme Singye Wangchuck, king since July 1972.

When King Jigme Singye Wangchuck ascended to the throne at age sixteen, after his father's death from a heart attack, he inherited a leadership plagued with conflicts that had been exacerbated by the involvement of his father's mistress. However, his reign as both chief of state and head of government was relatively stable. As king, he appoints a council of ministers to assist him. Bhutan also has a national assembly called the Tsongdu. Of the nearly 150 members of the Tsongdu, 70 percent are elected from villages, about 25 percent are selected by the king, and the remainder represent influential Buddhist monasteries.

By 1990 King Jigme Singye Wangchuck had developed a unique style of governing. Having studied in England, he was aware of worldwide issues. He felt the pressures of leading the Himalayas' last Buddhist monarchy and one of two remaining absolute monarchies in Asia. He sought to bring his isolated kingdom into the modern world while preserving its environment and culture.

In the late 1990s Jigme Singye Wangchuck announced his intentions to give the Bhutanese people greater participation in government. He surprised many by dismissing his ministerial appointees in 1998 and giving the Tsongdu the right to elect those council members. He also gave the Tsongdu the right to dismiss the king through a two-thirds vote. Wangchuck faced little risk of losing his throne, though, as the Tsongdu traditionally obeyed him on everything. Opponents of the king argued that the reforms did not grant Bhutanese a real role in governing themselves. Bhutan still had no political parties or constitution, and many protestors were in prison.

The king limited tourists to those who could afford to pay a $200 daily fee.

King Wangchuck worked to unify Bhutanese culture. He imposed a national language—Dzongkha—and forbade the teaching of minority languages in school. He also ordered all people to wear traditional Bhutanese clothes—the *gho* for men and the *kira* for women—or they must pay a fine. The king limited tourists to those who could afford to pay a $200 daily fee.

Jigme Singye Wangchuck married four sisters, a common practice in Bhutan, where property is inherited through daughters and families try to avoid splitting the inheritance. The king moved from the family palace, where his mother lives, to a two-room log cabin on a hillside overlooking Thimphu. His four queens live in a nearby compound with their ten children. Crown Prince Jigme Khesar Namgyal Wangchuck was sent to a preparatory school in the United States. The king entertains foreign guests at his mother's palace. Wangchuck played basketball in his youth and is a fan of American teams. He plays tennis and golf and drives Bhutan's mountain roads in a four-wheel-drive Toyota Land Cruiser.

Bhutan had about two million people at the end of the twentieth century, with only 30,000 in its capital city, Thimphu. Bhutan has no major highways, few phone lines, and villages that are isolated from each other. The Himalayan valleys still feature impressive dzongs, where red-robed monks study ancient texts. Nomads who wander the Himalayan plateaus come into the valleys to barter yak meat for grain. Most Bhutanese people farm or raise livestock. The king maintains the loyalty of most of his people, who display his portrait in homes and shops across the country. To some, he is a god. ◆

Wilhelm I

1797–1888 ● KAISER OF GERMANY

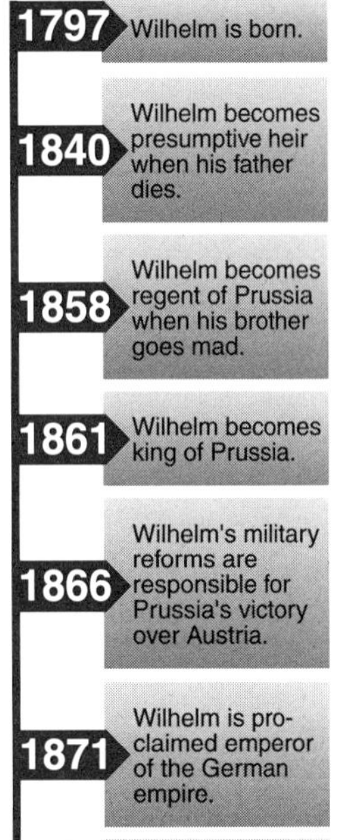

Wilhelm I was the first modern German emperor. Wilhelm, who united Germany and made it into the strongest European state of his time, was the second son of the Prussian king, Frederick William III. Wilhelm's passionate lifelong interest in military matters began early: he became an officer at ten, fought against France in the Napoleonic Wars at seventeen, and received the Iron Cross for personal bravery at eighteen. After the war his military rank and responsibilities steadily increased as an enlarged Prussia became part of the new confederation of German states.

When Wilhelm's father died in 1840, his childless older brother acceded to the throne and Wilhelm became heir presumptive. Prussia was not spared the 1848 rebellions that swept Europe with demands for liberalized government, with violent street mobs calling for revolution. Wilhelm was politically conservative but his wife, Augusta, was not, and Wilhelm agreed that adopting a constitution seemed wise. However, he loved order, and wanted it restored before making political reforms. When government troops fired into a mob of Berlin demonstrators he became the most hated man in Germany. A short vacation abroad seemed advisable and he took his family to England.

Britain's foreign policy focused on the adoption of British-type parliamentary governments by other countries, and Queen Victoria and the prince consort, Albert, approved of such liberal sentiments as Wilhelm expressed. They betrothed their daughter to Wilhelm's son (the future Frederick III) to help ensure that Prussia became a progressive ally for England. Upon Wilhelm's return to Berlin he gave a speech in the national assembly in favor of adopting a constitution—and used force to swiftly crush a rebellion.

In 1858 Wilhelm became regent of Prussia when his brother went mad, and was king from 1861. The opposition of Prussia's liberal parliament to his plan for reorganizing the army made Wilhelm feel that he had to choose between abdication and bringing in someone strong enough to crush the liberals. He chose to make Otto von Bismarck prime minister.

Wilhelm's great ambition was to unite Germany under Prussian rule. His military reforms were responsible for Prussia's

Neuschwanstein Castle

Neuschwanstein Castle, towering on a rock ledge in the Bavarian Alps of Germany, is one of three castles built by King Ludwig II of Bavaria. Ludwig (often referred to as "The Swan King" or "Mad Ludwig") modeled it after a medieval castle. Construction began in 1869, and it was still unfinished when Ludwig died mysteriously in 1886. He had been declared insane and was found drowned only a few days later. Ludwig intended the castle as a tribute to his favorite composer, Richard Wagner. One of the chief architects, Christian Jank, was actually a stage designer. Along with such "traditional" features as a walled courtyard and numerous towers, Ludwig also included the most up-to-date technology, such as central heating. The castle came to be called "Neuschwanstein" (new swan stone) shortly after Ludwig's death in honor of his favorite part of the castle, the swan grotto. Neuschwanstein Castle is now a major tourist attraction, owned by the German state of Bavaria. It reportedly served as the model for the castle in Fantasy World at Disney Land.

victory over Austria in 1866, which made Prussia the dominant German state, and over France in 1871, which made Germany the strongest country in Europe. He personally led Germany's army in several battles against France and was proclaimed emperor of the newly created, Prussian-controlled, German empire in 1871.

As king, Wilhelm had often disagreed with Bismarck although he usually ended up pursuing the latter's policies, either because he had come to agree with him or because Bismarck manipulated situations until Wilhelm had no choice. As emperor, Wilhelm was content to leave the running of the empire in Bismarck's hands, and for the rest of his life he was a figurehead whose upright and simple life made him respected and loved throughout Germany. Two socialist assassination attempts against him in 1878 were used by Bismarck as excuses to pass severe antisocialist laws. ◆

Wilhelm II

1859–1941 ● KAISER OF GERMANY

> *"For when the German has once learned to direct his glance upon what is distant and great, the pettiness which surrounds him in daily life on all sides will disappear."*
> Kaiser Wilhelm II, 1901

The grandson of Wilhelm I of Prussia and Prince Albert and Queen Victoria of England, Wilhelm was the product of a marriage arranged to promote Anglo-Prussian friendship. Albert hoped that the marriage of his eldest daughter Victoria with Crown Prince Frederick of Prussia would help Prussia. Prussia had adopted a democratic constitution in 1850 and was on the road to industrial efficiency and commercial liberalism; Albert hoped to unite the German kingdoms and create a modern, liberal ally for England in the heart of Europe. Wilhelm I favored the match because the connection with England greatly increased Prussia's prestige.

Wilhelm II's birth was difficult and it crippled him. His emotionally high-strung and domineering mother hated him for being deformed, called him "cripple" even in public, and tried to cure him with painful and unsuccessful treatments:

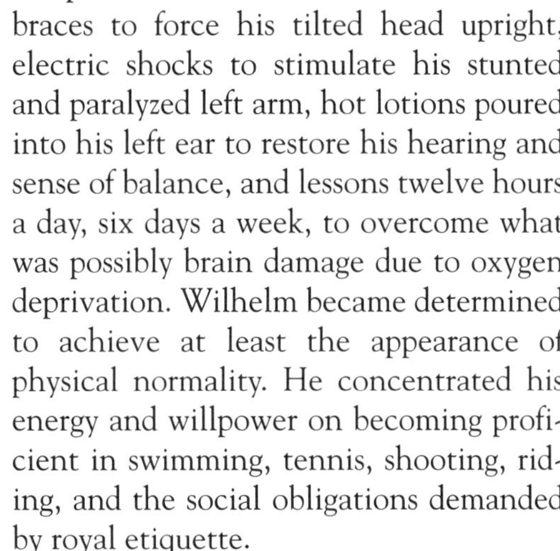

braces to force his tilted head upright, electric shocks to stimulate his stunted and paralyzed left arm, hot lotions poured into his left ear to restore his hearing and sense of balance, and lessons twelve hours a day, six days a week, to overcome what was possibly brain damage due to oxygen deprivation. Wilhelm became determined to achieve at least the appearance of physical normality. He concentrated his energy and willpower on becoming proficient in swimming, tennis, shooting, riding, and the social obligations demanded by royal etiquette.

When Otto von Bismarck reduced Wilhelm's father, who disliked his son, to a political cipher, Wilhelm responded by becoming closer to his adored grandfather, who groomed him, with Bismarck's help, to become king.

There were other influences on the future kaiser. His self-importance was inflated with ideas of personal rule and of a strong king leading Germany toward its destiny. As a lieutenant in the First Regiment of the Guards, he became fascinated with the trappings of military life, acquired a military bearing and bark, but was never exposed to military realities. His many intellectual interests did not include the art and literature his mother favored and his politics were conservative: he was almost hysterically opposed to any suggestion of English interference in German affairs and he was extremely suspicious of his uncle, Edward VII of England.

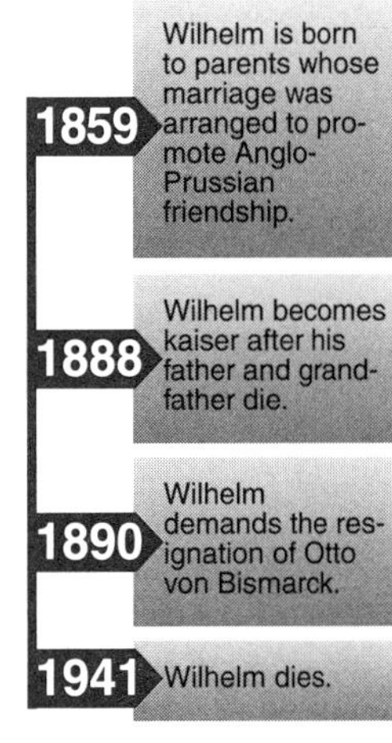

Wilhelm I and Frederick died in 1888, and Wilhelm II became kaiser. Bismarck had been the real ruler of Germany and this might have continued under the new monarch had Bismarck not openly challenged him by defeating the political parties backed by Wilhelm. The kaiser could not tolerate losing the appearance of power and authority and demanded Bismarck's resignation in 1890. Wilhelm was both an absolute and constitutional monarch; he never exceeded his constitutional authority but opposition to his policies resulted in exclusion from the court and all chances of social or career advancement.

The conservative Prussian aristocracy exercised an inordinate influence over Wilhelm. Three years of military service for all Germans became obligatory, spreading Prussian values of obedience to authority throughout Germany. A near-military discipline was extended to state schools, and the official state sponsored German culture was both patriotic and imperialistic. Wilhelm stated that "art which transgresses the laws and limits laid down by me can no longer be called art" and called any type of innovative artistic expression "gutter art."

"As head of the Empire I therefore rejoice over every citizen, whether from Hamburg, Bremen, or Lübeck, who goes forth with this large outlook and seeks new points where we can drive in the nail on which to hang our armor."
Kaiser Wilhelm II, 1901

Wilhelm's conduct of Germany's foreign policy was also erratic. He tended to babble unwisely and his self-important and condescending attitude alienated many; he abandoned old alliances and impetuously entered into new ones. Many of his actions were actually conducive to peace, but his belligerent posturings and speeches demanding Germany's "place in the sun" were not. Fear of German aggression caused England, France, and Russia to band together in a defensive alliance.

With the outbreak of World War I—which Wilhelm thought he could prevent with a word to his relatives, the other rulers of Europe—military rule was declared in Germany. The kaiser, discovering that he detested war, withdrew to his country estates and began suffering from psychosomatic illnesses. This did not stop anti-German propaganda from focusing on him—as Germany's Supreme War Lord—and caricaturing him in both picture and verse. "Little Willie," as he was called in England, played only a small, and typically inconsistent, role in the conduct of the war, first condemning, then condoning, unrestricted submarine warfare.

Wilhelm abdicated the day before the Armistice was declared and spent the rest of his life living quietly in the Netherlands, passing his time chopping wood on a country estate at Drom. He responded to the Nazis by behaving well to some of their victims, giving an archeology lecture in which he described the Nazi swastika as an ancient symbol of "night, misfortune, and death," and sending Hitler a congratulatory telegram when German armies entered Paris. ◆

William I, the Conqueror

C.1027–1087 ● KING OF NORMANDY AND ENGLAND

William was born in Falaise, Lower Normandy, the illegitimate son of Robert, duke of Normandy. With the death of his father in 1035 on a pilgrimage to Jerusalem, he succeeded to his father's title. Still a child, he was unable to exercise power and the country fell into a state of chaos and civil war. William was under the protection of guardians nominated from among his relatives, his life was thought to be in danger, and he often changed his residence.

> ***"Firstly that, above all things, he wishes one God to lie venerated throughout his whole kingdom, one faith of Christ always to be kept inviolate, peace and security to be observed between the English and the Normans."***
>
> Statutes of William the Conqueror

In 1047 he defeated in battle his cousin Count Guy, a rival claimant for the dukedom. The odds were against William in this contest and he was rescued by the intervention of King Henry I of France. Later this same monarch feared Normandy becoming too powerful and, allied with William's enemies, attempted to invade the dukedom but was rebuffed.

As William entered early manhood, his skills as a warrior and the sheer strength of his will and personality became apparent. Stronger than many other soldiers, even on horseback he could draw a bow weaker men could not use and, being 5 feet 10 inches in height, was tall for the times. He defeated challenges to his authority from both neighboring magnates and his own family. By 1049 his reputation was such that the count of Flanders agreed to allow him to marry his daughter, Mathilda. This was more than a strategic alliance; there was genuine attraction involved—at least on William's part. He pursued Mathilda for

Windsor Castle

A residence of Britain's monarchs, Windsor Castle is located on a thirteen-acre site along a ridge on the north bank of the Thames River, some 21 miles west of London, in the county of Berkshire in England. William the Conqueror began building a fortress and residence on the site about 1070, soon after his invasion of England and conquest of its Saxon inhabitants. The castle was expanded and fundamentally altered by later kings and queens to suit their needs and tastes.

At the end of the twentieth century, Windsor Castle is the largest castle in England and the royal family's most important residence outside London. The castle's most prominent feature is a 100-foot tower called the Round Tower, begun by Henry II and completed in 1528. The Round Tower stands between two collections of buildings: the lower ward to the west and the upper ward to the east. In the lower ward is the St. George's Chapel, built from 1473 to 1516 and renowned for its perpendicular architecture. Henry VIII (r. 1509–47), Charles I (r. 1625–49), and eight other British monarchs are buried there. Also in the lower ward is the Albert Memorial Chapel. Begun by Henry III in the thirteenth century, it was completed in its present form by Queen Victoria (r. 1837–1901). The upper ward includes the State Apartments; built in the early nineteenth century they serve as the monarch's residence. On November 20, 1992, a fire damaged much of the upper ward. Restoration was completed in November 1997.

seven years and eventually resorted to physical violence to get her to marry him. He was unusual among rulers of his time for remaining faithful to his wife. There is evidence she was just 4 feet 2 inches tall but still managed to bear twelve children.

William's firm rule in Normandy created stable conditions in which the economy flourished. He also brought surrounding territories into a Norman sphere of influence through skillful use of force of arms. He was a ruthless enemy, not hesitating to put to the torch the homes of those who stood in his way or mutilate those unlucky enough to fall into his hands. When he seized the neighboring territory of Maine, it is alleged that he had its ruler, Count Walter, and his wife murdered while they were his guests in Falaise.

However, he was careful to reward the nobles who supported him and he also cultivated good relations with the church. The building of abbeys and castles served as symbols of his power. By 1066 William was sufficiently secure to launch his most ambitious venture: the invasion of England.

The English ruler, Edward the Confessor, had promised the crown to William in 1051 but this prospect was not welcomed in England. When Harold succeeded Edward to the throne in 1066, William was doubly aggrieved: Edward's promise was violated and Harold had also behaved falsely, since a few years earlier, when shipwrecked on the Normandy coast, he became a guest at William's court and joined him in a campaign in Brittany, after which he swore an oath of allegiance to William.

William invaded England with a force of some seven thousand men, landing in Pevensey on the south coast. Harold's army, after defeating an invading Norwegian army in Yorkshire, was forced to march rapidly south to confront William, hoping to catch the Normans by surprise with the speed of their advance; however, the Normans were forewarned. The English forces put up a brave struggle, driving back Norman cavalry and infantry charges, and it seemed that they might win the day, but William rallied his troops. A hail of arrows rained down on Harold and his men as the Norman knights charged once more, King Harold was fatally injured (according to tradition, with an arrow in his eye), the English ranks broke and William had won a kingdom.

After suppressing the last elements of serious resistance he returned to France with a rich harvest of plunder. For the rest of his life Normandy remained William's chief residence. He would visit England in order to put down rebellious outbreaks, such as the uprising in the north in 1069, which he quashed with customary ruthlessness, sacking the city of York. When Danish invaders linked up with English rebels, William again marched north. He trapped the Danes on the banks of the River Humber, enforced his peace terms on them, and destroyed the country between York and Durham so that it was left unplowed for nine years.

Although unabashed at resorting to force, William was keen to show that his rule over England was a legitimate continuation from the reign of Edward the Confessor. He held his coronation in Westminster Abbey in December 1066 and two years later had Mathilda crowned queen. In 1070 there was a further coronation by papal legates. He soon replaced the existing aristocracy and clergy with those of his own choosing. William's Norman supporters were rewarded with impressive estates. His half brother Odo, already bishop of Bayeux, was made earl of Kent. Castles were built in strategic places to ensure the subjugation of hostile natives and the country was systematically exploited. Extensive areas were placed under draconian forest laws to preserve the game William loved to hunt. The Domesday survey of 1086 provided him with vital information for new tax assessments.

William I's last decade was troubled. The security of his dominions was undermined by family conflict. He had Bishop Odo arrested when his ambitions with regard to the papacy went a step too far. Then, his son Robert rebelled and joined his father's enemies bordering Normandy. He led raids across the frontier and in 1079 met William's forces in a battle in which Robert wounded his father in the hand. In 1080 a peace was concluded between them but this was not the end of William's problems. In reaction to raids from King Philip of France's territory, William led a punitive expedition across the border in 1087. While leading the sack of the town of Mantes, he was thrown from his horse and died of internal injuries. ◆

"We decree also that every free man shall affirm by compact and an oath that, within and without England, he desires to be faithful to king William, to preserve with him his lands and his honour with all fidelity, and first to defend him against his enemies."

Statutes of William the Conqueror

William I, the Silent

1533–1584 ● KING OF THE NETHERLANDS

William I, the Silent, was the leader of the Dutch rebellion against Spanish rule. He was the eldest son of William, count of Nassau-Dillenberg, whose religious tolerance enabled him to rule his domains throughout the religious wars of Emperor Charles V and remain on good terms with both Catholic and Protestant neighbors. He adopted Lutheranism without becoming intolerant of Catholicism and accepted Charles's condition that William, his eleven-year-old son, had to convert to Catholicism before inheriting his cousin

René of Orange's titles and lands, including the title of prince of the principality of Orange, in Provence, which included estates in the Low Countries.

Charles raised William as a Catholic prince, first making him his page, then a gentleman of his court. An astute statesman, Charles insisted that his favorite, William, be present at councils of state. William became a competent soldier and a superb statesman and when he was eighteen, Charles arranged his marriage with the wealthy heiress, Anne of Egmont. The couple had two children and the match was a happy one, even though William's duties left them little time together.

Charles's son, Philip II, became emperor and at first favored William with honors and position. This changed after the latter, now aged twenty-six, stayed with the king of France to ensure that France kept its peace treaty with Spain. The king, assuming that William knew about his secret agreement with Philip to use the Inquisition and the Spanish army to root out Protestantism in the Netherlands, began to talk about it. William did not reveal to the king his **aversion** to the plot but quickly organized the nobles of the Netherlands in opposition. His reticence on this occasion led to William—the most eloquent man of his day—being given the enduring nickname of "William the Silent."

Upon Anne's death, William insisted on marrying the Protestant heiress Anna of Saxony against both Catholic and Protestant opposition. He hoped to gain the powerful Lutheran nobles of central Germany as allies but they were not interested in helping the Dutch Calvinists. As a result, all William had to show for his ten years of marriage to an increasingly violent and abusive virago was two children; he eventually divorced Anna for adultery.

aversion: a feeling of repugnance toward something.

punitive: inflicting or involving punishment.

William wanted only to modify, not overthrow, Spanish rule of the Netherlands. He tried to accomplish this by urging the refusal of Philip's constant requests for funds unless Spanish troops were withdrawn. Philip, reluctant to drive his powerful nobles into armed rebellion, withdrew his army and appointed his half sister, Margaret of Parma, as regent of the Netherlands. Philip and William then entered into prolonged negotiations to gain time: Philip to prepare a **punitive** army, William to prevent armed intervention by moderating violent opposition. Calvinist extremists went on a church-sacking rampage in 1566, Margaret suspended the Inquisition and granted freedom of worship, William restored order, and an enraged Philip appointed the duke of Alba head of his army.

Realizing that the Netherlands could not win against Spain on its own, William unsuccessfully sought support from abroad. He also tried to maintain order but revolts broke out and the other nobles, refusing to bear arms against Philip, suppressed the outbreaks violently. William resigned his offices, withdrew his daughter from Margaret's court, and left for Germany.

William did not reveal to the king of France his aversion to the king's plot to use the Inquisition and Spanish army to root out Protestantism in the Netherlands.

Alba entered the Netherlands with his highly trained army and instituted a reign of terror. He outlawed William, seized William's eldest son, massacred thousands, executed those loyal to William, and easily defeated the armies of mercenaries and untrained rabble sent against him. Deprived of his estates and home, denounced as a rebel by Lutherans and Catholics alike, William was totally ruined and the rumor spread that he was dead.

In fact, he was working constantly to raise funds and organize resistance to Alba. However it was the privateer Sea Beggars' (Orangist exiles who had taken to the sea to combat the king of Spain from foreign bases) successful harassment of the Spanish that turned the tide. Popular risings were triggered throughout Holland and Zeeland when Sea Beggars captured the port of Briel and declared for William in 1572. When the land attacks led by him and his brothers Louis and Henry failed, William committed himself completely to Holland and Zeeland, returning there personally to lead the resistance against Spain and becoming a Calvinist, despite his aversion to Calvinistic Puritanism and intolerance.

The desperate and tenacious resistance he met as he massacred his way through the Netherlands drained Alba. Between 1573 and 1578 William achieved the upper hand and conducted extensive negotiations with Spain; these proved fruitless as neither side was willing to compromise on the three issues William had considered essential from the beginning: freedom of religion, withdrawal of Spanish soldiers, and restoration of the Netherlands' ancient rights. William also made many attempts to unite the Netherlands' seventeen provinces, which failed because of **irreconcilable** differences of race, religion, and interests.

irreconcilable: impossible to restore harmony.

In 1575 William married Charlotte of Bourbon-Montpensier, a relative of the king of France and a former abbess, who became a Protestant. His insistence on marrying her over the objections of friends and relatives gained him a happy marriage, a good mother for his children, a peaceful family life even when surrounded by defeat and war, and six daughters. Charlotte died in 1582, when the shock of an assassination attempt that left William severely wounded was too much for her in her weakened, postnatal condition.

In 1578 Alexander of Parma arrived with a Spanish army that swept through the Netherlands, leaving death and defeat in its wake. William spent the rest of his life hopelessly trying to keep the provinces united and get the foreign support he saw as essential, while successfully countering rivals brought in by different factions striving for ascendancy (each of whom William courteously welcomed, foiled, used, and politely persuaded to leave). Meanwhile the Netherlands formally abjured Philip as their king in 1581, declared their independence, and made William count (Stadholder) of Holland soon afterward.

William had been the target of assassination attempts for years, thanks to the rewards offered by Philip for his death. In 1583 William married Louise de Cologny, who gave birth to a son before the final assassination attempt was successful. William's sons continued to lead the rebellion against Spain for sixty-four more years before Spain recognized the Netherlands' independence with the Peace of Westphalia. His descendants rule the country to this day. ◆

William III

1650–1702 ● Dutch King of England

William was born in The Hague, Netherlands, to Princess Mary, widow of Prince William II of Orange and daughter of Charles I of England; his father died shortly before his birth.

"I have shewn, and will always shew, how desirous I am to be the common father of all my people."
William III, 1701

When France threatened to invade the Netherlands in 1672, William took command of Dutch forces. He was a fearless commander; under his direction Dutch forces were regrouped and succeeded in repelling the French and taking the war into Germany. War continued for most of that decade and William found fulfillment in leading his troops that made the routine of civil government pale in comparison.

In 1677 he married Mary, the fifteen-year-old daughter of James, duke of York, his uncle and future king of England. It was not a love match, but their relationship blossomed. Won over by his military reputation and the genuine regard in which his men held him, Mary became a doting wife. William was a far from ideal husband, preferring the company of his mistress, Elizabeth Villiers, but Mary's devotion remained steadfast.

William might have remained a relatively minor figure in European history but for the course of events in England. His uncle, Mary's father, came to the throne in 1685, becoming James II, and his favorable disposition toward Roman Catholicism alienated influential sections of his predominantly Protestant people. As Mary was next in line to the throne, it was felt that the future of Protestant England was secure in the long run, but in 1687 a son was born to James. Disaffected noblemen called on William to overthrow his uncle's regime and place Mary on the English throne. It was a priceless opportunity to free the Netherlands from the French threat by uniting the Dutch and English kingdoms.

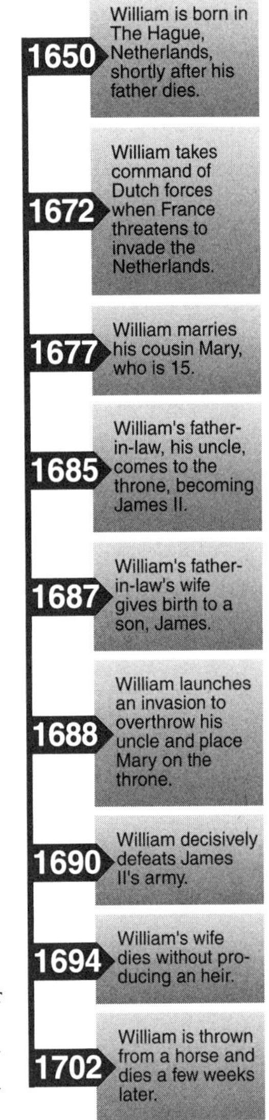

William launched his invasion in November 1688. His Dutch force was joined by English supporters and proceeded slowly toward London, uncertain of the reception awaiting them. James had no stomach for a fight and his supporters were not enthusiastic enough to put their lives at stake for his cause; and he was swept away in the "bloodless" or "glorious" revolution. William chose to enter London in a closed carriage via a route that would not attract public attention. He jealously guarded his privacy and had little interest in the pomp and ceremony of royalty. Mary, however, was drawn to pageantry, and arrived in her new capital by colorful procession along the river Thames.

Mary was the real heir to the kingdom and could have ruled alone with William as consort, but he held such a lofty place in her estimation that she insisted on a joint monarchy. William threatened to return to Holland if he were not granted equal status to the queen. Although he was regarded as the savior of Protestant England, his cold and secretive manner did not gain him the same popularity as his beautiful, extroverted wife. In the words of a contemporary, "He spoke little . . . he hated business of all sorts. Yet he hated talking, and all house games, more." His preference for all things Dutch and his awarding English earldoms to Dutch friends also had a negative effect on public sympathies.

For much of their five-year joint monarchy, William was out of the country with his armies. On July 12, 1690, he decisively defeated James II's Catholic army at the Battle of the Boyne in Ireland, an event that has become a legend. Irish Protestants

> ***"I should think it as great a blessing as could befall England, if I could observe you as much inclined to lay aside those unhappy fatal animosities, which divide and weaken you, as I am disposed to make all my subjects safe and easy as to any, even the highest offences, committed against me."***
>
> William III, address to Parliament, 1701

still celebrate the anniversary, with great enthusiasm for the memory of "King Billy." Having secured his British kingdom, William was able to turn his attention once more to fighting the French on the Continent.

Mary died in 1694 without having produced an heir and William was devastated by her death. He commanded a lavish funeral for her in recognition of the affection her subjects had for her. He then ruled alone for another eight years; his restraint in the exercise of royal power helped lay the foundation for the constitutional monarchy in Great Britain.

One of William's major ambitions had been the completion by Sir Christopher Wren of one of the country's finest palaces, Henry VIII's Hampton Court. The rebuilding was a triumph but the grounds were a setting for tragedy. In February 1702 his horse stumbled over a molehill and William was thrown, breaking his collarbone. The fracture did not heal and he died a few weeks later, little mourned by a people from whom he was distanced by character and nationality. Supporters of the house of James II, the Jacobites, drank toasts to "the little gentleman in black velvet"—the mole whose hill had caused the king's fatal fall. ◆

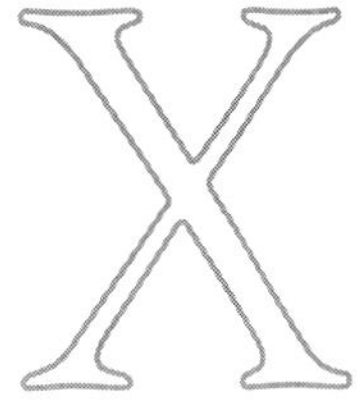

Xerxes I

C.519–465 B.C.E. ● KING OF PERSIA

Xerxes I was the son of Darius I, who had risen to power from the rank of spearbearer to Cambyses II, and Attosa, the daughter of Cyrus II (the Great). Xerxes was designated heir apparent in preference to his brother, Artabazanes, and had already been governor of Babylonia for over a decade by the time he acceded to the throne on his father's death in 486 B.C.E. He inherited from Darius an efficient system for the exploitation of the resources of his empire, which was organized into satrapies (provinces), each with its own governor and responsible for providing a certain levy of taxes, produce, ships, horses, and soldiers to the emperor.

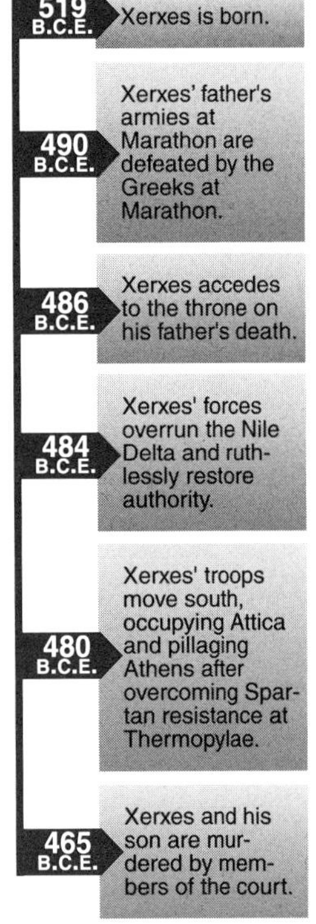

Soon after his accession Xerxes moved to pacify Egypt, where a usurper had been governing for two years: in 484 B.C.E. his forces overran the Nile Delta and ruthlessly restored imperial authority. He also violently suppressed a revolt in Babylonia: the rebels were tortured and slain; Babylon's city walls were destroyed; and the temple of Marduk, the largest and most prestigious in the oriental world, was razed to the ground.

Less tolerant of expressions of regional autonomy than his father, Xerxes was not prepared to brook any opposition to his status as absolute ruler. Zoroastrianism was the state religion and he regarded himself as the vice regent of its great god, Ahura Mazda. He was therefore keen to punish the Greek city-states for their participation in the Ionian revolt and the defeat of his father's armies at Marathon in 490 B.C.E. To this end, he

After the failure of his campaign to subdue the Greek states, Xerxes became more preoccupied with pomp rather than conquest and transformed Persopolis into one of the most monumentally grand cities of the known world.

embarked upon a diplomatic initiative that won him assurances of support from Carthage, Thessaly, Central Greece, Argos, and the Delphic Oracle. He then proceeded to muster a huge army; Herodotus claimed that it numbered five million men, although a more likely figure is three hundred and sixty thousand soldiers and some eight hundred ships. Xerxes' engineers oversaw massive engineering works to support its passage, bridging the Hellespont and digging a canal through the Athos peninsula.

After overcoming heroic Spartan resistance at the pass of Thermopylae in 480 B.C.E., Xerxes' troops moved southward, occupying Attica and pillaging Athens. Their Greek opponents were forced to retreat to their last line of defense, the Isthmus of Corinth. The wily Athenian leader, Themistocles, overcoming the disunity among his allies who feared for the safety of their own cities and homes, then lured the Persian navy into combat off the island of Salamis. There, despite their superior numbers, the Persians were defeated, losing some two hundred ships to ferocious ramming attacks from the Greek triremes (galleys). Xerxes was therefore forced to retreat for lack of a fleet large enough to supply his army. He left behind an occupying force in Thessaly under his brother-in-law Mardonius, but this too withdrew when the latter was killed.

The repulsion of Xerxes' attempt to subdue the rebel Greek states led to the defection of the Greeks of Asia Minor and signaled the onset of the decline of the Persian Empire. After the failure of this campaign, Xerxes became increasingly preoccupied with pomp rather than conquest, presiding over a vast and expensive construction program that developed his father's plans and transformed Persopolis into one of the most monumentally grand cities of the known world, although Susa remained the Persian Empire's administrative capital.

Xerxes distanced himself increasingly from affairs of state, becoming drawn into petty harem intrigues and leaving the administration of his realms to others, and information about his activities in the latter period of his reign is sparse. In the same year that the reconstruction of Persopolis was declared complete (an occasion marked by festivities, ceremonies, and the presence of tribute-bearing delegates from all parts of the empire, which stretched from the Caspian Sea to the Nile and from India to the Aegean), he and his eldest son were murdered by members of his court, among them his personal chief minister, Artabanus. ◆

Z

Mohammad Zahir

1914– ● King of Afghanistan

Born in Kabul, the capital of Afghanistan, Zahir attended Habibia and Istiqlal schools (1920–24), then accompanied his father, Mohammad Nadir Khan, to France where he continued his studies. Zahir's father was the second eldest and most influential of five Musahiban brothers, members of the Muhammadzai royal clan of the Barakzai Pakhtun (or Pashtun) tribe, who enjoyed considerable power in court during the 1910s and 1920s. During the turbulent rule of the modernizing King Amanullah Barakzai (1919–29), the Musahiban brothers fell into disfavor. In 1929, when popular rebellions forced Amanullah's abdication, followed by a nine-month interregnum of a non-Pakhtun ruler, Emir Habibullah II, Zahir's father returned to eastern Afghanistan from France. With assistance from the British in India, Pakhtun tribesmen, and religious leaders, Nadir Khan claimed the Afghan throne, declaring himself Muhammad Nadir Shah on October 15, 1929—thereby establishing the Musahiban dynasty.

Zahir Shah abdicated his throne without a fight and passively watched the suffering of his nation under Soviet occupation, communist rule, and civil war.

Zahir returned to Kabul in October 1930 and attended the Infantry Officers School for one year. In 1931, he married the daughter of Ahmad Shah, a court minister. The only surviving son of Nadir Shah, Crown Prince Zahir, at age seventeen was appointed assistant war minister (1932), then minister of education (1933). On November 8, 1933, following the assassination of his father, he was proclaimed King Mohammad Zahir Shah, with the religious title al-Mutawakkil ala Allah (he who puts his

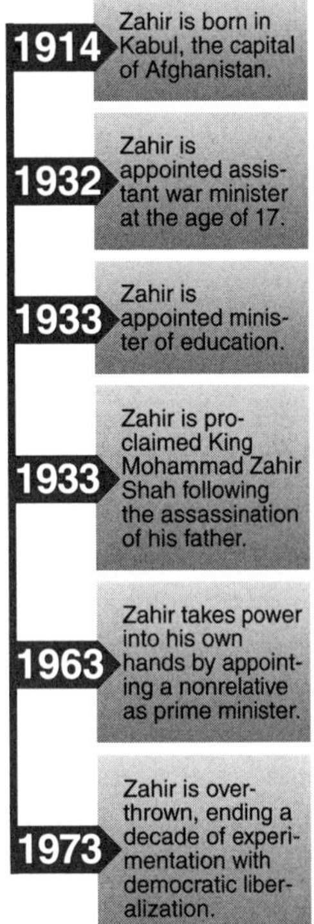

faith in Allah). To ensure the continuation of Musahiban rule, his accession to the throne was unopposed by his three surviving uncles. For the next thirty years, Zahir Shah simply reigned while two of his strong-willed and autocratic uncles held actual power as prime ministers, Sardar (Prince) Muhammad Hashim Khan (1933–47) and Sardar Shah Mahmud Khan (1947–53), followed by Zahir Shah's cousin and brother-in-law, the dictatorial prime minister Sardar Muhammad Daud (1953–63). During this period, although Afghanistan was officially a constitutional monarchy, power and decision making were monopolized by a few elder members of the Musahiban oligarchy; they maintained family unity through intermarriage, assuring continuation of their rule by stifling liberal expression and political freedoms with an oppressive police state.

Following a rift with Daud and his resignation as prime minister, Zahir Shah took power into his own hands in 1963 by appointing a nonrelative as prime minister. He then launched his program of *Demokrasy-i Now* (New Democracy)—a decade of experimentation with democratic liberalization that ended with his overthrow in 1973. During this decade, he encouraged the development of a new liberal constitution, supported relatively free elections, extended freedom of the press, and tolerated the formation of many political movements with diverse orientations. Indecisiveness and inaction on the passage of legislation governing political parties and his inability to prevent government interference by family members and friends undermined democratic experiments and by 1978 drove the country into Communist hands (by Nur Muhammad Taraki's coup of April 27) and Soviet intervention.

Zahir Shah is considered a mild-mannered, soft-spoken, kindly gentleman who lacks energy and is devoid of initiative. Deposed by his paternal cousin (and sister's husband), Sardar Muhammad Daud, he lives in exile in Italy. He abdicated his throne without a fight and passively watched the suffering of his nation under Soviet occupation, Communist rule, and civil war. Some Afghans, mostly his former associates and officials also living in exile, are advocating his return to Afghanistan, especially after the fall of the Communist regime. Most Islamist groups, however, strongly oppose the return of the monarchy, and Zahir Shah, by showing no interest in the throne, continues to disappoint his supporters. ◆

Suggested Reading

ABD AL-RAHMAN KHAN, KING OF AFGHANISTAN

Gurney, Gene. *Kingdoms of Asia, the Middle East, and Africa: An Illustrated Encyclopedia of Ruling Monarchs from Ancient Times to the Present.* Crown, 1986.

ABDULLAH IBN HASAYN, KING OF JORDAN

Fisher, Sidney Nettleton, and William Ochsenwald. *The Middle East: A History.* 5th ed. McGraw Hill, 1997.

Gurney, Gene. *Kingdoms of Asia, the Middle East, and Africa: An Illustrated Encyclopedia of Ruling Monarchs from Ancient Times to the Present.* Crown, 1986.

Shlaim, Avi. *The Politics of Partition: King Abdullah, the Zionists, and Palestine, 1921–1951.* Columbia University Press, 1990.

ABDULLAH II, KING OF JORDAN

Fisher, Sidney Nettleton, and William Ochsenwald. *The Middle East: A History.* 5th ed. McGraw Hill, 1997.

Embassy of Jordan Home Page, http://www.jordanembassyus.org/

AKBAR, MOGUL EMPEROR

Ganeri, Anita. *India Under the Mughal Empire, 1526–1858.* Raintree, 1998.

Gurney, Gene. *Kingdoms of Asia, the Middle East, and Africa: An Illustrated Encyclopedia of Ruling Monarchs from Ancient Times to the Present.* Crown, 1986.

Rothfarb, Ed. *In the Land of the Taj Mahal: The World of the Fabled Mughals.* Henry Holt, 1999.

AKHENATON (AKHENATEN), PHARAOH OF EGYPT

Aldred, Cyril. *Akhenaten, King of Egypt.* Thames and Hudson, 1991.

Clayton, Peter A. *Chronicle of the Pharaohs: The Reign-by-Reign Record of the Rulers and Dynasties of Ancient Egypt.* Thames and Hudson, 1994.

Redford, Donald B. *Akhenaten, the Heretic King.* Princeton University Press, 1984.

AKIHITO, EMPEROR OF JAPAN

Akihito, Emperor, and Empress Michiko. *Tomoshibi (Light): Collected Poetry.* Weatherhill, 1991.

Packard, Jerrold M. *Sons of Heaven: A Portrait of the Japanese Monarchy.* Scribner, 1987.

Embassy of Japan Home Page, http://www.embjapan.org/

ALARIC, KING OF THE VISIGOTHS

Heather, P. J. *The Goths*. Blackwell Publishers, 1996.

ALBERT II, KING OF BELGIUM

Embassy of Belgium Home Page, http://www.diplobel.org/usa/default.htm

ALEXANDER I, CZAR OF RUSSIA

Cate, Curtis. *The War of the Two Emperors: The Duel Between Napoleon and Alexander*. Random House, 1985.

Hartley, Janet M. *Alexander I*. Addison-Wesley, 1994.

Troyat, Henri. *Alexander of Russia, Napoleon's Conqueror*. Dutton, 1983.

ALEXANDER II, CZAR OF RUSSIA

Edmondson, Linda, and Olga Crisp, eds. *Civil Rights in Imperial Russia*. Clarendon Press, 1989.

Mosse, Werner Eugen. *Alexander II and the Modernization of Russia*. St. Martin's Press, 1992.

ALEXANDER III, CZAR OF RUSSIA

Edmondson, Linda, and Olga Crisp, eds. *Civil Rights in Imperial Russia*. Clarendon Press, 1989.

Lincoln, W. Bruce. *In War's Dark Shadow: The Russians Before the Great War*. Dial Press, 1983.

Naimark, Norman M. *Terrorists and Social Democrats: The Russian Revolutionary Movement Under Alexander III*. Harvard University Press, 1983.

ALEXANDER THE GREAT, KING OF MACEDONIA

Fox, Robin Lane. *Alexander the Great*. Penguin USA, reissue 1994.

Green, Peter. *Alexander of Macedon 356–323 B.C.: A Historical Biography*. University of California Press, reissue 1992.

Theule, Frederic. *Alexander and His Times*. Henry Holt and Co., 1996.

ALFRED, KING OF THE WEST SAXONS

Mapp, Alf Johnson. *The Golden Dragon: Alfred the Great and His Times*. Madison Books, 1991.

May, Robin. *Alfred the Great and the Saxons*. Bookwright Press, 1985.

Smyth, Alfred P. *King Alfred the Great*. Oxford University Press, 1996.

AMANOLLAH KHAN, KING OF AFGHANISTAN

Ali, Sharifah. *Afghanistan*. Benchmark Books, 1995.

Gurney, Gene. *Kingdoms of Asia, the Middle East, and Africa: An Illustrated Encyclopedia of Ruling Monarchs from Ancient Times to the Present*. Crown, 1986.

AMENHOTEP III, PHARAOH OF EGYPT

Bunson, Margaret. *Encyclopedia of Ancient Egypt*. Facts on File, 1991.

Clayton, Peter A. *Chronicle of the Pharaohs: The Reign-by-Reign Record of the Rulers and Dynasties of Ancient Egypt*. Thames and Hudson, 1994.

O'Connor, David B. *Amenhotep III: Perspectives on His Reign*. University of Michigan Press, 1998.

ARTHUR, KING OF ENGLAND

Malory, Thomas. *Le Morte D'Arthur: King Arthur and the Legends of the Round Table* (fiction). New American Library, revised ed. 1986.

Stewart, Mary. *The Crystal Cave* (fiction). Ballantine Books, 1996.

White, Terence Hanbury. *The Once and Future King* (fiction). Ace Books, reissue 1987.

ASOKA, EMPEROR OF INDIA

Allchin, Bridget. *The Rise of Civilization in India and Pakistan*. Cambridge University Press, 1982.

Galbraith, Catherine Atwater, and Rama Mehta. *India, Now and Through Time*. Houghton Mifflin, 1980.

Kanitkar, H. A. *Asoka and Indian Civilization*. Greenhaven Press, 1980.

ATAHUALPA, INCA EMPEROR

Hemming, John. *Conquest of the Incas*. Harcourt Brace, 1973.

Martell, Hazel. *Civilizations of Peru: Before 1535 (Looking Back)*. Raintree, 1999.

Schlesinger, Arthur M., ed. *The Ancient Incas*. Chelsea House, 1999.

ATTILA, KING OF THE HUNS

Howarth, Patrick. *Attila, King of the Huns: Man and Myth*. John Kallman, 1997.

Thompson, E. A. *The Huns*. Blackwell, 1996.

Vardy, Steven Bela. *Attila*. Chelsea House, 1991.

AUGUSTUS, EMPEROR OF ROME

Mellor, Ronald, ed. *From Augustus to Nero: The First Dynasty of Imperial Rome*. Michigan State University Press, 1991.

Shotter, D. *Augustus Caesar*. Routledge, 1991.

Southern, Pat. *Augustus*. Routledge, 1998.

BAJAZET (BAYEZID) II, SULTAN OF THE OTTOMANS

Goodman, Jason. *Lords of the Horizons: A History of the Ottoman Empire*. Henry Holt, 1999.

Wheatcroft, Andrew. *The Ottomans*. Viking, 1993.

BEATRIX, QUEEN OF THE NETHERLANDS

Ozer, Steven. *The Netherlands*. Chelsea House, 1990.

Embassy of the Netherlands Home Page, http://www.netherlands-embassy.org/

BHUMIBOL ADULYADEY, KING OF THAILAND

Gurney, Gene. *Kingdoms of Asia, the Middle East, and Africa: An Illustrated Encyclopedia of Ruling Monarchs from Ancient Times to the Present*. Crown, 1986.

Embassy of Thailand Home Page, http://www.thaiembdc.org/

BIRENDRA, KING OF NEPAL

Gurney, Gene. *Kingdoms of Asia, the Middle East, and Africa: An Illustrated Encyclopedia of Ruling Monarchs from Ancient Times to the Present*. Crown, 1986.

Royal Nepalese Consulate General Home Page, http://www.undp.org/missions/nepal/royal.htm

ROBERT BRUCE, KING OF SCOTLAND

Bingham, Caroline. *The Kings & Queens of Scotland*. Dorset Press, 1985.

Scott, Ronald McNair. *Robert the Bruce: King of Scots*. Carroll & Graf, reissue 1996.

CARL XVI, KING OF SWEDEN

Embassy of Sweden Home Page, http://www.swedenemb.org/

CATHERINE DE MÉDICIS, QUEEN OF FRANCE

Knecht, R. J. *Catherine de Médicis*. Addison-Wesley, 1998.

Strage, Mark. *Women of Power: The Life and Times of Catherine de Médicis*. Harcourt Brace Jovanovich, 1976.

CATHERINE II, EMPRESS OF RUSSIA

Alexander, John T. *Catherine the Great: Life and Legend*. Oxford University Press, 1988.

De Madariaga, Isabel. *Catherine the Great: A Short History*. Yale University Press, 1991.

Troyat, Henri. *Catherine the Great*. Meridian Books, 1994.

CHARLEMAGNE, KING OF THE FRANKS

Banfield, Susan. *Charlemagne*. Chelsea House, 1986.

Bulfinch, Thomas. *The Age of Chivalry and Legends of Charlemagne*. Dorset Press, 1991.

Bullough, Donald A. *The Age of Charlemagne*. 2d ed. Exeter Books, 1980.

CHARLES I, KING OF ENGLAND

Ashley, Maurice. *The Battle of Naseby and the Fall of King Charles I*. St. Martin's Press, 1992.

Hibbert, Christopher. *Cavaliers and Roundheads: The English at War, 1642–1649*. Maxwell Macmillan, 1993.

Morrill, J. S. *Revolt in the Provinces: The People of England and the Tragedies of War 1630–1648*. Longman, 1999.

CHARLES II, KING OF ENGLAND

Glassey, Lionel K. J., ed. *The Reigns of Charles II and James VII & II*. St. Martin's Press, 1997.

Hutton, Ronald. *Charles the Second, King of England, Scotland, and Ireland*. Clarendon Press, 1989.

Miller, John. *The Restoration and the England of Charles II*. Addison-Wesley, 1997.

CHARLES V, KING OF SPAIN (CHARLES I OF SPAIN; CHARLES V, HOLY ROMAN EMPEROR)

Bryce, James. *The Holy Roman Empire*. AMS Press, reissue 1978.

Wilson, Peter H. *The Holy Roman Empire, 1495–1806*. St. Martin's Press, 1999.

CHARLES VII, KING OF FRANCE

Curry, Anne. *The Hundred Years War*. St. Martin's Press, 1993.

Vale, Malcolm Graham Allan. *Charles VII*. University of California Press, 1974.

CHARLES XII, KING OF SWEDEN

Roberts, Michael, ed. *Sweden's Age of Greatness, 1632–1718*. St. Martin's Press, 1973.

CH'IEN-LUNG, EMPEROR OF CHINA

Paludan, Ann. *Chronicles of the Chinese Emperors: The Reign-by-Reign Record of the Rulers of Imperial China*. Thames and Hudson, 1998.

Peyrefitte, Alain. *The Immobile Empire*. Knopf, 1992.

Twitchett, Denis, and John K. Fairbank. *The Cambridge History of China*. Cambridge University Press, 1978.

CHRISTINA, QUEEN OF SWEDEN

Roberts, Michael, ed. *Sweden's Age of Greatness, 1632–1718*. St. Martin's Press, 1973.

Masson, Georgina. *Queen Christina*. Farrar, Straus & Giroux, 1969.

CLEOPATRA VII, QUEEN OF EGYPT

Grant, Michael. *Cleopatra.* Barnes & Noble Books, 1992.

Hoobler, Dorothy. *Cleopatra.* Chelsea House, 1986.

CLOVIS, KING OF THE FRANKS

Currier, John W. *Clovis, King of the Franks.* Marquette University Press, 1997.

James, Edward. *The Franks.* Blackwell, 1988.

CONSTANTINE I, EMPEROR OF ROME

Grant, Michael. *Constantine the Great: The Man and His Times.* Scribner, 1994.

Pohlsander, Hans A. *The Emperor Constantine.* Routledge, 1996.

Smith, John Holland. *Constantine the Great.* Scribner, 1971.

DARIUS I, KING OF PERSIA

Cook, J. M. *The Persian Empire.* Schocken Books, 1983.

Nardo, Don. *The Persian Empire.* Lucent Books, 1998.

Persians: Masters of the Empire. Time-Life Books, 1995.

DAVID, KING OF THE ISRAELITES

Cohen, Barbara. *David: A Biography.* Clarion Books, 1995.

Powell, Ivor C. *David: His Life and Times.* Kregel, 1990.

Segal, Lore Groszmann. *The Story of King Saul and King David.* Schocken Books, 1991.

JEAN JACQUES DESSALINES, EMPEROR OF HAITI

James, C. L. R. *The Black Jacobins: Toussaint L'Ouverture and the San Domingo Revolution.* Vintage Books, reissue 1989.

Nicholls, David. *From Dessalines to Duvalier: Race, Colour, and National Independence in Haiti.* Rutgers University Press, 1995.

ELIZABETH I, QUEEN OF ENGLAND

Erickson, Carolly. *The First Elizabeth.* St. Martin's Press, 1997.

Fraser, Antonia. *The Lives of the Kings and Queens of England.* University of California Press, reissue 1995.

Weir, Alison. *Life of Elizabeth I.* Ballantine Books, 1998.

ELIZABETH II, QUEEN OF ENGLAND

Bradford, Sarah. *Elizabeth: A Biography of Britain's Queen.* Farrar, Straus & Giroux, 1996.

Flamini, Roland. *Sovereign: Elizabeth II and the Windsor Dynasty.* Delacorte Press, 1991.

Pimlott, Ben. *The Queen: A Biography of Elizabeth II.* Wiley, 1997.

Monarchy in Britain Home Page (service of the British Embassy) http://www.britain-info.org/bis/monarchy/index.stm

FAHD, KING OF SAUDI ARABIA

Holden, David. *The House of Saud.* Holt, Rinehart, and Winston, 1982.

Lacey, Robert. *The Kingdom: Arabia and the House of Sa'ud.* Avon Books, 1983.

Embassy of Saudi Arabia Home Page, http://www.saudiembassy.net/

FAISAL I IBN HUSAYN, KING OF IRAQ

Cleveland, William L. *A History of the Modern Middle East.* Westview Press, 1994.

Fisher, Sidney Nettleton, and William Ochsenwald. *The Middle East: A History.* 5th ed. McGraw Hill, 1997.

Gurney, Gene. *Kingdoms of Asia, the Middle East, and Africa: An Illustrated Encyclopedia of Ruling Monarchs from Ancient Times to the Present.* Crown, 1986.

FAISAL IBN ABD AL-AZIZ AL SAUD, KING OF SAUDI ARABIA

Holden, David. *The House of Saud.* Holt, Rinehart, and Winston, 1982.

Lacey, Robert. *The Kingdom: Arabia and the House of Sa'ud.* Avon Books, 1983.

Stefoff, Rebecca. *Faisal.* Chelsea House, 1989.

FAROUK, KING OF EGYPT

McBride, Barrie St. Clair. *Farouk of Egypt; a Biography.* A. S. Barnes, 1968.

McLeave, Hugh. *The Last Pharaoh: Farouk of Egypt.* McCall Publishing, 1970.

Stadiem, William. *Too Rich: The High Life and Tragic Death of King Farouk.* Carroll & Graf, 1991.

FERDINAND I, HOLY ROMAN EMPEROR

Bryce, James. *The Holy Roman Empire.* AMS Press, reissue 1978.

Wilson, Peter H. *The Holy Roman Empire, 1495–1806.* St. Martin's Press, 1999.

FERDINAND II, HOLY ROMAN EMPEROR

Bryce, James. *The Holy Roman Empire*. AMS Press, reissue 1978.

Wilson, Peter H. *The Holy Roman Empire, 1495–1806*. St. Martin's Press, 1999.

FERDINAND II, KING OF ARAGON, CASTILE, SICILY, AND NAPLES

Fernandez-Armesto, Felipe. *Ferdinand and Isabella*. Dorset Press, 1991.

Wilkinson, Philip. *Statesmen Who Changed the World*. Chelsea House, 1994.

FREDERICK I, HOLY ROMAN EMPEROR

Bryce, James. *The Holy Roman Empire*. AMS Press, reissue 1978.

Munz, Peter. *Frederick Barbarossa: A Study in Medieval Politics*. Cornell University Press, 1969.

Wilson, Peter H. *The Holy Roman Empire, 1495–1806*. St. Martin's Press, 1999.

FREDERICK II, HOLY ROMAN EMPEROR

Abulafia, David. *Frederick II: A Medieval Emperor*. Oxford University Press, 1992.

Bryce, James. *The Holy Roman Empire*. AMS Press, reissue 1978.

Wilson, Peter H. *The Holy Roman Empire, 1495–1806*. St. Martin's Press, 1999.

FREDERICK II, KING OF PRUSSIA

Asprey, Robert B. *Frederick the Great: The Magnificent Enigma*. Ticknor & Fields, 1986.

Kittredge, Mary. *Frederick the Great*. Chelsea House, 1987.

Mitford, Nancy. *Frederick the Great*. Penguin, reissue 1995.

FREDERICK WILLIAM, KING OF PRUSSIA

Carsten, F. L. *The Origins of Prussia*. Greenwood Publishing, 1981.

Koch, H. W. *A History of Prussia*. Dorset Press, 1987.

Von Ranke, Leopold. *Memoirs of the House of Brandenburg, and History of Prussia*. Greenwood Publishing, 3 vols., 1970.

FUAD, KING OF EGYPT

Cleveland, William L. *A History of the Modern Middle East*. Westview Press, 1994.

Fisher, Sidney Nettleton, and William Ochsenwald. *The Middle East: A History*. 5th ed. McGraw Hill, 1997.

Goldschmidt, Arthur. *Modern Egypt: The Formation of a Nation-State*. Westview Press, 1988.

GALAWDEWOS, EMPEROR OF ETHIOPIA

Marcus, Harold G. *A History of Ethiopia*. University of California Press, 1994.

Pankhurst, Richard, and Barbara Pankhurst. *The Ethiopians*. Blackwell Publishers, 1998.

GENGHIS KHAN, MONGOL EMPEROR

Humphrey, Judy. *Genghis Khan*. Chelsea House, 1987.

Marshall, Robert. *Storm from the East: From Ghengis Khan to Khublai Khan*. University of California Press, 1993.

Severin, Timothy. *In Search of Genghis Khan*. Maxwell Macmillan International, 1992.

GEORGE III, KING OF ENGLAND

Brooke, John. *King George III*. McGraw-Hill, 1972.

Hibbert, Christopher. *George III: A Personal History*. Basic Books, 1998.

Lloyd, Alan. *The King Who Lost America; A Portrait of the Life and Times of George III*. Doubleday, 1971.

GUSTAVUS II ADOLPHUS, KING OF SWEDEN

Fletcher, C. R. L. *Gustavus Adolphus*. AMS Press, 1980.

Lee, Stephen J. *The Thirty Years War*. Routledge, 1991.

Roberts, Michael. *Gustavus Adolphus*. Addison-Wesley, 1992.

HADRIAN, EMPEROR OF ROME

Birley, Anthony Richard. *Hadrian: The Restless Emperor*. Routledge, 1997.

Perowne, Stewart. *Hadrian*. Barnes & Noble Books, 1996.

Yourcenar, Marguerite. *Memoirs of Hadrian*. Modern Library, 1984.

HAILE SELASSIE I, EMPEROR OF ETHIOPIA

Haile Selassie I. *My Life and Ethiopia's Progress*. Michigan State University Press, 1994.

Negash, Askale. *Haile Selassie*. Chelsea House, 1989.

Rasmussen, R. Kent. *Modern African Political Leaders*. Facts on File, 1998.

HAMAD IBN KHALIFA AL THANI, EMIR OF QATAR

Cleveland, William L. *A History of the Modern Middle East*. Westview Press, 1994.

Fisher, Sidney Nettleton, and William Ochsenwald. *The Middle East: A History*. 5th ed. McGraw Hill, 1997.

Rickman, Maureen. *Qatar*. Chelsea House, 1987.

Qatar Home Page (service of ArabNet), http://www.arab.net/qatar/qatar_contents.html

HAMMURABI, KING OF BABYLON

Gurney, Gene. *Kingdoms of Asia, the Middle East, and Africa: An Illustrated Encyclopedia of Ruling Monarchs from Ancient Times to the Present*. Crown, 1986.

Hammurabi, *The Code of Hammurabi*. Gaunt, 1994.

Landau, Elaine. *The Babylonians*. Millbrook Press, 1997.

HANS-ADAM II, PRINCE OF LIECHTENSTEIN

Kelly, Robert C., et al., eds. *Country Review, Liechtenstein 1998/1999*. Commercial Data International, 1998.

Liechtenstein Guide (service of Liechtenstein National Tourist Office), http://www.searchlink.li/tourist/guideeng/index.asp

HARALD V, KING OF NORWAY

Kagda, Sakina. *Norway*. Benchmark Books, 1996.

Zickgraf, Ralph. *Norway*. Chelsea House, 1997.

Embassy of Norway Home Page, http://www.norway.org/

HASSAN II, KING OF MOROCCO

Cleveland, William L. *A History of the Modern Middle East*. Westview Press, 1994.

Gurney, Gene. *Kingdoms of Asia, the Middle East, and Africa: An Illustrated Encyclopedia of Ruling Monarchs from Ancient Times to the Present*. Crown, 1986.

Morocco Home Page (service of ArabNet), http://www.arab.net/morocco/morocco_contents.html

HENRY IV, KING OF FRANCE

Briggs, Robin. *Early Modern France 1560–1715*. Oxford University Press, 1998.

Le Roy Ladurie, Emmanuel. *The Royal French State, 1460–1610*. Blackwell, 1994.

HENRY IV, KING OF GERMANY

Bryce, James. *The Holy Roman Empire*. AMS Press, reissue 1978.

Wilson, Peter H. *The Holy Roman Empire, 1495–1806*. St. Martin's Press, 1999.

HENRY V, KING OF ENGLAND

Allmand, C. T. *Henry V*. University of California Press, 1992.

Hutchison, Harold Frederick. *King Henry V: A Biography*. Hippocrene Books, 1990.

Shakespeare, William. *King Henry V* (play). Arden Shakespeare, 1998.

HENRY VI, KING OF GERMANY

Bryce, James. *The Holy Roman Empire*. AMS Press, reissue 1978.

Wilson, Peter H. *The Holy Roman Empire, 1495–1806*. St. Martin's Press, 1999.

HENRY VII, KING OF ENGLAND

Bacon, Francis. *The History of the Reign of King Henry the Seventh*. Cornell University Press, 1996.

Britnell, Richard. *The Closing of the Middle Ages: England, 1471–1529*. Blackwell Publishers, 1997.

HENRY VIII, KING OF ENGLAND

Dwyer, Frank. *Henry VIII*. Chelsea House, 1988.

Fraser, Lady Antonia. *Henry VIII*. Welcome Rain, 1998.

Ridley, Jasper Godwin. *Henry VIII*. Viking, 1985.

HERACLIUS, EMPEROR OF BYZANTIUM

Norwich, John Julius. *A Short History of Byzantium*. Knopf, 1997.

Ostrogorsky, George. *History of the Byzantine State*. Rutgers University Press, reissue 1986.

HEROD THE GREAT, KING OF JUDEA

Grant, Michael. *Herod the Great*. American Heritage Press, 1971.

Green, Robert. *Herod the Great*. Franklin Watts, 1996.

HIROHITO, EMPEROR OF JAPAN

Behr, Edward. *Hirohito: Behind the Myth*. Vintage Books, 1990.

Hoyt, Edwin Palmer. *Hirohito: The Emperor and the Man*. Praeger, 1991.

Packard, Jerrold M. *Sons of Heaven: A Portrait of the Japanese Monarchy*. Scribner, 1987.

HUSSEIN IBN TALAL, KING OF JORDAN

Lunt, James D. *Hussein of Jordan: Searching for a Just and Lasting Peace*. Morrow, 1989.

Matusky, Gregory. *King Hussein*. Chelsea House, 1987.

Salibi, Kamal S. *The Modern History of Jordan*. St. Martin's Press, 1993.

Embassy of Jordan Home Page, http://www.jordanembassyus.org/

ABD AL-AZIZ IBN SAUD, KING OF SAUDI ARABIA

Armstrong, H. C. *Lord of Arabia: Ibn Saud*. Kegan Paul Intl., 1998.

Holden, David. *The House of Saud*. Holt, Rinehart, and Winston, 1982.

Lacey, Robert. *The Kingdom: Arabia and the House of Sa'ud*. Avon Books, 1983.

ISA IBN SULMAN AL-KHALIFA, RULER OF BAHRAIN

Cleveland, William L. *A History of the Modern Middle East.* Westview Press, 1994.

Gurney, Gene. *Kingdoms of Asia, the Middle East, and Africa: An Illustrated Encyclopedia of Ruling Monarchs from Ancient Times to the Present.* Crown, 1986.

Bahrain Home Page (service of ArabNet), http://www.arab.net/bahrain/govt/bn_govtintro.html

ISABELLA I, QUEEN OF CASTILE

Fernandez-Armesto, Felipe. *Ferdinand and Isabella.* Dorset Press, 1991.

Liss, Peggy K. *Isabel the Queen: Life and Times.* Oxford University Press, 1992.

Rubin, Nancy. *Isabella of Castile: The First Renaissance Queen.* St. Martin's Press, 1991.

AGUSTIN DE ITURBIDE, EMPEROR OF MEXICO

Anna, Timothy E. *The Mexican Empire of Iturbide.* University of Nebraska Press, 1990.

Krauze, Enrique. *Mexico: Biography of Power; A History of Modern Mexico, 1810–1996.* HarperCollins, 1997.

IVAN III, GRAND PRINCE OF MOSCOW

Fennell, John. *Ivan the Great of Moscow.* St. Martin's Press, 1961.

Hartog, Leo de. *Russia and the Mongol Yoke: The History of the Russian Principalities and the Golden Horde, 1221–1502.* British Academic Press, 1996.

IVAN IV, CZAR OF RUSSIA

Bobrick, Benson. *Fearful Majesty: The Life and Reign of Ivan the Terrible.* Putnam, 1987.

Butson, Thomas G. *Ivan the Terrible.* Chelsea House, 1987.

Troyat, Henri. *Ivan the Terrible.* Dutton, 1984.

JABIR AHMAD AL SABAH, EMIR OF KUWAIT

Fisher, Sidney Nettleton, and William Ochsenwald. *The Middle East: A History.* 5th ed. McGraw Hill, 1997.

Gurney, Gene. *Kingdoms of Asia, the Middle East, and Africa: An Illustrated Encyclopedia of Ruling Monarchs from Ancient Times to the Present.* Crown, 1986.

Embassy of Kuwait Home Page, http://embassyofkuwait.com/

JAMES I (JAMES VI), KING OF SCOTLAND AND ENGLAND

Fraser, Antonia. *Faith and Treason: The Story of the Gunpowder Plot.* Doubleday, 1996.

Fraser, Antonia. *King James VI of Scotland, I of England.* Knopf, 1975.

Lee, Maurice. *Great Britain's Solomon: James VI and I in His Three Kingdoms.* University of Illinois Press, 1990.

JEAN, GRAND DUKE OF LUXEMBOURG

Sheehan, Patricia. *Luxembourg*. Benchmark Books, 1997.

Luxembourg National Tourist Office Home Page, http://www.visitluxembourg.com/

JOÃO VI, KING OF PORTUGAL

Birmingham, David. *A Concise History of Portugal*. Cambridge University Press, 1995.

JOHN, KING OF ENGLAND

Shakespeare, William. *The Life and Death of King John* (play). Cambridge University Press, 1995.

Turner, Ralph V. *King John*. Addison-Wesley, 1994.

Warren, W. L. *King John*. Yale University Press, 1998.

JOSEPH II, HOLY ROMAN EMPEROR

Bernard, Paul P. *Joseph II*. Twayne Publishers, 1968.

Bryce, James. *The Holy Roman Empire*. AMS Press, reissue 1978.

Wilson, Peter H. *The Holy Roman Empire, 1495–1806*. St. Martin's Press, 1999.

JUAN CARLOS, KING OF SPAIN

Powell, Charles. *Juan Carlos of Spain: Self-Made Monarch*. St. Martin's Press, 1996.

Embassy of Spain Home Page, http://www.spainemb.org/information/

JUSTINIAN I, EMPEROR OF BYZANTIUM

Evans, J. A. S. *The Age of Justinian: The Circumstances of Imperial Power*. Routledge, 1994.

Grant, Michael. *From Rome to Byzantium: The Fifth Century AD*. Routledge, 1998.

Moorhead, John. *Justinian*. Addison-Wesley, 1994.

KAMEHAMEHA I, KING OF HAWAII

Daws, Gavan. *Shoal of Time: A History of the Hawaiian Islands*. Macmillan, 1968; University of Hawaii Press, reissue 1989.

Seiden, Allan. *Hawai'i, the Royal Legacy*. Mutual Publishing, 1992.

KHALID IBN ABD AL-AZIZ AL SAUD, KING OF SAUDI ARABIA

Holden, David. *The House of Saud*. Holt, Rinehart, and Winston, 1982.

Lacey, Robert. *The Kingdom: Arabia and the House of Sa'ud*. Avon Books, 1983.

KUBLAI KHAN, MONGOL EMPEROR

Dramer, Kim. *Kublai Khan.* Chelsea House, 1990.

Rossabi, Morris. *Khublai Khan: His Life and Times.* University of California Press, 1987.

Silverberg, Robert. *Kublai Khan: Lord of Xanadu.* Bobbs-Merrill, 1966.

LEBNA DENGEL, KING OF ABYSSINIA

Jones, Arnold H. *A History of Abyssinia.* Greenwood Publishing, 1969.

LETSIE III, KING OF LESOTHO

Freeman-Grenville, G. S. P. *The New Atlas of African History.* Simon & Schuster, 1991.

Tonsing-Carter, Betty. *Lesotho.* Chelsea House, 1988.

Ungar, Sanford J. *Africa: The People and Politics of an Emerging Continent.* Simon & Schuster, 1986.

LILIUOKALANI, QUEEN OF HAWAII

Daws, Gavan. *Shoal of Time: A History of the Hawaiian Islands.* Macmillan, 1968; University of Hawaii Press, reissue 1989.

Guzzetti, Paula. *Liliuokalani, the Last Hawaiian Queen.* Benchmark Books, 1997.

Seiden, Allan. *Hawaii, the Royal Legacy.* Mutual Publishing, 1992.

LOUIS XI, KING OF FRANCE

Le Roy Ladurie, Emmanuel. *The Royal French State, 1460–1610.* Blackwell, 1994.

Potter, David. *A History of France, 1460–1560: The Emergence of a Nation State.* St. Martin's Press, 1995.

Tyrrell, Joseph M. *Louis XI.* Twayne, 1980.

LOUIS XIV, KING OF FRANCE

Bernier, Olivier. *Louis XIV: A Royal Life.* Doubleday, 1987.

Lossky, Andrew. *Louis XIV and the French Monarchy.* Rutgers University Press, 1994.

Mitford, Nancy. *The Sun King.* Penguin Books, 1994.

LOUIS XVI, KING OF FRANCE

Bernier, Olivier. *Words of Fire, Deeds of Blood: The Mob, the Monarchy, and the French Revolution.* Little, Brown, 1989.

Hardman, John. *Louis XVI.* Yale University Press, 1993.

Schama, Simon. *Citizens: A Chronicle of the French Revolution.* Vintage Books, 1990.

MAHMUD II, OTTOMAN SULTAN

Goodman, Jason. *Lords of the Horizons: A History of the Ottoman Empire.* Henry Holt, 1999.

Wheatcroft, Andrew. *The Ottomans.* Viking, 1993.

MANSU MUSA, EMPEROR OF MALI

Brooks, Larry. *Daily Life in Ancient and Modern Timbuktu* (Cities Through Time). Runestone Press, 1999.

Koslow, Philip. *Mali: Crossroads of Africa* (Kingdoms of Africa). Chelsea House Publishing, 1995.

Thompson, Carol. *The Empire of Mali* (African Civilizations). Franklin Watts, Incorporated, 1998.

MANUEL I, KING OF PORTUGAL

Bedini, Silvio A. *The Pope's Elephant.* J. S. Sanders & Co., 1998.

Sanceau, Elaine. *The Reign of the Fortunate King, 1495–1521.* Archon Books, 1969.

MARCUS AURELIUS, EMPEROR OF ROME

Birley, Anthony Richard. *Marcus Aurelius: A Biography.* Rev. ed. Yale University Press, 1987.

Marcus Aurelius. *Meditations.* Dorset Press, 1986.

MARGRETHE II, QUEEN OF DENMARK

Pateman, Robert. *Denmark.* Benchmark Books, 1995.

Embassy of Denmark Home Page, http://www.denmarkemb.org/

MARIA THERESA, QUEEN OF HUNGARY AND BOHEMIA

Bright, James. *Maria Theresa.* Ayer, 1971.

Bryce, James. *The Holy Roman Empire.* AMS Press, reissue 1978.

Wilson, Peter H. *The Holy Roman Empire, 1495–1806.* St. Martin's Press, 1999.

MARIE ANTOINETTE, QUEEN OF FRANCE

Bernier, Olivier. *Words of Fire, Deeds of Blood: The Mob, the Monarchy, and the French Revolution.* Little, Brown, 1989.

Erickson, Carolly. *To the Scaffold: The Life of Marie Antoinette.* Morrow, 1991.

Haslip, Joan. *Marie Antoinette.* Weidenfeld & Nicolson, 1988.

MARY I, QUEEN OF ENGLAND AND IRELAND

Erickson, Carolly. *Bloody Mary.* Griffin, reissue 1998.

Loades, D. M. *Mary Tudor: A Life.* Basil Blackwell, 1989.

Weir, Alison. *The Children of Henry VIII.* Ballantine Books, 1996.

MARY STUART, QUEEN OF SCOTLAND

Fraser, Lady Antonia. *Mary, Queen of Scots*. Delta, reissue 1993.

Ross, Stewart. *Long Live Mary, Queen of Scots*. Evans Brothers 1997.

Stepanek, Sally. *Mary Queen of Scots*. Chelsea House, 1987.

MAXIMILIAN, EMPEROR OF MEXICO

Haslip, Joan. *The Crown of Mexico; Maximilian and His Empress Carlota*. Holt, Rinehart, and Winston, 1972.

Ridley, Jasper Godwin. *Maximilian and Juarez*. Ticknor & Fields, 1992.

MAXIMILIAN I, HOLY ROMAN EMPEROR

Benecke, Gerhard. *Maximilian I (1459–1519)*. Routledge & Kegan Paul, 1982.

Bryce, James. *The Holy Roman Empire*. AMS Press, reissue 1978.

Wilson, Peter H. *The Holy Roman Empire, 1495–1806*. St. Martin's Press, 1999.

MENELIK II, EMPEROR OF ETHIOPIA

Marcus, Harold G. *A History of Ethiopia*. University of California Press, 1994.

Marcus, Harold G. *The Life and Times of Menelik II: Ethiopia 1844–1913*. Red Sea Press, 1995.

Pankhurst, Richard, and Barbara Pankhurst. *The Ethiopians*. Blackwell Publishers, 1998.

MOHAMMAD REZA PAHLAVI, SHAH OF IRAN

Cockcroft, James D. *Mohammed Reza Pahlavi, Shah of Iran*. Chelsea House, 1989.

Mohammed Reza Pahlavi. *Answer to History*. Stein and Day, 1980.

Zonis, Marvin. *Majestic Failure: The Fall of the Shah*. University of Chicago Press, 1991.

MOSHOESHOE, KING OF THE SOTHO

Mann, Kenny. *Monomotapa, Zulu, Basuto: Southern Africa* (African Kingdoms of the Past). Dillon Press, 1996.

Van Wyk, Gary. *Basotho*. Rosen Publishing Group, 1996.

MOTECUHZOMA I (MONTEZUMA), EMPEROR OF MEXICO

Davies, Nigel. *The Aztecs: A History*. Putnam, 1980.

Stein, R. Conrad. *The Aztec Empire*. Benchmark Books, 1996.

MOTECUHZOMA II (MONTEZUMA), EMPEROR OF MEXICO

Davies, Nigel. *The Aztecs: A History*. Putnam, 1980.

Stein, R. Conrad. *The Aztec Empire*. Benchmark Books, 1996.

Thomas, Hugh. *Conquest: Montezuma, Cortes, and the Fall of Old Mexico*. Simon & Schuster, 1993.

MSWATI II, KING OF SWAZILAND

Kuper, Hilda. *The Swazi: A South African Kingdom*. Holt, Rinehart, and Winston, 1986.

Oluikpe, Benson Omenihu A. *Swazi*. Rosen Publishing Group, 1997.

MSWATI III, KING OF SWAZILAND

Kuper, Hilda. *The Swazi: A South African Kingdom*. Holt, Rinehart, and Winston, 1986.

Oluikpe, Benson Omenihu A. *Swazi*. Rosen Publishing Group, 1997.

MUBARAK AL SABAH, KING OF KUWAIT

Fisher, Sidney Nettleton, and William Ochsenwald. *The Middle East: A History*. 5th ed. McGraw Hill, 1997.

Gurney, Gene. *Kingdoms of Asia, the Middle East, and Africa: An Illustrated Encyclopedia of Ruling Monarchs from Ancient Times to the Present*. Crown, 1986.

MUHAMMED V, KING OF MOROCCO

Porch, Douglas. *The Conquest of Morocco*. Knopf, 1983.

Seward, Pat. *Morocco*. Benchmark Books, 1995.

MUTSUHITO, EMPEROR OF JAPAN

Avakian, Monique. *The Meiji Restoration and the Rise of Modern Japan*. Silver Burdett Press, 1991.

Kornicki, Peter F. *Meiji Japan: Political, Economic and Social History, 1868–1912*. Routledge, 1998.

NAPOLEON I, EMPEROR OF FRANCE

Hamilton-Williams, David. *The Fall of Napoleon: The Final Betrayal*. Wiley, 1994.

Lyons, Martyn. *Napoleon Bonaparte and the Legacy of the French Revolution*. Macmillan, 1994.

Schom, Alan. *Napoleon Bonaparte*. HarperCollins, 1997.

NAPOLEON III, EMPEROR OF FRANCE

Bierman, John. *Napoleon III and His Carnival Empire*. St. Martin's Press, 1988.

Hugo, Victor. *Napoleon the Little*. Howard Fertig, reissue 1992.

McMillan, James F. *Napoleon III*. Addison-Wesley, 1991.

NEBUCHADNEZZAR, CHALDEAN KING

Landau, Elaine. *The Babylonians* (The Cradle of Civilization). Millbrook Press, 1997.

Oates, Joan. *Babylon*. Thames & Hudson, 1986.

Wiseman, Donald J. *Nebuchadnezzar and Babylon*. Oxford University Press, 1991.

NERO, EMPEROR OF ROME

Mellor, Ronald, ed. *From Augustus to Nero: The First Dynasty of Imperial Rome.* Michigan State University Press, 1991.

Shotter, D. C. A. *Nero.* Routledge, 1997.

Zoch, Paul A. *Ancient Rome: An Introductory History.* University of Oklahoma Press, 1998.

NICHOLAS II, CZAR OF RUSSIA

Kurth, Peter. *Tsar: The Lost World of Nicholas and Alexandra.* Little, Brown, 1995.

Massie, Robert K. *Nicholas and Alexandra.* Bantam Books, reissue 1995.

Massie, Robert K. *The Romanovs: The Final Chapter.* Ballantine Books, reissue 1996.

NOOR, QUEEN OF JORDAN

Salibi, Kamal S. *The Modern History of Jordan.* St. Martin's Press, 1993.

Embassy of Jordan Home Page, http://www.jordanembassyus.org/

OSMAN I, OTTOMAN EMPEROR

Goodwin, Jason. *Lords of the Horizons: A History of the Ottoman Empire.* Henry Holt, 1999.

Wheatcroft, Andrew. *The Ottomans.* Viking, 1993.

OTTO I, KING OF GERMANY

Henderson, Ernest F. *A History of Germany in the Middle Ages.* Haskell House, reissue 1968.

Reuter, Timothy. *Germany in the Early Middle Ages, C. 800–1056.* Addison-Wesley, 1991.

PACHACUTI, INCA EMPEROR

Hemming, John. *Conquest of the Incas.* Harcourt Brace, 1973.

Martell, Hazel. *Civilizations of Peru: Before 1535* (Looking Back). Raintree, 1999.

Schlesinger, Arthur M., ed. *The Ancient Incas.* Chelsea House, 1999.

PEDRO I, EMPEROR OF BRAZIL

Bethell, Leslie, ed. *Colonial Brazil.* Cambridge University Press, 1987.

Macaulay, Neill. *Dom Pedro: The Struggle for Liberty in Brazil and Portugal, 1798–1834.* Duke University Press, 1986.

PEDRO II, EMPEROR OF BRAZIL

Bernstein, Harry. *Dom Pedro II*. Twayne Publishers, 1973.

Bethell, Leslie, ed. *Colonial Brazil*. Cambridge University Press, 1987.

PETER I, CZAR OF RUSSIA

Hughes, Lindsey. *Russia in the Age of Peter the Great*. Yale University Press, 1998.

Massie, Robert K. *Peter the Great, His Life and World*. Ballantine Books, 1992.

McDermott, Kathleen. *Peter the Great*. Chelsea House, 1991.

PHILIP II, KING OF SPAIN

Kamen, Henry Arthur Francis. *Philip of Spain*. Yale University Press, 1997.

Parker, Geoffrey. *The Grand Strategy of Philip II*. Yale University Press, 1998.

Parker, Geoffrey. *Philip II*. Open Court Publishing, 1995.

PU YI, EMPEROR OF CHINA

Behr, Edward. *The Last Emperor*. Bantam Books, 1987.

Power, Brian. *The Puppet Emperor: The Life of Pu Yi, Last Emperor of China*. Universe Books, 1988.

Pu Yi. *The Last Manchu: The Autobiography of Henry Pu Yi, Last Emperor of China*. Pocket Books, 1987.

QABUS IBN SA'ID, SULTAN OF OMAN

Joyce, Miriam. *The Sultanate of Oman: A Twentieth Century History*. Praeger, 1995.

Oman Ministry of Information Home Page, http://www.omanet.com/

RAINIER III, PRINCE OF MONACO

Edwards, Anne, 1927. *The Grimaldis of Monaco*. Morrow, 1992.

Glatt, John. *The Royal House of Monaco: Dynasty of Glamour, Tragedy and Scandal*. St. Martin's Press, 1998.

Robinson, Jeffrey. *Rainier and Grace: An Intimate Portrait*. Atlantic Monthly Press, 1989.

Monaco Guide (service of Monaco Government Tourist Office), http://www.monaco.mc/monaco/index.html

RAMSES II, PHARAOH OF EGYPT

Ramses II: Magnificence on the Nile. Time-Life Books, 1993.

Tiano, Olivier. *Ramses II and Thebes*. Henry Holt, 1996.

Weeks, Kent R. *The Lost Tomb*. William Morrow, 1998.

RICHARD I, KING OF ENGLAND

Archer, Thomas A. *Crusade of Richard I, 1189–92*. AMS Press, 1989.

Gillingham, John. *Richard Coeur De Lion: Kingship, Chivalry and War in the Twelfth Century*. Hambledon Press, 1994.

Storr, Catherine. *Richard the Lion-Hearted*. Raintree, 1989.

RWABUGIRI, KING OF RWANDA

Davidson, Basil. *Modern Africa: A Social and Political History*. Addison-Wesley, 1994.

Newbury, Catharine. *The Cohesion of Oppression: Clientship and Ethnicity in Rwanda, 1860–1960*. Columbia University Press, 1989.

SARGON II, KING OF ASSYRIA

Landau, Elaine. *The Assyrians*. Millbrook Press, 1997.

Nardo, Don, ed. *The Assyrian Empire*. Lucent Books, 1998.

SAUL, KING OF ISRAEL

Segal, Lore Groszmann. *The Story of King Saul and King David*. Schocken Books, 1991.

Shamir, Ilana, and Shlomo Shavit, eds. *The Young Reader's Encyclopedia of Jewish History*. Viking Press, 1987.

SELIM III, OTTOMAN SULTAN

Goodman, Jason. *Lords of the Horizons: A History of the Ottoman Empire*. Henry Holt, 1999.

Wheatcroft, Andrew. *The Ottomans*. Viking, 1993.

SHAH JAHAN, EMPEROR OF INDIA

Ganeri, Anita. *India Under the Mughal Empire, 1526–1858*. Raintree, 1998.

Marshall, Julia, and Joan Ullathorne. *Shah Jahan and the Story of the Taj Mahal*. AMIDEAST Publications, 1996.

Rothfarb, Ed. *In the Land of the Taj Mahal: The World of the Fabulous Mughals*. Henry Holt, 1998.

SHIH HUANG TI, EMPEROR OF CHINA

Cotterell, Arthur. *The First Emperor of China: The Greatest Archeological Find of Our Time*. Holt, Rinehart, and Winston, 1981.

Geddes, Gary. *The Terra-cotta Army*. Oberon Press, 1985.

Guisso, R. W. L. *The First Emperor of China*. Carol Publishing Group, 1989.

NORODOM SIHANOUK, KING OF CAMBODIA

Kamm, Henry. *Cambodia: Report from a Stricken Land.* Arcade, 1998.

Norodom Sihanouk. *War and Hope: The Case for Cambodia.* Pantheon Books, 1980.

Osborne, Milton E. *Sihanouk: Prince of Light, Prince of Darkness.* University of Hawaii Press, 1994.

SOBHUZA I, KING OF SWAZILAND

Blauer, Ettagale. *Swaziland.* Children's Press, 1996.

Gillis, D. Hugh. *The Kingdom of Swaziland.* Greenwood Press, 1999.

SOLOMON, KING OF THE ISRAELITES

Gary, Romain. *King Solomon.* Harper & Row, 1983.

Shamir, Ilana, and Shlomo Shavit, eds. *The Young Reader's Encyclopedia of Jewish History.* Viking Press, 1987.

SÜLEYMAN THE MAGNIFICENT, OTTOMAN EMPEROR

Clot, Andre. *Suleiman the Magnificent.* New Amsterdam, 1992.

Goodwin, Jason. *Lords of the Horizons: A History of the Ottoman Empire.* Henry Holt, 1999.

Wheatcroft, Andrew. *The Ottomans.* Viking, 1993.

SUNDJATA KEITA (SUNDIATA KEITA), EMPEROR OF MALI

Mann, Kenny. *Ghana Mali Songhay: The Western Sudan* (African Kingdoms of the Past). Dillon Press, 1995.

McKissack, Pat. *The Royal Kingdoms of Ghana, Mali and Songhay: Life in Medieval Africa.* Henry Holt, 1995.

Niane, D. T. *Sundiata: An Epic of Old Mali.* Addison-Wesley, 1995.

TALAL IBN ABDULLAH, KING OF JORDAN

Cleveland, William L. *A History of the Modern Middle East.* Westview Press, 1994.

Salibi, Kamal S. *The Modern History of Jordan.* St. Martin's Press, 1993.

TÉWODROS, EMPEROR OF ETHIOPIA

Marcus, Harold G. *A History of Ethiopia.* University of California Press, 1994.

Pankhurst, Richard, and Barbara Pankhurst. *The Ethiopians.* Blackwell Publishers, 1998.

Pankhurst, Richard. *A Social History of Ethiopia: The Northern and Central Highlands from Early Medieval Times to the Rise of Emperor Tewodros II.* Red Sea Press, 1992.

THEODORIC THE GREAT, OSTROGOTH KING

Burns, Thomas S. *A History of the Ostrogoths*. Indiana University Press, reissue 1991.

Heather, P. J. *The Goths*. Blackwell Publishers, 1996.

THUTMOSE III, PHARAOH OF EGYPT

Bunson, Margaret. *Encyclopedia of Ancient Egypt*. Facts on File, 1991.

Clayton, Peter A. *Chronicle of the Pharaohs: The Reign-By-Reign Record of the Rulers and Dynasties of Ancient Egypt*. Thames and Hudson, 1994.

Silverman, David P., ed. *Ancient Egypt*. Oxford University Press, 1997.

TIBERIUS, EMPEROR OF ROME

Massie, Allan. *The Caesars*. F. Watts, 1984.

Mellor, Ronald, ed. *From Augustus to Nero: The First Dynasty of Imperial Rome*. Michigan State University Press, 1991.

Shotter, David. *Tiberius Caesar*. Routledge, 1993.

TRAJAN, EMPEROR OF ROME

Massie, Allan. *The Caesars*. F. Watts, 1984.

Mellor, Ronald, ed. *From Augustus to Nero: The First Dynasty of Imperial Rome*. Michigan State University Press, 1991.

Zoch, Paul A. *Ancient Rome: An Introductory History*. University of Oklahoma Press, 1998.

TUTANKHAMEN, PHARAOH OF EGYPT

Desroches-Noblecourt, Christiane. *Tutankhamen, Life and Death of a Pharaoh*. Viking Penguin, 1989.

Macdonald, Fiona. *The World in the Time of Tutankhamen*. Dillon Press, 1997.

Reeves, C. N. *The Complete Tutankhamun: The King, the Tomb, the Royal Treasure*. Thames and Hudson, reissue 1995.

TZ'U-HSI, EMPRESS DOWAGER OF CHINA

Paludan, Ann. *Chronicles of the Chinese Emperors: The Reign-by-Reign Record of the Rulers of Imperial China*. Thames and Hudson, 1998.

Twitchett, Denis, and John K. Fairbank. *The Cambridge History of China*. Cambridge University Press, 1978.

VICTOR EMMANUEL II, KING OF ITALY

Clark, Martin. *The Italian Risorgimento*. Longman Publishing Group, 1998.

Clark, Martin. *Modern Italy 1871–1995*. Addison-Wesley, 1996.

Smith, Dennis Mack. *Modern Italy: A Political History*. University of Michigan Press, 1998.

VICTORIA, QUEEN OF ENGLAND

Erickson, Carolly. *Her Little Majesty: The Life of Queen Victoria.* Simon & Schuster, 1997.

Hough, Richard Alexander. *Victoria and Albert.* St. Martin's Press, 1996.

Strachey, Lytton. *Queen Victoria.* Penguin USA, reissue 1997.

JIGME SINGYE WANGCHUCK, SULTAN OF BHUTAN

Aris, Michael. *The Raven Crown: The Origins of Buddhist Monarchy in Bhutan.* Weatherhill, 1995.

Crossette, Barbara. *So Close to Heaven: The Vanishing Buddhist Kingdoms of the Himalayas.* Alfred A. Knopf, 1995.

Kingdom of Bhutan Home Page (service of Bhutan Tourism Corporation), http://www.kingdomofbhutan.com/index.html

WILHELM I, KAISER OF GERMANY

Aronson, Theo. *The Kaisers.* Bobbs-Merrill, 1971.

Blackbourn, David. *The Long Nineteenth Century: A History of Germany, 1780–1918.* Oxford University Press, 1998.

WILHELM II, KAISER OF GERMANY

Massie, Robert. *Dreadnought: Britain, Germany, and the Coming of the Great War.* Ballantine Books, 1992.

Rohl, John C. G. *Young Wilhelm: The Kaiser's Early Life, 1859–1888.* Cambridge University Press, 1998.

Tuchman, Barbara. *The Guns of August.* Ballantine Books, 1994.

WILLIAM I, THE CONQUEROR, KING OF NORMANDY AND ENGLAND

Green, Robert. *William the Conqueror.* Franklin Watts, 1998.

Howarth, David. *1066: The Year of the Conquest.* Penguin USA, reissue 1981.

Lace, William W. *The Battle of Hastings.* Lucent Books, 1996.

WILLIAM I, THE SILENT, KING OF THE NETHERLANDS

Putnam, Ruth. *William the Silent.* AMS Press, 1997.

Wedgwood, C.V. (Cicely Veronica). *William the Silent, William of Nassau, Prince of Orange, 1533–1584.* Norton, 1968.

WILLIAM III, DUTCH KING OF ENGLAND

Rose, Craig. *England in the 1690s: Revolution, Religion, and War.* Blackwell Press, 1999.

Swisher, Clarice. *The Glorious Revolution.* Lucent Books, 1996.

XERXES I, KING OF PERSIA

Llywelyn, Morgan. *Xerxes*. Chelsea House, 1987.

Shepherd, W. (translator). *Herodotus: The Persian War*. Cambridge University Press, 1982.

MOHAMMAD ZAHIR, KING OF AFGHANISTAN

Ali, Sharifah Enayat. *Afghanistan*. Benchmark Books, 1995.

Girardet, Edward. *Afghanistan: The Soviet War*. St. Martin's Press, 1985.

Magnus, Ralph H., and Eden Naby. *Afghanistan: Mullah, Marx, and Mujahid*. Westview Press, 1998.

Glossary

abbey (ăb′ē) A religious house, containing sleeping quarters, places of worship, and often associated means of support, such as a farm. Similar to a monastery, but most often associated with nuns, or religious sisters.

abbot (ăb′ət) The title given to the leader, or superior, of a monastery.

abdicate (ăb′dĭ-kāt′) To formally relinquish power or responsibility. The term is often used to refer to political leaders who step down unexpectedly.

abrogate (ăb′rə-gāt′) Most often associated with a legal or authoritative act that abolishes, or does away with.

absolutism (ăb′sə-lo͞o′tĭz′əm) (also **absolutist**) In political theory, the practice or idea of all power being held by a single ruler or other unquestioned authority.

accession (ăk-sĕsh′ən) The act or fact of the attainment of rank or status. The term may also refer to the ceremony in which a royal figure is formally vested with his or her title and authority.

acumen (ə-kyo͞o′mən, ăk′yə-) A term often used to refer to exceptional perception, judgment, or insight. It implies an underlying understanding of factors and principles.

ad hoc (ăd hŏk′, hōk′) A Latin phrase meaning only for the specific case or situation at hand. It is also used to mean impromptu, or improvised.

adjudication The hearing and settling of a legal case by means of judicial procedure.

aggrandize (ə-grăn′dīz′, ăg′rən-) Literally, to make more grand, or larger in power, size, or stature, either physically or by rhetoric or exaggeration.

agrarian (ə-grâr′ē-ən) A sociological term used to refer to cultures or economies that are based on or derive their primary economic means from uses of the land, such as farming.

alchemy (ăl′kə-mē) A pseudo-science or scientific philosophy, prevalent in the Middle Ages, most commonly known for its acceptance of the possibility of the transmutation of elements from one to another. The term has also taken on a romantic and slightly sinister sense in modern usage, implying dark or secret magic.

allegory (ăl′ĭ-gôr′ē, -gōr′ē) A style of drama, fiction, or art in which specific elements or characters are used to represent abstract principles, ideas, or powers.

Allies (ə-lī′s) (also **Allied Forces**) The term given to the group of countries, consisting of the United States, Canada, Great Britain, France, and the USSR, that fought against the Axis powers during World War II.

ally (ə-lī′, ăl′ī) A friend or friendly association. In global international relations, most often used to refer to a nation with which one has mutually supportive treaties or common political interests.

ambassador (ăm-băs′ə-dər, -dôr′) The formal representative of one country or nation to another.

anarchy (ăn′ər-kē) A state of political disorder and confusion, with unclear or no political authority.

Anglican (ăng′glĭ-kən) An adherent of or relating to the Church or England or its associated churches.

annexation (ə-nĕks′āshən) The process of adding on to or joining various elements into a larger single unit.

annuity (ə-no͞o′ĭ-tē, ə-nyo͞o′-) A type of investment or other arrangement in which regular payments are made on a yearly, or annual, basis.

annul (ə-nŭl′) To declare invalid, or nullify, as in a marriage or law.

anoint (ə-noint′) Most often used to refer to a formal, often religious process in which an individual is recognized or consecrated as a ruler having the favor of the church.

antediluvian (ăn′tĭ-də-lo͞o′vē-ən) A term that refers literally to the time before the biblical Flood, commonly used to refer in general to something or someone who is very old or no longer relevant.

apathy (ăp′ə-thē) Lack of interest, concern, or caring.

apex (ā′pĕks) The top, or highest place.

apologist (ə-pŏl′ə-jĭst) A person who writes or speaks in defense of someone or something. The term is often used to refer to a person who seeks to justify the actions of another, or to reconcile behavior or beliefs with established principles.

apostate (ə-pŏs′tāt′, -tĭt) One who abandons his or her religious faith, principles, or cause.

arbitrate (är′bĭ-trāt′) To judge between or mediate between two conflicting parties.

aristocracy (ăr′ĭ-stŏk′rə-sē) From the Greek words *aristos*, meaning "best," and *kratos*, meaning "power," a term used either for a form of government ruled by an elite class or group, or to refer to the members of such a group.

Ark of the Covenant The chest where, according to legend and Old Testament scripture, the Hebrews stored the fragments of the Ten Commandments, which Moses brought down from Mt. Herod and smashed.

armistice (är′mĭ-stĭs) A truce or other temporary stop in fighting by the mutual agreement of the warring parties.

asp (ăsp) A collective term for a group of venomous snakes commonly found in Africa, Asia, or Europe.

assassinate (ə-săs′ə-nāt′) To murder. The term is most often used to refer to the killing of an important person, often for political reasons.

astrology (ə-strŏl′ə-jē) A pseudo-science or scientific philosophy that studies the positions, alignments, and other aspects of heavenly bodies in the belief that they have influences and effects on earthly and human affairs.

atrocities (ə-trŏs′ĭ-tēz) Specifically, acts of vicious cruelty, often used to refer to the killing of unarmed people or other depraved acts.

august (ô-gŭst′) An adjective that refers to something or someone that inspires a formal awe or majesty.

authoritarian (ə-thôr′ĭ-târ′ē-ən) A person or political system that enforces absolute obedience to authority.

autonomy (ô-tŏn′ə-mē) From the Greek word *autonomos*, meaning self-ruling, a person, group, or nation not controlled by others, or self-governing.

barbarous (bär′bər-əs) (also **barbarian** [bär-bâr′ē-ən]) From the Greek word *barbaros*, meaning "foreign," the term refers to primitive cultures lacking refinement and often marked by savage, brutal behavior.

bazaar (bə-zär′) A type of market, consisting of open-air shops and stalls.

beatify (bē-ăt′ə-fī′) Literally, to make blessedly happy, the term is most often used to refer to the public and formal proclamation by a religious institution that a deceased person is recognized as being worthy of respect and veneration. It is one of the steps in the process of recognizing a person as a saint in the Catholic church.

bedouin (bĕd′o͞oĭn, bĕd′wĭn) The collective name for the members of a number of the nomadic tribes of the Arabian or African deserts.

bevy (bĕv′ē) Literally, a group of animals or birds, the term is often used to refer to a large assemblage or group.

bicameral (bī-kăm′ər-əl) From the Latin *camera*, meaning chamber, something composed of two distinctive chambers or branches, such as the U.S. Congress or the human brain.

bigot (bĭg′ət) A person who is partial to or promotes his or her own group, such as a race or religion, as above all others, and is intolerant of those not a part of it.

booty Plunder taken from an enemy during a war, or stolen or seized goods.

bourgeois (bo͝or-zhwä′, bo͝or′zhwä′) Used interchangeably to refer both to those of the middle class, and to those whose philosophies and behaviors are influenced or may be characterized by conformity to the standards of the middle class.

boycott (boi′kŏt′) A form of protest in which a person or group refuses to buy products from or support companies, individuals, nations, or other groups with which they disagree. The intent of a boycott is to bring about or force change. It is used as a tool or weapon in labor disputes, by consumers, and in international affairs.

bureaucracy (byo͝o-rŏk′rə-sē) A general term for the employees and administrative structure of a company or organization, characterized by a specific hierarchy of authority or responsibility.

cabinet (kăb′ə-nĭ t) In political terms, the name used to refer to a formal group of advisors, or council, to the executive head of a parliamentary government. In the United States, the cabinet consists of fourteen different "secretaries," each responsible for a specific aspect of national policy. In addition, the vice president is considered part of the cabinet, and the president may give cabinet rank or status to other executive branch officials.

calamitous (kə-lăm′ĭ -təs) Something that involves or causes great harm or disaster.

Calvinism (kăl′vĭ -nĭ sm) A form of Christian belief or theology, a Protestant offshoot of the Catholic church, led by French reformer John Calvin (1509-64). It is characterized by belief in the absolute sovereignty of God, in predestination, and the absence of free will.

campaign (kăm-pān′) A series of military operations enacted to achieve a large-scale objective, or distinct phase, during a war.

canonize (kăn′ə-nī z′) (also **canonization**) The act or process of declaring someone a saint.

capitalism (kăp′ĭ -tl-ĭ z′əm) The overall term for the economic system in which individuals and companies produce and exchange goods and services through a network of prices and markets.

caste system (kăst sĭ s′təm) A type of social system arranged in hierarchical order, in which a person's status is determined by the caste, or level, into which he is born. A rigid caste system defines the worth or acceptability of an individual on the basis of his or her caste rather than individual merits or attributes, and personal advancement is often extremely difficult.

castigate (kăs′tĭ -gāt′) A term meaning to inflict severe punishment, often used to describe the inflicting of harsh verbal criticism.

castrate (kăs′trāt′) The removal of the testicles in a male or the ovaries in a female.

caul (kôl) A piece of the membranous sac in which the fetus resides, most often referring specifically to a portion that is covering the head.

chamberlain (chām′bər-lən) A servant or official responsible for the management of the household of a king or noble.

chateau (shă-tō′) A French castle or manor house.

chauvinism (shō′və-nĭ z′əm) Most often used to refer to a fanatical, sometimes prejudiced belief in the superiority of one's own group, such as gender, race, or religion.

chivalry (shĭ v′əl-rē) A rigid and clearly defined code of behavior that emphasizes the protection of women and the weak. It is often associated with the Arthurian legends and knightly orders.

circumcision (sûr′kəm-sĭ zh′ən) In males, the act of removing the loose fold of skin, known as the foreskin, that covers the glans of the penis. In females, the removal of the prepuce or a portion of the clitoris. Circumcision is often a religion ceremony.

claimant (klā′mənt) In royal politics or succession, one who advances a claim to the throne.

clan (klăn) A traditional social unit, originating from the Highlands of Scotland, that consists of a number of families claiming a common ancestor.

coalition (kō′ə-lĭ sh′ən) An alliance or union of two or more parties, usually temporary, established for the purpose of attaining goals favorable to those involved. The term is most often used to refer to political alliances.

codify (kŏd′ĭ -fī ′, kō′də-) To reduce to or organize into a coherent system of rules or laws.

colloquium (kə-lō′kwē-əm) An informal meeting or conference.

colonialism (kə-lō′nē-ə-lĭ z′əm) A political philosophy or policy by which a governing nation maintains control over its foreign colonies. The term is also used to refer to an attitude in which a citizen of the ruling country may view citizens of a subject nation with a certain disdain or sense of superiority.

commission (kə-mĭ sh′ən) A group or body, similar to a committee, assembled for the purpose of dealing with specific duties, tasks, or issues. Also used to refer to the legal document that confers the rank of military officer.

commoner (kŏm′ə-nər) A person who is not of noble rank or status.

communism (kŏm′yə-nĭ z′əm) A political theory and model for a government system in which all resources, businesses, and means of production are theoretically jointly owned by all members of the community, but in practice, administered and controlled by the central government.

compulsory (kəm-pŭl′sə-rē) Something that is obligatory, or required.

concession (kən-sĕsh′ən) Giving up or giving in, or something that is given up, or conceded.

concoct (kən-kŏkt′) To prepare or create, usually by mixing together ingredients or resources.

concordat (kən-kôr′dăt′) A formal agreement or contract, often used in connection with the Catholic church.

concubine (kŏng′kyə-bī n′) A woman who lives with a man. The term is often used to refer to a woman who has a sexual or conjugal relationship with a man outside of marriage.

confederacy (kən-fĕd′ər-ə-sē) A political union, or league.

Confucianism A philosophy or system of thought, most popular in and associated with China, based on the teachings and writings of Confucius and his disciples. It is characterized by a system of ethics and moral codes of behavior that stress goodness, integrity, and fair treatment of others.

conscription (kən-skrĭ p′shən) The process or practice of enrolling citizens in government service, most often in military forces.

conservative (kən-sûr′və-tĭ v) A term used to describe someone who is traditional in his or her views and values, and favors individualism rather than a central controlling authority.

consort (kŏn′sôrt′) A person who keeps company with another, often used to refer to the wife or husband of a monarch.

consortium (kən-sôr′tē-əm, -shē-əm) An association or cooperative arrangement between groups or interests.

conspiracy (kən-spîr′ə-sē) An agreement or plan between two or more individuals or organizations to perform an illegal or subversive act.

consternation (kŏn′stər-nā′shən) A state of severe or debilitating dismay or fear.

constitutionalism (kŏn′stĭ -tōō′shə-nə-lĭ z′əm, -tyōō′-) A form of government, or the political or philosophical belief in such, based on distributed power and limited by a central system of laws, such as a constitution, that must be obeyed by all, including rulers.

coronation (kôr′ə-nā′shən) The formal ceremony in which a sovereign, such as a king or queen, is formally crowned and invested with office.

count (kount) In the hierarchy of European nobility, a title used to denote a certain rank or status.

coup d'état (kōō dā-tä′) The quick and sometimes unexpected overthrow of a government by an often small group of people in or formerly in authority.

courtier (kôr′tē-ər, -tyər, kōr′-) A member of a group of attendants at a monarch's court. A courtier may be a figure of minor nobility, or a member of the gentry.

covenant (kŭv′ə-nənt) A binding agreement or treaty. The term is often used to indicate solemn or religious overtones.

covet (kŭv′ĭ t) A guilty or sinful desire for something that belongs to another person.

crown prince Of a king's sons or other heirs, one of princely rank who has been designated as the successor.

crusade (krōō-sād′) Originally referring to any of the military expeditions undertaken by the Christian leaders of Europe in the Middle Ages to recover the Holy Land from the Moslems, now commonly used to describe an organized, passionate campaign or movement for a specific cause. Its use is often meant to imply religious or spiritual overtones.

cuneiform (kyōō′nē-ə-fôrm′, kyōō-nē′-) A style of writing or symbolic depiction consisting of an arrangement of small, wedge-shaped elements or characters, used in certain ancient eastern writing.

czar (zär, tsär) Originally from the Latin *caesar*, meaning emperor, an autocratic leader, most often used to refer to the monarchs of imperial Russia. Also spelled "tsar."

dauphin (dô′fĭn) A term used from 1349 to 1830 to refer to the eldest son of the king of France.

de facto (dĭ făk′tō, dā) From the Latin, a phrase mean in reality or fact.

debauchery (dĭ-bô′chə-rē) An extreme indulgence or obsession with sensual pleasures.

decadent (dĕk′ə-dənt, dĭ-kād′nt) Self-indulgent or self-gratifying. Also used to refer to something or someone that is in decline, or is decayed.

decree (dĭ-krē′) An order or statement from a recognized authority that has the force of law.

deity (dē′ĭ-tē) A god or goddess.

delta (dĕl′tə) The fourth letter of the Greek alphabet. In geophysical terms, the triangular alluvial deposit found at the mouth of a river.

depose (dĭ-pōz′) To remove from authority or office, often by means of force.

depredation (dĕp′rĭ-dā′shən) A savage attack or raid. Also used to refer to long-term damage caused by outside forces such as enemies, or weather.

despotism (dĕs′pə-tĭz′əm) A form of government in which a single ruler has absolute power. Also called a tyranny.

dictator (dĭk′tā′tər, dĭk-tā′-) Originally the title of a magistrate in ancient Rome, appointed by the Senate in times of emergency, in modern times the term has come to refer to an individual who assumes sole and often absolute power over a country.

dignitary (dĭg′nĭ-tĕr′ē) A person of recognized rank or importance.

diocese (dī′ə-sĭs, -sēs′, -sēz′) In religious political structure, the collective churches and areas under the authority of a bishop.

diplomat (dĭp′lə-măt′) A person who is skilled in the practice of conducting international business or relations.

disarray (dĭs′ə-rā′) Disorder or confusion.

disavow (dĭs′ə-vou′) To deny knowledge of or responsibility for something.

disinherit (dĭs′ĭn-hĕr′ĭt) To exclude someone or something from inheriting or from the right to inherit.

disparate (dĭs′pər-ĭt, dĭ-spăr′ĭt) A term used to indicate a fundamental or very great difference or distinction between two parties.

dissent (dĭ-sĕnt′) To disagree or differ in feeling or opinion.

dissident (dĭs′ĭ-dənt) In a political sense, one who opposes governmental policies.

dissolution (dĭs′ə-lōō′shən) The fragmentation into many parts, or disintegration. Also used to refer to indulgence in pleasures of the flesh, or debauchery.

doctrine (dŏk′trĭn) The collective term for the body of principles, or beliefs, accepted by a religious, political, or philosophic group.

dominion (də-mĭn′yən) Something or someone that is controlled. Also refers to the exercise or fact of control.

dowager (dou′ə-jər) The legal term for a widow who holds titles or property that derives from her deceased husband. The term is also used to refer to an elderly woman of high social station.

draconic (drā-kŏn′ĭk) Meaning literally of or suggestive of a dragon, used to refer to conditions or measures that are seen as harsh or severe.

duchy (dŭch′ē) The territory, possessions, and subjects ruled by a duke or duchess.

dynasty (dī′nə-stē) A succession of rulers from the same family or group that maintains power over a period of years and generations. Often used to refer to political leaders.

dysentery (dĭs′ən-tĕr′ē) An inflammatory disorder of the lower intestinal tract, usually caused by a bacterial or parasitic infection and resulting in pain, fever, and severe diarrhea, often accompanied by the passage of blood and mucus.

ecclesiastical (ĭ-klē′zē-ăs′tĭ-kəl) Of or relating to a church or organized religion.

edict (ē′dĭkt′) A formal decree, pronouncement, or command, issued by an authority, having the force of law.

egalitarian (ĭ-găl′ĭ-târ′ē-ən-) The affirmation of one who professes political, economic, and social equality for all people.

emancipation (ĭ-măn′sə-pā′shən) Literally meaning to free from bondage, oppression, or restraint, most often used to refer to freedom from slavery, as in the Emancipation Proclamation.

embassy (ĕm′bə-sē) A building containing the offices of an ambassador and staff from a foreign country.

embryonic (ĕm′brē-ŏn′ĭk) Literally of or relating to an embryo, a term often used to refer to something in the early stages of development.

Enlightenment (ĕn-līt′n-mənt) A philosophical movement of the 18th century that emphasized the use of reason to question previously accepted practices.

entourage (ŏn′tŏŏ-räzh′) The group of servants, attendants, and hangers-on who often surround rich or famous people.

envoy (ĕn′voi′, ŏn′-) A government representative, sent to a particular place on a special diplomatic mission.

epilepsy (ĕp′ə-lĕp′sē) Collective name for any of a group of neurological disorders characterized by sudden fits, seizures, or spasms associated with the loss or malfunction of motor or sensory skills.

episcopal (ĭ-pĭs′kə-pəl) Of or relating to a bishop.

etiquette (ĕt′ĭ-kĕt′, -kĭt) A set of prescribed social rules, forms, or practices that constitute proper conduct and behavior in specific situations.

Eucharist (yōō′kər-ĭst) Also called the Lord's Supper or Holy Communion, the institution or sacrament of the Christian religion in which bread and wine are consecrated by an ordained minister, and then shared by the minister and members of the congregation. As commanded by Jesus at the Last Supper, the bread and wine symbolize the body and blood of Christ.

eulogy (yōō′lə-jē) A speech or written tribute to and in praise of someone who has died.

exacerbate (ĭg-zăs′ər-bāt′) To make worse, or increase the severity of something through actions; to aggravate.

excommunicate (ĕks′kə-myōō′nĭ-kāt′) In the Catholic church, to deny a person the sacraments and forbid him or her from participating in worship.

exemplar (ĭg-zĕm′plär′, -plər) A classification of something as a model or best example.

exhume (ĭg-zōōm′, -zyōōm′, ĭk-syōōm′, ĕks-hyōōm′) The removal of a corpse from a grave. Exhumation is sometimes done to determine a cause of death, or to establish the identity of a corpse.

exigency (ĕk′sə-jən-sē, ĭg-zĭj′ən-) An urgent or immediate situation requiring considerable effort or action.

exile (ĕg′zīl′, ĕk′sīl′) The involuntary removal from one's home country, or the person so removed.

expansionism (ĭk-spăn′shə-nĭz′əm) In political policy or action, the practice of expanding a nation's physical or economic boundaries.

expatriate (ĕk-spā′trē-āt′) A person who has left his or her native country, usually through banishment or exile, to live in another country.

faction (făk′shən) A group that separates itself within a larger group.

fascism (făsh′ĭz′əm) A system of government that follows the principles of a centralized authority under a dictator, strict economic controls, censorship, and the use of terror to suppress opposition.

fealty (fē′əl-tē) A formal and legal oath, owed by a vassal to his feudal lord under the feudal system prevalent in Europe during the Middle Ages. In contemporary usage, the term is often used to indicate a deep or more formal level of devotion or commitment to an individual or cause.

feudal (fyōōd′l) (also **feudal system**) Of or relating to the political and economic system known as feudalism, common in Europe in the Middle Ages, in which a landowner granted land to a vassal in exchange for fealty and military service.

fiasco (fē-ăs′kō, -ä′skō) A complete and utter failure.

figurehead (fĭg′yər-hĕd′) A person who appears to lead or control an organization or group, but who has little or no actual power.

fiscal (fĭs′kəl) Of or relating to economic issues.

friar (frī′ər) From the Middle English term *frere*, meaning brother, a member of a Roman Catholic order forbidden to own land, and dependent on alms and begging for support.

frontier (frŭn-tîr′) An international border. The term is often colorfully used to refer to the unexplored or mostly wild limits of expansion.

frugality (frōō-găl′ĭ-tē) A term referring to someone who is conservative in the expenditure of money or the use of material resources.

fugitive (fyōō′jĭ-tĭv) A person on the run or fleeing from authority.

galleon (găl′ē-ən, găl′yən) A type of sailing ship, characterized by three masts, a square rig, and often two or more decks. Galleons were in common use, especially in Spain, from the 15th through 17th centuries.

galvanize (găl′və-nīz′) To induce an awareness or action.

garrison (găr′ĭ-sən) A military post.

genealogy (jē′nē-ŏl′ə-jē, -ăl′-, jĕn′ē-) The record or account of the descent of a person, family, or group from a specific ancestor or group of ancestors.

gentry (jĕn′trē) The upper or ruling class of a society.

gladiator (glăd′ē-ā′tər) A term used in ancient Rome to refer to a professional fighter, captive, or slave trained to fight in the arena.

guerrilla (gə-rĭl′ə) From the Spanish word *guerra*, meaning war, a term used to refer to a soldier who is a member of a small, irregular military force that operates in small bands in hostile or occupied territory, harassing and working to undermine and disrupt the enemy. "Guerrilla warfare" refers to an organized campaign along these lines.

harpsichord (härp′sĭ-kôrd′, -kōrd′) A keyboard musical instrument, played by plucking strings with quills or the small pieces of metal, bone, or plastic known as plectrums.

havoc (hăv′ək) Widespread destruction or devastation.

heathen (hē′thən) A term used to describe members of a society or a religion that does not acknowledge the Judeo-Christian and Islamic God.

hedonism (hēd′n-ĭz′əm) The pursuit of or devotion to sensual pleasures.

hegemony (hĭ-jĕm′ə-nē, hĕj′ə-mō′nē) The predominant influence of one state over another.

heir (âr) The person designated by law or the terms of a will to inherit the hereditary rank, title, position, or estate of another.

heir apparent (âr ə-păr′ənt) A legal term referring to an heir whose right to inheritance cannot be changed by law provided he or she survives an ancestor.

hemophilia (hē′mə-fĭl′ē-ə, -fēl′yə) The collective name for a group of hereditary disorders characterized by the inability of blood to clot normally due to the deficiency or abnormality of one or more of the clotting factors. Hemophilia is a recessive trait found almost exclusively in males.

heresy (hĕr′ĭ-sē) An opinion or belief based in religion. Most often heresy refers to the denials of the Roman Catholic church by a follower or believer.

hierarchy (hī′ə-rär′kē) Most often used to refer to the structure of authority in a group or organization, ranked by authority or ability.

homage (hŏm′ĭj, ŏm′-) To pay tribute to or honor, especially in a public setting.

Huguenots (hyōō′gə-nŏt′s) Members of a French Protestant culture that flourished in the 16th and 17th centuries.

humane (hyōō-mān′) A trait characterized by kindness, mercy, and compassion.

humanitarian (hyōō-măn′ĭ-târ′ē-ən) Someone who is devoted to the promotion of the well-being of humans.

iconoclastic (ī-kŏn′ə-klăst′ĭk) A term used to describe an attack made as an attempt to overthrow traditional or popular ideas or institutions.

idealism (ī-dē′ə-lĭz′əm) The philosophy or practice of envisioning things in an ideal form. The term is often used to describe the subject of a piece of artwork or literature.

ideology (ī′dē-ŏl′ə-jē, ĭd′ē-) The collective term for the body of ideas and principles reflecting the social needs and aspirations of an individual, group, or culture.

idiom (ĭd′ē-əm) A literary term used to describe a word or expression that is peculiar to itself grammatically, or has no individual meaning.

idiosyncrasy (ĭd′ē-ō-sĭng′krə-sē) A peculiar or rare trait.

immigration (ĭm′ĭ-grāt′shən) The process of entering and settling into a country or region that is not one's native land.

imperialism (ĭm-pîr′ē-ə-lĭz′əm) The policy and practice by which a powerful nation extends and maintains economic and political control over weaker countries.

impunity (ĭm-pyōō'nĭ-tē) Exemption from punishment, penalty, or harm.

inaugurate (ĭn-ô'gyə-rāt') To induct a person, often a member of government, into office by a formal ceremony.

incognito (ĭn'kŏg-nē'tō, ĭn-kŏg'nĭ-tō') A term used for someone who has disguised him- or herself or otherwise concealed his identity.

indemnity (ĭn-dĕm'nĭ-tē) Compensation for, or insurance against, damage, loss, or injury.

industrialism (ĭn-dŭs'trē-ə-lĭz'əm) An economic and social system based on the development of large-scale industries and their productions. Other characteristics include mass production of inexpensive goods and the concentration of employment in urban factories.

inquisition (ĭn'kwĭ-zĭsh'ən) To inquire or investigate a matter.

insignia (ĭn-sĭg'nē-ə) A distinguishing sign or symbol, often a badge that denotes rank, office, or nationality.

insurgent (ĭn-sûr'jənt) A term used to describe someone who rebels against civil authority or a government.

intelligentsia (ĭn-tĕl'ə-jənsē'ə) The intellectual elite.

intercession (ĭn'tər-sĕsh'ən) A petition or plea in favor of another, most often a prayer or petition to God.

isolationism (ī'sə-lā'shə-nĭz'əm) A political policy or philosophy that advocates the belief that a nation's interests are best served by avoiding alliance or excessive contact with other nations.

janissaries (jăn'ĭ-sĕr'ēz) Members of a group of elite, highly loyal supporters. Specifically the term refers to members of an elite Turkish guard organized in the 14th century, and abolished in 1826.

Jesuit (jĕzh'ōō-ĭt, jĕz'ōō-, -yōō-) A member of the Society of Jesus, a religious order founded by Saint Ignatius of Loyola in 1534.

judiciary (jōō-dĭsh'ē-ĕr'ē, -dĭsh'ə-rē) A system of courts of law for the administration of justice.

khedive (kə-dēv') A term referring to one of several Turkish viceroys ruling in Egypt from 1867 to 1914.

knell (nĕl) A mournful or ominous sound, often a bell rung slowly for a funeral.

knighthood (nīt'hŏŏd') (also **knight**) In modern times, an honor by a nation or ruler that confers nobility on a person who has performed notable service. There are three distinct orders of knighthood: royal orders, generally limited to men and women of royal blood or the highest ranks of nobility; noble or family orders, open to members of the nobility in general; and orders of merit, which may be bestowed on persons from any class as a reward for distinguished service.

largesse (lär-zhĕs', -jĕs', lär'jĕs') The generous bestowal of money as a gift. The act is often done in a lofty or condescending manner.

leprosy (lĕp'rə-sē) (also **leper**) Also called Hansen's disease, a degenerative, chronic, infectious disease that affects primarily the skin, mucous membranes, and nerves. In biblical references, the term is used to refer to a variety of diseases, many not related to actual leprosy, that were considered a mark of defilement, or punishment from God for sin.

levy (lĕv'ē) To impose or collect, often referring to taxes.

liberal (lĭb'ər-əl, lĭb'rəl) A term used to describe someone who is not limited to traditional, orthodox, or authoritarian attitudes or views. The term also characterizes those favoring reform and new ideas, as well as being broadminded toward the behavior of others.

liberalism (lĭb'ər-ə-lĭz'əm, lĭb'rə-) A political theory based on the characteristics of being liberal.

lineage (lĭn'ē-ĭj) A line of descent, usually traced from a specific ancestor.

loot (lōōt) Valuables stolen in a time of war or disaster. The term also refers to the process of stealing or pillaging.

loyalist (loi'ə-lĭst) One who maintains political loyalty to the government or sovereign during a time of revolt.

Luftwaffe (lŏŏft'väf'ə) The German air force before and during World War II.

Lutheran (lōō'thər-ən) A Protestant religion based on the teachings of Martin Luther, characterized by opposition to the wealth and perceived corruption of the

Catholic church, and the belief that salvation would be granted on a basis of faith alone rather than by actions or membership in a specific church.

lyre (līr) A stringed instrument, prominently used in ancient Greece, that resembles a harp and is used to accompany poetry or song.

Machiavellian (măk′ē-ə-vĕl′ē-ən) A type of behavior originating from the works of Italian theorist Niccolò Machiavelli, characterized by expediency, deceit, and cunning as a means of achieving one's goals.

malcontent (măl′kən-tĕnt′) Someone who is dissatisfied with his or her existing conditions. The term can also be used to describe someone who rebels against the established government or system.

mandate (măn′dāt′) A law or command administered by a civil authority or ruler.

marksman (märks′mən) Someone who is skilled in shooting at a target.

martyr (mär′tər) Generally used to refer to a person who dies rather than renounce his or her religious principles, or one who makes great sacrifices for a cause.

massacre (măs′ə-kər) The act or an instance of killing a large number of human beings indiscriminately and cruelly.

maternal (mə-tûr′nəl) A term referring to characteristics most often associated with a mother or motherhood.

matrilineal (măt′rə-lĭn′ē-əl) A sociological term referring to a society whose descendants follow a maternal ancestral line.

matrimonial (măt′rə-mō′nē-əl) Of or relating to the marriage ceremony.

mediator (mē′dē-ā′tər) Someone who acts as a neutral party to assist others in resolving a dispute.

medieval (mē′dē-ē′vəl, mĕd′ē-) A term used to describe someone or something as belonging to, or a part of, the Middle Ages.

mercenaries (mûr′sə-nĕr′ēz) People who are motivated by a desire for monetary or material gain. The term is usually used to refer to freelance soldiers who are hired by a foreign army to supplement or assist in training local troops.

messiah (mĭ-sī′ə) A leader who is regarded as a savior or liberator. Within the Christian faith, the term refers to Jesus Christ, considered the Son of God.

Middle Ages The period in European history between the collapse of the Roman Empire and the Renaissance, often dated from C.E. 476 to 1453. It is also called the "Dark Ages."

militant (mĭl′ĭ-tənt) A person, political party, or course of action that is combative or aggressive, usually for a cause or to achieve a specific objective.

militarist (mĭl′ĭ-tə-rĭst) A person who actively promotes or glorifies in the ideals and traditions of the professional military class, or a person who believes that armed force is the solution to a great variety of international conflicts.

militia (mə-lĭsh′ə) The term used to describe an army made up of ordinary citizens rather than professional or career soldiers. A militia would be intended to function as a reserve or contingent force, available to be called on in case of emergency.

minority (mə-nôr′ĭ-tē, -nŏr′-, mī-) A racial, religious, political, national, or other group regarded as different from the larger group of which it is part.

missionary (mĭsh′ə-nĕr′ē) A member of a particular religious organization whose tradition is to "witness" by word and deed to the beliefs of his or her religion, so that others may come to know and understand it.

mobilization (mō′bə-lĭ-zā′shən) The process of moving, or making mobile, often referring to an army.

modernism (mŏd′ər-nĭz′əm) A state of being characterized by contemporary thought, character, or standards.

monarchist (mŏn′ər-kĭst) Someone who believes in and advocates the principles of the monarchy.

monarchy (mŏn′ər-kē, -är′-) (also **monarch**) A form of government in which the leader rules by hereditary right, or the nation that is governed. Monarchs include such rulers as kings, emperors, and czars.

monastery (mŏn′ə-stĕr′ē) A religious house, consisting of living quarters and places of worship, and often associated with some means of provender, such as a farm. The residence of monks.

Mongol (mŏng'gəl, -gōl', mŏn'-) A member of the nomadic society of Mongolia, for centuries an independent world power. Much of Mongolia was brought under Chinese control early in the 18th century, and remains mostly under Chinese rule.

monk (mŭngk) A Christian brother, living in a monastery, following a life devoted to rituals and disciplines defined by his "order."

monopoly (mə-nŏp'ə-lē) Exclusive control by one group to provide or produce a commodity or service.

monotheist (mŏn'ə-thē-ĭst) Someone who believes that there is only one God.

Moor (mo͝or) A member of a Moslem people of mixed Berber and Arab descent, now living chiefly in northwest Africa. Historically, a Moslem group who invaded Spain in the 8th century and established a civilization in Andalusia that lasted until the late 15th century.

mosque (mŏsk) A Moslem house of worship.

motto (mŏt'ō) A statement used to describe or represent a principle, goal, or ideal.

mulatto (mo͝o-lăt'ō, -lä'tō, myo͝o-) A term used to describe someone with one white parent and one black parent.

municipality (myo͞o-nĭs'ə-păl'ĭ-tē) A city or town that is locally self-governed. The term can also refer to the group of officials who manage the affairs of the government.

mutiny (myo͞ot'n-ē) An open rebellion against authority. It is most often used to refer to military personnel turning against a superior officer.

mysticism (mĭs'tĭ-sĭz'əm) A belief in or consciousness of a transcendent or higher reality, such as God or spirits.

nationalism (năsh'ə-nə-lĭz'əm) The devotion to the beliefs and interests of a specific nation.

nativist (nā'tĭ-vĭst) Someone who is a believer in nativism, a sociopolitical policy that favors the interests of native inhabitants over those of immigrants.

NATO (North Atlantic Treaty Organization) A regional defensive alliance, created by the signing of the North Atlantic Treaty in April 1949. Its purpose and intent is to provide security for its members through shared defensive resources.

neophyte (nē'ə-fīt') A beginner or novice.

noble (nō'bəl) Someone who possesses a hereditary rank in a political system or social class. The term is also used to describe someone who possesses the characteristics of honor, courage, and generosity.

nomadic (nō'măd') A term used to describe someone who is a member of a group of people who have no fixed home and move according to the seasons from place to place in search of food, water, and grazing land.

oath (ōth) A formal vow or declaration. An oath is held to have legal, spiritual, and moral weight.

oligarchy (ŏl'ĭ-gär'kē, ō'lĭ-) A government that is composed of a few members, usually a small faction or family.

opportunism (ŏp'ər-to͞o'nĭzm) The practice or trait of taking advantage of opportunities that present themselves, sometimes without regard for principles or consequences, in order to achieve a specific end.

oppression (ə-prĕsh'ən) To be kept down or denied rights through an unjust use of force or authority. The term is often used to refer to social and legal discrimination against certain ethic groups.

orthodoxy (ôr'thə-dŏk'sē) An accepted or established doctrine or creed, and the adherence to it. The term "orthodox" is also often used to refer to the most conservative or traditional element, especially of a religion.

pagan (pā'gən) A term used to characterize someone who is not Christian, Moslem, or Jewish. Also used to refer to someone who has no religion.

papal (pā'pəl) Of or relating to the Pope or papacy.

papal nuncio (pā'pəl nŭn'sē-ō') An ambassador or representative of the Pope.

paradigm (păr'ə-dīm', -dĭm') An example or incident that serves as a pattern or model for all that follows.

parliament (pär′lə-mənt) In some countries, a branch of government, similar to the U.S. Congress, that is responsible for enacting laws, levying taxes, and serving as the highest court of appeal.

patriarchal (pā′trē-är′kəl) A type of social system in which the father is the head of the household, and ancestry is determined through the paternal, or father's, line.

patrician (pə-trĭsh′ən) A person of refined upbringing, manners, and tastes. In some societies, the term also refers to a member of the aristocracy or ruling class.

patrilineal (păt′rə-lĭn′ē-əl) (also **paternal** [pə-tûr′nəl]) The determination or account of ancestry or lineage through the paternal line.

patrimony (păt′rə-mō′nē) An inheritance from a father or other ancestor.

patriotic (pā′trē-ŏt′ĭk) A term used to describe someone who expresses love and devotion to one's country.

patron (pā′trən) Someone who supports, protects, or champions an institution, event, or cause.

patron saint (pā′trən sānt) A saint who is regarded as the advocate in heaven of a specific nation, place, craft, activity, class, or person.

patronage (pā′trə-nĭj, păt′rə-) The support of a cause by means of financial assistance.

peasant (pĕz′ənt) A social class characterized by low status, often a farmer, laborer, or uneducated person.

pedigree (pĕd′ĭ-grē′) A documentable line of ancestors characterized by high social status or genetics.

penal code (pē′nəl kōd) A body of laws relating to crimes and offenses and the penalties for their actions.

penance (pĕn′əns) (also **penitent**) In the Christian faith, a voluntary act of contrition, or a sacrament performed for the forgiveness of sins.

pension (pĕn′shən) A sum of money paid regularly as a retirement benefit or as patronage for service.

pharaoh (fâr′ō) In ancient Egypt, the name originally used to refer to the palace of the king; it was later used to refer to the kings themselves.

philanthropy (fĭ-lăn′thrə-pē) In business, a term used to describe the ongoing practice or philosophy, usually of an individual, of giving to or establishing charitable or humanistic causes or foundations.

philosophy (fĭ-lŏs′ə-fē) In general terms, a speculative inquiry into the source and nature of human knowledge, or the system and ideas based on such thinking.

piety (pī′ĭ-tē) Strong religious devotion to and reverence of God.

pilgrim (pĭl′grəm) A person who travels to or visits a place of spiritual or political importance to seek refuge or insight.

pilgrimage (pĭl′grə-mĭj) The voyage taken by a pilgrim to a site of spiritual or political importance. Most often used to refer to a religious journey.

pious (pī′əs) Adamantly observant of religion and religious practices.

plebiscite (plĕb′ĭ-sīt′, -sĭt) A direct vote in which the entire electorate is invited to accept or refuse a proposal.

pluralism (plo͝or′ə-lĭz′əm) A philosophical belief that reality is made up of many different parts, and that no one theory or worldview is adequate for all aspects of life.

poll tax A type of tax levied on citizens when they are preparing to vote. It has occasionally been used as a political tool to prevent lower-income citizens from voting.

polygamy (pə-lĭg′ə-mē) A type of marriage made in which a husband or wife may have more than one spouse.

Pope (pōp) From the Latin word *papa*, meaning father, since the 8th century the title given to the bishop of Rome, the head of the Roman Catholic church.

populace (pŏp′yə-lĭs) The general public or citizens of a country or area.

populism (pŏp′yə-lĭz′əm) A political belief that governmental power should be in the hands of the people, or population, rather than royalty or the wealthy.

pragmatism (prăg′mə-tĭz′əm) The belief that the purpose of thought is to guide action, and that the effect of an idea is more important than its origin.

pretext (prē′tĕkst′) An excuse or rationale, often arrived at as a result of deliberate effort or strategy, taken as a reason to embark on a course of action.

prime minister The head of the a governmental cabinet, usually appointed by the ruler.

primogeniture (prī′mō-jĕn′ĭ-cho͝or′) The state of being the first-born, or eldest child of the same parents, often referring to the first-born heir to a monarchy; also the exclusive right of inheritance of the oldest son.

principality (prĭn′sə-păl′ĭ-tē) An area ruled by a prince, or the position, authority, or jurisdiction of a prince.

privatization (prī′və-tī zā′shən) The process of changing from governmental or public ownership to private enterprise.

profligacy (prŏf′lĭ-gə-sē) A term used to describe someone who is extremely wasteful or extravagant.

promulgate (prŏm′əl-gāt′, prō-mŭl′gāt′) To make known through a public declaration or official announcement.

propaganda (prŏp′ə-găn′də) Material that is distributed by people who advocate a specific belief or cause.

prophet (prŏf′ĭt) A person who speaks by divine inspiration, or as an interpreter for God.

prostrate (prŏs′trāt′) To bow or kneel in humility or adoration to a leader or ruler.

protectorate (prə-tĕk′tər-ĭt) An arrangement made between two countries to have the one with superior power protect the weaker country. The term also refers specifically to the country that is being protected.

Protestantism (prŏt′ĭ-stən-tĭz′əm) A religious term referring to a belief of the Protestant church, characterized by a belief that the Bible is the sole source of revelation and faith alone is justification to all believers. Protestantism is based on the theologies of Luther, Calvin, and Zwingli and was formed as a result of protest against the laws and practices of the Roman Catholic church.

protocol (prō′tə-kôl′) A code of conduct observed in a specific environment, often referring to diplomats and heads of state when in the presence of national leaders or rulers.

province (prŏv′ĭns) A territory governed as an administrative or political unit of a country or an empire.

purgatory (pûr′gə-tôr′ē) In Christian theology, a state of the afterlife, considered to be between heaven and hell, in which a soul is either cleansed of sins or endures a period of waiting that remains after the guilt of mortal sin has been remitted.

Quechua (kĕch′wə, -wä′) The language originally spoken by the Incas, now widely used throughout the Andes highlands from southern Colombia to Chile.

radical (răd′ĭ-kəl) A political term used to describe those who believe in extreme and revolutionary changes within a society or government.

radicalism (răd′ĭ-kə-lĭz′əm) A term that refers collectively to the actions or philosophies of radicals.

ransom (răn′səm) Payment of a demanded price for the release of a person or property.

rapprochement (rä′prôsh-mäɴ′) The process of reestablishing relations between two countries or other opposing parties.

reactionary (rē-ăk′shə-nĕr′ē) One who is opposed to progress, development, or new ideas.

realism (rē′ə-lĭz′əm) A philosophical discipline inclined toward truth and pragmatism. In art, the representation of objects as they actually appear.

reformer (rĭ-fôrm′ər) In political terms, a person who seeks to bring about change, often in laws and government policies, by means of the established political systems.

regatta (rĭ-gä′tə, -găt′ə) A boat race, or series of boat races.

regent (rē′jənt) A person who acts as a temporary ruler in the absence or disability of a monarch. A regent is also used when the heir to the throne is too young to hold the position of ruler.

regicide (rĕj′ĭ-sīd′) The killing of a ruling monarch.

regime (rā-zhēm′, rĭ-) A government or administration in power.

regimentation (rĕj′ə-məntā′shən) A military unit consisting of two battalions of ground troops, usually commanded by a colonel.

reign (rān) The period during which a monarch or other supreme leader rules and exercises his or her power.

relic (rĕl'ĭ k) In religion, a physical object of veneration that has some connection to a holy person or sacred site.

repression (rĭ -prĕsh'ən) In social or sociological terms, the deliberate denial of equal rights, usually to members of a minority.

republican (rĭ -pŭb'lĭ k-ən') A term used to describe someone who is in favor of a government that is not ruled by a monarch, often favoring a president as the head of state.

revolt (rĭ -vōlt') An attempt to overthrow the rule or control of a country, state, or other established authority.

rhetoric (rĕt'ər-ĭ k) The study or art of the use of language and persuasion.

rift (rĭ ft) A narrow crack in a rock. The term also refers to a break in friendly relations.

rivalry (rī 'vəl-rē) The act of competing, or attempting to surpass an opponent. The term may also refer to the competition itself.

royalist (roi'ə-lĭ st) A supporter of a government ruled by a monarch.

Sabbath (săb'əth) The first day of the week, Sunday, observed as the day of rest and worship by most Christians; the seventh day of the week observed by Jews from Friday evening to Saturday evening, also as a day of rest and worship.

sacrament (săk'rə-mənt) Any of several rites or liturgical actions in the tradition of the Christian church that are believed to be instituted by Jesus. They include marriage, the Eucharist, or communion, baptism, and Holy Orders, and are thought to communicate the grace or power of good through material objects and ritual.

sacred (sā'krĭ d) A term used to classify an object that is dedicated for the worship of a god.

sagacity (sə-găs'ĭ -tē) The quality of being discerning, sound in judgment, and far-sighted.

saint (sānt) In the Roman Catholic church, a person who is considered holy, and worthy of public veneration.

sanctions (săngk'shəns) In political terms, restrictions or prohibitions, usually economic, against dealings or interactions with other countries.

sanctuary (săngk'chōō-ĕr'ē) A sacred place, often a church, temple, or mosque. Sanctuary also refers to a place, often a church, where fugitives or criminals were immune to arrest.

satrap (sā'trăp', săt'răp') A governor of a province in ancient Persia.

Saxons (săk'səns) A Western Germanic tribal group that invaded Britain in the 5th and 6th centuries C.E. with the Angles and the Jutes.

scion (sī 'ən) A descendent or heir, usually from a noble or royal house.

secretariat (sĕk'rĭ -târ'ē-ĭ t) The department administered by a governmental secretary, especially for an international organization.

sect (sĕkt) A smaller, distinct unit, sometimes separated from a larger group or denomination by variations in common beliefs.

secular (sĕk'yə-lər) A term referring to an approach that does not relate to religious or spiritual views.

sedentary (sĕd'n-tĕr'ē) A term used to describe someone who spends the majority of his or her time sitting and seldom engaging in exercise.

separatist (sĕp'ər-ə-tĭ st) One who secedes or advocates separation, especially from an established church.

serf (sûrf) A member of the servile, feudal class of people of Europe, who were bound to the land and owned by the lord.

shah (shä) The title used for the hereditary monarch of Iran.

sheik (shēk, shāk) A leader of an Arab family or village. The term can also be used to refer to a religious official.

shogun (shō'gən) The hereditary commander of the Japanese army who, until 1867, exercised absolute rule under the nominal leadership of the emperor.

signatory (sĭ g'nə-tôr'ē, -tōr'ē) A person or nation that has signed a particular agreement. Also used to refer to the condition of being bound by an agreement.

sinecure (sī 'nĭ -kyŏŏr', sĭ n'ĭ -) A position or office that requires little work but still provides a salary.

smallpox (smôl′pŏks′) An acute, highly infectious, often fatal disease caused by a virus. The disease is characterized by high fever and aches with subsequent widespread eruption of pimples that blister, produce pus, and form pockmarks.

socialism (sō′shə-lĭ z′əm) A governmental system that maintains the beliefs that all goods are owned equally and controlled and distributed by the state, administered by a powerful central government.

sociology (sō′sē-ŏl′ə-jē, -shē-) The science or study of human social relations or group life and interaction. It examines the ways in which social structures, institutions, and social problems influence society. It is considered one of the social sciences, along with such studies and sciences as psychology, economics, and anthropology.

sovereignty (sŏv′ər-ĭ n-tē, sŏv′rĭ n-) A supreme political power free from external control.

Spartan (spär′tn) A citizen of the ancient city of Sparta in Greece.

status quo (stā′təs kwō) The state of affairs as they exist.

subaltern (sŭb-ôl′tərn, sŭb′əl-tûrn′) A term used to describe someone who is lower in rank or position.

subjugate (sŭb′jə-gāt′) To bring under control, or make subservient.

subsidy (sŭb′sĭ -dē) Monetary assistance given by a government to a person or group in support of a business that is regarded as being in the public interest.

subversive (səb-vûr′sĭ v, -zĭ v) Policies or actions that are intended to undermine, or subvert, established systems. The term is most often used to refer to oppositional or confrontational political activity.

subvert (səb-vûrt′) To destroy or ruin.

succession (sək-sĕsh′ən) A term referring to the act of following in sequence. The term often refers to the process of taking over for the previous monarch.

suffrage (sŭf′rĭ j) The right or privilege of voting.

sultanate (sŭl′tə-nāt′) (also **sultan**) The country or area ruled by a sultan, a Muslim title commonly used in the Ottoman empire.

summit (sŭm′ĭ t) A conference held by several government officials to reach a political agreement.

suzerainty (sōō′zər-ən-tē, -zə-rān′tē) The power or domain of a country that controls the international affairs of another country, but allows it domestic sovereignty.

taxation (tăk-sā′shən) The process or practice of being taxed.

technocrat (tĕk′nə-krăt′) A technical expert, usually in a managerial or administrative position.

temple (tĕm′pəl) A place of religious worship.

theocratic (thē′ə-krăt′ĭ k) A governmental style characterized by rules and laws being dictated by religious authority.

theology (thē-ŏl′ə-jē) A discipline that attempts to express the content of a religious expression in words that are contained in faith.

totalitarian (tō-tăl′ĭ -târ′ē-ən) A government based on the belief that political authority exercises complete and absolute control over all aspects of the citizens' lives.

transmigration (trăns′mī -grā′shən) The passing of a soul into another body after death.

treason (trē′zən) A term referring to the violation of allegiance toward one's own country or ruler.

treasury (trĕzh′ə-rē) A place, often within a government or company, where private and public funds are received, kept, managed, and distributed.

treatise (trē′tĭ s) An extensive narrative or dissertation on a subject.

treaty (trē′tē) A formal agreement between two or more states, often as a means of reaching peace or arranging trade.

tribunal A committee or organization appointed or created to investigate and judge a particular matter.

tuberculosis (tōō-bûr′kyə-lō′sĭ s, tyōō-) An infectious disease, characterized by the formation of small lumps within the body, most often the lungs.

tyrant (tī ′rənt) An absolute ruler. The term is most often used to refer to a cruel or oppressive dictator.

usurper (yo͞o-sûrp′r) A term used to describe someone who takes power by force, without legal authority.

vassal (văs′əl) (also **vassalage** [văs′ə-lĭ j]) A person who held land from a feudal lord and received protection in return for homage and allegiance.

viceroy (vī s′roi′) The political leader of a vassal or colonial country or province, who rules as a representative of the sovereign.

vizier (vĭ -zîr′, vĭ z′yər) A high officer in a Moslem government, especially in the Ottoman empire.

ziggurat (zĭ g′ə-răt′) A temple shaped like a terraced pyramid with successively receding storeys that were places of worship in ancient Assyria and Babylonia.

Zionism (zī ′ə-nĭ z′əm) A movement aimed at uniting the Jewish people of the exile and settling them in Palestine. Founded in the late 19th century by journalist Theodor Herzl, the organization eventually grew to settle the State of Israel in 1948. Their main goal of statehood was to defend and consolidate Israel and to justify its existence. In the 1970s and 1980s Zionist aid was extended to Soviet Jews and today guarantees a Jewish nationality to any Jew in need of it.

Zulu (zo͞o′lo͞o) A member of a Bantu people of southeast Africa, primarily inhabiting the northeastern province of Natal in South Africa.

Photo Credits

Akihito (page 13): Reuters/INA/Archive Photos
Albert II (page 18): Gamma Liaison/Lebrun-Photo News
Alexander the Great (page 26): CORBIS/Bettmann
Amenhotep (page 32): CORBIS/Roger Ressmeyer
Arthur (page 33): Gamma Liaison/Hulton Getty Picture Library
Atahualpa (page 37): Archive Photos
Beatrix (page 47): Reuters/Jerry Lampen/Archive Photo
Bhumibol Adulyadey (page 50): Archive Photos
Robert Bruce (page 54): CORBIS/Vottproamp Restelli
Charlemagne (page 64): CORBIS/Bettmann
Christina (page 79): Archive Photos
Cleopatra (page 82): CORBIS/Bettmann
Constantine (page 86): CORBIS/Araldo le Luca
David (page 93): Archive Photos
Elizabeth I (page 99): Archive Photos
Elizabeth II (page 103): Globe Photos
Elizabeth II (page 106): CORBIS/Hulton-Deutsch Collection
Elizabeth II (page 107): CORBIS
Fahd (page 112): Reuters/Frederic Neema/Archive Photos
Faisal (page 117): Thomas J. Abercrombie/National Geographic Image Collection
Farouk (page 125): Archive Photos
George III (page 148): CORBIS
Gustavus II Adolphus (page152): Culver Photos, Inc.
Haile Selassie (page 157): Culver Photos, Inc.
Harald V (page 165): Reuters/Jerry Lampen/Archive Photos
Hassan II (page 168): Cecile Treal/Gamma Liaison
Henry V (page 181): Archive Photos
Henry VIII (page 184): Archive Photos
Hirohito (page 192): CORBIS/Bettmann
Hussein (page 195): Luis Marden/National Geographic Image Collection
Isa ibn Sulman al-Khalifa (page 206): Reuters/Rick Wilking/Archive Photos
Isabella (page 208): Culver Pictures, Inc.
Ivan III (page 212): Archive Photos
Jean (page 223): Luxembourg National Tourist Office
Juan Carlos (page 231): George de Keerle/Gamma Liaison
Kamehameha I (page 238): CORBIS/Douglas Peebles
Letsie III (page 249): Reuters/Peter Andrews/Archive Photos
Liliuokalani (page 251): Culver Pictures, Inc.
Liliuokalani (page 252): CORBIS/Hulton-Deutsch Collection
Liliuokalani (page 253): CORBIS/Douglas Peebles
Louis XIV (page 257): CORBIS
Mahmud II (page 263): Archive Photos

Margrethe (page 274): Archive Photos
Maria Theresa (page 276): Archive Photos
Marie Antoinette (page 278): Culver Pictures, Inc.
Mary Stuart (page 284): Culver Pictures, Inc.
Maximilian (page 287): Culver Pictures, Inc.
Montecuhzoma I (page 298): Culver Pictures, Inc.
Mswati III (page 301): Reuters/Graham Williams/Archive Photos
Napoleon I (page 311): Culver Pictures, Inc.
Napoleon I (page 313): CORBIS/Robert Holme
Nicholas II (page 324): CORBIS/Bettmann
Nicholas II (page 325): CORBIS/Yogi, Inc.
Noor (page 329): Imapress/Archive Photos
Pachacuti (page 340): CORBIS/Tom Nebboa
Pedro II (page 343): Culver Pictures, Inc.
Pu Yi (page 350): Archive Photos
Qabus (page 354): Thomas J. Abercrombie/National Geographic Image Collection
Rainier (page 358): CORBIS/Bettmann
Rainier (page 359): Francis Apesteguy/Gamma-Liaison
Ramses II (page 362): Louis O. Mazzatenta/National Geographic Image Collection
Shah Jahan (page 377): CORBIS/Galen Rowell
Shih Huang Ti (page 380): CORBIS/Bettmann
Norodom Sihanouk (page 381): Reuters/Darren Whiteside/Archive Photos
Süleyman (page 388): Culver Pictures, Inc.
Tiberius (page 400): CORBIS/Archivo Iconografico, S. A.
Tupou (page 404): CORBIS/Jack Fields
Tutankhamen (page 406): CORBIS/Bettmann
Tz'u-Hsi (page 409): CORBIS/Bettmann
Victoria (page 415): Archive Photos/Popperfoto
Wangchuck (page 420): James L. Stanfield/ National Geographic Image Collection
Wilhelm I (page 423): CORBIS/Ric Ergenbright
Wilhelm II (page 424): Archive Photos
William the Conqueror (page 427): CORBIS/Corday Photo Library

Article Sources

Some of the articles in **Macmillan Profiles**: *Kings and Queens* were extracted from the following sources:

Encyclopedia of Africa South of the Sahara, Charles Scribner's Sons, 1997.
Encyclopedia of Latin American History and Culture, Charles Scribner's Sons, 1996.
Encyclopedia of the Modern Middle East, Macmillan Reference USA, 1996.
The Made History: A Biographical Dictionary, Simon & Schuster, 1993.

The article on King Norodom Sihanouk was extracted from the *Encyclopedia of Asian History*, prepared under the auspices of the Asia Society and published by Charles Scribner's Sons in 1988; it was updated and reprinted with the permission of the Asia Society.

The following writers contributed articles to **Macmillan Profiles**: *Kings and Queens*:

Abd al-Rahman Khan, king of Afghanistan	Ashraf Ghani
Abdullah ibn Husayn, king of Jordan	Jenab Tutunji
Abdullah II, king of Jordan	Mark LaFlaur
Akihito, emperor of Japan	Patty Ohlenroth
Albert II, king of Belgium	Laura Morelli
Amanollah Khan, king of Afghanistan	Ashraf Ghani
Atahualpa, Inca emperor	Kendall W. Brown
Beatrix, queen of the Netherlands	Laura Morelli
Bhumibol Adulyadey, king of Thailand	Patty Ohlenroth
Birendra, king of Nepal	Mary Carvlin
Carl XVI, king of Sweden	Laura Morelli
Jean Jacques Dessalines, emperor of Haiti	Thomas O. Otto
Elizabeth II, queen of England	Mark LaFlaur
Fahd ibn Abd al-Aziz Al Saud, king of Saudi Arabia	Malcolm C. Peck
Faisal I ibn Husayn, king of Iraq	Reeva S. Simon
Faisal ibn Abd al-Aziz Al Saud, king of Saudi Arabia	Malcolm C. Peck
Farouk, king of Egypt	Robert L. Tignor
Fuad, king of Egypt	Robert L. Tignor
Galawdewos, emperor of Ethiopia	Adrian Hastings
Hamad ibn Khalifa Al Thani, emir of Qatar	Fred H. Lawson
Hans-Adam II, prince of Liechtenstein	Mark LaFlaur
Harald V, king of Norway	Mark LaFlaur
Hassan II, king of Morocco	Remy Leveau
Hassanal Bolkiah, sultan of Brunei	Mary Carvlin
Herod the Great, king of Judea	Mary Carvlin
Hussein ibn Talal, king of Jordan	Peter Gubser
Isa ibn Sulman al-Khalifa, ruler of Bahrain	Fred H. Lawson
Jabir Ahmad Al Sabah, emir of Kuwait	Emile A. Nakhleh
Jean, grand duke of Luxembourg	Mark LaFlaur

João VI, king of Portugal	Maria Beatriz Nizza daSilva
John I, king of England	Michael Levine
Juan Carlos, king of Spain	Mark LaFlaur
Kamehameha I, king of Hawaii	Nancy Gratton
Khalid ibn Abd al-Aziz Al Saud, king of Saudi Arabia	Malcolm C. Peck
Lebna Dengel, king of Abyssinia	William A. Shack
Letsie III, king of Lesotho	Mary Carvlin
Liliuokalani, queen of Hawaii	Nancy Gratton
Mahmud II, Ottoman sultan	Avigdor Levy
Mansa Musa, emperor of Mali	Djibril Tamsir Niane
Manuel I, king of Portugal	Francis A. Dutra
Margrethe II, queen of Denmark	Laura Morelli
Marie Antoinette, queen of France	Michael Levine
Maximilian, emperor of Mexico	Brian Hamnett
Mohammad Reza Pahlavi, shah of Iran	Ahmad Ashraf
Mosheoshoe, king of the Sotho	Motlatsi Thabane
Motecuhzoma I, emperor of Mexico	Louise M. Burkhurst
Motecuhzoma II, emperor of Mexico	Susan Kellogg
Mswati II, king of Swaziland	Sarah Valdez
Mswati III, king of Swaziland	Mary Carvlin
Mubarak Al Sabah, king of Kuwait	Mary Ann Tetreault
Muhammed V, king of Morocco	Remy Leveau
Noor, queen of Jordan	Mark LaFlaur
Pachacuti, Inca emperor	Gordon F. McEwan
Pedro I, emperor of Brazil	Neill MacAulay
Pedro II, emperor of Brazil	Roderick J. Barman
Pu Yi, emperor of China	Patty Ohlenroth
Qabus ibn Sa'id, sultan of Oman	Donald Malcolm Reid
Ranier III, prince of Monaco	Mark LaFlaur
Rwabugiri, king of Rwanda	David Newbury
Salahuddin, king of Malaysia	Mary Carvlin
Saul, king of Israel	Mary Carvlin
Selim III, Ottoman sultan	I. Metin Kunt
Sobhuza I, king of Swaziland	Alan R. Booth
Sundjata Keita, emperor of Mali	Djibril Tamsir Niane
Talal ibn Abdullah, king of Jordan	Jenab Tutunji
Téwodros, emperor of Ethiopia	Donald E. Crummey
Tupou IV, king of Tonga	John Jones
Tutankhamen, pharaoh of Egypt	Mary Carvlin
Jigme Singye Wangchuck, sultan of Bhutan	Mary Carvlin
Mohammad Zahir, king of Afghanistan	M. Nazif Shahrani

Index

B

C

D

E

H

I

L

M

N

Q

R

T

U

Z